MAR CARIBE
Barranquilla
Cartagena
Maracaibo
Valencia
Caracas
Lago de Maracaibo
VENEZUELA
Medellín
Bogotá
Río Magdalena
Río Orinoco
COLOMBIA
GUAYANA
SURINAM (Holanda)
GUAYANA (Francia)
Quito
ECUADOR
Río Guayas
Guayaquil
CORDILLERA DE LOS ANDES
Río Marañón
Río Amazonas
Belém
BRASIL
PERÚ
Río Ucayali
Lima
Cuzco
Río Beni
Río Mamoré
ISLAS GALÁPAGOS (Ecuador)
Lago Titicaca
La Paz
Arequipa
BOLIVIA
Brasilia
Sucre
Lago Poopó
GRAN CHACO
PARAGUAY
Río de Janeiro
São Paulo
Antofagasta
Asunción
Villarrica
TRÓPICO DE CAPRICORNIO
OCÉANO PACÍFICO
San Miguel de Tucumán
OCÉANO ATLÁNTICO
Río Paraná
Río Uruguay
Porto Alegre
Córdoba
Santa Fe
URUGUAY
Valparaíso
Santiago
Mendoza
Rosario
Buenos Aires
Montevideo
Punta del Este
La Plata
Río de la Plata
Concepción
PAMPA
Río Bío-Bío
Mar del Plata
Río Colorado
Bahía Blanca
CHILE
ARGENTINA
AMÉRICA DEL SUR
0 600 Millas
0 600 Kilómetros
ISLAS MALVINAS
TIERRA DEL FUEGO
Estrecho de Magallanes
CABO DE HORNOS
ECUADOR

MODERN SPANISH

Third Edition

A PROJECT OF THE MODERN LANGUAGE ASSOCIATION

Working Committee: First Edition

Dwight L. Bolinger *Harvard University, Coordinator*
J. Donald Bowen *University of California, Los Angeles*
Agnes M. Brady *University of Kansas*
Ernest F. Haden *University of Texas, Austin*
Lawrence Poston, Jr. *University of Oklahoma*
Norman P. Sacks *University of Wisconsin, Madison*

Revisers: Second Edition

Dwight L. Bolinger *Harvard University*
Joan E. Ciruti *Mount Holyoke College*
Hugo H. Montero *Harvard University*

Reviser: Third Edition

Ronald C. Turner *Whitworth College*

MODERN SPANISH

Third Edition

A PROJECT OF THE MODERN LANGUAGE ASSOCIATION

HARCOURT BRACE JOVANOVICH, INC.
New York / Chicago / San Francisco / Atlanta

Picture credits and copyright acknowledgments appear on page 408.

ISBN: 0-15-563974-9

LIBRARY OF CONGRESS CATALOG CARD NUMBER: 72-93724

PRINTED IN THE UNITED STATES OF AMERICA

Contents

Preface to the Third Edition

In 1956 it became my duty to organize the conference of distinguished Hispanists who developed the guidelines for *Modern Spanish.* Subsequently, from 1956 to 1958, I served as MLA staff liaison to the Working Committee that, with support from the Rockefeller Foundation, produced *Modern Spanish.* Now, some sixteen years later, it is my privilege to preface the third edition.

The first edition, which appeared in 1960, turned out to be a landmark in foreign language teaching. The use of *Modern Spanish* has been overwhelming, and its general approach and techniques have been widely employed in other texts, both for schools and colleges. (Acknowledgments to the many people who participated in the creation of the first edition appear elsewhere.)

In 1966 the second edition appeared, with Donald D. Walsh, Director of the MLA Foreign Language Program from 1959–65, providing effective MLA staff liaison. While no radical alterations had to be made, the emphasis was on condensing and rewriting and on deleting the cultural readings and a variety of drills.

In 1970 Ronald C. Turner, Chairman of Modern Languages at Whitworth College, began work on this third edition, bringing a welcome youthful zeal and insight to the task (indeed, he was still a graduate student at Harvard University when the second revision was in progress). He was helped by an advisory committee consisting of Dwight L. Bolinger of Harvard University, J. Donald Bowen of the University of California, Los Angeles, Lawrence Poston, Jr. of the University of Oklahoma, and Norman P. Sacks of the University of Wisconsin. Further assistance was provided by Guillermo Segreda of Manhattanville College, who has reviewed portions of the manuscript and has commented on the authenticity of the new materials. Again, no major alterations were necessary. The following are the changes made in the third edition: (1) a completely rewritten Unit One, in which the discussion of the sounds of Spanish is less technical, speaks more directly to the student, and concentrates more on his problems as an English-speaker; (2) an entirely new Unit Six, with a new dialog, which contains part of the material from Unit Five of the previous edition (because of its density, this unit often presented problems before); (3) a completely new dialog for Unit Fifteen; (4) new "Guided Conversations" for each unit enabling students to engage in quasi-liberated conversations based on, but not limited to, the dialog sentences; (5) the elimination, through the use of a computer, of words in the drills not previously introduced in a dialog; (6) a completely new and expanded illustration program; and (7) a "streamlined" tape program, described in detail in the *Instructor's Manual.*

I cannot let pass this opportunity to note the warm cooperation this project has received from the publisher, Harcourt Brace Jovanovich, and in particular from William Pullin, its Vice President, for whom *Modern Spanish* has, from the beginning, been a personal enthusiasm. He too has helped make this a most durable project of the MLA. I commend the Third Edition to the profession.

KENNETH W. MILDENBERGER
Deputy Executive Secretary and Treasurer
Modern Language Association of America

Introduction to the First Edition

One of the most rewarding events in my term of office as President of the Modern Language Association of America was the development of the College Language Manual. It is now my privilege to introduce this long-awaited text to you. This is an exciting book, whose publication will mark a number of "firsts" in the history of foreign language study in the United States. The MLA, now seventy-six years old, has never before endorsed a textbook but is proud to sponsor this one, for reasons I want to explain.

"There are always new textbooks; what we need is a new *kind* of textbook." For years I have heard language teachers say this. What kind was rarely spelled out by the speaker, but the remark usually implied that foreign language study has become more important to all of us since World War II, that students now expect more of their language teachers (and can be expected, in turn, to do more than used to be asked of them), that a lot of important things have been learned in recent years about making language learning more efficient, and that these things should be more fully exploited in textbooks than has hitherto been the case. What the profession seemed to want was a beginning text that was bold, experimental, keyed throughout to the new spirit in language study. Here it is.

In a sense this is the profession's own book. I say this not because of its conference origin and multiple authorship, not even because it is sponsored by a professional society, but rather because its basic principles, once agreed upon (in May 1956), were widely publicized and talked about long before the book got written, and every Spanish teacher in the United States was invited to agree or disagree and to contribute of his own knowledge and experience. Many did. The reader should know also that the six authors of this book (and twenty-four members of an Advisory Committee) will receive no royalties. All royalties will go into an MLA fund to make possible the writing of other books, as teachers of other languages come forward in a similarly unselfish and cooperative spirit, desiring to achieve another "ideal" text.

Planning and writing a book in the way that this one was planned and written is an expensive, time-consuming matter. Anyone who has watched a committee struggle to compose a single paragraph may doubt that any committee should be entrusted with the writing of a whole book. However, thanks to a grant of $40,500 from the Rockefeller Foundation, and thanks also to the generosity and hospitality of the University of Texas, this committee was able to live and work together long enough to do the seemingly impossible. The adventure was undertaken only because a conference of seventeen veteran teachers of Spanish had agreed unanimously that the best textbook could be produced through *cooperative endeavor.* Since among these conferees were the authors of many of the successful textbooks already available, the argument was as convincing as it was surprising and inspiring.

Equally surprising was the agreement of these seventeen college and university teachers of Spanish (chosen to represent a variety of points of view) on criteria for a truly modern textbook. In arriving at these criteria they assumed these conditions: qualified instructors, students of college age with the usual spread in ability and motivation, a class of manageable size, and a course with a minimum of 300 hours spent in class, laboratory, and outside study. The general approach was then outlined to include the following points:

1. The course should concentrate at the beginning on the learner's *hearing* and *speaking* of Spanish, *whatever his objective.* (The Working Committee therefore developed a teaching tool that adequately presents and drills pronunciation—not the usual brief treatment of pronunciation in an introduction. Pronunciation exercises continue through the first eleven units, or weeks, with emphasis on contrasts within Spanish or comparison of Spanish sounds with English sounds.)

2. The text should make extensive use of *realistic dialogs,* which should also be *recorded*—in an acceptable standard for the Americas. (The Working Committee went further, trying to give the dialogs—and the readings too—*mature content,* interesting to learners of college age. It was decided that the student should *memorize all of these dialogs,* to make them immediately useful for conversational practice. Memorization has always been an indispensable part of language learning; but this book, instead of requiring the student to memorize vocabulary lists or verb paradigms or grammar rules, asks him to memorize full utterances in contextual relationships with each other—sentences one might actually want to speak someday outside the classroom.)

3. Grammar should be presented *inductively,* with summary statements given *after drill.* (The Working Committee therefore produced explanations of grammar that are both accurate and unambiguous, written in a style understandable to the student. It also produced grammar drills that give enough practice in the basic patterns of Spanish to enable the student to learn to use and respond to these patterns *automatically.* All exercise and drill materials are based on comparison of the structures of English and Spanish.)

4. Translation should be used sparingly as a device in teaching reading, since the goal is *direct reading,* without conscious item-by-item decoding. Consequently, although reading of previously heard and memorized material may begin early in the course, reading of previously unheard material should not begin until the student has reasonable control of the pronunciation and principal structural patterns involved in the material.

5. Visual and audio-visual aids should be used as auxiliaries to the text when possible.

6. In order to liberate the student from his single-culture limitations, Spanish and Spanish-American cultural values and patterns of behavior should form a significant part of the content of the linguistic material from the beginning—and at every stage.

This is the basic philosophy; the selection and organization of actual details came from a wealth of experience, cooperatively checked and double checked. The text is divided into thirty units of work, corresponding roughly to the weeks in an academic year. After the first unit, which emphasizes pronunciation and useful classroom phrases, each of the next twenty-three units consists of a *dialog* (*from which everything else in the unit is drawn*), a section of drills and grammar, and a section of readings. The last six units in the book are exclusively reading units, presenting few new points of grammar.

The drills are ingeniously designed to give the student the "feel" of Spanish as quickly as possible; having memorized a "frame sentence" from the basic dialog, he expands this through whatever range of vocabulary he controls, and soon has a considerable store of *complete utterances* he can use as occasion requires or suggests. The drills are of three main kinds: substitution drills, response drills, and translation drills (mostly structural oriented). Following each is a discussion of the pattern that has been drilled—not a set of rules to learn and follow, but a clear statement of how the pattern operates. Students should gain confidence rapidly through this *pattern assimilation* (each sentence having elements of novelty), but, if I may say so, they may need to be very patient with their teachers, for whom such *thorough* covering of familiar ground can become dull and tiring. (Drills are, however, for learners, not for teachers.) Teachers accustomed to traditional texts may even find the drills in this book deceptively easy. The variety of drill types has been intentionally limited: there are no paradigm recitations, no fill-the-blanks, no multiple choice, no conjugate-the-infinitives, no matching.

The readings are meant to be *read,* not translated. They are of two different kinds, with different functions. Units Three through Nine contain "reworked readings" (reintroducing situations, topics, vocabulary, and language patterns in somewhat different contexts and arrangements), whereas units Ten through Thirty contain "original readings" (nearly all produced for this text), the last six consisting of longer, more advanced readings. Questionnaires to check student comprehension follow all the original readings, which are designed to enlarge on the *cultural content* of the dialogs and hence to give the Spanish class the range of a liberal arts course on Hispanic society.

One of the most valuable lessons I learned when Director of the MLA's Foreign Language Program (1952–1956) was the potentiality of cooperative solutions to all sorts of problems vexing the profession. I can give many examples of how such solutions were found, but none so heart-warming, none involving the active participation of so many able people, as this book *Modern Spanish.* Since I was present at its inspiring beginning—having called the conference that recommended cooperative production of the book—it is most gratifying to be allowed now to commend the results to you.

Let me say finally that such wonderful cooperation should not end with publication. Having produced this unprecedented textbook, the profession will, I trust, see to it that it is later improved with each revision.

February, 1960

WILLIAM RILEY PARKER
Distinguished Service Professor of English
Indiana University

Acknowledgments for the First Edition

For a venture to which so many people have contributed, it is virtually impossible to make a complete list of acknowledgments. We wish to thank first, in the name of the MLA, the many Spanish teachers throughout the country who volunteered advice and constructive criticism. Our thanks go too to the Rockefeller Foundation and to the cooperating institutions:

University of Texas (host to writers working in residence)
Foreign Service Institute
University of Kansas
University of Oklahoma
University of Southern California

We owe a special debt of gratitude to the six members of the Working Committee, the twenty-four members of the Advisory Committee, the editors of *Hispania,* Kenneth W. Mildenberger (Director of Programs of MLA and chiefly responsible for MLA liaison in the critical months of the project), and to all those whose names are listed below.

Special Services

Richard Beym *Defense Language Institute*
D. Lincoln Canfield *University of Rochester*
Odette Scott (Chile) *University of Kansas*
Jack L. Ulsh *Foreign Service Institute*
Howard Walker *University of Kansas*

Informants and Critics

Omar Arias (Chile)
Ramón Martínez López (Spain) *University of Texas*
Hugo H. Montero (Venezuela) *Harvard University*
Oldemar Mora (Costa Rica)
Laudelino Moreno (Spain) *University of Southern California*
Francisca Paz (Mexico)
Olga Petesch (Mexico)

Informants and Critics (continued)

Carmen Rodríguez Rosada (Puerto Rico)
Marta Santillana (Mexico)
Rodrigo Solera (Costa Rica) *Pennsylvania State University*
Gerald P. Sullivan *University of Southern California*

Working Committee

Dwight L. Bolinger *Harvard University*
J. Donald Bowen *University of California, Los Angeles*
Agnes M. Brady *University of Kansas*
Ernest F. Haden *University of Texas*
Lawrence Poston, Jr. *University of Oklahoma*
Norman P. Sacks *University of Wisconsin*

Authors of Dialogs and Original Readings

Domingo Ricart (Spain) *University of Kansas* (*readings*)
Guillermo Segreda (Costa Rica) *Manhattanville College* (*dialogs*)
Ismael Silva-Fuenzalida (Chile) *Foreign Service Institute* (*dialogs*)

Consultants

Daniel N. Cárdenas *University of Chicago*
Rodger A. Farley *U.S. Naval Academy*
S. N. Treviño *Foreign Service Institute*

Advisory Committee

Frederick B. Agard *Cornell University*
Richard Armitage *Ohio State University*
Ralph S. Boggs *University of Miami*
D. Lincoln Canfield *University of Rochester*
John A. Crow *University of California, Los Angeles*
Rodger A. Farley *U.S. Naval Academy*
Lewis U. Hanke *Columbia University*
Francis Hayes *University of Florida*
Hayward Keniston *University of Michigan* (*Emeritus*)
Robert Lado *Georgetown University*
J. Kenneth Leslie *Northwestern University*
George E. McSpadden *George Washington University*
Robert G. Mead, Jr. *University of Connecticut*
Sarah M. Pereira *West Virginia State College*
Ruth Richardson *Adelphi College* (*Emeritus*)
Hilario S. Sáenz *University of Nebraska*

Advisory Committee
(continued)

Sol Saporta *University of Washington*
William H. Shoemaker *University of Illinois*
Robert K. Spaulding *University of California, Berkeley*
Charles N. Staubach *University of Arizona*
Robert P. Stockwell *University of California, Los Angeles*
S. N. Treviño *Foreign Service Institute*
Laurel H. Turk *DePauw University*
Donald D. Walsh *Director of the MLA Foreign Language Program, 1959–65*

Critics for the Second Edition

J. Donald Bowen *University of California, Los Angeles*
Mills F. Edgerton, Jr. *Bucknell University*
Roger Hadlich *University of Hawaii*
Allan Kulakow *Peace Corps*
Rudolph Morgan *Stanford University*
Robert P. Stockwell *University of California, Los Angeles*

MODERN SPANISH

Third Edition

A PROJECT OF THE MODERN LANGUAGE ASSOCIATION

UNIT 1

Foreword to the Student

What kind of Spanish?

First, spoken before written. Writing is important, but pronunciation should be learned first. All the exercises in this book are intended to be spoken.

Second, a particular variety. There is no "general Spanish" any more than there is a general English. Some differences between ways of speaking a language need not concern you as a student seeking to learn an acceptable variety. The way—that is, the dialect—adopted for this book is American Spanish. It is different from Castilian, the dialect most widely accepted as a standard in Spain, but the differences are slight. Mostly they affect a sound or two and here and there a word. The grammars are virtually the same.

How do you learn pronunciation?

First, know the mechanisms used in pronouncing your own language; be aware that when you make the sound [b] you are using your lips and when you pronounce [k] you are bringing the back of the tongue up against the velum (diagrams for the speech organs appear later in this unit). Next, apply this awareness to adopting the right position and manner for Spanish sounds, some of which either differ appreciably from their English counterparts or do not exist in English.

In the following section, listen to your teacher (or to the voice on the tape) and then pronounce the phrases according to the instructions given, imitating what you hear as accurately as you can. As you read the explanations on the pages that follow, apply them to the **Frases útiles** in order to improve your pronunciation.

Mexico City: Chapultepec Park

Useful Phrases

P. *Professor* S. *Student (male or female)*
E. *Elenita Vásquez, a visitor*

P. Come in. Sit down. Good morning [ladies and gentlemen].

S. Good morning, Mr. Freitas.

* * *

P. Mr. Huerta, shut the door, please.

S. Yes, sir, be glad to [with much pleasure].

P. Thanks.

S. You're welcome.

* * *

P. How are you, Miss Arjona?

S. I'm fine, thanks; how are [and] you?

P. Very well, thanks.

* * *

P. Aurelio, how do you say *book* in Spanish?

S. You say *libro.*

* * *

P. Do you have a pencil and paper, Raimundo?

S. Yes, I do [have].

Frases útiles

P. *Professor* A. *Alumno (o Alumna)*
E. *Elenita Vásquez, una visitante*

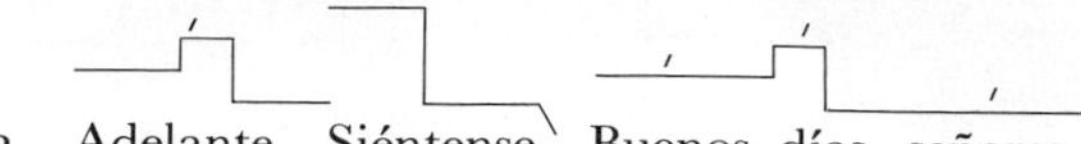

P. Adelante. Siéntense. Buenos días, señores.

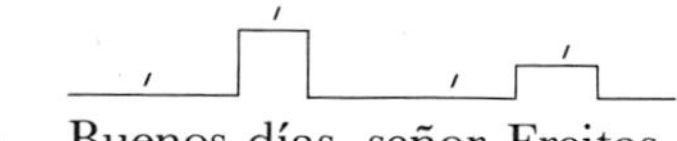

A. Buenos días, señor Freitas.

* * *

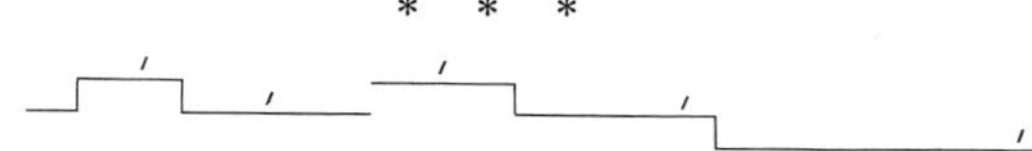

P. Señor Huerta, cierre la puerta, por favor.

A. Sí, señor, con mucho gusto.

P. Gracias.

A. De nada.

* * *

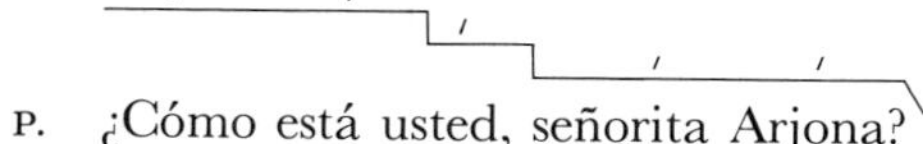

P. ¿Cómo está usted, señorita Arjona?

A. Estoy bien, gracias, ¿y usted?

P. Muy bien, gracias.

* * *

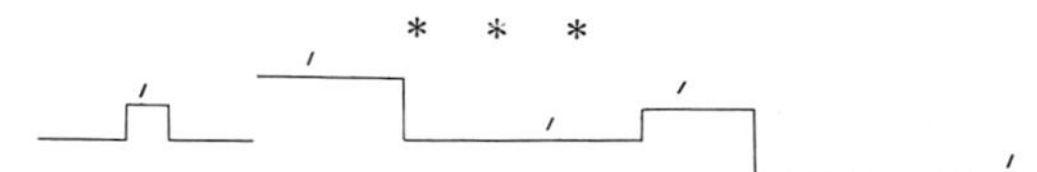

P. Aurelio, ¿cómo se dice *book* en español?

A. Se dice *libro.*

* * *

P. ¿Tiene lápiz y papel, Raimundo?

A. Sí tengo.

P. Do you have a pen? | P. ¿Tiene pluma?

S. No, I don't. | A. No, no tengo.

* * *

P. I'm very sorry. | P. Lo siento mucho.

S. That's okay. | A. Está bien.

* * *

P. I'd like to introduce [to you] Mrs. Elenita Vásquez. | P. Quiero presentarle a[1] la señora Elenita Vásquez.

S. Glad to meet you. | A. Mucho gusto.

E. Glad to meet you, too [Equally], thanks. | E. Igualmente, gracias.

* * *

P. Excuse me [With permission]. | P. Con permiso.

S. Certainly. | A. Cómo no.

* * *

S. Are you leaving already? | A. ¿Ya se va?

E. Yes, I'm leaving [now]. | E. Sí, ya me voy.

S. Pleased to have met you. | A. Mucho gusto en conocerla.

E. Same here. Goodbye. | E. Igualmente, señor. Adiós.

S. Goodbye, see you [until] tomorrow. | A. Adiós, hasta mañana.

[1]This a is not to be translated. It will be explained in a later unit.

1 The Sounds of Spanish

To sound like a native when you speak a language you must do more than articulate individual sounds precisely. That is, of course, a necessary part of the total impression; but one could play each note of a piece of music with exactly the right pitch and pressure and still produce something that no musical ear would accept—for example, if the sounds were not combined with the right phrasing and rhythm. The sounds of language are combined in the act of speech in ways typical of each language. Our first task is to get an understanding of these combinations in Spanish, for they are the framework that encloses and connects the individual sounds. This framework has three elements: RHYTHM, the way successive syllables are fitted together; STRESS, the way certain syllables are made more prominent; and INTONATION, the way syllables are set to the tune of speech.

Rhythm

Pronounce the following sentence several times. As you repeat the sentence, tap your foot to establish a beat like that of a metronome.

Líons róar.

Continue tapping your foot and pronounce the next three sentences.

The líons are róaring.
The líonesses are róaring.
The líonesses interféred.

Notice that with little exaggeration the sequence *-onesses inter-* can be compressed to occupy roughly the same amount of time as *-ons are* in the first sentence. On the other hand, *li-* and *-fered* must be compressed slightly only in the last sentence. These sentences demonstrate that English almost always squeezes short syllables between long ones.

Occasionally a whole sentence is made up of evenly timed syllables, as in the advertisement *Gets out dirt plain soaps can't reach.* This sentence is rhythmically somewhat unusual for English, but the pattern of evenly timed syllables is the normal one for Spanish. What is not normal in Spanish is the shortening of syllables that one finds in a different version of the advertisement, which can be compared with the first:

Gets	out	dirt	plain	soaps	can't	reach
Takes a-	way the	dirt that	com-mon	soaps can	nev-er	reach

After *takes, -way, dirt, com-, soaps,* and *nev-* there are syllables containing a "reduced" vowel (called *schwa*) that borrows approximately enough time from the syllable preceding it so that both together take about as long as the single syllable in the first version. Thus *Gets* and *Takes a-* have equal length, and so do *out* and *-way the,* and so on. Schwa does not occur in Spanish and is shorter than Spanish vowels normally are, thus producing a very short syllable. Avoiding schwa should help you to regularize the rhythm of your Spanish; try also to regularize the rhythm consciously, which will help you to avoid schwa. The two things go together.

› PRONUNCIATION EXERCISE

Pronounce the English words *photograph* and *photography.* Note carefully (1) the relative length of syllables in each word and (2) the quality of the vowel in each syllable. Observe in the corresponding syllables of each word that when the syllable is stressed it is longer, and its vowel has a more distinctive quality. On the other hand, a syllable that is unstressed is much shorter, and its vowel has the quality of schwa.

Now repeat the **Frases útiles,** making sure (1) that the syllables are evenly timed and (2) that all vowels are clearly distinguishable in quality one from the other (unlike those in English). This pronunciation may seem exaggerated to you at first, but these two principles are the main components of a "Spanish accent" and are quite foreign to English. They are habits which must be acquired at the outset of your study in order for your pronunciation of Spanish to be readily understood.

Stress

Words in both English and Spanish each have one major, or stressed, syllable. Each word may also have one or more minor, or unstressed, syllables. A stressed syllable is one that is highlighted in a sentence when we want to give importance to the word that contains it; the other syllables of the important word receive no more prominence than do the syllables of the unimportant words surrounding the stressed syllable. Consider a sentence like *The mistáke was uninténtional.* The words *mistake* and *unintentional* are the important ones, and their stressed syllables, *–take* and *–ten–*, are made prominent, while the other syllables form a sort of low-intensity background.

The highlighting is done mostly by changing the pitch, as when we say

take ten
The mis was unin tional.

making the stressed syllables stand out by raising their pitch. A syllable may also be made prominent by dropping its pitch below the reference line:

ten
The mis was unin tional.
take

There are certain affective differences, but the same result—that of making the stressed syllable stand out—is achieved by either kind of pitch change.

Spanish has the same system of highlighting or accenting stressed syllables in a phrase or sentence. Listen to the pronunciation of the following sentence and be conscious of the abrupt changes in pitch that make the stressed syllables stand out:

Quiero tarle ñora nita Vás
presen a la se Ele quez.

READING ALOUD

For reading aloud in any language, it is necessary to know which syllable of each word is the stressed one. There are three patterns of stress placement in Spanish:

1. The most common stress pattern is on the next-to-last syllable of a word. Words ending in a vowel or in *n* or *s* are pronounced in this manner: **buenos, señorita, Elenita, tienen.**
2. A less frequent pattern is to stress the last syllable. Words ending in a consonant other that *n* or *s* are so pronounced: **español, favor, usted.**
3. If the placement of word stress does not follow the two rules above, a written accent is included in the normal spelling.[2] There are three possibilities:
   a. Violation of rule 1 (words ending in a vowel, *n*, or *s*, but stressed on the last syllable): **aquí, está, jardín, inglés.**

[2]The written accent is usually omitted with capital letters.

b. Violation of rule 2 (words ending in a consonant other than *n* or *s* but stressed on the next-to-last syllable): **lápiz, Vásquez, cónsul.**

c. Words stressed three or more syllables from the last[3]: **rápido, siéntense, dígamelo.**

› PRONUNCIATION EXERCISE

Cover the right-hand column and read aloud the following list of words. Check after each word to see whether you have placed the stress on the correct syllable.

buenos	*bue*nos	está	es*tá*
conocerla	cono*cer*la	Elenita	Ele*ni*ta
señorita	seño*ri*ta	lápiz	*lá*piz
español	espa*ñol*	papel	pa*pel*
gusto	*gus*to	adelante	ade*lan*te
presentarle	presen*tar*le	siéntense	*sién*tense
favor	fa*vor*	cierre	*cie*rre
mañana	ma*ña*na	puerta	*puer*ta

Intonation

Besides the jumps in pitch that highlight individual syllables, there are broader sweeps of pitch that we call intonation, generally organized around two especially prominent syllables, one at the beginning and the other at the end of the phrase or sentence. Pronounce the English command *Describe your operation to me* and the English request *Then why don't we all go together,* as shown:

Des cribe your opera tion to me. Then why don't we all go toge ther.

Now pronounce the statements *He described his operation to me* and *They all went together.*

He des cribed his oper a tion to me. They all went to ge th e r.

Notice how in the command and the request the first main accent (*-cribe* and *why*) reaches a high pitch, and then there is a very gradual drop to the last main accent (*-a-* and *-ge-*), followed by a steep drop, while in the statements the first main accent (*-cribed* and *all*) goes up only a little way, after which there is a drop that holds until the steep jump on the last main accent (*-a-* and *-ge-*), followed again by a drop. These are characteristic intonational curves for English. They are not the only ways of saying those sentences, but they are the most usual ones. If we were to pronounce most of our statements the way we pronounce most of our commands, the total impression that our speech would make on the ear would be quite different.

Yet that is exactly what Spanish does. The commonest form of statement in Spanish resembles the commonest form of the command in English. This is one of the very few marked differences in intonation between the two languages.[4] We shall see the others in a later unit.

---

[3]The written accent has other functions, which will be discussed in a later unit.

[4]In English statements that are too short to show the two-accent pattern there is only one accent, and the two languages are the same:

He knows it. **Lo sa be.**

Pronounce

Mucho gusto en conocerla.

and be conscious of putting the highest pitch on the first main accent, lowering the pitch thereafter.

For convenience we have shown intonation in later units by horizontal lines whose relative height above the line of type represents the height of the pitch. For Spanish it is sufficient to recognize three heights—high, middle, and low. The horizontal lines are connected by vertical ones to show phrasing, and slant lines are used to show pitch that glides up or down. For example:

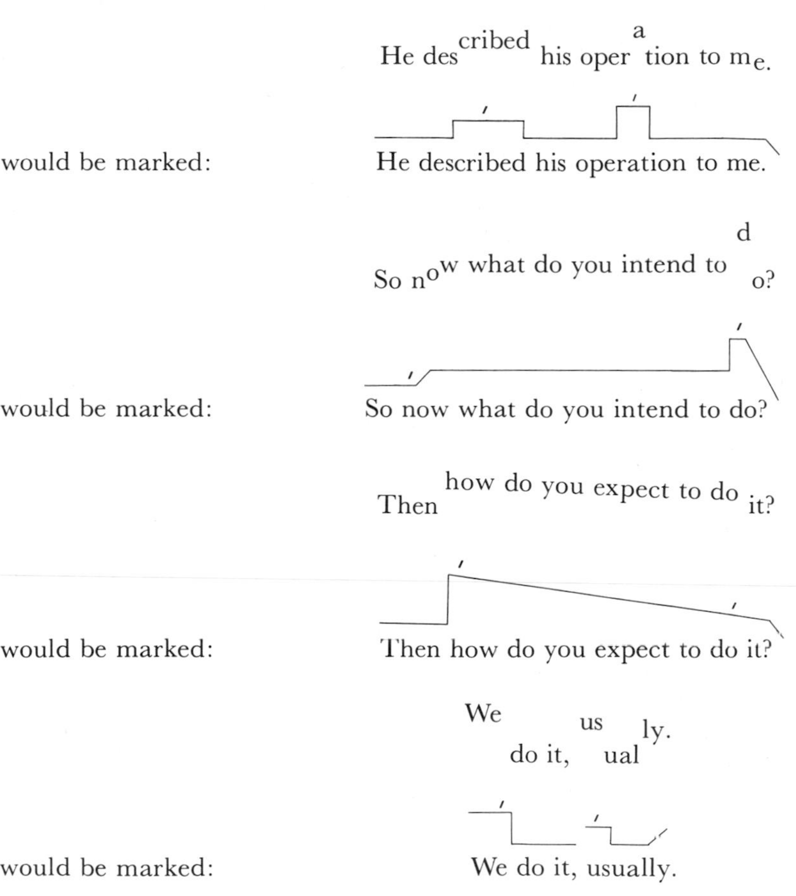

Description of sounds

In this section and in special pronunciation exercises within the next ten units of the book it will be necessary to refer to specific speech sounds. Unfortunately, the letters of the alphabet, whether Spanish or English letters, are not altogether adequate for this purpose, since they often either blur important distinctions in pronunciation or make spelling distinctions which do not exist in pronunciation. Furthermore, since the correspondences between sound and spelling in Spanish are different from those in English, it is best to refer to sounds by means of a system that is both unambiguous and economical. This section will serve as a useful reference guide for later work on specific pronunciation problems.

While each of the distinctive sounds of a language has its own peculiarities, most of them can be put into certain groups that share a family resemblance. Families of sounds are best described in terms of PLACE, where they are produced; MANNER, how they are produced; and VOICE, whether or not the vocal cords are vibrating. This threefold system of description is needed mainly for consonants; all vowels may be described simply by reference to place, as we shall observe shortly.

PLACE

Study Diagram 1 and learn the positions of the speech organs and the terms that refer to the sounds produced at each position:

(1) BILABIAL, involving both lips—for example, [p];
(2) LABIODENTAL, involving the lower lip and upper teeth, as in [f];
(3) DENTAL, involving the tongue tip and upper teeth, as in [t];
(4) ALVEOLAR, involving the gum ridge directly back of the upper front teeth—for instance, [s];
(5) PALATAL, involving the tongue blade and palate, as in [y]; and
(6) VELAR, involving the back of the tongue and the velum (soft palate), as in [k].

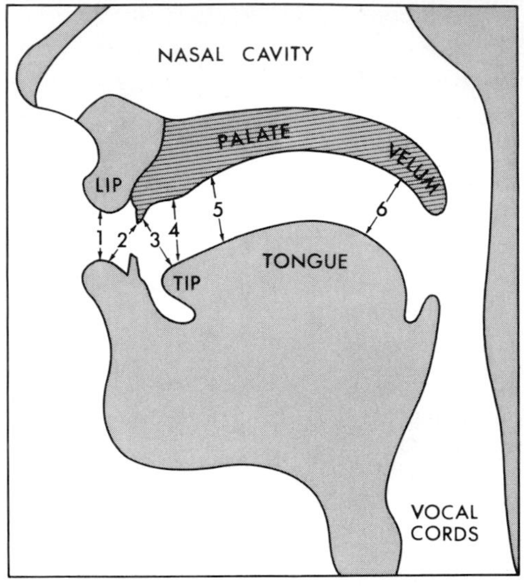

DIAGRAM 1

MANNER

In addition to specifying which portions of the speech organs are used to produce a particular sound, it is necessary to describe how those organs interact with the air used to produce the sound. The names that classify sounds in terms of manner suggest this interaction: (1) STOP, in which the flow of air is momentarily halted from passing through the mouth and then released, such as [p]; (2) SPIRANT, in which the flow of air is squeezed or only partially stopped—for instance, *th* of *they;* (3) FRICATIVE, in which the escaping air is heard with a noticeable friction noise, such as [f]; (4) NASAL, in which the air escapes not through the mouth but through the nose—[m], for example; (5) LATERAL, in which the air escapes around the edges of the tongue, such as [l]; (6) TRILL, in which the tongue vibrates rapidly against the alveolar ridge (trills are not used in American English); (7) TAP, in which the tip of the tongue only momentarily strikes the roof of the mouth, such as the consonant sound in the middle of *butter.*

VOICE

The factor of voice (vocal cord vibration) plays a major role in all speech that is not a whisper. In normal speech, voice occurs with all the vowels and with some of the consonants: with the sound [m], for example, and the sound [z], but not with [f] or [s]. We thus have *voiced* consonants and *voiceless* consonants. (In order to hear the contrast between voicing and voicelessness, pronounce these sounds with your hands covering your ears.)

PHONEMES AND ALLOPHONES

Now refer to Diagram 2, which categorizes the sounds of Spanish. Do not be alarmed by the odd-looking symbols. This is not the writing alphabet of Spanish but only a set of symbols selected to represent its sounds. Note the boxes around certain groups of sounds, [s] and [z], for example. Within each box the sounds are different; they are indicated by the "same" letter, but which specific sound we use is determined by where the sound occurs in a word or phrase. A particular grouping is referred to as a *phoneme,* designated by / /, and the specific sounds are called *allophones,* designated by [ ]. So Spanish [s] and [z] are allophones of the phoneme /s/, with [z] used directly before a voiced consonant and [s] elsewhere.

The Sounds of Spanish

PHONEMES AND ALLOPHONES

	PLACE											
	Bilabial		*Labiodental*		*Dental*		*Alveolar*		*Palatal*		*Velar*	
	voice-less	*voiced*	*voice-less*	*voiced*	*voice-less*	*voiced*	*voice-less*	*voiced*	*voice-less*	*voiced*	*voice-less*	*voiced*
Consonants												
MANNER: Stop	p	b			t	d			č		k	g
Spirant		ƀ				đ						ǥ
Fricative			f				s	z			x	
Nasal		m				n		n		ñ		ŋ
Lateral								l				
Trill								rr				
Tap								r				
Semiconsonants										y		w

Vowels	*Front*	*Central*	*Back*
High	i		u
Mid	e		o
Low		a	

DIAGRAM 2

Practice using Diagram 2 by locating the *voiced bilabial stop* [b]. Now locate the following consonant sounds: *voiced palatal nasal* [ñ], *voiceless labiodental fricative* [f], and *voiceless dental stop* [t].

As for the classification of vowels in Spanish, they are specified by tongue height (*high, mid,* or *low*) and by whether the position of the arched portion of the tongue is front (nearer the palatal region), back (nearer the velar region), or *central* (between the two). Thus /e/ is the *mid-front* vowel phoneme and /a/ is the *low-central* one. The semiconsonants /y/ and /w/, related to the vowels, occur directly before or directly after vowels.

Distinctive sounds in Spanish

Some Spanish sounds are enough like English sounds to be rather easily understood and pronounced, but some are not. The most important of these are covered here and reviewed in later chapters.

VOWELS

Listen to the following Spanish-English pairs as they are pronounced by your instructor or by the voice on the tape. How would you describe the main difference in pronunciation of each pair?

mi (*my*)	me
tú (*you*)	too
de (*of, from*)	day
me (*to me*)	may
no	know

The words in each pair are somewhat similar in their pronunciation, but the significant difference is that while in Spanish simple vowel sounds are used, English uses diphthongs (a vowel sound followed by a glide). Listen again as the contrasts from the two languages are pronounced somewhat slowly to emphasize the difference.

In English if a syllable does not end in a consonant we normally turn the vowel into a diphthong. Thus we may have *met* (with a simple vowel) or *mate* (with a diphthong) in a word that ends in a /t/. But removing the /t/ from *mate* produces *may,* while removing the /t/ from *met* produces a non-English form. The deeply ingrained habit of turning a final vowel into a diphthong will make the correct Spanish pronunciation difficult for you. It may even sound a bit strange until you become accustomed to it. Now repeat the Spanish words above, exerting special effort not to add a glide to the vowels. It might be helpful to use a mirror for this exercise in order to prevent movement of the jaw, lips, and tongue, all of which are in motion for English diphthongs. Remember that individual Spanish vowels are simple vowels, not glided diphthongs.

STOPS

This is a family of sounds represented by the symbols /p, t, k/. As their name implies, they are formed by briefly stopping the air from passing through the mouth, but the obstruction is quickly removed and the air is then suddenly released. These sounds are voiceless, since the vocal cords are not vibrating during their production. There are certain features of Spanish stops which are unlike English and which you must learn to reproduce for basic competence in your pronunciation.

Listen to this series of contrasting pairs and notice the difference between the initial sounds in each pair:

polo (*polo*)	polo
tú (*you*)	too
qué (*what*)	Kay

All three of the English sounds /p, t, k/ are accompanied by a puff of air, enough to blow out a lighted match or move a sheet of paper held near the lips. In Spanish the sound is unaspirated. The aspiration that occurs after initial stops is automatic in English; it is part of our phonological system. It is therefore a difficult habit to break in acquiring a Spanish accent.

The other major feature which is unlike English is the position of the tongue for /t/. In Spanish this is a dental sound, made with the tip of the tongue against the inner surface of the upper front teeth rather than farther back on the alveolar ridge as in English.

Listen now to the stop sounds contrasted in the following English phrases:

/p/	Fill a pail	Philip Ayle
/t/	See Ted	Seat Ed
/k/	See Candy	Seek Andy

Since /p, t, k/ in the second column lack aspiration (because they come at the end rather than at the beginning of a syllable), these stop sounds are like their Spanish counterparts. The important distinction between Spanish and English here is that the Spanish stops are never aspirated, even at the beginning of words.

Practice these unaspirated sounds in **polo, tú,** and **qué.** Make certain that /t/ is pronounced with the tongue against the upper teeth.

The sound /k/ is spelled either **c** (as in **con** *with*), **qu** (as in **qué** *what*), or occasionally **k** (as in **kilo** *kilogram*).

STOP-SPIRANTS

This family carries a double label because the sounds occur in two varieties according to their surroundings. There are three, /b, d, g/, and in their stop variety they are simply the voiced counterparts of the three voiceless stops /p, t, k/. This means that Spanish /d/, like /t/, is made with the tip of the tongue on the inner surface of the upper front teeth rather than farther back as in English. The symbols [b, d, g] are used for the stop variety of this family.

Pronounce the voiced stops [b, d, g] in the words **bien, días,** and **gracias.** Make sure that [d] is pronounced with the tongue against the upper teeth.

The spirant variety of the stop-spirant family, [ƀ, đ, ǥ], is more frequent and occurs whenever any one of these sounds is between vowels. This variety is the same as the first except that the obstruction that stops the air is incomplete, with the result that a certain amount of air keeps coming through. The symbols [ƀ, đ, ǥ] are used for these sounds, not ordinarily heard in English.

Listen to the following paired groups of words and phrases taken from the **Frases útiles** and notice the difference between the two varieties of /b, d, g/ in the two columns.

/b/	**bien, Vásquez**	**se va, me voy**
/d/	**días, de**	**se dice, nada**
/g/	**gracias, tengo**	**mucho gusto, igualmente**

In the second column, the sounds /b, d, g/ occur between vowels and are produced as spirants [ƀ, đ, ǥ]. [Remember that / / designates the sound-unit (phoneme), whereas the symbol [ ] designates the particular variant that occurs in a given environment (allophone).]

Practice the distinction between [b, d, g] and [ƀ, đ, ǥ] using the phrases above.

The sound /b/ (referring to both [b] and [ƀ]) is spelled **b** in some words and **v** in others. The sound /g/ is **g** (as in **gas** *gas,* **gusto** *pleasure*) or **gu** (as in **guerra** *war,* **guía** *guide*), depending on what follows.

FRICATIVE /x/

Set your tongue in position to pronounce the English sound /k/. Now release your tongue very slightly, allowing some air to pass. This is the sound of the Spanish fricative /x/. In many dialects, Spanish /x/ is quite relaxed, resembling English /h/ without any appreciable friction noise.

The sound /x/ is spelled **j** (anywhere, as in **jefe** *boss,* **justicia** *justice*) or **g** (before **e** or **i,** as in **general** *general,* **gigante** *giant*).[5]

PALATALS

The Spanish sound /y/ is somewhat different from its English counterparts. As a semiconsonant it is pronounced tensely, with a hint of the buzzing sound in the English words *measure, leisure,* and *vision.* It is spelled **y** (as in **ya** *already*) and **ll** (as in **valle** *valley*).

Spanish /ñ/ is pronounced something like the *ny* of *canyon.* Try to say *–nyon* as a single syllable, holding the tip of the tongue against the lower teeth.

Practice the palatal sounds /y/ and /ñ/ in the phrase **la señora Villegas.**

THE SOUNDS /r/ AND /rr/

The sound /r/ in Spanish is similar to a sound that is common in American English as a variant of English /t/ or /d/ between vowels when word stress precedes; speakers who make the words *latter* and *ladder* or *kitty* and *kiddy* sound the same use this variant. The tip of the tongue is flapped up against the front of the roof of the mouth, producing a brief, unprolongable tap.

Listen to the Spanish word **aro** (*hoop*) and the English word *Otto* spoken by someone who uses this American English variety of /t/. Notice the quick tapping of the tongue in both. Listen also for the similarity between the Spanish word **tarde** (*late*) and the English nonsense phrase *totter they* pronounced rapidly.

Practice the tapped /r/, pronouncing the Spanish words **señorita, señora, quiero, señor, puerta,** and **permiso.**

The sound /rr/ is a trill consisting of a succession of two or more /r/-like taps, a sound comparable to a little boy's simulation of the noise of a racing car. American English has no speech sound produced in this manner, but speakers who use the tapped variety of /t, d/ in English can produce a vaguely similar analogy by pronouncing rapidly the nonsense English word *petter-o* as a step to saying the Spanish word **perro** (*dog*).

Practice pronouncing /rr/ in the Spanish words **cierre** and **Raimundo.**

The spelling of /rr/ is **r** at the beginning of words and **rr** between vowels.

DIPHTHONGS

As emphasized earlier under the discussion of vowels, it is extremely important to pronounce simple Spanish vowels without a following glide. However, diphthongs are very frequent in Spanish; they are connected sounds consisting of a vowel plus /w/ or /y/.[6] (The /w/ is more firmly rounded than in English; the /y/ has a high-front tongue position but is without the friction described above for /y/.) The automatic result of attaching them to a vowel is that they give the overall effect of a glide in which the /w/ and /y/ elements do not lose any of their identity. English glides tend to be lax:

[5] However, in America **x** is preferred to **j** in the spelling of the words **México** and **mexicano.**

[6] The /w/ or /y/ may either precede or follow a vowel in a diphthong. When it *follows,* the diphthong is quite unlike English; only this type of diphthong will be discussed here.

the tongue moves toward the position of /w/ or /y/ but only part of the way. The Spanish glides are more tensely pronounced, and the tongue goes almost all the way to the position of /w/ or /y/.

Listen to the Spanish word **soy** (*I am*) and the English word *soy* and notice how much higher, how much closer to /i/, the tongue moves in the Spanish word. Notice this same difference as you listen to the following pairs: **grey** (*flock*) and *grey,* **ley** (*law*) and *lay,* **vaivén** (*wavering*) and *buy Ben,* **laude** (*tombstone*) and *loud.* Listen to the glide in **deuda** (*debt*) and **Europa** and note that English has no parallel.

Say the Spanish words **Freitas** and **Aurelio.**

The /w/ of the diphthong is always spelled **u** (**miau** *meow*), but the /y/ is spelled **i** in the interior of words (**baile** *dance*) and **y** at the end of a word (**ley, soy**).

Buenos Aires: Avenida 9 de Julio

UNIT 2

Cecilia's Family

P. *Pablo* M. *Julio's mother* J. *Julio, Pablo's friend* B. *Betty* C. *Cecilia, Julio's sister* S. *Susana*

P. Good afternoon, Doña Mercedes. Is Julio in?

M. Yes, he must be in the kitchen or in the patio. Julio, Pablo's here!

J. Come on in, Pablo! I'm in here, in my room.

P. Excuse me, ma'am.

M. Of course.

* * *

P. Who are the two girls [who are] in the living room?

La familia de Cecilia

P. *Pablo* M. *Madre de Julio* J. *Julio, amigo de Pablo* B. *Betty* C. *Cecilia, hermana de Julio* S. *Susana*

P. Buenas tardes, doña (1) Mercedes. ¿Está Julio?

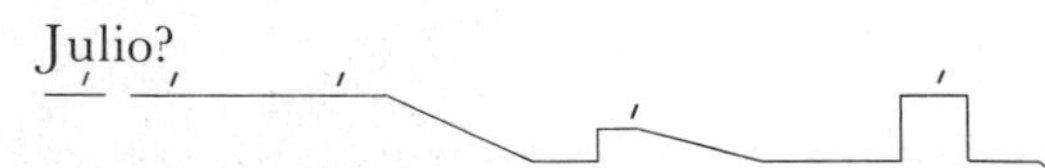

M. Sí, debe estar en la cocina o en el patio. ¡Julio, aquí está Pablo!

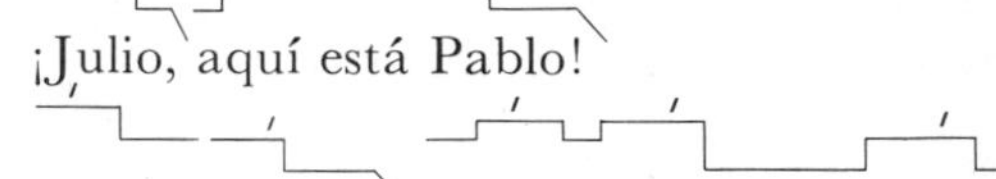

J. ¡Entra, Pablo! Estoy aquí, en mi cuarto.

P. Con permiso, señora.

M. Cómo no.

* * *

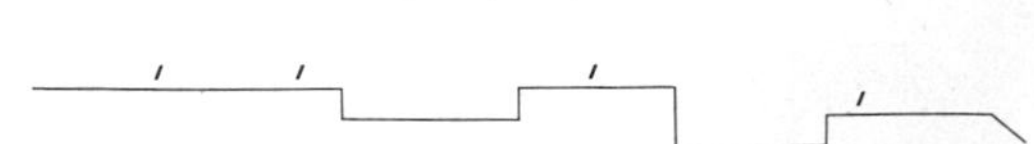

P. ¿Quiénes son las dos chicas que están en la sala?

Paipa, Colombia:
Colonial house

J. A couple of my sister's schoolmates [companions of school of my sister]. Why? Do you like them [they appeal to you]?

J. Compañeras de escuela de mi hermana.

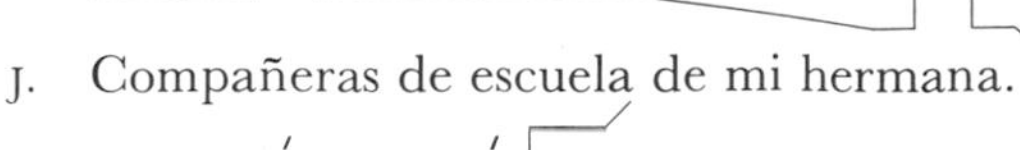

¿Por qué? ¿Te gustan?

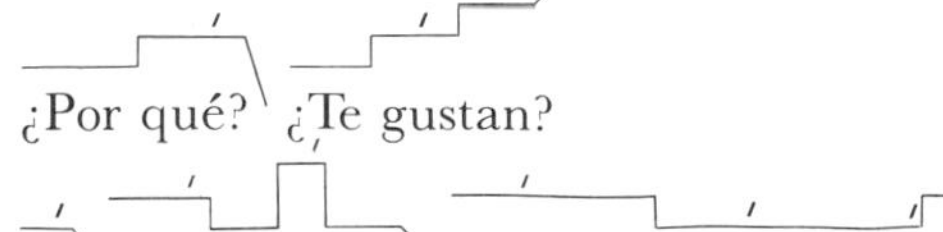

P. Yes, they're really [how] pretty! You [are] a friend of theirs [them]?

P. Sí, ¡qué bonitas! ¿Tú eres amigo de ellas?

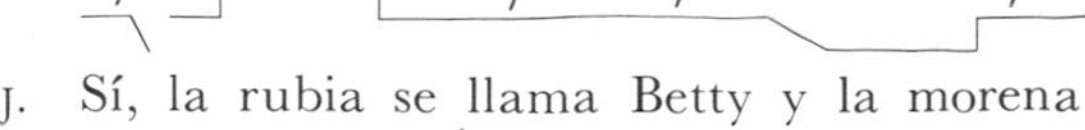

J. Yes, the blonde's name is [calls herself] Betty, and the brunette's Susana. They're cousins.

J. Sí, la rubia se llama Betty y la morena Susana. Son primas.

P. Where are they from?

P. ¿De dónde son?

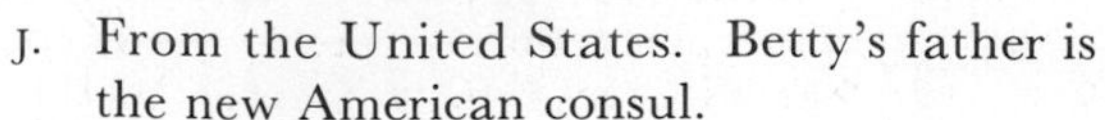

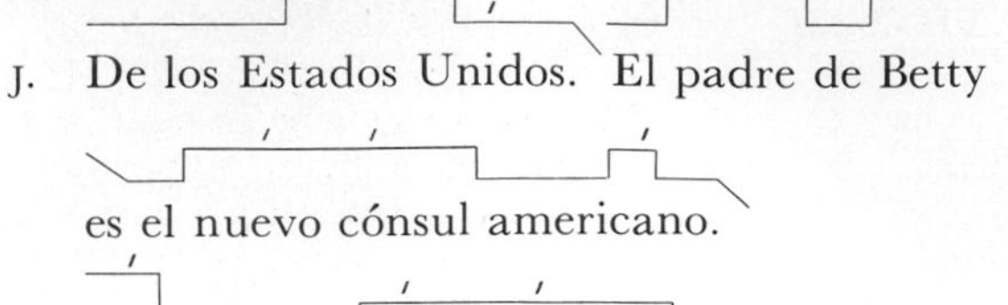

J. From the United States. Betty's father is the new American consul.

J. De los Estados Unidos. El padre de Betty es el nuevo cónsul americano.

P. Too bad I don't speak English.

P. Lástima que yo no hablo inglés.

J. You don't need to know any English; they speak [know] Spanish perfectly.

J. No necesitas saber inglés; ellas saben español perfectamente.

P. Then, what are we waiting for? Let's go talk to [with] them first. We'll study later.

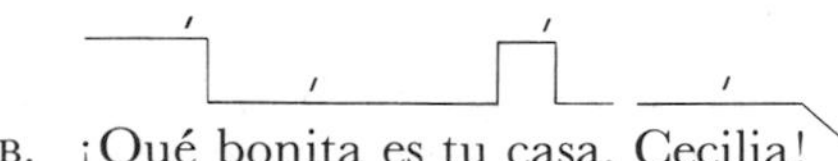

P. Entonces, ¿qué esperamos? Vamos a hablar con ellas primero. Después estudiamos.

* * *

B. Your house is so nice [How pretty your house is], Cecilia.

B. ¡Qué bonita es tu casa, Cecilia!

C. Thanks, you're very kind.

C. Gracias, eres muy amable.

S. And so [how] big, too.

S. Y qué grande también.

C. It's because we're a big family [many]: Dad, Mom, ten children, my grandmother, and an aunt.

C. Es que somos muchos: papá, mamá, diez hijos, mi abuela y una tía.

B. Fourteen altogether! That many! You have nine brothers and sisters?

B. ¡Catorce en total! ¡Tantos! ¿Tú tienes nueve hermanos?

C. Yes, five brothers and four sisters. I'm the youngest.

C. Sí, cinco hermanos y cuatro hermanas. Yo soy la menor.

S. My gosh! What a family!

S. ¡Dios mío! (2) ¡Qué familia!

cultural notes

(1) **Doña,** from Latin *domina* 'mistress,' is a title of respect used with the given name of a woman, generally one who is married, older, or distinguished. As a form of address **doña** with the given name is a common substitute for **señora** (*Mrs.*) with the family name; e.g., Mrs. Mercedes López might be addressed as **doña Mercedes** or as **señora López.** This title, once reserved for the upper strata of society, has come to be used in some regions of Spain and America to address any woman of a certain age and social position, while elsewhere it may be used for women of all classes.

(2) The use of sacred words in exclamations, such as **Dios, Jesús,** and **María,** is common even among women and does not imply profanity as the English equivalents might.

Introductory Note to the Student

The drills in this book are designed for oral recitation in class with books closed. This closed-book performance is the goal toward which you must work in all preparation outside class. You can best prepare yourself for recitation by doing the drills in the language laboratory without referring to the text. Tape recordings have been made for this purpose. If no laboratory is available, use the written directions in the text; but when you do this, cover any answers that may be there. Always remember that your goal is to be able to perform the drills easily with the book closed.

A few simple direction words will be used to cue the drill procedures. Some of these are:

ADDRESSING ONE STUDENT	ADDRESSING MORE THAN ONE STUDENT	
repita	**repitan**	*repeat*
conteste	**contesten**	*answer*
traduzca	**traduzcan**	*translate*
cambie	**cambien**	*change*
escuche	**escuchen**	*listen*

Some additional words, such as **palabra** *word,* and some references to grammatical categories, for example, **singular** *singular,* **plural** *plural,* will be needed. As other terms are needed they will be introduced.

The drills will move fast. Answers should be given without hesitation, and preparation is not complete until this can be done. If the basic dialogs have been properly memorized, the drills should be done very easily.

› PRONUNCIATION EXERCISE (Reread "Rhythm" in Unit I, Section I, "The Sounds of Spanish.")

Minimal vowel contrasts in unstressed syllables. INSTRUCTIONS: The teacher will read the following pairs of words. The student will repeat them just as he hears them.

/a/	/e/	/a/	/i/	/a/	/o/	/a/	/u/
mesas	meses	pañal	piñal	cara	caro	lagar	lugar
sobras	sobres	matad	mitad	habla	hablo	pajar	pujar
marcado	mercado	pasar	pisar	derecha	derecho	cañada	cuñada
preguntas	preguntes	charlar	chirlar	esposas	esposos	sabido	subido
españolas	españoles	paquete	piquete	hermanas	hermanos	palidez	pulidez

/e/	/i/	/e/	/o/	/e/	/u/
pecar	picar	deje	dejo	lechar	luchar
pesar	pisar	vine	vino	legar	lugar
remar	rimar	hable	hablo	temor	tumor
rezar	rizar	leche	lecho	pechero	puchero
pesada	pisada	quiere	quiero	retina	rutina

/i/	/o/	/i/	/u/	/o/	/u/
mirar	morar	ligar	lugar	bocal	bucal
timó	tomó	mirar	murar	morar	murar
imito	omito	birlar	burlar	plomero	plumero
mirada	morada	pintar	puntar	motilar	mutilar
pisada	posada	pidiendo	pudiendo	acosar	acusar

All the above pairs involve minimal vowel contrasts in unstressed syllables. You have noticed that two words may be differentiated in Spanish by an unstressed vowel. Since this feature is not characteristic of English, it is important that you develop the habit of saying the Spanish vowels clearly. Slurring the vowels or reducing them to the schwa sound may distort the meaning.

2 Subject pronouns

EXAMPLES

1. **Yo** soy la menor.
2. ¿**Tú** eres amigo de ellas?
3. ¿**Usted** es amigo de ellas?
4. Pasen **ustedes.** *Come in.*
5. **Ellas** saben español perfectamente.

SINGULAR		PLURAL	
I	**yo**	we	**nosotros** (**nosotras,** *feminine*)
you you	**tú** **usted**	you	**ustedes**
he she	**él** **ella**	they	**ellos** (**ellas,** *feminine*)

› **DISCUSSION**

In the singular there are two equivalents of *you,* **usted** and **tú,** which call for different forms of the verb (see the conjugations of **ser** and **hablar** below). **Usted** is used when the speaker is on terms equivalent to "Mr.," "Mrs.," or "Miss" with a person: *You, Mr. Gómez, sit here* **Usted, señor Gómez, siéntese aquí. Tú** may be used when the speaker is on an intimate footing with his hearer, beginning at approximately the point at which in English he begins to address the person by his first name: *You, Juan, sit here* **Tú, Juan, siéntate aquí.** In the plural, however, no distinction is made by Spanish-American speakers, and **ustedes** serves for both.[1]

Gender is distinguished in **él** and **ella, ellos** and **ellas,** and **nosotros** and **nosotras. Ellos** and **nosotros** refer either to male beings alone or to a mixed group. Many nouns behave similarly: **alumnos,** either *men students* or *men and women students;* **hermanos,** either *brothers* or *brother(s) and sister(s).*

[1] English at one time had this same distinction between intimate *thou* and formal *you.* In Spain the distinction between intimate and formal applies to the plural as well as to the singular, with **vosotros,–as** as opposed to **ustedes.** While these forms are not treated in the grammar sections of this book, the entire set of **vosotros** verb forms appears in the Appendix, immediately following Unit 24.

Present tense[2] forms of *ser*, to be

EXAMPLES

1. Yo **soy** la menor.
2. **Eres** muy amable.
3. El padre de Betty **es** el cónsul.
4. **Somos** muchos.
5. ¿Quiénes **son** las dos chicas?

ser *to be*			
yo	soy	nosotros,-as	somos
tú	eres		
usted él ella Cecilia	es	ustedes ellos,-as Betty y Susana	son

The present tense of **ser** is irregular. Each form must be learned separately. The subject pronouns are not required except for emphasis.

PERSON-NUMBER SUBSTITUTION DRILL

INSTRUCTIONS: The teacher will say the model sentence and ask a student to repeat it. Then the teacher will give a word to be substituted for a word in that sentence. If the student has any difficulty in making the new sentence, the teacher should prompt, using a stage whisper. The students' books are closed during class recitation.

	TEACHER	STUDENT
A.	1. *Ellos* son de los Estados Unidos. *Repita.*	**Ellos son de los Estados Unidos.**
	2. El ________	El es de los Estados Unidos.
	3. Yo ________	Yo soy de los Estados Unidos.
	4. Ustedes ________	Ustedes son de los Estados Unidos.
	5. Susana y yo ________	Susana y yo somos de los Estados Unidos.
	6. Tú ________	Tú eres de los Estados Unidos.
	7. El señor Martínez ________	El señor Martínez es de los Estados Unidos.
	8. Ellas ________	Ellas son de los Estados Unidos.
B.	1. ¿De dónde son *ellos?* *Repita.*	**¿De dónde son ellos?**
	2. ________ él	¿De dónde es él?
	3. ________ ustedes	¿De dónde son ustedes?
	4. ________ usted	¿De dónde es usted?
	5. ________ ellas	¿De dónde son ellas?
	6. ________ tú	¿De dónde eres tú?
	7. ________ Pablo	¿De dónde es Pablo?
	8. ________ Pablo y Julio	¿De dónde son Pablo y Julio?
	9. ________ la señora de Arjona	¿De dónde es la señora de Arjona?
	10. ________ nosotros	¿De dónde somos nosotros?

[2] The term *tense* as used here covers all those changes in the verb that relate to time and aspect (how the action is viewed) and includes the constructions that are usually referred to as compound tenses. Examples of various tenses in English are: *he works* (present), *he worked* (past), *he will work* (future), *he has worked* (present perfect).

PATTERNED RESPONSE DRILL

INSTRUCTIONS: The teacher will ask questions and prompt the answers that fit the student's status. Only one of several possible answers is given for each question.

	TEACHER	STUDENT
A.	1. ¿Qué es usted, americano? *Conteste.*	**Sí, yo soy americano.**
	2. ¿Qué son ustedes, americanos?	Sí, nosotros somos americanos.
	3. ¿Qué es él, americano?	Sí, él es americano.
	4. ¿Qué eres tú, americano?	Sí, yo soy americano.
	5. ¿Qué son ellos, americanos?	Sí, ellos son americanos.
	6. ¿Qué son ellas, americanas?	Sí, ellas son americanas.
	7. ¿Qué soy yo, americano?	Sí, usted es americano.
	8. ¿Qué somos Jaime y yo, americanos?	Sí, ustedes son americanos.
B.	1. ¿De dónde es usted? *Conteste.*	**¿Yo? Soy de los Estados Unidos.**
	2. ¿De dónde es ella?	¿Ella? Es de los Estados Unidos.
	3. ¿De dónde eres tú?	¿Yo? Soy de los Estados Unidos.
	4. ¿De dónde son ellas?	¿Ellas? Son de los Estados Unidos.
	5. ¿De dónde son ustedes?	¿Nosotros? Somos de los Estados Unidos.
	6. ¿De dónde es él?	¿El? Es de los Estados Unidos.
C.	1. ¿Es usted morena o rubia? *Conteste.*	**Yo soy rubia.**
	2. ¿Soy yo moreno o rubio?	Usted es rubio.
	3. ¿Es ella rubia o morena?	Ella es morena.
	4. ¿Eres tú rubio o moreno?	Yo soy moreno.
	5. ¿Son ustedes primos o amigos?	Nosotros somos amigos.
	6. ¿Son ellas primas o amigas?	Ellas son amigas.
	7. ¿Somos Julio y yo primos o amigos?	Ustedes son amigos.
	8. ¿Son ellos hermanos o compañeros de escuela?	Ellos son compañeros de escuela.
	9. ¿Son ustedes hermanos o compañeros de escuela?	Nosotros somos compañeros de escuela.
D.	1. ¿Cómo es ella, morena? *Conteste.*	**Sí, ella es morena.**
	2. ¿Cómo es él, moreno?	Sí, él es moreno.
	3. ¿Cómo es ella, rubia?	Sí, ella es rubia.
	4. ¿Qué son ellos, amigos?	Sí, ellos son amigos.
	5. ¿Qué son ustedes, amigos?	Sí, nosotros somos amigos.
	6. ¿Qué son ellas, primas?	Sí, ellas son primas.
	7. ¿Qué son ustedes, compañeros de escuela?	Sí, nosotros somos compañeros de escuela.
	8. ¿Qué soy yo, profesor?	Sí, usted es profesor.
	9. ¿Qué son ustedes, alumnos?	Sí, nosotros somos alumnos.

DISCUSSION

Verb endings carry more information in Spanish than in English. Thus, in **Nosotros hablamos** we can omit the **nosotros** and still know that *we* is understood as the subject; but if *we* is omitted in *We speak,* all reference to *we* is lost.

In English, however, there are two ways of PRONOUNCING the subject pronouns, depending on whether they are used merely for reference or for emphasis. This can be seen most clearly with the pronoun *he.* When we use it just for meaning we not only de-emphasize it (give it no accent, no stress) but even, most of the time, drop the /h/; listen to the tape recording of *Why didn't* ***he*** *do it? Because 'e didn't want to.* The other subject pronouns do not drop their consonant, but the same de-emphasis can occur; listen to the recording of *Why didn't* ***they*** *do it? Because they didn't want to.* If for any reason—contrast, clarity, or whatever—the pronoun has to be highlighted, the resulting emphasis causes it to be pronounced distinctly (including restoration of the /h/ of *he*). Listen to the tape recording of *They* (a married couple) *didn't go to the movies because he didn't want to,* appearing first with full *he* as the sense requires and then with *'e;* note that the latter sounds odd.

When English completely de-emphasizes the pronouns, Spanish omits them altogether. When English emphasizes them (to whatever degree), Spanish uses them: **Yo soy la menor** corresponds to *I'm the youngest,* with a slight emphasis on *I'm.* An example is the use of the subject pronouns in Spanish when the subject might otherwise be unclear, as in the ***he*** *didn't want to* example above.

4 Present tense forms of -*ar* verbs

EXAMPLES

1. No **hablo** inglés (from **hablar** *to speak*).
2. No **necesitas** saber inglés (from **necesitar** *to need*).
3. El profesor **llega** a la clase (from **llegar** *to arrive*). *The professor arrives at the class.*
4. ¿Qué **esperamos** (from **esperar** *to wait for*)?
5. Ellos **trabajan** mucho aquí (from **trabajar** *to work*). *They work a lot here.*

hablar *to speak*			
habl-		**habl-**	
yo	**-o**	**nosotros, -as**	**-amos**
tú	**-as**		
usted / él / ella	**-a**	**ustedes / ellos, -as**	**-an**

The present tense of **-ar** verbs is formed by replacing **-ar** with the above endings.[3] The subject pronouns are not required except for emphasis.

› PERSON-NUMBER SUBSTITUTION DRILL

	TEACHER	STUDENT
A. 1.	*Yo* no hablo inglés. *Repita.*	**Yo no hablo inglés.**
2.	Nosotros ________	Nosotros no hablamos inglés.
3.	El ________	El no habla inglés.
4.	Ellas ________	Ellas no hablan inglés.
5.	Usted ________	Usted no habla inglés.
6.	Usted y yo ________	Usted y yo no hablamos inglés.
7.	La señorita Flores ________	La señorita Flores no habla inglés.
8.	Ustedes ________	Ustedes no hablan inglés.
9.	Tú ________	Tú no hablas inglés.
10.	Mi abuela ________	Mi abuela no habla inglés.
11.	Pablo y Julio ________	Pablo y Julio no hablan inglés.
12.	Ella ________	Ella no habla inglés.

[3]These verb forms appear in the Appendix under "Regular Verbs."

TEACHER	STUDENT
B. 1. No necesitas saber inglés. *Repita.*	**No necesitas saber inglés.**
2. (usted) ________	No necesita saber inglés.
3. (nosotros) ________	No necesitamos saber inglés.
4. (él) ________	No necesita saber inglés.
5. (ellos) ________	No necesitan saber inglés.
6. (el profesor) ________	No necesita saber inglés.
7. (yo) ________	No necesito saber inglés.
8. (ella) ________	No necesita saber inglés.
9. (nosotras) ________	No necesitamos saber inglés.
10. (ellas) ________	No necesitan saber inglés.
C. 1. *Pablo* llega a la clase. *Repita.*	**Pablo llega a la clase.**
2. Yo ________	Yo llego a la clase.
3. Tú ________	Tú llegas a la clase.
4. Nosotros ________	Nosotros llegamos a la clase.
5. Ellas ________	Ellas llegan a la clase.
6. Usted ________	Usted llega a la clase.
7. Pablo y yo ________	Pablo y yo llegamos a la clase.
8. Ellos ________	Ellos llegan a la clase.
9. El padre de Betty ________	El padre de Betty llega a la clase.
D. 1. *Yo* trabajo mucho aquí. *Repita.*	**Yo trabajo mucho aquí.**
2. El ________	El trabaja mucho aquí.
3. Nosotros ________	Nosotros trabajamos mucho aquí.
4. Pablo ________	Pablo trabaja mucho aquí.
5. Tú ________	Tú trabajas mucho aquí.
6. El y yo ________	El y yo trabajamos mucho aquí.
7. Ellos ________	Ellos trabajan mucho aquí.
8. Nosotras ________	Nosotras trabajamos mucho aquí.
9. El cónsul ________	El cónsul trabaja mucho aquí.
E. 1. ¿Qué esperamos? *Repita.*	**¿Qué esperamos?**
2. (usted) ________	¿Qué espera?
3. (yo) ________	¿Qué espero?
4. (ellas) ________	¿Qué esperan?
5. (usted y él) ________	¿Qué esperan?
6. (ella) ________	¿Qué espera?
7. (ustedes) ________	¿Qué esperan?
8. (nosotras) ________	¿Qué esperamos?
9. (él) ________	¿Qué espera?
F. 1. Después estudiamos. *Repita.*	**Después estudiamos.**
2. (yo) ________	Después estudio.
3. (usted) ________	Después estudia.
4. (ustedes) ________	Después estudian.
5. (él) ________	Después estudia.
6. (nosotros) ________	Después estudiamos.
7. (tú) ________	Después estudias.
8. (ellos) ________	Después estudian.

PATTERNED RESPONSE DRILL

INSTRUCTIONS: The teacher will ask the question and prompt the answer.

	TEACHER	STUDENT
A.	1. ¿Qué estudia usted? *Conteste.*	**Estudio español.**
	2. ¿Qué estudia ella?	Estudia español.
	3. ¿Qué estudian ellos?	Estudian español.
	4. ¿Qué estudias tú?	Estudio español.
	5. ¿Qué estudian ustedes?	Estudiamos español.
	6. ¿Qué estudia Jaime?	Estudia español.
	7. ¿Qué estudian las chicas?	Estudian español.
B.	1. ¿Qué hablamos nosotros en la clase? *Conteste.*	**Hablamos español.**
	2. ¿Qué hablan ellos en la clase?	Hablan español.
	3. ¿Qué habla usted en la clase?	Hablo español.
	4. ¿Qué hablamos él y yo en la clase?	Hablan español.
	5. ¿Qué habla ella en la clase?	Habla español.
	6. ¿Qué hablas tú en la clase?	Hablo español.
	7. ¿Qué habla el profesor en la clase?	Habla español.
	8. ¿Qué hablan los alumnos en la clase?	Hablan español.
C.	1. ¿Dónde trabaja él? *Conteste.*	**Trabaja aquí.**
	2. ¿Dónde trabaja usted?	Trabajo aquí.
	3. ¿Dónde trabajan ustedes?	Trabajamos aquí.
	4. ¿Dónde trabajamos ella y yo?	Trabajan aquí.
	5. ¿Dónde trabajas tú?	Trabajo aquí.
	6. ¿Dónde trabajan ellos?	Trabajan aquí.
	7. ¿Dónde trabajan las señoritas?	Trabajan aquí.
	8. ¿Dónde trabaja Susana?	Trabaja aquí.
D.	1. ¿Qué necesita saber el cónsul? *Conteste.*	**Necesita saber inglés.**
	2. ¿Qué necesitan saber los profesores?	Necesitan saber inglés.
	3. ¿Qué necesita saber la señora?	Necesita saber inglés.
	4. ¿Qué necesitan saber las alumnas?	Necesitan saber inglés.
	5. ¿Qué necesita saber el señor Arjona?	Necesita saber inglés.
E.	1. ¿Habla ella bien el español o el inglés? *Conteste.*	**Habla bien el inglés.**
	2. ¿Hablan ustedes bien el español o el inglés?	Hablamos bien el inglés.
	3. ¿Hablan ellas bien el español o el inglés?	Hablan bien el inglés.
	4. ¿Habla usted bien el español o el inglés?	Hablo bien el inglés.
	5. ¿Habla Susana bien el español o el inglés?	Habla bien el inglés.
	6. ¿Hablas tú bien el español o el inglés?	Hablo bien el inglés.
F.	1. ¿Usted trabaja o estudia? *Conteste.*	**Estudio.**
	2. ¿Ustedes trabajan o estudian?	Estudiamos.
	3. ¿Ellos trabajan o estudian?	Estudian.
	4. ¿Tú trabajas o estudias?	Estudio.
	5. ¿Ellos trabajan o estudian?	Estudian.
	6. ¿El trabaja o estudia?	Estudia.

Santiago de Chile: Girl's school

5 Articles, gender of nouns

MASCULINE		FEMININE	
el *the*	el patio el padre el cónsul	la *the*	la familia la cocina la sala
un *a, an* (*one*)	un patio	una *a, an* (*one*)	una tía

MASCULINE FOR MALE	FEMININE FOR FEMALE
abuelo	abuela
alumno	alumna
amigo	amiga
compañero	compañera
chico	chica
hermano	hermana
hijo	hija
primo	prima
tío	tía
profesor	profesora
señor	señora

ITEM SUBSTITUTION DRILL

	TEACHER	STUDENT
A.	1. Estamos con el *cónsul.* *Repita.*	**Estamos con el cónsul.**
	2. ______ hermano	Estamos con el hermano.
	3. ______ papá	Estamos con el papá.
	4. ______ tía	Estamos con la tía.
	5. ______ mamá	Estamos con la mamá.
	6. ______ compañera	Estamos con la compañera.
	7. ______ padre	Estamos con el padre.
	8. ______ señor	Estamos con el señor.
	9. ______ señorita	Estamos con la señorita.
	10. ______ amigo	Estamos con el amigo.
	11. ______ señora	Estamos con la señora.
	12. ______ prima	Estamos con la prima.
	13. ______ abuelo	Estamos con el abuelo.
	14. ______ tío	Estamos con el tío.
	15. ______ alumna	Estamos con la alumna.
B.	1. ¿Tú tienes un *hermano?* *Repita.*	**¿Tú tienes un hermano?**
	2. ______ abuela	¿Tú tienes una abuela?
	3. ______ hermana	¿Tú tienes una hermana?
	4. ______ primo	¿Tú tienes un primo?
	5. ______ hijo	¿Tú tienes un hijo?
	6. ______ hija	¿Tú tienes una hija?
	7. ______ amiga	¿Tú tienes una amiga?
	8. ______ abuelo	¿Tú tienes un abuelo?
	9. ______ alumna	¿Tú tienes una alumna?
	10. ______ profesor	¿Tú tienes un profesor?
	11. ______ profesora	¿Tú tienes una profesora?
	12. ______ clase	¿Tú tienes una clase?
	13. ______ libro	¿Tú tienes un libro?
	14. ______ cuarto	¿Tú tienes un cuarto?
C.	1. La *chica* está en la *sala.* *Repita.*	**La chica está en la sala.**
	2. ______ clase	La chica está en la clase.
	3. __ chico ______	El chico está en la clase.
	4. ______ cuarto	El chico está en el cuarto.
	5. __ chica ______	La chica está en el cuarto.
	6. ______ patio	La chica está en el patio.
	7. __ chico ______	El chico está en el patio.
	8. ______ cocina	El chico está en la cocina.
	9. __ chica ______	La chica está en la cocina.
	10. ______ escuela	La chica está en la escuela.
	11. __ chico ______	El chico está en la escuela.
	12. ______ casa	El chico está en la casa.
	13. __ chica ______	La chica está en la casa.

DISCUSSION

Every noun in Spanish falls into one of two classes traditionally called "masculine" and "feminine." The relatively few nouns that have a sex connotation usually assign masculine gender to male beings and feminine gender to female. Among these nouns with sex connotation are most of the familiar names of relatives and the like; given a masculine word such as **hijo** *son,* it is usually safe to infer a feminine **hija** *daughter,* and vice versa (**tía** *aunt,* **tío** *uncle*).

A large proportion of nouns have endings that indicate their genders. Nouns ending in **-o** and **-or** are almost all masculine, and nouns ending in **-a** are usually feminine. With other nouns it is helpful to learn the article as a reminder of the gender (for example, **la clase** *the class,* **el total** *the total*).

The definite article (equivalent to *the*) is **el** with masculine nouns and **la** with feminine nouns. The indefinite article (equivalent to *a, an*) is **un** with masculine nouns and **una** with feminine nouns. In Spanish the indefinite article is the same as the adjective meaning *one* (just as in English *an* and *one* used to be the same word).

Number: the plural

MASCULINE		FEMININE	
SINGULAR	PLURAL	SINGULAR	PLURAL
el { **estado**, **padre**, **cónsul**	los { **estados**, **padres**, **cónsules**	la { **chica**, **clase**, **pared**[4]	las { **chicas**, **clases**, **paredes**

› **NUMBER SUBSTITUTION DRILL**

TEACHER	STUDENT
1. ¿Tú tienes el *libro?* *Repita.*	**¿Tú tienes el libro?**
Plural.	**¿Tú tienes los libros?**
2. ¿Tú tienes la *casa?* *Repita.*	¿Tú tienes la casa?
Plural.	¿Tú tienes las casas?
3. ¿Tú tienes el *cuarto?* *Repita.*	¿Tú tienes el cuarto?
Plural.	¿Tú tienes los cuartos?
4. ¿Tú tienes la *pluma?* *Repita.*	¿Tú tienes la pluma?
Plural.	¿Tú tienes las plumas?

› **ITEM SUBSTITUTION DRILL**

TEACHER	STUDENT
A. 1. ¿Quiénes son las dos *chicas?* *Repita.*	**¿Quiénes son las dos chicas?**
2. ________ señoras	¿Quiénes son las dos señoras?
3. ________ alumnos	¿Quiénes son los dos alumnos?
4. ________ americanos	¿Quiénes son los dos americanos?
5. ________ profesoras	¿Quiénes son las dos profesoras?
6. ________ cónsules	¿Quiénes son los dos cónsules?
7. ________ señoritas	¿Quiénes son las dos señoritas?
8. ________ señores	¿Quiénes son los dos señores?
9. ________ chicos	¿Quiénes son los dos chicos?
10. ________ compañeras de escuela	¿Quiénes son las dos compañeras de escuela?

[4] **pared** *wall*

TEACHER	STUDENT
B. 1. El *padre* de Betty es de aquí. *Repita.*	**El padre de Betty es de aquí.**
2. — abuela ______________	La abuela de Betty es de aquí.
3. — amigo ______________	El amigo de Betty es de aquí.
4. — compañera ______________	La compañera de Betty es de aquí.
5. — abuelos ______________	Los abuelos de Betty son de aquí.
6. — padres ______________	Los padres de Betty son de aquí.
7. — hermanas ______________	Las hermanas de Betty son de aquí.
8. — amigas ______________	Las amigas de Betty son de aquí.
9. — primos ______________	Los primos de Betty son de aquí.
10. — compañeros ______________	Los compañeros de Betty son de aquí.
11. — hijos ______________	Los hijos de Betty son de aquí.
12. — tías ______________	Las tías de Betty son de aquí.
13. — profesores ______________	Los profesores de Betty son de aquí.

› DISCUSSION

The meanings of singular and plural are the same in Spanish and English: singular = 'one' and plural = 'two or more.'

In Spanish, if the singular of a noun ends in a vowel (**estado, chica, clase**), the plural is formed by adding **-s** (**estados, chicas, clases**). If the singular ends in a consonant (**cónsul, pared**), the plural is formed by adding **-es** (**cónsules, paredes**).

7 Adjectives: agreement with nouns

EXAMPLES

1. El **nuevo** cónsul americano.
2. Los Estados **Unidos.**
3. ¡Qué **bonita** es tu casa!
4. **Buenas** tardes.

SINGULAR	PLURAL
(M) el cuart**o** bonit**o** (*ending* **-o**) (F) la cocin**a** bonit**a** (*ending* **-a**)	(M) los cuart**os** bonit**os** (*ending* **-os**) (F) las cocin**as** bonit**as** (*ending* **-as**)

Adjectives agree in number and gender with the nouns they modify. The majority of adjectives show agreement by the four endings listed above.

› GENDER-NUMBER SUBSTITUTION DRILL

TEACHER	STUDENT
A. 1. ¿La casa? ¡Qué bonita! *Repita.*	**¿La casa? ¡Qué bonita!**
2. ¿El cuarto? ______________	¿El cuarto? ¡Qué bonito!
3. ¿La sala? ______________	¿La sala? ¡Qué bonita!
4. ¿La chica? ______________	¿La chica? ¡Qué bonita!
5. ¿Las primas? ______________	¿Las primas? ¡Qué bonitas!
6. ¿Las morenas? ______________	¿Las morenas? ¡Qué bonitas!
7. ¿Los cuartos? ______________	¿Los cuartos? ¡Qué bonitos!
8. ¿Las rubias? ______________	¿Las rubias? ¡Qué bonitas!
B. 1. ¿El libro? ¡Qué bueno! *Repita.*	**¿El libro? ¡Qué bueno!**
2. ¿La escuela? ______________	¿La escuela? ¡Qué buena!
3. ¿Los lápices? ______________	¿Los lápices? ¡Qué buenos!
4. ¿Las plumas? ______________	¿Las plumas? ¡Qué buenas!

	TEACHER	STUDENT
C. 1.	¿La cocina? ¡Qué nueva! *Repita.*	**¿La cocina? ¡Qué nueva!**
2.	¿El cuarto? ________	¿El cuarto? ¡Qué nuevo!
3.	¿El libro? ________	¿El libro? ¡Qué nuevo!
4.	¿La casa? ________	¿La casa? ¡Qué nueva!
5.	¿Los libros? ________	¿Los libros? ¡Qué nuevos!
6.	¿Las plumas? ________	¿Las plumas? ¡Qué nuevas!
D. 1.	Es *el cónsul* americano. *Repita.*	**Es el cónsul americano.**
2.	__ la prima ________	Es la prima americana.
3.	__ el amigo ________	Es el amigo americano.
4.	__ la escuela ________	Es la escuela americana.
5.	__ los tíos ________	Son los tíos americanos.
6.	__ las chicas ________	Son las chicas americanas.
7.	__ los profesores ________	Son los profesores americanos.
8.	__ las señoras ________	Son las señoras americanas.
9.	__ los primos ________	Son los primos americanos.
10.	__ las profesoras ________	Son las profesoras americanas.
E. 1.	*El patio* es muy bonito. *Repita.*	**El patio es muy bonito.**
2.	La sala ________	La sala es muy bonita.
3.	Los hijos ________	Los hijos son muy bonitos.
4.	Las primas ________	Las primas son muy bonitas.
5.	La profesora ________	La profesora es muy bonita.
6.	Las rubias ________	Las rubias son muy bonitas.
7.	La española ________	La española es muy bonita.

EXAMPLES
1. La chica **inglesa.** *The English girl.*
2. **Mis** amigos **españoles.** *My Spanish friends.*
3. Las hermanas **menores.** *The younger sisters.*

SINGULAR			PLURAL		
MASCULINE		FEMININE	MASCULINE		FEMININE
bonito		**bonita**	**bonitos**		**bonitas**
	mi			**mis**	
	menor			**menores**	
	grande			**grandes**	
	amable			**amables**	
inglés		**inglesa**	**ingleses**		**inglesas**
español		**española**	**españoles**		**españolas**

Adjectives whose masculine singular does not end in **-o** are the same in masculine and feminine, except that adjectives of nationality whose masculine ends in a consonant add **-a** for the feminine. Adjectives form their plurals in the same way that nouns form theirs.

› GENDER-NUMBER SUBSTITUTION DRILL

	TEACHER	STUDENT
A. 1.	¿La sala? ¡Qué grande! *Repita.*	**¿La sala? ¡Qué grande!**
2.	¿La clase? ________	¿La clase? ¡Qué grande!

TEACHER	STUDENT
3. ¿El patio? ________	¿El patio? ¡Qué grande!
4. ¿La escuela? ________	¿La escuela? ¡Qué grande!
5. ¿Los cuartos? ________	¿Los cuartos? ¡Qué grandes!
6. ¿Las clases? ________	¿Las clases? ¡Qué grandes!
7. ¿La familia? ________	¿La familia? ¡Qué grande!
8. ¿Las puertas? ________	¿Las puertas? ¡Qué grandes!
9. ¿La cocina? ________	¿La cocina? ¡Qué grande!
B. 1. ¿La rubia? ¡Qué amable! *Repita.*	**¿La rubia? ¡Qué amable!**
2. ¿El tío? ________	¿El tío? ¡Qué amable!
3. ¿Las chicas? ________	¿Las chicas? ¡Qué amables!
4. ¿Los hermanos? ________	¿Los hermanos? ¡Qué amables!
5. ¿El cónsul? ________	¿El cónsul? ¡Qué amable!
6. ¿Los tíos? ________	¿Los tíos? ¡Qué amables!
7. ¿La familia? ________	¿La familia? ¡Qué amable!
8. ¿Las morenas? ________	¿Las morenas? ¡Qué amables!
9. ¿Los hijos? ________	¿Los hijos? ¡Qué amables!
C. 1. ¿El patio? ¡Qué grande! *Repita.*	**¿El patio? ¡Qué grande!**
2. ¿Las tías? ________	¿Las tías? ¡Qué amables!
3. ¿La sala? ________	¿La sala? ¡Qué grande!
4. ¿La morena? ________	¿La morena? ¡Qué amable!
5. ¿Los abuelos? ________	¿Los abuelos? ¡Qué amables!
6. ¿Los cuartos? ________	¿Los cuartos? ¡Qué grandes!
7. ¿La puerta? ________	¿La puerta? ¡Qué grande!

› GENDER-NUMBER SUBSTITUTION DRILL

TEACHER	STUDENT
A. 1. *Es la señorita* española. *Repita.*	**Es la señorita española.**
2. Es el cónsul ________	Es el cónsul español.
3. Son los chicos ________	Son los chicos españoles.
4. Es el amigo ________	Es el amigo español.
5. Es la chica ________	Es la chica española.
6. Son las amigas ________	Son las amigas españolas.
7. Son los señores ________	Son los señores españoles.
8. Son las señoritas ________	Son las señoritas españolas.
B. 1. *Es el profesor* inglés. *Repita.*	**Es el profesor inglés.**
2. Es el señor ________	Es el señor inglés.
3. Son las señoras ________	Son las señoras inglesas.
4. Son los amigos ________	Son los amigos ingleses.
5. Es la señorita ________	Es la señorita inglesa.
6. Son los señores ________	Son los señores ingleses.
7. Es la chica ________	Es la chica inglesa.
8. Son las señoritas ________	Son las señoritas inglesas.
C. 1. Es que somos *muchos compañeros.* *Repita.*	**Es que somos muchos compañeros.**
2. ________ tantos ________	Es que somos tantos compañeros.
3. ________ hijas ________	Es que somos tantas hijas.
4. ________ muchas ________	Es que somos muchas hijas.
5. ________ hijos ________	Es que somos muchos hijos.

TEACHER	STUDENT
6. ________ tantos ________	Es que somos tantos hijos.
7. ________ compañeras ___	Es que somos tantas compañeras.
8. ________ muchas ________	Es que somos muchas compañeras.
D. 1. ¡Qué *bonita* es tu *casa!* *Repita.*	**¡Qué bonita es tu casa!**
2. ________ cuarto	¡Qué bonito es tu cuarto!
3. ____ grande ____	¡Qué grande es tu cuarto!
4. ________ clase	¡Qué grande es tu clase!
5. ____ buena ____	¡Qué buena es tu clase!
6. ________ profesor	¡Qué bueno es tu profesor!
7. ____ amable ____	¡Qué amable es tu profesor!
8. ________ mamá	¡Qué amable es tu mamá!
9. ____ bonita ____	¡Qué bonita es tu mamá!
10. ________ prima	¡Qué bonita es tu prima!
11. ____ buena ____	¡Qué buena es tu prima!
12. ________ libro	¡Qué bueno es tu libro!

Numerals 1-10

EXAMPLES
1. **Un** nuevo amigo. *One (A) new friend.*
2. **Una** o **dos** chicas. *One or two girls.*
3. **Cinco** hermanos y **cuatro** hermanas.
4. ¿Tú tienes **nueve** hermanos?
5. **Diez** hijos.

SINGULAR	1	(M) **un chico**	(F) **una chica**
PLURAL	2	**dos**	**chicos** / **chicas**
	3	**tres**	
	4	**cuatro**	
	5	**cinco**	
	6	**seis**	
	7	**siete**	
	8	**ocho**	
	9	**nueve**	
	10	**diez**	

The numeral *one,* which is the same as the articles *a* and *an,* has separate forms for masculine and feminine. The other numerals have only one form. (*Zero* is **cero.**)

un AND **uno**	
one (a) friend	**un amigo**
one (a) new friend	**un nuevo amigo**
one of my friends	**uno de mis amigos**
one or two friends	**uno o dos amigos**

The numeral *one* (or article *a* or *an*) when masculine is **un** directly before a noun (or with an intervening adjective) but **uno** elsewhere.

Bogotá, Colombia: Universidad de los Andes

➤ COUNTING DRILL

TEACHER	STUDENT
1. Cuente[5] de uno a cinco.	uno, dos, tres, cuatro, cinco
2. Cuente de seis a diez.	seis, siete, ocho, nueve, diez
3. Cuente de uno a diez.	uno, dos, tres, cuatro, cinco, seis, siete, ocho, nueve, diez

➤ ITEM SUBSTITUTION DRILL

TEACHER		STUDENT
1. ¿Son ustedes *diez* hijos en total?	*Conteste.*	**Sí, yo tengo nueve hermanos.**
2. ______ seis ______		Sí, yo tengo cinco hermanos.
3. ______ cinco ______		Sí, yo tengo cuatro hermanos.
4. ______ nueve ______		Sí, yo tengo ocho hermanos.
5. ______ cuatro ______		Sí, yo tengo tres hermanos.
6. ______ siete ______		Sí, yo tengo seis hermanos.
7. ______ ocho ______		Sí, yo tengo siete hermanos.
8. ______ tres ______		Sí, yo tengo dos hermanos.
9. ______ dos ______		Sí, yo tengo un hermano.

[5] **Cuente(n)** *Count*

UNIT 3

A Telephone Conversation

O. *Olga* J. *José María* M. *María Elena* A. *María Elena's aunt*

O. Fine thing [What a pity]! The record player's broken [bad].

J. Why don't we call María Elena? She has a portable [one].

O. Good idea. Do you know her [the] number?

J. I think it's 17–26–58, if I'm not mistaken. Can I use your [the] telephone?

O. Yes, sure. It's over there, by the diningroom door [at the entrance of the diningroom].

* * *

Una conversación por teléfono

O. *Olga* J. *José María* M. *María Elena* T. *Tía de María Elena*

O. ¡Qué lástima! Está malo el tocadiscos.

J. ¿Por qué no llamamos a María Elena? Ella tiene uno portátil.

O. Buena idea. ¿Sabes el número?

J. Creo que es el diecisiete, veintiséis, cincuenta y ocho, si no estoy equivocado. ¿Puedo usar el teléfono?

O. Sí, claro. Está ahí, a la entrada del comedor.

* * *

J.	Hello. Is this [Am I speaking with] Dr. Fernández' house?	J.	¿Aló? (1) ¿Hablo con la casa del doctor Fernández?
A.	Yes. Who do you want to speak to?	T.	Sí, señor. ¿Con quién desea hablar?
J.	María Elena, please. Are you her mother, may I ask?	J.	Con María Elena, por favor. Perdón, (2) ¿Es usted la mamá?
A.	No, this is her aunt [you're talking with the aunt]. María Elena just left [finishes leaving], but she'll be back [returns] in [inside of] ten minutes. Would you like [do you wish] to leave a [some] message?	T.	No, habla con la tía. María Elena acaba de salir (3) pero regresa dentro de diez minutos. ¿Desea usted dejar (3) algún recado?

Mexico City: Record shop

J.	No, thanks. I'll call later [more late].	J.	No, gracias, señora. Yo llamo más tarde.
A.	Who may I say is calling [On behalf of whom, in order to tell her]?	T.	¿De parte de quién, para decirle?
J.	José María Romero, thank you [please, if you do me the favor].	J.	De José María Romero (4), si me hace el favor.

* * *

M.	Hi, Pepe. Where are you? What's all that noise I hear [Where are you that I hear so much noise]?	M.	¿Qué tal, Pepe? (5) ¿Dónde estás que oigo tanto ruido?
J.	We're all at Olga's house [at house of Olga]. Why don't you come over? She's got some new records.	J.	Estamos todos en casa de Olga. ¿Por qué no vienes? Tiene unos discos nuevos.
M.	Oh, I'd love to [what desires of going]. But you know Mom . . .	M.	Ay, qué ganas de ir. Pero tú conoces a mamá...
J.	Yes, but your dad . . .	J.	Sí, pero tu papá...
M.	No, not him; her—Mom. She says I have to stay with my aunt. But [However, Still], maybe I can come. What time is it?	M.	No, él no; ella, mi mamá. Dice que tengo que estar con mi tía. Sin embargo, tal vez puedo ir. (6) ¿Qué hora es?
J.	It's three-thirty [and a half]. If you come, can you bring your record player? We'll come by for you.	J.	Son las tres y media. Si vienes, ¿puedes traer tu tocadiscos? Nosotros pasamos por ti.

M.	Don't you have one there?	M.	¿No tienen ustedes uno allá? (7)
J.	Yes, but it isn't working [is broken].	J.	Sí, pero está descompuesto.
M.	Oh, so that's how come [because of that] the invitation, huh?	M.	Ah, por eso la invitación, ¿eh?
J.	No, girl. What crazy ideas you have!	J.	No, chica, ¡qué ideas tienes!

cultural notes

(1) The Spanish equivalents of the English telephone greeting, *Hello,* are several: in Spain, **Diga** or **Dígame;** in Mexico, **Bueno;** in Cuba, **Oigo** or **¿Qué hay?;** in Colombia, **A ver;** in Argentina, **Holá;** and in most other Spanish-speaking countries, **¿Aló?**

(2) One-for-one equivalents in meaning, like the Spanish equivalents of *Hello* explained above, are rare between any two languages (see footnote 8, p. 56). The use of **perdón** in this dialog and **con permiso** in the previous one, both translated as *excuse me,* illustrate the fact that one word or phrase in English often covers a range of meanings requiring more than one equivalent in Spanish. (The reverse is also true.) Thus, in excusing oneself from people with whom one is speaking, in passing in front of someone at a theater, or in making one's way through a crowded elevator or public conveyance, **con permiso** is normally used; but in interrupting a conversation to inquire about something, **perdón** is one of the commonly used expressions.

(3) Another instance of the lack of one-to-one correspondence is **salir** and **dejar,** both translated *to leave,* but one meaning *to depart* and the other *to leave behind:* **Sale de la casa** *She leaves (departs from) the house,* **Deja el recado** *She leaves the note.*

(4) The name **María** is not uncommon as the second element of a male double name, as in the case of José María Morelos, the Mexican patriot, and Carlos María Ocantos, the Argentine novelist.

(5) **Pepe** is a nickname for **José,** which in Old Spanish is **Josep.** The form **Pepe** is just a reduplicated syllable (cf. English *knickknack, wishy-washy, chitchat*).

(6) When English takes the point of view of the person spoken to in the choice of *go* and *come,* Spanish takes that of the speaker: *"Why don't you come over?" "Maybe I can come."* But from the speaker's own standpoint he is *going,* not *coming;* therefore in Spanish one says: **"¿Por qué no vienes?" "Tal vez puedo ir."**

(7) There are three Spanish adverbs corresponding to English *there:* **ahí, allí,** and **allá.** In general **allá** indicates greater remoteness from the speaker and often a less precise location than do the other adverbs. In Spanish America **ahí** has tended to crowd out **allí** so that the former distinction (**ahí** referring to something nearer the person addressed, and **allí** to something distant from either speaker in a conversation) has to some extent been lost, though it is still preserved in Spain.

› PRONUNCIATION EXERCISE (Reread "Stop-spirants" in Unit 1, Section 1.)

A. The variants [b] and [ƀ]. INSTRUCTIONS: Repeat the following pairs of words just as you hear them.

[b]	[ƀ]	[b]	[ƀ]
vez	la vez	un **bus**	este **bus**
voz	la voz	un **baile**	este **baile**
vaca	la vaca	un **banco**	este **banco**
boca	la **b**oca	un **v**aso	este **v**aso
vista	la vista	un velo	este velo

[b]	[ƀ]	[b]	[ƀ]
banca	la **b**anca	un **b**alcón	este **b**alcón
banda	la **b**anda	un **v**erano	este **v**erano
bocina	la **b**ocina	un **b**illete	este **b**illete

In the above pairs the first column has the stop [b], which occurs at the beginning of an utterance (i.e., when preceded by silence) or after [m]; the second column has the fricative [ƀ], which is found everywhere else. The letters **b** and **v** represent the same sound, and the letter **n** when it occurs before a /b/ represents the sound [m]: **un bus** [um bus].

B. The variants [d] and [đ].

[d]	[đ]	[d]	[đ]	[d]	[đ]
día	ese **d**ía	un **d**ía	este **d**ía	el **d**ios	la **d**iosa
disco	ese **d**isco	un **d**isco	este **d**isco	el **d**anés	la **d**anesa
deporte	ese **d**eporte	un **d**ólar	este **d**ólar	el **d**icho	la **d**icha
desfile	ese **d**esfile	un **d**eporte	este **d**eporte	el **d**ucho	la **d**ucha
dinero	ese **d**inero	un **d**esfile	este **d**esfile	el **d**iestro	la **d**iestra
discurso	ese **d**iscurso	un **d**iscurso	este **d**iscurso	el **d**ichoso	la **d**ichosa
despacho	ese **d**espacho	un **d**espacho	este **d**espacho	el **d**iscreto	la **d**iscreta
director	ese **d**irector	un **d**irector	este **d**irector	el **d**irector	la **d**irectora

In the above pairs the first column has the stop [d], which occurs at the beginning of an utterance (i.e., when preceded by silence) or after [n] and [l]; the second column has the fricative [đ], which is found everywhere else.

C. The variants [g] and [ǥ].

[g]	[ǥ]	[g]	[ǥ]
gato	este **g**ato	un **g**algo	mi **g**algo
gaucho	este **g**aucho	un **g**anso	mi **g**anso
globo	este **g**lobo	un **g**asto	mi **g**asto
golpe	este **g**olpe	un **g**ato	mi **g**ato
gordo	este **g**ordo	un **g**lobo	mi **g**lobo
grito	este **g**rito	un **g**rupo	mi **g**rupo
grupo	este **g**rupo	un **g**usto	mi **g**usto
gusto	este **g**usto	un **g**alón	mi **g**alón

In the above pairs the first column has the stop [g], which occurs at the beginning of an utterance (i.e., when preceded by silence) or after /n/, which here has the sound [ŋ]. The second column has the fricative [ǥ], which is found everywhere else.

Interrogative words

EXAMPLES

1. **¿Cuándo** pasa lista? *When does he call the roll?*
2. **¿Cómo** estudian los alumnos? *How do the students study?*
3. **¿Por qué** no llamamos a María Elena?
4. ¿Con **quién** desea hablar?
5. **¿Cuál** es el cónsul? *Which one is the consul?*
6. **¿Cuáles** amigos vienen? *Which friends are coming?*
7. **¿Cuánto** es? Es un dólar. *How much is it? It's a dollar.*
8. **¿Cuántas** hermanas tienes? *How many sisters do you have?*

when?	**¿cuándo?**
how?[1]	**¿cómo?**
why?	**¿por qué?**
who, whom?	**¿quién?** (*plural,* **¿quiénes?**)
which, which one?	**¿cuál?** (*plural,* **¿cuáles?**)
how much?	**¿cuánto? -a?**
how many?	**¿cuántos? -as?**

› TRANSLATION DRILL[2]

A. 1. When is the lady arriving?
2. How is the lady arriving?
3. Why is the lady arriving?
4. With whom is the lady arriving?

B. 1. Who is arriving?
2. Who all[3] are arriving?
3. Which one is arriving?
4. Which ones are arriving?
5. Which family is arriving?
6. Which families are arriving?
7. How much is arriving?
8. How many are arriving?

C. 1. Who is he?
2. Who are they?
3. Which is it?
4. Which are they?
5. How much is it?
6. How many are they?

› CONSTRUCTION SUBSTITUTION DRILL

	TEACHER	STUDENT
1.	Pregúntele[4] al señor cómo se llama.	¿Cómo se llama, señor?
2.	Pregúntele al señor cuándo viene.	¿Cuándo viene, señor?
3.	Pregúntele al señor cómo viene.	¿Cómo viene, señor?
4.	Pregúntele al señor por qué viene.	¿Por qué viene, señor?
5.	Pregúntele al señor con quién viene.	¿Con quién viene, señor?
6.	Pregúntele al señor con quiénes viene.	¿Con quiénes viene, señor?
7.	Pregúntele al señor cuál viene.	¿Cuál viene, señor?
8.	Pregúntele al señor cuáles vienen.	¿Cuáles vienen, señor?
9.	Pregúntele al señor quién viene.	¿Quién viene, señor?
10.	Pregúntele al señor quiénes vienen.	¿Quiénes vienen, señor?
11.	Pregúntele al señor cuántos vienen.	¿Cuántos vienen, señor?

EXAMPLES
1. ¿A **qué** hora estudia usted? *At what time do you study?*
2. ¿**Qué** hora es?
3. ¿**Qué** hacen los alumnos? *What are the students doing?*

---

[1] In addition, Spanish uses **¿cómo?** to ask for a repetition of what someone has just said; compare English *How was that?* (*What did you say?*).

[2] In order to present more drills in the space available, instructions and answers will appear in this and in subsequent units only when needed, for example, when a new type of drill is introduced.

[3] English expressions with *all* will be used in the drills to cue a plural when the English form does not show plurality: e.g., *who all* and *you all.* If the teacher prefers, he can give this cue with a gesture that indicates he is talking to more than one person.

[4] **Pregunte(n)** *Ask*

What? BEFORE NOUN	*What?* BEFORE VERB
¿qué { **clase?** / **día?** / **libros?**	¿qué { **hacen?** / **esperamos?** / **dice?**

ITEM SUBSTITUTION DRILL

A. 1. ¿Qué día es?
2. ____ hora ____
3. ____ libro ____
4. ____ disco ____
5. ____ clase ____
6. ____ discos ____
7. ____ plumas ____

B. 1. ¿Qué dice?
2. ____ deja?
3. ____ espera?
4. ____ hace?
5. ____ necesita?
6. ____ desea?
7. ____ tiene?

EXAMPLES
1. **¿Dónde** está Julio?
2. **¿De dónde** son?
3. **¿Para dónde** van? *Where are they headed for?*
4. **¿Adónde** desea ir? *Where do you wish to go?*

where? where from? for where? etc.	**¿dónde?** **¿de dónde?** **¿para dónde?** **etc.**

where? where to?	**¿adónde?**

CONSTRUCTION SUBSTITUTION DRILL

A. 1. TEACHER: Pregúntele adónde desea ir.
STUDENT: **¿Adónde desea ir?**
2. Pregúntele adónde tiene que ir.
3. Pregúntele adónde tiene que llamar.

B. 1. Pregúntele dónde está.
2. Pregúntele dónde trabaja.
3. Pregúntele dónde estudia.

C. 1. Pregúntele de dónde es.
2. Pregúntele de dónde viene.

DISCUSSION

Most English interrogative words have just one equivalent in Spanish. *Where?,* however, has two possibilities: when it means *where to?* it is translated **¿adónde?** (meaning, literally, *to where?*), but the rest of the time it is translated **¿dónde?** *Where are you going?* therefore calls for **¿adónde?**, *Where are you?* for **¿dónde?**, and *Where are you from?* for **¿de dónde?**

English *what?* followed directly by a noun calls for **¿qué?** The same is usually true of English *what?* followed by a verb.

10 Word order in questions

QUESTIONS WITH INTERROGATIVE WORDS		
INTERROGATIVE WORD	VERB	SUBJECT (IF ANY)
¿Cómo	estudian	los alumnos?
¿Quiénes	son	las chicas?
¿Qué	esperamos?	
¿De dónde	son?	
¿Con quién	desea hablar?	

In this pattern the subject, if any, follows the verb, and any preposition understood with the interrogative word precedes it.

› **TRANSLATION DRILL**

A. 1. Where is Julio from?
2. Who is she?
3. Which ones are they?
4. How much is it?
5. When is it?
6. What is it?
7. Which is it?

B. 1. Where are you working?
2. When are you coming?
3. Why are you studying?
4. What are you waiting for?
5. What is he saying?

C. 1. Why does he study?
2. What does he have?
3. When does he come by for you?
4. What do you want?
5. Which one do you need?

SUBJECT	VERB	SUBJECT	REMAINDER (IF ANY)
	¿Sabes		el número?
	¿Puedes traer		tu tocadiscos?
¿Tú	eres		amigo de ellas?
¿Tú	tienes		nueve hermanos?
¿Julio	está?		
	¿Es	usted	la mamá?
	¿Llega	el profesor	a la clase?
	¿No tienen	ustedes	uno allá?
	¿Está	Julio?	

Questions, like other sentences, do not need an expressed subject. When the subject is expressed, it may go either before or after the verb, as in English *Julio is here?* and *Is Julio here?*

› **CONSTRUCTION SUBSTITUTION DRILL**

INSTRUCTIONS: Repeat the question as you hear it. Then change the order of the subject and verb.

A. 1. TEACHER: ¿Tú eres amigo de ellas?
STUDENT: **¿Eres tú amigo de ellas?**
2. ¿Tú tienes nueve hermanos?
3. ¿Usted es el señor Arjona?
4. ¿Usted estudia español?
5. ¿Pablo está en la clase?
6. ¿Ustedes son catorce en total?

B. 1. ¿Es usted la mamá?
2. ¿Tienen ustedes uno allá?
3. ¿Tiene la casa un patio grande?
4. ¿Vamos todos a casa de Olga?
5. ¿Son ellos compañeros de escuela?

INSTRUCTIONS: Repeat the question as you hear it. Then repeat it again, omitting the subject.

C. 1. TEACHER: ¿Tú eres amiga de las dos chicas?
STUDENT: **¿Eres amiga de las dos chicas?**
2. ¿Ellas son compañeras de escuela?
3. ¿Ella tiene un tocadiscos?
4. ¿Usted desea hablar con Olga?
5. ¿Yo soy la menor?

D. 1. ¿Llegan los alumnos a la clase?
2. ¿Está Julio en la cocina?
3. ¿Son ellos primos?
4. ¿Puedo yo usar el teléfono?
5. ¿Regresa Olga dentro de diez minutos?

VERB	SUBJECT	REMAINDER	SUBJECT
¿Está **¿Llega**	**el recado** **el profesor**	**ahí?** **a la clase?**	←EMPHATIC REMAINDER ↙EMPHATIC SUBJECT
¿Está **¿Llega**		**ahí** **a la clase**	**el recado?** **el profesor?**

Emphasis may be on either the subject or the remainder, depending on which is at the end of the sentence. **¿Está el recado ahí?** means *Is the message* ***there?*** **¿Está ahí el recado?** means *Is the* ***message*** *there?*

› TRANSLATION DRILL

INSTRUCTIONS: Translate the following paired sentences, placing the emphasized words last in your Spanish sentence.

1. Is *the record player* broken?
Is the record player *broken?*
2. Is *everybody* here? (Are all here?)
Is everybody *here?*
3. Does *Cecilia* have lots of friends?
Does Cecilia have *lots of friends?*
4. Don't *you* have one?
Don't you have *one?*
5. Are *the students* arriving at the class?
Are the students arriving *at the class?*
6. Is the *professor* present?
Is the professor *present?*
7. Do *you* have a sister?
Do you have *a sister?*

› DISCUSSION

In questions with interrogative words the subject normally comes after the verb. In other questions it may precede or follow the verb, with effects similar to those in English: **¿Es usted la mamá?** *Are you her mother?* **¿Usted es la mamá?** *You are her mother?* (The words *do* and *did,* as used in questions like *Do you like it?* and negations like *He didn't want to,* have no parallel in Spanish: the question *Do you have the invitation?* appears in the same order as *Have you the invitation?* **¿Tiene usted la invitación?**)

When Spanish omits the subject there is no problem of word order. Whether **¿Puedes traer tu tocadiscos?** means *You can bring your record player?* or *Can you bring your record player?* depends on context and intonation.

English emphasizes a word by stressing it. Spanish emphasizes a word both by stressing it and, more often than is possible in English, by shifting it to the end of the sentence.

11 Placement of *no* with verbs

EXAMPLES
1. **No** necesitas saber inglés.
2. Si **no** estoy equivocado.
3. ¿Por qué **no** vienes?
4. **¿No** puedes traer tu tocadiscos?

no	+	*verb*

When **no** accompanies a verb, it is placed directly before the verb.

› CONSTRUCTION SUBSTITUTION DRILL

INSTRUCTIONS: Repeat the following sentences. Then say them again, making the verbs negative.

A. 1. TEACHER: Los alumnos llegan a la puerta.
STUDENT: **Los alumnos no llegan a la puerta.**
2. Debe estar en la cocina.
3. Son primas.
4. El padre de Betty es el nuevo cónsul americano.
5. Ellas saben español perfectamente.
6. Después estudiamos.
7. Eres muy amable.
8. Yo soy la menor.
9. Está malo el tocadiscos.
10. Ella tiene uno portátil.
11. No, habla con la tía.
12. ¿Está Julio?
13. ¿Sabes el número?

12 Intonation[5]

EXAMPLES

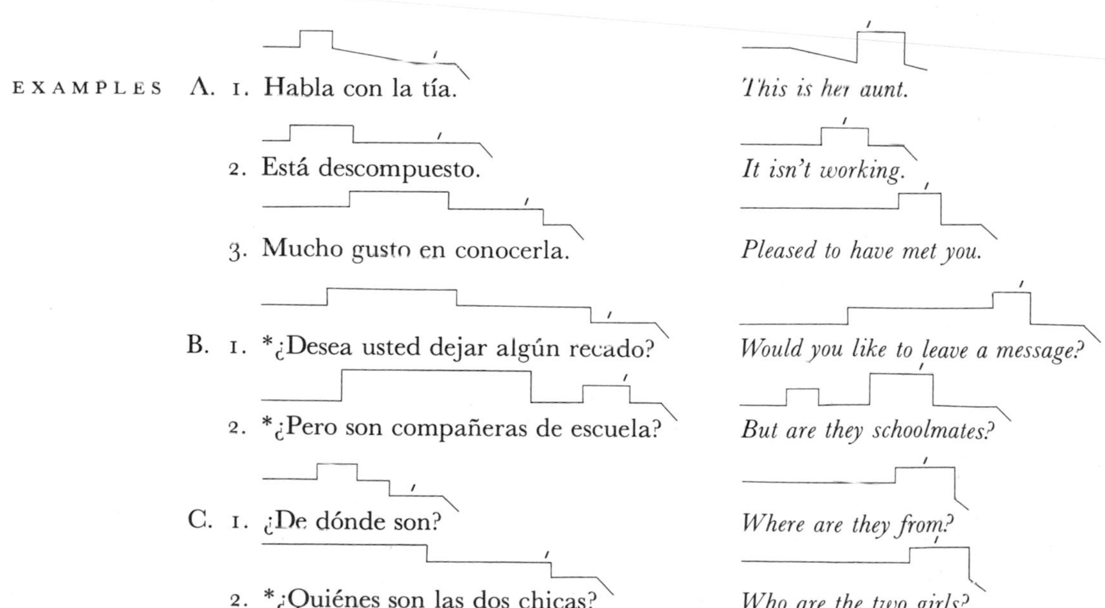

[5] The examples, with contrasting Spanish and English intonation patterns, have been recorded. You will understand the explanations better if you listen to the recording as you read the examples and diagrams.

(NOTE: In the diagrams, broken lines show the location of certain unstressed syllables that may or may not be present. The accent mark indicates the main stress. The starred examples are included to show possibilities of intonation that do not actually occur in the dialogs.)

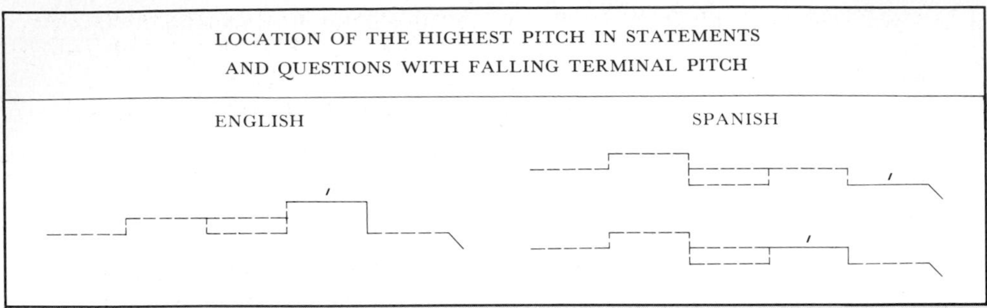

In statements and questions that end with a falling pitch, Spanish tends to put the highest pitch somewhere BEFORE the main stress while English tends to put it AT the main stress.

PRONUNCIATION DRILL

INSTRUCTIONS: Repeat the following English sentences and their Spanish equivalents, using the normal intonations shown. Be aware of the high-to-low in Spanish.[6]

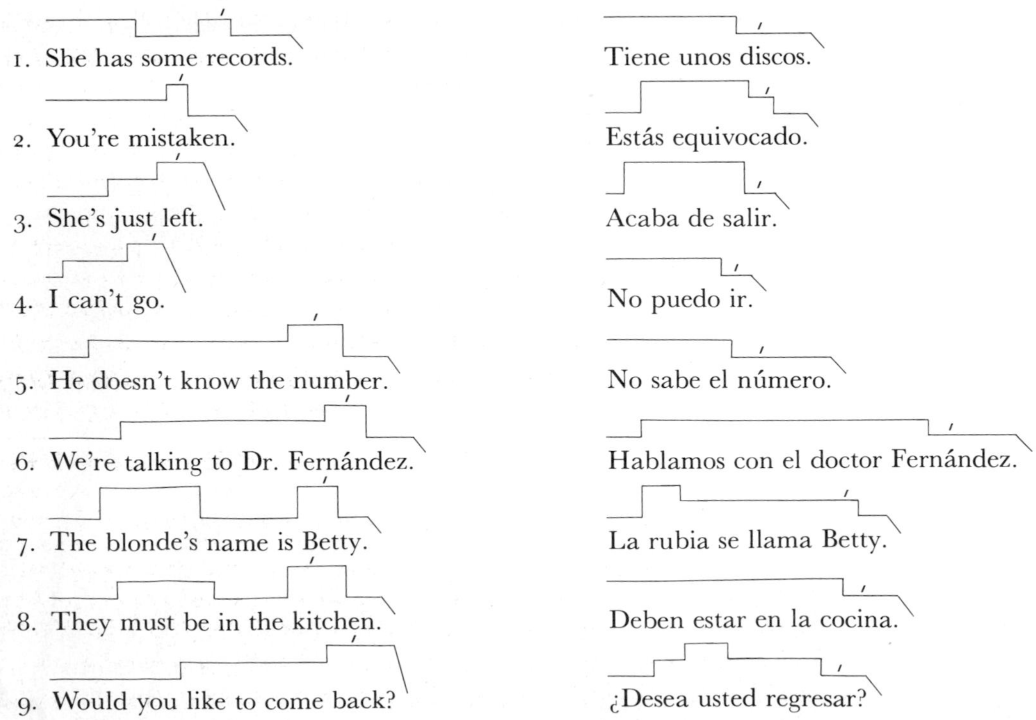

[6] You should not worry about trying to follow rigidly the levels as shown. The important thing is not to put the highest pitch on the main stress in Spanish. For example, in **Estás equivocado** the syllable **-ca-** might be brought to level 1 instead of level 2.

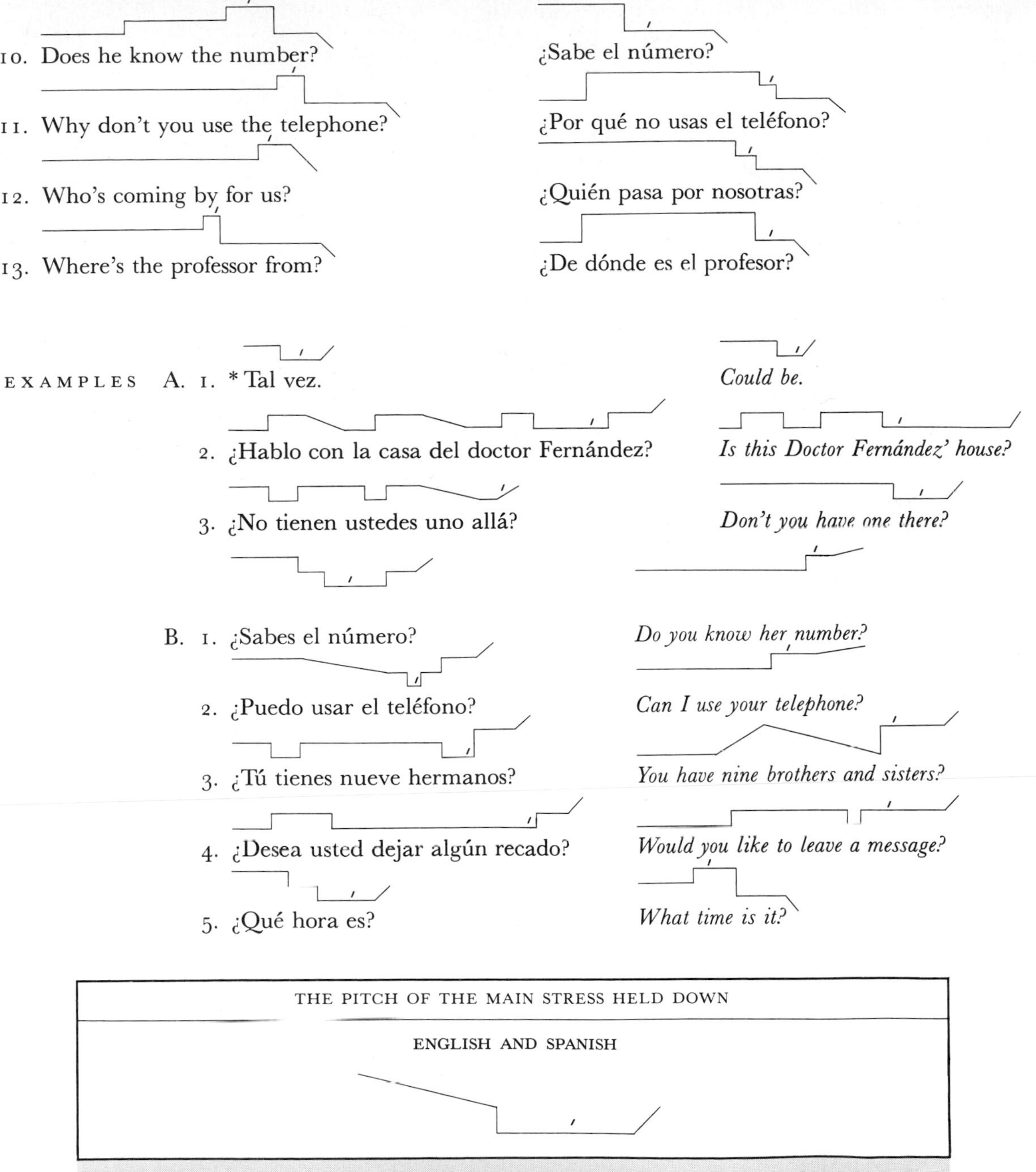

10. Does he know the number? — ¿Sabe el número?

11. Why don't you use the telephone? — ¿Por qué no usas el teléfono?

12. Who's coming by for us? — ¿Quién pasa por nosotras?

13. Where's the professor from? — ¿De dónde es el profesor?

EXAMPLES A. 1. * Tal vez. — *Could be.*

2. ¿Hablo con la casa del doctor Fernández? — *Is this Doctor Fernández' house?*

3. ¿No tienen ustedes uno allá? — *Don't you have one there?*

B. 1. ¿Sabes el número? — *Do you know her number?*

2. ¿Puedo usar el teléfono? — *Can I use your telephone?*

3. ¿Tú tienes nueve hermanos? — *You have nine brothers and sisters?*

4. ¿Desea usted dejar algún recado? — *Would you like to leave a message?*

5. ¿Qué hora es? — *What time is it?*

THE PITCH OF THE MAIN STRESS HELD DOWN

ENGLISH AND SPANISH

Holding down is the opposite of excitement: the main stress is at the lowest pitch, followed by a rise at the end. The attitude is one of considerateness toward the hearer: the speaker is ingratiating (as when asking a question of a total stranger, example A2), coaxing (as with a child), or restrained (as in the politely restrained exclamation in the Spanish of B3). In questions, particularly of the yes-no type, Spanish favors restraint more than English does (see the B examples).

Mexico City:
"Los Yaquis,"
student musical group

› PRONUNCIATION DRILL

INSTRUCTIONS: Repeat the following English sentences and their Spanish equivalents, using the intonations shown. In the A examples the main stress is held down in both Spanish and English; be aware of the tone of considerateness (ingratiation, coaxing, restraint, etc.). In B the main stress is held down in Spanish but not in English; this gives the Spanish an air of greater reserve and the English an air of greater uninhibitedness.

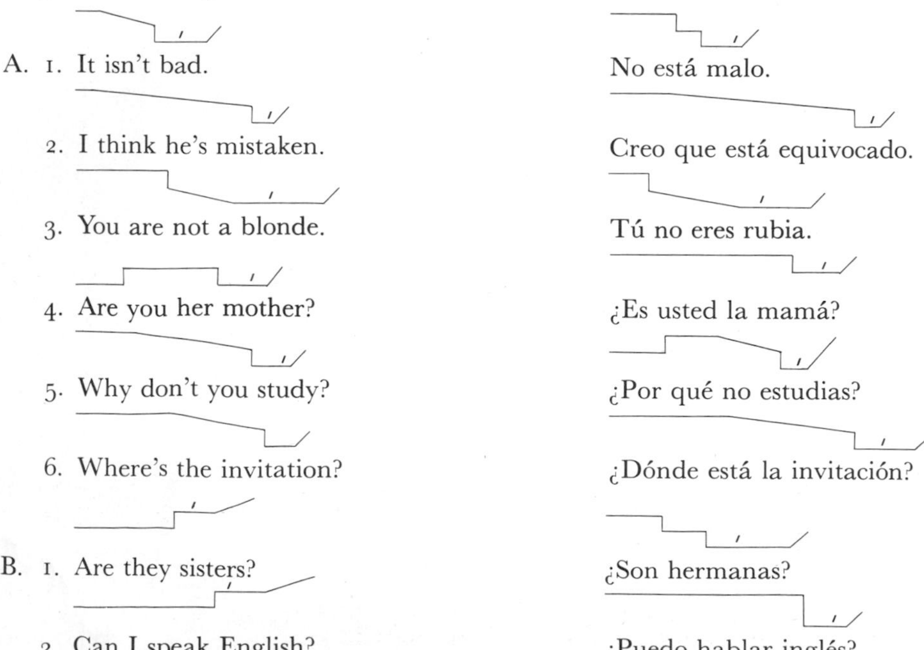

A. 1. It isn't bad. — No está malo.

2. I think he's mistaken. — Creo que está equivocado.

3. You are not a blonde. — Tú no eres rubia.

4. Are you her mother? — ¿Es usted la mamá?

5. Why don't you study? — ¿Por qué no estudias?

6. Where's the invitation? — ¿Dónde está la invitación?

B. 1. Are they sisters? — ¿Son hermanas?

2. Can I speak English? — ¿Puedo hablar inglés?

3. Can you bring your record player? — ¿Puedes traer tu tocadiscos?

4. Who's going to call? — ¿Quién va a llamar?

5. Why don't you wait for her? — ¿Por qué no la esperas?

6. Who's the invitation from? — ¿De quién es la invitación?

EXAMPLES

A. 1. ¡Qué familia! — *What a family!*

2. Buena idea. — *Good idea.*

B. 1. *¿Desea usted dejar algún recado? — *Would you like to leave a message?*

2. *¿Pero son compañeras de escuela? — *But are they schoolmates?*

C. 1. ¿Por qué no llamamos a María Elena? — *Why don't we call María Elena?*

2. ¿Qué esperamos? — *What are we waiting for?*

HIGHEST PITCH ON THE MAIN STRESS UNDER EXCITEMENT

ENGLISH AND SPANISH

Both languages put the highest pitch on the main stress to show emphasis, enthusiasm, a sudden bright idea, etc.

›PRONUNCIATION DRILL

INSTRUCTIONS: Repeat the thirteen sentences of the next-to-the-last preceding drill as you will now hear them, exaggerating the range in English somewhat and making the pitch of the main stress in the Spanish as high as or higher than anything that precedes, for example:

Tiene unos discos. or Tiene unos discos.

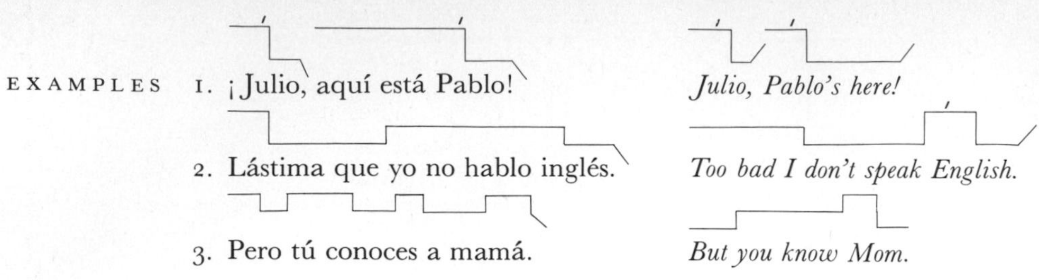

EXAMPLES

1. ¡Julio, aquí está Pablo! — *Julio, Pablo's here!*
2. Lástima que yo no hablo inglés. — *Too bad I don't speak English.*
3. Pero tú conoces a mamá. — *But you know Mom.*

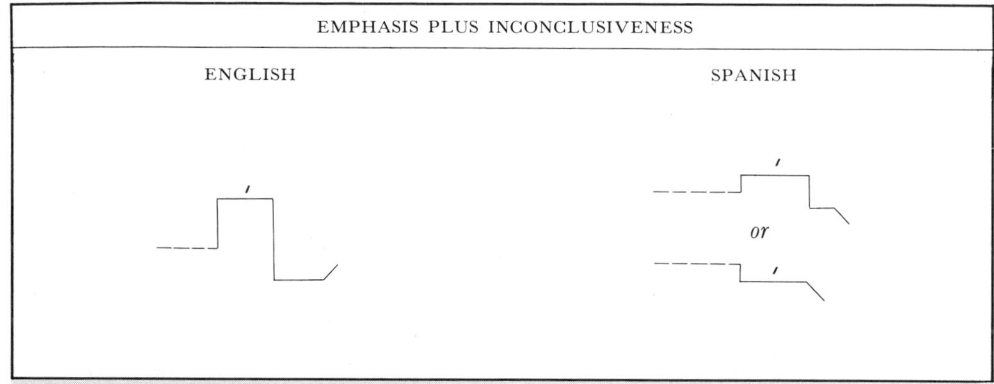

To show emphasis plus inconclusiveness (by this we mean a statement that is "left up in the air" at the end), American English regularly uses a rising-falling-rising pitch curve starting at the main stress. Spanish treats most such utterances as if they were conclusive.

› PRONUNCIATION DRILL

INSTRUCTIONS: Repeat the following English sentences and their Spanish equivalents, using the intonations shown, which in English will show emphasis plus inconclusiveness but in Spanish will be the normal intonation. Be conscious of the English intonation as one that is much less used in Spanish.

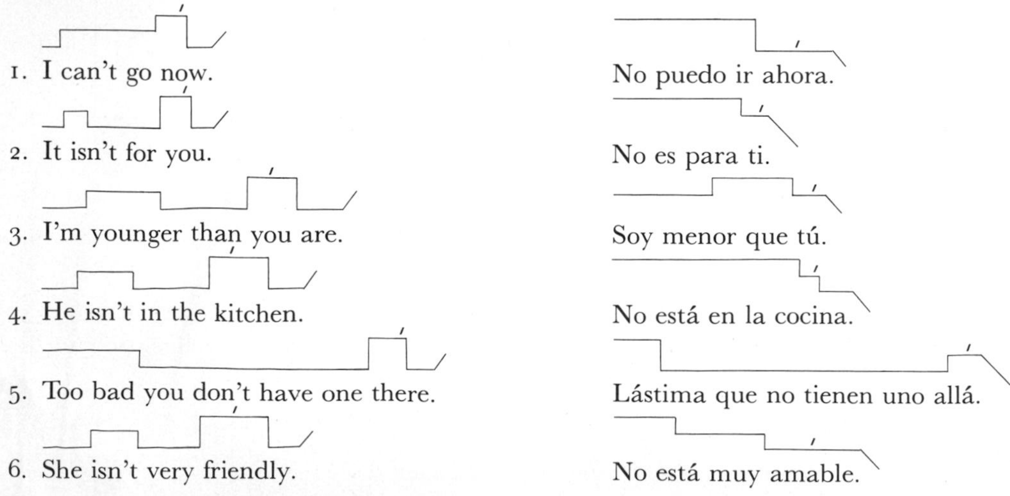

1. I can't go now. — No puedo ir ahora.
2. It isn't for you. — No es para ti.
3. I'm younger than you are. — Soy menor que tú.
4. He isn't in the kitchen. — No está en la cocina.
5. Too bad you don't have one there. — Lástima que no tienen uno allá.
6. She isn't very friendly. — No está muy amable.

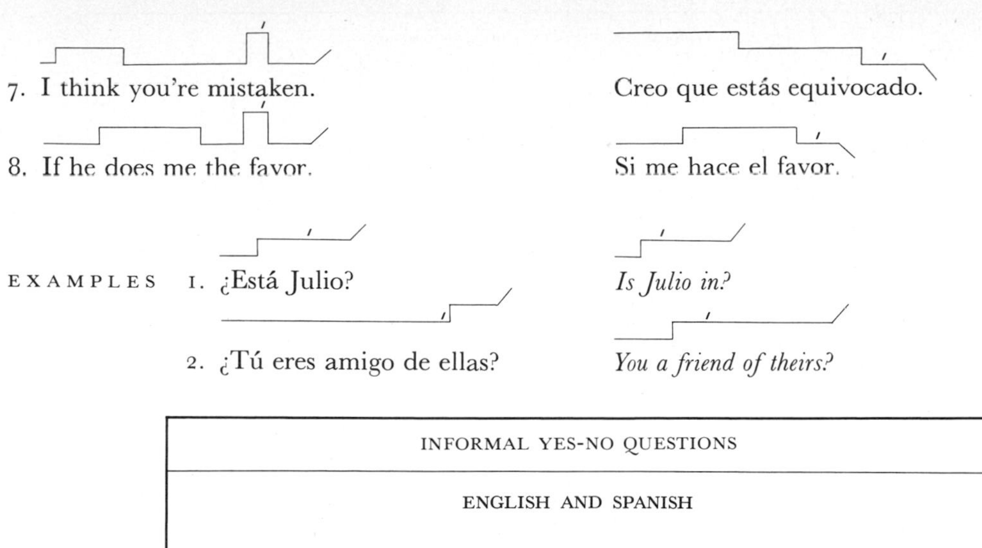

7. I think you're mistaken. — Creo que estás equivocado.

8. If he does me the favor. — Si me hace el favor.

EXAMPLES

1. ¿Está Julio? — *Is Julio in?*

2. ¿Tú eres amigo de ellas? — *You a friend of theirs?*

INFORMAL YES-NO QUESTIONS

ENGLISH AND SPANISH

In offhand, informal yes-no questions both languages use the same simple rise in pitch at the end.

› PRONUNCIATION DRILL

INSTRUCTIONS: Repeat the following English sentences and their Spanish equivalents, using the same intonation in both, as shown.

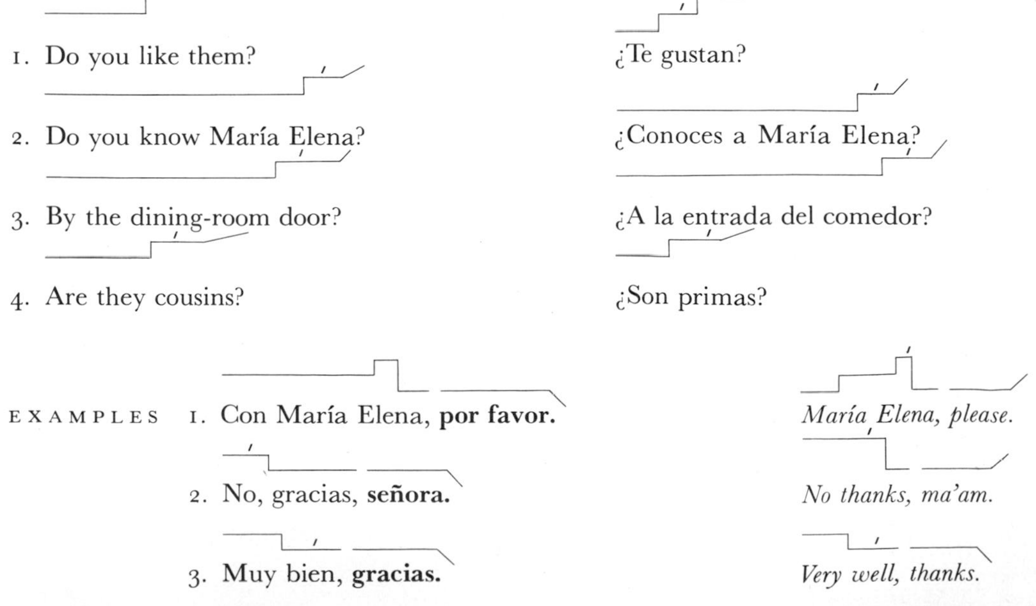

1. Do you like them? — ¿Te gustan?

2. Do you know María Elena? — ¿Conoces a María Elena?

3. By the dining-room door? — ¿A la entrada del comedor?

4. Are they cousins? — ¿Son primas?

EXAMPLES

1. Con María Elena, **por favor.** — *María Elena, please.*

2. No, gracias, **señora.** — *No thanks, ma'am.*

3. Muy bien, **gracias.** — *Very well, thanks.*

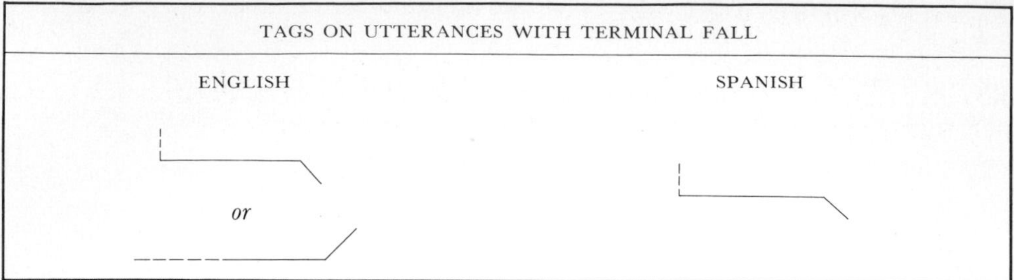

If, supposing one had the same utterance without the tag, the utterance were one that ended in a falling pitch, then the tag in Spanish would simply become part of that falling pitch. The tag in English may do the same, or it may rise.

› PRONUNCIATION DRILL

A. INSTRUCTIONS: Repeat the following sentences, using the intonations shown. Be conscious of the rising pitch at the end of the tags in English and the falling pitch at the end of those in Spanish.

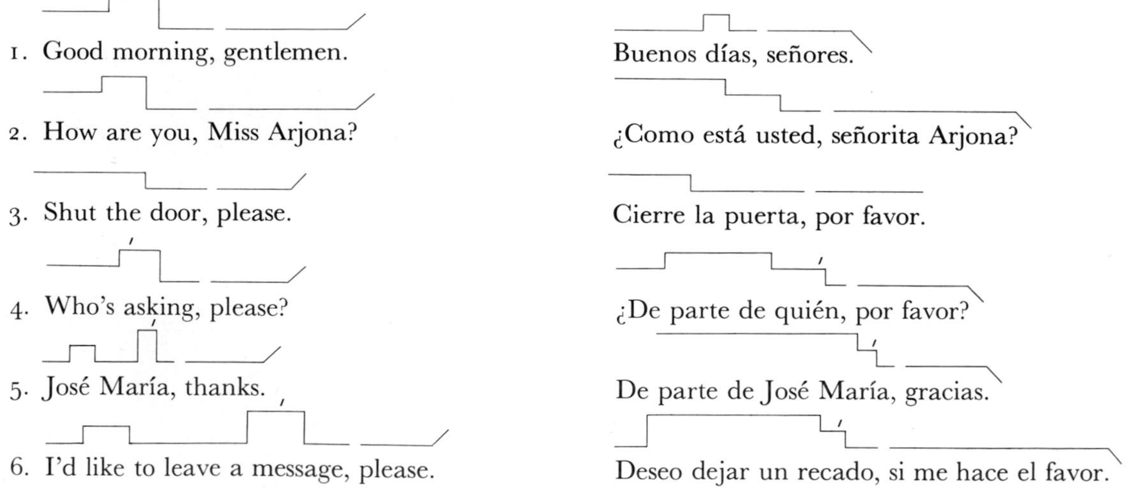

1. Good morning, gentlemen. — Buenos días, señores.
2. How are you, Miss Arjona? — ¿Como está usted, señorita Arjona?
3. Shut the door, please. — Cierre la puerta, por favor.
4. Who's asking, please? — ¿De parte de quién, por favor?
5. José María, thanks. — De parte de José María, gracias.
6. I'd like to leave a message, please. — Deseo dejar un recado, si me hace el favor.

B. INSTRUCTIONS: Repeat the following sentences, using the intonations shown. The tag rises in both English and Spanish because without the tag the utterance would still rise at the end.

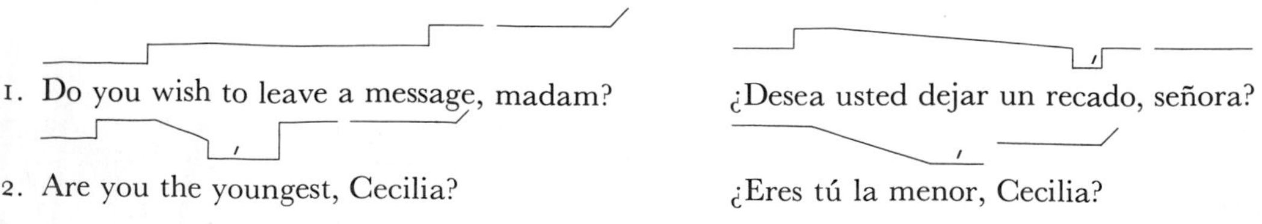

1. Do you wish to leave a message, madam? — ¿Desea usted dejar un recado, señora?
2. Are you the youngest, Cecilia? — ¿Eres tú la menor, Cecilia?

C. INSTRUCTIONS: Repeat A above, making the tag in English fall as it does in Spanish.

A. INSTRUCTIONS: The following questions will be asked and answered on the tape with the intonations shown. Questions 1–4 are informal yes-no questions with simple rising pitch.

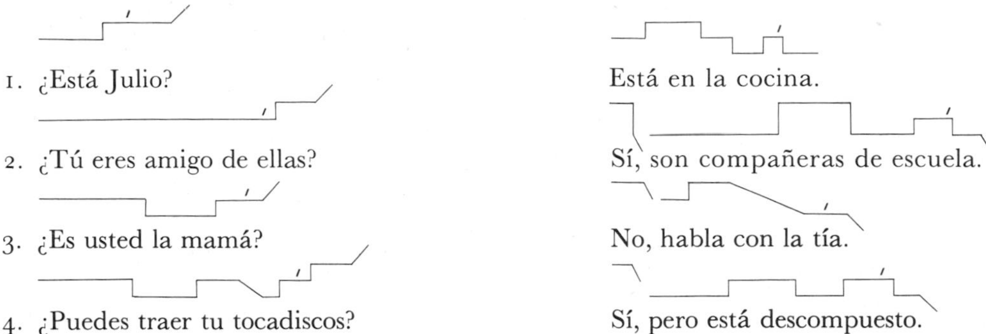

1. ¿Está Julio? — Está en la cocina.
2. ¿Tú eres amigo de ellas? — Sí, son compañeras de escuela.
3. ¿Es usted la mamá? — No, habla con la tía.
4. ¿Puedes traer tu tocadiscos? — Sí, pero está descompuesto.

Questions 5–9, in contrast to English, use the restrained pattern, in which the pitch of the main stress is held down.

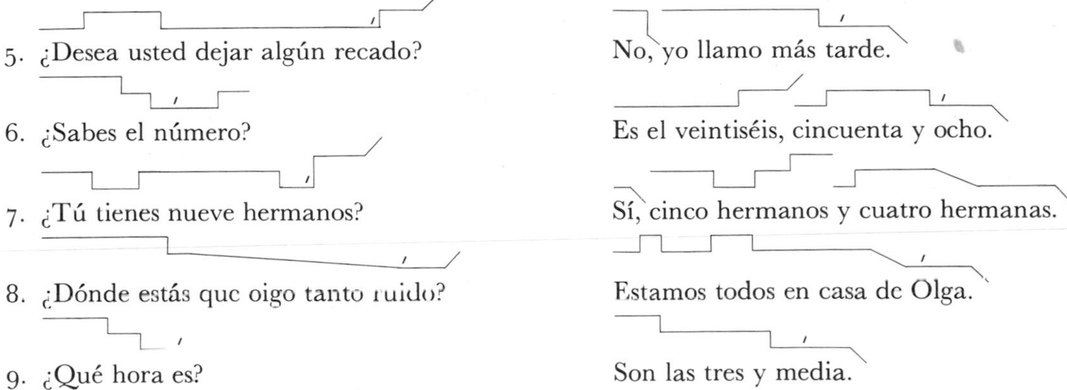

5. ¿Desea usted dejar algún recado? — No, yo llamo más tarde.
6. ¿Sabes el número? — Es el veintiséis, cincuenta y ocho.
7. ¿Tú tienes nueve hermanos? — Sí, cinco hermanos y cuatro hermanas.
8. ¿Dónde estás que oigo tanto ruido? — Estamos todos en casa de Olga.
9. ¿Qué hora es? — Son las tres y media.

B. INSTRUCTIONS: Questions 1–7 of drill A will be asked again, using the more restrained intonation, as indicated for question 1 below. In the questions the drop should be on the main stress (the syllable in bold type). The answers have the same intonation as before.

1. ¿Está **Ju**lio? — Está en la cocina.
2. ¿Tú eres amigo de **e**llas? — Sí, son compañeras de escuela.
3. ¿Es usted la ma**má?** — No, habla con la tía.
4. ¿Puedes traer tu toca**dis**cos? — Sí, pero está descompuesto.
5. ¿Desea usted dejar algún re**ca**do? — No, yo llamo más tarde.
6. ¿Sabes el **nú**mero? — Es el veintiséis, cincuenta y ocho.
7. ¿Tú tienes nueve her**ma**nos? — Sí, cinco hermanos y cuatro hermanas.

C. INSTRUCTIONS: The following questions will be asked first with the intonation shown in the example on the left and then with the more emphatic intonation shown in the example on the right.

1. ¿Qué esperamos?	¿Qué esperamos?
2. ¿De dónde **son?**	¿De dónde **son?**
3. ¿Por qué no lla**ma**mos?	¿Por qué no lla**ma**mos?
4. ¿Dónde es**tás?**	¿Dónde es**tás?**
5. ¿Por qué no **vie**nes?	¿Por qué no **vie**nes?
6. ¿Cómo es**tá** usted?	¿Cómo es**tá** usted?

› **DISCUSSION**

The intonation of Spanish differs from that of American English because it has: (1) a tendency to put the highest pitch toward the beginning of the sentence rather than on the main stress, which is usually at or near the end. Both languages favor this intonation with commands, e.g.,

Hand me that chisel. Help me to lift this. Shut the door, please. **Cierre la puerta, por favor.**

but Spanish favors it generally. (2) A more sparing use of upward glides at the end of anything that is not a question and very little use of the typically English rise-fall-rise. (3) A somewhat greater preference for yes-no questions with a drop to the main stress before the final rise.

The effect of Spanish intonation on American ears is one of greater restraint, sobriety, or even gruffness, whereas that of American English on Spanish ears is one of overexcitement or overemphasis. English also gives a gliding impression as opposed to the crisp and angular impression of Spanish. This is partly due to word order. English syntax more often forces the main stress well back from the end, with the result that the upward or downward glides at the end are drawn out. In **¿Hablo con la casa del Dr. Fernández?** the stressed word **Fernández** comes at the end; but in *Is this Dr. Fernández' house?* English has to make room at the end for *house,* and the upward glide is extended over it.

13 Confirmation tags

EXAMPLES

1. Por eso la invitación, **¿eh?**
2. Tiene uno portátil, **¿no?** (**¿verdad?**) *She has a portable one, hasn't (doesn't) she?*
3. No regresa, **¿verdad?** *She isn't coming back, is she?*

statement	+	*tag*

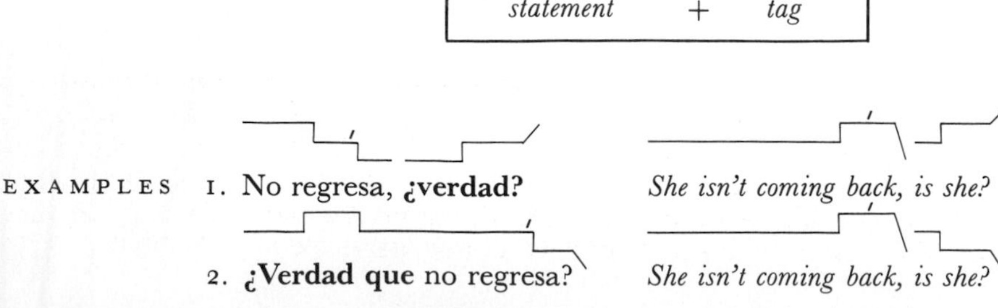

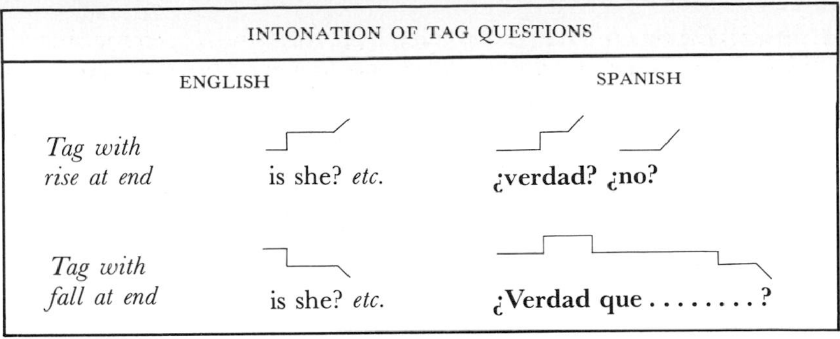

› CONSTRUCTION SUBSTITUTION DRILL

A. INSTRUCTIONS: Repeat the following statements; then repeat them again and make them tag questions by adding **¿no?** or **¿verdad?**

1. Son primas.
2. El padre de Betty es el nuevo cónsul.
3. Después estudiamos.
4. Ella tiene uno portátil.
5. Pero tú conoces a mamá.
6. Son las tres y media.
7. Pero está malo.

B. INSTRUCTIONS: Repeat the following negative statements. Then make them tag questions by adding **¿verdad?**

1. No está Julio.
2. Tú no sabes el número.
3. Ella no es la menor.
4. Las chicas no saben español.
5. No tienes que estar en casa.
6. No está el Dr. Fernández.

› PRONUNCIATION DRILL

INSTRUCTIONS: Repeat the following statements. Then repeat them again as questions with **verdad que,** along with the English equivalents, using the intonation shown in the first example.

1. Está descompuesto el tocadiscos.

   ¿Verdad que está descompuesto el tocadiscos? The record player's broken, isn't it?
2. No sabes el número.
3. María acaba de salir.
4. Ella no es la menor.
5. Tiene que estar con su tía.
6. Ella no habla español.

› DISCUSSION

¿Eh? is equivalent to English *right? huh? hm?* and the like as a tag or an independent question.

¿No? or **¿no es verdad?** (after an affirmative) and **¿verdad?** (after either an affirmative or a negative) correspond to the English tags in *You don't like it, do you? You like it, don't you? He won't eat it, will he? He'll eat it, won't he?* etc., all with rising pitch at the end. Where English puts a falling pitch at the end, Spanish does not use a tag at all but starts the utterance with **¿Verdad que?** and ends it with a falling pitch. This occurs with questions that do not really ask.

14 Present tense forms of *estar*, to be

EXAMPLES
1. **Estoy** aquí.
2. ¿Dónde **estás?**
3. Pedro **está** enfermo. *Peter is sick.*
4. **Está** ahí, a la entrada del comedor.
5. Aquí **estamos** todos.
6. Las muchachas **están** contentas. *The girls are happy.*

I am	**estoy**	we are	**estamos**
you are	**estás**		
you are he, she, it is	**está**	you are they are	**están**

› PERSON-NUMBER SUBSTITUTION DRILL

1. *Las chicas* están en la sala.
   (mi hermano, nosotros, Julio, tú y yo, ellos, usted, ustedes, él, yo)[7]
2. ¿Dónde está *el profesor?*
   (los alumnos, papá, los tíos, el recado, la invitación, los cónsules, tú)
3. *¿Yo?* Estoy contento.
   (Pablo, Betty y Susana, nosotros, ellos, Cecilia, todos, Julio y yo, los chicos)

› PATTERNED RESPONSE DRILL

	TEACHER	STUDENT
A.	1. ¿Cómo están los alumnos? *Conteste.*	**Están bien.**
	2. ¿Cómo está el profesor?	Está bien.
	3. ¿Cómo está la rubia?	Está bien.
	4. ¿Cómo está el cónsul?	Está bien.
	5. ¿Cómo están los profesores?	Están bien.
B.	1. ¿Está el teléfono en la sala o en el comedor? *Conteste.*	**Está en el comedor.**
	2. ¿Están los discos en el cuarto o en la sala?	Están en la sala.
	3. ¿Está el tocadiscos en la cocina o en la sala?	Está en la sala.
	4. ¿Está Julio en el patio o en el cuarto?	Está en el cuarto.
	5. ¿Dónde está el teléfono?	Está en el comedor.
	6. ¿Dónde están los discos?	Están en la sala.
	7. ¿Dónde está el tocadiscos?	Está en la sala.
C.	1. ¿Está usted bien? *Conteste.*	**Sí, estoy bien.**
	2. ¿Están ustedes bien?	Sí, estamos bien.
	3. ¿Están ellos bien?	Sí, están bien.

[7] In order to present more drill material in the space available, the substitution items are listed in parentheses following the sentence. These items replace the words in italics in the model. The drill is conducted in the same way as similar drills in Unit 2.

	TEACHER	STUDENT
4.	¿Cómo estás tú?	Estoy bien.
5.	¿Cómo está ella?	Está bien.
6.	¿Cómo están ellos?	Están bien.
7.	¿Estás tú contenta?	Sí, estoy contenta.
8.	¿Están ellas contentas?	Sí, están contentas.
9.	¿Estamos Jaime y yo contentos?	Sí, están contentos.
10.	¿Cómo está usted?	Estoy contento.
11.	¿Cómo están ustedes?	Estamos contentos.
12.	¿Cómo está él?	Está contento.
13.	¿Está él enfermo?	No, no está enfermo.
14.	¿Están ustedes enfermos?	No, no estamos enfermos.
15.	¿Están ellos enfermos?	No, no están enfermos.

15 *Ser* versus *estar*

ser	estar
LINKING SUBJECTS WITH NOUNS, PRONOUNS	
A. 1. Yo **soy** la menor. 2. ¿Tú **eres** amigo de ellas? 3. El padre de Betty **es** el nuevo cónsul. 4. **¿Es** usted la mamá? 5. **Somos** muchos. 6. **Son** primas. 7. ¿Quiénes **son** las dos chicas?	
LINKING SUBJECTS WITH ADJECTIVES	
B. 1. Juan **es** listo. *John is clever (ready-witted).* 2. Ese cuento **es** sucio. *That story is dirty.* 3. La modelo **es** hermosa. *The model is beautiful.*	**C.** 1. El desayuno **está** listo. *Breakfast is ready.* 2. Ese coche **está** sucio. *That car is dirty.* 3. Anita **está** hermosa con su nuevo vestido. *Annie's (all) beautiful in her new dress.*
LOCATION	
	D. 1. **¿Está** Julio? 2. Debe **estar** en la cocina. 3. **Estoy** aquí, en mi cuarto.
ORIGIN AND POSSESSION WITH **de**	
E. 1. ¿De dónde **son?** 2. ¿De quién **es** la casa? *Whose house is it?* 3. **Es** de Cecilia. *It's Cecilia's.*	
TIME OF DAY	
F. 1. ¿Qué hora **es?** 2. **Son** las tres y media.	

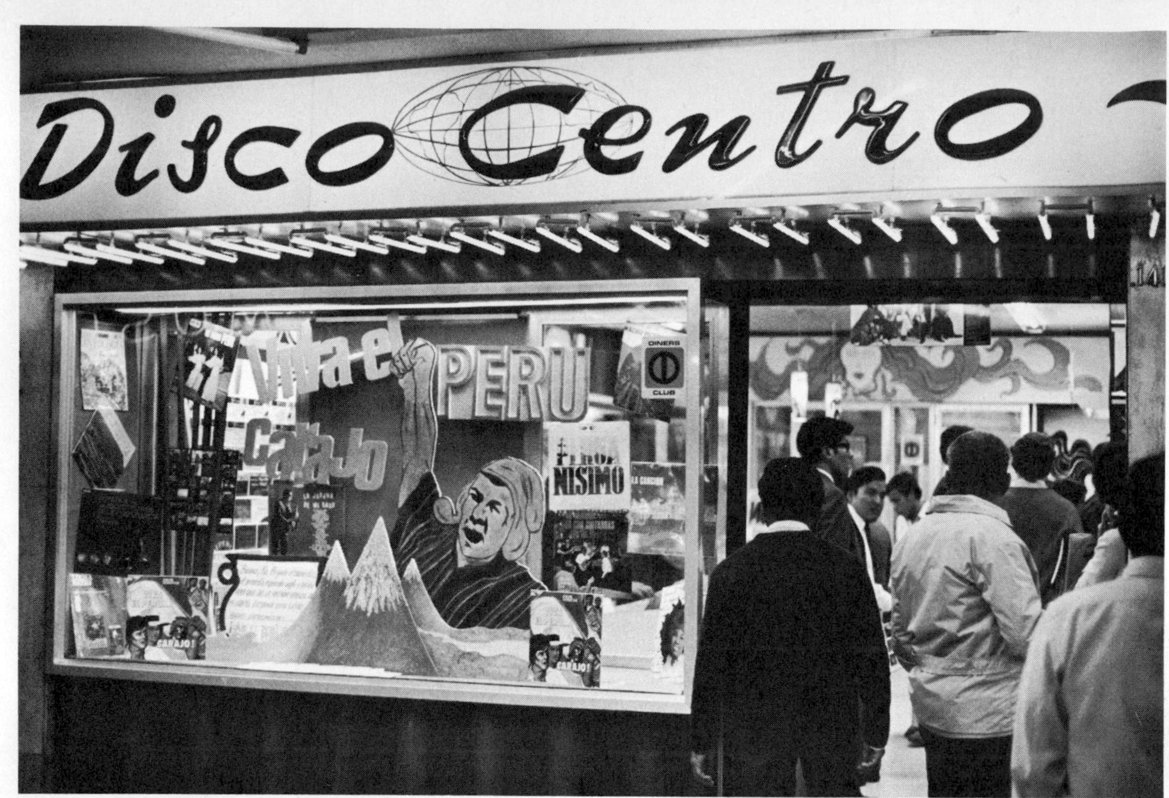

Lima, Peru: Record shop

PERSON-NUMBER SUBSTITUTION DRILL

1. *Pablo* es de Chile, pero está en los Estados Unidos.
   (yo, mi tía, ellos, nosotros, Cecilia, tú, Susana y yo, mis padres, él)
2. *Los alumnos* son amables, pero están equivocados.
   (el profesor, mi tía, ellos, los abuelos, usted, tú)
3. *Yo* no soy profesor, pero estoy contento.
   (Julio, nosotros, mis tíos, ustedes, tú, ellas, la señora)

QUESTION DRILL

INSTRUCTIONS: The teacher will read the following questions. The student will answer with **ser** or **estar,** whichever is appropriate.

TEACHER	STUDENT
1. ¿El profesor? ¿Equivocado? *Conteste.*	**Sí, el profesor está equivocado.**
2. ¿El tocadiscos? ¿Descompuesto?	Sí, el tocadiscos está descompuesto.
3. ¿El padre de Betty? ¿El nuevo cónsul?	Sí, el padre de Betty es el nuevo cónsul.
4. ¿Julio? ¿Enfermo?	Sí, Julio está enfermo.
5. ¿Las dos chicas? ¿Primas?	Sí, las dos chicas son primas.
6. ¿Susana? ¿De los Estados Unidos?	Sí, Susana es de los Estados Unidos.
7. ¿Todos? ¿En casa de Olga?	Sí, todos están en casa de Olga.

TEACHER	STUDENT
8. ¿La tía? ¿Amable?	Sí, la tía es amable.
9. ¿Qué hora? ¿Las tres?	Sí, son las tres.
10. ¿Doña Mercedes? ¿Bien?	Sí, doña Mercedes está bien.
11. ¿Olga y Cecilia? ¿Contentas?	Sí, Olga y Cecilia están contentas.
12. ¿La casa? ¿Bonita?	Sí, la casa es bonita.
13. ¿El tocadiscos? ¿Portátil?	Sí, el tocadiscos es portátil.
14. ¿Julio? ¿En su cuarto?	Sí, Julio está en su cuarto.
15. ¿La familia? ¿Grande?	Sí, la familia es grande.
16. ¿Los abuelos? ¿En Chile?	Sí, los abuelos están en Chile.

› TRANSLATION DRILL

1. Betty is in the dining room.
   She is pretty.
2. It's two-thirty.
   The students are here.
3. The records are Spanish.
   The record player is broken.
4. How is Mrs. del Valle?
   Where is she from?
5. Where are you (*plural*) from?
   Are you all right here?
6. You are not mistaken.
   The consul is my father.
7. Where is the professor?
   What time is it?
8. Mr. Arjona is my uncle.
   He is in Chile.
9. Who is the blonde?
   Is she here?
10. My family is in the living room.
    The living room is big.
11. The girls are Americans.
    They are very happy.
12. Cecilia is very kind.
    What a pity! She is sick.
13. The record player is a portable.
    It's in the living room.

› PATTERNED RESPONSE DRILL

TEACHER	STUDENT
1. ¿Está mi primo? Es Pedro González.	**¿Quién es su primo? No, no está aquí.**
2. ¿Está mi prima? Es Elena Fernández.	¿Quién es su prima? No, no está aquí.
3. ¿Está mi tío? Es Julio Arjona.	¿Quién es su tío? No, no está aquí.
4. ¿Está mi tía? Es Mercedes Flores.	¿Quién es su tía? No, no está aquí.
5. ¿Está mi profesor? Es José María Martínez.	¿Quién es su profesor? No, no está aquí.
6. ¿Está mi profesora? Es María Romero.	¿Quién es su profesora? No, no está aquí.

› DISCUSSION

The two verbs **ser** and **estar** cover most of the meanings of *to be.*

The verb *to be* links something to the subject of the sentence. In the sentences *John is sick, John is a lawyer,* and *John is here, is* ties *sick, lawyer,* and *here* to *John.*

With **estar** the things linked are thought of as not really "belonging to" the subject. The speaker already has an impression of the subject, and **estar** adds something from outside. So **estar** is used to tell *where* the subject is (section D in the box above) or the *state* or *condition* the subject is in (section C above).

Ser tells *what* the subject is, so it is used for tying the subject to: (1) nouns or pronouns (section A in the box above), (2) adjectives when they are thought of as belonging to the subject and not added to it (section B above), and (3) expressions of origin and possession (section E above). Time of day is a special case (section F above).

It is sometimes difficult in English to distinguish between *what* something is and the *state* or *condition* it is in, especially when adjectives are used. Consider these two sentences:

My tools are handy; I wouldn't have any other kind.
My tools are handy; they're right here in the kit.

The first sentence refers to the *nature* of the tools. Perhaps they have sturdy handles or are made to be used for more than one purpose. The second sentence refers to the *state* that the tools are in—the interest is in their condition, or location.

When English wants to be very precise about a difference like this, it may use two different adjectives. Though *ready* is sometimes used in the sense 'quick-witted' (*He's a ready chap*), we normally use a different adjective, *clever,* for this meaning, reserving *ready* for 'in a state of readiness.' In Spanish it is very easy to use the same adjective for both purposes, since the distinction is made in the verb:

Juan is clever.	**Juan es listo.**
Breakfast is ready.	**El desayuno está listo.**

Spanish is not only *able* to make the distinction; it *insists* on it wherever it occurs.[8] So where English just trusts to the context to clear up any confusion, Spanish requires the proper verb to be selected:

That story is dirty.	**Ese cuento es sucio.**
That car is dirty.	**Ese coche está sucio.**

If a story is dirty, it can only be so by nature. Clean it up and it is not the same story any more. If a car is dirty, it can only be so by state or condition. It can be cleaned and will still be the same car.

As a speaker of English you have learned to make this distinction with the word *all* when it is used as an intensifier. Notice that in the cases above where **estar** is used, *all* may appear in English, but where **ser** is used, it may not:

ACCEPTABLE	UNACCEPTABLE
Breakfast is all ready.	John is all clever.
That car is all dirty.	That story is all dirty.
Look, mama! Annie's all beautiful in her new dress!	We hired the model because she was all beautiful.

In the last pair above, the model is beautiful by nature; Annie is beautiful in the state or condition of wearing a new dress: **La modelo es hermosa; Anita está hermosa con su nuevo vestido.**

The notion of *change* to a state or condition, expressed with **estar,** can be made evident by paraphrasing the English examples in section C with *has become:*

Breakfast has become ready.
The car has become dirty.
Annie has become beautiful in her new dress.

Since telling *where* something is never refers to the nature of the thing itself, **estar** is used:

Brazil is in South America.	**Brasil está en Sudamérica.**
Joe is with me.	**Pepe está conmigo.**

[8] A foreign language often forces you to make distinctions that seem irrelevant or unnecessary in your own language. **Ser** and **estar** compel you to see "being" from two points of view and to decide between them. English compels similar "unnecessary" distinctions from the point of view of Spanish-speakers: for example, in place of one word **hacer,** English requires a choice between *make* and *do.*

UNIT 4

The Saint's Day

F. *Francisco* R. *Don Rafael, friend of Francisco*

F. I'm hungry [have hunger]; I'm going to go eat something. Won't you come with me, Don Rafael?

R. I can't right now, thanks. However, since you're going, can you send me up a cup of coffee?

F. Of course. Be glad to.

* * *

F. (*a short time later*) Are you writing to someone, Don Rafael?

R. Yes, to my niece who lives in Mexico. I'm writing to congratulate her on her birthday this month.

El día del santo

F. *Francisco* R. *Don Rafael, amigo de Francisco*

F. Tengo hambre; voy a ir a comer algo. ¿No quiere venir conmigo, don (1) Rafael?

R. Ahora no puedo, gracias. Sin embargo, ya que va, ¿puede mandarme una taza de café?

F. Cómo no. Con mucho gusto.

* * *

F. (*un rato después*) ¿Le escribe a alguien, don Rafael?

R. Sí, a mi sobrina que vive en México. Le escribo para felicitarla por su cumpleaños este mes.

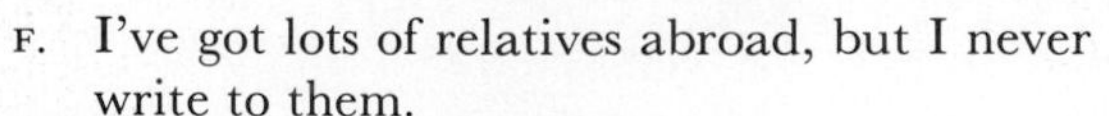

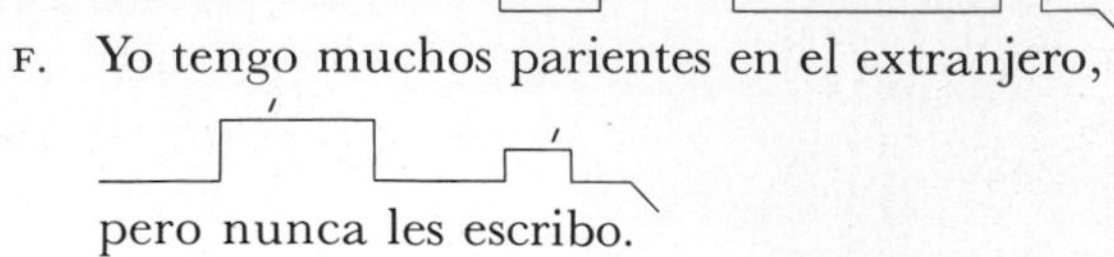

F. I've got lots of relatives abroad, but I never write to them.

F. Yo tengo muchos parientes en el extranjero, pero nunca les escribo.

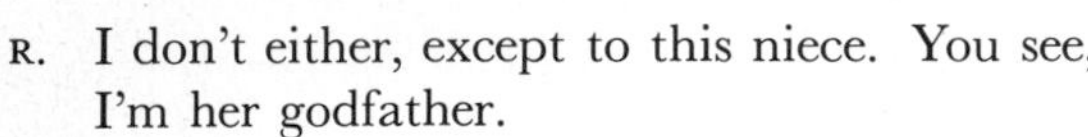

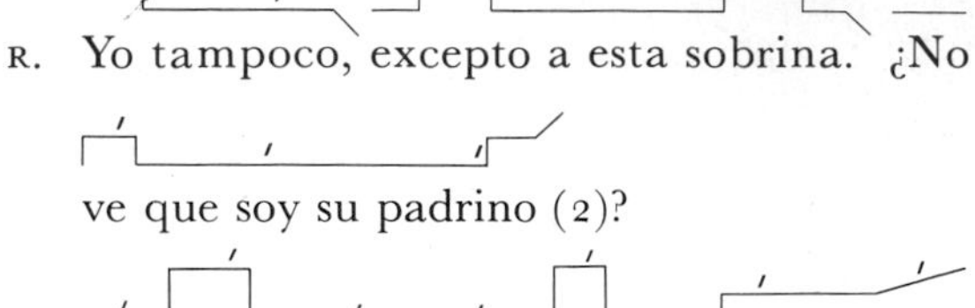

R. I don't either, except to this niece. You see, I'm her godfather.

R. Yo tampoco, excepto a esta sobrina. ¿No ve que soy su padrino (2)?

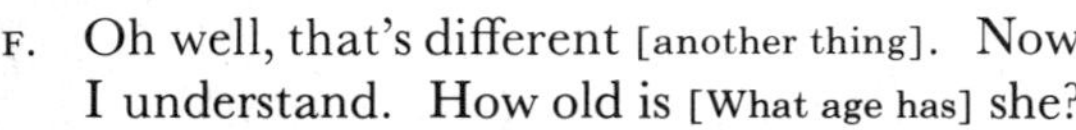

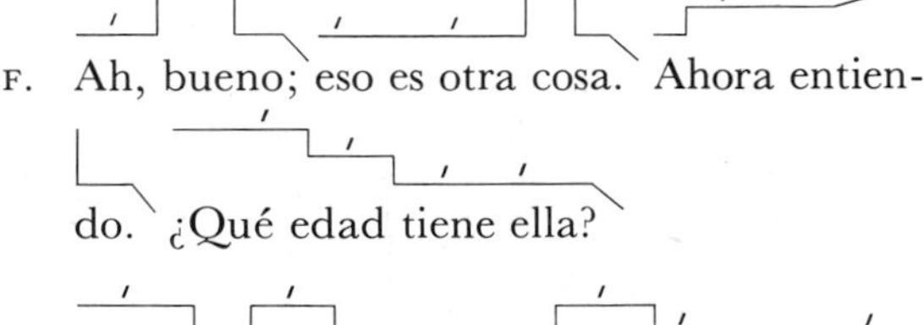

F. Oh well, that's different [another thing]. Now I understand. How old is [What age has] she?

F. Ah, bueno; eso es otra cosa. Ahora entiendo. ¿Qué edad tiene ella?

R. She must be around twenty-one [have some twenty-one years]. She's been living there about four years.

R. Debe tener unos veintiún años. Hace como cuatro años que vive allá.

* * *

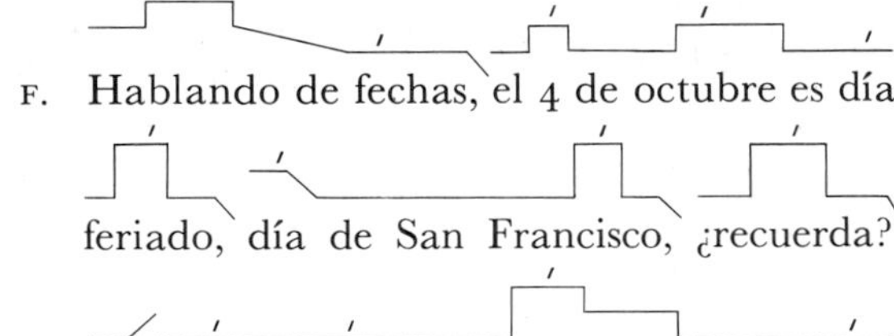

F. Speaking of dates, the 4th of October is a holiday, St. Francis' Day, remember?

F. Hablando de fechas, el 4 de octubre es día feriado, día de San Francisco, ¿recuerda?

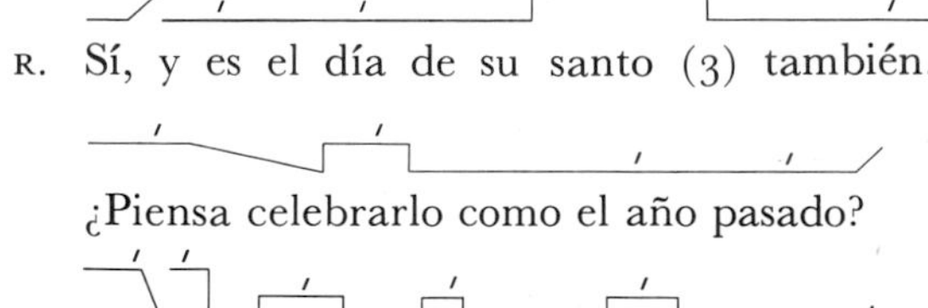

R. Yes, and it's your saint's day, too. Do you expect to celebrate like last year?

R. Sí, y es el día de su santo (3) también. ¿Piensa celebrarlo como el año pasado?

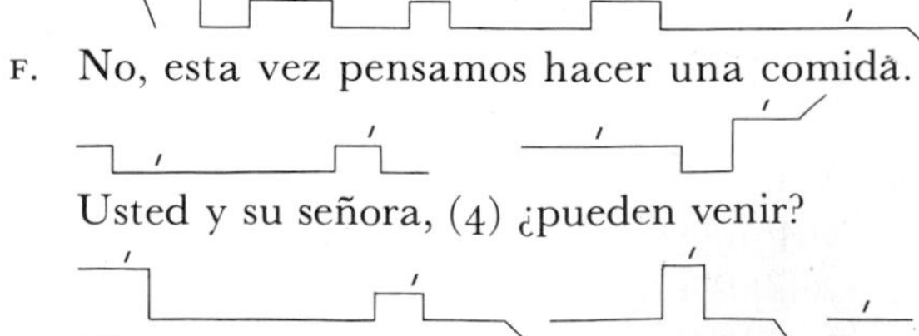

F. No, this time we're planning to have [make] a dinner. How about you and your wife, can you come?

F. No, esta vez pensamos hacer una comida. Usted y su señora, (4) ¿pueden venir?

R. Sure we can; delighted. But it's still two weeks off [are lacking]. What day is it [does it fall]?

R. Claro que podemos; encantados. Pero todavía faltan dos semanas. ¿Qué día cae?

Lima, Peru: Avenida Arequipa

F. Wednesday. You know where we live?

R. I know that you live near Central Park, but I don't remember the exact address.

F. Very easy; it's not far. You go [follow; continue] straight up [along] North Avenue till you come to Twentieth Street, and then . . .

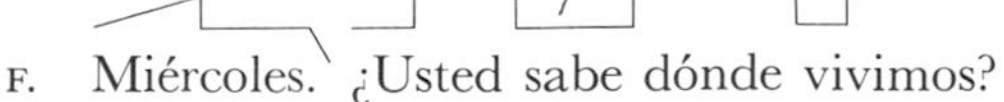

F. Miércoles. ¿Usted sabe dónde vivimos?

R. Yo sé que viven cerca del Parque Central, pero no recuerdo la dirección exacta.

F. Muy fácil; no está lejos. Usted sigue derecho por la Avenida Norte hasta llegar a la

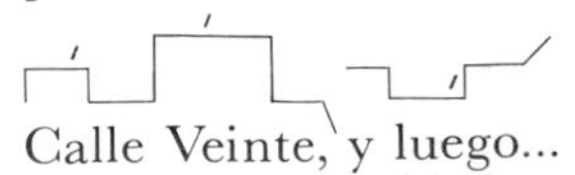

Calle Veinte, y luego...

Lima, Peru: Private residence

R. Now I remember: then I turn right and go [continue] three more blocks, the last house on the left, right?

R. Ya recuerdo: ahí doblo a la derecha y sigo tres cuadras más, la última casa a la izquierda, ¿verdad?

F. That's it, a small green house [that is] on the corner.

F. Exactamente, una casita verde que está en la esquina.

cultural notes

(1) **Don** is a title of respect used with a man's given name. As a form of address its use parallels that of the feminine **doña** (see Unit 2, Cultural Note 1).

(2) A **padrino** is the sponsor for a child at baptism. A regular feature of Hispanic life, the relationship of the **padrino** to his godchild (**ahijado** or **ahijada**) may vary from the merely nominal to the actual assumption of certain responsibilities toward the child. A set of specific family relationships with the child's parents may also be found.

(3) The Catholic calendar is full of saints' days, and people who are named for saints ordinarily celebrate their saint's day. In practice this means that all men bearing the given name Francisco, for example, will celebrate **el día de San Francisco** (St. Francis' Day, October 4). Certain saints' days are recognized as national holidays in some countries.

(4) The equivalents for *wife* are **señora, esposa,** and **mujer.** When referring to his own wife a gentleman often uses **esposa** and sometimes **mujer.** When referring to someone else's wife he is likely to use the more formal **señora.**

› PRONUNCIATION EXERCISE (Reread "Stop-spirants" and "The sounds /r/ and /rr/" in Unit 1, Section 1.)

A. /d/ and /r/ between vowels. INSTRUCTIONS: Repeat the following pairs of words just as you hear them.

[đ]	[r]	[đ]	[r]	[đ]	[r]
cada	cara	modo	moro	todo	toro
codo	coro	mudo	muro	oda	hora
lodo	loro	pida	pira	hada	ara
mida	mira	seda	sera		

The Spanish fricative [đ] is similar to the voiced *th* in English *this,* though pronounced much more laxly. Spanish [r] resembles English [t] and [d] in words like *latter* and *ladder, kitty* and *kiddy, mutter* and *mudder* for those speakers who make these pairs of words sound virtually the same. A stop [d] rather than a fricative [đ] between vowels in a Spanish word might be interpreted by the Spanish ear as an [r] sound. Thus Spanish **todo** (*all, every*), if incorrectly pronounced with a stop [d] between vowels, might be heard by a native Spanish speaker as **toro** (*bull*). To avoid this kind of misunderstanding be sure to use the fricative [đ] between vowels in Spanish.

B. /r/ and /rr/. INSTRUCTIONS: Repeat the following pairs of words just as you hear them.

[r]	[rr]	[r]	[rr]	[r]	[rr]
caro	carro	para	parra	amara	amarra
cero	cerro	pero	perro	serete	se rete
coro	corro	vara	barra	seraje	se raje
foro	forro	fiero	fierro	seronda	se ronda
mira	mirra	torero	torrero	serosa	se rosa

The Spanish voiced alveolar tap [r] is spelled **r** between vowels, whereas the voiced alveolar multiple trill [rr] is spelled **rr,** as in the preceding list of words. When initial in a word, or when following [n], [l], or [z] (i.e., the variant of /s/ before the voiced consonant), only the multiple trill [rr] is found, and in these positions it is spelled **r.**

At the end of a syllable either [r] or [rr] may be heard, both of which are spelled **r.** (You may sometimes hear a fricative type of alveolar sound [ɹ] at the beginning or at the end of a word. The multiple trill [rr] can always be substituted for the fricative sound.)

16 Present tense forms of *–er* and *–ir* verbs

EXAMPLES

A. 1. **Creo** que es el diecisiete (from **creer** *to think, believe*).
2. Nunca les **escribo** (from **escribir** *to write*).

B. 1. **Debe** estar en la cocina (from **deber** *must, ought*).
2. ¿Le **escribe** a alguien, don Rafael?
3. Mi sobrina que **vive** en México (from **vivir** *to live*).

C. 1. **Comemos** en el restorán. *We eat at the restaurant.*
2. ¿Usted sabe dónde **vivimos?**

D. 1. **Viven** cerca del Parque Central.
2. ¿Por qué no **abren** la puerta (from **abrir** *to open*)?

	comer *to eat* com–	vivir *to live* viv–
I	–o	–o
you	–es	–es
you, he, she, it	–e	–e
we	–emos	–imos
you, they	–en	–en

Except in the forms corresponding to *we,* **–er** and **–ir** verbs have the same endings in the present tense.[1]

› PERSON-NUMBER SUBSTITUTION DRILL

1. *Rafael* nunca come en el restorán.
   (ellos, nosotros, usted, tú, él, Pepe, mi señora y yo, Cecilia)
2. *Yo* creo que es la última vez.
   (Olga, mis abuelos, nosotros, ustedes, Susana, tú, ellos)
3. Debo estar equivocado esta vez.
   (él, tú, Julio, Susana, nosotros, ellos, nosotras, ellas, alguien)
4. *Ella* vive muy cerca del parque.
   (Francisco y su señora, yo, mis padres, mi padrino, tú, ella, mi señora y yo, la profesora)
5. Le escribo a un pariente en el norte.
   (él, nosotros, mi papá, Francisco, ellos, mi compañero de escuela)
6. *Jaime* nunca abre la puerta.
   (yo, ellos, doña Mercedes, ustedes, nosotros, tú, usted)

› CHOICE-QUESTION RESPONSE DRILL

INSTRUCTIONS: Answer the following questions by selecting one of the alternatives proposed in each question.

1. TEACHER: ¿Usted come en el restorán o en casa?
   STUDENT: **Como en casa.**
2. ¿Usted cree que son dos cuadras o tres?
3. ¿Usted vive en una calle o en una avenida?
4. ¿Viven ustedes cerca o lejos del parque?
5. ¿Vive su sobrina aquí o en el extranjero?
6. ¿Le escribe usted a su padrino para su cumpleaños o para el día de su santo?
7. ¿Abre usted primero el libro de inglés o el libro de español?

17 Verbs with changes in the stem: *o → ue, e → ie, e → i*

EXAMPLES A. 1. No **recuerdo** el color exacto.
I don't remember the exact color.
2. Tal vez **puedo** ir.
3. Ahora **entiendo.**

[1]These verb forms appear in the Appendix under "Regular Verbs."

B. 1. **¿Puedes** traer tu tocadiscos?
2. ¡Qué ideas **tienes!**
3. ¿Por qué no **vienes?**

C. 1. Es día de San Francisco, **¿recuerda?**
2. **¿Puede** mandarme una taza de café?
3. **¿Piensa** celebrarlo como el año pasado?
4. ¿No **quiere** venir conmigo, don Rafael?
5. Ella **tiene** uno portátil.

D. 1. Claro que **podemos.**
2. Esta vez **pensamos** hacer una comida.

E. 1. Usted y su señora, **¿pueden** venir?
2. ¿No **tienen** ustedes uno allá?
3. Ellos **prefieren** leche. *They prefer milk.*

recordar *to remember*	poder *can, to be able*	pensar *to intend, think about*	preferir *to prefer*	querer *to wish, want*
recuerdo recuerdas recuerda recordamos recuerdan	puedo puedes puede podemos pueden	pienso piensas piensa pensamos piensan	prefiero prefieres prefiere preferimos prefieren	quiero quieres quiere queremos quieren

In certain verbs the last vowel of the stem is changed when it is stressed, giving **o → ue** and **e → ie.**[2]

tener *to have*	venir *to come*
tengo tienes tiene tenemos tienen	vengo vienes viene venimos vienen

The verbs **tener** and **venir** are like the other verbs with changes in the stem, except that in the first-person singular (the form corresponding to **yo** *I*) they have a different kind of irregularity.

EXAMPLES A. 1. **Sigo** tres cuadras más.
2. Te **pido** un favor. *I'm asking you a favor.*
3. Usted **sigue**[3] derecho por la Avenida Norte.
4. Los muchachos **siguen** enfermos. *The boys are still sick.*

B. 1. **Digo** que es extranjera. *I say that she is a foreigner.*
2. **¿Dices** que no está lejos? *You say it's not far?*

[2] See Appendix, "Stem-Changing Verbs."

[3] The spelling **gu** before **e** and **i** represents the same sound as the spelling **g** before **a, o,** or **u.** That is to say, the **u** in the spellings **gue** and **gui** is "silent" as in the English words *guess, rogue,* and *beguile.*

A.[4] pedir *to request, ask for*	B. decir *to say, tell*
pido pides pide pedimos piden	digo dices dice decimos dicen

A few **-ir** verbs change **e** to **i** in the forms shown. Note that the **yo** form of **decir** also has an irregularity similar to that of **tener** and **venir.**

PERSON-NUMBER SUBSTITUTION DRILL

A. 1. *Nosotros* no recordamos el número.
(Julio, ellos, yo, mi profesor, ustedes, tú, Gloria)
2. *Nosotros* podemos celebrarlo con una comida.
(tú, don Rafael, mis tíos, yo, Pepe y yo, ella, ellas)

B. 1. Pensamos regresar un rato después.
(yo, él, tú, Pablo y yo, Pablo y usted, Susana, ellos)
2. Entendemos algo, pero no todo.
(el señor, tú, María Elena, yo, Olga y yo, él, ustedes)
3. Queremos comer algo.
(yo, mi señora, tú, Cecilia, ustedes, usted, mi señora y yo)
4. *Nosotros* nunca cerramos la puerta.
(el señor Arjona, yo, ustedes, él, tú, mi hermano y yo)

C. 1. Hoy no tengo mucha hambre.
(tú, ellos, mi hijo, nosotros, usted, ustedes, ella)
2. Vengo el cuatro de octubre.
(él, ellos, doña Mercedes, nosotros, tú, mi hermana, ellas)

D. 1. Después de un rato seguimos.
(yo, ellos, el señor Flores, él y yo, tú, ustedes, él)
2. Pedimos una taza de café.
(tú, él, mis padres, yo, ustedes, ella, alguien)
3. *Ellos* prefieren leche.
(Paquito, nosotros, tú, yo, ustedes, mi prima)
4. *Francisco* dice buenos días al profesor.
(ellos, mi sobrina y yo, tú y Olga, yo, la rubia, ustedes)

CHOICE-QUESTION RESPONSE DRILL

A. 1. ¿Puede usted comer en diez minutos o en media hora?
2. ¿Recuerda usted el número del teléfono o el número de la casa?

B. 1. ¿Quiere estudiar o escribir?
2. ¿Piensa estar en México una semana o un mes?
3. ¿Entienden ustedes una parte o todo?
4. ¿Quieren ustedes ir primero o después?
5. ¿Piensa doblar a la izquierda o a la derecha?
6. ¿Cierra usted primero o después?

C. 1. ¿Tiene que ir a la casa o a la escuela?
2. ¿Su hija tiene cuatro años o cinco?
3. ¿Viene la muchacha ahora o más tarde?

D. 1. ¿Piden ustedes un libro o un disco?
2. ¿La muchacha sigue enferma o ya está bien?

[4] Letters appearing with grammatical material in boxes refer to the specific examples associated with that material.

18 Present tense with future meaning

EXAMPLES A. 1. **¿Abro** la puerta? *Shall I open the door?*
2. ¿Le **mandamos** una taza de café? *Shall we send you up a cup of coffee?*

B. 1. Después **estudiamos.**
2. Yo **llamo** más tarde.
3. Nosotros **pasamos** por ti.
4. Ellos lo **hacen,** entonces. *They'll do it, then.*

FUTURE	PRESENT
A. shall I . . . ?	**-o**
shall we . . . ?	**-amos** / **-emos** / **-imos**

In Spanish the present tense of the first person is used when English uses *shall* with a future meaning to ask instructions.

FUTURE	PRESENT
B. we'll study	**estudiamos**
I'll call	**llamo**
we'll come by	**pasamos**
he'll eat	**come**
they'll write	**escriben**
etc.	**etc.**

The present tense is also used when the speaker offers or agrees to a future action.

› TRANSLATION DRILL

A. 1. But she'll be back in ten minutes.
Pero regresa dentro de diez minutos.
2. But she'll call in ten minutes.
3. But she'll arrive in ten minutes.
4. But she'll open the door in ten minutes.
5. But she'll send the message in ten minutes.
6. But she'll write the invitation in ten minutes.

B. 1. Shall I go in with you, Don Rafael?
¿Entro con usted, don Rafael?
2. Shall I eat with you, Don Rafael?
3. Shall I wait with you, Don Rafael?
4. Shall I go with you, Don Rafael?
5. Shall I return with you, Don Rafael?
6. Shall I celebrate with you, Don Rafael?
7. Shall I speak with you, Don Rafael?

C. 1. We'll (*I propose that we*) study later.
Estudiamos más tarde.
2. We'll celebrate later.
3. We'll talk later.
4. We'll eat later.
5. We'll write later.
6. We'll come by for you later.
7. We'll bring the record player later.
8. We'll send the coffee later.

› DISCUSSION

The present tense is used more frequently in Spanish than in English to express a future meaning:

1. As regularly as in English for a planned future action: *She's returning* (*she'll be back*) *in ten minutes* **Regresa dentro de diez minutos;** *I work* (*plan to work, am working*) *here tomorrow* **Trabajo aquí mañana.**

2. Regularly, and hence more often than in English, to ask for instructions (examples A): *What do I* (*shall I*) *ask for now?* **¿Qué pido ahora?** *Shall we* (less likely, *do we*) *send you up a cup of coffee?* **¿Le mandamos una taza de café?**

3. Regularly, and hence unlike English, for unplanned actions that one proposes or offers on the spur of the moment (examples B). The English meaning *can* is appropriate here: *I'll call* (*I can just as well call*) *later* **Yo llamo más tarde;** *We'll study* (*we can study*) *later* **Después estudiamos.**

The present tense is possible here because the context makes the future meaning clear. Note the frequency of adverbs of time such as **más tarde, después, mañana** *tomorrow,* etc.

19 With-verb pronouns

EXAMPLES

A. Déje**me** ver. *Let me see.*

B. **Te** felicito. *I congratulate you.*

C. 1. ¿Puede mandar**lo?** *Can you send it?*
2. Le escribo para felicitar**la.**

D. **Nos** conocen. *They know us.*

E. 1. **Los** invita a entrar. *He invites them to come in.*
2. No **las** recuerdo. *I don't remember them.*

DIRECT OBJECT					
me		**me**	us		**nos**
you		**te**			
you / him / it	*masculine*	**lo**	you / them	*masculine*	**los**
you / her / it	*feminine*	**la**	you / them	*feminine*	**las**

With-verb pronouns are always joined, in speech, to a verb. Normally they precede the verb, but with the infinitive and with affirmative commands they follow. (In writing, a with-verb pronoun that follows a verb is always attached to it.)

› CONSTRUCTION SUBSTITUTION DRILL

A. INSTRUCTIONS: Repeat the following sentences just as you hear them. Then say them again, substituting a with-verb pronoun for the appropriate noun.

1. TEACHER: Pablo ve *la casa.* *Repita.*
STUDENT: **Pablo ve la casa.**
TEACHER: *Cambie.*
STUDENT: **Pablo la ve.**
Pablo ve el número.
Pablo lo ve.
Pablo ve las calles.
Pablo las ve.
Pablo ve los colores.
Pablo los ve.
2. Yo no tengo *el recado.*
(la invitación, el tocadiscos, el lápiz, el café, la dirección, las tazas, los discos)
3. Tampoco necesitas *el libro.*
(la dirección, el café, las tazas, la clase, los cuartos, la sala, el total)
4. No recuerdo *el número.*
(la fecha, la edad, el día, las semanas, la avenida, las calles, la dirección)
5. Quiero ver *el libro.*
(las calles, la avenida, los discos, las invitaciones, el patio, las casas, los cuartos)
6. Rafael va a dejar *los libros.*
(el número, la dirección, el recado, las tazas, los discos, la invitación, el tocadiscos)

B. INSTRUCTIONS: The teacher will make the following comments to various students, who will respond with the appropriate comment as indicated in the model.

TEACHER: Yo no tengo *el libro*. STUDENT: **Tampoco lo tengo yo.**
(la invitación, los discos, las cosas, el número, los cafés, las tazas, el recado)

› PERSON-NUMBER SUBSTITUTION DRILL

1. Si *ella* no viene, no la invitan.
   (yo, él, Julio y Olga, nosotros, ellas, tú)
2. Si *yo* no llego a las tres, no me esperan.
   (nosotros, tú, él, Pablo, ellos, Cecilia)
3. Si *Olga* llama, la felicitan.
   (yo, nosotros, doña Mercedes, ellos, tú, él)
4. Si *ellos* pasan, déjelos entrar, si me hace el favor.
   (ella, Julio, nosotros, Olga y Francisco, la señora, Cecilia y su mamá)

› PATTERNED RESPONSE DRILL

INSTRUCTIONS: Give negative answers to the following questions, using a with-verb pronoun to refer to the noun in the question.

A. 1. TEACHER: ¿Recuerda la dirección?
   STUDENT: **No, no la recuerdo.**
2. ¿Celebra su cumpleaños?
   No, no lo celebro.
3. ¿Abre la puerta?
4. ¿Quiere el teléfono?
5. ¿Entiende el libro?
6. ¿Manda los discos?
7. ¿Pide la comida?
8. ¿Entiende la idea?

B. 1. ¿Puede traer el tocadiscos?
   No, no puedo traerlo.
2. ¿Quiere ver la puerta?
   No, no quiero verla.
3. ¿Piensa estudiar el libro?
4. ¿Desea dejar la invitación?
5. ¿Va a celebrar el cumpleaños?
6. ¿Necesitas saber la dirección?

EXAMPLES

1. Si **me** hace el favor.
2. **Me** parece bueno. *It looks OK (to me).*
3. No puedo mandar**te** el café. *I can't send you the coffee.*
4. ¿Qué **te** parece el libro? *How do you like the book?* (*How does the book seem to you?* [from **parecer**]).
5. **Le** escribo para felicitarla. *I'm writing (her) to congratulate her.*
6. No quieren hablar**nos**. *They don't want to talk to us.*
7. ¿**Les** abro la puerta? *Shall I open the door for them?*

INDIRECT OBJECT			
me	**me**	us	**nos**
you	**te**		
you, him, her, it	**le**	you, them	**les**

The indirect object expresses a relationship that is usually expressed with *to* or *for* in English. Indirect-object pronouns combine with the verb in the same way as direct-object pronouns.

❯ PATTERNED RESPONSE DRILL

NOTE TO TEACHER: The teacher will ask questions and indicate the correct reply by pointing to different students in the class, and those called on will respond accordingly. The students will respond with *me* if the teacher points to only one; with *nos* if to the student and another; with *les* if to two other persons, and so on.

NOTE TO STUDENTS: In the laboratory students should do this drill with books open, visualizing the teacher's gestures.

		TEACHER	STUDENT
A.	1.	¿Qué le parece el libro? (*Teacher points to one student*)	Me parece bueno.
		¿Le gusta?	Sí, me gusta mucho.
	2.	¿Qué les parece el libro? (*Points to the student and another*)	Nos parece bueno.
		¿Les gusta?	Sí, nos gusta mucho.
	3.	¿Qué les parece el libro? (*To two others*)	Les parece bueno.
		¿Les gusta?	Sí, les gusta mucho.
	4.	¿Qué le parece el libro? (*To one other*)	Le parece bueno.
		¿Le gusta?	Sí, le gusta mucho.
	5.	¿Qué me parece el libro? (*To himself*)	Le parece bueno.
		¿Me gusta?	Sí, le gusta mucho.
	6.	¿Qué nos parece el libro? (*To the whole class and himself*)	Nos parece bueno.
		¿Nos gusta?	Sí, nos gusta mucho.
	7.	¿Qué nos parece el libro? (*To himself and one other*)	Les parece bueno.
		¿Nos gusta?	Sí, les gusta mucho.
B.	1.	¿Qué le parecen los libros? (*To one student*)	Me parecen buenos.
		¿Le gustan?	Sí, me gustan mucho.
	2.	¿Qué les parecen los libros? (*To the student and another*)	Nos parecen buenos.
		¿Les gustan?	Sí, nos gustan mucho.
	3.	¿Qué les parecen los libros? (*To two others*)	Les parecen buenos.
		¿Les gustan?	Sí, les gustan mucho.
	4.	¿Qué le parecen los libros? (*To one other*)	Le parecen buenos.
		¿Le gustan?	Sí, le gustan mucho.
	5.	¿Qué me parecen los libros? (*To himself*)	Le parecen buenos.
		¿Me gustan?	Sí, le gustan mucho.
	6.	¿Qué nos parecen los libros? (*To the whole class and himself*)	Nos parecen buenos.
		¿Nos gustan?	Sí, nos gustan mucho.
	7.	¿Qué nos parecen los libros? (*To himself and one other*)	Les parecen buenos.
		¿Nos gustan?	Sí, les gustan mucho.
C.	1.	¿Quién le habla en español? (*To one student*)	El profesor me habla en español.
		¿Qué le dice?	Me dice buenos días.
	2.	¿Quién les habla en español? (*To the student and another*)	El profesor nos habla en español.
		¿Qué les dice?	Nos dice buenos días.
	3.	¿Quién les habla en español? (*To two others*)	El profesor les habla en español.
		¿Qué les dice?	Les dice buenos días.
	4.	¿Quién le habla en español? (*To one other*)	El profesor le habla en español.
		¿Qué le dice?	Le dice buenos días.
D.	1.	¿Quién me escribe? (*To himself*)	Le escribe don Pablo.
	2.	¿Quién les escribe? (*To two others*)	Les escribe don Pablo.

TEACHER	STUDENT
3. ¿Quién le escribe? (*To one student*)	Me escribe don Pablo.
4. ¿Quién les escribe? (*To the student and another*)	Nos escribe don Pablo.
5. ¿Quién nos escribe? (*To himself and another student*)	Les escribe don Pablo.

E. 1. ¿Qué piensa hacerle Susana? (*To one other*)	Piensa hacerle una comida.
2. ¿Qué piensa hacernos Susana? (*To the whole class and himself*)	Piensa hacernos una comida.
3. ¿Qué piensa hacerles Susana? (*To the student and another*)	Piensa hacernos una comida.
4. ¿Qué piensa hacerle Susana? (*To one student*)	Piensa hacerme una comida.
5. ¿Qué piensa hacerme Susana? (*To himself*)	Piensa hacerle una comida.

F. 1. ¿Qué quiere decirme Olga? (*To himself*)	Quiere decirle la verdad.
2. ¿Qué quiere decirnos Olga? (*To the whole class and himself*)	Quiere decirnos la verdad.
3. ¿Qué quiere decirle Olga? (*To one other*)	Quiere decirle la verdad.
4. ¿Qué quiere decirnos Olga? (*To himself and another student*)	Quiere decirles la verdad.
5. ¿Qué quiere decirles Olga? (*To the student and another*)	Quiere decirnos la verdad.
6. ¿Qué quiere decirle Olga? (*To one student*)	Quiere decirme la verdad.

SUMMARY CHART OF OBJECT PRONOUNS

DIRECT			INDIRECT
me	⟵	**me** ⟶	me
you	⟵	**te** ⟶	you
you, him, it (*masculine*)	**lo**	**le**	you, him, her, it
you, her, it (*feminine*)	**la**		
us	⟵	**nos** ⟶	us
you, them (*masculine*)	**los**	**les**	you, them
you, them (*feminine*)	**las**		

Direct- and indirect-object pronouns are the same in the **me, te,** and **nos** forms and different in the **l-** forms.

› TRANSLATION DRILL

1. I write (to) him.
   Le escribo.
   I write (to) her.
   Le escribo.
   I write it.
   Lo (la) escribo.
   I write (to) them.
   Les escribo.
   I write them (books, words, etc.).
   Los (las) escribo.

2. I say to (tell) him.
   I say to her.
   I say it.
   I say to them.
   I say them.

3. I speak to him.
   I speak to her.
   I speak it.
   I speak to them.
   I speak them.

PRONOUN SUBSTITUTION DRILL

1. **Le escribe para felicitarlo.**
2. Les escribe ______________
3. ______________ felicitarte
4. Nos escribe ______________
5. ______________ felicitarla
6. Les escribe ______________
7. ______________ felicitarme
8. Te escribe ______________
9. ______________ felicitarlas
10. Le escribe ______________

DISCUSSION

The English pronouns used as objects of prepositions are the same as those used as objects of verbs: *Let's follow him, Let's get a description of him.* But in Spanish a distinction is made between with-*verb* and with-*preposition* pronouns. With-preposition pronouns will be studied in a later unit.

Spanish is like English, however, in having two types of objects, DIRECT and INDIRECT. English distinguishes direct and indirect objects mostly by POSITION. Thus in *Show me them* we know that *me* means "to me" because it precedes *them,* whereas in *Show them me* we know that *them* means "to them" because it precedes *me.* Spanish, on the other hand, distinguishes on the basis of FORM in the case of the third-person pronouns: **lo**(**s**) and **la**(**s**) for direct, **le**(**s**) for indirect. For **me, te,** and **nos,** which are the same whether direct or indirect, the distinction is often made by CONTEXT.

In the third-person pronouns agreement in gender and number follows a pattern similar to that of adjectives (see Unit 2, Section 7). The proper gender must be used even if the noun referred to is a thing rather than a person. Thus *I have it* referring to *cup* (**taza**) is **La tengo,** but *I have it* referring to *coffee* (**café**) is **Lo tengo.**

In English we can usually tell when an object is indirect by determining whether we can add *to* or *for* to it. Thus in *I am writing* (*to*) *her to congratulate her* the first *her* is an indirect object and the second is a direct object; and in *If you will do* (*for*) *him the favor* we know that *him* is indirect.

In writing, the with-verb pronouns are attached to the verb when they follow it. When they precede they are written as separate words.

20 Possessive adjectives

EXAMPLES

A. 1. Estoy aquí, en **mi** cuarto.
2. Compañeras de escuela de **mi** hermana.
3. Vienen **mis** parientes. *My relatives are coming.*

B. 1. Sí, pero **tu** papá...
2. ¡Qué bonita es **tu** casa!
3. ¿Puedo ver **tus** discos? *May I see your records?*

C. 1. Soy **su** padrino.
2. Usted y **su** señora, ¿pueden venir?
3. ¿Cecilia? Ella siempre trae **sus** libros a clase. *Cecilia? She always brings her books to class.*

D. 1. **Nuestro** profesor está ahí. *Our teacher is over there.*
2. **Nuestras** casas están en la misma calle. *Our houses are on the same street.*

E. Cierren **sus** libros. *Close your books.*

ONE POSSESSOR	ONE THING POSSESSED	MORE THAN ONE THING POSSESSED	MORE THAN ONE POSSESSOR	ONE THING POSSESSED	MORE THAN ONE THING POSSESSED
my	**mi cuarto** **mi casa**	**mis cuartos** **mis casas**	our	**nuestro cuarto** **nuestra casa**	**nuestros cuartos** **nuestras casas**
your	**tu cuarto** **tu casa**	**tus cuartos** **tus casas**			
your his her its	**su cuarto** **su casa**	**sus cuartos** **sus casas**	your their	**su cuarto** **su casa**	**sus cuartos** **sus casas**

Possessive adjectives agree in number with the noun. (**Nuestro** has in addition the form **nuestra** to show agreement in gender.)

ITEM SUBSTITUTION DRILL

1. ¿Dónde tienes tu *libro?*
   (casa, discos, cosas)
2. Aquí está mi *cuarto.*
   (sala, invitaciones, recados)
3. Su *sobrina* está en la casa.
   (hijo, padres, tías)
4. Nuestro *papá* es de los Estados Unidos.
   (abuela, tíos, primas)

PATTERNED RESPONSE DRILL

INSTRUCTIONS: Answer the questions as shown.

	TEACHER	STUDENT
A.	1. Señor, ¿dónde está mi libro?	¿Su libro? Está en el cuarto.
	2. Señor, ¿dónde está su libro?	¿Mi libro? Está en el cuarto.
	3. Señor, ¿dónde están mis tíos?	¿Sus tíos? Están en el cuarto.
	4. Señor, ¿dónde están sus tíos?	¿Mis tíos? Están en el cuarto.
B.	1. Señores, ¿dónde está mi invitación?	¿Su invitación? Está en el cuarto.
	2. Señores, ¿dónde está su invitación?	¿Nuestra invitación? Está en el cuarto.
	3. Señores, ¿dónde están mis discos?	¿Sus discos? Están en el cuarto.
	4. Señores, ¿dónde están sus discos?	¿Nuestros discos? Están en el cuarto.
C.	1. Señores, ¿dónde está nuestra invitación?	¿Nuestra invitación? Está en el cuarto.
	2. Señores, ¿dónde está nuestro cónsul?	¿Nuestro cónsul? Está en el cuarto.
	3. Señores, ¿dónde están nuestros compañeros?	¿Nuestros compañeros? Están en el cuarto.
	4. Señores, ¿dónde están nuestras amigas?	¿Nuestras amigas? Están en el cuarto.

21 Possession with *de*

EXAMPLES

A. 1. Compañeras de escuela **de** mi hermana.
   2. En casa **de** Olga.

B. 1. ¿Tú eres amigo **de** ellas?
   2. ¿De parte **de** quién?

A. POSSESSION WITH NOUNS	
The friend of my niece. My niece's friend.	**El amigo de mi sobrina.**
A friend of my niece. A friend of my niece's.	**Un amigo de mi sobrina.**

B. POSSESSION WITH STRESSED PRONOUNS	
It's *her* friend (not his). A friend of hers.	**Es el amigo de ella.** **Un amigo de ella.**

› TRANSLATION DRILL

A. 1. My uncle's house is near the park.
2. My friend's school is near the park.
3. My brother's house is near the park.
4. My cousin's restaurant is near the park.

B. 1. They're friends of my sister's.
2. They're companions of my son's.
3. They're students of my uncle's.
4. They're daughters of my professor's.

C. 1. We're in Rafael's living room.
2. We're in my cousin's room.
3. We're in my family's restaurant.
4. We're at Olga's house.

D. 1. Is he a friend of theirs?
2. Is he a friend of yours?
3. Is he a friend of hers?
4. Is he a friend of his?

› DISCUSSION

Spanish has no device like the *'s* of English. Its place is taken by a construction with the preposition **de.**

The possessive adjective **su, sus** is rarely stressed in Spanish. When emphasis is desired (*He's* ***her*** *friend; He's a friend of* ***hers***), **su** and **sus** are replaced by **de** plus one of the stressable forms **él, ella, usted, ellos, ellas,** or **ustedes.**[5]

› TRANSLATION REVIEW DRILL

The construction **acabar de** plus infinitive.

A. 1. TEACHER: She just left.
STUDENT: **Acaba de salir.**
2. She just arrived.
3. She just entered.
4. She just spoke.
5. She just passed.
6. She just returned.

B. 1. We just arrived.
2. We just entered.
3. We just passed.
4. We just returned.

C. 1. She just arrived.
2. We just arrived.
3. You just arrived.
4. I just arrived.
5. He just arrived.
6. They just arrived.

D. 1. She just opened the door.
2. She just used the telephone.
3. She just brought the coffee.
4. She just left the message.
5. She just studied the book.

E. 1. She just ate it.
2. She just remembered it.
3. She just sent it.
4. She just wrote it.
5. She just left it.

[5]A comparable substitution for **mi** and **tu** is treated in Unit 12, Section 62.

reading

El teléfono

J. *Juanito* P. *Papá*

J. Papá, Pablo dice que el teléfono tiene mucha importancia.
P. Es verdad, hijo.
J. ¿Y por qué es el teléfono de tanta importancia?
P. Porque hay muchas cosas que uno puede hacer y decir por teléfono. Por ejemplo: si estoy malo, puedo llamar al doctor Fernández.
J. ¿Y qué haces si el doctor Fernández no puede venir?
P. Llamo a otro doctor.
J. ¿Y si no puede venir el otro tampoco?
P. Entonces... Juanito, ¿no ves que estoy muy ocupado?
J. Perdón, papá. ...¿Papá?
P. ...Sí, Juanito.
J. Cuando dos hombres hablan por teléfono, habla primero uno y después el otro. Uno habla y el otro escucha. Cuando mamá y tía Julia hablan por teléfono, las dos hablan al mismo tiempo, y ninguna escucha. Pero creo que se entienden perfectamente. ¿Cómo puede ser eso?
P. Es que... es que las señoras son... son... muy inteligentes, hijo.
J. Papá, Pablo dice también que el teléfono es un servicio público. ¿Cómo sabemos eso?
P. Sabemos que eso es verdad porque... porque la compañía de teléfonos lo dice.

al = **a** + **el**

hombres *men*
escuchar *to listen*
al... tiempo *at the same time*
ninguna *neither* **se entienden** *they understand each other*

UNIT 5

The Life of a Housewife

B. *Doña Beatriz* R. *Rosa, Doña Beautriz' maid*
J. *Josefina, maid*

B. What day is today, Rosa, Thursday or Friday?

R. Friday, ma'am. We're having guests tonight, remember?

B. Oh, of course. Then I'm going to the beauty shop. So I can't go to the market today. You better go alone.

R. All right, ma'am. What shall I get [bring]?

B. Here's the list: beans, meat, bread, butter, a dozen eggs, and some fruit.

Vida de una dueña de casa

B. *Doña Beatriz* R. *Rosa, criada de doña Beatriz*
J. *Josefina, criada*

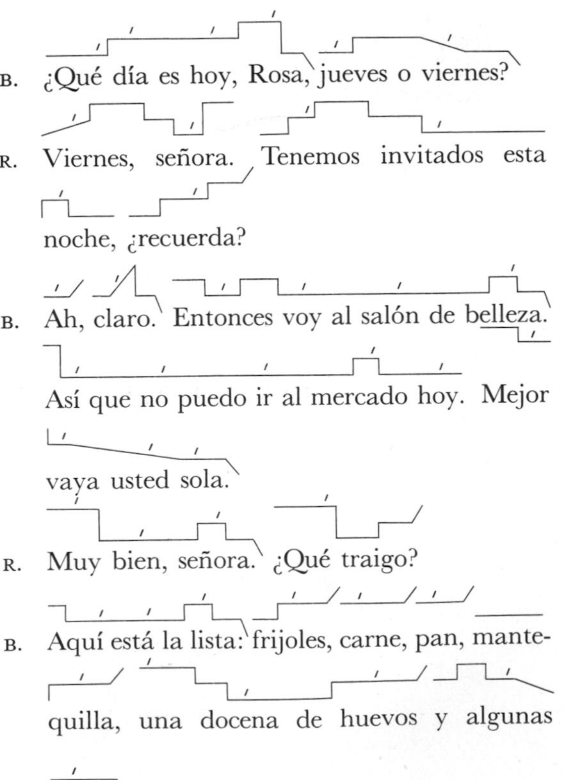

B. ¿Qué día es hoy, Rosa, jueves o viernes?

R. Viernes, señora. Tenemos invitados esta noche, ¿recuerda?

B. Ah, claro. Entonces voy al salón de belleza. Así que no puedo ir al mercado hoy. Mejor vaya usted sola.

R. Muy bien, señora. ¿Qué traigo?

B. Aquí está la lista: frijoles, carne, pan, mantequilla, una docena de huevos y algunas frutas.

Lima, Peru: Supermarket

R. Shall I put down rice, too?

R. ¿Pongo arroz también?

B. All right, put down two kilos. Take the money; look here—this is [note that it is (see that they are)] fifty pesos. Don't lose it.

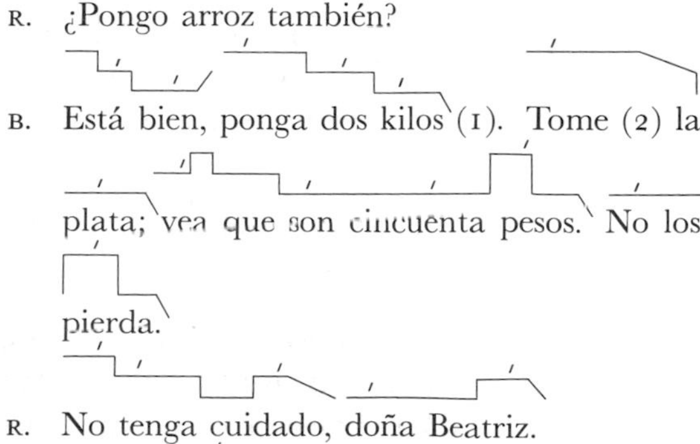

B. Está bien, ponga dos kilos (1). Tome (2) la plata; vea que son cincuenta pesos. No los pierda.

R. Don't worry, Doña Beatriz.

R. No tenga cuidado, doña Beatriz.

J. Ma'am, [there] outside there's a man who is buying old clothes.

J. Señora, ahí afuera hay un hombre que compra ropa vieja.

B. I have some things to sell, but not today. Tell him some other [another] day. Monday maybe, or Tuesday. And you, Rosa, listen, another thing: don't let them put anything over on you [don't let yourself be given a cat for a hare]. Do as I do; if you don't, [even with] a *hundred* pesos won't be enough [it won't reach].

B. Tengo algunas cosas para vender, pero hoy no. Dígale que otro día. El lunes tal vez, o el martes. Y usted, Rosa, oiga, otra cosa: no se deje dar gato por liebre (3). Haga como yo; si no, no alcanza ni con cien pesos.

R. Don't worry, ma'am; when it comes to bargaining, nobody beats me [wins on me].

R. No se preocupe, señora, que para regatear (4), a mí nadie me gana.

B. All right, don't be long [delay much]. Get back as soon as you can [the soonest possible].

B. Bueno, no tarde mucho. Vuelva lo más pronto posible.

* * *

Yaracuy, Venezuela: Open air market

J.	Ma'am, the gentleman says that he'll come back Wednesday. And now, shall I sweep down here in the dining room first?	J.	Señora, dice el señor que vuelve el miércoles. Y ahora, ¿barro primero aquí abajo en el comedor?
B.	Yes, and dust all that furniture well. Be careful not to break anything.	B.	Sí, y sacuda bien todos esos muebles. Tenga cuidado de no romper nada.
J.	And the toys?	J.	¿Y los juguetes?
B.	Take them to the garden. Paquito will have (has) to play there.	B.	Llévelos (2) al jardín. Paquito tiene que jugar ahí.
J.	And what'll I do with these clothes they just brought? Shall I take them upstairs?	J.	¿Y qué hago con esta ropa que acaban de traer? ¿La llevo arriba?
B.	What? I can't hear anything. Please, Josefina, don't turn that radio up so loud! Better turn it off.	B.	¿Cómo? No oigo nada. ¡Por favor, Josefina, no ponga ese radio tan fuerte! Mejor apáguelo.

cultural notes

(1) The metric system is employed throughout the Hispanic world. Thus weight is in **kilos** (kilograms) rather than *pounds,* distance is in **metros** or **kilómetros** rather than *yards* or *miles,* and the quantity of a liquid is in **litros** rather than *quarts* or *gallons.*

(2) **Tomar** is *take* in the sense 'to lay hold of': "He took the pill," "Take the train on Track 5," "He took (grasped) her by the hand." **Llevar** is *take* in the sense to 'transport, carry, wear': "I'll take the box upstairs," "You'd better take a hat (along)—it looks like rain." Hence *We take a train that takes us to Madrid* **Tomamos un tren que nos lleva a Madrid.**

(3) In **no se deje dar gato por liebre** (lit., don't allow yourself to be given a cat for a hare), the infinitive **dar** has passive force. Compare the English *too tough to eat* = *too tough to be eaten.* This construction is common after the verb **dejar.**

(4) **Regatear** *to bargain, haggle,* to bring down the price of an article below the figure quoted by a storekeeper. Haggling is a common practice, especially in markets and small stores and among sidewalk vendors where fixed prices are not taken seriously.

(5) Two Spanish adverbs correspond to English *here:* **aquí** and **acá. Aquí,** the one more commonly used, is more definite in its reference; **acá** (**acá** resembles English *over here*) is often found in set phrases with the command forms of **venir.** See Cultural Note 7 in Unit 3.

PRONUNCIATION EXERCISE (Reread "Vowels" in "Distinctive sounds in Spanish," Unit 1, Section 1.)

A. English and Spanish vowels. INSTRUCTIONS: Listen for the difference between the English and the Spanish vowels as an English speaker and a Spanish speaker say alternately the English and Spanish words.

English /ey/	*Spanish* /e/	*English* /ow/	*Spanish* /o/
day	de	low	lo
Fay	fe	no	no
Kay	que	so	so
lay	le	dough	do
may	me		
say	sé		

English /iy/	*Spanish* /i/	*English* /uw/	*Spanish* /u/
bee	vi	boo	bu
Dee	di	coo	cu
knee	ni	moo	mu
me	mí	pooh	pu
see	sí	too	tu
tea	ti	Sue	su

In some positions, English vowels are automatically followed by a glide or semivowel. The related Spanish vowels are always short, simple, and tense. The preceding pairs illustrate the difference.

B. English and Spanish /l/. INSTRUCTIONS: Listen for the difference between the English and the Spanish [l] as an English speaker and a Spanish speaker say alternately the English and Spanish.

English /l/	*Spanish* /l/
feel	fil
el	él
dell	del
hotel	hotel
tall	tal
coal	col
tool	tul

The principal difference between the English and the Spanish /l/ is that in the Spanish /l/ the back of the tongue is high in the mouth, but in the English /l/ it is usually low.

22 Present tense forms of irregular verbs

EXAMPLES A. 1. **¿Pongo** arroz también?
2. ¿Qué **traigo?**
3. ¿Qué **hago** con esta ropa?
4. Yo **sé** que viven cerca del Parque Central.
5. **Voy** a ir a comer.

B. 1. Tú **conoces** a mamá.
2. **¿Sabes** el número de su casa? *Do you know the number of his house?*

C. 1. ¿Qué le **parece** el libro? *How does the book seem to you?*
2. **Cae** en miércoles.
3. ¿No **ve** que soy su padrino?
4. ¿Usted **sabe** dónde vivimos?
5. Ya que **va,** ¿puede traerme una taza de café?

D. ¿Qué **hacemos** ahora? *What shall we do now?*

E. ¿Qué **hacen** los alumnos? *What are the students doing?*

conocer *to know*	**parecer** *to seem*	**poner** *to put*	**salir** *to leave, depart*
conozco	parezco	pongo	salgo
conoces	pareces	pones	sales
conoce	parece	pone	sale
conocemos	parecemos	ponemos	salimos
conocen	parecen	ponen	salen

caer *to fall*	**traer** *to bring*	**hacer** *to make, do*	**ver** *to see*	**saber** *to know*
caigo	traigo	hago	veo	sé
caes	traes	haces	ves	sabes
cae	trae	hace	ve	sabe
caemos	traemos	hacemos	vemos	sabemos
caen	traen	hacen	ven	saben

A number of verbs, most of them ending in **-er,** are regular in all forms of the present tense except the first-person singular.[1]

dar *to give*	**ir** *to go*
doy	voy
das	vas
da	va
damos	vamos
dan	van

Dar is also irregular only in the first-person singular, and **ir** resembles it. Compare **soy** from **ser** and **estoy** from **estar.**

› PERSON-NUMBER SUBSTITUTION DRILL

1. *Tú* no conoces a nadie en el extranjero.
(yo, ella, nosotros, usted, ustedes, nadie)
2. *Pablo* no parece español.
(él, yo, usted, tú, ellos)
3. *Mi mamá* nunca pone frutas en la lista.
(mi tía, usted, nosotros, ella, yo, ustedes)
4. *Don Rafael* sale el miércoles a las tres.
(mi hermano y yo, tú, yo, Julio, usted, ellos)

[1] See Appendix, "Irregular Forms of Verbs."

5. No trae mantequilla del mercado.
(yo, la muchacha, tú, ellas, nosotros, ella)
6. ¿Qué hacemos ahora?
(mi mamá, yo, Susana, ellas, Ana y yo, usted)
7. No veo nada en la última cuadra.
(ellos, nosotros, él, tú, ella, ustedes)
8. *Yo* no sé si está arriba o abajo.
(Olga, ellas, tú, María, las chicas, usted)
9. *Mi mamá* nunca le da café a Paquito.
(ella, yo, mi abuela, nosotros, tú, ellos)
10. *Ellos* van allá para los días feriados.
(Rosa, nosotros, usted, ustedes, tú, él)

› PATTERNED RESPONSE DRILL

A. 1. TEACHER: ¿Sabe usted si está descompuesto?
STUDENT: **No, no sé nada.**
2. ¿Ve usted ese radio viejo?
3. ¿Trae usted plata?
4. ¿Sabe usted si el cuatro de octubre es feriado?
5. ¿Hace usted algo por la tarde?
6. ¿Pone usted muebles en el patio?
7. ¿Da usted mucha ropa vieja?

B. 1. Pregúntele si usted los conoce.
¿Yo los conozco?
2. Pregúntele si usted parece un loco.
¿Yo parezco un loco?
3. Pregúntele si usted sale mucho.
4. Pregúntele si usted hace la comida.
5. Pregúntele si usted la pone ahí.
6. Pregúntele si usted lo ve todo.
7. Pregúntele si usted lo sabe.

C. 1. TEACHER: Pregúntele si él los conoce.
STUDENT 1: **¿Tú los conoces?**
STUDENT 2: **Claro que los conozco.**
2. Pregúntele si él parece un loco.
3. Pregúntele si él sale mucho.
4. Pregúntele si él hace la comida.
5. Pregúntele si él lo pone ahí.
6. Pregúntele si él lo ve todo.
7. Pregúntele si él lo sabe.

EXAMPLES 1. No **oigo** nada.
2. **¿Incluyen** el café? *Do they include the coffee?*

oir *to hear, listen*	**incluir** *to include*
oigo	incluyo
oyes	incluyes
oye	incluye
oímos	incluímos
oyen	incluyen

A few other verbs have additional irregularities.

› PERSON-NUMBER SUBSTITUTION DRILL

1. *Yo* no oigo nada con tanto ruido.
(nosotros, usted, ellos, tú, él, ustedes, ella)
2. *Yo* no incluyo pan en la lista.
(él, ellos, nosotros, tú, usted, ustedes, ella)

› PATTERNED RESPONSE DRILL

A. 1. TEACHER: ¿Qué oye usted?
STUDENT: **¿Yo? No oigo nada.**
2. ¿Qué oyes tú?
3. ¿Qué oyen ustedes?
4. ¿Qué oye él?
5. ¿Qué oyen ellos?
6. ¿Qué oye ella?

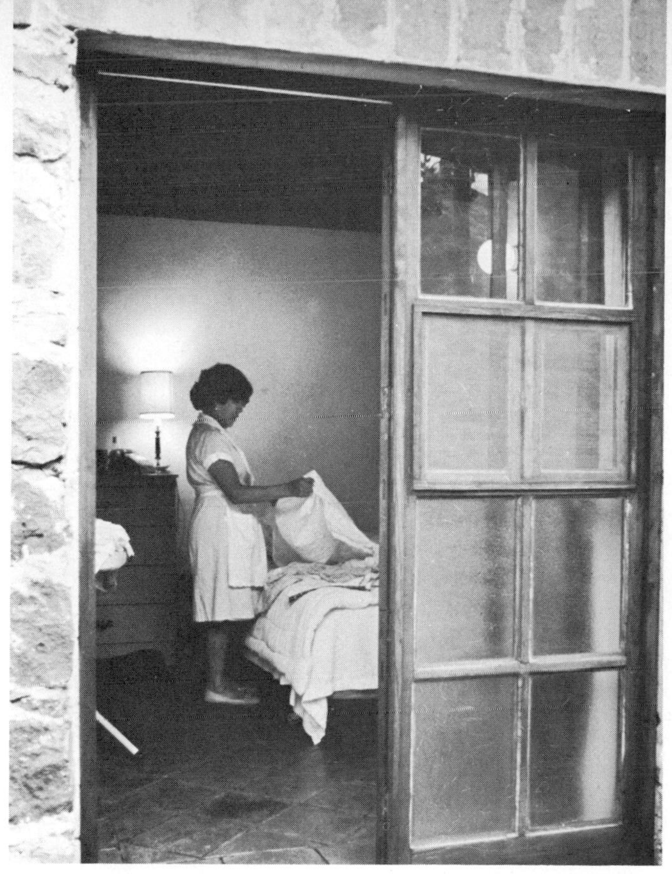

Pedregal, Mexico: Private residence

B. 1. ¿Qué incluyen ellos?
No incluyen nada.
2. ¿Qué incluyes tú?
3. ¿Qué incluyen ustedes?
4. ¿Qué incluye él?
5. ¿Qué incluye usted?
6. ¿Qué incluye Pablo?

› DISCUSSION

"Irregular" in this section refers to verb changes other than the systematic vowel shifts in the stem-changing verbs studied in Unit 4, Section 17. When an irregularity occurs in the present tense, it is most often in the first person singular. The verbs **tener** (with **tengo**) and **venir** (with **vengo**), studied in Unit 4, are members of this group of verbs.

Certain of the irregularities are systematic; for example, practically all verbs ending in **-ecer** and **-ducir** have the same irregularity in the first-person singular as **parecer: merecer** *to deserve, win* (with **merezco**), **pertenecer** *to belong* (with **pertenezco**), **producir** *to produce* (with **produzco**), etc. There are also derivatives, identical except for a prefix with the verbs studied: **hacer** → **deshacer** *to undo* (**hago** → **deshago**), **poner** → **componer** *to compose, repair* (**pongo** → **compongo**), etc.

23 Direct commands: the *usted, ustedes* forms

EXAMPLES A. 1. **Tome** la plata.
2. No se **deje** dar gato por liebre.
3. No **tarde** mucho.
4. No se **preocupe.**
5. **Pasen** ustedes.

B. 1. No **coma** tanto. *Don't eat so much.*
   2. **Sacuda** todos los muebles (from **sacudir** *to dust*).
   3. **Abran** sus libros, por favor. *Open your books, please.*
   4. **Barran** todos los cuartos, por favor. *Sweep all the rooms, please* (from **barrer**).

C. 1. **Recuerde** que esta noche tenemos invitados.
   2. **Cierre** la puerta, por favor.

D. 1. **Vuelva** lo más pronto posible.
   2. No los **pierda.**
   3. No **pida** eso. *Don't ask for that.*

E. 1. No **tenga** cuidado. (*Don't have worry.*)
   2. **Ponga** dos kilos.
   3. **Haga** como yo.
   4. **Vea** que son cincuenta pesos.

F. 1. No **sea** tan aburrido. *Don't be so boring.*
   2. Mejor **vaya** usted sola.

REGULARLY FORMED COMMANDS					
	INFINITIVE	FIRST-PERSON SINGULAR PRESENT		SINGULAR COMMAND **(usted)**	PLURAL COMMAND **(ustedes)**
A. *Regular* **–ar**	**hablar**	**habl–**	**–o**	**–e**	**–en**
B. *Regular* **–er** *and* **–ir**	**comer** **vivir**	**com–** **viv–**	**–o**	**–a**	**–an**
C. –ar *with stem changes*	**recordar** **cerrar**	**recuerd–** **cierr–**	**–o**	**–e**	**–en**
D. –er, –ir *with stem changes*	**volver** **perder** **pedir**	**vuelv–** **pierd–** **pid–**	**–o**	**–a**	**–an**
E. *Verbs irregular in the first-person singular*	**conocer** **parecer** **tener** **venir** **poner** **salir** **caer** **traer** **hacer** **decir** **oir** **ver**	**conozc–** **parezc–** **teng–** **veng–** **pong–** **salg–** **caig–** **traig–** **hag–** **dig–** **oig–** **ve–**	**–o**	**–a**	**–an**

In almost all verbs the **usted** command is based on the first-person singular of the present tense: in **–ar** verbs the **–o** is replaced by **–e,** and in **–er** and **–ir** verbs the **–o** is replaced by **–a.** The plural, or **ustedes,** command adds **–n** to the singular.

F. IRREGULARLY FORMED COMMANDS		
INFINITIVE	SINGULAR COMMAND	PLURAL COMMAND
dar	**dé**	**den**
estar	**esté**	**estén**
ser	**sea**	**sean**
ir	**vaya**	**vayan**
saber	**sepa**	**sepan**

The irregular first-person singulars **doy, estoy, soy, voy,** and **sé** are matched by irregular command forms.

› CONSTRUCTION SUBSTITUTION DRILL

INSTRUCTIONS: Repeat each statement as you hear it. Then make a command, following the models given.

A. 1. TEACHER: El señor[2] habla con el cónsul.
STUDENT: **Señor, hable con el cónsul.**
2. La señora acaba pronto.
3. La señorita pasa a la sala.
4. El señor celebra su cumpleaños.
5. La señora dobla a la izquierda.
6. La señorita apaga el radio.
7. El señor estudia inglés.
8. La señora habla muy fuerte.
9. La señorita pasa por Susana.
10. El señor regresa el jueves.
11. La señora toma la plata.
12. La señorita usa el teléfono.

B. 1. La señora no llega tarde.
Señora, no llegue tarde.
2. La señorita no regatea tanto.
3. El señor no tarda mucho.
4. La señora no trabaja tanto.
5. La señorita no apaga ese radio.

C. 1. Los señores pasan por los invitados.
Señores, pasen por los invitados.
2. Las señoras celebran sus cumpleaños.
3. Las señoritas regresan dentro de cinco minutos.
4. Las señoras no esperan la comida.
5. Las señoritas no estudian los martes.

D. 1. El señor come en el restorán.
Señor, coma en el restorán.
2. La señora sacude los muebles.
3. La señorita barre aquí abajo.
4. El señor vende la casa.
5. La señora vive con nosotros.

E. 1. El señor no come tanto.
Señor, no coma tanto.
2. La señora no cree eso.
3. La señorita no rompe nada.
4. El señor no vende pan.

F. 1. Los señores abren los libros.
Señores, abran los libros.
2. Las señoras comen algo.
3. Los señores no escriben tanto.

G. 1. El señor recuerda la fecha.
Señor, recuerde la fecha.
2. La señora vuelve más tarde.
3. El señor piensa bien.
4. La señora no pierde la plata.
5. La señorita no cierra la puerta.
6. Los señores entienden bien.
7. Las señoras siguen derecho.
8. Las señoritas piden una docena de huevos.

H. 1. El señor no pone los pies en los muebles.
Señor, no ponga los pies en los muebles.
2. La señora viene ahora.
3. La señorita tiene mucho cuidado.
4. Los señores traen café.
5. Las señoras no hacen ruido.
6. Los señores saben el número exacto.
7. El señor está aquí a las tres.
8. La señora no oye discos malos.

[2] For the purpose of drilling commands, **señor, señora, señorita,** etc. will be used to cue the **usted, ustedes** forms.

› PATTERNED RESPONSE DRILL

INSTRUCTIONS: Answer each of the following questions with a command.

A. 1. TEACHER: ¿Espero yo?
STUDENT: **Sí, espere usted.**
2. ¿Hablo yo?
3. ¿Llego yo?
4. ¿Estudio yo?
5. ¿Regateo yo?
6. ¿Barro yo?
7. ¿Escribo yo?
8. ¿Vengo yo?
9. ¿Voy yo?
10. ¿Vuelvo yo?

B. 1. TEACHER: ¿Hablamos nosotros?
STUDENT: **Sí, hablen ustedes.**
2. ¿Llegamos nosotros?
3. ¿Estudiamos nosotros?
4. ¿Regateamos nosotros?
5. ¿Esperamos nosotros?
6. ¿Barremos nosotros?
7. ¿Escribimos nosotros?
8. ¿Venimos nosotros?
9. ¿Vamos nosotros?

C. 1. TEACHER: ¿Tengo que llamar?
STUDENT: **Sí, llame.**
2. ¿Tengo que llegar?
3. ¿Tengo que regresar?
4. ¿Tengo que cerrar?
5. ¿Tengo que estudiar?
6. ¿Tengo que barrer?
7. ¿Tengo que volver?

D. 1. TEACHER: ¿Tenemos que trabajar?
STUDENT: **Sí, trabajen.**
2. ¿Tenemos que esperar?
3. ¿Tenemos que regatear?
4. ¿Tenemos que volver?
5. ¿Tenemos que comer?
6. ¿Tenemos que venir?
7. ¿Tenemos que ir?

› DISCUSSION

The **usted** command is used in situations that call for **usted** rather than **tú.** (See Unit 2, Section 2.)

The subject pronouns **usted** and **ustedes** need not accompany the verb, but do accompany it more frequently than *you* accompanies the command in English. Using them makes the command somewhat less abrupt; for example, **Pasen ustedes.** The usual position is after the verb.

Personal *a*

EXAMPLES

A. 1. ¿Por qué no llamamos **a** María Elena?
2. Tú conoces **a** mamá.

B. 1. Tome la plata.
2. Sacuda todos los muebles.

C. ¿Tú tienes nueve hermanos?

A.	*verb*	+ **a**	+	*personal noun*
B.	*verb*		+	*nonpersonal noun*
C.	**tener**		+	*any noun*

The preposition **a** is put before a *direct-object* noun that refers to a definite person. The verb **tener,** however, does not usually require it.

› ITEM SUBSTITUTION DRILL

1. TEACHER: Tengo que ver a la *criada*. *Repita.*
STUDENT: **Tengo que ver a la criada.**

TEACHER: ________________ *liebre.*
STUDENT: **Tengo que ver la liebre.**
(profesora, escuela, alumna, casa, compañeros, clase)

2. Voy a esperar a mi *prima.*
(clase, cumpleaños, compañero, cosas, hijo, abuelo, tía, ropa)
3. No conozco el *parque.*
(rubia, restorán, español, invitados, lugar, mercado)
4. No veo a *Paquito.*
(la casa, la plata, el número, las chicas, la ropa, los muchachos, la carne)

› DISCUSSION

The nouns in examples A and B above are all direct objects of verbs. Those in example A, however, refer to definite persons. Spanish identifies objects of this kind by putting the preposition **a** before them.

The verb **tener** does not call for **a.** It does not matter whether the object is personal or nonpersonal.[3]

25 *Saber* and *conocer*

EXAMPLES

A.
1. No necesitas **saber** inglés.
2. **Sé** ese sistema. *I know that system (can perform the operations).*
3. **¿Sabe** trabajar? Sí, **sabe.** *Does he know how to work? Yes, he knows how.*
4. **¿Sabes** el número?
5. ¿Usted **sabe** dónde vivimos?
6. Yo **sé** que viven cerca del Parque Central.

B.
1. Pero tú **conoces** a mamá...
2. **Conozco** ese sistema. *I know that system (am aware of its existence and characteristics.)*
3. **Conozco** mis faltas. *I know (am aware of, recognize) my faults.*

THE EQUIVALENTS of *know*			
CONTROL: **saber**		AWARENESS: **conocer**	
skill	**Sé inglés.** **Sé ese sistema.** **Sé trabajar.**	*acquaintance*	**Conoces a mamá.** **Conozco ese sistema.**
communicable knowledge	**Sé el número.** **Sé dónde viven.** **Sé que viven aquí.**	*recognition*	**Conozco mis faltas.**

Saber represents knowledge that is learned and can be acted out (verbalized or performed). **Conocer** represents degrees of awareness, from acquaintance to mere recognition.

[3] The meaning of **tener,** like that of English *have,* often emphasizes "existence" rather than "possession." When the speaker says **Tengo una sobrina** *I have a niece* he calls attention to the existence of this person so related to him: "There is a niece where I am concerned." But if the speaker views the object as someone whose existence is already established, **a** is called for: **Tengo a mi sobrina conmigo** *I have my niece with me.*

❯ PATTERNED RESPONSE DRILL

A. 1. TEACHER: ¿Conoce al señor Arjona?
STUDENT: **No, no conozco al señor Arjona.**
TEACHER: ¿Sabe dónde vive?
STUDENT: **No, no sé dónde vive.**

2. ¿Conoce el mercado?
¿Sabe dónde está?
3. ¿Conoce a mi hija?
¿Sabe dónde trabaja?
4. ¿Conoce a la rubia?
¿Sabe cuándo llegó?
5. ¿Conoce al profesor?
¿Sabe cómo se llama?
6. ¿Conoce el mercado?
¿Sabe regatear?

B. 1. TEACHER: ¿Conoce a la señora de Martínez?
STUDENT: **Sí, la conozco.**
TEACHER: ¿Sabe su número de teléfono?
STUDENT: **Sí, lo sé.**

2. ¿Conoce la escuela?
¿Sabe la dirección?
3. ¿Conoce México?
¿Sabe español?

❯ DISCUSSION

The range of meaning covered by *know* is divided between **saber** and **conocer. Saber** implies control: the knower can put all his knowledge into words or can act it out. It is knowledge that can be communicated, taught, and learned. **Conocer** implies that the knower is aware of the thing known. He may be closely acquainted with it or may merely be conscious of its existence. **Sé las calles de Madrid** *I know the streets of Madrid* means that I can name them. **Conozco las calles de Madrid** *I know the streets of Madrid* means that their existence and characteristics are known to me. Referring to a game of cards one might say **Conozco ese sistema pero no lo sé** *I know that system* (*it is present to my mind*) *but I don't know it* (*can't play it*).

Three important particular cases are: *to know a person,* which calls for **conocer** (*They know John* **Conocen a Juan**); *to know a fact,* which calls for **saber** (*I know that it's true* **Sé que es verdad**); and *to know how to do something,* which calls for **saber** (*They know how to write* **Saben escribir,** *It's easy when you know how* **Es fácil cuando uno sabe**).

❯ PATTERNED RESPONSE REVIEW DRILL

Present with future meaning. INSTRUCTIONS: Answer as in the model.

1. TEACHER: Pague usted ahora.
STUDENT: **Ahora no, pago mañana.**
2. Vaya usted ahora.
3. Barra usted ahora.
4. Llame usted ahora.
5. Pregunte usted ahora.
6. Escriba usted ahora.

❯ TRANSLATION REVIEW DRILL

Noun-adjective agreement.

1. It's a bad dinner.
It's a bad coffee.
2. It's a pretty house.
It's a pretty patio.
3. It's a new entrance.
It's a new market.
4. It's an old cup.
It's an old plate.
5. It's a foreign thing.
It's a foreign book.
6. It's an American school.
It's an American record.
7. It's a broken pen.
It's a broken pencil.

reading

Conversación en un restorán

PAQ. *Paquito* P. *Papá* M. *Mamá* MO. *Mozo*

mozo *waiter*

PAQ. Papá, tengo mucha hambre; quiero arroz, rosbif, frijoles, tres huevos...

P. ¡Dios mío, Paquito, tú no te vas a comer todo eso!

no te vas *aren't going*

PAQ. ¿Por qué no, papá?

P. Porque te vas a enfermar.... En primer lugar, no debes pedir tantos huevos. Quieres ser tan grande como yo, ¿verdad?

te... enfermar *you'll get sick* **lugar** *place*

PAQ. No, papá.

P. ¿No? ¿Y por qué?

PAQ. Tú estás muy gordo.

muy gordo *too fat*

M. ¡Paco, no hables así a tu padre!

así *like that*

PAQ. Pero, mamá, tú le dices siempre que...

siempre *always*

M. Yo a papá, sí, pero tú eres un niño, y... ya viene el mozo, gracias a Dios...

niño *child*

MO. Buenas tardes, señores.

M. Buenas tardes. El menú, por favor. Pero primero, leche para el niño, que tiene mucha hambre.

MO. Muy bien, señora.

PAQ. Mamá, ¿quién es esa señora bonita?

M. ¿Cuál?

PAQ. La señora que mira a papá.

P. Pues... ejem.

pues *well*

M. Hmm...

PAQ. Papá, ¿por qué miran los hombres a las señoritas bonitas?

P. (*mirando a Mamá*) Bueno... como admiran una pintura ...es cuestión de arte... Ah, aquí viene el mozo. Yo también tengo mucha hambre.

pintura *painting*

Caracas, Venezuela: Restaurant

UNIT 6

The Debts

O. *Octavio, head of the household* Y. *Yolanda, servant*
A. *Alfredo, friend of Octavio*

O. Someone's [They're] knocking at the door, Yolanda! Go [to] see who it is.

Y. I [can] see him from here. It's another bill collector.

O. Tell [to] him the same thing as [to] the other one: that I'm not here.

Y. You tell him, sir. I hate [it gives me pain] to lie so much.

O. Do you think I'm [believe me] crazy? I'm not going out to tell him that I'm not here. Go on [run], or he'll knock the door down.

* * *

Las deudas

O. *Octavio, señor de la casa* Y. *Yolanda, sirvienta*
A. *Alfredo, amigo de Octavio*

O. ¡Están tocando a la puerta, Yolanda! Ve a ver quién es.

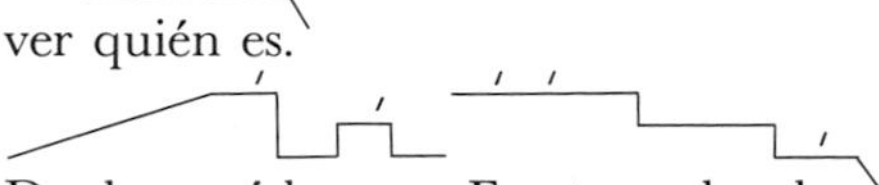

Y. Desde aquí lo veo. Es otro cobrador.

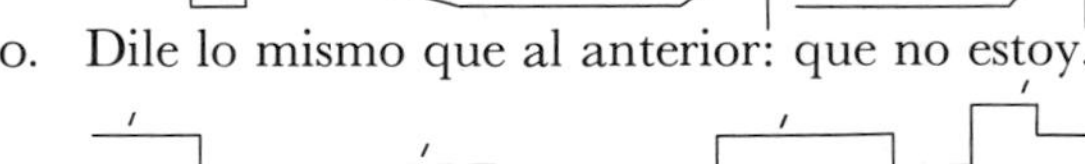

O. Dile lo mismo que al anterior: que no estoy.

Y. Dígale (1) usted, señor. A mí me da pena mentir tanto.

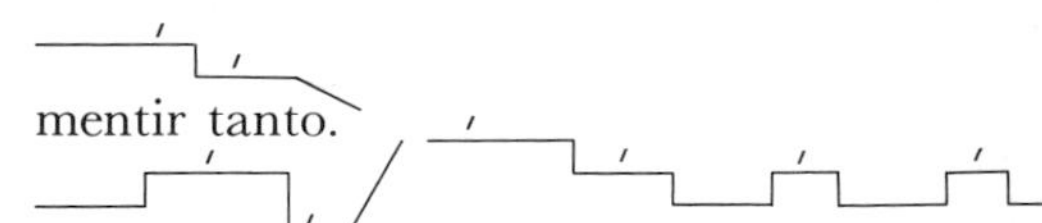

O. ¿Me crees loco? Yo no voy a salir a decirle

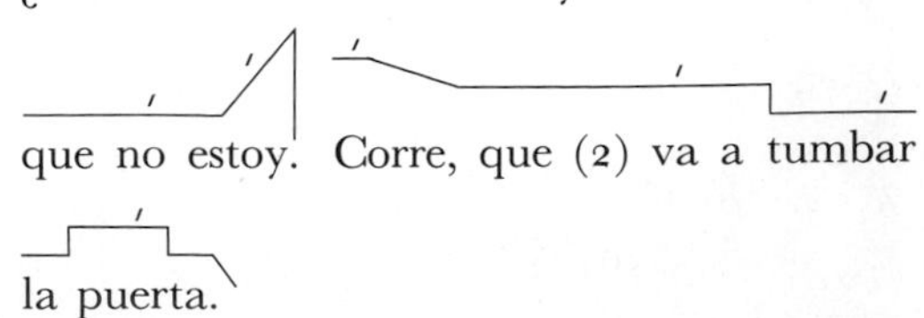

que no estoy. Corre, que (2) va a tumbar la puerta.

* * *

Buenos Aires: Business street

Y. The telephone is ringing too. Shall I answer it?

Y. El teléfono está sonando también. ¿Contesto?

O. No, let me. Yes? Hello? Who? Yes, Octavio Cruz [is] speaking. Ah, Alfredo, how nice [what a pleasure] to hear you. What? Speak louder; I can barely [almost cannot] hear you.

O. No, déjame. ¿Bueno? (3) ¿Aló? ¿Quién? Sí, habla Octavio Cruz. ¡Ah, Alfredo, qué gusto oirte! ¿Qué? Habla más alto, que casi no te oigo.

A. Listen, Octavio, I desperately need the three hundred you owe me. And don't tell me that you can't.

A. Oye, Octavio, necesito urgentemente los trescientos que me debes. Y no me digas que no puedes.

O. Of course not, Alfredo; don't worry. But be patient [have patience]. Give me a few days.	O. Claro que no, Alfredo, no te preocupes. Pero ten paciencia. Dame unos días.
A. I can't! They'll take my car away from me if I don't pay the bank. Put yourself in my place, please.	A. ¡No puedo! Me quitan el coche si no le pago al banco. Ponte en mi lugar, hazme el favor.
O. OK, come (over) here. But don't come right now because I'm going to go out. Come this afternoon. Yes, I swear to you that I'll be here. So long [till then].	O. Está bien, ven acá (4). Pero no vengas ahora mismo porque voy a salir. Ven esta tarde. Sí, te juro que voy a estar aquí. Hasta luego.

* * *

Y. Sir, when is the *señora* coming back from Europe? I'd just like to know [It's in order to know] when you're going to pay me [my wages]. You owe me two hundred fifty, for two months' back pay.	Y. Señor, ¿cuándo vuelve la señora de Europa? Es para saber cuándo me van a pagar mi sueldo. Me deben doscientos cincuenta, de dos meses.
O. I don't know; don't ask me! Leave me alone [in peace] now!	O. ¡No sé, no me preguntes! ¡Déjame en paz ahora!
Y. Yes, sir, sorry. Shall I bring your [you the] dessert?	Y. Sí, señor, perdón. ¿Le traigo el postre?
O. No, don't bring me anything. Or rather, bring me a couple of aspirins. What a headache!	O. No, no me traigas nada. O mejor, tráeme un par de aspirinas. ¡Qué dolor de cabeza!

cultural notes

(1) The maid talks to Octavio in the **usted** form, while he addresses her in the **tú** form. Recall that the use of **tú** is analogous to addressing a person by his first name in English (Unit 2, Section 2). Similar situations are frequently encountered in English—between professor and student or employer and employee, for example—in which the higher ranking person would address the other by his first name and the person of lower rank would address his superior using some sort of title such as *Mister.* (**Usted** itself is a fossilized title, the descendant of Old Spanish **vuestra merced** *your grace.*)

(2) The use of **que** to begin a sentence without a preceding verb is very common in Spanish.

(3) See Cultural Note 1 in Unit 3.

(4) Two Spanish adverbs correspond to English *here:* **aquí** and **acá. Aquí,** the one more commonly used, is more definite in its reference; **acá,** which resembles English *over here,* is often found in set phrases with the command forms of **venir.** See Cultural Note 7 in Unit 3.

› PRONUNCIATION EXERCISE (Reread "Stress" in Unit 1, Section 1.)

A. Minimal stress contrasts. INSTRUCTIONS: The teacher will read the following pairs of words. The student will repeat them just as he hears them.

calle (street) — callé (I was quiet)
jugo (juice) — jugó (he played)
hablo (I speak) — habló (he spoke)
esta (this) — está (is)
peso (monetary unit) — pesó (he weighed)
libro (book) — libró (he freed)
pico (peak) — picó (it stung)
abra (open) — habrá (there will be)
ara (altar) — hará (he will do)

In Spanish it is essential that the stresses be correctly placed when you speak. A misplaced stress is apt to give either a radically different meaning or nonsense.

B. Cognate stress patterns. INSTRUCTIONS: Listen for the difference in stress between the English and the Spanish cognates as an English speaker and a Spanish speaker say alternately the English and Spanish words.

1. *English* (–́–) — *Spanish* (––́)
action — acción
actual — actual
altar — altar
brutal — brutal
civil — civil
color — color
favor — favor
metal — metal

2. *English* (–́––) — *Spanish* (–––́)
animal — animal
capital — capital
criminal — criminal
cultural — cultural
doctoral — doctoral
general — general
liberal — liberal
natural — natural

3. *English* (––́–) — *Spanish* (–––́)
commission — comisión
conversion — conversión
decision — decisión
informal — informal
judicial — judicial
official — oficial
production — producción
professor — profesor

4. *English* (––́––) — *Spanish* (––––́)
activity — actividad
barbarity — barbaridad
conformity — conformidad
facility — facilidad
particular — particular

5. *English* (–––́–) — *Spanish* (––––́)
artificial — artificial
universal — universal
constitution — constitución
opposition — oposición
revolution — revolución

6. *English* (–––́––) — *Spanish* (–––––́)
opportunity — oportunidad
possibility — posibilidad
probability — probabilidad
semicircular — semicircular
sensibility — sensibilidad

The English and Spanish cognates given above illustrate a striking difference between the stress patterns of the two languages. Spanish tends to favor the latter part of a word, English the earlier part. Note also that in the Spanish words only one syllable is stressed and that the stressed syllable is not lengthened the way it is in English.

 Direct commands: the affirmative *tú* form

EXAMPLES

A.
1. **Ten** paciencia.
2. **Ven** esta tarde.
3. **Dile** lo mismo.
4. **Ve** a ver quién es.

B.
1. **Habla** más alto.
2. **Dame** unos días.
3. No, **déjame.**
4. **Corre,** que va a tumbar la puerta.

A. IRREGULARLY FORMED AFFIRMATIVE COMMANDS

INFINITIVE	STEM	COMMAND
tener	**ten–**	**ten**
venir	**ven–**	**ven**
poner	**pon–**	**pon**
salir	**sal–**	**sal**
hacer	**hac–**[1]	**haz**[1]
decir		**di**
ser		**sé**
ir		**ve**

Most verbs that are irregular in the **tú** command form simply use the stem as it appears in the infinitive. **Decir, ser,** and **ir** are exceptions.

B. REGULARLY FORMED AFFIRMATIVE COMMANDS

THIRD-PERSON SINGULAR PRESENT = **Tú** COMMAND

habla	**recuerda**	**conoce**
toma	**piensa**	**cae**
come	**vuelve**	**trae**
cree	**pierde**	**ve** (*from* **ver**)
vive	**pide**	**oye**
escribe	**sigue**	**da**
		está
		sabe

Regular **tú** command forms are the same as the third-person singular present. This includes verbs with stem changes and verbs that are in other respects irregular.

› CONSTRUCTION SUBSTITUTION DRILL

INSTRUCTIONS: Repeat each statement as you hear it. Then make a command, following the models given.

A.
1. Ana[2] viene acá.
   Ana, ven acá.
2. María tiene cuidado.
3. Julio sale pronto.

[1] Both **hac–** and **haz** represent the same pronunciation [ás]. See Unit 12, Writing Exercise.

[2] For the purpose of drilling commands, given names will be used to cue the **tú** forms.

4. Josefina pone los juguetes en el cuarto.
5. Cecilia dice la verdad.
6. María Elena es buena.
7. Olga va al jardín.

B. 1. Josefina habla fuerte.
Josefina, habla fuerte.
2. Pablo entra por aquí.
3. Julio pasa a mi cuarto.
4. Rosa espera un minuto.
5. Pepe cierra la puerta.
6. Ana recuerda la dirección.
7. Paquito juega en el jardín.
8. María está aquí a las cinco.

C. 1. Pepe come carne.
Pepe, come carne.
2. Olga escribe más.
3. Josefina barre aquí abajo.
4. Rosa sacude los muebles.
5. Pablo vive con los abuelos.
6. Ana ve la avenida.
7. Mercedes oye bien.

27 Direct commands: the negative *tú* form

EXAMPLES
1. No me **preguntes.**
2. No me **traigas** nada.
3. No **vengas** ahora mismo.
4. No me **digas** que no puedes.

NEGATIVE COMMANDS	
NEGATIVE OR AFFIRMATIVE **usted** COMMAND	NEGATIVE **tú** COMMAND
(no) **pase**	**no pases**
(no) **cierre**	**no cierres**
(no) **abra**	**no abras**
(no) **vuelva**	**no vuelvas**
(no) **haga**	**no hagas**
(no) **sea**	**no seas**
(no) **dé**	**no des**

Without exception the negative **tú** command is the same as the **usted** command with an added **-s.**

CONSTRUCTION SUBSTITUTION DRILL

INSTRUCTIONS: Repeat each statement as you hear it. Then make a negative command, following the models given.

A. 1. Rosa no habla tanto.
Rosa, no hables tanto.
2. Susana no apaga el radio.
3. Betty no usa ese color.
4. María no viene el viernes.
5. Olga no trae fruta.
6. Cecilia no sigue derecho.

B. 1. Ana no barre el lunes.
Ana, no barras el lunes.
2. Mercedes no pone el radio.
3. Susana no escribe en el libro.
4. Rosa no pierde la plata.

C. 1. Josefina no viene este mes.
Josefina, no vengas este mes.
2. Rosa no sale hasta el martes.
3. Olga no hace eso tampoco.
4. Paquito no dice eso nunca.
5. Julio no va tan lejos.
6. Pablo no pone la ropa en el comedor.

INSTRUCTIONS: Repeat each of the following affirmative commands. Then make them negative.

D. 1. Entra en la sala.
No entres en la sala.
2. Lleva la ropa.
3. Dobla en esa esquina.
4. Cierra la puerta.
5. Vuelve a las cinco y media.
6. Trae a tus parientes.

E. 1. Pon tus juguetes en el jardín.
No pongas tus juguetes en el jardín.
2. Haz la comida ahora.
3. Ten cuidado.
4. Di la verdad.
5. Sal a las seis.
6. Ve allá ahora.
7. Ven conmigo.

INSTRUCTIONS: Repeat each of the following negative commands. Then make them affirmative.

F. 1. No hables con las chicas.
Habla con las chicas.
2. No juegues en el patio.
3. No llames a María Elena.
4. No comas ahora.
5. No abras la puerta.
6. No vendas ese libro.

G. 1. No vengas esta noche.
Ven esta noche.
2. No digas esas cosas.
3. No salgas con tu hermana menor.
4. No hagas la comida hoy.
5. No vayas a la escuela.
6. No tengas cuidado.
7. No traigas todas estas cosas.

› DISCUSSION

The **tú** commands are required in situations that call for **tú** rather than **usted.** The subject pronoun **tú** itself, however, is not commonly used with the verb unless it is emphasized, as in **Habla tú** ***You*** *talk* (***You*** *do the talking*).

In the plural, only the **ustedes** command form is used in Spanish America. The **vosotros** forms, used in Spain (see Unit 2, Section 2), are given in the Appendix.

28 With-verb pronouns in commands

EXAMPLES A. 1. **Siéntense.**[3]
2. Mejor **apáguelo.**
3. **Dígale** que otro día.
4. **Llévelos** al jardín.
5. **¡Déjame** en paz ahora!
6. **Tráeme** un par de aspirinas.
7. **Enséñeme** la lista. *Show me the list.*

B. 1. No **los pierda.**
2. No **se preocupe.**
3. No **me traigas** nada.
4. No **me preguntes.**
5. No **me digas** que no puedes.
6. No **nos enseñe** inglés. *Don't teach us English.*

[3] In writing, the with-verb pronouns are attached to the verb when they follow but not when they precede it. Also in writing, when the pronoun is attached to a verb whose stress is not on its last syllable, the accent mark is placed over the stressed syllable. This reflects the fact that the stress stays on that syllable.

A. AFFIRMATIVE	
verb	*pronoun*

B. NEGATIVE		
no	*pronoun*	*verb*

The with-verb pronouns follow the verb in affirmative commands and precede the verb in negative commands. Only a with-verb pronoun can intervene between **no** and the verb.

›CONSTRUCTION SUBSTITUTION DRILL

INSTRUCTIONS: Repeat each statement as you hear it. Then make a command, following the models given.

A. 1. El señor me deja pasar.
Señor, déjeme pasar.
2. La señora me espera en la esquina.
3. La señorita me enseña español.
4. La señorita me felicita por mi cumpleaños.
5. El señor me manda una taza de café.
6. La señorita me escribe pronto.
7. La señora me cree.

B. 1. Paquito me deja en paz.
Paquito, déjame en paz.
2. Ana me lleva al parque.
3. Mamá me da cinco centavos.
4. Elena me llama a las cinco.
5. Cecilia me invita el domingo.
6. José María me escribe todos los días.
7. Olga me quiere mucho.
8. Pablo me dice la verdad.

INSTRUCTIONS: Repeat each of the following affirmative commands. Then make them negative.

C. 1. Déjeme solo.
No me deje solo.
2. Piénselo más.
3. Llévenos a la escuela.
4. Póngalos en la cocina.
5. Tráigalo el domingo.
6. Enséñeles el libro.
7. Apáguelo.
8. Pídales perdón.
9. Dígale que no hay.
10. Déjenlos aquí.
11. Tráigalas el viernes.
12. Celébrenlo como el año pasado.

D. 1. Háblame en inglés.
No me hables en inglés.
2. Tráelos ahora.
3. Apágalo, por favor.
4. Dile que no hay nada.
5. Felicítanos por la invitación.
6. Hazlo otra vez.
7. Ponlo todo en su lugar.
8. Siéntate aquí.

Mexico City: Night view of northern section

PATTERNED RESPONSE DRILL

INSTRUCTIONS: Answer each question with an affirmative command and then with a negative command.

A. 1. TEACHER: ¿Traigo la lista o no, señor?
STUDENT: **Tráigala. No la traiga.**
2. ¿Llevo los frijoles o no, señor?
3. ¿Cierro las puertas o no, señor?
4. ¿Pongo el radio o no, señor?
5. ¿Vendo el tocadiscos o no, señor?
6. ¿Traemos el café o no, señor?
7. ¿Rompemos los discos viejos o no, señor?
8. ¿Sacudimos los muebles o no, señor?
9. ¿Damos las gracias o no, señor?

B. 1. ¿Traigo los centavos o no, Pablo?
Tráelos. No los traigas.
2. ¿Estudio el libro o no, Ana?
3. ¿Celebro mi cumpleaños o no, Mercedes?

C. 1. ¿Te escribo o no, Julio?
Escríbeme. No me escribas.
2. ¿Te hablo o no, Olga?
3. ¿Te dejo o no, María?
4. ¿Te enseño o no, Josefina?
5. ¿Te espero o no, Rosa?
6. ¿Te felicito o no, Betty?
7. ¿Te llamo o no, Francisco?
8. ¿Te llevo o no, Elena?
9. ¿Te creo o no, José?
10. ¿Te digo o no, Ana?
11. ¿Te oigo o no, Pablo?
12. ¿Te sigo o no, Mercedes?
13. ¿Te traigo o no, Susana?
14. ¿Te veo o no, Olga?

29 Cardinal numerals above ten

COUNTING FORMS, 11–99		
	20 veinte	**uno**
11 once	**21 veintiuno**	**30 treinta** … **dos**
12 doce	**22 veintidós**	**40 cuarenta** … **tres**
13 trece	**23 veintitrés**	**50 cincuenta** … **cuatro**
14 catorce	**24 veinticuatro**	**60 sesenta** } **y** { **cinco**
15 quince	**25 veinticinco**	**70 setenta** … **seis**
16 dieciséis	**26 veintiséis**	**80 ochenta** … **siete**
17 diecisiete	**27 veintisiete**	**90 noventa** … **ocho**
18 dieciocho	**28 veintiocho**	**nueve**
19 diecinueve	**29 veintinueve**	

Within the tens from 30 up the units are merely added with **y;** for example, 35 is **treinta y cinco;** 78 is **setenta y ocho.**

COUNTING FORMS, 100–999	
100 cien	
200 doscientos	
300 trescientos	**uno**
400 cuatrocientos	**100 ciento** … **dos**
500 quinientos	**200 doscientos** … **veintiuno**
600 seiscientos	**300 trescientos** … **cuarenta**
700 setecientos	**etc.** … **noventa y cinco**
800 ochocientos	**etc.**
900 novecientos	

The units and tens are added directly to the hundreds without **y.** When a number smaller than 100 is added to 100, **cien** becomes **ciento.**

COUNTING FORMS, 1000–999,999	
1.000[4] mil 2.000 dos mil 21.000 veintiún mil 44.000 cuarenta y cuatro mil 100.000 cien mil 300.000 trescientos mil etc.	uno dos veintiuno cincuenta y seis cien trescientos sesenta y cinco quinientos cuatro etc.

Smaller numbers are added to 1000 and its multiples. The word **mil** is not pluralized here.

› COUNTING DRILL

A. 1. Cuente de uno a veinte.
2. Cuente de veintiuno a cuarenta.
3. Cuente de cuarenta y uno a sesenta.
4. Cuente de sesenta y uno a ochenta.
5. Cuente de ochenta y uno a cien.

B. Cuenten en rotación.[5]

C. 1. Cuente de dos en dos[6] hasta veinte.
2. Cuente de tres en tres hasta treinta.
3. Cuente de cinco en cinco hasta cincuenta.
4. Cuente de diez en diez hasta cien.

D. 1. Cuente de cien en cien hasta mil.
2. Cuente de mil en mil hasta veinticinco mil.

EXAMPLES

A. 1. ¿Cuántos años tiene?—**Veintiuno.** *How old is she (How many years does she have)?—Twenty-one.*
2. ¿Cuánto cuesta?—**Veintiún** dólares. *How much does it cost?—Twenty-one dollars.*
3. ¿Cuántas veces lo hizo?—**Veintiuna.** *How many times did you do it?—Twenty-one.*
4. Lo hice **veintiuna** veces. *I did it twenty-one times.*

B. 1. ¿Cuántos dólares cuesta?—**Doscientos.** *How many dollars does it cost?—Two hundred.*
2. ¿Cuántas pesetas cuesta?—**Doscientas.** *How many pesetas does it cost?—Two hundred.*
3. ¿Costó **doscientos** dólares o **doscientas** pesetas? *Did it cost two hundred dollars or two hundred pesetas?*

MODIFYING FORMS OF **uno** AND **–cientos** BEFORE NOUN			
21 years	**veintiún años**	200 years	**doscientos años**
21 hours	**veintiuna horas**	200 hours	**doscientas horas**
31 years	**treinta y un años**	320 years	**trescientos veinte años**
31 hours	**treinta y una horas**	320 hours	**trescientas veinte horas**
101 years	**ciento un años**	721 years	**setecientos veintiún años**
101 hours	**ciento una horas**	721 hours	**setecientas veintiuna horas**

Numerals ending in *one* and multiples of 100 agree in gender with the noun they modify. When a number ending in *one* precedes the noun it modifies, **uno** shortens to **un.**

[4] Arabic numerals are usually punctuated with the period in Spanish where the comma is used in English. The comma is used as a decimal point.

[5] *Count off* [6] *Count by twos*

MULTIPLE NUMERAL MODIFYING FORMS			
101,000 dollars 101,000 pesetas	**ciento un mil dólares** **ciento un mil pesetas**	200,000 years 200,000 hours	**doscientos mil años** **doscientas mil horas**
21,000 years 21,000 hours	**veintiún mil años** **veintiún mil horas**	500,020 years 500,020 hours	**quinientos mil veinte años** **quinientas mil veinte horas**

When a number terminating in *one* multiplies a following number, the masculine **un** (**–ún**) is always used, regardless of the noun modified. When one of the **–cientos** numbers multiplies a following thousand, the feminine **–cientas** is used if the noun modified is feminine.

› READING DRILL

INSTRUCTIONS: Read the following sentences aloud.

1. Necesitamos 21 horas más.
   Necesitamos 21 años más.
2. Es necesario esperar 101 horas.
   Es necesario esperar 101 años.
3. Cuesta 200 pesos.
   Cuesta 200 pesetas.
4. Cuesta 521 pesos.
   Cuesta 521 pesetas.
5. Cuesta 761 pesos.
   Cuesta 761 pesetas.
6. Cuesta 991 pesos.
   Cuesta 991 pesetas.
7. Tengo que hacer 21.000 cosas.
   Tengo que hacer 21.000 discos.
8. Necesitamos 300.000 casas.
   Necesitamos 300.000 libros.

EXAMPLES
1. ¿Cuántos **millones** tiene? *How many million(s) does he have?*
2. Tiene veinte **millones de** pesos. *He has twenty million pesos.*

COUNTING FORMS, 1,000,000–	
1.000.000 un millón **2.000.000 dos millones** **21.000.000 veintiún millones** **200.000.000 doscientos millones** **etc.**	**uno** **dos** **veintiuno** **ochenta y seis** **cien** **mil** **dos mil seiscientos tres** **etc.**

The multiples of **millón** unlike those of **mil** use a plural, **millones.** Whereas English *million* modifies a noun directly, Spanish **millón** adds **de.**

› READING DRILL

A.
1. Tiene 1.000.000 de dólares.
2. Tiene 3.000.000 de dólares.
3. Tiene 10.000.000 de dólares.
4. Tiene 100.000.000 de dólares.

B.
1. Tienen 2.000.000 de pesos.
2. Tienen 11.000.000 de pesos.
3. Tienen 21.000.000 de pesos.
4. Tienen 200.000.000 de pesos.

C.
1. 1.000.223
2. 1.001.500
3. 1.020.700
4. 1.050.986
5. 1.111.654
6. 2.654.275
7. 10.275.837

▸ **ITEM SUBSTITUTION REVIEW DRILL**

Gender of nouns ending in **-e.**

1. ¿Cuál es el café?
2. ________ juguete
3. ________ calle
4. ________ padre
5. ________ clase
6. ________ noche
7. ________ parte
8. ________ pariente
9. ________ liebre
10. ________ mueble
11. ________ tarde
12. ________ madre

reading

Conversación en el aeropuerto

O. *Octavio, señor de la casa* I. *Isabel, su esposa* — **esposa** *wife*

O. ¡Isa, qué bueno verte! ¿Cómo estás? ¿Qué tal el vuelo? — **vuelo** *flight*
I. ¡Ay, Octavio! Por favor, no me hables de vuelos.
O. ¿Y por qué no? ¿Mal tiempo? — **tiempo** *weather*
I. No, son los pasajeros. Yo, sentada con dos señoritas que hablaban sólo de sus novios... secretarias, yo creo. — **pasajeros** *passengers* **sentada** *seated* **sólo** *only* **novios** *boyfriends*

Lima, Peru: Jorge Chavez airport

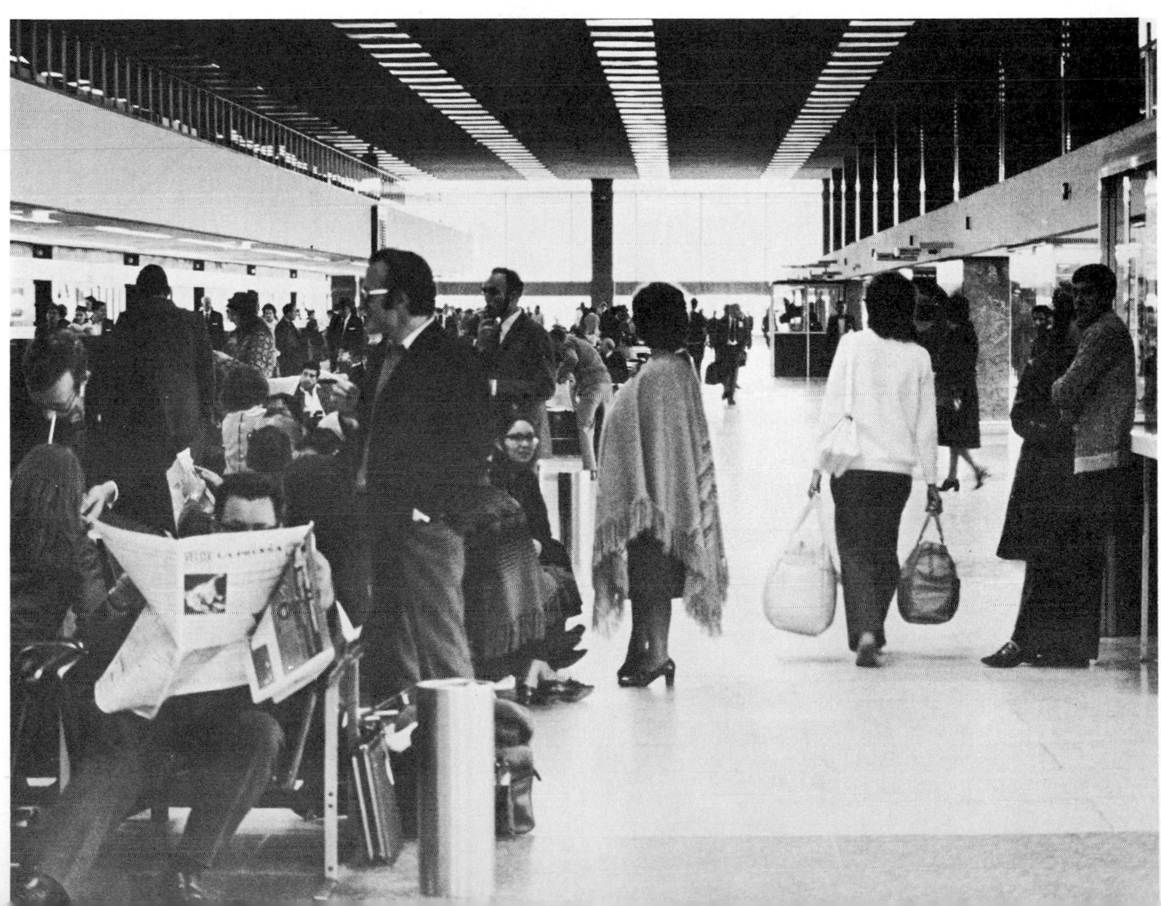

O. ¿Pero son tan malas las secretarias?

I. Es que esa gente no comprende nada de cosas artísticas, culturales: el teatro, la pintura...

O. Pero Isa, hay muy pocos que tienen los gustos tan... tan refinados.

I. Pues de aquí en adelante yo sólo voy en primera clase. Octavio, ¿por qué estamos esperando un taxi?

O. Es que el coche está... en el garaje. Una que otra reparación, nada más.

I. ¡Qué bueno comer en casa otra vez! Y Yolanda prepara tan bien la comida.

O. Sí... lástima que ya no está con nosotros.

I. ¡Cómo que no está! Octavio, ¿qué pasa? Dímelo en seguida.

O. Pues ¿recuerdas los doscientos mil que debemos?

I. Sí, al Banco Central.

O. Dicen que nos quitan la casa si no pagamos ahora.

I. Pueden esperar.

O. No, ya no esperan más.

I. Entonces... ¿el coche?

O. Está vendido. Y también el televisor, los radios, el piano, las pinturas, los muebles...

I. No me digas más, Octavio. Vamos a un restorán y te muestro el regalo que te compré en París.

esa gente *those people*
teatro *theater* **pintura** *painting*
pocos *few* **gustos** *tastes*
Pues...adelante *Well from now on*
estamos esperando *are we waiting for*
Una...reparación *A few repairs*
ya no *no longer*
Cómo que *What d'ya mean* **¿qué pasa?** *What's going on?* **en seguida** *this instant*
Está vendido *It's sold*
muestro *I'll show* **regalo** *gift* **compré** *I bought*

UNIT 7

Traffic Mixup

F. *Fernando* R. *Roberto, Fernando's friend* M. *Don Miguel, Traffic Chief* P. *Patricio, Don Miguel's brother-in-law*

F. Did you get some bad news? Is that why you're looking so glum [that I see you with that face so sad]?

R. I'm not glum; I'm mad. I've just had a big mixup with the police.

F. Don't tell me! What happened this time?

R. I went the wrong way on a one-way street [put myself on a street against the traffic].

F. What! Where?

R. At that darned [blessed] corner by the National Theater. I didn't see the arrow.

F. Calm down, boy. That's nothing serious.

Lío de tráfico

F. *Fernando* R. *Roberto, amigo de Fernando* M. *Don Miguel, Jefe de Tránsito* P. *Patricio, cuñado de don Miguel*

F. ¿Recibiste alguna mala noticia, que te veo con esa cara tan triste?

R. No estoy triste, estoy furioso. Acabo de tener un tremendo lío con la policía. (1)

F. No me digas. ¿Qué pasó esta vez?

R. Es que me metí en una calle en contra del tránsito.

F. ¡Cómo! ¿En qué parte?

R. En esa bendita esquina del Teatro Nacional. (2) No vi la flecha.

F. ¡Cálmate, chico! Eso no es nada serio.

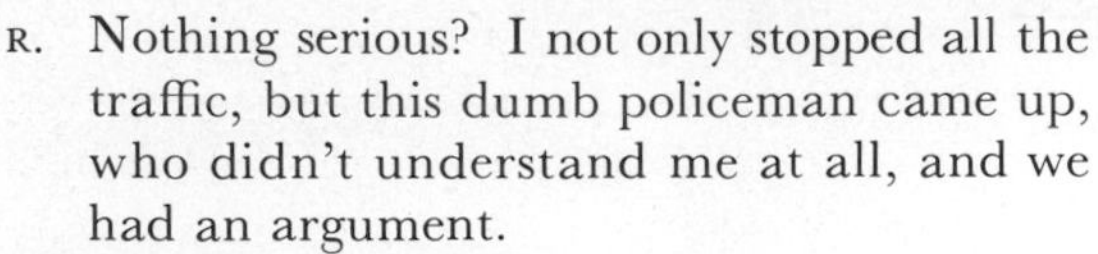

R.	Nothing serious? I not only stopped all the traffic, but this dumb policeman came up, who didn't understand me at all, and we had an argument.	R.	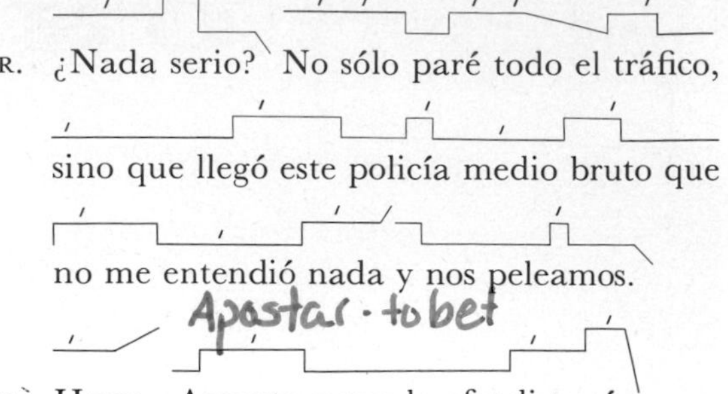 ¿Nada serio? No sólo paré todo el tráfico, sino que llegó este policía medio bruto que no me entendió nada y nos peleamos.
F.	Hmm. I bet you offended *him*.	F.	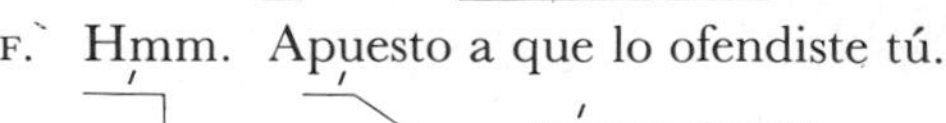 Hmm. Apuesto a que lo ofendiste tú.
R.	Maybe so. Anyway [Be that as it may], we didn't understand each other. And it was all his fault.	R.	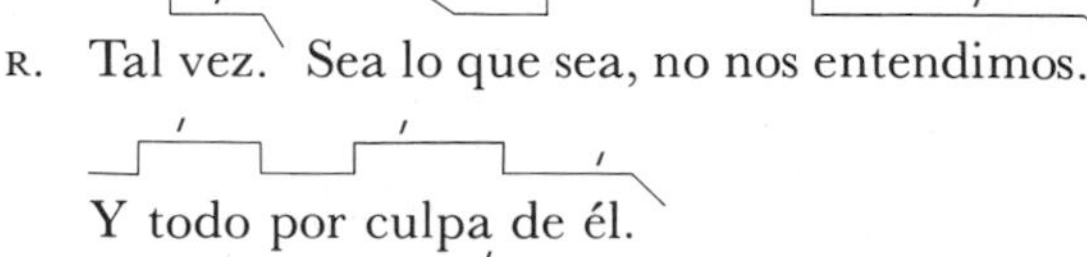 Tal vez. Sea lo que sea, no nos entendimos. Y todo por culpa de él.
F.	Well, but what else happened?	F.	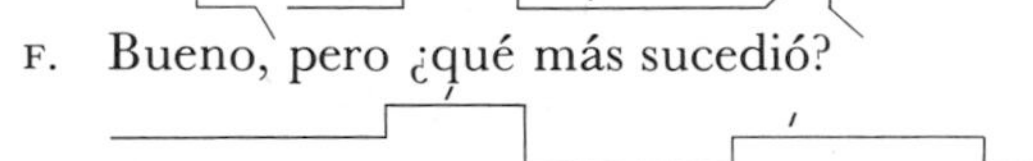 Bueno, pero ¿qué más sucedió?
R.	They took [from me] all my papers and fined me [demanded of me a fine]. What a system!	R.	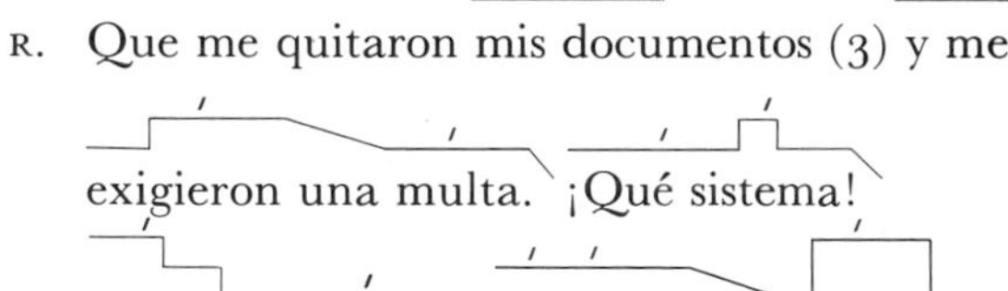 Que me quitaron mis documentos (3) y me exigieron una multa. ¡Qué sistema!
F.	Don't worry. I have a friend who's related to [a relative of] the Traffic Chief. I'll call him this afternoon.	F.	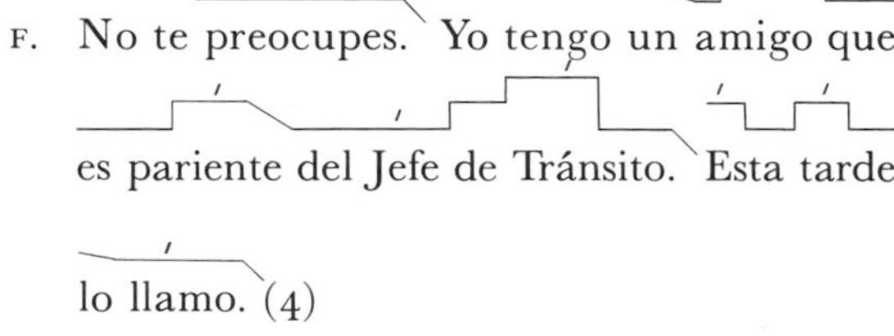 No te preocupes. Yo tengo un amigo que es pariente del Jefe de Tránsito. Esta tarde lo llamo. (4)

* * *

P.	Hello. I'd like to speak to [With] the Traffic Chief, please. This is his brother-in-law speaking.	P.	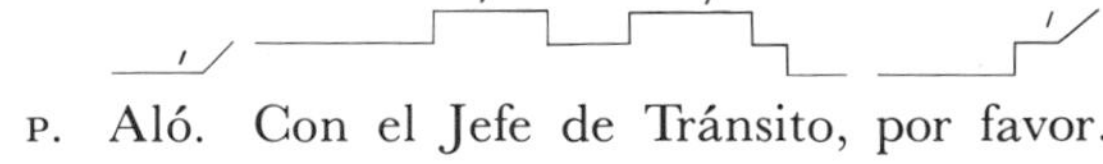 Aló. Con el Jefe de Tránsito, por favor. 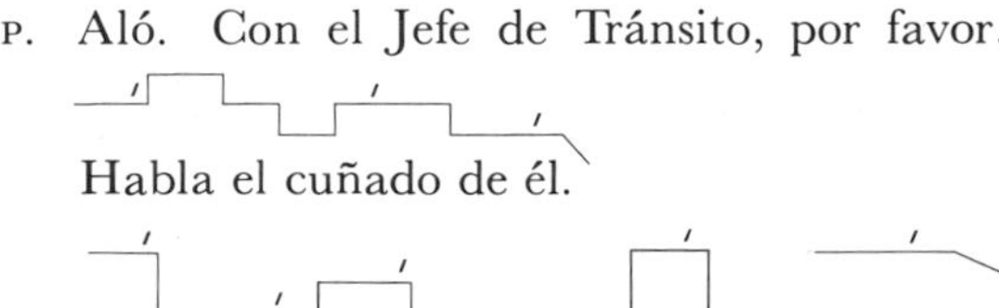 Habla el cuñado de él.
M.	Hello, I'm glad [how good that] you called. When can I have a talk with you? A friend of mine wants to get a job at the Ministry.	M.	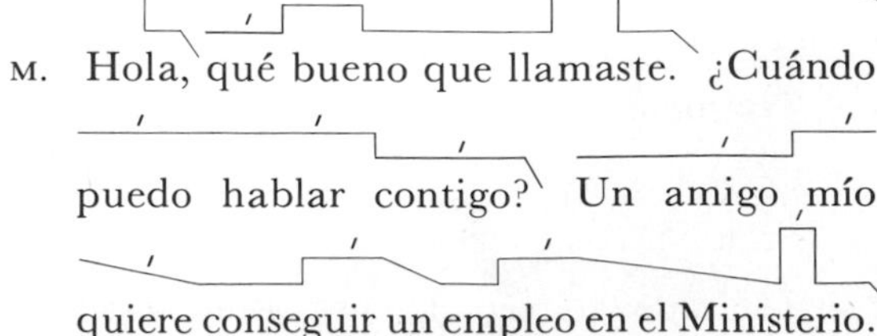 Hola, qué bueno que llamaste. ¿Cuándo puedo hablar contigo? Un amigo mío quiere conseguir un empleo en el Ministerio.

Managua, Nicaragua: Traffic policeman

P. Okay. Then what do you say we have dinner together tonight? By the way, I'm calling to ask you a favor.	P. Muy bien. Entonces, ¿qué te parece si comemos juntos esta noche? A propósito, te llamo para pedirte un favor.
M. Glad to help you [At your service].	M. A tus órdenes.
P. It seems that a boy who is a friend of mine, Roberto Salazar, had his papers taken away from him [from a young fellow (who is) a friend of mine they took from him the papers] and he has to pay a fine. He was just thoughtless [It was a piece of foolishness].	P. Es que a un muchacho amigo mío, Roberto Salazar, le quitaron los documentos y tiene que pagar una multa. Fue una tontería.
M. Well, if you say so... I'll take care of [arrange] it [this].	M. Bueno, si tú lo dices... Yo voy a arreglar esto.

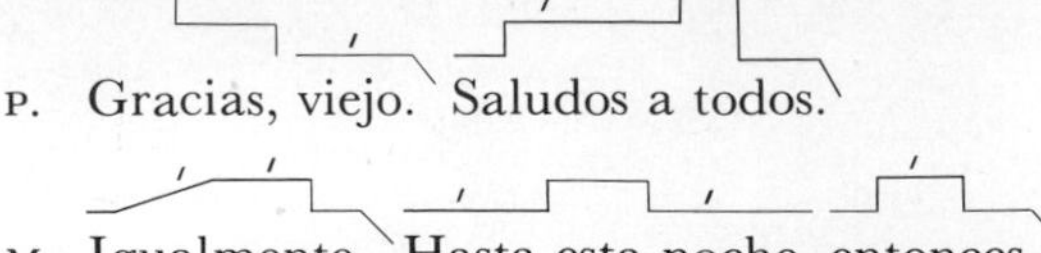

P. Thanks, old man. Give my regards to everybody.

P. Gracias, viejo. Saludos a todos.

M. Same for me. See you tonight then.

M. Igualmente. Hasta esta noche, entonces.

cultural notes

(1) **La policía** means *the police* (i.e., police force); **el policía** means *the policeman.* There are a number of feminine nouns in Spanish, all ending in **-a,** which, when used with the article **el** or other masculine determiners (e.g., **un, este,** etc.), refer to a male person. Examples, in addition to **policía,** are: **la guardia** *the guard* (as a corps) vs. **el guardia** *the guard* (guardsman); **la escolta** *the escort* (e.g., a group of ships or airplanes accompanying, say, a convoy) vs. **el escolta** *the escort* (i.e., a man who accompanies a woman in public); **la ayuda** *the aid* (i.e., assistance) vs. **el ayuda** *the aide* (i.e., assistant).

(2) In the Hispanic world it is considered quite normal for the government to subsidize cultural institutions such as the theater and the orchestra. The **Teatro Nacional** is an example.

(3) It is usual for Latin-American countries to require foreign visitors to carry a number of documents or papers which in addition to a passport might include a police certificate and an identification card. The police certificate, which a person generally carries with him whether or not he leaves the country, serves as proof of good conduct.

(4) Working through contacts rather than through regular channels is sometimes termed **amiguismo** ("friend-ism"). In the political sphere it is termed **personalismo.**

› PRONUNCIATION EXERCISE (Reread "Stops" in Unit 1, Section 1.)

A. The stops [p] and [b]. INSTRUCTIONS: Repeat the following pairs of words just as you hear them.

[p]	[b]	[p]	[b]
paño	**baño**	**peso**	**beso**
pago	**vago**	**pida**	**vida**
peca	**beca**	**pino**	**vino**
pelo	**velo**	**poca**	**boca**
pena	**vena**	**pesar**	**besar**

The first and third columns have the Spanish stop [p], which differs from its English counterpart in that it is unaspirated (i.e., not followed by a puff of breath). Thus Spanish [p] is often heard by English speakers as [b].

B. The stops [t] and [d]. INSTRUCTIONS: Repeat the following pairs of words just as you hear them.

[t]	[d]
tos	**dos**
tía	**día**
teja	**deja**
trama	**drama**
tomar	**domar**

The first column has the Spanish stop [t], which differs from its English counterpart in that it is unaspirated and consequently is often heard by English speakers as [d]. Both Spanish [d] and Spanish [t] are dental, whereas English [d] and [t] are alveolar.

C. The stops [k] and [g].

[k]	[g]
callo	gallo
casa	gasa
coma	goma
cura	gura
cordura	gordura

The first column has the Spanish stop [k], which differs from its English counterpart in that it is unaspirated. Thus Spanish [k] is often heard by English speakers as [g].

30 Preterit of regular verbs and *dar*

EXAMPLES A. 1. **Paré** todo el tráfico.
2. Qué bueno que **llamaste.**
3. ¿Qué **pasó** esta vez?
Llegó este policía.
4. Nos **peleamos.**
5. Me **quitaron** mis documentos.

B. 1. Me **metí** en una calle en contra del tránsito.
No **vi** la flecha.
2. Tal vez lo **ofendiste** tú.
¿**Recibiste** alguna mala noticia?
3. ¿Qué más **sucedió?**
4. No nos **entendimos.**
5. Me **exigieron** una multa.

C. Ayer me **dieron** diez pesos. *Yesterday they gave me ten pesos.*

A. -ar VERBS		B. -er AND -ir VERBS		C. dar	
hablar		comer	vivir	d-	
habl-		com-	viv-		
-é	-amos	-í	-imos[1]	-i	-imos
-aste		-iste[1]		-iste	
-ó	-aron	-ió[2]	-ieron[2]	-io	-ieron

[1] In writing, verbs with stem ending in a vowel place the accent mark over the **i** of **-iste** and **-imos** as, for example, **creíste, creímos,** from **creer** with stem **cre-**. This indicates that stress is on **i** and not on **e.**

[2] On verbs with stem ending in a vowel the **-ió** and **-ieron** are spelled **-yó** and **-yeron** as, for example, **creyó, creyeron** (from **creer**), **oyó, oyeron** (from **oir**), **incluyó, incluyeron** (from **incluir**). This does not reflect any necessary difference in sound, though some speakers of Spanish do produce a more fricative sound in **creyó,** for example, than in **comió.**

➤ PERSON-NUMBER SUBSTITUTION DRILL

1. Entré en el cuarto de Julio.
   (José, nosotros, tú, don Rosario, ustedes, Pepe y yo, mis padres)
2. *Francisco* les mandó una taza de café.
   (yo, tú, usted, nosotros, la muchacha, ellos, él)
3. Ayer llamamos a María Elena.
   (yo, él, ellos, el jefe, tú, ella, ustedes)
4. La semana pasada *Rosa* llevó a Paquito al mercado.
   (nosotros, la muchacha, yo, ellos, tú, él, alguien)
5. *Yo* no comí mucho arroz en los Estados Unidos.
   (Paquito, ellas, Betty, tú, nosotros, Susana, ustedes)
6. *Pablo* no vendió los muebles.
   (la muchacha, ella, nosotros, tú, yo, la criada, usted, Paquito y José)
7. Después volvieron al Teatro Nacional.
   (yo, el señor Salazar, tú, nosotros, los señores, Patricio, ustedes)
8. *El jefe* no entendió el problema.
   (mi mamá, nosotros, doña Mercedes, yo, él, ellos, tú)
9. Ayer perdí esos benditos documentos.
   (Paco y yo, ellos, tú, nosotros, Josefina, ustedes, ella)
10. Ayer *la chica* rompió todas las tazas.
    (las criadas, tú, usted, yo, María, nosotros, alguien)
11. Escribió para pedir un empleo.
    (ellos, Rafael, nosotros, usted, yo, tú, los alumnos)
12. *Don José* vivió dos años en esa casa.
    (nosotros, ellos, tú, yo, usted, mi señora y yo, un loco)
13. Mamá le dio diez centavos.
    (yo, un señor, tú, ellos, nosotros, ella, ustedes)

➤ TENSE SUBSTITUTION DRILL

INSTRUCTIONS: Repeat the following sentences just as you hear them. Then repeat each again, changing the present tense verb to preterit.

A. 1. TEACHER: No *alcanza* ni con cien pesos. *Repita.*
   STUDENT: **No alcanza ni con cien pesos.**
   TEACHER: *Cambie.*
   STUDENT: **No alcanzó ni con cien pesos.**
2. Rosa no se *deja* dar gato por liebre.
3. Josefina no *tarda* mucho en volver.
4. Esta tarde lo *llamo.*
5. Las madres *calman* a los chicos.
6. Una tontería, pero lo *arreglo.*
7. Todos *miramos* a las chicas bonitas.

B. 1. La cosa *parece* fácil.
2. Casi me *vuelves* loca.
3. Los policías *corren* al banco.
4. Las criadas *barren* abajo y afuera.
5. *Entendemos* muy bien al profesor.
6. Fernando *pierde* los documentos.
7. *Sacudimos* muy bien todos los muebles.
8. Le *doy* dos pesos.

INSTRUCTIONS: Repeat the following sentences just as you hear them. Then repeat each again, changing the preterit forms to present tense.

C. 1. La criada *apagó* el radio.
2. Me *quitaron* los documentos.
3. *¿Pagaste* la multa?
4. ¡Qué bueno que *llamaste!*
5. Sea lo que sea, no nos *entendimos.*
3. ¿No *viste* la flecha?
4. Este policía no me *entendió.*
5. Sea lo que sea, no nos *entendimos.*
6. ¿Por qué no *salimos* juntos?
7. Me *dieron* el radio.

D. 1. Los chicos *comieron* frijoles.
2. El cónsul *vivió* en la Calle Veinte.

› PATTERNED RESPONSE DRILL

A. 1. ¿Cuándo llamó?
Llamé ayer.
2. ¿Cuándo estudió?
3. ¿Cuándo jugó?
4. ¿Cuándo pagó?
5. ¿Cuándo barrió?
6. ¿Cuándo salió?

B. 1. ¿Cuándo llamaron?
Llamamos ayer.
2. ¿Cuándo estudiaron?
3. ¿Cuándo jugaron?
4. ¿Cuándo pagaron?
5. ¿Cuándo barrieron?
6. ¿Cuándo salieron?

C. 1. ¿Qué recordaron?
Recordaron todo.
2. ¿Qué pagaron?
3. ¿Qué creyeron?
4. ¿Qué perdieron?
5. ¿Qué vendieron?
6. ¿Qué vieron?
7. ¿Qué escribieron?

D. 1. ¿Dónde dejaste el documento?
Lo dejé en el ministerio.
2. ¿Dónde usaste el documento?
3. ¿Dónde perdiste el documento?
4. ¿Dónde vendiste el documento?
5. ¿Dónde viste el documento?

E. 1. ¿Cuándo recibiste las tazas?
Las recibí la semana pasada.
2. ¿Cuándo llevaste las tazas?
3. ¿Cuándo mandaste las tazas?
4. ¿Cuándo rompiste las tazas?
5. ¿Cuándo viste las tazas?

F. 1. ¿Ya pagó usted?
Sí, ya pagué.
2. ¿Ya estudiaron ustedes?
3. ¿Ya pagaste tú?
4. ¿Ya pagaron ellos?
5. ¿Ya pagué yo?
6. ¿Ya escribiste tú?
7. ¿Ya comió usted?
8. ¿Ya barrieron ellas?
9. ¿Ya estudió ella?
10. ¿Ya comieron ustedes?
11. ¿Ya comió él?
12. ¿Ya salieron ellos?

INSTRUCTIONS: A student will make each of the following statements; another student will pretend he has not understood and will call for a repetition, as in the models.

G. 1. Llamé ayer.
¿Cuándo llamó?
2. Estudié ayer.
3. Pagué ayer.
4. Jugué ayer.
5. Barrí ayer.
6. Salí ayer.
7. Escribí ayer.

H. 1. Llamamos ayer.
¿Cuándo llamaron?
2. Estudiamos ayer.
3. Pagamos ayer.
4. Jugamos ayer.
5. Barrimos ayer.
6. Salimos ayer.
7. Escribimos ayer.

› DISCUSSION

Following are examples of the English past tense occurring in affirmative, negative, and interrogative contexts compared with the present tense in the same contexts:

CONTEXT	PAST		PRESENT	
affirmative	I went. He went.	I ran. He ran.	I go. He goes.	I run. He runs.
negative	I didn't go. He didn't go.	I didn't run. He didn't run.	I don't go. He doesn't go.	I don't run. He doesn't run.
interrogative	Did I go? Did he go?	Did I run? Did he run?	Do I go? Does he go?	Do I run? Does he run?

Spanish has *two* past tenses, differing in meaning, that cover different aspects of the English past tense above. The preterit is one of them. Until the other past tense is explained (the imperfect, in Unit 10) only those past meanings that are translatable by the preterit will appear in the drills and written exercises.

There is no difference between the preterit endings of regular **-er** verbs and those of regular **-ir** verbs. The irregular **-ar** verb **dar** takes these same endings.

In the *we* (**nosotros**) form, **-ar** and **-ir** verbs are the same in present and preterit. Thus **hablamos** means either *we speak* or *we spoke*. The two meanings are distinguished by context.

31 Demonstratives

EXAMPLES

A. 1. Llegó **este** policía medio bruto.
2. ¿Qué pasó **esta** vez?
3. Hasta **esta** noche. (*Until this night.*)
4. Yo voy a arreglar **esto.** (*I'm going to arrange this.*)

B. 1. No ponga **ese** radio tan fuerte.
2. Te veo con **esa** cara tan triste.
3. Sacuda bien todos **esos** muebles.
4. **Eso** no es nada serio.

GENDER	SINGULAR this	PLURAL these	SINGULAR that	PLURAL those
masculine	**este**	**estos**	**ese**	**esos**
feminine	**esta**	**estas**	**esa**	**esas**
neuter	**esto**		**eso**	

ITEM SUBSTITUTION DRILL

INSTRUCTIONS: Repeat the following sentences just as you hear them. Then substitute the items listed for the emphasized nouns. When **esto** or **eso** is the item substituted it replaces both the demonstrative and the noun: **este arroz** becomes **esto.**

1. Este *arroz* es muy bueno.
   (carne, escuela, frutas, esto)
2. Este *comedor* es muy grande.
   (sala, cuartos, puertas, esto)
3. Dame un poquito de este *pan.*
   (carne, arroz, mantequilla, esto)
4. Tenga cuidado de no romper ese *juguete.*
   (taza, huevo, radio, puerta, disco, mueble, tocadiscos, teléfono, eso)
5. Ese *juguete* es muy típico.
   (arroz, frijoles, cosas, eso)
6. Ese *lugar* es mejor.
   (criada, mercados, clases, eso)
7. ¿De quién son estos *frijoles?*
   (frutas, centavos, pesos, listas, huevos, cosas)
8. ¿Dónde están esos *libros?*
   (listas, muebles, documentos, noticias, amigas, alumnos, invitaciones)

PATTERNED RESPONSE DRILL

INSTRUCTIONS: Answer the questions below, following the pattern of the models given. The teacher should make an appropriate gesture to indicate the position referred to.

A. 1. ¿De quién es este libro?
¿Cuál? ¿Ese?
Sí, éste.[3]
Es mío.
2. ¿De quién es esta lista?
3. ¿De quién es este lápiz?
4. ¿De quién es esta plata?
5. ¿De quién es este centavo?

B. 1. ¿De quién son estos libros?
¿Cuáles? ¿Esos?
Sí, éstos.
Son míos.
2. ¿De quién son estas listas?
3. ¿De quién son estos lápices?
4. ¿De quién son estas cosas?
5. ¿De quién son estos pesos?

C. 1. ¿De quién es ese libro?
¿Cuál? ¿Ese?
Sí, ése.
Es de Roberto.
2. ¿De quién es esa flecha?
3. ¿De quién es ese café?
4. ¿De quién es esa taza?
5. ¿De quién es ese disco?

D. 1. ¿De quién es ese libro?
¿Cuál? ¿Este?
Sí, ése.
Es mío.
2. ¿De quién es esa lista?
3. ¿De quién es ese documento?
4. ¿De quién es esa ropa?
5. ¿De quién es ese juguete?

E. 1. ¿De quién son esos libros?
¿Cuáles? ¿Estos?
Sí, ésos.
Son míos.
2. ¿De quién son esas listas?
3. ¿De quién son esos lápices?
4. ¿De quién son esas cosas?
5. ¿De quién son esos juguetes?

F. 1. ¿De quién son esos libros?
¿Cuáles? ¿Esos?
Sí, ésos.
Son de Fernando.
2. ¿De quién son esas cosas?
3. ¿De quién son esos documentos?
4. ¿De quién son esas listas?
5. ¿De quién son esos huevos?

› DISCUSSION

The demonstratives are singular or plural, masculine or feminine, to agree with the noun that they modify or to which they refer.

In addition to masculine and feminine there is a neuter gender that refers to actions, generalities, or unidentified things. For example, to ask *What is that?* the speaker will say **¿Qué es eso?** since the thing is unidentified. For *Don't do that,* he will say **No hagas eso,** since the reference is to an action, not to a noun with its specific gender and number. And to say *Shall I put that (that stuff) on the list too?* he will say **¿Pongo eso en la lista también?** because the things referred to, though they may have been identified, are thought of vaguely and generally and hence are summarized by a neuter form. The neuter has no plural.

The phrase **esta noche** translates both *this evening* and *tonight.*

32 The conjunctions *e* in place of *y* and *u* in place of *o*

EXAMPLES

A. 1. Hablan de libros **e** ideas. *They're talking about books and ideas.*
2. Fernández **e** Hijo. *Fernández and Son.*
3. Es española **e** inglesa. *She's Spanish and English.*
4. Tengo siete **u** ocho. *I have seven or eight.*
5. Quieren verlo **u** oirlo. *They want to see it or hear it.*
6. ¿Son muchachos **u** hombres? *Are they boys or men?*

[3]When the demonstratives appear by themselves, functioning as nouns, they are written with the accent mark. (See Unit 12, Section 61.) But the rule that the written accent does not usually appear over capital letters applies here as well.

B. 1. Hablan de nuevos libros **y** de nuevas ideas. *They're talking about new books and new ideas.*

2. Tengo siete **o** tal vez ocho. *I have seven or maybe eight.*

3. Quieren oirlo **o** verlo. *They want to hear it or see it.*

EQUIVALENTS OF *and*	
DIRECTLY BEFORE A WORD BEGINNING WITH [i]	ELSEWHERE
e	**y**

EQUIVALENTS OF *or*	
DIRECTLY BEFORE A WORD BEGINNING WITH [o]	ELSEWHERE
u	**o**

› CONSTRUCTION SUBSTITUTION DRILL

A. 1. TEACHER: Dice izquierda y derecha. *Repita y cambie.*
STUDENT: **Dice izquierda y derecha.**
Dice derecha e izquierda.
2. Dice hijo y sobrino.
3. Dice inglés y español.
4. Dice ideas y libros.
5. Dice invitaciones y recados.
6. Dice invitados y compañeros.
7. Dice ir y venir.
8. Dice hija y madre.

B. 1. TEACHER: Dice hombres o muchachos. *Repita y cambie.*
STUDENT: **Dice hombres o muchachos.**
Dice muchachos u hombres.
2. Dice ocho o siete.
3. Dice octubre o ahora.
4. Dice oir o ver.
5. Dice horas o minutos.

C. 1. TEACHER: Dice ideas y libros. *Repita y cambie.*
STUDENT: **Dice ideas y libros.**
Dice libros e ideas.
2. Dice invitaciones y compañeros.
3. Dice ir y venir.
4. Dice horas o minutos.
5. Dice oir o ver.
6. Dice octubre o ahora.
7. Dice inglés o español.
8. Dice invitados o parientes.

33 Contraction of *a* plus *el* to *al*

EXAMPLE Ve a jugar **al** jardín.

a + el → al
When **a** and the article **el** come together they fuse to form **al.**[4]

[4] In writing, the fusion of **de** plus **el** is also recognized, with the spelling **del.** In speech the occurrence of the same fusion in, for example, **de e**ste or **le e**scribe does not affect the spelling.

› ITEM SUBSTITUTION DRILL

1. Voy a la *sala.*
   (patio, cocina, cuarto, entrada)
2. Vemos a la *tía.*
   (cónsul, morena, alumnos, amigas)
3. ¿Le escribe a la *muchacha?*
   (mexicano, americanos, españoles)
4. Las chicas llegaron a la *escuela.*
   (parque, casa, Estados Unidos, clases)

34 The article with classifying nouns

EXAMPLES

A. 1. ¿Hablo con la casa **del** doctor Fernández?
2. Invitamos **al** padre Roberto. *We're inviting Father Robert.*
3. ¿Conoces a **los** señores Arjona? *Do you know Mr. and Mrs. Arjona?*
4. Usted sigue derecho por **la** Avenida Norte hasta llegar a **la** Calle Veinte.
5. Con don Rosario, por favor. *I'd like to speak to Don Rosario, please.*

B. 1. Señor Huerta, cierre la puerta, por favor.
2. De nada, profesor Alvarez. *You're welcome, Professor Alvarez.*
3. No tenga cuidado, doña Beatriz.
4. ¿No quiere venir conmigo, don Rafael?

A. SPEAKING *about* A PERSON OR THING			
el, la, los, las	+	*classifying noun (esp. title)*	*proper name*

B. SPEAKING *to* A PERSON	
title	*proper name*

A common noun that classifies an immediately following proper name calls for the definite article. The typical examples are titles with names of persons. The article is not used, however, when the person is addressed directly, nor is it used at any time with the titles **don** and **doña.**

› TRANSLATION DRILL

A. 1. Good morning, Mr. Arjona.
2. Good morning, Mrs. Arjona.
3. Good morning, Miss Arjona.
4. Good morning, Professor Arjona.
5. Good morning, Doctor Arjona.
6. Good morning, Father Arjona.

B. 1. Where's Mr. Arjona?
2. Where's Mrs. Arjona?
3. Where's Miss Arjona?
4. Where's Professor Arjona?
5. Where's Dr. Arjona?
6. Where's Father Arjona?

C. 1. Good afternoon, Mr. Arjona. How's Mrs. Arjona?
2. Good afternoon, Mr. Martínez. How's Mrs. Martínez?
3. Good afternoon, Mr. Flores. How's Mrs. Flores?
4. Good afternoon, Professor Romero. How's Mrs. Romero?
5. Good afternoon, Dr. Fernández. How's Mrs. Fernández?

› DISCUSSION

In combinations of classifying nouns and proper names, English sometimes uses the article (*the Santa Fe Trail, the Atlantic Ocean, the Ozark Mountains, the Messrs. Jones and Reed*), sometimes not (*Santa Fe Street, Lake Mead, Mount Whitney, Mr. Jones*). Spanish uses the article whenever the thing or person is spoken *about* but not when the person is spoken *to*. The commonest classifying nouns are the personal and professional titles. **Don** and **doña** are exceptions in that they never call for the article (nor do the words **San, Santo,** and **Santa** used as titles equivalent to English *Saint*).

35 The article with things possessed

EXAMPLES

A. 1. Es el día de **su** santo también.
2. Sí, pero **tu** papá...
3. **Sus** zapatos están sucios. *Your shoes are dirty.*
4. A **tus** órdenes.

B. 1. Le quitaron **los** documentos.
2. ¿Qué tienes en **las** manos? *What do you have on* (or *in*) *your hands?*
3. ¿Es usted **la** mamá? No, habla con **la** tía.

A.	B.
POSSESSOR NOT OTHERWISE OBVIOUS	POSSESSOR OTHERWISE OBVIOUS
possessive adjective + *noun*	*article* + *noun*

When it is obvious who the possessor is, Spanish generally uses the article rather than a possessive adjective.

› TRANSLATION DRILL

A. 1. Your hands are very dirty.
Tienes las manos muy sucias.
2. Your face is very dirty.
3. Your clothes are very dirty.
4. Your things are very dirty.
5. Your book is very dirty.
6. Your room is very dirty.

B. 1. What do I have on my face?
2. What do I have in my cup?
3. What do I have on my shoes?

› DISCUSSION

By comparison with Spanish, English overworks its possessive adjectives. It is not normal in Spanish to insist as English does on a routine possessive adjective in a sentence like **Habla con las manos** *He speaks with his hands,* since one cannot speak with someone else's hands.[5] If a possessive adjective is used under these circumstances, it is for some special effect (when the speaker in the dialog says **Me quitaron *mis* documentos** he is probably thinking of the trespass on *his* property).

[5] Clothing and parts of the body are the most typical examples of nouns which in Spanish call for the article rather than the possessive adjective. This discussion is resumed in Unit 14, Section 78.

Tú commands.

A. Answer each question with an affirmative command.

1. FIRST STUDENT: ¿Traigo la lista?
   SECOND STUDENT: **Sí, tráela ahora.**
2. ¿Quito los documentos?
3. ¿Pago la multa?
4. ¿Llamo al jefe?
5. ¿Pido el favor?
6. ¿Sacudo los muebles?

B. Now respond with a negative command to each of the above questions.

1. FIRST STUDENT: ¿Traigo la lista?
   SECOND STUDENT: **No, no la traigas hasta las tres y media.**

reading

"The Policeman's Lot"

(*El policía acaba de volver a casa. Va a la sala y se sienta en el sofá. Espera la comida que su esposa le prepara en la cocina.*)

P. *Policía* E. *Esposa* V. *Visitante*

P. ¡Ay, caramba! ¡Me matan los pies!

E. ¡Pobre muchacho!

P. Dime, Rafaela, ¿quién fue el poeta que escribió que la vida del policía es muy triste?... Debió pensar en mis pies.

E. ¿Pasó algo hoy?

P. Sí, con uno de esos benditos extranjeros que infestan nuestro país, en vez de quedarse en su casa. Cada día que vienen a nuestra...

E. Sí, sí; ya sé... Pero sigue; dime qué sucedió.

P. Bueno, allí estaba yo, en la esquina del Teatro Nacional, y ese extranjero se metió en la calle en contra del tránsito. Me acerqué a él y le pregunté: "¿No ve usted esa flecha ahí en la pared?" Y el bruto me dijo que no; que ¿qué flecha?... ¿Hay algo más estúpido? ¿Por qué no miró?

E. ¿Paró el tráfico?

P. Claro, ¡cómo no!... Luego nos peleamos. Un tremendo lío. Y todo por culpa de él. Le quité los documentos... Después le exigieron una multa.

E. ¿Va a tener que pagarla?

P. ¿Qué crees tú? Te apuesto a que no.

E. ¿Por qué?

matan *are killing* **pies** *feet*
vida *life*
Debió pensar *He must have been thinking*
país *country*
en vez...casa *instead of staying at home*
Me...a *I went up to* **pared** *wall*
Te...no *I'll bet you he won't*

Quito, Ecuador: Colonial street

P. Porque debe tener amigos que son amigos de la esposa de algún primo del Jefe, que va a arreglarlo todo. Hasta pueden darme una reprimenda. Estoy acostumbrado a eso. Pero lo que me pone más furioso es que estos extranjeros, que hablan muy mal nuestra lengua, y ni llevan nombres españoles... (*Llaman a la puerta.*)

E. Ya voy. (*Va a la puerta.*)

V. ¿Es aquí donde vive el señor O'Reilly?

E. Sí, señor, pase usted... Terencio, preguntan por ti.

Hasta *Even*

pone *makes* **lengua** *language*

ni llevan *don't even have* **nombres** *names*

UNIT 8

Topic for the Day

B. *Barber* A. *Mr. Alonso*

B. Mr. Alonso, you're next. Do you want it short this time?

A. No, cut off just [scarcely] a little in back, and on the sides very little. And don't touch the sideburns. They're all right the way they are.

B. All right. Well, Mr. Alonso, what are they saying about the coming Pan-American Olympic Games in Peru? They're going to be great, aren't they?

A. Yes, where I work that's all they're talking about. They're already getting up a group to go, but a trip that long costs a lot of money. Ouch!! You pulled my hair!

B. I'm sorry. It's the clippers [little machine]; I don't know what's the matter with them. I'd better use the scissors.

* * *

B. Who do you think's going to win the games? The Americans?

A. Probably. They have very good athletes and they're going to send quite a large team, as usual [always].

B. We're going to compete in football, basketball, swimming, boxing, the marathon race . . . What else?

Tema del día

B. *Barbero* A. *Señor Alonso*

B. Señor Alonso, usted sigue. ¿Lo quiere corto esta vez?

A. No, córteme apenas un poquito atrás, y a los lados muy poco. Y no me toque las patillas. Están bien así.

B. Muy bien. Bueno, señor Alonso, y ¿qué se dice de los próximos Juegos Olímpicos Panamericanos en Perú? Van a estar fantásticos, ¿verdad?

A. Sí, donde yo trabajo, sólo de eso se habla. Ya se está organizando un grupo para ir, pero cuesta mucho dinero un viaje tan largo. ¡¡Ay!! ¡que me tiró del pelo!

B. Perdón, es la maquinilla; no sé qué tiene. Mejor uso las tijeras.

* * *

B. ¿Quién cree usted que va a ganar los juegos? ¿Los americanos?

A. Probablemente. Ellos tienen muy buenos atletas y van a mandar un equipo muy grande, como siempre.

B. Nosotros vamos a participar en fútbol (1), básquetbol, natación, boxeo, en la carrera de maratón... ¿en qué más?

Soccer: Chile vs. Brazil

A. Nothing else, but unfortunately we're going to lose in everything. With countries like the United States, Brazil, and Argentina, the competition is too stiff.

A. En nada más, pero desgraciadamente vamos a perder en todo. Con países como Estados Unidos, Brasil y Argentina, la competencia es muy grande.

* * *

A. Another thing I'd like to see, if I go to the games, is a good bullfight.

A. Otra cosa que tengo ganas de ver, si voy a los juegos, es una buena corrida de toros.

B. In Peru? Isn't it just Spain and Mexico where they have [there are] bullfights?

B. ¿En Perú? ¿No es sólo en España y México donde hay corridas?

A. No sir! In Peru, Colombia, Ecuador, Venezuela, and Panama they also have them.

A. ¡No, hombre! En Perú, Colombia, Ecuador, Venezuela y Panamá también hay.

B. That's one sport I don't know beans about [about which I don't even know potato].

B. Ese es un deporte del que yo no sé ni papa.

A. It's something terrific. And don't say sport. Bullfighting is considered a real art.

A. Es algo fenomenal. Y no diga "deporte." El toreo se considera como un verdadero arte (2).

B. That's the nice thing about my job; every day you learn something new. OK, that's it.

B. Esto es lo bueno de mi profesión; cada día se aprende algo nuevo. Bueno, ya está.

A. Thanks. Lend me the comb. I'll comb it myself.

A. Gracias. Présteme el peine. Yo me peino.

cultural notes

(1) Baseball is highly popular in Mexico and Cuba, whereas **fútbol** is the favorite sport in most South-American countries. **Fútbol,** popular throughout the Hispanic world, is what we call *soccer.* In Spain this kind of football has even come to rival the bullfight in popularity.

(2) The bullfight is not considered a sport in the sense that **fútbol, jai-alai,** and baseball are. It is rather a combination of pageant, ritual, and art, dramatizing the Spaniard's courage and feeling for the tragedy of life in the face of brute force.

PRONUNCIATION EXERCISE

A. Alveolar [n] and bilabial [m]. INSTRUCTIONS: Repeat the following pairs just as you hear them.

[n]	[m]	[n]	[m]	[n]	[m]
ni	mi	nodo	modo	cana	cama
napa	mapa	nudo	mudo	lana	lama
noche	moche	nene	neme	gana	gama

Spanish /n/ is normally alveolar except when it assimilates to the following consonant. The bilabial nasal is [m].

B. Dental [n] and bilabial [m]. INSTRUCTIONS: Repeat the following pairs just as you hear them.

[n]	[m]	[n]	[m]
canto	campo	contar	comprar
contra	compra	entender	emprender
ponto	pompo	un taco	un paco
entero	empero	un techo	un pecho

[n]	[m]	[n]	[m]
un tío	un pío	sin dar	sin par
un tomo	un pomo	cintra	cimbra
un tuerto	un puerto	en tiento	en viento
ronda	rompa	indicar	invitar

Spanish /n/ assimilates to a following dental consonant ([t], [d]) and becomes dental itself. The Spanish nasal consonant which precedes a bilabial consonant ([p], [b], [m]) is always [m], no matter how it is spelled (i.e., the spelling may be **m** or **n**). Note also that the voiced bilabial stop [b] may be spelled either **b** or **v.**

C. Dental [n] and velar [ŋ]. INSTRUCTIONS: Repeat the following pairs just as you hear them.

[n]	[ŋ]	[n]	[ŋ]	[n]	[ŋ]	[n]	[ŋ]
cinto	cinco	tondo	tongo	en taza	en casa	un dato	un gato
junto	junco	monta	monja	un tarro	un carro	un dañón	un gañón
manda	manga	entero	engero	un teso	un queso	un terco	un huerco
manto	manco	entibar	engibar	un tío	un quío	un teso	un hueso
mando	mango			un tope	un cope	un tiro	un huiro
				un tubo	un cubo		

Spanish /n/ becomes velar [ŋ] before a velar consonant ([k], [g], [w], [x]). The striking characteristic of /n/ is its readiness to assimilate to any consonant that follows it.

D. English and Spanish [nt]. INSTRUCTIONS: Listen for the difference between the English and the Spanish [nt] as an English speaker and a Spanish speaker say alternately the English and Spanish words.

English [nt]	*Spanish* [nt]
canto	canto
junta	junta
pinto	pinto
Santa	santa
Tonto	tanto

In English the [nt] combination is usually yoked so that the [t] sounds almost like [d]. In Spanish both the [n] and the [t] are clearly pronounced, the [n] being resonated through the nose before the [t] begins, and the [t] retaining its voiceless quality.

36 Infinitive after another verb

EXAMPLES

1. No necesitas plata. *You don't need money.*
   No necesitas **saber** inglés.
2. ¿Desea unas vacaciones? *Do you desire a vacation?*
   ¿Desea **dejar** algún recado?
3. ¿No quiere la oportunidad? *Don't you want the opportunity?*
   ¿No quiere **venir** conmigo?
4. Prefiero una corrida de toros. *I prefer a bullfight.*
   Prefiero **usar** las tijeras. *I prefer to use the scissors.*
5. Espera más dinero. *He expects more money.*
   Espera **trabajar.** *He expects (hopes) to work.*
6. Si consigo el empleo. *If I get (achieve) the job.*
   Si consigo **salir.** *If I manage to get (achieve getting) out.*
7. ¿Recordaste la lista? *Did you remember the list?*
   ¿Recordaste **hacerlo?** *Did you remember to do it?*
8. Ellas saben español.
   Ellas saben **hablar.** *They know (how) to talk.*

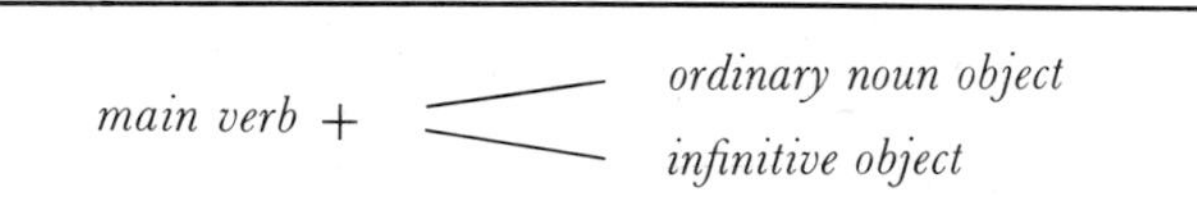

In Spanish, as in English, a verb may take an infinitive object just as it may take a noun object.

› ITEM SUBSTITUTION DRILL

1. *Desea* tomar unas vacaciones.
   (necesita, prefiere, quiere, espera, piensa)
2. *Queremos* hacer un viaje.
   (sabemos, deseamos, esperamos, pensamos)
3. *Esperan* participar en fútbol, natación y boxeo.
   (quieren, piensan, prefieren, desean, necesitan, saben)
4. Si *prefieres* volver a la profesión, está bien.
   (piensas, recuerdas, quieres, consigues, necesitas, deseas, esperas)

› CONSTRUCTION SUBSTITUTION DRILL

INSTRUCTIONS: Repeat each sentence just as you hear it. Then change it by inserting the infinitive after the verb form.

1. Espero unas vacaciones.
   (tener, conseguir, tomar)
2. No queremos una competencia de esta clase.
   (hacer, traer, organizar, quitar)
3. Necesita el peine.
   (usar, llevar, conseguir, prestar)
4. Prefieren el equipo de básquetbol.
   (ver, llevar, mandar, conocer)
5. ¿Recordaste la lista?
   (mandar, traer, conseguir)
6. Si consigo el empleo, está bien.
   (dejar, pedir, ganar)
7. El sabe la noticia.
   (arreglar, dar, exigir, cortar)
8. Ellas no piensan ahora.
   (entrar, venir, jugar, pelear)

EXAMPLES
1. **Debe estar** en la cocina.
2. **¿Pueden venir?**
3. **Déjeme peinarme** yo mismo. *Let me comb it myself* (*comb myself, myself*).

I must go (I ought to go).	**Debo ir.**
I can go (I am able to go).	**Puedo ir.**
Let me go (allow me to go).	**Déjeme ir.**

Deber, poder, and **dejar** take infinitive objects.

› ITEM SUBSTITUTION DRILL

1. *Déjeme* ver la maquinilla.
   (puedo, debo)
2. *Debe* estar en el país.
   (déjelo, puede)
3. *Podemos* mandar saludos a la familia.
   (debemos, déjenos)
4. *Piensa* trabajar como el año pasado.
   (puede, debe, déjelo)
5. *Esperamos* ir juntos al Teatro Nacional.
   (podemos, debemos, déjenos)

EXAMPLES
1. Viene gente **a la casa.** *People are coming to the house.*
   Viene gente **a comer.** (*People are coming to eat.*)
2. Ve **al jardín.** *Go to the garden.*
   Ve **a jugar.** (*Go to play.*)
3. El profesor los invita **a la clase.** *The teacher invites them to the class.*
   El profesor los invita **a entrar.** *The teacher invites them in.*
4. Pasaron **a la casa.** *They went on to the house.*
   Pasaron **a vernos.** *They went on* (*in*) *to see us.*
5. Entró **a mi cuarto.** *He came into my room.*
   Entró **a llamarme.** *He came in to call me.*

main verb + *preposition* + < *noun object* / *infinitive object*

Where the main verb would call for a preposition before a noun object, it calls for the same preposition before an infinitive. Typical examples are verbs of motion, calling for *to* (**a**).

ITEM SUBSTITUTION DRILL

1. *Llegaron* a ver el patio.
   (pasaron, regresaron, entraron, salieron, volvieron)
2. Los *invitaron* a comer frijoles.
   (llevaron, llamaron)
3. *Viene* la señora extranjera a pasar unos días.
   (llega, regresa, sale, vuelve)
4. *Ve* a jugar al jardín.
   (sal, ven, vuelve)

PATTERNED RESPONSE DRILL

A. 1. TEACHER: ¿Por qué entraron?
STUDENT: **Entraron a ver los muebles.**
TEACHER: ¿Qué quieren?
STUDENT: **Quieren ver los muebles.**
2. ¿Por qué llegaron?
¿Qué desean?
3. ¿Por qué volvieron?
¿Qué necesitan?

B. 1. TEACHER: ¿Por qué pasaron?
STUDENT: **Pasaron a vernos.**
TEACHER: ¿Qué quieren?
STUDENT: **Quieren vernos.**
2. ¿Por qué entraron?
¿Qué desean?
3. ¿Por qué llegaron?
¿Qué necesitan?

DISCUSSION

The infinitive (the form of the verb that appears after *to* in English) functions as a noun. Like other nouns it may serve as object of a verb (examples in this unit), subject or predicate noun (**Ganar a veces es perder** *To win is sometimes to lose*), and object of a preposition (object of **a** in this unit; other prepositions will be given in Unit 9).

Whereas English does not distinguish between *He wants to see me* and *He comes to see me,* using *to* with the infinitive in both, Spanish does distinguish between **Quiere verme** and **Viene a verme,** using an **a** in the latter. This **a** is the same directional *to* that is used with **venir** and other similar verbs to link them to a following noun, as in English *come* (*go, run, walk, hurry, crawl,* etc.) *to the house.* English *He wants the house* vs. *He comes to the house* is like Spanish **Quiere verme** vs. **Viene a verme.** We might say that **Viene a verme** means *He is heading **toward** the act of seeing me.*

When in addition to an infinitive after the verb of motion there is also a noun referring to the destination of the motion, Spanish normally repeats the **a: Ve *a* jugar *a*l jardín.** This is true whether the corresponding English is *Go play **in** the yard* or *Go **to** the yard to play.*

37 *Ir a* plus infinitive

EXAMPLES

A. 1. **Ve a ver** quién es.
2. Si **vamos a verlos** hoy, podemos traer a mamá a casa con nosotros.
If we go see them today, we can bring Mother home with us.

B. 1. **Voy a arreglar** esto.
2. ¿Quién cree usted que **va a ganar** los Juegos?
3. **Vamos a perder** en todo.
4. **Van a estar** fantásticos.

C. **Vamos a hablar** con ellas.

THREE USES OF **ir a** PLUS INFINITIVE		
MEANING	EXAMPLES	POSSIBLE FORMS OF **ir**
A. To go (to)	**Ve a ver.** **Vamos (allí) a verlos.**[1]	*unlimited*
B. To be going to (*future time*)	**Voy a ir.** **Vamos a perder.** **Van a estar fantásticos.**	*present tense*[2]
C. Let's	**Vamos a hablar con ellas.**	**vamos** *only; affirmative sentences*[3]

Besides the basic *to go (to)* meaning, **ir a** is used like English *to be going (to)* to indicate future time. Also, in the one form **vamos a** it can mean *let's.*

› PERSON-NUMBER SUBSTITUTION DRILL

1. *Ellos* van a traer muy buenos atletas.
   (Chile, nosotros, usted, los Estados Unidos, yo)
2. *El* va a quererlo muy corto atrás.
   (ustedes, nosotros, Pablo, yo, tú, ellos)
3. Mañana voy a estar en tu casa.
   (él, nosotros, ella, ellos, Rafael y yo, el barbero)
4. Esta tarde vas a ver esa esquina.
   (usted, nosotros, él, yo, María, ustedes)
5. *Tú* vas a trabajar en el Ministerio.[4]
   (Francisco, yo, el señor Alonso, nosotros, ellos, usted, Patricio y don Rosario)

› CONSTRUCTION SUBSTITUTION DRILL

INSTRUCTIONS: Repeat the following sentences just as you hear them. Then repeat them again, substituting an appropriate **ir a** construction for the verb of the original sentence.

A. 1. TEACHER: El viaje cuesta mucho dinero. *Repita.*
   STUDENT: **El viaje cuesta mucho dinero.**
   TEACHER: *Cambie.*
   STUDENT: **El viaje va a costar mucho dinero.**
2. Olga está encantada de conocerlo.
3. La carrera es algo fenomenal.
4. Cierran la escuela a las nueve y media.
5. Los juegos están fantásticos, ¿eh?
6. De esto yo no sé ni papa.

B. 1. TEACHER: El policía le exigió una multa. *Repita.*
   STUDENT: **El policía le exigió una multa.**
   TEACHER: *Cambie.*
   STUDENT: **El policía le va a exigir una multa.**
2. Le quitaron todos los documentos.
3. El habló perfectamente bien.
4. Pero desgraciadamente perdieron en todo.
5. Me metí en una calle en contra del tránsito.
6. ¡Qué bueno que llamaste!

[1] *We're going (there) to see them.*

[2] *Was going* will be treated in Unit 11.

[3] *Let's not* will be treated in Unit 18, Section 104.

[4] If this were *to go to* (motion) rather than *to be going to* (future action), it would be **Tú vas a trabajar al Ministerio** *You're going (are on your way) to work at the Ministry.* See Section 36.

› PATTERNED RESPONSE DRILL

TEACHER	STUDENT
1. ¿Quiere hablar con ella?	Sí, vamos a hablar con ella.
2. ¿Quiere salir con ella?	Sí, vamos a salir con ella.
3. ¿Quiere comer ahora?	Sí, vamos a comer ahora.
4. ¿Quiere pagar ahora?	Sí, vamos a pagar ahora.
5. ¿Quiere estudiar en el comedor?	Sí, vamos a estudiar en el comedor.
6. ¿Quiere trabajar en el comedor?	Sí, vamos a trabajar en el comedor.

› DISCUSSION

In place of the future tense (*I'll buy it*) English often substitutes the verb *go* (*I'm going to buy it*). Spanish uses **ir a** in the same way.

38 *Al* plus infinitive

EXAMPLES

1. Hay que cerrar la puerta **al entrar.** *You have to shut the door when you go in.*
2. **Al pasar** por el parque, miramos los juegos. *As we passed through the park, we looked at the games.*
3. **Al llegar** a la Calle Veinte, doblaron a la derecha. *When they got to Twentieth Street, they turned right.*

on, at the moment of	–ing

al	*infinitive*

Al plus the infinitive expresses an action simultaneous with another action. The closest English equivalent is the literary *on* plus *–ing,* e.g., *On arriving at Twentieth Street, they turned right.*

› ITEM SUBSTITUTION DRILL

1. Al *salir,* te llamo.
   (llegar, acabar, regresar)
2. Al *entrar a* la casa, recordé la dirección.
   (salir de, volver a, pensar en)
3. Al *llegar a* la escuela, me lo dijeron.
   (salir de, llamar a, entrar a)
4. Al *mandar el café,* me llamaron.
   (doblar la esquina, pasar por ahí, abrir la puerta)
5. Al *decir eso,* algo pasó.
   (volver a la casa, recibir la noticia)

› DISCUSSION

Appearing with the infinitive, the contraction **al** for **a + el** (see Unit 7, Section 33) means *at the* (*moment of*). It is used under the same conditions as English *on* plus *–ing* (*on arriving, on getting up, on discovering the mistake,* etc.), though the conversational English equivalent is normally with *when, as,* or *as soon as.* This is to say that it refers to an action viewed as virtually simultaneous with another action and relatively brief.

39 The verb *haber*, there to be

EXAMPLES A. 1. En México **hay** corridas de toros. *In Mexico there are bullfights.*
2. **¿Hay** huevos? *Are there any eggs?*

B. 1. Debe **haber** un teléfono aquí. *There must (ought to) be a telephone here.*
2. ¿Cuántos números puede **haber?** *How many numbers can there be?*

there is there are	**hay**

Haber has the form **hay** *there is, there are* in the present tense.

there	seems, seem has, have is (are) able, can ought, must	(to) be	**parece** **tiene que** **puede** **debe**	**haber**

Any other verb (**debe, parece,** etc.) combined with **haber** is used in the third person singular.

CONSTRUCTION SUBSTITUTION DRILL

INSTRUCTIONS: Repeat each sentence just as you hear it. Then repeat it again, substituting **está el** (**están los**) for **hay un** (**hay unos**) or vice versa.

A. 1. TEACHER: Aquí hay un libro. *Repita.*
STUDENT: **Aquí hay un libro.**
TEACHER: *Cambie.*
STUDENT: **Aquí está el libro.**
2. Aquí hay una lista.
3. Aquí hay unos documentos.
4. Aquí hay unas noticias.

B. 1. ¿Dónde está el restorán?
2. ¿Dónde está la fruta?
3. ¿Dónde están los frijoles?
4. ¿Dónde están las tazas de café?

C. 1. Ya hay un profesor aquí.
2. Ya hay una profesora aquí.
3. Ya hay unos alumnos aquí.
4. Ya hay unas criadas aquí.

D. 1. ¿Está el café a la izquierda?
2. ¿Está la casa a la izquierda?
3. ¿Están los teatros a la izquierda?
4. ¿Están las flechas a la izquierda?

VERB TRANSFORMATION DRILL

1. TEACHER: Hay muchos números. *Repita.*
STUDENT: **Hay muchos números.**
TEACHER: Debe.
STUDENT: **Debe haber muchos números.**
2. Hay un buen sistema.
(debe, tiene que, puede, parece)
3. Hay un policía en la esquina.
(parece, debe, puede, tiene que)
4. Hay mucha competencia.
(tiene que, puede, parece, debe)

› PATTERNED RESPONSE DRILL

INSTRUCTIONS: The student will answer each question according to the situation in the class.

A. 1. ¿Hay señoritas en la clase?
Sí, sí hay (**No, no hay**).
¿Cuántas hay?
Hay dos.
2. ¿Hay señoras en la clase?
3. ¿Hay rubias en la clase?
4. ¿Hay mexicanos en la clase?
5. ¿Hay abuelos en la clase?
6. ¿Hay morenas en la clase?
7. ¿Hay policías brutos en la clase?

B. 1. ¿Atletas en la clase?
No, no hay (**Sí, sí hay**).
2. ¿Extranjeros en la clase?
3. ¿Barberos en la clase?
4. ¿Juguetes en la clase?
5. ¿Señores en la clase?

Mexico City: Opening parade of the corrida

Reflexives with nonpersonal subjects

EXAMPLES A. 1. Cada día **se aprende** algo nuevo.
2. Cada día **se aprenden** cosas nuevas. *Every day new things are learned (you learn, one learns, new things).*

B. 1. **Se está organizando** un grupo para ir.
2. **Se están organizando** grupos para ir. *Groups are being organized (They're getting up groups) to go.*

ENGLISH MEANINGS		SPANISH EQUIVALENTS
NORMAL	LITERAL	
The game is (gets) organized.	The game organizes itself.	**Se organiza el juego.**
The games are (get) organized.	The games organize themselves.	**Se organizan los juegos.**
A cup of coffee was sent (up). They sent (up) a cup of coffee.	A cup of coffee sent itself (up).	**Se mandó una taza de café.**
Two cups of coffee were sent (up). They sent (up) two cups of coffee.	Two cups of coffee sent themselves (up).	**Se mandaron dos tazas de café.**
The door came open. The door opened.	The door opened itself.	**Se abrió la puerta.**
The doors came open. The doors opened.	The doors opened themselves.	**Se abrieron las puertas.**
The record got broken. The record broke.	The record broke itself.	**Se rompió el disco.**
The records got broken. The records broke.	The records broke themselves.	**Se rompieron los discos.**
The traffic was (got) stopped. The traffic stopped.	The traffic stopped itself.	**Se paró el tráfico.**

To show an action performed on something without regard to who or what performs it, Spanish uses **se** with the third person singular and plural of the verb.

EMPHASIS	
STRESS IN ENGLISH	POSITION IN SPANISH
The **radio** was turned off.	**Se apagó el radio.**
The radio was **turned off.**	**El radio se apagó.**

As with questions (see Unit 3, Section 10), the element being emphasized tends to be placed last.

› NUMBER SUBSTITUTION DRILL

INSTRUCTIONS: Repeat the following sentences just as you hear them. Then repeat them again, substituting a plural (or singular) noun as subject of the reflexive verb.

A. 1. TEACHER: Se acabó la corrida. *Repita.*
STUDENT: **Se acabó la corrida.**
TEACHER: *Cambie.*
STUDENT: **Se acabaron las corridas.**
2. Se cerró la puerta.
3. Se oyó un ruido.
4. Se paró el juego.

B. 1. Se va a organizar un grupo.
2. Se va a hacer un viaje.
3. Se va a aprender una cosa nueva.
4. Se va a necesitar una casa nueva.

C. 1. Se ve la flecha.
2. El teatro se usa mucho.
3. La multa se paga aquí.
4. Esta cosa se considera buena.

D. 1. Se mandaron dos tazas de café.
2. Se abrieron los libros.
3. Se dejaron los recados.
4. Se vieron las calles.

E. 1. Se van a llevar los documentos.
2. Se van a necesitar unos muebles nuevos.
3. Se van a vender unas docenas de huevos.

F. 1. Se celebran los días feriados.
2. Se barren los cuartos de arriba.
3. Se comen muchas frutas.
4. Se sacuden los muebles.

› TRANSLATION DRILL

A. 1. You say "Thank you."
Se dice "Gracias".
2. You say "You're welcome."
3. You say "Excuse me."
4. You say "Of course."
5. You say "My gosh."
6. You say "At your service."

B. 1. They say he's coming.
Se dice que viene.
2. They say he's arriving.
3. They say he's leaving.
4. They say he's returning.
5. They say he's studying.
6. They say he's speaking.
7. They say he's participating.

C. INSTRUCTIONS: Translate the following paired sentences, placing the equivalents of the emphasized English items last in the Spanish sentence.

1. The *traffic* was stopped.
The traffic was *stopped.*
2. The *door* opened.
The door *opened.*
3. A *group* is being organized.
A group is being *organized.*
4. The *message* was left.
The message was *left.*
5. The *document* was taken away.
The document was *taken away.*
6. The *arrow* was lost.
The arrow was *lost.*
7. The *market* closed.
The market *closed.*
8. Every day *new things* are learned.
Every day new things are *learned.*
9. The *record player* was turned off.
The record player was *turned off.*

EXAMPLES 1. Sólo de eso **se habla.**
2. **Se vive** bien en Cuba. *You can live well (One lives well) in Cuba.*
3. **Se sigue** por esta calle. *You keep on down this street.*

4. No **se juega** con él. *You don't fool around (One doesn't play [around]) with him.*

5. No **se regatea** aquí. *There's no bargaining here (You can't bargain here, One doesn't bargain here).*

ACTION-GOING-ON
se + *third-person singular of any verb*

To show an action as merely going on, without any grammatical subject, **se** is used with the third-person singular of the verb.

› TRANSLATION DRILL

A. 1. One eats well here.
2. One lives well here.
3. One works well here.

B. 1. One studies a lot here.
2. One plays a lot here.
3. One learns a lot here.

C. 1. There's no haggling here.
2. There's no learning here.
3. There's no talking here.

› DISCUSSION

The uses of the reflexive pronoun **se** (*yourself, yourselves, oneself, himself, herself, itself, themselves*) are complex.

One highly frequent use is equivalent to a variety of indefinite expressions in English. The doer of the action is disregarded. In fact the purpose is often to picture the action as happening of itself. We sometimes find a parallel use of *itself* in English: *The bullet* ***flattened itself*** *(got flattened, was flattened, flattened) against the stone where it struck.*

Where English takes an object and turns it into a subject, leaving the verb exactly the same, Spanish adds **se:**

Something opened the door—The door *opened:* **se abrió.**
Something stopped the traffic—The traffic *stopped:* **se paró.**
Someone combs hair—Straight hair *combs* well: **se peina.**
Someone dusts furniture—It *dusts* easily: **se sacude.**

A special case is that of **se** with the third person singular (never plural) of any verb to indicate merely action-going-on: **se habla** *there is talking,* **se regatea** *there is bargaining,* **se come** *there is eating* (**Se come bien aquí** *There's good eating here, One eats well here, Good food is served here*).

› GUIDED CONVERSATION

INSTRUCTIONS: Fill in the blanks of the following conversation as amply as possible with appropriate passages from the main dialog.

B. *Barbero* A. *Señor Alonso*

B. Bueno, señor Alonso, y ¿cómo lo quiere esta vez?
A. Como siempre: ______________
B. Bueno, y ¿se habla mucho de los juegos panamericanos donde usted trabaja?
A. Sí, y ¡cómo hablan! Ya se está ______________
B. La radio[5] dice que van a ganar los americanos.

[5]The Spanish word **radio** can be either masculine or feminine. Considered as an appliance, it is masculine: **No ponga ese radio tan fuerte.** But when it refers to the transmitting station and its broadcasts, the word is feminine.

A. Yo creo que sí, porque ellos tienen ______
B. ¿Y en qué deportes vamos a participar nosotros?
A. ______
B. ¿Pero por qué dice usted que vamos a perder en todo?
A. Porque con países como ______
B. El mismo programa de radio habló de los toros, pero ¿no es sólo en España y México donde hay corridas de toros?
A. No, hombre. En ______
B. Pero ése es un deporte totalmente[6] diferente de los otros, ¿no es verdad?
A. Hombre, no diga "deporte." El toreo ______

› REVIEW DRILLS

Some additional verbs with stem changes.

A. Substitution drill.

1. Le apostamos a que ganamos en fútbol. (yo, Pablo, Julio y Pablo, Julio y yo, tú, ella, ustedes)
2. Por eso juegas fútbol. (ellos, Francisco, nosotros, usted, yo, los muchachos, él)
3. Siempre vuelve dentro de diez minutos. (Elena y María, tú, ella, nosotros, usted, yo, Paquito)
4. Es que nunca perdemos. (Rafael, Patricio y Rosario, nosotros, él, yo, tú, las chicas)
5. *Roberto* prefiere no pagar la multa. (nosotros, usted, tú, Fernando y él, yo, mi padre, ellos)
6. Nunca consigo ganar en las carreras. (Cecilia, ellos, tú, ustedes, nosotros, él, mis hermanos)
7. La criada sigue por la avenida. (yo, las muchachas, el barbero, nosotros, ellos, tú)

B. Translation drill.

1. The boy plays a lot.
2. The man bets a lot.
3. My nephew loses a lot.
4. I prefer the brunette.
5. I return with the blonde.
6. I play with the team.
7. I bet with the boss.

reading

Paquito y la relatividad

PAQ. *Paquito* P. *Papá*

PAQ. Papá, voy a escribir una composición sobre los deportes. ¿Quieres ayudarme? — **ayudar** *to help*
P. Muy bien, Paquito. ¿Cuáles deportes?
PAQ. Todos, papá: fútbol, básquetbol, beisbol, boxeo, toreo...
P. ¡Por Dios, Paquito, no vas a describirlos todos! ¿Por qué no tratas sólo uno o dos? — **tratar** *to treat, discuss*
PAQ. Porque si hablo de todos no es necesario saber tanto de cada uno...
P. Hmm... Bueno, vamos a trabajar.

[6] *totally*

Valencia, Spain:
Toreros in action

PAQ. Pues aquí tengo algo que quiero leerte. (*Lee.*) "El juego de fútbol es muy conocido en Latinoamérica. También en los Estados Unidos. Pero allá se juega una clase de fútbol muy diferente. En Sudamérica se toca el balón sólo con los pies y la cabeza. En los Estados Unidos se pueden usar también las manos. Pero en los Estados Unidos el juego es muy cruel, tan cruel que los jugadores tienen que llevar ropa especial como protección, porque en los Estados Unidos, en vez de dar puntapiés al balón, se dan puntapiés a los atletas del otro equipo..."

leer *to read*
conocido *well-known*
tocar *to touch* **balón** *ball*
cabeza *head*
jugadores *players*
dar...al *kicking the*

P. ¡Ja, ja, ja!... Ejem. Pero, hijo, ¿de dónde te vienen tales ideas?

PAQ. De mi primo Roberto, que vive en El Paso. El ve muchos juegos de fútbol.

P. Pues, es verdad que el fútbol americano es muy diferente del nuestro, pero...

PAQ. Sí, sí, papá. Roberto me dice también que sufren tantos golpes que muchas veces hay que llevarlos al hospital.

golpes *injuries*

P. Mira, Paquito. Eso de la crueldad es muy relativo. Hay millones de norteamericanos que creen que nuestro toreo es cruel.

PAQ. Eso es una tontería, papá. El toro no es más que un animal.

P. Muy bien, Paquito: eso decimos nosotros, pero los norteamericanos consideran al toro como algo humano... que vive, que tiene un corazón... Nosotros también somos animales... animales humanos.

corazón *heart*

PAQ. Entonces, papá, nosotros creemos que los norteamericanos son crueles, y ellos creen que nosotros somos crueles. ¿Quiénes tienen razón?

tienen razón *are right*

P. Los dos, digo, ni unos ni otros.

PAQ. No entiendo, papá.

P. Yo tampoco, Paquito. Para entender esto, hay que ser filósofo.

hay...filósofo *one must be a philosopher*

UNIT 9

A Respectable Man

A. *Alfredo* B. *Bernardo, friend of Alfredo*

A. What are you doing with those tools?
B. I'm changing the tires on the car.
A. But that's a very complicated job.

B. Nonsense! It's very simple.
A. But very dirty.
B. Phooey. I'll wash afterwards.
A. Are you crazy! You, a respectable, professional man . . .
B. Those are old-fashioned ideas.
A. OK, OK, let's not argue.

* * *

A. Incidentally, you know that tomorrow's the official opening of the petroleum refinery?

B. Sure; I'd really like to go. You going?

A. I have two invitations; do you want to go along? They say it's a magnificent plant.
B. Too bad it's costing the country such a lot of money in dollars.
A. What of it [does it matter]? It'll be the most up-to-date plant in Latin America.
B. But, listen, man . . .
A. You've got to think about progress once in a while.

* * *

Hombre respetable

A. *Alfredo* B. *Bernardo, amigo de Alfredo*

A. ¿Qué estás haciendo con esas herramientas?
B. Estoy cambiando las llantas del auto.
A. Hombre, pero eso es un trabajo muy complicado.
B. ¡Qué va! Es muy sencillo.
A. Pero muy sucio.
B. Bah, después me lavo.
A. ¡Qué cosa más ridícula! Tú que eres hombre respetable... profesional... (1)
B. Esas son ideas anticuadas.
A. Bueno, bueno, no discutamos.

* * *

A. Pasando a otro tema, ¿sabes que mañana es la inauguración de la refinería de petróleo?
B. Sí, hombre; tengo muchas ganas de ir. ¿Tú vas?
A. Yo tengo dos invitaciones; ¿quieres ir conmigo? Dicen que es una planta magnífica.
B. Lástima que al país le cuesta una cantidad astronómica de dólares. (2)
A. Y eso ¿qué importa? Va a ser la planta más moderna de Latinoamérica. (3)
B. Pero, hombre...
A. Hay que pensar en progresar alguna vez.

* * *

Colombia: Petroleum refinery

B. I suppose a lot of important people are going.

A. Yes, of course: doctors, lawyers, and technicians, and also some business men, not to mention high government officials.

B. Let's go in my car, [since] there's always something wrong with yours: the battery, the carburetor, the brakes, the steering . . .

A. Nonsense! Don't exaggerate. In any case, the horn never fails.

B. Supongo que va a ir mucha gente importante.

A. Sí, claro: médicos, abogados y técnicos,[1] también algunos hombres de negocios, sin mencionar altos funcionarios del gobierno.

B. Vamos en mi coche, ya que el tuyo siempre tiene algo malo: la batería, el carburador, los frenos, la dirección...

A. ¡Qué va! No exageres. En todo caso, la bocina nunca falla.

[1] The first c of **técnicos** is pronounced [g̸].

cultural notes

(1) The middle- and upper-class Spaniard and Spanish American have long regarded manual labor as a symbol of lower-class status. As the dialog suggests, the pattern is changing.

(2) An important index of the economic health and growth of other nations is the amount of foreign exchange, especially of American dollars, that they have. For countries whose economies depend upon exporting raw materials dollars are essential for buying the machinery and manufactured goods that they do not produce themselves.

(3) Hitherto unindustrialized countries tend to view industrialization as a symbol of progress.

› PRONUNCIATION AND WRITING EXERCISE

(Reread "Vowels," "Stops," and "Stop-spirants" in Unit 1, Section 1.)

A. Vowels and consonants in similar-sounding words. INSTRUCTIONS: Listen for the difference between the sounds indicated as an English speaker and a Spanish speaker say alternately the English and Spanish words.

English /a/	*Spanish* /o/	*English* /æ/	*Spanish* /a/	*English* /z/	*Spanish* /s/
October	octubre	admirable	admirable	rose	rosa
occupied	ocupado	attack	ataque	use	usar
office	oficina	class	clase	result	resultar
opportunity	oportunidad	pass	pasa	present	presente
doctor	doctor	Spanish	español	president	presidente

B. The written representation of /k/ by **c** and **qu.** INSTRUCTIONS: Write the following lists of words from dictation.

1	2	3	4	5	6
cara	codo	cura	que	quipos	creer
casa	como	curso	queso	quince	crédito
cama	copo	cuna	quebrar	quise	criatura
carta	cosa	cuyo	quedar	química	clásico
casi	corto	culpa	quemar	quitar	clarinete
cada	comer	culto	querer	quizá	acto
campo	común	cubrir			

You have noted that the Spanish phoneme /k/ is written **qu** before the sounds [e] and [i] (but **c** everywhere else). Exceptions are occasional words borrowed from other languages using **k** as, e.g., **kilo.**

C. The written representation of /g/ by **g** and **gu.** INSTRUCTIONS: Write the following lists of words from dictation.

1	2	3	4		5	6
gana	goma	gusto	pagué	pague	guía	granizo
gato	golfo	gula	regué	riegue	guija	gratis
ganga	gota	gura	vagué	vague	guincho	glotón
ganso	gorra	gusano	jugué	juegue	guiño	gloria
ganar	golpe	gutural	llegué	llegue	guisa	agricultor
gastar	gordo	gustar	entregué	entregue	guión	digno

You have noted that the Spanish phoneme /g/ with its variants [g] and [ǥ] is written **gu** before the sounds [e] and [i] (but simply **g** everywhere else).

Infinitive after prepositions

EXAMPLES

1. En vez **de ir,** llame. *Instead of going, call.*
2. **Sin mencionar** altos funcionarios de gobierno. (*Without mentioning high government officials.*)
3. Hay que pensar **en progresar.** (*It is necessary to think about progressing.*)
4. Tengo muchas ganas **de ir.** (*I have many desires of going.*)
5. **Por hablar** tanto no oyes nada. *Because of talking so much you don't hear anything.*
6. Usted sigue derecho **hasta llegar** a la Calle Veinte. (*You keep straight ahead until arriving at Twentieth Street.*)

ENGLISH *preposition* + -ing	=	SPANISH *preposition* + *infinitive*
without mentioning		**sin mencionar**

English preposition plus verb ending *-ing* corresponds to Spanish preposition plus infinitive.

› ITEM SUBSTITUTION DRILL

1. Tengo muchas ganas de *ir.*
   (salir, venir, volver, seguir, participar, comer, ganar)
2. No puede hacerlo sin *trabajar* un poquito.
   (estudiar, saber, pagar, apostar, perder, exigir, pelear)
3. Hay que pensar en *progresar* alguna vez.
   (cambiar, trabajar, participar, jugar, pagar, vender, vivir)
4. Por *hablar* tanto, no oyes nada.
   (discutir, pelear, llamar, regatear, pedir)
5. Siga usted hasta *acabar*lo.
   (alcanzar, arreglar, conseguir, recibir, ver, oir, traer)
6. En vez de *pensar* tanto, apueste.
   (organizar, discutir, hablar, escribir, esperar)
7. Para *regatear,* Rosa es muy buena.
   (organizar, exagerar, apostar, pelear, discutir, vender)
8. Después de *traer* el auto, va a la refinería.
   (conseguir, pedir, arreglar, usar, lavar, pagar)

› TRANSLATION DRILL

A. 1. Bring[2] the coffee instead of sending it.
   2. Bring the coffee instead of selling it.

B. 1. Without seeing the doctor, I can't.
   2. Without speaking to the professor, I can't.

C. 1. They can't win without participating.
   2. They can't progress without organizing.

D. 1. I don't like the idea of lending my comb.
   2. I don't like the idea of selling my tools.

E. 1. I have no desire for studying.
   2. I have no desire for eating.

F. 1. Before eating, he goes to the plant.
   2. Before studying, he goes to the park.

G. 1. After working, he goes to the café.
   2. After playing, he goes to the patio.

H. 1. Don't leave until you see (until seeing) the marathon race.
   2. Don't leave until you congratulate the football team.

I. 1. Because of being a professional athlete, he can't come.
   2. Because of playing basketball, he can't come.

[2] In translation drills such as this, unless **tú** is specifically called for use the **usted** form.

EXAMPLES A. 1. ¿De parte de quién, **para decir**le?
2. Le escribo **para felicitar**la.

B. 1. Tengo algunas cosas **para vender.**
2. Es una herramienta **para cambiar** llantas. *It's a tool for changing tires.*

ENGLISH	
(in order) to	congratulate
for	changing

SPANISH	
para	**felicitar**
para	**cambiar**

(In order) to plus the infinitive and *for (the purpose of)* plus verb ending in *-ing* are both equivalent to **para** plus infinitive in Spanish.

ITEM SUBSTITUTION DRILL

1. Mamá, ven acá para *ver* una cosa. (arreglar, oir)
2. Viene mañana para *dejar* los muebles. (arreglar, cambiar, pagar, sacudir)
3. Dice un señor que si hay ropa para *vender.* (lavar, llevar, mandar)
4. Se está organizando un grupo para *ir.* (jugar, participar, discutir, estudiar)

CHOICE-QUESTION RESPONSE DRILL

1. TEACHER: ¿Viene usted para estudiar o para trabajar?
   STUDENT: **Para estudiar.**
2. ¿Quiere usted la ropa para usarla o para venderla?
3. ¿Vienen los técnicos para organizar la planta o para hacer competencia?
4. ¿Quiere los juguetes para usarlos o para venderlos?
5. ¿Va al ministerio para discutir o para oir?
6. ¿Quieres a tu mamá para decirle algo o para pedirle algo?
7. ¿Le escribe a su sobrina para felicitarla o para calmarla?

DISCUSSION

English has two verbal nouns (forms of verbs used in noun functions), the infinitive and the *-ing* form.[3] In most situations there is little practical difference between them, as may be seen in the virtual identity of meaning in *I prefer* ***to wait*** and *I prefer* ***waiting.*** The main difference is in *where* the two forms are permitted to occur. After prepositions only the *-ing* is found.

The one exception to this is the preposition *to* itself, when used in the sense of "purpose." Thus we may say either *a tool* ***to change*** *tires* or *a tool* ***for changing*** *tires.* The *to* here is more than the sign of the infinitive; it is equivalent to the *for* of purpose and is so translated to Spanish: **una herramienta *para cambiar* llantas.** (*To* as the sign of the infinitive is actually dropped in cases like *You don't need* ***to worry*** → *You needn't* ***worry.***) We must therefore watch out for the difference between *to* as merely the sign of the infinitive and *to* as an indication of purpose.

42 Infinitive after verb-plus-relator

EXAMPLES 1. **Tengo que estar** con mi tía.
2. Mañana **tiene que pagar** una multa.

[3] The *-ing* form has other uses, however: adverbial, as in *You can't make friends arguing (by arguing) all the time,* and adjectival, as in *a losing fight.*

3. Ahora **hay que trabajar.**
4. María Elena **acaba de salir.**
5. **Acabo de tener** un tremendo lío.

tener que **haber que** **acabar de**	+ *infinitive*

Certain combinations of verb and relator words (**que** and prepositions) function as units.

EXAMPLES 1. Tiene una multa que pagar. *He has a fine to pay.*
2. Hay unos documentos que arreglar. *There are some documents to arrange.*

VERB	NOUN	INFINITIVE
He has	a fine	to pay.
There are	some documents	to arrange.

VERB	NOUN	**que** + INFINITIVE
Tiene	**una multa**	**que pagar.**
Hay	**unos documentos**	**que arreglar.**

With **tener que** and **haber que** the noun may come directly after the verb as in English.

ITEM SUBSTITUTION DRILL

1. *Acaban de* cortarle el pelo.
   (tienen que, piensan en, hay que)
2. *Tienen que* discutir la profesión del toreo.
   (piensan en, hay que, acaban de)
3. *Piensan en* hacer un viaje a Perú.
   (hay que, acaban de, tienen que)
4. *Hay que* cambiar las llantas.
   (acaban de, tienen que, piensan en)

PATTERNED RESPONSE DRILL

A. 1. ¿Tiene usted que pagar una multa? — Sí, tengo que pagar una multa.
¿Tiene usted una multa que pagar? — Sí, tengo una multa que pagar.
2. ¿Tiene usted que decir algo? — Sí, tengo que decir algo.
¿Tiene usted algo que decir? — Sí, tengo algo que decir.
3. ¿Tiene usted que traer ropa? — Sí, tengo que traer ropa.
¿Tiene usted ropa que traer? — Sí, tengo ropa que traer.
4. ¿Tiene usted que apostar dinero? — Sí, tengo que apostar dinero.
¿Tiene usted dinero que apostar? — Sí, tengo dinero que apostar.
5. ¿Hay que sacudir unos muebles? — Sí, hay que sacudir unos muebles.
¿Hay unos muebles que sacudir? — Sí, hay unos muebles que sacudir.
6. ¿Hay que arreglar unos documentos? — Sí, hay que arreglar unos documentos.
¿Hay unos documentos que arreglar? — Sí, hay unos documentos que arreglar.

B. 1. ¿Ya recibió usted el recado?
Sí, acabo de recibirlo.
2. ¿Ya recibieron ellos el recado?
3. ¿Ya recibieron ustedes el recado?
4. ¿Ya recibiste tú el recado?
5. ¿Ya recibió Olga el recado?

C. 1. ¿En qué piensa Fernando?
Piensa en hacer un viaje.
2. ¿En qué piensan ustedes?
3. ¿En qué piensa la gente importante?
4. ¿En qué piensas tú?
5. ¿En qué piensa ella?

▸ DISCUSSION

Like the auxiliary verbs in Unit 8 certain combinations of verb–plus–relator take infinitive objects. They must be learned separately.

Que as an indicator of obligation admits of two arrangements, **Tiene que cambiar una llanta** *He has to change a tire* and **Tiene una llanta que cambiar** *He has a tire to change,* as in English. (If there is no obligation, **que** is not used: **Tiene pan para comer** *He has bread to eat* means that he has it for food, not that his mother expects him to eat it.)

43 The *-ndo* form

EXAMPLES

A.
1. **Hablando** de fechas, el 4 de octubre es día feriado.
2. **Pasando** a otro tema.
3. Me tiró del pelo **cortando** con la maquinilla. *He pulled my hair, cutting with the clippers.*
4. Vimos dos equipos **jugando.** *We saw two teams playing.*
5. **Volviendo** a casa vi a Josefina. *Returning home (When I was returning home, On my way home) I saw Josefina.*
6. **Viviendo** en los Estados Unidos nunca vamos a tener la oportunidad de ver una corrida de toros. *Living (Since, If we live) in the United States, we're never going to have a chance to see a bullfight.*

B.
1. **¿Diciendo** qué? *Saying what?*
2. No **pudiendo,** no entré. *Not being able to, I didn't go in.*

C.
1. **Yendo** contigo, veo más. *Going (By going) with you, I see more.*
2. **Oyéndolo,** recordamos. *Hearing it, we remembered.*

A. *regular verbs*	**hablar**	**habl-**	**-ando**
	comer **vivir**	**com-** **viv-**	**-iendo**
B. *irregular verbs*	**venir** **decir** **poder**	**vin-** **dic-** **pud-**	**-iendo**
C. *the verb* **ir**	**ir**		**yendo**[4]
verbs with stem ending in a vowel	**traer** **caer** **creer** **oir** **incluir**	**tra-** **ca-** **cre-** **o-** **inclu-**	**-yendo**[4]

Nearly all verbs that are irregular elsewhere are regular in the **-ndo** form; e.g., **hacer, haciendo,** and **ser, siendo.** The three irregulars listed above are among the few exceptions.[4]

[4] See footnote 2 p. 95 for the **y** of **trayendo.** The **y** in the forms that have it is merely a variant spelling for some speakers, while for others it indicates a more fricative sound than the **i** in **-iendo.**

-ndo-	-le -las -nos etc.

With-verb pronouns follow the **-ndo** form.[5]

› ITEM SUBSTITUTION DRILL

1. *Pensando en* eso, no podemos seguir. (pasando a, hablando de)
2. *Hablando de autos,* pensamos hacer un viaje. (mencionando baterías, pasando a frenos, hablando de llantas)
3. *Volviendo a casa,* tuve una magnífica idea. (yendo a la escuela, jugando en el jardín, oyendo esos discos)
4. *Viviendo en Cuba,* se aprende mucho. (haciendo un viaje a Chile, apostando, arreglando este trabajo, practicando)
5. *Trayéndolas* nosotros, no pagamos tanto. (escribiéndola, haciéndolos, pagándole, hablándoles)

› DISCUSSION

The **-ndo** form of the verb points to a HAPPENING that is actually TAKING PLACE at the time referred to. If either of these conditions is not met, we do not normally have an **-ndo:**

1. No happening: In *a house* ***standing*** *on the corner, a box* ***containing*** *paper, the figure* ***leaning*** *against the wall* we have verbs that, at least as used in these phrases, denote a steady state, not a happening or a potentially fluctuating condition. They do not normally take **-ndo** in Spanish.

2. A happening, but not tied to a time and a place: In ***Working*** *is good for the health, He's fond of* ***playing*** *golf, People* ***living*** *in the tropics are more exposed to disease* we have hypothetical or nonspecific actions. The first two examples we recognize as verbal nouns—these are infinitives in Spanish. The third is a restrictive modifier; here Spanish uses the equivalent of *People* ***who live.*** Neither admits an **-ndo.**

This leaves us with two kinds of English *-ings* that equate with Spanish **-ndo.** The first is adverbial and covers all the examples in Section 43. It shows something going on, usually at the same time as the action of the main verb. Just as in English, the two actions are loosely associated with a *when, because of, if,* etc., frequently implied in their relationship. The second is the *-ing* of the progressive, given in the next section.

44 Present progressive: temporary action

EXAMPLES

A.
1. **Estoy cambiando** las llantas del auto.
2. ¿Qué **estás haciendo** con esas herramientas?
3. **Estamos aprendiendo** español. *We are learning Spanish.*
4. **Están llegando.** *They are arriving.*

B.
1. **Sigue sucediendo.** *It keeps on happening.*
2. Para **seguir participando,** necesitamos otro equipo. *To keep on taking part, we need another team.*

[5] Also, in writing with-verb pronouns are attached to **-ndo** forms, as they are to infinitives and affirmative command forms. See Section 19.

A. FORM OF **estar**		**–ndo** FORM OF VERB
estoy **estás** **está** **estamos** **están**	+	**hablando** **comiendo** **viviendo** **diciendo** **trayendo**

The present progressive portrays what is going on just for the time being.

B. FORM OF **seguir**		**–ndo** FORM OF VERB
sigo **sigues** **sigue** **seguimos** **siguen**	+	**hablando** **comiendo** **viviendo** **diciendo** **trayendo**

Seguir is typical of several verbs of motion which combine with the **–ndo** form to make a kind of progressive that is colored with the meaning of the verb of motion.

PERSON-NUMBER SUBSTITUTION DRILL

1. Estoy cambiando las llantas del auto.
   (Bernardo, tú, ellos, usted, nosotros, él, Pablo y yo)
2. Por eso *Julio* está trabajando.
   (yo, Elena, tú, las chicas, nosotros, Alfredo, ellas)
3. Están comiendo en la cocina.
   (nosotros, María, las criadas, Patricio, tú, ellos, yo)
4. *¿Ellas?* Están sacudiendo los muebles.
   (Josefina, nosotros, ella, yo, tú, las criadas, Rosa)

CONSTRUCTION SUBSTITUTION DRILL

INSTRUCTIONS: Repeat the following sentences just as you hear them. Then repeat them again, making the verbs progressive.

1. TEACHER: *Hablo* con un hombre respetable. *Repita.*
   STUDENT: **Hablo con un hombre respetable.**
   TEACHER: *Cambie.*
   STUDENT: **Estoy hablando con un hombre respetable.**
2. *Haces* una cosa ridícula.
3. *Pensamos* en algo diferente.
4. *Estudiamos* español.
5. *Escribo* mucho en la clase.
6. *Hablo* con la casa del Dr. Arjona.
7. *Trae* el auto a la escuela.
8. *Organizan* un grupo para ir.
9. Bernardo *hace* un trabajo muy sencillo.
10. Tú *exageras* mucho.

PATTERNED RESPONSE DRILL

A. 1. TEACHER: ¿Qué está haciendo Bernardo?
   STUDENT: **Está cambiando las llantas del auto.**
2. ¿Qué están haciendo ellos?
3. ¿Qué estás haciendo tú?
4. ¿Qué están haciendo ustedes?
5. ¿Qué está haciendo usted?
6. ¿Qué estoy haciendo yo?
7. ¿Qué estamos haciendo nosotros?

B. 1. ¿Qué está vendiendo Olga?
   Está vendiendo unos discos nuevos.
2. ¿Qué está vendiendo Pepe?
3. ¿Qué están vendiendo los chicos?
4. ¿Qué está vendiendo usted?
5. ¿Qué están vendiendo ustedes?
6. ¿Qué estás vendiendo tú?
7. ¿Qué estoy vendiendo yo?
8. ¿Qué estamos vendiendo nosotros?

C. 1. TEACHER: ¿Está usted trabajando o estudiando?
STUDENT: **Estoy estudiando.**
TEACHER: ¿Sigue estudiando? (trabajando)
2. ¿Están ellos trabajando o estudiando? ¿Siguen estudiando? (trabajando)
3. ¿Estás tú jugando o trabajando? ¿Sigues trabajando? (jugando)
4. ¿Está él jugando o trabajando? ¿Sigue trabajando? (jugando)
5. ¿Están ustedes barriendo o comiendo? ¿Siguen comiendo? (barriendo)
6. ¿Están ellas barriendo o comiendo? ¿Siguen comiendo? (barriendo)
7. ¿Está el abogado escribiendo o discutiendo? ¿Sigue discutiendo? (escribiendo)
8. ¿Está el jefe escribiendo o discutiendo? ¿Sigue discutiendo? (escribiendo)

› DISCUSSION

English uses its "simple present" tense for happenings that are viewed as more or less fixed or habitual as, for example, *He lives in New York, He smokes a pipe.* If the happening is viewed as temporary, going on just for the time being, or unexpected (hence liable to change), English requires the present progressive as, for example, *He is living in New York, He is smoking a pipe.*

The Spanish progressive is even more restricted to temporariness. It is avoided in instances like *He is wearing a blue tie*—to use it there would sound like saying in English *He is having on a blue tie* rather than *He has on a blue tie.* In writing a letter one would say for *I'm asking you for more time* **Le pido más tiempo** (the written words are permanent). To say *He is teaching Spanish* in the sense *He is a Spanish teacher,* **Enseña español** would be the normal thing, but **Está enseñando español** could be used to suggest a temporary job, surprise at his holding the job, or something of the kind. Of course, if he is in the act of teaching Spanish right at the moment, **Está enseñando español** is normal.

The progressive shares with previously studied uses of **estar** (Unit 3, Section 15) the notion of comparison, change, instability.

There is no parallel in Spanish to the English use of the present progressive to express a PLANNED FUTURE action, as in *They are coming to dinner tonight.* (See Unit 4, Section 18).

45 Position of the with-verb pronouns in verb constructions

EXAMPLES

A. 1. **Fuimos a verla.**
2. **La fuimos a ver.** — *We went to see her.*
3. **Vamos (Van) a hablarle.**
4. **Le vamos (van) a hablar.** — *We (They) are going to speak to him.*
5. **Puede cortarme** un poco.
6. **Me puede cortar** un poco. — (*You can cut a little for me.*)
7. **¿Piensa celebrarlo?**
8. **¿Lo piensa celebrar?** — (*Do you expect to celebrate it?*)
9. **Acaba de hacerlo.**
10. **Lo acaba de hacer.** — *He has just done it.*
11. **Tengo que decirlo.**
12. **Lo tengo que decir.** — *I have to say it.*

B. 1. **Están haciéndolas.** 2. **Las están haciendo.** } *They're making them.*
3. Ya se **está organizando** un grupo para ir.

C. 1. **Vamos a hablarle.** *Let's speak to him.*
2. **Hay que traerlos.** *It is necessary to bring them.*

MOST COMMON VERBS THAT ARE COUPLED WITH INFINITIVE OR **-ndo**				
PRONOUN	CONJUGATED FORM OF VERB	RELATOR IF ANY	INFINITIVE OR **-ndo**	PRONOUN
A.	**Fuimos**	**a**	**ver-**	**-la.**
La	**fuimos**	**a**	**ver.**	
	Piensa		**celebrar-**	**-lo.**
Lo	**piensa**		**celebrar.**	
	Acaba	**de**	**hacer-**	**-lo.**
Lo	**acaba**	**de**	**hacer.**	
B.	**Están**		**haciéndo-**	**-las.**
Las	**están**		**haciendo.**	

In most constructions with infinitive and **-ndo** (progressive) the pronoun may go with either verb.

Vamos a (let's) AND **hay que**			
CONJUGATED FORM OF VERB	RELATOR	INFINITIVE	PRONOUN
C. Vamos	**a**	**hablar-**	**-le.**
Hay	**que**	**traer-**	**-los.**

With **hay que,** and with **vamos a** when it means *let's,* the pronoun goes with the infinitive.

› CONSTRUCTION SUBSTITUTION DRILL

INSTRUCTIONS: Repeat the following sentences just as you hear them. Then repeat them again, changing the position of the with-verb pronoun as indicated by the models.

A. 1. TEACHER: Le vamos a hablar. *Repita.*
STUDENT: **Le vamos a hablar.**
TEACHER: *Cambie.*
STUDENT: **Vamos a hablarle.**
2. Las van a traer.
3. Esta tarde lo voy a esperar.
4. Lo vamos a perder entonces.
5. La van a quitar de aquí.
6. Lo vamos a estudiar después.
7. Me voy a peinar.

B. 1. ¿Me puede cortar un poco arriba?
¿Puede cortarme un poco arriba?
2. ¿Lo piensa celebrar este año?
3. ¿Lo acaban de mandar?
4. ¿Lo piensa discutir?
5. Los esperamos ver.
6. La quiero invitar.
7. Le acaba de escribir.
8. Lo sabe decir.

C. 1. Están organizándolo.
Lo están organizando.
2. Estoy cambiándolas.
3. Está sacudiéndolos.
4. Estamos escribiéndole.
5. Estás haciéndolo.
6. Está mirándola.

INSTRUCTIONS: Repeat the following sentences just as you hear them. Then repeat them again, substituting a verb construction for the verb, as indicated by the models.

D. 1. TEACHER: Le hablo todos los días. *Repita.*
STUDENT: **Le hablo todos los días.**
TEACHER: *Cambie.*
STUDENT: **Voy a hablarle todos los días.**
2. Las traen mañana.
3. Lo dejo en la escuela.
4. La quitan dentro de diez minutos.
5. Lo estudiamos más tarde.
6. Los tienen en casa.
7. Las venden ahora.

E. 1. Los organizan ahora.
Los están organizando ahora.
2. Me hace un favor.
3. Me cierran las puertas.
4. Nos traen dos tazas de café.
5. Lo perdemos entonces.
6. Los aprendo muy bien.

DISCUSSION

Constructions in which an infinitive or an **-ndo** form depends on a preceding verb allow some freedom in placing the object pronoun. In general it may go with either verb, according to the norms of placement explained in Unit 4, Section 19—**Lo puedo decir** or **Puedo decirlo** *I can say it;* **para poderlo decir** or **para poder decirlo** *in order to be able to say it;* **Lo estoy arreglando** or **Estoy arreglándolo** *I'm arranging it;* **Le sigues hablando** or **Sigues hablándole** *You keep on talking to him.* There are, however, a few constructions with the infinitive that permit only end-position of the pronoun. Among these are **hay que** (**Hay que mostrarlos** *It is necessary to show them*) and **vamos a** with the meaning *let's* (**Vamos a verla** *Let's go see her*). With other meanings of **ir a** either position is possible (**Vamos a verla** or **La vamos a ver,** both meaning either *We're going to see her* or *We go to see her*).

GUIDED CONVERSATION

A. *Alfredo* B. *Bernardo*

A. Hombre, ¿qué es ese trabajo tan sucio que estás haciendo?
B. Estoy ______________
A. ¿Pero no es muy complicado... y sucio?
B. ¡Qué va! ______________
A. Lástima que mi coche está malo.
B. El tuyo siempre tiene algo malo: ______________
A. No exageres. Es que tengo dos invitaciones para la inauguración.
B. ¿De la refinería de petróleo? Vi en *La Tribuna* que va a ir mucha gente importante: ______________
A. Pues ¿quieres ir conmigo... en tu coche?
B. Sí, hombre, ______________
B. Debe ser una planta magnífica.
B. Sí, pero es lástima que ______________
A. Pero hay que pensar en progresar alguna vez.

➤ VERB REVIEW DRILL

Contrast between **usted** commands and preterit through stress placement.

A. 1. TEACHER: *Hable* usted como yo *hablé.*
STUDENT: **Hable usted como yo hablé.**
TEACHER: Pagar.
STUDENT: **Pague usted como yo pagué.**[6]
2. *Enseñe* usted como yo *enseñé.*
(doblar, estudiar, ganar, llamar, regatear, trabajar, parar, entrar)

B. 1. TEACHER: No *hablo* como él *habló.*
STUDENT: **No hablo como él habló.**
TEACHER: Esperar.
STUDENT: **No espero como él esperó.**
2. No *tardo* como él *tardó.*
(enseñar, progresar, exagerar, trabajar, estudiar, regatear, esperar, apostar)

Present tense forms of **decir.**

C. 1. ¿Qué dicen ustedes?
Decimos que no.
2. ¿Qué dicen ellos?
3. ¿Qué dice Alicia?
4. ¿Qué dices tú?
5. ¿Qué dicen ellas?
6. ¿Qué dice él?

[6]The spelling **gu** before **e** and **i** represents the same sound as **g** before **a, o,** or **u.** (See Unit 4, footnote 3.)

San José, Costa Rica: Barber shop

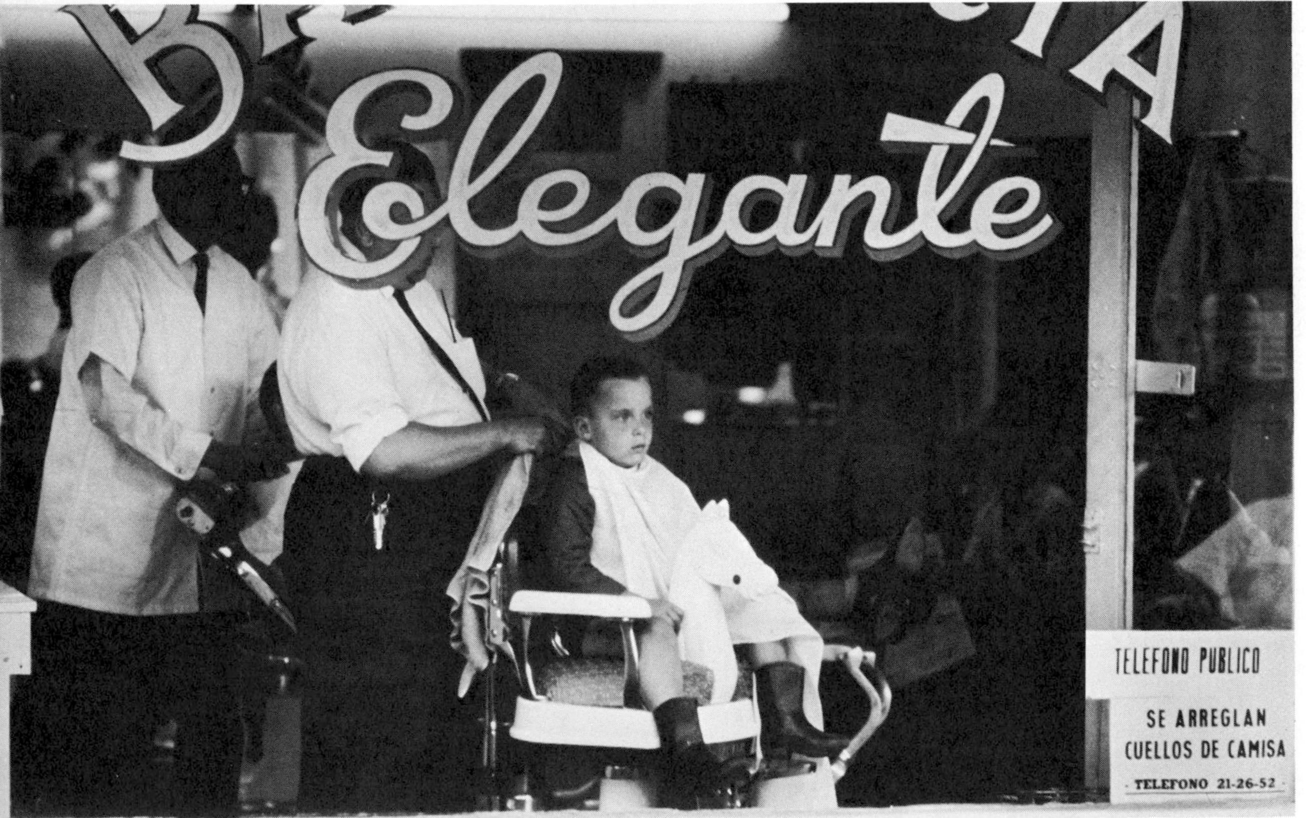

reading

Juanito en la barbería

B. *Barbero* J. *Juanito* S. *Señor Suárez, padre de Juanito*

B. Muy bien, Juanito, tú sigues. Siéntate aquí, por favor. ¿Lo quieres corto, como siempre?

J. Esta vez, señor Alonso, lo quiero largo a los lados y atrás, como los actores en el cine mexicano, ¿verdad?

B. (*al padre de Juanito*) ¿Está bien, señor Suárez, si se lo corto como quiere?

se = le *for him* (See Unit 12, Section 59)

S. (*que está muy ocupado mirando las fotos de una revista*) Sí, Pablo; hágalo como él quiere.

mirar *to look at* **revista** *magazine*

J. Pero en la coronilla, señor Alonso, lo quiero como el pelo de papá, con un círculo en medio.

coronilla *on top*

S. ¡Juanito, el señor Alonso sabe cortar el pelo! No digas tonterías.

B. Ya sé, señor Suárez; Juanito siempre...

J. ¡¡Ay!!

D. ¿Qué te pasa?

¿Qué...pasa? *What's the matter?*

J. ¡Que me tiró del pelo!

B. Lo siento, Juanito. Esta maquinilla no funciona muy bien; voy a usar las tijeras. ...Bueno, Juanito, ¿quién va a ganar los Juegos Olímpicos?

J. ...Señor Alonso.

B. ¿Eh?

J. ¿Por qué no tienen barba las mujeres?

barba *a beard*

B. Pues... hmm... No es fácil explicarte eso.

explicar *to explain*

J. Es que tienen más pelo en la cabeza, ¿verdad? Mi tío tiene una barba muy larga pero no tiene pelo en la cabeza. Su cabeza brilla como un melón.

brillar *to shine*

B. (*que también tiene cabeza que brilla como un melón*) Bueno, Juanito, esto de no tener pelo tiene sus ventajas; por ejemplo, no hay que peinarse...

ventajas *advantages*

J. Es verdad, señor Alonso, pero vea usted que hay una gran desventaja en no tener pelo en la cabeza.

vea usted *bear in mind*

B. ¿Y cuál es, Juanito?

J. ¡Es que cuando uno se lava la cara no sabe dónde parar!

UNIT 10

In a Café

A. *Alvaro* F. *Felipe* C. *Chalo*

A. This is a first-rate café [What a good café this is]!

F. You're right. For good coffee there's no place like this one. Hey! pst! pst! Two black coffees, good and hot.

A. Here [There] comes Carlos Francisco. What a glum look he has [bad face he brings]! What's new, Chalo? Sit down.

F. Why didn't you go to school yesterday? We had an exam in philosophy.

C. I meant to go, but I couldn't. I had a bad day. I was sick.

* * *

C. How was the exam?

A. Pretty good. I got almost everything.

F. I memorized all that stuff about Socrates, but they only asked questions about Plato. I don't even know when he died.

C. What a break [luck] I didn't go, then! Philosophy is too hard.

A. It's just like all the other subjects. It's a question of learning them by heart. What a bore!

C. I don't know what I'm going to do. We still have [There still remain to us] algebra, Spanish, physics, chemistry, and biology.

A. By the way, did you know there was a meeting of the Student Council yesterday? They came from all the schools.

F. And what did they say? Was anything done?

En un café

A. *Alvaro* F. *Felipe* C. *Chalo*

A. ¡Qué buen café es éste!

F. Tienes razón. Para café bueno no hay como este lugar. ¡Mire, pst, pst! (1) Dos cafés negros bien calientes.

A. Ahí viene Carlos Francisco. ¡Qué mala cara trae! ¿Qué hay, Chalo? (2) Siéntate.

F. ¿Por qué no fuiste al colegio ayer? Tuvimos examen en filosofía.

C. Quise ir, pero no pude. Tuve un mal día. Estuve enfermo.

* * *

C. ¿Cómo estuvo el examen?

A. Bastante bien. Supe casi todo.

F. Yo aprendí de memoria lo de Sócrates, pero sólo hicieron preguntas sobre Platón. No sé ni cuándo murió.

C. ¡Qué suerte que no fui, entonces! La filosofía es demasiado difícil.

A. Es igual que todas las demás materias. Es cuestión de aprenderlas de memoria. ¡Qué aburrido!

C. Yo no sé qué voy a hacer. Todavía nos quedan álgebra, castellano, (3) física, química y biología. (4)

A. A propósito, ¿supiste que ayer hubo una reunión del Consejo Estudiantil? Vinieron de todos los colegios. (5)

F. ¿Y qué dijeron? ¿Se hizo algo?

Guatemala City: Student coffee shop

A. They asked to have the number of courses per year reduced.
C. And what if the Ministry of Education doesn't accept?
F. Then there's no way out except a general strike.
C. Well, let's go; here's the check [bill].
A. Where'd I put my wallet? Did either of you bring any money?
C. I didn't even bring a dime.
F. Well, I'll pay, as usual.

A. Se pidió acortar el número de materias por año.
C. ¿Y si el Ministerio de Educación no acepta?
F. Entonces, no hay más remedio que hacer una huelga general. (6)
C. Bueno, vámonos; aquí está la cuenta.
A. ¿Dónde puse mi cartera? ¿Alguno de ustedes trajo plata?
C. Yo no traje ni un diez.
F. Bueno, yo pago, como de costumbre.

cultural notes

(1) It is quite common in Hispanic countries to attract someone's attention with a hissing noise (**pst, pst**). To call a waiter sometimes a clap of the hands is used.

(2) **Chalo** is a nickname for several names, especially for **Carlos,** and is sometimes equivalent to *Mac,* as in *Hey, Mac!*

(3) **Castellano** is widely used as a synonym of **español** in the sense of *Spanish language.*

(4) The curriculum of the Latin-American secondary school (variously called **colegio, liceo, escuela secundaria, instituto**) is basically academic and aims to prepare the student for the university. Learning is primarily verbal, and memorization of much factual material rather than manipulation is emphasized. Though sciences form part of the curriculum, laboratory and field work are not stressed. On the other hand, the emphasis upon the traditional humanities and the handling of ideas and abstractions enable the Latin-American

student at the secondary school level to discuss philosophical and literary matters with a skill that American students of the same age can rarely match.

(5) **Colegio** here refers to the secondary school with the rigidly prescribed academic curriculum mentioned in the preceding Note. Upon graduation from a **colegio** a student receives the **bachillerato** or bachelor's degree. In some countries the **bachillerato** is a university entrance examination. The **colegio** roughly corresponds to an American high school plus the first two years of college in the sense that both are primarily concerned with general education rather than specialized training.

(6) Latin-American students do not hesitate to air their grievances—political as well as academic—by striking.

› PRONUNCIATION EXERCISE

A. Identical vowel fusion. INSTRUCTIONS: Repeat the following phrases and sentences just as you hear them.

1.

Fusion of /e/'s

la clase de español
¿Qué es eso?
Paré el tráfico.
porque es la verdad
Tengo que estudiar.
compañera de escuela
Vive en México.
¿Qué edad tiene ella?
Se ensucia la pared.
Habla el cuñado de él.
Ya se está organizando.
¿Qué mejor oportunidad que ésta?
porque en los Estados Unidos
¿Qué estás haciendo?
Tú que eres hombre respetable.

2.

Fusion of /a/'s

Va a hablar.
Se lo doy a aquel hombre.
Llega a la puerta.
¿Qué va a hacer?
Está abierta.
la puerta abierta
Voy a arreglar esto.
Va a ir mucha gente.
esta vida agitada
Necesitaba a alguien.
La cuenta está algo baja.
Va a aceptar.
La última casa a la izquierda
Llama a la policía.
¿Quién va a hablar?

3.

Fusion of /e/'s and of /a/'s

el hombre que está aquí
¿Le escribe a alguien?
Decían que era a mediodía.

When two or more like vowels of different words come together in a breath group they contract so that only one vowel is pronounced. In the great majority of instances the vowels at the end and the beginning of words in the same breath group are /e/ and /a/. In an earlier period in the history of the Spanish language some contractions were shown in writing; e.g., **de este** was written **deste,** and **de él** was written **dél.** Today only the contraction of **de** and **el** (definite article) is represented in writing; the only other contraction shown in written Spanish, namely the fusion of **a** and **el** to **al,** involves unlike vowels (see Unit 7, Section 33.)

B. The written accent mark (**acento gráfico**).[1]

1. The syllable.

	A.	B.	C.	D.
EXAMPLES	id*ea*lista	v*iu*da	camb*ia*r	tonter*ía*s
	cr*ea*n	f*ui*	ac*ue*rdo	ingenier*ía*
	corr*eo*	c*iu*dad	camb*ie*mos	guaran*íe*s
	s*ea*n	c*ui*dado	pl*ei*to	R*aú*l
	Latin*oa*mérica		estud*io*s	p*aí*s

[1]For a general treatment of stress and the written accent mark see pp. 7–8.

a. Usually in Spanish there are as many syllables as there are vowels. In **política,** for example, there are four vowels—**o, í, i,** and **a**—and therefore four syllables—**po-, -lí-, -ti-,** and **-ca.**

b. When two vowels come together they are sometimes in the same syllable, sometimes in different syllables. (1) The vowels **a, e,** and **o** are called strong vowels. When they occur together they go in different syllables. The word **correo,** for example, divides **co-rre-o** (see Examples A above). (2) The vowels **i** and **u** are called weak vowels. When they occur together they go in the same syllable, and the second one is normally more prominent than the first (see Examples B).[2] (3) When a weak vowel stands next to a strong vowel they go either in the same syllable (Examples C) or in separate syllables (Examples D). In the latter case the weak vowel is written with the accent mark: **í, ú.** In Spanish two vowels occurring together in a single syllable make a diphthong.

2. The accent mark.

EXAMPLES	digas	medicina	ideal	joven
	jamás	política	difícil	jóvenes
	papa	contigo	acabar	
	papá	único	fácil	

a. There are two main classes of words: (1) Words ending in **-n, -s,** or a vowel. These are regularly stressed on the next to the last syllable and when so stressed are written without the accent mark: ***di*gas, *pa*pa, medi*ci*na, con*ti*go, *jo*ven.** But if any other syllable is stressed, that syllable carries the accent mark: **ja*más*, pa*pá*, po*lí*tica, *ú*nico, *jó*venes.** (2) Words ending in a consonant other than **-n** or **-s.** These are regularly stressed on the last syllable and when so stressed are written without the accent mark. But if any other syllable is stressed, that syllable carries the accent mark: **di*fí*cil, *fá*cil.**

b. To conform to these rules it often happens that one form of a word will carry the accent mark while another does not. Thus **joven** needs no accent mark because it ends in **-n** and is stressed on the next to the last syllable: ***jo*ven.** But the plural **jóvenes** does need the accent mark because it is stressed on the same syllable **jo-,** now no longer the next to the last syllable.

c. There are pairs of words that though otherwise pronounced the same differ in that one member of the pair is normally highlighted (stressed or accented, raised in pitch, etc.) while the other is not. The one normally highlighted is written with the accent mark whether actually highlighted in the given instance or not: **tú, tu; qué, que; él, el.**

d. The accent mark is written over vowels, never over consonants. In the case of a diphthong, if an accent mark is needed, it is written on the more prominent of the two vowels: on the strong vowel if one of the two vowels is strong **(cuáquero [cuá-que-ro], murciélago [mur-cié-la-go], láudano [láu-da-no], periódico [pe-rió-di-co]),** or on the second of the two vowels if both are weak **(cuídalo [cuí-da-lo], veintiún [vein-tiún]).** No accent mark is written on the **-ir** infinitive ending though it is always stressed and in a separate syllable: **oir (o-ir), reir (re-ir).**

› WRITING EXERCISE

INSTRUCTIONS: Write the following lists of words or phrases from dictation.

A. In this group the vowel of the stressed syllable of each word bears a written accent mark.

1.		2.		3.	
algún	lección	demás	francés	café	habló
ningún	sesión	detrás	inglés	está	comí
perdón	también	después	adiós	papá	comió
razón		interés		hablé	

[2] **Flúido** *fluid* is an exception.

4. cárcel útil
cónsul difícil
fácil portátil
fértil

5. fábrica música
fósforo química
médico sábado
lástima

B. In this group are paired forms. In the first group the written accent mark occurs in the plural but not in the singular; in the second group the written accent mark occurs in the singular but not in the plural.

1.		2.	
crimen	crímenes	razón	razones
germen	gérmenes	sesión	sesiones
joven	jóvenes	lección	lecciones
margen	márgenes	cortés	corteses
orden	órdenes	inglés	ingleses
virgen	vírgenes	portugués	portugueses

C. In this group a weak vowel forms a syllable separate from that of the strong vowel that precedes or follows it and therefore bears a written accent mark.

1.	2.
lío	maíz
rubíes	país
todavía	raíz
policía	caída
continúa	baúl
actúe	Raúl

D. In this group are pairs of words pronounced alike; the member of the pair that is highlighted bears a written accent mark. To make the stress evident the words are used in phrases.

1. ¿Qué es eso?
   El libro que me dio.
2. ¿Eres tú?
   Tengo tu libro.
3. Sí, señor.
   Si viene, lo veré.
4. A mí me gusta.
   Mi hermano está aquí.
5. ¿Cómo estás?
   Haga como yo.
6. ¿Cuándo llega Pepe?
   Lo veo cuando viene.
7. ¿Dónde está tu hermano?
   En la casa donde vive.
8. Es él.
   No tengo el libro.
9. Sólo Juan está aquí.
   Juan está aquí solo.

46 Irregular preterits

EXAMPLES

A. 1. **Estuve** enfermo.
2. **Tuve** un mal día.
3. ¿Dónde **puse** mi cartera?
4. **Supe** casi todo.
5. **Quise** ir pero no **pude.**
6. No **traje** ni un diez.

B. **¿Supiste** que ayer hubo una reunión?

C. 1. ¿Cómo **estuvo** el examen?
2. ¿Se **hizo** algo?
3. ¿Alguno de ustedes **trajo** plata?

D. **Tuvimos** examen en filosofía.

E. 1. **Anduvieron** hasta el parque. *They walked as far as the park.*
2. Sólo **hicieron** preguntas sobre Platón.
3. **Vinieron** de todos los colegios.
4. ¿Qué **dijeron?**
5. **Produjeron** más ese año. *They produced more that year.*

THE UNSTRESSED **-e, -o** PRETERITS		
estar **andar** **tener** **poder** **poner** **saber** **querer** **hacer** **venir**	**estuv-** **anduv-** **tuv-** **pud-** **pus-** **sup-** **quis-** **hic-**[3] **vin-**	**-e** **-iste** **-o** **-imos** **-ieron**
traer **decir** **producir**	**traj-** **dij-** **produj-**	**-e** **-iste** **-o** **-imos** **-eron**

Both stem and ending are irregular in these verbs. Note that the **-e** and **-o** endings are not stressed as in the regular verbs.

EXAMPLES 1. ¿Por qué no **fuiste** al colegio ayer? 2. **Fue** una tontería.

THE PRETERIT OF **ser** AND **ir**	
fui	**fuimos**
fuiste	
fue	**fueron**

These two verbs are identical in the preterit.

EXAMPLES 1. Ayer **hubo** una reunión. 2. No **hubo** Juegos Olímpicos en ese año. *There were no Olympic Games in that year.*

FORMS OF **haber** *there to be*	
present	**hay** there is (are)
preterit	**hubo** there was (were)

› **PERSON-NUMBER SUBSTITUTION DRILL**

1. *Yo* estuve equivocado.
   (usted, tú, ellos, mi profesor, nosotros, Susana, mis padres)
2. *Pablo* anduvo en el parque todo el día.
   (ellos, María Elena, tú, nosotros, yo, él, Pepe y yo)
3. Hoy tuvimos examen en álgebra.
   (yo, Betty y Susana, Julio y yo, tú, Carlos Francisco, ellos, usted)
4. ¿Dónde pusiste el libro de física?
   (yo, Josefina, ellos, mamá, nosotros, usted, ustedes)

[3]Spelled **hiz-** in the form **hizo.**

5. No pudieron aceptar la invitación.
   (el Ministerio de Educación, los profesores, yo, nosotros, usted, ustedes)
6. No supe lo de Sócrates.
   (nosotros, Alvaro, las chicas, tú, Felipe, ustedes, él)
7. *Nosotros* no quisimos acortar esa parte.
   (el Consejo Estudiantil, yo, ellos, tú, los técnicos, Patricio y yo, usted)
8. *Mi mamá* hizo la comida.
   (tú, ellos, yo, usted, nosotros, ella, mis padres)
9. *Los señores* vinieron a la inauguración.
   (yo, usted, los funcionarios de gobierno, nosotros, él, tú, ellos)
10. ¿Por qué no trajo una nueva batería?
    (ustedes, tú, ellos, nosotros, él, los chicos, Bernardo)
11. *Yo* no dije nada.
    (él, nosotros, ella, ustedes, el Consejo Estudiantil, ellos, tú)
12. Produjeron más arroz que frutas.
    (nosotros, tú, él, estos países, usted, yo, ellos)
13. *Don Alonso* fue un gran jefe.
    (tú, él, usted, Julio)
14. ¿Por qué no fuiste a la refinería ayer?
    (usted, ustedes, él, ellos, nosotros, los abogados, yo)
15. Quise ir pero no pude.
    (nosotros, ellos, usted, los alumnos, ella, tú, ellas)

› TENSE SUBSTITUTION DRILL

INSTRUCTIONS: Repeat the following sentences just as you hear them. Then repeat them again, substituting a preterit for the present-tense verb form, or vice versa.

A. 1. El carburador y la dirección *están* descompuestos.
   El carburador y la dirección estuvieron descompuestos.
2. Arreglar los frenos *es* demasiado complicado.
3. Ellos no *pueden* ir a la reunión.
4. Yo nunca *tengo* razón en esto.
5. ¿Qué *puede* importar lo de Platón?
6. No *hay* más remedio que hacer una huelga.
7. Esta tarde *tengo* exámenes en biología y castellano.
8. *Es* cuestión de aprenderlos de memoria.
9. Esas *son* ideas modernas.
10. Yo no *sé* nada de negocios.
11. ¿De dónde *trae* ese tocadiscos portátil?
12. ¿Quién *dice* "Si me hace el favor"?
13. No *quiero* ir a ver al médico.

B. 1. Mi hermano *estuvo* enfermo.
   Mi hermano está enfermo.
2. ¿Por qué no *fuiste* al colegio hoy?
3. Yo *tuve* un examen de biología.
4. No *supimos* nada de castellano.
5. No *hubo* nadie en la reunión.
6. Ellos no *pudieron* faltar a la clase de química.
7. Sólo *hicieron* preguntas sobre Sócrates.
8. *Anduvieron* hasta la esquina.
9. ¿Dónde *puse* mi cartera?
10. Yo no *quise* ir a física.
11. ¿Alguno de ustedes *trajo* plata?
12. ¿Quién *dijo* "Vámonos"?
13. Eso *fue* una cosa fácil.
14. ¿Quiénes *vinieron* a la planta?

› CHOICE-QUESTION RESPONSE DRILL

A. 1. ¿Fuiste a biología o no tuviste clase hoy?
2. ¿Pudiste pagar o no trajiste plata?
3. ¿Estuviste en el examen o no pudiste ir?
4. ¿Viniste a la escuela o anduviste en el parque?
5. ¿Hiciste la comida o no quisiste hacerla?
6. ¿Anduviste en el parque o fuiste a la casa?

B. 1. ¿Fue usted a ver al médico o no quiso?
2. ¿Hizo usted lo mismo o dijo que no?
3. ¿Trajo usted la cartera aquí o la puso arriba?
4. ¿Tuvo el examen o no fue a clase hoy?
5. ¿Estuvo usted enfermo o pudo ir al teatro?
6. ¿Vino usted ayer o hubo otra reunión?

› **DISCUSSION**

The unstressed **-e, -o** preterits all have the same endings except that those with preterit stem ending in **j** have **-eron** rather than **-ieron** in the third-person plural.

Numerous derivatives are identical except in the prefix. For example, all verbs ending in **-ducir** are like **producir: reducir** *to reduce* is **reduje, redujimos,** etc.; **detener** *to stop* is like **tener: detuve, detuvimos,** etc.

The verb **hubo** *there was, there were* is normally found only in the third person singular. (See Unit 8, Section 39).

47 Preterit and *-ndo* forms of *-ir* stem-changing verbs

EXAMPLES

A. 1. No sé ni cuándo **murió.**
2. **Pidió** dos cafés negros. *He asked for (ordered) two black coffees.*

B. 1. **Durmieron** siete horas anoche. *They slept seven hours last night.*
2. **Siguieron** hablando. *They kept on talking.*

C. Lo vi **durmiendo.** *I saw him sleeping.*

	dormir	**pedir**
preterit	**dormí** **dormiste** **durmió** **dormimos** **durmieron**	**pedí** **pediste** **pidió** **pedimos** **pidieron**
-ndo *form*	**durmiendo**	**pidiendo**

All the **-ir** verbs that have stem changes in the present tense (see Unit 4, Section 17) also have the **o → u** and **e → i** changes in the above three forms.

› **PERSON-NUMBER SUBSTITUTION DRILL**

1. *El* murió el año pasado.
(ellos, ella, mis abuelos, ellas, la profesora)
2. *Nosotros* no dormimos bien anoche.
(ella, tú, Francisco, yo, ellos, Chalo y yo, los otros)
3. *Yo* preferí un trabajo profesional.
(usted, nosotros, ellos, Julio y yo, Pablo, tú, ustedes)
4. No le pedimos una cosa difícil ni ridícula.
(ustedes, tú, Carlos, yo, Betty y Susana, nosotros, ella)
5. *Yo* seguí diez minutos después.
(ellos, Mercedes y yo, ella, tú, ustedes, nosotros, usted)
6. Conseguimos una criada magnífica.
(mamá, yo, ellos, Beatriz y yo, doña Mercedes, tú, usted)

› TENSE SUBSTITUTION DRILL

INSTRUCTIONS: Repeat the following sentences just as you hear them. Then repeat them again, changing each present-tense verb to preterit or vice versa.

A. 1. Se *muere* de hambre.
2. Ellos *duermen* ocho horas en total.
3. ¡Qué va! Ella *prefiere* una clase de filosofía.
4. ¿Por qué *piden* ustedes el único documento?
5. Usted *sigue* hasta llegar a la Avenida Norte.
6. Ellos no *consiguen* un empleo en la refinería.

B. 1. Se *murieron* de hambre.
2. Paquito *durmió* en el patio.
3. Los altos funcionarios de gobierno *prefirieron* no hacer nada.
4. Roberto *pidió* un trabajo más importante.
5. Ellos *siguieron* con esa costumbre anticuada.
6. Su padrino no *consiguió* el negocio.

› CONSTRUCTION SUBSTITUTION DRILL

INSTRUCTIONS: Repeat the following sentences just as you hear them. Then repeat them again, changing the present-tense verb forms to progressive.

A. 1. Aquí no se *muere* nadie.
2. Mi hermana menor *duerme* en la sala.
3. Una señorita muy amable me *pide* un favor ahora.
4. El *sigue* enfermo.
5. Alvaro *consigue* autos nuevos sin pagar.

B. 1. ¿Qué *dice* el profesor?
2. *Vienen* de Perú para participar en los juegos.
3. *Dicen* la verdad exacta.
4. *Viene* el amigo de Felipe.

48 Limiting adjectives

EXAMPLES

A. 1. Tengo **dos** invitaciones.
2. Aquí están los **mismos cuatro** señores. *Here are the same four men.*
3. Es igual que las **demás** materias.
4. Es el **nuevo** cónsul americano.

B. 1. Me hizo **otras tres** preguntas. *He asked me three other questions.*
2. Me hizo **otras muchas** (**muchas otras**) preguntas. *He asked me many other questions.*

C. Los **cien primeros** (**primeros cien**) días. *The first hundred days.*

D. 1. Tengo dos invitaciones **más.** *I have two more invitations.*
2. Cuesta un dólar **menos.** *It costs one dollar less.*

E. 1. Estuve aquí **todo el** día. *I was here all day (the whole day).*
2. **Todo el** examen fue así. *The whole exam was like that.*
3. Es igual que **todas las** demás materias.

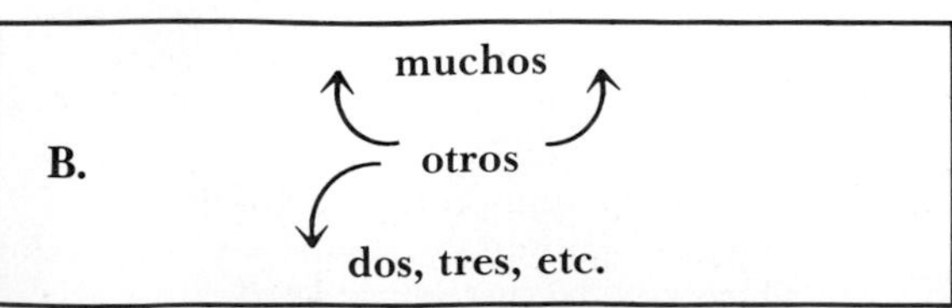

Otros may either precede or follow **muchos** but may only precede a cardinal numeral.

C.	primeros (segundos, etc.) ↘ dos, tres, etc. ↙

Ordinal numerals usually follow cardinal numerals but may precede them.

D.	**más, menos** ↘	
dos, tres, etc.	*noun*	

Más and **menos** must come after the combination of cardinal numeral plus noun.

E.	the whole / all the	**todo el, toda la** / **todos los, todas las**

Todo *all* precedes the article, as in English, and also precedes in the sense of *whole.*

ITEM SUBSTITUTION DRILL

A. 1. **Es tanta ropa.**
2. __ mucha ____
3. _____ dinero
4. __ poco ____
5. _____ plata
6. __ tanta ____
7. _____ fruta
8. Son ______
9. __ muchas ____
10. _____ recados
11. __ algunos ____
12. _____ llantas

B. 1. **Hay otros dos chicos en la clase.**
2. _____ tres ______
3. _____ chicas ____
4. __ otros ______
5. _____ alumnas ____
6. _____ cinco ______
7. __ otros ______
8. _____ muchas ______
9. __ muchas otras ____
10. __ primeros cuatro __
11. __ próximos ____
12. __ _____ cosas
13. __ cuatro próximas __
14. __ cinco ______

4. _____ seis ____
5. __ primeras ____
6. _____ tres ____
7. __ tres primeras ____
8. _____ papeles
9. __ cuatro ______

C. 1. **Hay muchos otros libros.**
2. __ algunos ____
3. ______ lista
4. __ algunas ____
5. ______ documentos
6. __ tantos ____
7. _____ nuevos __

D. 1. **Las dos últimas casas.**
2. __ últimas dos ____
3. __ mismas ____

E. 1. **Todas las demás noches estuvimos ahí.**
2. ______ días ______
3. _____ primeros ______
4. ______ tarde ______
5. _____ otras ______
6. ______ meses ______

TRANSLATION DRILL

A. 1. There are two more kilos.
2. There are five more pesos.
3. There are three more cats.
4. There's one more egg.
5. There's one dozen more.

La Paz, Bolivia: Instituto Americano

B. 1. He was here all day.
2. He was here all night.
3. He was here all month.
4. He was here all week.
5. He was here the whole day.
6. He was here the whole night.
7. He was here the whole month.
8. He was here the whole week.
9. He was here the whole hour.

› DISCUSSION

Adjectives that relate the noun to its environment (to its possessor, as with *my, his;* to its position relative to other things, as with *this, that, third, last;* to itself, as with *other, same,* etc.) and adjectives that quantify the noun (*more, many, some, eight,* etc.), normally come before the noun in Spanish, as in group A of the examples above. Their positions relative to each other are not always the same as in English.

Ordinal numerals

EXAMPLES A. 1. ¿Barro **primero** aquí abajo?
2. Vamos a hablar con ellas **primero.**[4]
3. Es la **primera** clase del día. *It's the first class of the day.*
4. Fue el **primer** ruido que oí. *It was the first noise I heard.*
5. Los veinte **primeros** días fueron buenos. *The first twenty days were good.*
6. Fue el **primer** buen día que tuvimos. *It was the first good day we had.*

[4]As an adverb **primero** is invariable.

B. 1. El **segundo** juego fue casi tan malo. *The second game was almost as bad.*
2. Mi **segunda** dirección está en la lista. *My second address is on the list.*

C. 1. ¿Cuál examen? ¿El **tercero?** *Which exam? The third (one)?*
2. La **tercera** cuenta se perdió. *The third bill got lost.*
3. El **tercer** recado fue de Pablo. *The third note was from Pablo.*
4. Fue el **tercero** o cuarto cónsul que fue allá. *He was the third or fourth consul who went there.*

D. El **tercer** Felipe; Felipe **Tercero.** *The third Philip; Philip the Third.*

E. 1. El cuarto **doce.** *Room Twelve, the twelfth room.*
2. La casa **veintiuna.** *The twenty-first house.*

THE ORDINALS, *first* TO *tenth*				
	MASCULINE BEFORE NOUN	MASCULINE ELSEWHERE	FEMININE	
first	**primer**	**primero**	**primera**	
second	**segundo**		**segunda**	
third	**tercer**	**tercero**	**tercera**	
fourth	**cuarto**		**cuarta**	*plurals regularly formed with* **-os, -as**
fifth	**quinto**		**quinta**	
sixth	**sexto**		**sexta**	
seventh	**séptimo**		**séptima**	
eighth	**octavo**		**octava**	
ninth	**noveno**		**novena**	
tenth	**décimo**		**décima**	

These are uniformly **-o** for masculine and **-a** for feminine, except for the two shortened forms **primer** and **tercer** used before masculine singular nouns when nothing more than another adjective intervenes.

› ITEM SUBSTITUTION DRILL

1. Mi número está en la *primera* lista. (segunda, tercera, cuarta, quinta, sexta, séptima, octava, novena, décima)
2. El *primer* auto es de Julio. (segundo, tercero, cuarto, quinto, sexto, séptimo, octavo, noveno, décimo)
3. Estoy en la primera *clase.* (juego, clases, juegos)
4. Yo vi la segunda *pregunta.* (toro, preguntas, toros)
5. Jugamos la tercera *noche.* (día, hora, lunes)
6. Supongo que el cuarto *exámen* es fácil. (materia, tema, carrera)
7. Es el quinto *cónsul* que viene hoy. (muchacha, señor, señora)
8. Es la sexta *puerta* a la derecha. (cuarto, casa, número)
9. Es la séptima *semana.* (mes, hora, día)
10. ¿Dónde está el octavo *libro?* (lista, juguete, calle)
11. ¿Cuál es la novena *cosa?* (color, cuadra, estado)
12. Vaya usted a la décima *cuadra.* (cuarto, calle, jardín)

› TRANSLATION DRILL

1. Which is the first?
2. Where is the second?
3. Who has the third?
4. First, dust down there.
5. Second, sweep up here.

› DISCUSSION

The ordinal numerals from *first* to *tenth* are among the adjectives that normally precede rather than follow the noun. They follow in titles (**Felipe Tercero** *Philip the Third,* **Calle Segunda** *Second Street,* **Libro Primero** *Book First*) and in a few set phrases like **prima segunda** *second cousin.*

Most speakers of Spanish are agreed on the ordinal numerals from first to tenth. From *eleventh* on, however, there is considerable variation with different speakers and in different contexts.[5] A safe compromise is to use the cardinal numerals and put them after the noun, for example, **el cuarto trece** *Room Thirteen,* substituting for *the thirteenth room.* Numerals that can differentiate the feminine normally do so with feminine nouns; thus *the thirty-first list* and *the two-hundredth list* are respectively **la lista treinta y una** and **la lista doscientas.**

Days, months, years

EXAMPLES

A. 1. ¿Qué día es hoy, **jueves** o **viernes?**
2. Vuelve el **miércoles.**
3. El **lunes** tal vez, o el **martes.**

B. 1. Antes del 4 de **octubre.** *Before the fourth of October.*
2. Fue el **23** (**veintitrés**) **de agosto de 1771** (**mil setecientos setenta y uno**). *It was the 23rd (twenty-third) of August, 1771.*

C. 1. **¿A cuánto** (**del mes**) **estamos?** *What day (of the month) is it?*
2. **Estamos a primero** (**dos, tres,** etc.). *It's the first (second, third, etc.).*

Sunday	**domingo**
Monday	**lunes**
Tuesday	**martes**
Wednesday	**miércoles**
Thursday	**jueves**
Friday	**viernes**
Saturday	**sábado**

January	**enero**
February	**febrero**
March	**marzo**
April	**abril**
May	**mayo**
June	**junio**
July	**julio**
August	**agosto**
September	**setiembre**
October	**octubre**
November	**noviembre**
December	**diciembre**

› TRANSLATION DRILL

A. 1. The first Sunday in (of) May.
2. The second Thursday in August.
3. The third Saturday in January.
4. The fourth Tuesday in March.

[5] *Eleventh,* for example, may be **undécimo, décimo primero, onceavo,** or simply **once.**

B. 1. Friday, July 4, 1776.
2. Monday, October 12, 1492.
3. Wednesday, August 15, 1588.
4. Thursday, November 11, 1918.
5. Sunday, February 22, 1732.

C. 1. December 25, 1977.
2. April 29, 1968.
3. June 10, 1951.
4. September 18, 1938.
5. March 11, 1923.
6. April 1, 1899.

› DISCUSSION

The days of the month are designated by cardinal numerals (**diez, doce, veintiuno,** etc.), except for the first (**primero**).

The standard formula for asking the day of the month, as shown in group C of the examples above, is **¿A cuánto** (**del mes**) **estamos?** literally, *At how much (of the month) are we?* The reply is **Estamos a siete** (**veintiséis,** etc.).

Normally the preposition **de** appears twice in a complete date: **el 23 de agosto de 1771** *August 23, 1771.* Thousands are not represented as multiples of hundreds: *eighteen twenty-six* is **mil ochocientos veintiséis.**

51 Plural of nouns with singular ending in [s]

EXAMPLES 1. Nos queda un **tocadiscos.** *We have one record player left.*
2. Practican los **jueves** y juegan los **viernes.** *They practice (on) Thursdays and play (on) Fridays.*

SINGULAR				PLURAL			
one	birthday record player Thursday Monday	un	**cumpleaños** **tocadiscos** **jueves** **lunes**	two	birthdays record players Thursdays Mondays	dos	**cumpleaños** **tocadiscos** **jueves** **lunes**
one	Saturday Sunday	un	**sábado** **domingo**	two	Saturdays Sundays	dos	**sábados** **domingos**
one	Englishman country month	un	**inglés** **país** **mes**	two	Englishmen countries months	dos	**ingleses** **países** **meses**

Almost all nouns whose last syllable is an unstressed syllable ending in [s] in the singular have the same form for the plural.

› TRANSLATION DRILL

1. I celebrate my birthday here.
I celebrate my birthdays here.
2. I haven't got my record player here.
I haven't got my record players here.
3. We need one more Friday.
We need two more Fridays.
4. We have one Monday left.
We have two Mondays left.
5. There's one more Tuesday this month.
There are two more Tuesdays this month.

52 Shortened forms of adjectives

EXAMPLES

A. 1. ¡Qué **buen** café es éste!
2. Para café **bueno,** no hay como este lugar.
3. **Buena** idea.

B. 1. Tuve un **mal** día.
2. El tuyo siempre tiene algo **malo.**
3. ¡Qué **mala** cara trae!

C. 1. Fue un **gran** jefe. *He was a great boss.*
2. Ayer hubo una reunión **grande.** *Yesterday there was a big meeting.*

D. 1. ¿Desea dejar **algún** recado? (*Do you wish to leave some message?*)
2. ¿Quieres traerme **algún** buen libro? *Will you bring me some good book?*
3. **¿Alguno** de ustedes trajo plata?
4. Hay que pensar en progresar **alguna** vez.

E. 1. **Ningún** extranjero puede. *No foreigner is able to.*
2. No tuvieron **ninguna** reunión. *They didn't have any meeting.*

BEFORE SINGULAR NOUN			ELSEWHERE
MASCULINE		FEMININE	
buen		**buena**	**bueno, -a, -os, -as**
mal		**mala**	**malo, -a, -os, -as**
	gran		**grande, -s**
algún		**alguna**	**alguno, -a, -os, -as**
ningún		**ninguna**	**ninguno, -a, -os, -as**
un		**una**	**uno, -a, -os, -as**
primer		**primera**	**primero, -a, -os, -as**
tercer		**tercera**	**tercero, -a, -os, -as**

Except for **grande** the shortening takes place only in the masculine singular when the adjective precedes the noun and nothing more than another adjective intervenes.

EXAMPLES

1. Venga **cualquier** día. *Come any day.*
2. ¿Cuál desea usted?—**Cualquiera** (de los dos). *Which one do you wish?—Either one (of the two).*
3. ¿Cuál desea usted?—**Cualquiera** (de los tres). *Which one do you wish?—Any one (of the three).*

any man any woman	**cualquier hombre** **cualquier mujer**	either one any one }	**cualquiera**

The shortened form **cualquier** is used before a singular noun, either masculine or feminine. **Cualquiera** is used independently of the noun.

ITEM SUBSTITUTION DRILL

1. Aquí no hay ninguna *profesora.*
   (profesor, tijeras, frijoles)
2. ¿Desea dejar algún *recado?*
   (cosa, libros, herramientas)
3. ¡Qué buena *carne!*
   (café, frijoles, comidas)
4. Tuve una mala *idea.*
   (día, preguntas, exámenes)
5. Aquí hay un *médico.*
   (planta, funcionarios, refinerías)
6. No puedo venir la primera *semana.*
   (día, tarde, mes)
7. ¿Dónde está el tercer *libro?*
   (noticia, documento, cuenta)
8. Es un gran *médico.*
   (señora, jefes, profesores)
9. Deme cualquier *libro* de éstos.
   (cartera, lápiz, pluma)
10. La *batería* está mala.
    (carburador, llantas, frenos)
11. Este *café* es muy bueno.
    (carne, huevos, frutas)
12. La *muchacha* ya está muy grande.
    (muchacho, muchachas, muchachos)
13. Primero vienen *Susana y Betty.*
    (Julio, Cecilia, Pablo y Roberto)
14. ¿Cualquier *colegio* le gusta? ¿Cualquiera?
    (materia, lugar, tema, negocio)

DISCUSSION

Only a limited number of adjectives, the majority of which are listed above, undergo shortening. Shortening characteristically occurs in the masculine singular when the adjective stands directly before the noun it modifies (or with nothing more than some additional adjective between it and its noun). A very few adjectives are shortened under other circumstances. Among these are certain of the numerals studied in Unit 6: **cien** is the regular form for *one hundred,* shortened from **ciento,** the latter being used only when some smaller numeral follows, as in **ciento dos,** and in the plural multiples **doscientos,** etc.; **veintiún** (**treinta y un,** etc.) is shortened from **veintiuno** (**treinta y uno,** etc.), and is used under conditions like those of the other shortened adjectives except that it is, of course, always plural in meaning (there is no such form as **veintiunos**).

Cualquier(a) means *any* (*one*) (*either* if there are just two choices) in the sense *any whatsoever.* It does not change for gender. Its plural, **cualesquier(a)**, is no longer generally used in conversation.

GUIDED CONVERSATION

V. *Vicente* E. *Eduardo*

V. Hay buen café aquí, ¿verdad?
E. Tienes razón. ______________
V. ¿Y por qué no fuiste al colegio ayer?
E. Quise ir ______________
V. Tuvimos examen en filosofía.
E. ¡Qué suerte ______________
V. Pero no fue tan difícil el examen. Sin embargo yo tuve que aprender muchas cosas de memoria.
E. Es igual ______________
V. Tienes razón. Debe haber una reforma de este sistema tan anticuado.
E. En mi opinión, no hay más remedio que ______________
V. Cálmate chico, no es tan grave la cosa.
E. Recuerda que todavía nos quedan ______________
V. Pero esta tarde hay una conferencia entre[6] el presidente del Consejo Estudiantil y el director del colegio. Vamos a ver qué pueden hacer ellos.

[6] *between*

› QUESTION REVIEW DRILL

Usage of **ser** and **estar.**

INSTRUCTIONS: The teacher will read several two-part questions. The student will make a single sentence from each of them, choosing the correct or more probable form to express *to be.*

TEACHER	STUDENT
1. ¿El examen? ¿Importante?	Sí, el examen es importante.
2. ¿Pablo? ¿Triste?	Sí, Pablo está triste.
3. ¿Las plantas? ¿Modernas?	Sí, las plantas son modernas.
4. ¿Ellos? ¿Atletas?	Sí, ellos son atletas.
5. ¿Roberto? ¿Furioso?	Sí, Roberto está furioso.
6. ¿La cartera? ¿Negra?	Sí, la cartera es negra.
7. ¿Las materias? ¿Difíciles?	Sí, las materias son difíciles.
8. ¿Alvaro y Felipe? ¿En el equipo?	Sí, Alvaro y Felipe están en el equipo.
9. ¿La ropa? ¿Sucia?	Sí, la ropa está sucia.
10. ¿Las herramientas? ¿En el comedor?	Sí, las herramientas están en el comedor.
11. ¿El Ministerio? ¿Lejos?	Sí, el Ministerio está lejos.
12. ¿El pelo de Ana? ¿Muy corto?	Sí, el pelo de Ana está muy corto.
13. ¿El cuatro de octubre? ¿Día feriado?	Sí, el cuatro de octubre es día feriado.
14. ¿Las criadas? ¿Morenas?	Sí, las criadas son morenas.
15. ¿Bernardo? ¿Un hombre respetable?	Sí, Bernardo es un hombre respetable.
16. ¿Don Rafael? ¿El padrino?	Sí, don Rafael es el padrino.
17. ¿El trabajo? ¿Sencillo?	Sí, el trabajo es sencillo.
18. ¿Las invitaciones? ¿Equivocadas?	Sí, las invitaciones están equivocadas.
19. ¿Los abogados? ¿Hombres de negocios?	Sí, los abogados son hombres de negocios.
20. ¿El café de México? ¿Bueno?	Sí, el café de México es bueno.
21. ¿El café? ¿Caliente?	Sí, el café está caliente.
22. ¿La cuenta? ¿Aquí?	Sí, la cuenta está aquí.
23. ¿La casita? ¿Verde?	Sí, la casita es verde.
24. ¿Fernando? ¿Abogado?	Sí, Fernando es abogado.

› TRANSLATION REVIEW DRILL

Contrasts of **ser** and **estar.**

A. 1. He's serious, but he's wrong (mistaken) now.
2. He's strong, but he's sick now.
3. He's simple, but he's furious now.
4. He's kind, but he's sad now.

B. 1. It's magnificent, but it's not here.
2. It's pretty, but it's out of order (bad).
3. It's antiquated, but it's not there.

C. 1. It's not portable, but it's okay.
2. It's not modern, but it's dirty.
3. It's not important, but it's here.

reading

Lección de aritmética[7]

J. *Juanito* PAQ. *Paquito* P. *Papá de Paquito*

J. ¡Hola, Paquito! ¿Qué estás haciendo?
PAQ. Papá me está enseñando las lecciones de aritmética.

[7] The first **t** in **aritmética** is pronounced [d].

Mexico City:
Father and son in park

P. ¿Qué tal, Juanito? ...Sí, hay que estudiar para progresar en la escuela... Vamos a ver, Paquito, si tienes un peso, y te doy tres pesos más, ¿cuántos pesos vas a tener en total?

PAQ. Tres, papá.

P. ¿Tres no más?

PAQ. Sí.

P. Mira, Paquito: ya tienes un peso que te di...

PAQ. ¡No, papá! No me diste nada.

P. ¡Suponlo, suponlo! ...Ahora, ¿cuántos pesos tienes?

PAQ. Cuatro.

P. ¿Cuatro qué?

PAQ. Cuatro no más.

P. Mira, hijo: pesos y pesos son pesos; huevos y huevos son huevos; gatos y gatos son gatos. Para ser exacto, hay que dar la unidad... es decir, hay que mencionar la cosa de que se trata. ¿Entiendes?

de...trata *in question*

PAQ. Sí, papá.

P. Bueno: otra vez... Si tengo dos coches y compro tres coches más, ¿cuántos tengo?

PAQ. (*contando con los dedos*) Cinco.

dedos *fingers*

P. ¡¿Cinco qué, por Dios?!

PAQ. ¡Ah, cinco autos!

P. Cinco coches, sí... y si tomo dos cafés negros y más tarde cuatro cafés negros, ¿cuántos cafés negros tomo en total?

PAQ. Seis... cafés negros... Pero la última vez que tomaste tanto café, no dormiste en toda la noche, y mamá dijo que...

P. (*con prisa*) A Juanito no le puede interesar lo que dijo mamá... Bueno, vamos a tomar un helado.

con prisa *hastily*
helado *ice cream*

J. No traigo dinero, don Rafael.

P. Yo pago, Juanito... como de costumbre.

UNIT 11

The Country and the City

M. *Mario* L. *Luis, friend of Mario*

M. I heard you were going to work in the country. How awful! I can't even stand looking at a picture of it [to me not even in painting].

L. Why? I'm crazy about [appeals to me very much] the country: pure air, mountains, clouds, blue sky, trees, simple people . . .

M. What ranch are you going to?

L. To the Hacienda El Alamo, Don Pepe's ranch, [at] about forty kilometers from here.

M. And what do they grow there?

L. Wheat, lentils, corn, potatoes, onions, and things like that.

M. I heard [They told me that] Don Pepe had a lot of livestock on that ranch.

L. Yes, he still does [has]. And a lot of the cows and bulls are imported.

M. I imagine they must have sheep and hogs, too.

L. Yes, mainly for wool, hides, and meat.

* * *

M. And when did you accept that job? As manager, right?

L. Yes. Just the night before last we met at the Union Club. While we were eating, Don Pepe told me he needed someone.

El campo y la ciudad

M. *Mario* L. *Luis, amigo de Mario*

M. Supe que usted se iba a trabajar al campo. ¡Qué horror! A mí ni en pintura.

L. ¿Por qué? A mí me gusta muchísimo el campo: aire puro, montañas, nubes, cielo azul, árboles, gente sencilla...

M. ¿A qué finca va?

L. A la Hacienda El Alamo, la finca de don Pepe, como a cuarenta kilómetros de aquí.

M. ¿Y qué producen allí?

L. Trigo, lentejas, maíz, papas, cebollas y cosas por el estilo.

M. Me dijeron que don Pepe tenía mucho ganado en esa finca.

L. Sí, todavía tiene. Y muchas de las vacas y de los toros son importados. (1)

M. Me imagino que deben tener ovejas y cerdos también.

L. Sí, principalmente para lana, cueros y carne.

* * *

M. ¿Y cuándo aceptó ese trabajo? De administrador, (2) ¿verdad?

L. Sí. Sólo anteanoche nos encontramos en el Club de la Unión. Mientras comíamos, don Pepe me contó que necesitaba a alguien.

Argentina: The pampa

M. And then he offered you the job, I suppose.
L. That's how it was. I was all excited [got enthusiastic] and promised to give him an answer the next day.
M. And what did your wife say to all this?
L. She said it was fine, if it was necessary, but that she and the children had to stay in the city this winter on account of school.
M. What's it like? Good salary?
L. It sure is! *And* what's more, he promised to give me part of the profits.
M. Well, I congratulate you! Apparently farmers don't do so bad, eh?
L. A little [Somewhat] better than a bank clerk, my friend, a little better . . .

M. Y entonces le ofreció el puesto, me imagino.
L. Así fue. Yo me entusiasmé y le prometí contestarle al otro día.
M. Y su señora, ¿qué dijo a todo esto?
L. Dijo que estaba bien, si era necesario, pero que ella y los niños tenían que quedarse en la ciudad este invierno por el colegio.
M. ¿Y qué tal? ¿Buen sueldo?
L. Ya lo creo. Además prometió darme parte de la ganancia.
M. Hombre, lo felicito. Por lo visto, los agricultores (3) no la pasan mal, (4) ¿eh?
L. Algo mejor que un empleado de banco, mi amigo, algo mejor...

cultural notes

(1) A livestock breeder may import purebred stock as much for prestige as for building up his herd.

(2) Only a man of fairly high social position is eligible for the post of tenant administrator of a large ranch.

(3) *Farmer* in the sense of peasant or one who cultivates ground as a tenant is **campesino** in Spanish; a landed farmer, one who owns or manages a farm, is **agricultor.**

(4) The feminine object pronoun **la** is used in a number of idiomatic expressions without reference to a specific antecedent. Sometimes it is equivalent to an indefinite *it* in English (e.g., *We've made a fine mess of it!* **¡Buena la hemos hecho!**), but often there is no specific equivalent.

➤ PRONUNCIATION EXERCISE

A. The variants [s] and [z].[1] INSTRUCTIONS: Repeat the following pairs of words and phrases just as you hear them.

[s]	[z]	[s]	[z]
esposo	esbozo	de este	desde
rascar	rasgar	estado	es dado
buscar	juzgar	este	es de
fisco	fisgo	es francés	es mexicano
descaro	desgarro	es todo	es lodo
discurso	disgusto	es té	es rey[2]
escribir	esgrimir	es falso	es verdad
desteñir	desdeñar	es paca	es vaca
asco	asno	es Paco	es Baco
misto	mismo	es paqueta	es baqueta

Spanish [s] and [z] are variants of a single phoneme /s/; consequently, they do not distinguish words as they do in English (cf. *seal* and *zeal*). The voiced variant [z] occurs in Spanish when /s/ is final in a syllable before a voiced consonant /b, d, g, m, n, l, rr/. Everywhere else the voiceless variant [s] occurs. The occurrence of the voiced variant [z] before a voiced consonant is an instance of *assimilation.*

B. The variants [s] and [h]. INSTRUCTIONS: Listen to the variant pronunciations of /s/ in the following sets of words:

[s]	[s]	[h]	[s]	[s]	[h]
ese	este	este	mesa	mesta	mesta
esa	esta	esta	misa	mista	mista
asa	hasta	hasta	pasa	pasta	pasta
casa	caspa	caspa	pisa	pista	pista
quiso	quisto	quisto	pese	peste	peste
cosa	costa	costa	caso	casco	casco

In some dialects of Spain and Spanish America /s/ at the end of a syllable becomes a mere aspiration, represented phonetically by [h]. (It is less fricative than the voiceless velar /x/, which is represented in writing by **j** or **g.**) You should be able to recognize but not necessarily imitate the pronunciations under [h].

➤ WRITING EXERCISE

INSTRUCTIONS: Write the following lists of words from dictation.

1. **gu**apo, **gu**ante, **gu**ardia, **Gu**alterio, **gu**anaco, **Gu**atemala, **gu**agua, **gu**ardar, **gu**adaña, **Gu**araní, **Gu**adalupe, **gu**ajolote, **gu**acamole, a**gu**antar, a**gu**a, len**gu**a

[1] Note that we are now talking about *sounds,* not spellings. The spelling of letter **z** will be treated in Unit 12.

[2] The combination [srr] is frequently articulated as a slightly prolonged trill of which the first portion is voiceless (i.e., the [s] "turns into" a voiceless trill by assimilation to the [rr]).

2. amenguo	antiguo	3. amengüe	pingüe
apaciguo	ambiguo	apacigüe	bilingüe
averiguo	exiguo	averigüe	güiro
			vergüenza
			lingüístico

The sequence [gw] is written **gu** when followed by [a] or [o] and is written **gü** when followed by [e] or [i]. See Unit 9, page 134 for the spelling of /g/ elsewhere (compare **pingue** with **pingüe**).

53 Imperfect

EXAMPLES

1. Dijo que **estaba** bien, si **era** necesario, pero que ella y los niños **tenían** que quedarse en la ciudad.
2. Mientras **comíamos,** don Pepe me contó que **necesitaba** a alguien.
3. Antes don Pepe **tenía** mucho ganado. *Don Pepe had a lot of livestock before.*
4. Se **iba** a trabajar al campo.
5. Yo no **sabía** que usted **hablaba** español. *I didn't know that you spoke Spanish.*
6. Todos los días le **mandaban** una taza de café. *Every day they sent him a cup of coffee.*

IMPERFECT OF REGULAR VERBS			
hablar		**comer**	**vivir**
habl-		**com-**	**viv-**
-aba	**-ábamos**	**-ía**	**-íamos**
-abas		**-ías**	
-aba	**-aban**	**-ía**	**-ían**

The imperfect indicates "unstopped action" in the past. English *I used to work* (*play, live,* etc.) and *I was working* (*playing, living,* etc.) are among its equivalents.

IMPERFECT OF **ser, ir,** AND **ver**					
ser		**ir**		**ver**	
era	**éramos**	**iba**	**íbamos**	**veía**	**veíamos**
eras		**ibas**		**veías**	
era	**eran**	**iba**	**iban**	**veía**	**veían**

These three verbs are the only ones that are irregular in the imperfect.

› PERSON-NUMBER SUBSTITUTION DRILL

1. Antes *usted* hablaba español, ¿verdad? (ustedes, nosotros, Luis, tú, yo)
2. *Don Pepe* necesitaba a alguien. (ellos, yo, tú, nosotros, él)
3. *Yo* trabajaba en el Ministerio de Educación. (nosotros, ella, tú, ustedes, Mario)
4. Siempre comíamos en ese restorán. (ellos, yo, tú, él, Fernando y yo)

5. Antes vivían en el extranjero.
   (yo, nosotros, ella, tú, el administrador)
6. *Los niños* tenían que volver a la ciudad.
   (el consejo estudiantil, nosotros, Rosa, usted, alguien)
7. *Yo* veía a las chicas en el parque.
   (tú, ellos, usted, nosotros, los muchachos)
8. *Yo* iba al campo todos los días.
   (nosotros, ellos, usted, tú, los agricultores)
9. En esos días *él* era un gran atleta.
   (Rosa, tú, yo, nosotros, ellos, Pablo y yo)

› TENSE SUBSTITUTION DRILL

INSTRUCTIONS: Repeat the following sentences just as you hear them. Then repeat them again, changing the present tense verb forms to the imperfect tense.

A. 1. Carlos siempre *contesta* mis preguntas fáciles.
2. Sólo *faltan* tres días, ¿verdad?
3. Por lo visto los empleados de banco no la *pasan* mal.
4. Como de costumbre me *da* algo.
5. Siempre *dobla* a la derecha en esa esquina.
6. *Estudiamos* álgebra, biología y castellano.

B. 1. *Producen* cebollas, lentejas y maíz.
2. *Vivimos* cerca de la Hacienda El Alamo.
3. No *hay* aire puro.
4. Esas casas no *tienen* comedor.
5. Yo no *quiero* vivir en la ciudad.
6. Siempre *trae* a los niños.
7. No *hay* más remedio que hacer una huelga.
8. La casa *tiene* un patio.

C. 1. Lo *veo* casi todos los días en el Club de la Unión.
2. *Voy* a tener exámenes en física.
3. Mi cuñado *va* a su finca en el campo casi todos los días.
4. Eso *es* lo bueno de mi profesión.
5. Las vacas *son* para vender.
6. *Es* cuestión de aprenderlas de memoria.

› CHOICE-QUESTION RESPONSE DRILL

A. 1. Antes de entrar a la clase, ¿usted estudiaba o dormía?
2. Antes de entrar a la clase, ¿usted escribía o jugaba?
3. Antes de vivir aquí, ¿ustedes trabajaban o estudiaban?
4. Antes del invierno, ¿le gustaba el campo o tenía que trabajar demasiado?

B. 1. Cuando usted vivía ahí, ¿comía en la casa o iba a un restorán?
2. Cuando usted vivía ahí, ¿aprendía o enseñaba español?
3. Cuando ustedes vivían ahí, ¿estudiaban o trabajaban?
4. Cuando ustedes vivían ahí, ¿les gustaba el aire puro del campo o preferían la ciudad?
5. Cuando ustedes vivían ahí, ¿les gustaba el cielo azul del campo o preferían el ruido de la ciudad?

C. 1. ¿Usted no tenía hambre o no quería volver a la casa?
2. ¿Ustedes no tenían dinero o no querían pagar?
3. ¿Usted estudiaba química o prefería castellano?
4. ¿Usted era amigo de Pablo o no lo conocía?

› CUED RESPONSE DRILL

1. TEACHER: ¿Qué hacía usted cuando vivía en Venezuela? (hablar español)
   STUDENT: **Cuando vivía en Venezuela hablaba español.**
2. Cuando usted y sus amigos estaban en la universidad, ¿qué hacían? (siempre estudiar)

3. ¿Qué hacía don Pepe cuando viajaba por Hispanoamérica? (comer bien)
4. ¿Qué decía usted cuando hablaba con el empleado de banco todos los días? (la verdad)
5. ¿Qué decían ustedes cuando llegaban a clase tarde? ("buenas noches")
6. ¿Qué hacía yo cuando estaba en el hospital? (dormir mucho)
7. Usted y yo, ¿qué hacíamos en el campo? (trabajar siempre)
8. ¿Por qué ganaban los mismos países todos los años? (mandar equipos grandes)
9. ¿Qué hacían sus profesores en las demás clases? (siempre hacer preguntas)

54 Imperfect versus preterit

EXAMPLES

1. No sé ni cuándo **murió.**
2. Me **tiró** del pelo.
3. **¿Recibiste** alguna mala noticia?
4. Me **quitaron** los documentos.

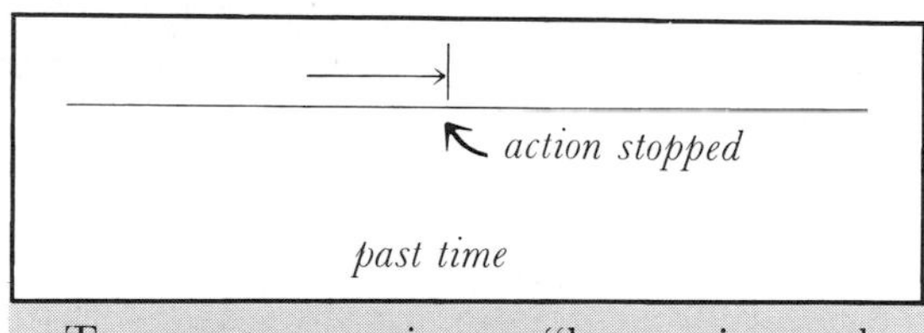

To report an action as "happening and then over with" the preterit is used.

› TENSE SUBSTITUTION DRILL

INSTRUCTIONS: Repeat the following sentences just as you hear them. Then repeat them again, changing the present tense verb forms to preterit.

1. ¿Recibes alguna mala noticia?
2. Me quitan los documentos.
3. La criada pierde el dinero.
4. Entonces don Pepe le ofrece el puesto.
5. Me felicitan por el día de mi santo.
6. Les damos la invitación.
7. Llego a la clase de español.
8. Roberto menciona a un pariente suyo.
9. Apago el radio.
10. Prometemos pasar por el cónsul.
11. Después sucede algo tremendo.
12. El barbero me tira del pelo.

EXAMPLES

A. 1. **Tuvimos** examen en filosofía.
   2. Don Pepe **tenía** mucho ganado.

B. 1. ¿Por qué no **fuiste** al colegio ayer?
   2. Se **iba** a trabajar al campo.

C. 1. ¿Cómo **estuvo** el examen? (*How did it **turn out?***)
   2. Dijo que **estaba** bien.

D. 1. **Fue** una tontería. (***What happened** was only a trifle.*)
   2. Dijo que estaba bien, si **era** necesario.

E. 1. Quise ir pero no **pude.** (*I **failed** to.*)
   2. Dijo que no **podía.** *He said he couldn't (lacked the power or ability).*

F. 1. **Tuvieron** que quedarse aquí. *They had to stay here (and did).*
2. **Tenían** que quedarse aquí. (*They felt obliged to.*)

G. 1. **Costó** mucho. *It (an actual purchase) cost a lot.*
2. **Costaba** mucho. No lo compré. *The price was high. I didn't buy it.*

H. 1. ¿Supiste que ayer **hubo** una reunión? (*A meeting* ***took place.***)
2. **Había** mucha gente en el comedor. *There were a lot of people in the dining room (they were on hand, doing whatever they were doing).*

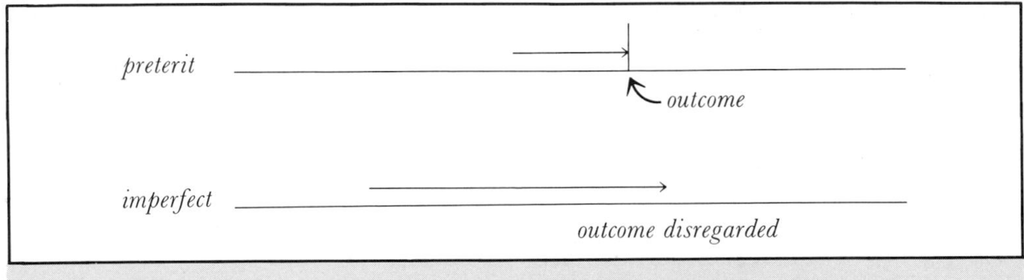

The preterit concentrates on the *outcome*. The imperfect ignores it.

▸ ITEM SUBSTITUTION DRILL

INSTRUCTIONS: Repeat the following sentences just as you hear them. Then repeat them again, substituting the words or phrases suggested and changing the verb from imperfect to preterit or vice versa.

1. TEACHER: *Antes* producía mucho trigo. *Repita.*
   STUDENT: **Antes producía mucho trigo.**
   TEACHER: El año pasado ______
   STUDENT: **El año pasado produjo mucho trigo.**
2. *Siempre* me ofrecían un puesto con buen sueldo.
   Anteanoche ______
3. *Muchas veces* él salía encantado.
   Después de un rato ______
4. *Antes* yo lo veía con horror.
   Anteanoche ______
5. *Ayer* tuvimos examen en física.
   Casi todos los días ______
6. *El año pasado* tuve un coche.
   En esos días ______
7. Comió carne *todo el día.*
   ______ todos los días.
8. *Ayer* comimos en el Club de la Unión.
   Siempre ______

▸ TRANSLATION DRILL

INSTRUCTIONS: The following paired sentences are designed as equivalents of Spanish sentences requiring preterit in the first and imperfect in the second sentence of the pair. Since context beyond the sentence frequently gives the cue that determines the choice, these cues are occasionally presented here parenthetically; the hints in parentheses are not to be translated.

1. How was the exam (did it turn out)?
   How was the professor?
2. He went to do it.
   He was going to do it.
3. They had to stay home (and did).
   They had to stay home (felt they should).
4. It cost too much (but was purchased).
   It cost too much (and therefore was not purchased).
5. I managed to win.
   I was able to win.

6. I worked at the Ministry (for a time).
   I was working at the Ministry (at that time).
7. I went to the theater (once).
   I went to the theater (customarily).
8. Yesterday there was a meeting.
   Many times there used to be meetings.
9. I got very enthusiastic (when she told me).
   I was very enthusiastic (whenever she told me).
10. I wrote very little (that time).
    I wrote very little (as a rule).

EXAMPLES A. 1. Anoche **tuve** una idea. *Last night I had an idea (it popped into my head).*
2. Yo **tenía** otras ideas. *I had other ideas (held to a different opinion).*

B. 1. Ayer **conocí** a su hermano. *Yesterday I met (got to know, got acquainted with) your brother.*
2. Le hablé porque lo **conocía.** *I spoke to him because I knew him (was acquainted with him).*

C. 1. ¿Cuándo lo **supiste?** *When did you find it out (get to know it)?*
2. Ya lo **sabía.** *I already knew it (possessed the knowledge).*

D. 1. **Estuve** allí a las seis. *I was (got) there at six.*
2. **Estaba** allí a las seis. *I was (already) there at six.*

E. 1. **Comprendieron** por qué. *They realized (caught on) why.*
2. **Comprendían** por qué. *They understood why.*

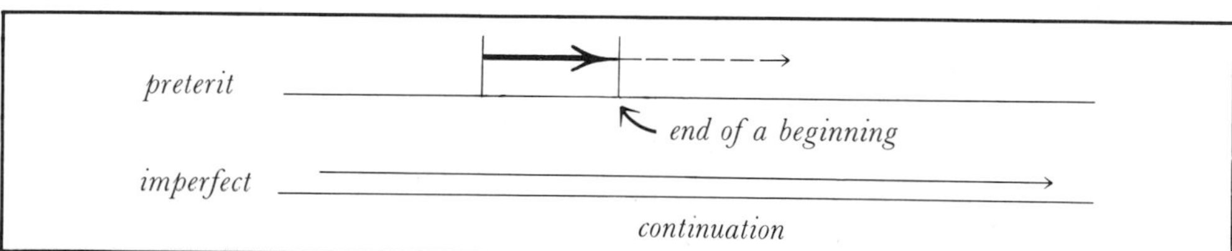

The preterit completes the "get-going" phase of an action. The imperfect implies continuation.

› TRANSLATION DRILL

1. Then I learned about the saint's day.
   I already knew about the saint's day.
2. Then I caught on to the idea.
   I understood the idea.
3. I preferred (picked out) the other cat.
   I preferred (liked most) the other cat.
4. We met Mr. Arjona in Panama.
   We knew Mr. Arjona in Panama.
5. They were here (got here) at eleven o'clock.
   They were already here at eleven o'clock.
6. (I tried but) I wasn't able to open the door.
   (I knew that) I wasn't able to open the door.
7. I had a mix-up (it happened) yesterday.
   I had the money yesterday.

EXAMPLES 1. Nos **encontramos** en el club. Mientras **comíamos,** don Pepe me **contó** que **necesitaba** a alguien.
2. **Dijo** que **estaba** bien.
3. Como **estaba** algo escaso de dinero, yo mismo **cambié** las llantas y después **lavé** el auto. *As I was a little short of money, I changed the tires myself and then washed the car.*

Mexico: Wheat harvest in Yaqui Valley

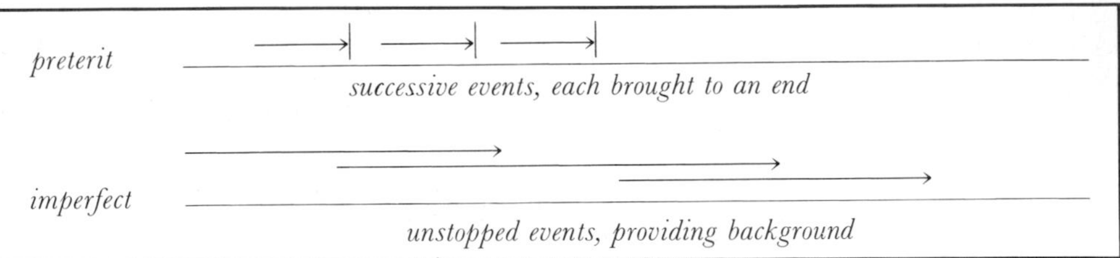

In combinations of preterit and imperfect the preterit pictures the successive events while the imperfect gives the background or the unfinished business, i.e., the events "going on" at the time.

› PERSON-NUMBER SUBSTITUTION DRILL

INSTRUCTIONS: Repeat the following sentences just as you hear them. Then repeat them again, substituting the subjects suggested. Note that in these sentences both verbs (in preterit and imperfect tenses) have the same subject.

1. *Don Pepe* le contó que necesitaba a alguien.
   (yo, ellos, nosotros, tú, él)
2. ¿*Ellos* dijeron que estaban bien?
   (él, yo, tú, nosotros, usted)
3. Dijo que iba a hablar sobre los empleados.
   (nosotros, tú, ellos, yo, él)
4. *Yo* no quería, pero tuve que hacerlo.
   (ella, nosotros, ustedes, Mario, tú)
5. Cuando tenía once años, fui a las montañas.
   (ella, ellos, tú, María Elena, nosotros)
6. Hablé con la chica que quería conocer.
   (Luis, tú, mis sobrinos, nosotros, él)
7. Mientras comíamos, hablamos de nuestros parientes.
   (ellos, yo, él, tú, Alfredo)
8. Cuando *yo* estaba en México, fui a ver al doctor Arjona.
   (nosotros, ella, ellos, tú, usted)

› TENSE SUBSTITUTION DRILL

INSTRUCTIONS: Repeat each sentence just as you hear it. Then repeat it again, changing the present tense verbs in group A to preterit and imperfect, as indicated in the model sentence, and those in group B to imperfect and preterit.

A. 1. TEACHER: Dice que va a hablar más tarde. *Repita.*
STUDENT: **Dice que va a hablar más tarde.**
TEACHER: *Cambie.*
STUDENT: **Dijo que iba a hablar más tarde.**
2. Dice que hay muchas nubes.
3. Veo una casa que está a dos kilómetros de aquí.
4. Josefina barre el cuarto que está sucio.
5. Salgo con una chica que no habla inglés.
6. Vemos a la señora que quiere la casa.

B. 1. Como estoy algo escaso de dinero, yo mismo lavo el auto.
2. Ya que tengo la oportunidad, consigo el empleo.
3. Como voy para arriba, llevo la ropa.
4. Cuesta mucho; por eso no la compro.

› TENSE SUBSTITUTION DRILL

INSTRUCTIONS: Repeat each sentence just as you hear it, changing the present tense verbs to the appropriate past tense, either preterit or imperfect, as in the model sentence. Each drill narrates a brief story.

A. 1. TEACHER: Roberto va en su coche. *Cambie.*
STUDENT: **Roberto iba en su coche.**
2. Piensa ir a ver a su hermana.
3. Toma la avenida principal de la ciudad.
4. Hay muchos automóviles en la avenida.
5. Dobla en la esquina.
6. Se mete en contra del tránsito.
7. Para todo el tráfico.
8. Tiene un tremendo lío con la policía.
9. El policía le quita los documentos,
10. y Roberto está furioso.
11. Llama tres veces al Jefe del Tránsito.
12. Por fin el Jefe contesta,
13. y pronto arregla la cuestión de la multa.

B. 1. María Elena vive en la Calle Veinte.
2. Es una chica bonita y amable.
3. Una tarde algunos amigos vienen a su casa.
4. Ella siempre invita a sus amigos a su casa.
5. Esta vez los amigos quieren oir unos discos nuevos.
6. Pero el tocadiscos está malo.
7. Luego María Elena tiene una idea.
8. Invita a su amigo Francisco.
9. Sabe que él puede arreglar el tocadiscos.
10. Deja su trabajo con mucho gusto,
11. y se va a la casa de María Elena.
12. En diez minutos él puede arreglar el tocadiscos.
13. Todos se quedan hasta la hora de comer.

EXAMPLES

A. 1. Entre enero y junio, le **escribí** todos los días. *Between January and June, I wrote him every day (and then I stopped writing).*
2. Eramos amigos. Le **escribía** todos los días. *We were friends. I wrote (used to write) him every day.*

B. 1. Al principio la **llamé** cada dos o tres días y luego fui a verla unas pocas veces. *At first I called her every two or three days, and then I went to see her a few times.*
2. La **llamaba** cada dos o tres días. *I called (used to call, was calling) her every two or three days.*

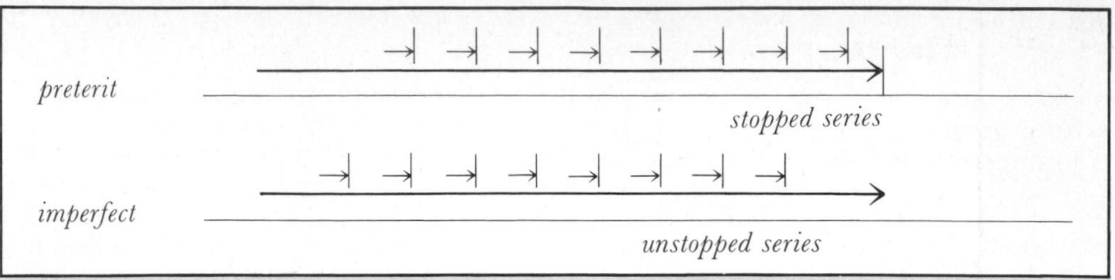

When a series of repeated acts (each terminated within itself) is viewed by the speaker as terminated, the preterit is used. If the series is not viewed as terminated, the imperfect is used.

TRANSLATION DRILL

1. I wrote him every day (until Christmas, when I stopped).
   I wrote (used to write) him every day.
2. I called her every three days (until she left the hospital).
   I called her every three days (at that time).
3. We went four times.
   We used to go often (many times).
4. They argued every week (last year).
   They were arguing every week.

DISCUSSION

The preterit and imperfect represent two different ways of looking at events in the past. The preterit is like an on–off switch, while the imperfect just lets things run. The preterit focuses on the termination; whatever the event is, however long it lasted or however many times it was repeated, we picture it as having come to an end. Since actions of brief duration are the ones that we most typically think of in these terms—an act like *it burst,* for example, is hard to view in any other way than as happening and terminating at once—they are the ones most commonly met in the preterit: *he said, it fell, I sneezed, the ship sank,* etc. Nevertheless, any event may be so viewed and is then preterit: *I lived thirty years in Palma and then went to Rome* **Viví treinta años en Palma y después fui a Roma.** The example **Estuve enfermo** implies that I got over it or at least that that particular period of illness came to an end; **Estaba enfermo** tells us that at a certain time in the past I was ill but is noncommittal about the outcome.

English makes similar contrasts but organizes them differently. The English past tense forms listed in Unit 7, Section 30 give us no clue—without context they can be equivalent to either preterit or imperfect. But when English uses *used to* (*He used to have cattle there* **Tenía ganado allí**), *would* as a synonym of *used to* (*When we played, I would lose in order to please him* **Cuando jugábamos, yo perdía para darle gusto**), and generally when it uses *was* (*were*) . . . *–ing* (*I was working for Don Pepe* **Trabajaba para don Pepe**), Spanish uses the imperfect. These are the English devices for picturing a past action as in progress and disregarding its termination.

Spanish does with a number of verbs what English does with very few: It makes the same verb serve for both the "get-going" and the "continuing" phase of an action. An English example is the verb *to have: I had an idea yesterday* normally means *It occurred to me* (since I probably still *have* it, the past form *had* refers to the act of *getting* it). But in *He asked me what ideas I had on the subject,* the same *I had* means *I was carrying in my head.* For the "get-going" phase, i.e., to show the "end of a beginning," Spanish uses the preterit and is able to do the same with several other verbs where English has to use an entirely different verb. For example, *How come he knew it?—He found it out through a friend* becomes **¿Cómo lo *sabía*?—Lo *supo* por un amigo.**

The preterit does not necessarily refer to the "get-going" phase of these verbs—this depends on context. Thus **Lo supe** might mean *I knew it and then forgot it,* or it might mean *I learned* (*grasped*) *it;* in either case the action is carried through to its end.

55 Past progressive[3]

EXAMPLES

A. 1. **Estuve trabajando** allí hasta ayer. *I was working there until yesterday.*
2. **Estuviste hablando** muy fuerte ahí por un minuto, amigo. *You were talking pretty loud there for a minute, friend.*

B. 1. **Estaba comiendo** y no podía[4] hablar. *I was eating and couldn't talk.*
2. ¿Qué **estaban haciendo** con esas herramientas? *What were they doing with those tools?*

preterit progressive

imperfect progressive

With the preterit of **estar** the progressive shows action continuing up to a cutoff point. The imperfect of **estar** shows it as continuing.

› TRANSLATION DRILL

INSTRUCTIONS: Preterit progressive should be used in the first sentence of each pair and imperfect progressive should be used in the second.

1. He was celebrating his birthday until 1 o'clock.
   He was celebrating his birthday at 1 o'clock.
2. We were waiting on the corner until six.
   We were waiting on the corner yesterday.
3. I was studying until yesterday.
   I was studying in Spain.

› TENSE SUBSTITUTION DRILL

INSTRUCTIONS: Repeat each sentence just as you hear it. Then repeat it again, substituting imperfect progressive for present progressive, as in the model sentence.

A. 1. TEACHER: *Estoy* estudiando para la clase de castellano. *Repita.*
STUDENT: **Estoy estudiando para la clase de castellano.**
TEACHER: *Cambie.*
STUDENT: **Estaba estudiando para la clase de castellano.**
2. *Estamos* hablando con el doctor Fernández.
3. Tampoco *está* trabajando hoy.
4. Paquito se *está* peinando.
5. *Están* pensando en algo igual.

B. 1. Le *estoy* escribiendo a mi tío.
2. ¿Por qué *están* comiendo en la cocina?
3. *Está* haciendo otra pregunta.
4. Le *están* cortando el pelo.
5. *Estamos* haciendo una cosa ridícula en vez de estudiar.

› DISCUSSION

The past progressive with the imperfect of **estar** differs from the simple imperfect in the same way that the present progressive differs from the simple present. It is not used for something future to the past time referred to, that is, for something *planned.* **Se iba a trabajar al campo** cannot be expressed with **estaba yendo.** But elsewhere it may replace the simple imperfect whenever the

[3]See also present progressive, Unit 9, Section 44.

[4]**No pude hablar** would mean that I *failed* to speak when the impulse hit me or at the moment I was expected to.

speaker wishes to emphasize comparison or temporariness; **mientras comíamos** could appear as **mientras estábamos comiendo,** hinting more strongly that the persons involved might be or would presently be doing something else. *He was wearing a blue tie* would be unlikely in the progressive unless the speaker had expected something else.

The preterit of **estar** does here just what the preterit does elsewhere: brings the action to a conclusion.

56 With-preposition pronouns

EXAMPLES

A. 1. **A mí** ni en pintura.
2. **A mí** me gusta muchísimo el campo. ([*To me*] *the country appeals to me a lot.*)
3. ¿Quieres ir **conmigo?**

B. 1. Nosotros pasamos **por ti.**
2. ¿Cuándo puedo hablar **contigo?**

C. 1. No tengo nada **en contra de usted.** *I don't have anything against you.*
2. Todo por culpa **de él.**
3. Le gusta tanto el café (la carne) que casi no puede vivir **sin él** (**sin ella**). *She likes coffee* (*meat*) *so much that she can hardly live without it.*
4. Nos vamos **sin ella.** *We're going off without her* (or *without it*).

D. ¿Es **para nosotros?** *Is it for us?*

E. 1. ¿Alguno **de ustedes** trajo plata?
2. Fue **a ellos** y les habló. *He went up to them and spoke to them.*
3. Vamos a hablar **con ellas.**

AFTER **con**		AFTER ANY OTHER PREPOSITION
-migo		**mí**
-tigo		**ti**
	usted	
	él	
	ella	
	nosotros, -as	
	ustedes	
	ellos	
	ellas	

Aside from **mí** and **ti** (and the special forms **conmigo** and **contigo**) the pronouns used after prepositions are identical to those used as subjects.

› ITEM SUBSTITUTION DRILL

1. A *mí,* ni en pintura.
(él, ellos, nosotros, ti, usted)
2. Y todo por culpa de *él.*
(ella, ellos, nosotros, mí, ustedes)
3. Pablo no tiene nada en contra de *usted.*
(ellos, nosotros, ti, ella, mí)
4. Pasan por *ti* a las ocho.
(ustedes, usted, mí, ellas, nosotros)
5. ¿El maíz es para *nosotros?*
(mí, él, ustedes, ellas, ti)
6. Van a salir sin *ella.*
(nosotros, ti, ustedes, mí, nosotras)
7. Quieren ir *con nosotros.*
(con ellos, con ella, con usted, conmigo, contigo)

Mexico: Hacienda in Uxmal, Yucatán

› CHOICE-QUESTION RESPONSE DRILL

A. 1. ¿Fue esa tontería por culpa de él o de ella?
2. ¿Vas a pasar por él o por ella?
3. ¿Vamos a hablar con ella o con ellos?
4. ¿Salieron sin ella o sin él?

B. 1. ¿Los saludos son para mí o para ella?
2. ¿Va usted conmigo o con ellos?
3. ¿Esto es para mí o para ti?
4. ¿Quieres hablar conmigo o con todos nosotros?
5. ¿Ellos quieren comer con nosotros o con ustedes?

› TRANSLATION DRILL

A. 1. They asked questions about him.
2. They asked questions about you all.
3. They asked questions about her.
4. They asked questions about them.

B. 1. Do you want to go with them?
2. Do you want to go with us?
3. Do you want to go with her?
4. Do you want to go with me?

C. 1. The bread is from us.
2. The bread is from her.
3. The bread is from them.
4. The bread is from you.

D. 1. Here's the bread. Don't go off without it.
2. Here's the meat. Don't go off without it.
3. Here's the tire. Don't go off without it.
4. Here they are. Don't go off without them.

With-preposition pronouns as objects with *a*

EXAMPLES

1. —¿Quieres traer a Olga y a José María? *"Will you bring Olga and José María?"*
   —Sí, y **a ti** también. *"Yes, and you too."*
2. —¿La profesora? La vimos ayer. Vamos a verla hoy. *"The teacher? We saw her yesterday. We're going to see her today."*
   —¿Y los alumnos? *"And the students?"*
   —Sí, **a ellos** también. *"Yes, them too."*
3. **A mí** ni en pintura.

	la	vimos
ver-	-la	
	a ella	

With-verb pronouns are used only with verbs; therefore, when no verb is present the with-preposition pronoun (introduced by **a**) is used.

› PATTERNED RESPONSE DRILL

INSTRUCTIONS: Answer the following questions according to the models given.

1. TEACHER: A mí me gusta muchísimo el campo. ¿Y a ella?
   STUDENT: **A ella también.**
   ¿Y a ellos?
   ¿Y a usted?
   ¿Y a ustedes?
   ¿Y a nosotros?
   ¿Y a mí?

2. A ella no le gusta nada la química. ¿Y a él?
   A él tampoco.
   ¿Y a ellos?
   ¿Y a ellas?
   ¿Y a ustedes?
   ¿Y a usted?
   ¿Y a nosotros?
   ¿Y a mí?

EXAMPLES

1. **A mí me** gusta muchísimo el campo.
2. **Me** gusta **a mí.** (***I*** *like it.*)
3. Para regatear, **a mí** nadie **me** gana.
4. De los dos, **lo** prefiero **a él.** (*Of the two, I prefer* ***him.***)

a	WITH–PREPOSITION PRONOUN	WITH–VERB PRONOUN	VERB	a	WITH–PREPOSITION PRONOUN
A	mí	me	gusta.		
		Me	gusta	a	mí.

The with-verb pronouns are always unstressed. Therefore, when the speaker wishes to add emphasis he uses the with-preposition pronoun (introduced by **a**) IN ADDITION TO the with-verb pronoun.

PERSON-NUMBER SUBSTITUTION DRILL

1. Para regatear, a *ella* nadie le gana.
   (mí, las señoras, nosotros, ustedes, ti)
2. A *él* le falta dinero para el viaje.
   (mí, nosotros, ella, ti, ustedes)
3. A *nosotros* nos pasó exactamente lo mismo.
   (ellos, él, ustedes, ti, mí)
4. A *mí* me parece un poco mejor.
   (ella, ustedes, ti, ellos, nosotros)
5. Pero no la veo a *ella.*
   (él, ellas, ellos, usted, ti)
6. Los prefiere a *ellos.*
   (ellas, ella, ti, nosotros, mí)

DISCUSSION

Stress is achieved by adding the with-preposition pronoun to the with-verb pronoun. As in English, whether it is put before the verb or after the verb depends on where the speaker wants the stress. Thus **A mí me gusta** is similar to *As for* **me,** *I like it* (answering the question *What about* ***you?***), while **Me gusta a mí** is similar to *The one who likes it is* **me** (answering the question *Who likes it?*).

58 With-verb pronouns that repeat indirect-object nouns

EXAMPLES

1. **A un muchacho amigo mío le** quitaron los documentos.
2. **Al país le** cuesta una cantidad astronómica.
3. **Les** escribo **a mis primos.** *I'm writing to my cousins.*
4. **¿A quién le** dieron el dinero? *Who did they give the money to?*

Les | **escribo** | **a mis primos.**

A mis primos | **les** | **escribo una carta muy larga.**

With an indirect-object noun (introduced by **a**) the corresponding with-verb pronoun is usually added.

EXAMPLES

1. No **les** gusta (a ellos). *They don't like it (It doesn't appeal to them).*
2. ¿Qué **le** parece (a ella)? *What does she say to it? (How does it seem to her? How does she like it)?*
3. **Le** gané a Juan. *I beat Juan.*
4. **¿Te** falta algo? *Are you lacking something? (Is something lacking to you)?*
5. No **le** pasó nada a Roberto. *Nothing happened to Roberto.*

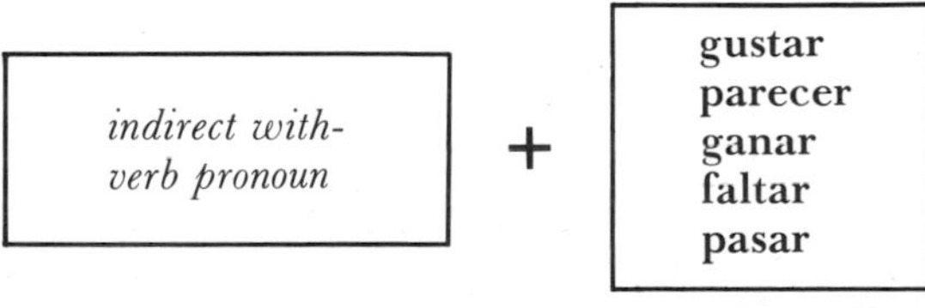

With the meanings given these verbs take indirect objects.

EXAMPLES 1. ¿Qué **le** parece **a María?** *What does María say to it (How does it seem to María? How does María like it)?*

2. No **les** gusta **a los otros.** *The others don't like it (It doesn't appeal to the others).*

3. **Le** gané **a Juan.**

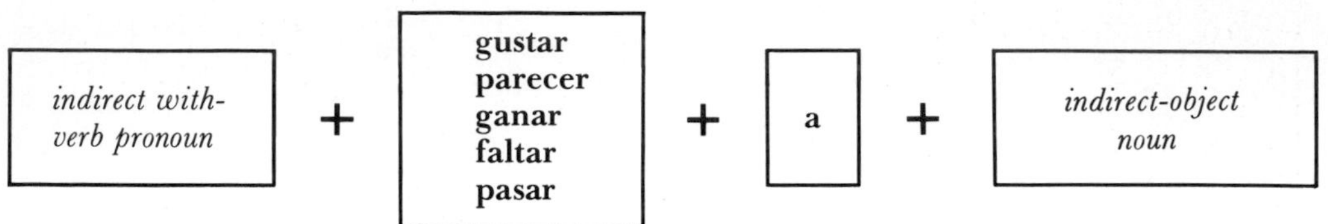

When these verbs have a noun object they add the with-verb pronoun object as well.

❯ PERSON-NUMBER SUBSTITUTION DRILL

1. A *Felipe* le parece muy bien.
   (los muchachos, Olga, las chicas)
2. ¡Cuidado! A los *señores* no les gusta discutir.
   (policía, muchacha, señoritas)
3. No le falta nada a mi *amigo.*
   (cuñados, sobrina, tíos)
4. A los *otros* les parece un poco lejos.
   (jefe, profesoras, cónsul)
5. Vámonos; nadie les gana a las *criadas.*
   (empleado, agricultores, abogado)
6. ¿Le pasó algo al *profesor?*
   (médicos, barbero, técnicos)
7. Ya lo creo; le gusta muchísimo a *Mario.*
   (Luis y Mario, todo el equipo, los viejos)

❯ DISCUSSION

There is a small class of verbs, represented by **gustar** *to appeal,* **parecer** *to seem,* **ganar** *to beat,* **faltar** *to be lacking (to be missing),* and **pasar** *to happen,* which when they carry special meanings call for indirect objects. Thus **Le gané** means *I beat him* (got-the-advantage over-him, won-out on-him), while **Lo gané** means *I won it.* When a noun object accompanies one of these verbs with its special meaning, the with-verb pronoun is added: **Le gané a Juan** *I beat Juan (in the competition).*

❯ GUIDED CONVERSATION

L. *Luis* P. *Don Pepe*

L. ¡Qué horror! ¡A mí ni en pintura! Cuando usted me invitó a comer no dijo nada de un puesto en su finca.
P. ¿Pero no le gusta el campo: ________________
L. Claro que sí, pero...
P. Además producimos un gran número de cosas importantes: ________________
L. Pero El Alamo está muy lejos de aquí.
P. No está tan lejos, sólo ________________
L. Pero un trabajo tan sucio... Yo no sé.
P. Hombre, es un puesto administrativo. Además, prometo ________________
L. ¡Administrativo! ¡Ah, bueno, eso es otra cosa!
P. Lo malo es que no hay escuela en la finca. Su señora y los niños ________________
L. Entonces voy a hablar con ella. Le prometo contestarle mañana, don Pepe.
P. Muy bien. Y recuerde usted que los agricultores ________________

Final vowels in present tense verb forms.

A. 1. He works and eats a lot.
2. He studies and learns a lot.
3. He talks and writes a lot.
4. He enters and leaves a lot.
5. He bargains and sells a lot.
6. He waits and offers a lot.
7. He plays and sleeps a lot.
8. He bets and loses a lot.

B. 1. We work and eat a lot.
2. We study and learn a lot.
3. We bargain and sell a lot.
4. We wait and offer a lot.
5. We bet and lose a lot.
6. We play and sleep a lot.
7. We talk and write a lot.
8. We enter and leave a lot.

reading

La familia Alvarez va a la feria[5]

P. *Papá* M. *Mamá* PAQ. *Paquito* L. *Luisa*

P. Bueno, aquí estamos en la feria. Muchos animales, muchas cosas que ver...

M. Sí, pero hay mucha gente... te apuesto a que no vemos nada. ¡Uf!

P. No fue idea mía, María, que...

PAQ. ¡Mamáaa! Tengo hambre.

M. Ay, Paquito, acabamos de llegar. Siempre estás pensando en el estómago. Tuvimos una buena comida y...

L. ¡Mamáaa! Quiero ver las ovejas.

P. Sí, sí: vamos a ver los animales. Están por aquí, a la derecha... Aquí están. Me dijeron que había mucho ganado en esta feria... Sí, mira a este toro, Paquito. Qué cabeza tan grande, ¿no? ¡Qué...!

L. ¡Quiero ver las ovejas! ¡Quiero ver las ovejas!

M. Paciencia, hija; no se puede ver todo a la vez.

a...vez *at the same time*

* * *

P. Y ahora, aquí están las ovejas, Luisa. ¡Mira qué bonitas y qué blancas!

blancas *white*

L. ¡Ah sí! ¿Puedo tocarlas, papá?

P. ¡Claro que sí!
M. ¡Claro que no!

P. Mira, María, no van a hacerle daño.

hacerle daño *to hurt her*

[5] Hereafter only the more difficult words will be glossed. Before looking for a word in the end vocabulary try to infer its meaning from the context, just as you would do with most new words in English. An intelligent guess is often the only clue you need.

M. ¡No se trata de eso! Es que se va a ensuciar. ...¡Ay Jesús, Luisa, tócalas con las manos, pero no con la cara! ¡Vámonos!

se...ensuciar *she's going to get dirty*

L. ¿Adónde, mamá?

M. Vamos a... ¿Dónde está Paquito? (*llamando*) ¡Paquitoo! ¡Paquitooo!

PAQ. (*gritando*) ¡Aquí estoy, mamá!

gritando *shouting*

M. ¿Qué estás haciendo?

PAQ. Estoy jugando con los cerdos. ¿No son...?

M. (*escandalizada*) ¿Con los cerdos? ¿Con esos sucios animales? Ay, ¡ese chico va a volverme loca!

L. Yo lo voy a buscar, mamá. (*Va corriendo adonde está su hermano. Corto silencio. Entonces se oye un grito formidable.*) ¡Mamáaa! ¡Papáaa! ¡Paquito me tiró del vestido y me caí...!

buscar *to look for*

vestido *dress* **me caí** *I fell down*

PAQ. ¡No le hice nada, no le hice nada! ¡Fue culpa de Luisa! ¡Me tiró del pelo!

P. ¡LUISA! ¡PACO!

M. ¡Jesús, María y José! ¡Denme paciencia! (*Con un poco de dificultad separan a los dos chicos ya muy sucios y se van en busca de los baños.*)

baños *washrooms*

Buenos Aires: Palermo cattle show

UNIT 12

At the Cleaner's

C. *First clerk* M. *Maid* A. *Doña Ana*
CL. *Second clerk*

C. What can I do for you?
M. I've got a bundle of [package with] clothes here.
C. That one?
M. No, these are shoes; *this* one.
C. How soon [For when] do you want them?
M. The underwear and the shirts by Tuesday and the bed linen by Saturday.
C. All right. Anything else?
M. Oh, this lady's dress and this man's suit. Can you have them ready for me by tomorrow?
C. Of course. We'll send them to you at five o'clock.
M. Can I count on that [Without fail]?
C. Yes, yes. Don't worry.

* * *

(*two days later*)

A. Young lady, we didn't get back a suit and a dress that you promised [agreed] to send yesterday.
CL. Impossible, ma'am. Did you bring them in yourself?
A. No, the maid did [came].
CL. Oh, then she didn't say it was for yesterday.
A. But here are the receipts.
CL. Let's see . . . But there's no address here.

En la tintorería (1)

D. *Dependiente* C. *Criada* A. *Doña Ana*
DA. *Dependienta*

D. ¿Qué se le ofrece?
C. Aquí traigo un paquete con ropa.
D. ¿Ese?
C. No, éstos son unos zapatos; éste.
D. ¿Para cuándo la quiere?
C. La ropa interior y las camisas para el martes y la de cama para el sábado.
D. Muy bien. ¿Nada más?
C. Ah, este vestido de la señora y este traje del señor. (2) ¿Me los puede tener para mañana?
D. Cómo no. Se los mandamos a las cinco.
C. ¿Sin falta?
D. Sí, sí, no tenga cuidado.

* * *

(*dos días después*)

A. Señorita, no recibimos un traje y un vestido que ustedes quedaron en mandar ayer.
DA. Imposible, señora. ¿Usted misma nos los trajo?
A. No, vino la criada.
DA. Ah, entonces ella no dijo que era para ayer.
A. Pero aquí están los recibos.
DA. A ver... Pero aquí no hay dirección.

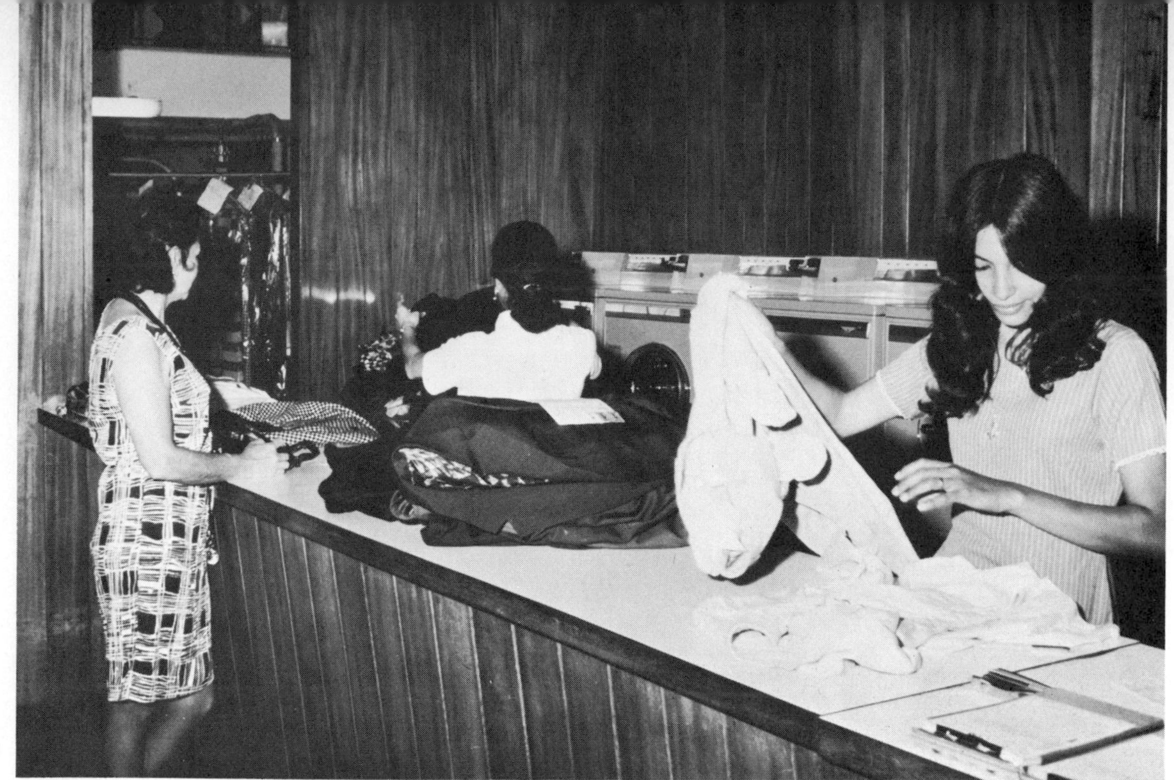

Guatemala City: Dry cleaning shop

A. And why didn't you ask her for it?
CL. I don't know [Who knows], ma'am. I wasn't the one that took these clothes.
A. What nonsense [barbarity]!

* * *

CL. Is this [Are these] your suit and dress?
A. No, they're [those are] not mine. That green one and that blue one over there.
CL. All right, wait until I wrap them up for you. That's four seventy-five.
A. This is the first and last time I come here.
CL. I'm sorry, ma'am, but it isn't our fault.

A. ¿Y por qué no se la preguntaron?
DA. Quién sabe, señora. Yo no fui la que recibí esta ropa.
A. ¡Qué barbaridad!

* * *

DA. ¿Son éstos los trajes suyos?
A. No, ésos no son míos; aquel (3) verde y aquel azul que están allá.
DA. Muy bien, espere para envolvérselos. Son cuatro setenta y cinco.
A. Primera y última vez que vengo aquí.
DA. Lo siento, señora, pero no es culpa nuestra.

cultural notes

(1) This dialog illustrates the casualness of certain business relationships.

(2) In this context **señora** and **señor** refer to the mistress and the master of the house.

(3) There are two commonly used demonstratives corresponding to English *that:* **ese** and **aquel** (the forms of **aquel** are **aquel** *m. sing.*, **aquella** *f. sing.*, **aquellos** *m. pl.*, and **aquellas** *f. pl.*). **Ese** refers to something near the person addressed or not far from either speaker in a conversation; **aquel** suggests greater remoteness from both speakers. Thus the distinction between **ese** and **aquel** is merely a matter of comparative distance. The tendency in Spanish America has been to disregard this distinction, as English does, with **ese** crowding out **aquel,** so that for the most part the meaning *that* is translated by **ese.** See Unit 7, Section 31, on demonstratives and Unit 3, Cultural Note 7.

› WRITING EXERCISE

The written representation of /s/ by **c** and **z.**[1] INSTRUCTIONS: Write the following lists of words from dictation.

A.			
zanco	cinco	caza	cace
zona	cena	plaza	place
zumo	cimo	gozo	goce
zurdo	cerdo	trozo	trece
zarzuela	ciruela	empieza	empiece
zurrido	cerrado	rezó	recé

B.			
faz	faces	cruz	cruces
haz	haces	tez	teces
paz	paces	pez	peces
hoz	hoces	juez	jueces
voz	voces	vez	veces
luz	luces	lápiz	lápices

In American Spanish the letter **z** represents the same sound as the letter **s.** The letter **c** represents this same sound before [e] or [i]. Note that in the words in B the final **z** of a noun or adjective is changed to **c** before adding the plural ending.

Spanish spelling is not always consistent. There are a few words with variant spellings. Examples: **zinc** or **cinc, zenit** or **cenit, zimo** or **cimo.**

59 Two with-verb pronoun objects

EXAMPLES

1. **¿Me los** puede tener para mañana?
2. ¿Usted misma **nos los** trajo? (*Did you yourself bring them to us?*)
3. Quiero enseñá**rtelo.** *I want to show it to you.*

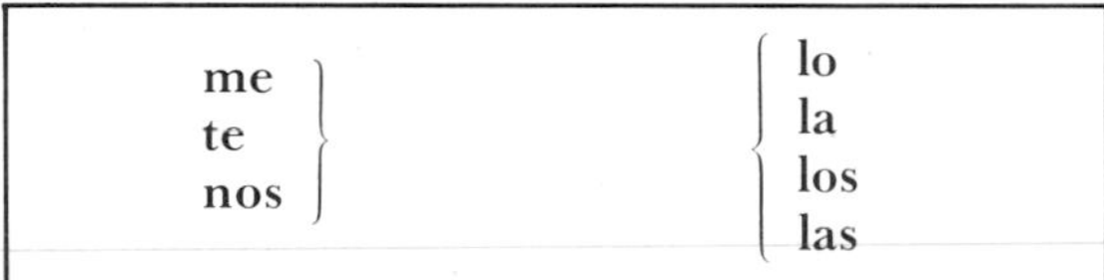

In combinations of two with-verb pronouns, the forms beginning with **l-** follow the forms **me, te,** and **nos.**

› CONSTRUCTION SUBSTITUTION DRILL

INSTRUCTIONS: Repeat the following sentences just as you hear them. Then repeat them again, substituting an appropriate with-verb pronoun for the direct-object noun (and any modifiers it has).

A. 1. TEACHER: Mario me enseñó la *finca* ayer. *Repita.*
STUDENT: **Mario me enseñó la finca ayer.**
TEACHER: *Cambie.*
STUDENT: **Mario me la enseñó ayer.**
2. Don Pepe me enseñó *el trigo* ayer.
3. Luis me enseñó *los cerdos* ayer.
4. Francisco me enseñó *las cebollas.*
5. El dependiente me vendió *el arroz.*
6. La dependienta me vendió *la mantequilla.*
7. La dependienta me prometió *las camisas* para mañana.
8. ¿Me puede tener *estos vestidos* para mañana?
9. La dependienta no me dio *el recibo.*
10. La dependienta no me dijo *la verdad.*

[1] This refers to the letter **z** rather than the sound [z], which was treated in Unit II.

B. 1. Mario nos enseñó *la hacienda* ayer.
2. Don Rosario nos enseñó *el maíz* ayer.
3. El empleado nos vendió *la carne.*
4. Josefina nos va a traer *el pan.*
5. Don Rafael nos consiguió *ese buen puesto.*
6. Alberto nos dio *estos cueros.*
7. Antonio nos dejó *esta lana.*
8. La empleada nos mandó *esta* lista.

C. 1. ¿Mario te enseñó *el Club de la Unión?*
2. Antonio no te quitó *el empleo.*
3. Por lo visto el administrador te prestó *un peso.*
4. A ver, ¿quién te dio *el trabajo?*
5. Queremos darte *este traje.*
6. Queremos enseñarte *este árbol.*

EXAMPLES 1. **Se los** mandamos a las cinco.
2. Espere para envolvér**selos.**
3. ¿Por qué no **se la** preguntaron? (*Why didn't you ask it of* [*address the question to*] *her?*)

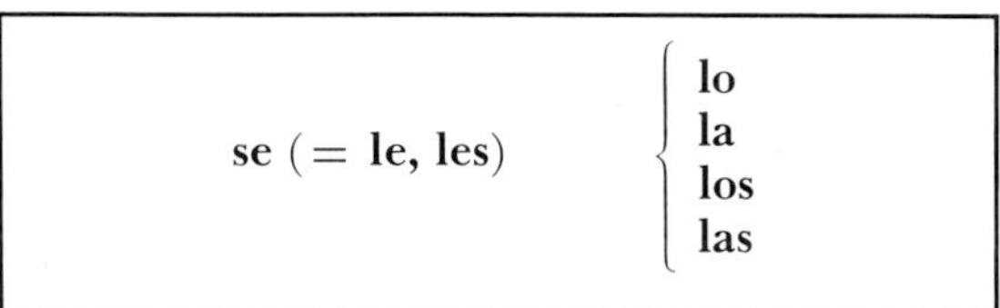

se (= **le, les**) { **lo** / **la** / **los** / **las**

Se replaces **le** and **les** before the other pronouns beginning with **l–;** it always comes first.

› CONSTRUCTION SUBSTITUTION DRILL

INSTRUCTIONS: Repeat the following sentences just as you hear them. Then repeat them again, substituting an appropriate with-verb pronoun for the direct-object noun (and any modifiers it has); this cues the replacement of **le** or **les** with **se.**

A. 1. TEACHER: Le mandamos *los trajes* a las cinco. *Repita.*
STUDENT: **Le mandamos los trajes a las cinco.**
TEACHER: *Cambie.*
STUDENT: **Se los mandamos a las cinco.**
2. Le traemos *las papas* esta tarde.
3. ¿Le enseño *las ovejas* el próximo invierno?
4. Le vendo *la hacienda* en octubre.
5. Yo le enseñé *este árbol viejo* a Paquito.
6. Entonces le presté *el peine.*
7. Después le mandamos *la cuenta.*
8. Le vendí *el coche* al señor que está ahí afuera.
9. Le ofrecimos *el puesto* a Luis.
10. Le di *las maquinillas* al barbero.

B. 1. Les di *los centavos* a mis sobrinas.
2. Yo les arreglé *el carburador.*
3. ¿Les mandaste *los paquetes* a tus padres?
4. Les dieron *una lista* a los estudiantes.
5. Les prestaron *las tijeras* a las señoras.
6. Les prometí *un viaje* a los niños.
7. El policía les enseñó *la flecha.*
8. Les dimos *la ganancia* a los empleados.
9. Les quitamos *los juguetes* a los niños.

› PATTERNED RESPONSE DRILL

A. 1. ¿Le presté el libro?
Sí, me lo prestó.
¿Cuándo se lo presté?
Me lo prestó ayer.
2. ¿Le presté los centavos?
¿Cuándo se los presté?
3. ¿Le presté las herramientas?
¿Cuándo se las presté?

4. ¿Le enseñé la flecha?
¿Cuándo se la enseñé?
5. ¿Le apagué el radio?
¿Cuándo se lo apagué?
6. ¿Le prometí los documentos?
¿Cuándo se los prometí?
7. ¿Le di la invitación?
¿Cuándo se la di?
8. ¿Le di el examen?
¿Cuándo se lo di?
9. ¿Le vendí los autos?
¿Cuándo se los vendí?
10. ¿Le vendí el arroz?
¿Cuándo se lo vendí?
11. ¿Le traje los paquetes?
¿Cuándo se los traje?
12. ¿Le traje el recado?
¿Cuándo se lo traje?

B. 1. ¿Me prestó el libro?
Sí, se lo presté.
¿Cuándo me lo prestó?
Se lo presté ayer.
2. ¿Me prestó las herramientas?
¿Cuándo me las prestó?
3. ¿Me prestó los pesos?
¿Cuándo me los prestó?
4. ¿Me enseñó la pintura?
¿Cuándo me la enseñó?
5. ¿Me apagó el radio?
¿Cuándo me lo apagó?
6. ¿Me dio la invitación?
¿Cuándo me la dio?
7. ¿Me dio la orden?
¿Cuándo me la dio?
8. ¿Me prometió los documentos?
¿Cuándo me los prometió?
9. ¿Me vendió la lana?
¿Cuándo me la vendió?
10. ¿Me trajo las llantas?
¿Cuándo me las trajo?

C. 1. ¿Te presté el libro, Juan?
Sí, me lo prestaste.
¿Cuándo te lo presté?
Me lo prestaste ayer.
2. ¿Te prometí el coche, Cecilia?
¿Cuándo te lo prometí?
3. ¿Te vendí la vaca, Alberto?
¿Cuándo te la vendí?
4. ¿Te rompí las tazas, Elena?
¿Cuándo te las rompí?
5. ¿Te traje la invitación, Roberto?
¿Cuándo te la traje?

D. 1. ¿Me prestaste el libro, Susana?
Sí, te lo presté.
¿Cuándo me lo prestaste?
Te lo presté ayer.
2. ¿Me ofreciste el puesto, Olga?
¿Cuándo me lo ofreciste?
3. ¿Me prometiste las ovejas, Alfredo?
¿Cuándo me las prometiste?
4. ¿Me trajiste la noticia, Mercedes?
¿Cuándo me la trajiste?

INSTRUCTIONS: Indicate with appropriate gestures that the questions in the following two sections, although intended to be answered by one individual, are actually directed to a group of two or more.

E. 1. ¿Les presté el libro?
Sí, nos lo prestó.
¿Cuándo se lo presté?
Nos lo prestó ayer.
2. ¿Les llevé las noticias?
¿Cuándo se las llevé?
3. ¿Les pagué la cuenta?
¿Cuándo se la pagué?
4. ¿Les vendí los muebles?
¿Cuándo se los vendí?
5. ¿Les traje el dinero?
¿Cuándo se lo traje?
6. Les dije la pregunta?
¿Cuándo se la dije?

F. 1. ¿Nos prestó el libro?
Sí, se lo presté.
¿Cuándo nos lo prestó?
Se lo presté ayer.
2. ¿Nos arregló los frenos?
¿Cuándo nos los arregló?
3. ¿Nos vendió las ovejas?
¿Cuándo nos las vendió?
4. ¿Nos pagó la cuenta?
¿Cuándo nos la pagó?
5. ¿Nos trajo las frutas?
¿Cuándo nos las trajo?

INSTRUCTIONS: Indicate with appropriate gestures that the questions in the following two sections are asked (in G) or answered (in H) by one individual who is speaking for a group of two or more.

G. 1. ¿Le prestamos el libro?
Sí, me lo prestaron.
¿Cuándo se lo prestamos?
Me lo prestaron ayer.
2. ¿Le enseñamos la pintura?
¿Cuándo se la enseñamos?
3. ¿Le escribimos las preguntas?
¿Cuándo se las escribimos?
4. ¿Le conseguimos el auto?
¿Cuándo se lo conseguimos?
5. ¿Le hicimos la comida?
¿Cuándo se la hicimos?

H. 1. ¿Me prestaron el libro?
Sí, se lo prestamos.
¿Cuándo me lo prestaron?
Se lo prestamos ayer.
2. ¿Me enseñaron las fincas?
¿Cuándo me las enseñaron?
3. ¿Me lavaron el coche?
¿Cuándo me lo lavaron?
4. ¿Me vendieron la lana?
¿Cuándo me la vendieron?
5. ¿Me ofrecieron el puesto?
¿Cuándo me lo ofrecieron?

INSTRUCTIONS: Indicate with appropriate gestures that the questions in the two sections following are exchanges between two groups of two or more individuals each.

I. 1. ¿Les prestamos el libro?
Sí, nos lo prestaron.
¿Cuándo se lo prestamos?
Nos lo prestaron ayer.
2. ¿Les pagamos la cuenta?
¿Cuándo se la pagamos?
3. ¿Les vendimos las casas?
¿Cuándo se las vendimos?
4. ¿Les enseñamos los toros?
¿Cuándo se los enseñamos?

J. 1. ¿Nos prestaron el libro?
Sí, se lo prestamos.
¿Cuándo nos lo prestaron?
Se lo prestamos ayer.
2. ¿Nos prometieron los trajes?
¿Cuándo nos los prometieron?
3. ¿Nos dieron la plata?
¿Cuándo nos la dieron?
4. ¿Nos trajeron los vestidos?
¿Cuándo nos los trajeron?

60 Meaning of the indirect object

EXAMPLES

A. 1. Yo tampoco, excepto **a esta sobrina.**
2. Espera para envolvér**se**los.
3. Córte**me** apenas un poquito atrás.

B. 1. **A un muchacho amigo mío** le quitaron los documentos.
2. **Me** exigieron una multa.
3. No **me** entendió nada. (*He didn't understand anything* ***from me*** [*or* ***for me***].)
4. **Le** compré una casa. *I bought a house* ***from him*** (*or* ***for him***).

C. 1. **Nos** apagaron el radio. *They turned the radio off* ***on us.***
2. No **me** los pierda. *Don't lose them* ***for me*** (***on me***).

D. 1. ¿Por qué no **se** la preguntaron?
2. ¿Qué **te** pidieron? *What did they ask* ***of you?***

VERB	INDIRECT OBJECT
action	*a person (occasionally, a thing) who is interested in the action or who stands to gain or lose by it*

The indirect object includes meanings that are translated by English *from* (group B of the examples above), *on* (C), and *of* (D), as well as the more usual *to* and *for* (A). (See Unit 4, Section 19.)

TRANSLATION DRILL

A. 1. TEACHER: He gave the money to me.
STUDENT: **Me dio el dinero.**
2. He changed the money on me.
Me cambió el dinero.
3. He took the money from me.
Me quitó el dinero.
4. He won the money off me.
Me ganó el dinero.
5. He arranged the money for me.
Me arregló el dinero.

B. 1. She gave the book to me.
2. She changed the book on me.
3. She took the book from me.
4. She won the book off me.
5. She arranged the book for me.

C. 1. They gave the furniture to her.
2. They changed the furniture on her.
3. They took the furniture from her.
4. They won the furniture off her.
5. They arranged the furniture for her.

D. 1. They gave the car to us.
2. They changed the car on us.
3. They took the car from us.
4. They won the car off us.
5. They arranged the car for us.

E. 1. They gave the pesos to my father.
2. They changed the pesos on my father.
3. They took the pesos from my father.
4. They won the pesos off my father.
5. They arranged the pesos for my father.

EXAMPLES

A. 1. No puedo ir **al mercado** hoy.
2. Me llevaron **a ella.** *They took me to her (to where she was).*

B. 1. Compré un tocadiscos **para mi sobrina.** *I bought a record player for my niece.*
2. Trabajo **para la refinería.** *I work for the refinery.*

C. Nosotros pasamos **por ti.**

D. El recado es **de Rafael.** *The message is from Rafael.*

		POINT OF VIEW		TARGET OR SOURCE
to (*terminus of motion*)	= a	●	——————→	■
for (*aim*)	= para	●	——→	■
for (*to get*)	= por	●	←——————⊃	■
from (*source*)	= de	●	←——	■

The more literal meanings of *to, for,* and *from* do not call for the indirect object in Spanish.

› TRANSLATION DRILL

1. TEACHER: They passed the money to us.
   STUDENT: **Nos pasaron el dinero.**
   TEACHER: The money passed to us.
   STUDENT: **El dinero pasó a nosotros.**
2. They passed the meat to us.
   The meat was passed to us.
3. I took the record player from her.
   I took the record player from the living room.
4. I took her a book.
   I took the book for her.
5. They passed the money to Mario.
   The money passed to Mario.
6. We bought the tools from Carlos.
   We bought the tools (intended) for Carlos.

› DISCUSSION

Although *to* and *for* are the meanings most commonly associated with the indirect object (see Unit 4, Section 19), actually the range of meanings is much wider. Except in a few relics like *He played* **us** *a dirty trick* (played a trick ON US), *His recklessness cost* **him** *his life* (took his life FROM HIM), *It took* **me** *an hour* (took an hour of my time FROM ME), English must use prepositions for these broader meanings. Spanish, however, is free to use the indirect object to indicate a loose sort of involvement in the action not necessarily implying anything more than an interest in it. A more accurate translation of **Le quitaron los documentos** is *They took the papers where-he-was-concerned* or *with-respect-to-him.* One who loses as well as one who benefits may therefore appear as an indirect object. **Le compré una casa** means only that he was involved in the purchase; it covers the more specific meanings of *from,* i.e., *I bought the house from him* (he benefited by getting the money), or *for,* i.e., *I bought the house for him* or *I bought him the house* (he benefited by the service I performed for him or even by getting the house). The precise meaning depends on the context. The meaning of the verb is usually enough to tell us in what sense to take the indirect object; thus **quitar,** *to take* or *to take away* in the sense of *remove,* suggests *from* or *off:* **Le quitaron el dinero** *They took the money from him.*

The underlying meaning of **para** is *toward.* For this reason **para** is used rather than the indirect object if the speaker implies nothing as to whether the person at the receiving end derives any benefit (or loss). English makes this distinction, rather loosely, with some verbs: *I brought my niece a record player* **Le traje a mi sobrina un tocadiscos** versus *I brought a record player for my niece* **Traje un tocadiscos para mi sobrina.** In the first we imply that she benefited, but in the second nothing is implied as to whether she received it or even knew about it. With other verbs English has to express both ideas with *for,* but Spanish continues to make the distinction: *I wrapped the package for them* is either **Les envolví el paquete** (I did them this favor, and they benefited) or **Envolví el paquete para ellos** (the package was for them, or the act was aimed in their direction, but nothing is implied as to whether they wanted the favor, received the package, or otherwise benefited).

Para is required in two special cases: (1) employment (impersonal; no favor or disfavor is done)—**Trabajo para la refinería** *I work for the refinery,* **Estudio para mis clases** *I study for my classes;* and (2) if no ACT is mentioned from which a benefit (or loss) can be derived—**Es un tocadiscos para mi sobrina** *It's a record player for my niece.*

61 Nominalization

EXAMPLES

A.
1. **La rubia** se llama Betty y **la morena** Susana.
2. Yo soy **la menor.**
3. Había trajes en el primer paquete y camisas en **el segundo.** *There were suits in the first bundle and shirts in the second (one).*
4. Estas refinerías no son **las principales.** *These refineries are not the main ones.*

B. 1. La ropa interior para el martes y **la de cama** para el sábado. (*The underclothing by Tuesday and the [clothing] of bed by Saturday.*)

2. Los empleados del club y **los del banco.** *The employees of the club and those of the bank.*

C. 1. Ella no fue **la que recibió esta ropa.** *She wasn't the one who received these clothes.*

2. **Los que me gustan más** son importados. *The ones I like best are imported.*

NOMINALIZATION WITH THE ARTICLE

NOUN EXPRESSED		NOUN OMITTED	
A. the blonde girl the youngest sister the second bundle the main refineries	**la muchacha rubia** **la hermana menor** **el segundo paquete** **las refinerías principales**	the blonde the youngest the second (one) the main ones	**la rubia** **la menor** **el segundo** **las principales**
B. the bedclothing the bank employees	**la ropa de cama** **los empleados del banco**	that of the bed those of the bank	**la de cama** **los del banco**
C. the employee who received the bulls I like	**la empleada que recibió** **los toros que me gustan**	the one who received the ones I like	**la que recibió** **los que me gustan**

Modifiers of nouns (these include adjectives, **de** phrases, and **que** clauses) may function as nouns when combined with the definite article. Thus **las principales** is an abbreviated way of saying **las refinerías principales; refinerías** is understood from the context.

› CONSTRUCTION SUBSTITUTION DRILL

INSTRUCTIONS: Repeat the following sentences just as you hear them. Then repeat them again, omitting the noun indicated, thus nominalizing the accompanying modifiers.

A. 1. TEACHER: La *muchacha* rubia se llama Betty. *Repita.*
STUDENT: **La muchacha rubia se llama Betty.**
TEACHER: *Cambie.*
STUDENT: **La rubia se llama Betty.**

2. Yo soy la *hermana* menor.
3. ¿Dónde están los *alumnos* españoles?
4. La próxima *semana* no puedo ir.
5. Salió la *señora* enferma.
6. ¿Tiene usted el mismo *libro?*
7. Es el mejor *equipo* del Perú.
8. Esta es la *casa* más moderna que tenemos.
9. ¿Quién tiene el *tocadiscos* portátil?
10. Es el último *documento* que tenemos.
11. La *muchacha* bonita paró el tráfico.
12. Los *hombres* importantes comieron juntos.
13. Los nuevos *juguetes* están abajo.
14. El *examen* primero fue más fácil.
15. La *señora* amable es doña Marta.

B. 1. Quiero la *ropa* de cama para el sábado.
2. Los *empleados* del banco están celebrando el día feriado.
3. La *chica* del vestido azul es mi compañera de clase.
4. El *muchacho* del colegio tuvo un tremendo lío con la policía.
5. El *señor* del Ministerio dijo que no era nada serio.

C. 1. Ella fue la *empleada* que recibió esta ropa.
2. Los *trajes* que me gustan más son importados.
3. Estas son las *tijeras* que me prestó el barbero.
4. Esta es la *finca* que produce arroz, trigo y cosas por el estilo.
5. Y tú eres el *muchacho* que dijo "imposible".

› CHOICE-QUESTION RESPONSE DRILL

A. 1. ¿Cuál traje quiere, el negro o el azul?
2. ¿Cuál profesor es, el americano o el mexicano?
3. ¿Cuál lista tiene, la nueva o la vieja?
4. ¿Cuál hijo es, el segundo o el menor?
5. ¿Cuál pregunta tiene, la fácil o la difícil?
6. ¿Cuál casa compró, la moderna o la anticuada?
7. ¿Cuál auto es más sucio, el verde o el negro?

B. 1. ¿Cuál funcionario es, el del ministerio o el de la escuela?
2. ¿Cuál muchacha es, la del restorán o la de la tintorería?
3. ¿Cuál clase es más difícil, la de física o la de química?

C. 1. ¿Cuál cuarto es más grande, el que está arriba o el que está abajo?
2. ¿Cuál profesor le gusta más, el que acaba de salir o el que viene ahora?
3. ¿Cuál coche es más nuevo, el que está aquí o el que está allí?
4. ¿Cuál árbol es más alto, el que está en el patio o el que está en la calle?

EXAMPLES 1. No, **éstos**[2] son unos zapatos; **éste.**
2. ¿A **cuál** de las fincas de don Pepe va? *Which of Don Pepe's ranches are you going to?*
3. **Ese** es un deporte del que yo no sé ni papa.

NOMINALIZED DEMONSTRATIVES AND **¿cuál?**			
this (one)	**éste** **ésta**	that (one)	**ése** (**aquél**) **ésa** (**aquélla**)
these (ones)	**éstos** **éstas**	those (ones)	**ésos** (**aquéllos**) **ésas** (**aquéllas**)
which (one)?	**¿cuál?**	which (ones)?	**¿cuáles?**

The demonstratives and **¿cuál?** function like nouns without adding the equivalent of the nominalizing *one* in English.

EXAMPLES 1. **Aquel verde** y **aquel azul** que están allá.
2. **¿Cuál verde? ¿Ese que usted tiene?** *Which green one? That (one) that you have?*

NOMINALIZATION WITH DEMONSTRATIVES AND **¿cuál?**			
NOUN EXPRESSED		NOUN OMITTED	
that green suit this invitation from Olga those exams I lost which green suit?	**ese traje verde** **esta invitación de Olga** **esos exámenes que perdí** **¿cuál traje verde?**	that green one this one from Olga those I lost which green one?	**ese verde** **ésta de Olga** **ésos que perdí** **¿cuál verde?**

The demonstratives and **¿cuál?** may be used to nominalize in the same way as the article.

[2] Recall that when they are themselves nominalized, the demonstratives are written with the accent mark, although this accent is usually omitted when the demonstrative is capitalized; and that the neuter forms **esto, eso,** and **aquello** are never written with the accent mark. (See Unit 7, Section 31.)

› CONSTRUCTION SUBSTITUTION DRILL

INSTRUCTIONS: Repeat the following sentences just as you hear them. Then repeat them again, omitting the noun indicated, thus nominalizing the accompanying demonstrative or other adjective.

A. 1. TEACHER: Esa *muchacha* es mi prima. *Repita.*
STUDENT: **Esa muchacha es mi prima.**
TEACHER: *Cambie.*
STUDENT: **Esa es mi prima.**
2. Esa *docena* es para nosotros.
3. Esta *criada* nunca tarda mucho.
4. Este *dinero* alcanza para toda la semana.
5. Estos *muchachos* tienen las camisas muy sucias.
6. Esta *chica* quiere comprar unos zapatos.
7. Me imagino que estos *toros* son importados.
8. ¿Cuál *señor* es el español?

B. 1. Esa *muchacha* rubia es mi prima.
Esa muchacha rubia es mi prima.
Esa rubia es mi prima.
2. Este *traje* negro es para mí.
3. Esos *hombres* respetables no tienen deudas.
4. Déme ese *traje* azul.
5. ¿De quién es este *vestido* verde?
6. Estos *señores* americanos van a salir pronto.
7. Ese mismo *señor* me lo contó.
8. ¿Cuál *señor* extranjero quiere verme?

C. 1. Esta *invitación* de Olga acaba de llegar.
2. Ese *señor* del traje negro le está esperando.
3. ¿Cuál *camisa* de las dos quiere?

D. 1. Esta *invitación* que acaba de llegar es de Olga.
2. Esos *libros* que perdí eran para ustedes.

› DISCUSSION

The adjectives in English that can be freely used like nouns, without the addition of something to show the noun function, are comparatively few. The most familiar examples are the demonstratives (*This book is new:* ***This*** *is new*), the adjectives of order (*Here is the last copy: Here is the* ***last***), and the superlatives (*The biggest fellow was over two hundred pounds: The* ***biggest*** *was over two hundred pounds*). Normally it is necessary to add the word *one, ones,* or replace with *that, those—The pretty girl was elected queen,* repeated without *girl,* calls for *one: The pretty one was elected queen. The cards you gave me* repeated without *cards* calls for *ones* or *those: the ones you gave me, those you gave me.*

In Spanish almost any adjective can be nominalized without adding anything provided there is an accompanying definite article, demonstrative, or **¿cuál?** *The pretty one,* referring to *girl,* is **la bonita,** and *the pretty ones,* referring to *girls,* is **las bonitas;** *the pretty ones,* referring to *shoes,* is **los bonitos.** *Those portable ones,* referring to *tools,* is **esas portátiles.** *Those I lost,* referring to *books,* is **los que perdí** if *those* is just another way of saying *the ones* (*the ones I lost*), or **esos que perdí** if *those* has its full demonstrative meaning (*those over there,* as if one were pointing at them).

62 Possessives that do not precede nouns

EXAMPLES

A. No, ésos no son **míos.**

B. La culpa no es **nuestra.** *The fault isn't ours.*

C. ¿Es **tuyo** éste? *Is this one yours?*

D. 1. Creo que es **suyo.** *I think it's yours (his, hers, theirs).*
2. ¿Es **de usted?** —No, es **de ella.** *Is it yours? —No, it's hers.*

POSSESSIVES BEFORE NOUNS	POSSESSIVES NOT BEFORE NOUNS	
SHORT FORM	LONG FORM	ALTERNATE CONSTRUCTION WITH **de**
mi	**mío, -a, -os, -as**	
nuestro, -a, -os, -as	**nuestro, -a, -os, -as**	
tu	**tuyo, -a, -os, -as**	
su	**suyo, -a, -os, -as**	**de usted** **de ustedes** **de él** **de ellos** **de ella** **de ellas**

In all positions except before the noun, the forms in the second and third columns are used. The forms with **de** are sometimes needed where **suyo** would be ambiguous.

› ITEM SUBSTITUTION DRILL

1. Esa *batería* no es mía.
   (traje, camisas, peines)
2. ¿Es tuyo este *vestido?*
   (ropa, paquetes, llantas)
3. Lo siento, pero la *culpa* no es nuestra.
   (dinero, ideas, trajes)
4. ¿Son suyas estas *tijeras?*
   (zapatos, plata, coche)

› PERSON-NUMBER SUBSTITUTION DRILL

1. *Yo* digo que este libro no es mío.
   Yo digo que este libro no es mío.
   El ______________________________
   El dice que este libro no es suyo.
   (nosotros, ellos, tú, usted, ustedes)
2. *Usted* dice que tampoco es suyo.
   (yo, ellos, nosotros, ella, tú)
3. *Pablo* dice que la lista no es de él.
   (ellos, ella, ellas, usted, ustedes, yo, tú, nosotros)

› PATTERNED RESPONSE DRILL

A. 1. ¿Es tuyo este libro?
   No, no es mío.
2. ¿Es tuya esta cartera?
3. ¿Es tuyo este auto?
4. ¿Son tuyas estas llantas?
5. ¿Son tuyos estos juguetes?

B. 1. ¿Es suya esta refinería?
   Sí, es nuestra.
2. ¿Es suyo este mercado?
3. ¿Es suyo este jardín?
4. ¿Son suyos estos discos?
5. ¿Son suyas estas tijeras?
6. ¿Es suya esta idea?

EXAMPLES 1. Un amigo **mío** quiere conseguir un empleo.
2. No es culpa **nuestra.** *It isn't* ***our*** *fault* (*It's no fault of ours*).

POSITION FOR ***of mine, of his,*** ETC.[3]	
noun	*possessive*

› ITEM SUBSTITUTION DRILL

1. Hay un *amigo* mío aquí.
   (compañera, primos, sobrinas)
2. Compraron unas *casas* nuestras.
   (restoranes, finca, negocio)
3. ¿Un *pariente* tuyo está en México?
   (tía, alumnos, profesoras)
4. Vino una *prima* nuestra.
   (sobrino, tías, cuñados)

› DISCUSSION

The essential difference between the **mi-tu-su** possessives and the **mío-tuyo-suyo** possessives is one of stress. The short forms are normally unstressed; they correspond to the possessive in an English phrase such as *my* ***brother,*** in which the stress occurs on the noun. (There is one situation in which they may be stressed: where the possessive is contrastive and the noun, being merely repeated from what has been said before, is de-stressed: *She wants to be close to* ***her*** *family* [*not mine*] **Ella quiere estar cerca de *su* familia.**)

In the usual positions of stress the longer forms are required. The two most frequent are after the verb **ser,** as in **Es mío** *It's mine,* and in the sense *of mine, of his,* etc., as in **un hermano mío** *a brother of mine.* But other occasions of stress (apart from the contrastive one above) also call for the longer forms, as in **Todo por culpa de él,** which could also be said **Todo por culpa suya,** corresponding to English *It was* ***his fault,*** with stress on both possessive and noun.

There are sizable areas of the Spanish-speaking world in which **de nosotros** replaces **nuestro.** To use **de mí** for **mío,** or **de ti** for **tuyo,** however, is regarded as substandard.

For many speakers of Spanish the **su, suyo** forms are more normally taken in the sense *your, yours* than in the sense *his, her(s), its, their(s).* For the latter meanings the **de** constructions are more usually substituted by these speakers and do not necessarily indicate emphasis: **Habla el cuñado de él.**

63 Nominalized possessives

EXAMPLES

1. Si tu café no está caliente, toma **el mío.** *If your coffee isn't hot, take mine.*
2. ¿Vas en tu coche o en **el nuestro?** *Are you going in your car or in ours?*
3. **El tuyo** siempre tiene algo malo.
4. Estas herramientas son mías. ¿Dónde están **las suyas?** *These tools are mine. Where are yours?*
5. Nuestra madre no es como **la de ellos.** *Our mother isn't like theirs.*

mine (my one)	**el mío, la mía**
mine (my ones)	**los míos, las mías**
yours (your one)	**el suyo, la suya** (**el, la de usted**)
yours (your ones)	**los suyos, las suyas** (**los, las de usted**)
etc.	**etc.**

The long possessives (**mío, tuyo, nuestro, suyo,** and the forms with **de**) nominalize in the same way as other adjectives (see Section 61). When English *mine, ours,* etc., function as nouns, the nominalized form must be used in Spanish.

[3] See Unit 4, Section 21.

› ITEM SUBSTITUTION DRILL

1. Si tu *café* no está aquí, toma el mío.
   (carne, centavos, frutas)
2. Ahí está mi *camisa,* pero ¿dónde está la tuya?
   (traje, lápices, tazas)
3. No tengo mis *recibos,* pero los suyos están en la sala.
   (camisas, documento, invitación)
4. Nuestro *coche* está aquí, pero no sé dónde está el de ustedes.
   (batería, exámenes, plumas)

› PATTERNED RESPONSE DRILL

A. 1. ¿Es tuyo este libro?
   No, el mío está en la sala.
2. ¿Es tuya esta cartera?
3. ¿Es tuyo este peine?
4. ¿Son tuyos estos zapatos?
5. ¿Es tuyo este café?
6. ¿Son tuyos estos documentos?
7. ¿Es tuya esta lista?

B. 1. ¿Son suyos estos discos?
   No, ya tenemos los nuestros.
2. ¿Son suyas estas tijeras?
3. ¿Es suyo este libro?
4. ¿Son suyos estos trajes?
5. ¿Es suya esta plata?
6. ¿Son suyos estos zapatos?
7. ¿Es suya esta invitación?

› TRANSLATION DRILL

A. 1. My car is the green one; how about yours?
   Mi coche es el verde; ¿y el suyo?
2. My shirts are the blue ones; how about his?
3. My shoes are the old ones; how about yours?

B. 1. Here's your comb; where's mine?
2. Here's your invitation; where's his?
3. Here's your coffee; where's ours?
4. Here's your milk; where's hers?

64 Telling time

EXAMPLES

A. 1. ¿Qué hora es?
2. Son las tres y media.
3. Es la una y cuarto. *It's a quarter past one.*
4. Son las cinco menos veinte. *It's twenty minutes to five (five minus twenty).*
5. Eran las doce y diez. *It was ten past twelve.*

B. 1. **¿A qué hora** llegan? *When do they arrive?*
2. Llegan **a la una menos cuarto.** *They arrive at a quarter to one.*
3. Llegan **a las nueve de la mañana (noche).** *They arrive at nine in the morning (at night).*
4. Llegan **por la tarde.** *They arrive in the afternoon.*

	VERB	HOUR	FRACTION BEFORE THE HOUR		FRACTION AFTER THE HOUR	PERIOD OF THE DAY
present	**Es** **Son**	**la una** **las dos** **las tres** **etc.**	**menos diez** **menos cuarto** **menos veinte** **etc.**	*or*	**y diez** **y cuarto** **y veinte** **etc.** **y media**	**de la mañana.** **de la tarde.** **de la noche.**
past	**Era** **Eran**					

TRANSLATION DRILL

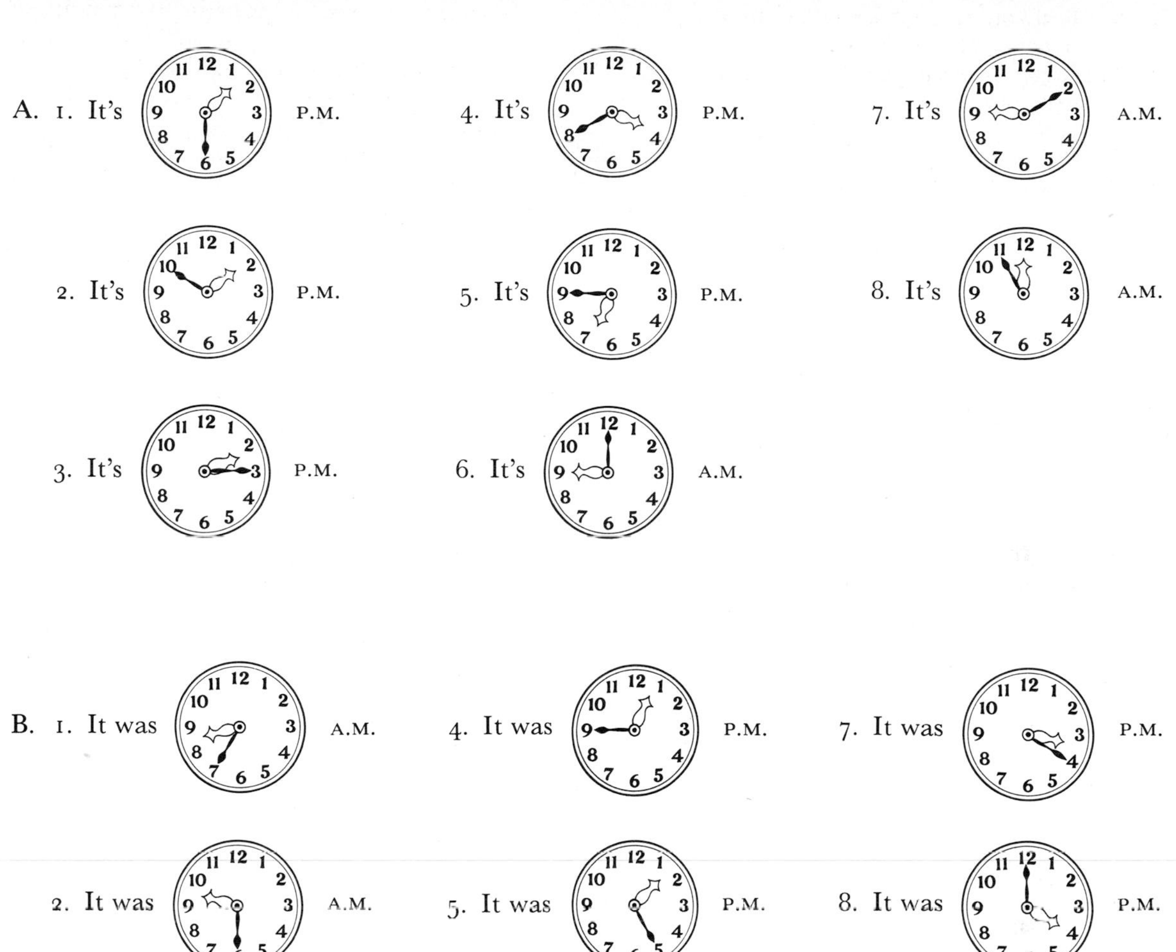

C. 1. It's going to be eight-fifteen.
Van a ser las ocho y cuarto.
It seems to be about eight-fifteen.
Parecen ser como las ocho y cuarto.
It must be eight-fifteen.
Deben ser las ocho y cuarto.
It has to be eight-fifteen.
Tienen que ser las ocho y cuarto.
It can't be eight-fifteen.
No pueden ser las ocho y cuarto.

2. It's going to be twenty-five to nine.
It seems to be about twenty-five to nine.
It must be twenty-five to nine.
It has to be twenty-five to nine.
It can't be twenty-five to nine.

3. It's going to be four o'clock.
It seems to be about four o'clock.
It must be four o'clock.
It has to be four o'clock.
It can't be four o'clock.

D. 1. It was going to be one-thirty.
Iba a ser la una y media.
It seemed to be about one-thirty.
Parecía ser como la una y media.
It must have been one-thirty.
Debía ser la una y media.
It had to be one-thirty.
Tenía que ser la una y media.
2. It was going to be ten-ten.
It seemed to be about ten-ten.
It must have been ten-ten.
It had to be ten-ten.
3. It was going to be nine o'clock.
It seemed to be about nine o'clock.
It must have been nine o'clock.
It had to be nine o'clock.

E. 1. They arrived at six o'clock in the morning.
They arrived in the morning.
2. They arrive at five-thirty in the afternoon.
They arrive tomorrow (in the) afternoon.
3. He came at eight-fifteen in the evening (night).
He came back in the evening (night).

› DISCUSSION

It is and *It was* appear in the forms **es, son,** and **era, eran.** (The time is almost always "background," and therefore the preterit is rarely used here. See page 174.) One o'clock (plus or minus fractions) calls for the singular, and hours later than one o'clock call for the plural.

The feminine article (agreeing with **hora, horas** understood) is required with the numeral.

Fractions appear as simple addition (**y** *plus,* hence *past*) and subtraction (**menos** *minus,* hence *before, to, till, of*).

Period of the day is introduced by **de** when the hour is specified, otherwise by **por.**

Spanish does not recognize a period corresponding to *evening;* it may be translated according to the lateness of the hour by either **tarde** or **noche.** Just as in English many speakers do not make a precise division (compare *I'll see you at five tonight*), there is no clear-cut division between **tarde** and **noche;** but generally **tarde** corresponds to daylight hours.

65 Anticipation of number and person

EXAMPLES

A. 1. **Son** las tres y media.
2. Vea que **son** cincuenta pesos.
3. **Son** cuatro setenta y cinco.
4. La cuestión principal **eran** las huelgas. *The main problem was the strikes.*

B. 1. La alumna que habla mejor **eres** tú. *The student who talks best is you.*
2. No **fui** yo. *It wasn't me.*

A.	SINGULAR NOUN	ser *to be*	PLURAL NOUN
ENGLISH	problem	was	strikes
SPANISH	**cuestión**	**eran**	**huelgas**

Ser is normally plural if it has a plural predicate noun.

B.	THIRD-PERSON NOUN	ser *to be*	FIRST- OR SECOND-PERSON PRONOUN
ENGLISH	student	is	you me
SPANISH	**alumna**	**eres** **soy**	**tú** **yo**

Ser is normally first or second person if it has a first- or second-person predicate pronoun.

› TRANSLATION DRILL

A. 1. The main thing was the strike.
La cosa principal era la huelga.
2. The main thing was the strikes.
La cosa principal eran las huelgas.
3. The main thing was the debt.
4. The main thing was the meetings.
5. The main thing was the plant.
6. The main thing was the refineries.
7. The main thing was the inauguration.

B. 1. The trouble is the document.
Lo malo es el documento.
2. The trouble is the scissors.
3. The trouble is the car.
4. The trouble is the wheat.
5. The trouble is the beans.
6. The trouble is the traffic.
7. The trouble is the streets.

C. 1. The package? It was the suits.
¿El paquete? Eran los trajes.
2. The package? It was the shirt.
3. The package? It was the dresses.
4. The package? It was the suit.
5. The package? It was the shoes.

D. 1. It's three shirts.
Son tres camisas.
2. It's one suit.
3. It's one pair of shoes.
4. It's one dress.
5. It's four o'clock.
6. It's one o'clock.
7. It's eight o'clock.
8. It's one-thirty.
9. It's fifty pesos.
10. It's one peso.
11. It's four seventy-five.

E. 1. It wasn't me.
No fui yo.
2. It wasn't him.
3. It wasn't you (**tú**).
4. It wasn't you.
5. It wasn't us.
6. It wasn't them.
7. It wasn't her.

F. 1. The lawyer was Francisco.
El abogado fue Francisco.
2. The lawyer was me.
3. The lawyer was you.
4. The lawyer was you (**tú**).
5. The lawyer was him.
6. The lawyer was Don Rafael.

G. 1. The one who does it best is you.
El que lo hace mejor eres tú.
2. The one who does it best is him.
3. The one who does it best is Rosario.
4. The one who does it best is me.
5. The one who does it best is you.

› DISCUSSION

At an earlier period in the history of English, constructions like *It* ***am*** *I, That man* ***wert*** *thou* (modern *It's me* or *It's I, That man was you*) were regular: the verb *be* took its person not from the subject but from the predicate. Present-day Spanish equivalents parallel this older English form: ***Soy*** **yo** (note the absence of an equivalent of *It*—discussed in Unit 2, Section 3), **Ese hombre *eras* tú.**

Similarly, in Spanish, with NUMBER: when English says *Your life* ***is*** *all the things you do,* Spanish says **Tu vida *son* todas las cosas que haces.** (English sometimes wavers: *The only thing I never forget* ***is*** *(**are**) the keys.*) The result is that if there is a plural on EITHER side of the verb *be,* the verb in Spanish is plural: *The strikes were the main problem* **Las huelgas *eran* la cuestión principal;** *The main problem was the strikes* **La cuestión principal *eran* las huelgas.**

› GUIDED CONVERSATION

D. *Dependienta* A. *Doña Ana*

D. ¿Qué se le ofrece, señora?
A. Señorita, no recibimos ______________
D. Déjeme ver los recibos. Pero aquí no hay dirección.
A. ¿Y por qué no ______________
D. No sé señora. Pero primero dígame para cuándo quería la otra ropa.
A. La ropa interior ______________
D. Estos que tengo aquí sin número, ¿no son los trajes suyos?
A. No, ésos no son ______________
D. Muy bien, ¿se los envuelvo entonces?
A. No, no me ______________
D. Está muy bien, señora. Son cuatro setenta y cinco.

› PATTERNED RESPONSE REVIEW DRILL

Possessive constructions.

A. 1. Yo conozco a Pablo. ¿Usted es el hijo?
Sí, yo soy el hijo de Pablo.
2. Yo conozco a Francisco. ¿Usted es la tía?
3. Yo conozco a Roberto. ¿Usted es la hermana?
4. Yo conozco a doña Beatriz. ¿Usted es la criada?
5. Yo conozco a Susana. ¿Usted es el cuñado?

B. 1. Don Rafael está vendiendo su casa. ¿Es nueva?
Sí, la casa de don Rafael es nueva.
2. María está vendiendo su tocadiscos. ¿Es portátil?
3. Don Pepe está vendiendo su finca. ¿Es grande?
4. Bernardo está vendiendo su coche. ¿Es azul?
5. Rosa está vendiendo su traje. ¿Es verde?

reading

Fragmento de una conferencia sobre la etimología hispánica

conferencia *lecture*

...La mayor parte de las palabras españolas vienen del latín. Puedo demostrárselo a ustedes sin ninguna dificultad. Por ejemplo, voy a leerles algunas líneas de la primera parte del diálogo "En la tintorería", que acabamos de estudiar. Se las voy a leer, como digo, pero si llego a una palabra *no* latina, en vez de la palabra

palabras *words*

Mexico City: Book store

voy a hacer una pausa. Escuchen ustedes con mucho cuidado (*leyendo*):

cuidado *care*

—¿Qué se le ofrece?
—Aquí traigo un... con...
—¿Ese?
—No, éstos son unos...; éste.
—¿Para cuándo la quiere?
—La... interior y las camisas para el martes y la dc cama para el sábado. Ah, este vestido de la señora y este traje del señor. *Etcétera, etcétera.*

Si ustedes siguen leyendo hasta el final y buscan los orígenes de las otras palabras en el gran diccionario de Corominas,[4] van a hallar solamente una palabra de origen no latino: la palabra *azul,* que deriva del árabe... Es una demostración... ejem... muy clara, ¿verdad? Y hay que notar también que las palabras no latinas son todas, o casi todas, sustantivos, o nombres. *Paquete,* por ejemplo, es palabra tomada directamente del francés; la palabra francesa es de origen neerlandés. *Ropa* tiene el mismo origen que *robar,* de origen germánico; su sentido primitivo era "despojos, botín". *Zapato* es de origen incierto: puede ser árabe. Se puede añadir que *cama, camisa* y *sábado,* aunque pasando al español por medio del latín, tienen orígenes diferentes: el de *cama* es oscuro; *camisa* viene del céltico, y *sábado* es hebreo en su origen más remoto. *Traje* no es una forma del pretérito de *traer;* es más bien un préstamo del portugués, aunque la forma portuguesa está relacionada con el verbo español...

hallar *to find*

nombres *nouns*

sentido *sense, meaning* **despojos** *spoils* **botín** *booty*
añadir *to add*
aunque *although* **por medio de** *by means of*

más bien *rather* **préstamo** *loanword*

[4] Joan Corominas is the author of the *Diccionario crítico etimológico de la lengua castellana,* published in Madrid in four volumes that appeared successively from 1954 to 1957.

UNIT 13

The University and Politics

A. *Don Antonio* R. *Ricardo* P. *Paperboy*

A. Ricardo! Ricardo! Come here. What's going on? Why's everybody running?

R. The police fired on [against] a student demonstration; it was something awful.

A. How terrible! Did they kill anyone?

R. I don't know if there were any killed, but I know there are more than ten wounded.

A. Murderers! Cowards! There's never been [existed] a government as bad as this one! But they'll pay for it all right.

R. Sh . . . calm down, Don Antonio, somebody'll [they can] hear you. Let's go inside and talk.

* * *

R. You know that today is the anniversary of the death of the university leader, Gustavo Díaz.

A. Yes, sure, and his comrades went to put flowers on his tomb. What's so bad about that?

R. Nothing, an admirable gesture. But it was also a pretext for speeches against the President.

La universidad y la política

A. *Don Antonio* R. *Ricardo* V. *Vendedor*

A. ¡Ricardo! ¡Ricardo! Venga acá. ¿Qué pasa? ¿Por qué anda toda la gente corriendo?

R. La policía disparó contra una manifestación de estudiantes, (1) algo horrible.

A. ¡Qué barbaridad! ¿Mataron a alguno?

R. No sé si hubo muertos pero sé que hay más de diez heridos.

A. ¡Asesinos! ¡Cobardes! ¡Un gobierno tan malo como éste jamás ha existido! Pero ya la pagarán. (2)

R. Sh..., cálmese, don Antonio, que lo pueden oir. Vamos a hablar adentro.

* * *

R. Usted sabe que hoy es el aniversario de la muerte del líder universitario, Gustavo Díaz.

A. Sí, claro, y sus compañeros fueron a ponerle flores a su tumba. ¿Qué hay de malo en eso?

R. Nada, un gesto admirable. Pero fue también un pretexto para discursos contra el Presidente.

Tegucigalpa, Honduras: Students and police

A. It serves him right [Very well done]. That tyrant deserves them. And then what? I suppose the police made onc of their shameful attacks upon them [attacked them infamously].

A. Muy bien hecho. Ese tirano se los merece. Y entonces ¿qué? La policía los atacó infamemente.

R. Yes, and without respecting the sacred place they were in, they broke up the demonstration with clubs and guns [shots].

R. Sí, y sin respetar el lugar sagrado donde estaban, disolvió la manifestación a palos y a tiros.

A. Scoundrels! I tell you things can't go on like this. Something's got to be done.

A. ¡Infames! Yo le digo a usted que esta situación no puede seguir así. Hay que hacer algo.

R. It's a good thing the elections are coming up soon. The opposition has a much stronger party than the government [the government's].

R. Menos mal que las elecciones vienen pronto. La oposición tiene un partido mucho más fuerte que el del gobierno.

A. But is it possible you still believe in free elections? Don't be so simple-minded. Only a revolution can carry us to power.

A. ¿Pero es que usted todavía cree en elecciones libres? No sea tan inocente. Sólo una revolución puede llevarnos al poder.

* * *

* * *

P.	Extra! Extra!! All about [With] the trouble [events] this morning at the cemetery! E-e-extra!!! Extra, sir?	V.	¡Extra! ¡¡Extra!! ¡Con los acontecimientos de esta mañana en el cementerio! ¡¡¡E-e-extra!!! ¿Extra, señor?
A.	Look at those headlines, Ricardo.	A.	Mire usted, Ricardo, esos titulares del periódico.
R.	Let's buy it, just so we can read the lies put out by the government.	R.	Vamos a comprarlo, no más para leer las mentiras del gobierno.

cultural notes

(1) Latin-American university students play a much more active role in the political life of their countries than do American college students. The university is regarded as an institution that provides informal apprenticeship in politics. Political leaders seek the support of the students. Students often cooperate with workers in labor strikes, and at times student demonstrations and uprisings have led to the fall of dictatorial regimes.

(2) See Unit 11, Cultural Note 4, for an explanation of indefinite **la.**

WRITING EXERCISE

A. The written representation of /s/ by **s** or **c** before **e** or **i.** INSTRUCTIONS: As the teacher dictates the following list, write each word in two ways (note that **z** does not occur in any of these words).

sien	cien	sebo	cebo	sera	cera	segar	cegar
seso	ceso	siervo	ciervo	sidra	cidra	coser	cocer
sima	cima	seda	ceda	sierra	cierra	sesión	cesión
sena	cena	sepa	cepa	serrar	cerrar	resiente	reciente
siento	ciento						

B. The written representation of /s/ by **s** or **z** before **a, o,** or **u.** INSTRUCTIONS: As the teacher dictates the following list, write each word in two ways (note that **c** does not occur in any of these words).

vos	voz	tasa	taza	rosa	roza	sueco	zueco
ves	vez	baso	bazo	poso	pozo	sonado	zonado
rasa	raza	laso	lazo	saga	zaga	asar	azar
masa	maza			sumo	zumo		

You have noted that the pairs of words in each double column of the exercises above are identical in pronunciation though spelled differently. Consequently, without a context there is no way of knowing how to spell them when you hear them.

In Castilian pronunciation, however, the letter **c** before **e** or **i,** and the letter **z** wherever it occurs, represent the voiceless interdental fricative [θ], corresponding to the voiceless *th* in English *thin.* Therefore, the pairs of words in each double column of A and B are pronounced differently and can be correctly differentiated in spelling when heard, whether or not a context is provided.

Before a consonant the variant [s] may be spelled **s** or **z** (e.g., **viscoso, vizconde, mescal, mezcla**), and the variant [z] may also be spelled **s** or **z** (e.g., **lesna, lezna, resma, rezno**). Whatever the spelling, the variant that occurs before a voiceless consonant is [s], and the variant that occurs before a voiced consonant is [z]. This is another instance of *assimilation.* (See also the discussion of the variants [s] and [z] in Unit 11.)

That Spanish spelling is not always consistent may be shown by the existence of such variants as **mesquite** and **mezquite, bisnieto** and **biznieto, cusma** and **cuzma, piesgo** and **piezgo,** etc. (See also Unit 12, Writing Exercise, page 185.)

C. The written representation of /s/ before a consonant by **s** or **x**. INSTRUCTIONS: Write the words in the following list as the teacher dictates them, remembering that /s/ before a consonant in the first word of each pair is written **s** and in the second word of the pair is written **x.**

esperar	explicar	estreno	extremo
espuela	expuesto	estraperlo	extranjero
espeso	expreso	escarpa	excava
espejar	expeler	misto	mixto
espolada	explanada		

The letter **x** in Spanish is normally found before a voiceless consonant or between vowels. Before a voiceless consonant **x** usually represents the sound [s]; between vowels **x** represents the sound group [gs] or [ks] as in **examen, existencia, taxi.** In a few words **x** between vowels represents the sound [s], e.g., **exacto** and **auxilio.**

To sum up, the phoneme /s/ in Spanish is written **s, z, c,** or **x;** the variant [z] may be written **s** or **z.**

Position of negative words other than *no*

EXAMPLES A. 1. A mí **nadie** me gana.
2. A mí **no** me gana **nadie.** } (*Nobody gets the better of me.*)

B. 1. **Nunca** les escribo.
2. **No** les escribo **nunca.** } *I never write to them.*

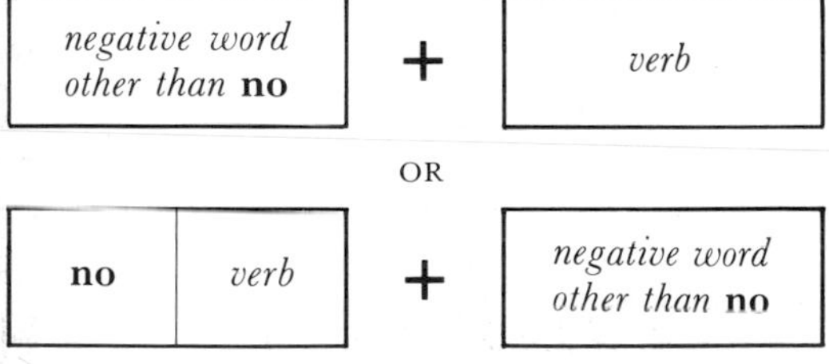

> The negative word other than **no** may be placed either before or after the verb that it negates. If after, **no** is added before the verb. (See Unit 3, Section 11.)

› ITEM SUBSTITUTION DRILL

INSTRUCTIONS: Repeat the following sentences just as you hear them. Then repeat them again, substituting **nunca** for **no.**

A. 1. *No* sé qué voy a hacer.
2. *No* estoy equivocado.
3. *No* puedo ir al mercado.
4. *No* participamos en natación.
5. *No* piensas en progresar.
6. *No* se la preguntaron.

B. 1. Paquito *no* me deja en paz.
2. Los agricultores *no* la pasan mal, ¿eh?
3. Yo *no* les escribo.
4. Ellos *no* hablan inglés.
5. Ellos *no* me entienden nada.

› CONSTRUCTION SUBSTITUTION DRILL

INSTRUCTIONS: Repeat the following sentences just as you hear them. Then repeat them again, moving **nunca** to a position after the verb, which requires adding **no** before the verb.

A. 1. TEACHER: Ellos *nunca* regatean. *Repita.*
STUDENT: **Ellos nunca regatean.**
TEACHER: *Cambie.*
STUDENT: **Ellos no regatean nunca.**
2. Yo *nunca* corrí.
3. *Nunca* disparamos.
4. *Nunca* digas eso.
5. *Nunca* trabaje usted aquí.

B. 1. El abogado *nunca* exagera.
2. Los alumnos *nunca* duermen.
3. La policía *nunca* ataca.
4. Los profesores *nunca* discuten.

› DISCUSSION

The negative words other than **no,** unlike **no** itself (whose position relative to the verb is fixed, see Unit 3, Section 11), are relatively free as to position. For effects similar to those in English—for example, *I never write to them* vs. *I don't write to them ever* (*at any time*)—the negative words may precede or follow the verb. When they follow, **no** is placed before the verb.

67 Negative words (other than *no*) and their affirmative counterparts

EXAMPLES

A. 1. Me contó que necesitaba a **alguien.**
Para regatear, a mí **nadie** me gana.
2. Hay que hacer **algo.**
No oigo **nada.**
3. Es **algo** fenomenal.
No es **nada** serio.
4. **Algún día** voy allá. *Some day I'm going there.*
Nunca les escribo.
Un gobierno tan malo como éste **jamás** ha existido.
5. ¿Recibiste **alguna** mala noticia?
No recibí **ninguna.** *I didn't receive any.*
6. ¿Pongo arroz **también?**
Yo tengo muchos parientes en el extranjero, pero nunca les escribo. —Yo **tampoco.**
7. ¿Qué día es hoy, jueves **o** viernes?
Hoy no es **ni** jueves **ni** viernes. *Today is neither Thursday nor Friday.*

B. 1. **Ninguna** otra profesión es posible.
No es posible **ninguna** otra profesión. } *No other profession is possible.*
2. **Nada** puede entrar.
No puede entrar **nada.** } *Nothing can get in.*
3. **Ni** Juan **ni** Pablo pueden[1] hacerlo.
No puede hacerlo **ni** Juan **ni** Pablo. } (*Neither Juan nor Pablo can do it.*)
4. **Tampoco** lo creo yo. (*Neither do I believe it.*)
No lo creo yo **tampoco.** (*I don't believe it either.*)

[1] Singular nouns joined by **o** or **ni** and preceding the verb normally take a plural verb.

AFFIRMATIVE		NEGATIVE	
*some*one	**alguien**	no one, not *any*one	**nadie**
*some*thing	**algo**	nothing, not *any*thing	**nada**
*some*day	**algún día**	never, not ever, not at *any* time	**nunca** / **jamás**
some, either (one)	**alguno(s), -a(s)**	no, none, not *any,* neither (one)	**ninguno, -a**[2]
also	**también**	neither, not either	**tampoco**
either . . . or	**o . . . o**	neither . . . nor	**ni . . . ni**

The affirmative-negative contrast in Spanish is like the *some-any* contrast in English. All these Spanish negative words have the choice of positions discussed in Section 66.

› CONSTRUCTION SUBSTITUTION DRILL

INSTRUCTIONS: Repeat the following sentences just as you hear them. Then repeat them again, substituting the negative counterpart of the emphasized form and adding **no** before the verb.

A. 1. TEACHER: Hay *alguien* adentro. *Repita.*
STUDENT: **Hay alguien adentro.**
TEACHER: *Cambie.*
STUDENT: **No hay nadie adentro.**
2. La manifestación es *algo* serio.
3. Vamos al cementerio *algún día.*
4. ¿Es *alguna* manifestación?
5. Yo tengo un discurso *también.*
6. El presidente es *o* tirano *o* cobarde.

B. 1. Necesitaban a *alguien.*
2. Pero se puede hacer *algo.*
3. Debe conocer al presidente *algún día.*
4. ¿Recibiste *alguna* mala noticia?
5. Pongo flores en la lista *también.*
6. Ellos son *o* cobardes *o* asesinos.

› ITEM SUBSTITUTION DRILL

INSTRUCTIONS: Repeat the following sentences just as you hear them. Then repeat them again, making the negative words affirmative.

A. 1. TEACHER: La policía nunca ataca. *Repita.*
STUDENT: **La policía nunca ataca.**
TEACHER: *Cambie.*
STUDENT: **La policía algún día ataca.**
2. *Ninguno* pudo disparar.
3. *Nada* horrible va a pasar.
4. *Nadie* es tan inocente.
5. *Tampoco* tenemos elecciones libres.
6. *Ni* Carlos *ni* Pablo son inocentes.
7. *Jamás* va a haber un gobierno tan malo.

B. 1. *Tampoco* fue un gesto admirable.
2. *Nadie* tiene el poder.
3. *Ninguno* fue atacado infamemente.
4. *Jamás* hay que pensar en progresar.
5. *Nada* puede disolver esta manifestación.
6. Los estudiantes *ni* hicieron una huelga *ni* atacaron al gobierno.

[2] The plurals **ningunos, -as** rarely appear except in reference to mass plurals such as *leaves, grains, hairs,* or plural stereotypes such as *trousers, shears, pliers,* etc.: **ningunas tijeras** *no scissors.* For *no lessons* Spanish prefers *no lesson:* **ninguna lección.**

❯ CONSTRUCTION SUBSTITUTION DRILL

INSTRUCTIONS: Repeat the following sentences just as you hear them. Then repeat them again, placing the negative word or phrase at the end, which will require adding **no** before the verb.

1. TEACHER: *Nadie* lo merece. *Repita.*
   STUDENT: **Nadie lo merece.**
   TEACHER: *Cambie.*
   STUDENT: **No lo merece nadie.**
2. *Nada* puede llevarlo al poder.
3. *Ninguno de ustedes* viene mañana.
4. *Nunca* veo los titulares.
5. *Tampoco* lo dice el líder.
6. *Ni Alfredo ni Roberto* están en el partido.

❯ TRANSLATION DRILL

INSTRUCTIONS: Translate the following pairs of sentences, placing the emphasized elements last in the Spanish.

1. TEACHER: Nobody *deserves it.*
   STUDENT: **Nadie lo merece.**
   TEACHER: *Nobody* deserves it.
   STUDENT: **No lo merece nadie.**
2. Neither Alfredo nor Roberto *is in the party.*
   Neither Alfredo nor Roberto is in the party.
3. Nothing *can happen to you.*
   Nothing can happen to you.
4. None of you *want to come tomorrow?*
   None of you want to come tomorrow?
5. Never do I see *the headlines.*
   I don't *ever* see the headlines.

❯ DISCUSSION

The negative words in the box above are not permitted after the verb unless a negative also precedes the verb.

Although changing the position of the negative word produces effects similar to those in English (see Section 66), the restrictions on word order in English often make the comparison difficult to see. The second sentence Example in B3 above, for example, requires us to say something like *It can't be done by either Juan or Pablo* in order to maneuver *Juan or Pablo* to the end so as to get a parallel contrast with *Neither Juan nor Pablo can do it;* English does not permit *No can do it either Juan or Pablo.*

Ninguno differs from **cualquier(a)** (see Unit 10, Section 52) in that it is merely the negative of *some,* whereas **cualquier(a)** means *just any:* **No compre ninguna pintura** *Don't buy any painting* (*Buy no painting*), **No compre cualquier pintura** *Don't buy any* (*just any*) *painting* (*Be particular about what painting you buy*). English makes this distinction by means of intonation, using a terminal fall plus rise when the sense is **cualquier(a).**

The **alguien-nadie** pair differs from the **alguno-ninguno** pair in that the latter normally refers to a member of a group already held in mind. For example, **¿Alguno de ustedes trajo plata?** refers to a member of the known **ustedes** group; **¿Mataron a alguno?** in the dialog refers to a member of a known group of demonstrators: *any one of them.*

Since **alguno** may refer to one of a group of two as well as one of a group of more than two, it may be translated by *either* (e.g., *either of you two*) as well as by *some* (*some one of you three*).

68 Negatives other than *no* both before and after the verb

EXAMPLES

A. 1. **Nadie** dijo **nada.** *Nobody said anything.*
2. **Tampoco** vi a **nadie.** *I didn't see anybody either.*
3. **Nadie nunca** dice **nada.** *Nobody ever says anything.*

B. 1. Entró **sin** pagar **nada.** *She got in without paying anything.*
2. **Sin** llamar a **nadie.** *Without calling anyone.*

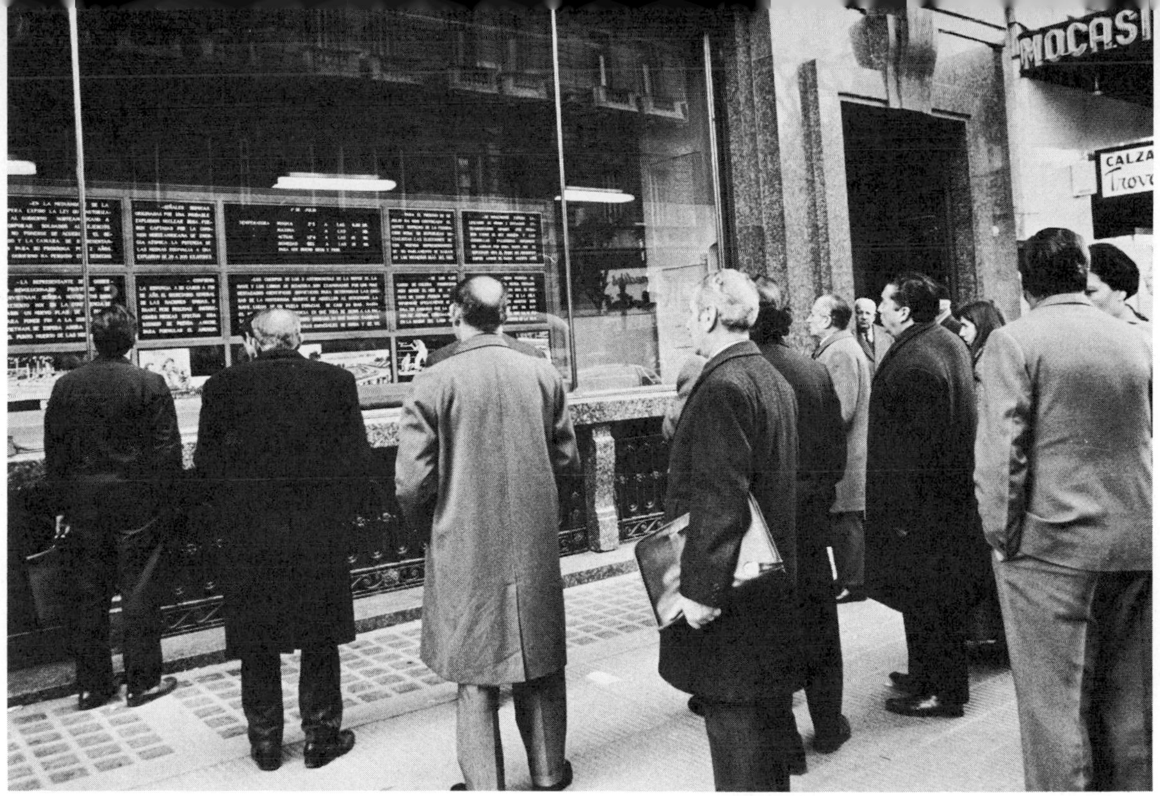

Buenos Aires: Offices of *La Prensa*

C. 1. **No** dijo **nadie nada.** *Nobody said anything.*
2. Yo **no** vi a **nadie tampoco.** *I didn't see anybody either.*
3. **No** dice **nadie nunca nada.** *Nobody ever says anything.*

negative word other than **no**	+	*verb*	+	*negative word other than* **no**

no *verb*	+	*negative word other than* **no**	+	*negative word other than* **no**

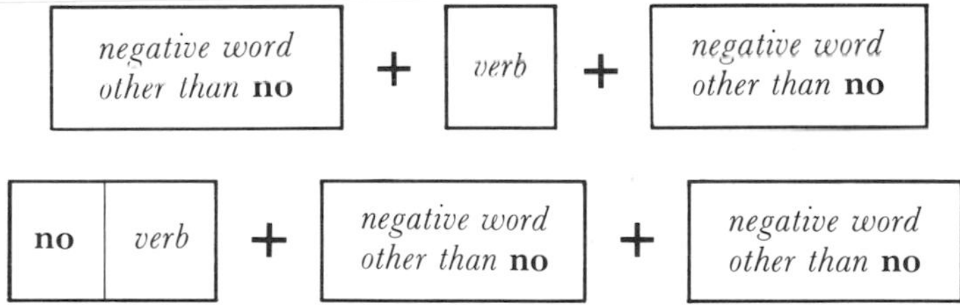

It is necessary to add **no** before the verb if the other negative words follow the verb, but not if at least one precedes the verb. (For the latter purpose an implied negative such as **sin** is sufficient.)

› TRANSLATION DRILL

1. Nobody said anything.
2. Never does anything happen.
3. Neither of you is going to come, ever.
4. Neither of them saw anybody.
5. Nobody believes that either.
6. Neither is there any employee.
7. Nobody left any message for you.
8. Never is there anything bad there.

› DISCUSSION

The "implied negatives" referred to under the table are parallel to the words in English that call for *any* rather than *some:* compare *We* ***hardly*** *need* ***anything*** and *We* ***surely*** *need* ***something.***

Position of *no* in contradictions and reservations

EXAMPLES

1. Sí, pero tu papá...
   No, él **no;** ella, mi mamá.
2. ¿Quieres ir conmigo al restorán?
   Sí, pero esta vez **no** sin plata, hombre. (*Yes, but this time not without money, old boy.*)

CONTRADICTIONS		
FIRST SPEAKER	X	
SECOND SPEAKER	X	**no**

RESERVATIONS		
FIRST SPEAKER		X
SECOND SPEAKER	**no**	X

To repeat and contradict something that another has just said, **no** is normally placed after it; to express a reservation, **no** is placed before it.

TRANSLATION DRILL

A. 1. TEACHER: Is he coming?
STUDENT: **¿Viene él?**
TEACHER: No, he's not, she is.
STUDENT: **No, él no; ella.**
2. Is the record player broken?
No, not the record player; the car.
3. Do you want wheat?
No, not wheat; rice.
4. Do I have to sit down?
No, not sit down; stay in the city.
5. And was it a meeting?
No, not a meeting; a demonstration.
6. Did she go upstairs?
No, not upstairs; downstairs.

B. 1. Shall I bring my brothers?
¿Traigo a mis hermanos?
Yes, but not the youngest.
Sí, pero no al menor.
2. Do you want the books?
Yes, but not the green one.
3. Tomorrow is your saint's day?
Yes, but not my birthday.
4. Is that your party?
Yes, but not my group.
5. Do you like the idea?
Yes, but not the excuse.

DISCUSSION

End position is favored for things that are new or strange to the context. In **él no, él** (**tu papá**) has already been mentioned. (If the speaker had said **no él,** it would be like an exclamation, **¡No él!** *Anybody but him!* as if the whole idea were outlandish.) In **no sin plata** the **sin plata** is new to the context.

There is a suggestion of "yes, but" in reservations, although the words may not necessarily be expressed. Thus in answer to *Shall I bring my brothers?* **¿Traigo a mis hermanos?** the reply would be **No al menor** to imply "It's all right so long as the youngest isn't included" but **Al menor, no** to imply "If you mean the youngest the answer is no." In the first, **el menor** occurs to the speaker as an exception, a new idea; in the second, **el menor** is assumed to be something that the other person already has in mind. The same contrast can be observed in English where the word order is flexible enough to permit it, e.g., to the question *Do you get much work done?* one might answer *At home, hardly ever* or *Hardly ever at home.* Elsewhere the contrast is shown by intonation: **Al menor, no** and **No al menor,** in the above example would be, respectively

not / the / young / est   not / the / young / est

The "new idea" (*youngest*) in the second pattern is characteristically spoken with a high pitch.

70 Personal *a* with indefinites

EXAMPLES

1. ¿Mataron **a alguno?**
2. No mataron **a ninguno.** *They didn't kill any (any one of the known group).*
3. Necesitaba **a alguien.**
4. No vi **a nadie.** *I didn't see anybody.*

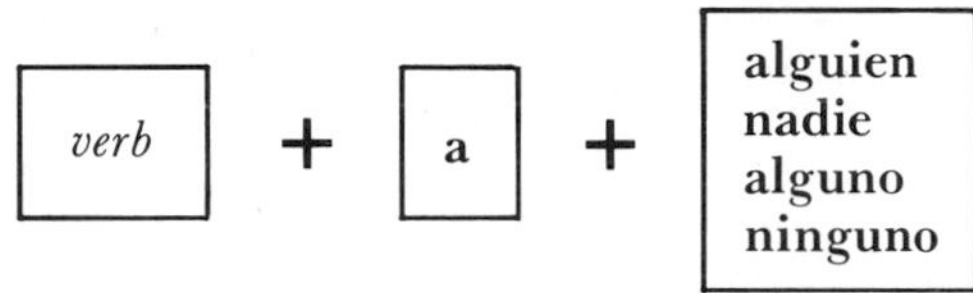

As object of a verb the indefinite words **alguien, nadie, alguno,** and **ninguno** call for the personal **a.**

EXAMPLES

1. Necesito **un médico.** *I need a doctor (any doctor).*
2. Trajeron **muchos heridos.** *They brought in a lot of wounded.*
3. Van a mandar **un equipo** muy grande.

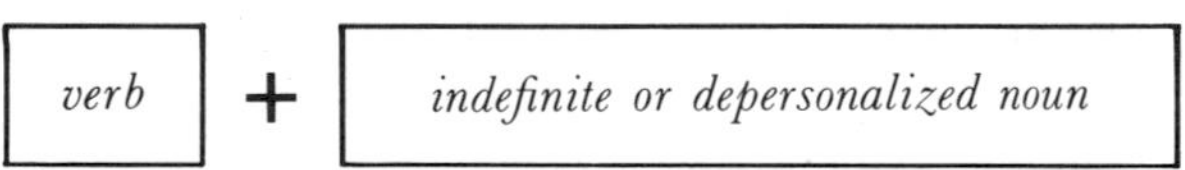

When a noun that does not refer to a definite person or persons, or one that refers to people in the mass as if they were things, is the direct object of a verb, no personal **a** is used.

› TRANSLATION DRILL

A. 1. I don't see anybody.
   2. I see someone.
   3. I don't see any of them.
   4. I see some of them.
   5. Do you need anybody?
   6. I don't need anyone.
   7. Do you want to meet some of them?
   8. I don't want to meet any of them.

B. 1. I need a doctor.
   2. I need a lawyer.
   3. I need a business man.
   4. I need a technician.
   5. I need a maid.
   6. I need an administrator.
   7. I need a leader.

C. 1. They're going to send a big team.
   2. They're going to send a big group.
   3. They're going to discuss a Ministry.
   4. They're going to organize a party.

› DISCUSSION

Indefiniteness in general makes it possible to use a personal noun as direct object of a verb without introducing it with the personal **a.** The four indefinites **alguien, nadie, alguno,** and **ninguno,** however, do call for the **a.**

71 Indefinites in affirmative questions

EXAMPLES
1. ¿Mataron a **alguno?**
2. ¿Le escribe a **alguien,** don Rafael?
3. ¿Vio usted a **alguien?** *Did you see someone (anyone)?*
4. ¿Tiene usted **algo?** *Do you have something (anything)?*
5. ¿Va usted allí **alguna** vez? *Are you going there sometime (any time, ever)?*

some –one –body –thing etc. any –one –body –thing etc.	**alguno**(s), **–a**(s) **alguien** **algo** **etc.**

Spanish does not make the distinction in affirmative questions that are made between *some* and *any* in English.

› PATTERNED RESPONSE DRILL

INSTRUCTIONS: Answer the following questions with short answers, omitting nouns, adverbs, and with-preposition pronouns.

1. ¿Necesita algo ahora?
   No, no necesito nada.
2. ¿Necesita algún libro?
   No, no necesito ninguno.
3. ¿Conoce a alguien en la ciudad?
4. ¿Quiere algo aquí?
5. ¿Vio a alguno de ellos?
6. ¿Dejó algo para mí?
7. ¿Hay alguna noticia?
8. ¿Está llamando a alguien?
9. ¿Ganó alguno de ustedes?
10. ¿Desea ver algún periódico?
11. ¿Necesita algunas tijeras?

› TRANSLATION DRILL

A. 1. Did you see some of them?
2. Did you write to someone?
3. Did you leave something?
4. Did you ever go there (Did you go there sometime)?

B. 1. Did you see any of them?
2. Did you write to anyone?
3. Did you leave anything?
4. Did you go there any time?

72 Definite article for "definite wholes"

EXAMPLES A. 1. ¿Tiene **ganado?** *Does he have (any) livestock?*
2. Va a vender **el ganado que tiene.** *He's going to sell the livestock he has.*

B. 1. Un poco menos **cebolla,** si me hace el favor. *A little less onion, please.*
2. ¿Dónde puse **las cebollas?** *Where did I put the onions?*

C. 1. A mí me gusta muchísimo el campo: **aire puro, montañas, nubes, cielo azul, árboles, gente sencilla...**
2. Hoy es **el aniversario** de **la muerte del líder.**

el, la, los, las	*all of a single thing or set of things*

English and Spanish are alike in using the definite article to specify a single thing or set of things and in omitting it to suggest *some*, *any*, or an indefinite mass.

EXAMPLES
1. **Los agricultores** no la pasan mal, ¿eh?
2. **La filosofía** es demasiado difícil.
3. **La cebolla** es buena con **la carne.** *Onion is good with meat.*
4. No discutamos **del dinero.** *Let's not argue about money.*
5. No me gustan **las ciudades grandes.** *I don't like big cities.*

el, la, los, las	*an entire mass or collectivity*

Spanish, unlike English, uses the definite article to refer to all of something.

› TRANSLATION DRILL

A. 1. Good meat costs a lot.
2. Rice is good.
3. Money is necessary.
4. Death is horrible.
5. People are simple.
6. Petroleum is important.

B. 1. Children are innocent.
2. New ideas are important.
3. Anniversaries are ridiculous.
4. Tyrants are infamous.
5. Old cemeteries are sacred.
6. Spanish furniture is pretty.
7. Portable record players are bad.

C. 1. They tell lies.
They don't respect lies.
2. We're paying in pesetas.
We believe in pesetas.
3. The university needs students.
The university thinks about students.
4. The country needs leaders.
Let's not argue about leaders.
5. They are demanding elections.
They are attacking elections.
6. They ask the leader for speeches.
They tell him that they like speeches.

EXAMPLES
1. **Toda la carne** cuesta mucho. *All (the) meat costs a lot.*
2. **Todas las huelgas** fueron inútiles. *Every strike was (All the strikes were, Every one of the strikes was) useless.*
3. **Toda huelga** es inútil. (*Every [Any] strike is useless.*)

all		**todo(s), –a(s)**	**el, la, los, las**	
every (*all of a limited number*)	*noun*	**todos, –as**	**los, las**	*noun*
every (*unlimited totality*)		**todo, –a**		

When *every* is used in a universal sense, the Spanish equivalent is **todo, –a** (singular) without the article. The equivalent of *all* is normally **todo, –a, –os, –as** with the article.

› TRANSLATION DRILL

A. 1. All meat costs a lot.
   2. All rice is good.
   3. All money is useless.
   4. All opposition is difficult.

B. 1. Every class was difficult.
   2. Every day was long.
   3. Every hour was necessary.
   4. Every school is modern.
   5. Every receipt was important.

C. 1. Every subject is important.
   2. Every professor is half crazy.
   3. Every election is different.
   4. Every man is complicated.
   5. Every new idea is admirable.

› DISCUSSION

In most respects the definite article has the same uses in Spanish as in English. In both languages it is used to specify particular things; note the difference between *They threw it in the water* (a particular body of water) and *They threw it in water.* But Spanish goes farther in calling for the definite article also to specify all of something. English does this sporadically (*He likes the movies* vs. *He likes television*); Spanish does it consistently.

More often than not, when a noun would be used in English without the article but in Spanish with the article, it will be found to be a subject noun rather than an object noun. This is because we ordinarily do not operate on wholes but on parts: in **Como carne** *I eat meat,* one eats only as much meat as he has within reach. One can *discuss* meat as a whole, but not *eat* it as a whole, and most verbs are like *eat* rather than like *discuss.* When a noun is the subject there is no such problem: **La carne es buena** *Meat is good* clearly refers to the whole.

Since *all* normally specifies wholes, it normally calls for the article in Spanish whether the article does occur (*all the money*) or does not occur (*all money*) in English. But Spanish *todo* translates not only *all* but also *every.* In the latter sense we must distinguish between a limited *every* (*Every member present voted = All the members present voted*) and an unlimited *every* (*Every election should be honest*). The latter calls for **todo, –a** in the singular without the article.

73 Definite article with places

EXAMPLES

A. 1. Nos encontramos en **el Club de la Unión.**
   2. Se iba a trabajar **al campo.**

B. 1. ¿Por qué no fuiste **al colegio** ayer?
   2. Hay cientos en **la cárcel.** *There are hundreds in jail.*

3. Voy **al mercado.** *I'm going to (the) market.*
4. Viene **del trabajo.** *He's coming from work.*

C. 1. Voy a **clase.** *I'm going to class.*
2. Está en **casa.** *He's (at) home.*

from (*and other prepositions*)	A. the country, the ranch, the club (*and most other nouns*)	
	B. school, jail, market	(*and a few other nouns*)
	C. class, home	

de (*and other prepositions*)	**A. el campo, la finca, el club**	(*and most other nouns*)
	B. el colegio, la cárcel, el mercado	
	C. clase, casa	

In prepositional phrases most nouns indicating place, such as *office, store, club,* etc., require the article in both English and Spanish. With the few for which English omits it, such as *jail, town, school,* Spanish usually requires it. *Class* and *home* are exceptions in that both English and Spanish omit the article.

› TRANSLATION DRILL

A. 1. I'm going to the country.
2. I'm going to the inauguration.
3. I'm going to the cleaner's.
4. I'm going to the Ministry.
5. I'm going to the bullfight.
6. I'm going to the bank.
7. I'm going to the meeting.
8. I'm going to the demonstration.

B. 1. I'm going to school.
2. I'm going to market.

C. 1. He's coming from class.
2. He's coming from home.

› DISCUSSION

Both English and Spanish have nouns of the *home, school, class* type for which one or the other language, or both languages, do not require the article. They are nouns that refer to places where some activity goes on, and the reference is as much to the activity as to the place; for example, *to go to church* refers to the SERVICE at the church; *to go to class* means to participate in the class SESSION, etc. The difficulty is that English and Spanish do not usually agree on which nouns to regard in this way. **Voy a clase** is *I'm going to class,* and **Voy a la clase** is *I'm going to the class;* the contrast of usage and meaning is the same in Spanish as in English. **Estoy en casa** *I'm at home* and **Estoy en la casa** *I'm at (in) the house* again show a similar contrast. If you are unsure, usually it is safer to add the article in Spanish: *I'm going to (the) lab* **Voy al laboratorio.**

The definite article was traditionally used with certain geographical names in Spanish such as **el Canadá, el Brasil, la Argentina,** etc. (compare English *the Argentine, the Congo, the Yukon*). This practice is fading, with the result that instances either with or without the article may be found; for example, in the dialogs we have both **países como Estados Unidos** and **de los Estados Unidos.**

74 Articles with days of the week

EXAMPLES

A. 1. El trece de marzo fue domingo. *The thirteenth of March was (a) Sunday.*
2. ¿Hoy es martes? *Is today Tuesday?*

B. 1. Llegó el jueves. *He arrived (on) Thursday.*
2. Llegó un jueves. } *He arrived on a Thursday.*
3. Llegó en un jueves. }

C. 1. El sábado es el día que me gusta más. *Saturday is the day I like best.*
2. Los domingos aquí son muy tranquilos. *Sundays here are very quiet.*
3. Los viernes no trabajo. *(On) Fridays I don't work.*

A. IDENTIFICATIONS

Today is Tomorrow is Day after tomorrow is Yesterday was Day before yesterday was The second of May was (a)	Sunday. Monday. Tuesday. Wednesday. Thursday. Friday. Saturday.	**Hoy es** **Mañana es** **Pasado mañana es** **Ayer fue** **Anteayer fue** **El dos de mayo fue**	**domingo.** **lunes.** **martes.** **miércoles.** **jueves.** **viernes.** **sábado.**

B. HAPPENINGS

definite day	He arrived on Thursday.	**Llegó el jueves.**
indefinite day	He arrived on a Thursday.	**Llegó** { **un** / **en** / **en un** } **jueves.**

C. GENERALIZATIONS

Tuesday is the third day of the week. Wednesdays I stay home.	**El martes es el tercer día de la semana.** **Los miércoles me quedo en casa.**

› PATTERNED RESPONSE DRILL

INSTRUCTIONS: Answer the questions, following the models given.

A. 1. Después del domingo, ¿qué día es?
Es lunes.
2. Después del martes, ¿qué día es?
3. Después del sábado, ¿qué día es?
4. Después del lunes, ¿qué día es?
5. Después del viernes, ¿qué día es?
6. Después del miércoles, ¿qué día es?
7. Después del jueves, ¿qué día es?

B. 1. ¿Qué días viene usted a clase?
Vengo el lunes, el martes...
Vengo los lunes, los martes...

C. 1. ¿Qué día es hoy?
Hoy es martes.
2. ¿Qué día es mañana?
3. ¿Qué día es pasado mañana?
4. ¿Qué día fue ayer?
5. ¿Qué día fue anteayer?

TRANSLATION DRILL

A. 1. My birthday was on Friday.
The strike is going to be on a Wednesday.
2. That dinner was on Saturday.
The demonstration is going to be on a Thursday.
3. Our exams are on Mondays.
The game is going to be on a Wednesday.

B. 1. Is today Saturday?
2. The meeting was on Friday.
3. Sundays, she used to call us at nine.
4. The eleventh of December was (a) Tuesday.
5. Thursday is the day I like best.
6. Mondays here are very sad.
7. (On) Wednesdays I don't go to class.

DISCUSSION

English regards the names of the days of the week as proper nouns. Spanish regards them as common nouns and uses the definite and indefinite articles with them in much the same ways as with other common nouns.

To match a day of the month—or any one of the special words **hoy, mañana, pasado mañana, ayer,** and **anteayer**—with a day of the week no article is used: **Hoy es jueves, El dos de julio es sábado,** etc.

To name the day on which something happens the definite article is used for a definite day and the indefinite article (or **en** or both combined) is used for an indefinite day. English similarly uses the indefinite article for indefiniteness, *He arrived on a Monday* **Llegó un** (**en, en un**) **lunes,** but uses no article at all for definiteness: *He arrived* (*on*) *Monday* (on *the* Monday of this week) **Llegó el lunes;** *He's going to arrive* (*on*) *Monday* (on *the* Monday of next week) **Va a llegar el lunes;** *He arrived last Monday* **Llegó el lunes pasado.**

To generalize about every Sunday, for example, or about all Sundays the definite article is used, as explained in Section 72: *Sunday* (every Sunday) *is a day of rest* **El domingo es día de descanso;** *I go* (*on*) *Mondays* (Mondays in general are my days for going) **Voy los lunes.**

GUIDED CONVERSATION

A. *Arturo* E. *Enfermera*[3]

A. ¿Dónde estoy? ¿Por qué me duele[4] tanto la cabeza?
E. Señor, usted está en la clínica central con algunos de sus compañeros.
A. Ya recuerdo. La tumba... La policía ______________
E. ¿Pero qué hacían ustedes en el cementerio?
A. ¿No recuerda usted que hoy es ______________
E. Sí, pero el periódico menciona algo de discursos contra el Presidente.
A. Muy bien hecho. ______________
E. Sh..., cálmese, señor.
A. ¡Cómo puedo calmarme! Yo le digo a usted ______________
E. Pero no olvide usted que muy pronto vienen las elecciones y que la oposición tiene un partido muy fuerte.
A. ¿Pero es que usted ______________
E. Señor, tenga la bondad de calmarse. Hay más de diez heridos graves aquí. Usted no es el único.[5]
A. ¡Asesinos! ______________

[3] *nurse* [4] *hurts* [5] *only one*

Word order in information questions.

A. 1. When did *he* come?
2. Where did *he* go?
3. Why did *he* leave?
4. How did *he* eat?
5. How much did *he* pay?
6. How many did *he* bring?
7. Which did *he* see?
8. What did *he* do?

B. 1. When did John come?
2. Where did John go?
3. Why did John leave?
4. How did John eat?
5. How much did John pay?
6. How many did John bring?
7. Which did John see?
8. What did John do?

reading

Dos puntos de vista

I

Todo el mundo sabe ahora los tristes resultados de la manifestación de estudiantes que se hizo anteanoche en el cementerio. Con el pretexto de celebrar el aniversario de la muerte de su "líder martirizado" Gustavo Díaz, cuyas actividades eran bien conocidas de la policía de la ciudad, cientos de estos estudiantes, en vez de quedarse en sus casas estudiando para sus carreras, fueron a poner flores en la tumba de Díaz, según dijeron. No sabemos exactamente cómo empezó el lío, pero parece que algunos estudiantes llevaban palos y revólveres, y que se enfrentaron a la policía en el propósito de ejercer su deber de mantener el orden público. Al ser atacada la policía, tuvo que defenderse y unos pocos estudiantes resultaron levemente heridos. También fue necesario llevar a unos cuantos estudiantes a la cárcel para aclarar detalles del acontecimiento. En fin, creemos que un gobierno tiene que gobernar y que la policía debe mantener el orden. De otra manera no puede existir ninguna democracia. (Editorial de *El Conservador,* 17 de agosto de 1972.)

cuyas *whose*
según *according to what*
empezar *to begin*
enfrentarse a *to interfere with*
propósito de *attempts to*
deber *obligation* **Al...policía** *When the police were attacked*
levemente *slightly*
cárcel *jail*

II

La brutal acción de la policía, al disparar anteanoche contra una manifestación de estudiantes en el cementerio, donde se hallaban reunidos para celebrar el aniversario de la muerte del héroe y mártir Gustavo Díaz, casi no tiene paralelo en los anales históricos de nuestra patria. Fue acción de cobardes y asesinos. Los estudiantes estaban allí sólo para rendir homenaje a la memoria de un gran hombre. Sin respetar el sagrado lugar donde estaban, la policía los atacó infamemente y disolvió la manifestación a palos y a tiros.

patria *country, fatherland*

Mexico City: University students on strike

Doce estudiantes quedaron gravemente heridos y tres de ellos están para morir. Cientos fueron llevados a la cárcel. Acabamos de oir que los otros están declarando una huelga general en todo el país.

para morir *on the point of death*

La situación no puede seguir así. El gobierno debe poner en libertad a los estudiantes que están en la cárcel. A los heridos hay que darles las mejores atenciones médicas, a costa del gobierno. Por último recordamos a nuestros lectores que las elecciones vienen pronto. El partido liberal va a ser bastante más fuerte a consecuencia de estos acontecimientos, y el triunfo de este partido es necesario para la restitución de nuestras instituciones democráticas. (Editorial de *El Liberal,* 17 de agosto de 1972.)

a costa de *at the expense of*
lectores *readers*

UNIT 14

A Medical Appointment

R. *Ricardo* N. *Nurse* D. *Doctor*

R. Good morning, ma'am [miss].
N. Good morning. Do you want to see the doctor?
R. Yes, ma'am. I have an appointment with him for eleven o'clock.
N. Your name, please?
R. Ricardo Mendoza.
N. Of course. Now I remember. Come right in.

* * *

D. Come in [Forward, Ahead], Mr. Mendoza. How are you?
R. Just so-so.
D. Please [Have the goodness to] sit down. Tell me what seems to be the trouble [you feel].
R. I think I've got the flu, doctor. I ache all over [All the body aches on me].
D. With this winter weather everybody's got a cold. They've all got a headache and a sore throat [To them all the head and the throat ache].
R. What should I do, doctor?
D. Let's see. First tell me how long [how much time it makes that] you've been feeling this way.
R. About three days.
D. Are you taking anything?
R. Yes, aspirin. Yesterday I took five.
D. Take off your shirt and tie. Put this thermometer under your tongue.

* * *

Una visita al médico

R. *Ricardo* E. *Enfermera* M. *Médico*

R. Buenos días, señorita.
E. Buenos días. ¿Quiere ver al doctor?
R. Sí, señorita. Tengo hora con él para las once.
E. ¿Su nombre, por favor?
R. Ricardo Mendoza.
E. Ah, claro. Ahora me acuerdo. Pase usted.

* * *

M. Adelante, Sr. Mendoza. ¿Cómo está usted?
R. Así, así, regular.
M. Tenga la bondad de sentarse. Dígame qué siente.
R. Creo que tengo gripe, doctor. Me duele todo el cuerpo.
M. Con este invierno todo el mundo está resfriado. A todos les duele la cabeza y la garganta.
R. ¿Y qué debo hacer, doctor?
M. A ver. Primero dígame cuánto tiempo hace que se siente así.
R. Como tres días.
M. ¿Está tomando algo?
R. Sí, aspirinas. Ayer me tomé cinco.
M. Quítese la corbata y la camisa. Póngase este termómetro debajo de la lengua.

* * *

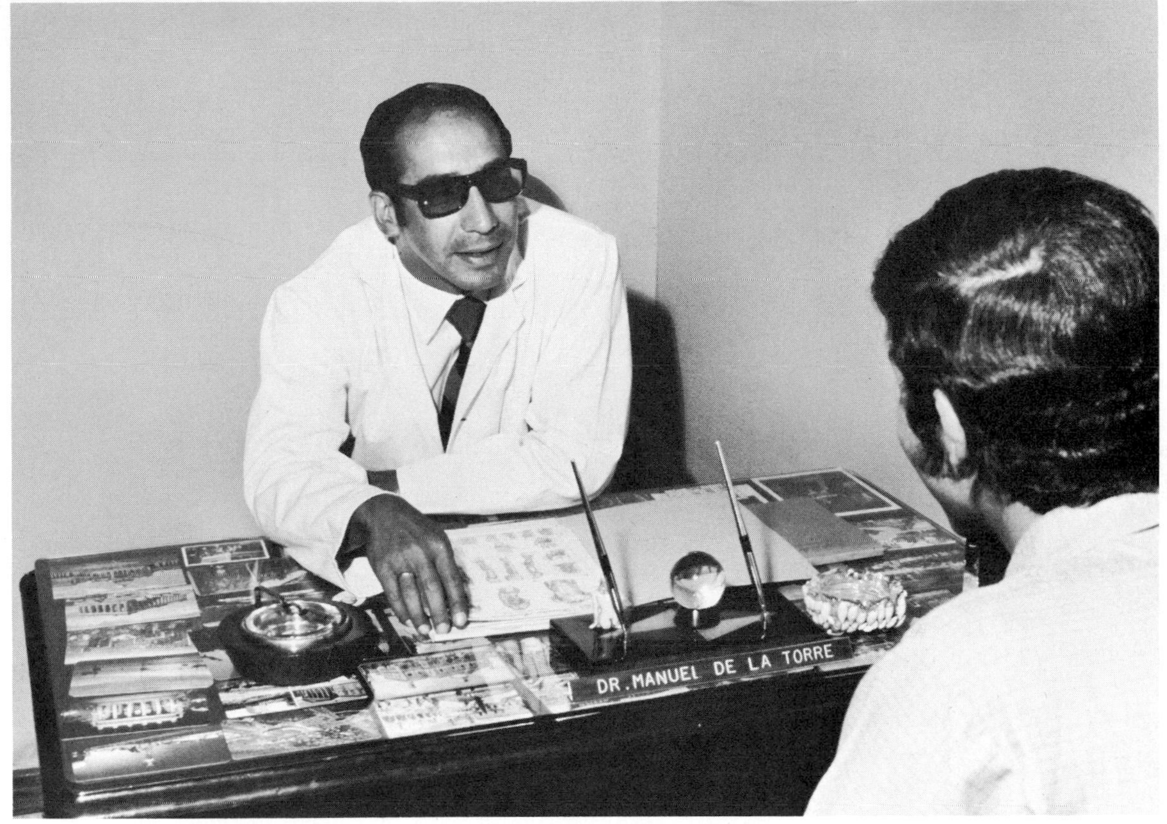

Mexico City: Doctor's office

R. Do I have a fever?
D. Just a little. You must go home and go to bed. Take this prescription with you.
R. Go to bed?
D. Yes, and when you get home, take these pills with a hot lemonade. And don't take a bath [bathe yourself] tomorrow.
R. But, doctor, I have to get up tomorrow.
D. My friend, there're no buts about it [there's no but that is worth (while)].

R. ¿Tengo fiebre?
M. Sí, un poquito. Tiene que irse a su casa y acostarse. Llévese esta receta.
R. ¿Acostarme?
M. Sí, y al llegar, tómese estas pastillas con una limonada bien caliente. Y mañana no se bañe.
R. Pero doctor, tengo que levantarme mañana.
M. Mi amigo, no hay pero que valga.

› WRITING EXERCISE

The written representation of /x/ by **g** or **j**. INSTRUCTIONS: Write the following lists of words from dictation.

jarra	joven	junto	gente	gis
jaula	jota	jugo	gesto	Gil
jarabe	jobo	julio	genio	giro
jarana	joya	junio	género	gigante

jalea	joropo	jueves	gerente	ginebra
jamás	jornada	jurar	gemelo	gitano
jardín	joroba	jugar	geografía	giralda
jabón	jocoso	justicia	geometría	ginesta
jamón	jornal	judío	general	gimnasio
Japón	José		gestión	girasol

You have noted that the Spanish phoneme /x/ is written **j** before **a, o,** or **u** and written **g** before **e** or **i.**

That Spanish spelling is not always consistent may be shown by a number of words in which the [x] sound before **e** or **i** is written **j,** for example, **jefe, jinete,** and **jifa.** There are also variant spellings of certain words, such as **gira** and **jira, giga** and **jiga,** etc.

75 Descriptive adjectives

EXAMPLES

1. El nuevo cónsul **americano.**
2. Los Juegos **Olímpicos.**
3. El Consejo **Estudiantil.**
4. La ropa **interior.**
5. Una huelga **general.**
6. Una casita **verde.**
7. Dos cafés **negros.**
8. Dice un señor si hay ropa **vieja.**
9. Esas son ideas **anticuadas.**
10. No recuerdo la dirección **exacta.**
11. Aire **puro,** cielo **azul,** gente **sencilla.**
12. Va a ir mucha gente **importante.**
13. Una cantidad **astronómica.**
14. Es una planta **magnífica.**
15. Para café **bueno,** no hay como este lugar.

noun	+	*differentiating adjective*

Descriptive adjectives, when used to differentiate, follow the noun. Differentiation ranges from CLASSIFICATION according to nationality, position, official status, etc., to CONTRAST, i.e., "x rather than y," important rather than trivial, huge rather than small, etc. The examples above are roughly scaled from classification (1 . . .) to contrast (. . . 15).

› ITEM SUBSTITUTION DRILL

A. 1. **Es un cónsul americano.**
2. _____ disco _________
3. __________ fantástico
4. _____ planta _________
5. __________ importante
6. _____ huelga _________
7. __________ general
8. _____ idea _________
9. __________ anticuada
10. _____ coche _________
11. __________ verde
12. _____ casita _________
13. __________ sencilla
14. _____ materia _________
15. __________ difícil
16. _____ cosa _________
17. __________ vieja

B. 1. **¿Hay gente importante?**
2. __________ extranjera
3. _____ muebles _________
4. __________ importados
5. _____ ropa _________
6. __________ negra
7. _____ café _________
8. __________ caliente
9. _____ arroz _________
10. __________ bueno

11. ____ mantequilla ____
12. ________ pura
13. ____ aire ________

C. 1. **Este juego es fenomenal.**
2. ________ fantástico
3. ____ escuela ________
4. ________ magnífica
5. ____ grupo ________
6. ________ fuerte
7. ____ batería ________
8. ________ regular
9. ____ finca ________
10. ________ grande
11. ____ refinería ________
12. ________ fenomenal
13. ____ tocadiscos ________
14. ________ complicado
15. ____ cosa ________
16. ________ imposible
17. ____ competencia ________
18. ________ buena
19. ____ equipo ________

EXAMPLES
1. Muchas[1] de las vacas y de los toros son **importados.**
2. Médicos y enfermeras **extranjeros.**
3. Tenemos una casa y un jardín **magníficos.** *We have a wonderful house and garden.*
4. El carburador y la batería están **descompuestos.** *The carburetor and battery are out of order.*

noun + *noun* + *plural masculine adjective*

one or both masculine, singular or plural

When an adjective modifies and follows two or more nouns of different genders, it is plural and masculine.

ITEM SUBSTITUTION DRILL

A. 1. **Hay vacas y ovejas importadas.**
2. ____ cerdos y ovejas ________
3. ________ enfermos
4. ____ abogados y médicos ____
5. ________ viejos
6. ____ frijoles y trigo ____
7. ____ fincas y haciendas ____

B. 1. **Hay cerdos y toros malos.**
2. ____ carne y frutas ____
3. ____ café y lentejas ____
4. ________ buenos
5. ____ fruta y frijoles ____
6. ____ lentejas y fruta ____
7. ____ trigo y cebollas ____

EXAMPLES
1. Esa cara **tan triste.**
2. Este policía **medio bruto.** (*This half-brute policeman.*)
3. Una limonada **bien caliente.** (*A thoroughly hot lemonade.*)

noun	+	*modified adjective*

Descriptive adjectives that are themselves modified normally follow the noun.

[1] An adjective *preceding* two or more nouns agrees with the noun nearest it.

ITEM SUBSTITUTION DRILL

A. 1. **¡Qué chicos tan tristes!**
2. _____ muchachas _____
3. _______________ amables
4. _____ gente _________
5. ___________ más _____
6. _______________ sencilla

B. 1. **Es un policía medio bruto.**
2. ___________ muy _______
3. _____ enfermera _________
4. _______________________ loca
5. ______________ bien _______
6. _____ funcionario ________

C. 1. **Quiero una limonada bien caliente.**
2. ______________________ menos _____
3. ______________________________ fuerte
4. ___________ café _______________
5. ______________________ igualmente __
6. ______________________________ puro
7. ______________________ más _______

EXAMPLES

A. 1. **¿Buen** sueldo?
2. ¿Qué **mejor** oportunidad que ésta? *What better opportunity than this?*
3. El toreo es considerado como un **verdadero** arte.
4. Sin mencionar **altos** funcionarios de gobierno.
5. Fue un **gran** hombre. *He was a great man.*

B. 1. Tuve un **mal** día.
2. ¿Recibiste alguna **mala** noticia?
3. Esa **bendita** esquina del Teatro Nacional.
4. Acabo de tener un **tremendo** lío con la policía.

enhancing adjective	+	*noun*

Descriptive adjectives that enhance rather than differentiate normally precede their nouns. Typically these adjectives express value judgments, referring to goodness (Examples A) or badness (Examples B).

TRANSLATION DRILL

1. I had a big *mix-up.*
   Tuve un tremendo lío.
   I had a *big* mix-up.
   Tuve un lío tremendo.
2. I have a good *group.*
   I have a *good* group.
3. It's considered a real *art.*
   It's considered a *real* art.
4. We had a bad *day.*
   We had a *bad* day.
5. There were high *officials.*
   There were *high* officials.
6. He's a good *student.*
   He's a *good* student.
7. He's my old *friend.*
   He's my *old* friend.
8. We sold our best *bed.*
   We sold our *best* bed.
9. I lost that dirty *receipt.*
   I lost that *dirty* receipt.

Descriptive adjectives are typically those that tell something about the nature of the thing they describe. In this they differ from the adjectives treated in Unit 10, Section 48: **mi coche** *my car* relates the car to its environment (specifically, to me), but tells nothing about the car itself—its make, color, size, efficiency, etc. On the other hand, **buen coche** *good car,* **coche negro** *black car,* **coche fenomenal** *wonderful car,* etc., do tell something about the nature of the car.

Descriptive adjectives include some—such as those of nationality (*American, Costa Rican*), affiliation in society (*Masonic, Methodist, social, medical, Democratic, financial*), scientific or technical classification (*oxalic, radioactive, metrical*), etc.—that almost always follow the noun in Spanish. They also include many that may appear in Spanish either after the noun (the more usual position) or before it.

The basis for the distinction is what might be termed the "relative informativeness" of the noun and the adjective. When we say, for example, **No es leal amigo** *He isn't a loyal friend* we are saying, essentially, that he is not a *friend,* loyalty being something one expects of friends. But when we say **No es amigo leal** *He isn't a loyal friend,* we are not denying that he is a friend, but we are saying that he may be a fair-weather friend; we are denying his loyalty.

English (and Spanish also) does much the same with verb and adverb as Spanish does with noun and adjective. The distinction in English between *Can we easily lift it?* (*Can we lift it?*) and *Can we lift it easily?* (*Will it be easy?*) parallels the distinction between **leal amigo** and **amigo leal.**

Most instances of a descriptive adjective occurring before a noun are those in which the adjective is used for enhancement, that is, to suggest a good quality or a bad quality; the speaker is being complimentary or uncomplimentary about the thing described. In **viejo amigo** *old friend* the adjective **viejo** means "tried and true"—it is a compliment. In **bendita esquina** *darned corner* the adjective **bendita** tells us little about **esquina** but a lot about the speaker's feelings. This is why **buen(o)** and **mal(o)** (see Unit 10, Section 52, for shortening of adjectives) more often precede the noun than follow it, even sometimes when **bueno** or **malo** is itself modified (**Tienen muy buenos atletas**); but when used in a differentiating sense as in **Para café bueno no hay como este lugar** *For* ***really good*** *coffee there's no place like this one,* they follow the noun.

76 Position of limiting adjectives

EXAMPLES

A. 1. Es **pura** imaginación. *It's just imagination.*
2. Es imaginación **pura.** *It's sheer imagination.*
3. Es leche **pura.** *It's pure milk.*

B. 1. La **nueva** criada acaba de llegar. *The new maid has just arrived.*
2. Nos gusta más la criada **nueva.** *We like the new maid better.*
3. Este peso **nuevo** es muy bonito. *This new peso is very pretty.*

C. 1. La **próxima** casa que visitamos fue la de don Enrique. *The next house we visited was Don Enrique's.*
2. No venga esta semana; venga la semana **próxima.** *Don't come this week; come next week.*
3. Vive en la casa **próxima.** *He lives in the house next door.*

D. 1. Es el **único** hijo que no se parece a su padre. *He's the only son that doesn't resemble his father.*
2. No es un hijo **único.** *He's not an only son.*
3. Es un médico muy **único.** *He's a very unique doctor.*

LIMITING USE OF ADJECTIVE	NOUN
pura **nueva** **próxima**	**imaginación** **criada** **semana**

NOUN	EMPHATIC OR CONTRASTIVE USE OF ADJECTIVE
imaginación **criada** **semana**	**pura** **nueva** **próxima**

NOUN	LITERAL USE OF ADJECTIVE
leche **peso** **casa**	**pura** **nuevo** **próxima**

TRANSLATION DRILL

1. There goes the new *maid.*
   There goes the *new* maid.
   There goes the brand-new car.
2. It's his only suit.
   It's his one and only suit.
   It's his unique suit.
3. It's pure (*nothing but*) air.
   It's pure (*uncontaminated*) air.
4. What are they bringing, just milk?
   What are they bringing, pure milk?

DISCUSSION

A number of adjectives can be regarded as either LIMITING (See Unit 10, Sections 48 and 49) or DESCRIPTIVE. *New,* for example, can be used merely to distinguish a present something from a former something; it tells us that the thing referred to is new on the scene, not new in itself: e.g., *Are these your new antiques* (the ones you have just bought)?—*How delightfully old they are!* On the other hand, *new* can describe something that is bright and fresh, literally new, such as a newly minted coin. When an adjective of this kind has its literal and concrete descriptive meaning (Examples numbered 3 above), Spanish favors position after the noun, e.g., **agua pura** *pure water.* When it has its limiting meaning, position before the noun is favored: **pura agua** *just water.* As *pure* and *just* illustrate, English often has to use an entirely different adjective to get this same effect: *only* vs. *unique, next* vs. *next-door* or *neighboring, mere* vs. *pure.*

If the speaker wishes to make the limiting sense emphatic or contrastive, he again places the adjective after the noun (Examples numbered 2): *We like the* ***new*** *maid, not the one we had before; That is* ***sheer*** *(out-and-out) nonsense!* Contrast as well as literalness and concreteness makes the adjective more informative and calls for placement after the noun.

If an adjective is used in an enhancing sense (i.e., for goodness-badness), it may precede, as has already been explained: **La pura agua de las montañas** *The pure* ("sweet, good") *water of the mountains.*

77 Reflexive with-verb pronouns

EXAMPLES

1. **Me** dije que no podía ser. *I told (said to) myself that it was impossible.*
2. ¿**Te** cortaste? *Did you cut yourself?*
3. Tenga la bondad de sentar**se.** (*Have the goodness to seat yourself.*)

myself, to (for) myself	**me**
ourselves, to (for) ourselves	**nos**
yourself, to (for) yourself	**te**
yourself, to (for) yourself yourselves, to (for) yourselves himself, to (for) himself herself, to (for) herself itself, to (for) itself themselves, to (for) themselves	**se**

Except for **se,** the reflexive pronouns are the same as the nonreflexive.

› PERSON-NUMBER SUBSTITUTION DRILL

1. ¿Cómo se llama *usted?*
   (tú, él, ellas, ella, ustedes)
2. *Yo* me llamo Mario (María).
   (él, nosotros, ellos, tú, ella)
3. ¿Dónde puedo sentarme?
   (él, tú, ellas, nosotros, usted)
4. ¿Por qué te preocupas tanto?
   (ellos, usted, yo, ella, nosotros)
5. *Rosa* no se dejó dar gato por liebre.
   (las criadas, tú, ustedes, yo, nosotros)
6. *Yo* me metí en una calle en contra del tránsito.
   (ustedes, nosotros, Roberto, ellos, tú)
7. *El muchacho* no pudo calmarse.
   (nosotros, ella, tú, ellos, yo)
8. *Yo* me puedo imaginar el gran lío que sucedió.
   (ustedes, tú, usted, nosotros, ellas)
9. Es difícil, pero me levanto a las seis.
   (nosotros, ellos, tú, ella, ustedes)
10. Casi me muero de hambre.
    (Paquito, nosotros, ustedes, tú, María Elena)
11. *Las chicas* se acostaron muy tarde anteanoche.
    (Pablo, ustedes, nosotros, tú, yo)
12. No quieren bañarse por la mañana.
    (la muchacha, tú, ella, nosotros, usted)
13. En realidad, no me acordé del juego.
    (el equipo, los atletas, nosotros, él, tú)
14. Es que *Paquito* no sabe peinarse bien.
    (las niñas, el chico, tú, yo, nosotros)
15. *Yo* me siento así así, regular.
    (Olga, Pablo y yo, las alumnas, tú, usted)
16. Se cayeron en esa bendita esquina.
    (yo, mi abuela, tú, ellos, nosotros)
17. Tuvo que quitarse hasta los zapatos.
    (nosotros, los chicos, tú, yo, él)
18. Tenemos que irnos al campo.
    (ustedes, tú, usted, yo, ellos)
19. *Ellos* se quedaron a ver el boxeo.
    (usted, los muchachos, yo, tú, nosotros)
20. *Ricardo* se tomó las pastillas.
    (yo, ellos, nosotros, usted, tú)

› DISCUSSION

The *-self* words in English, like the Spanish reflexives to which they correspond, are unemphatic; the English to which **¿Te cortaste?** corresponds is *Did you* **cut** *yourself?* with the verb stressed but *-self* unstressed. The emphatic *-self* word in Spanish is **mismo, -a, -os, -as,** as in the example **Déjeme peinarme yo mismo** *Let me comb myself* ***I myself.***

The multiple meanings of **se** given here do not cause confusion because **se** merely repeats the subject, and the subject may always be expressed; thus **El se cortó** means *He cut himself* and **Usted se cortó** means *You cut yourself.*

In the reflexive pronouns there is no difference between direct and indirect objects. Example 1 above is indirect (**me** *to myself*), whereas Example 2 is direct.

Reflexive constructions, direct object

EXAMPLES

1. ¿Por qué no **llamamos a María Elena?**
   La rubia **se llama** Betty.
2. **Lo mataron.** *They killed him.*
   El pobre **se mató.** *The poor fellow killed himself.*
3. El barbero **me peinó.** *The barber combed me (combed my hair).*
   Déjeme **peinarme** yo mismo.
4. **Metí la plata** en la cartera *I put (stuck) the money in the wallet.*
   Me metí en una calle en contra del tránsito.
5. La madre **acostó a sus hijos.** *The mother put her children to bed (put to bed her children).*
   ¡¿Acostarme?! *(Put myself to bed?)*
6. La madre **bañó a sus hijos.** *The mother bathed her children.*
   Mañana no **se bañe.**

	DIRECT OBJECT, REFLEXIVE OR NONREFLEXIVE	VERB
I wash them	**los**	**lavo**
I wash (myself)	**me**	**lavo**
we seat them	**los**	**sentamos**
we seat ourselves (sit down)	**nos**	**sentamos**
he raises it	**lo**	**levanta**
he raises himself (gets up)	**se**	**levanta**

Any verb that may take a nonreflexive direct object may take a reflexive direct object, as in English. The best English translation, however, does not always have a reflexive pronoun.

› TRANSLATION DRILL

1. We call her Betty.
   She calls herself Betty.
2. They killed him.
   He killed himself.
3. The barber combs my hair (combs me).
   I comb my hair (comb myself).
4. We seated them at one side.
   They sat down (seated themselves) at one side.
5. The mother put them to bed.
   The mother went to bed.
6. She bathed her.
   She took a bath (bathed herself).
7. I put them in their place.
   I put myself in their place.
8. He raises it.
   He gets up (raises himself).
9. She cut it.
   She cut herself.
10. We washed it.
    We washed ourselves.

EXAMPLES

1. **¡Cálmate,** chico!
2. Yo **me entusiasmé.**
3. No **te preocupes.**
4. Ellos **se ofendieron.** *They took offense.*

to calm (someone or something) to calm down	**calmar** **calmarse**
to thrill, excite (someone) to be thrilled, get excited	**entusiasmar** **entusiasmarse**
to worry (someone) to worry, be (get) worried	**preocupar** **preocuparse**
to offend (someone) to take offense	**ofender** **ofenderse**

Most verbs signifying a change in the subject's state call for the reflexive pronoun. The English equivalent often carries the verb *get: get worried, get sore, get upset, get scared, get worse.*

EXAMPLES A. 1. ¡Ese hombre **me pone** tan furiosa! *That man makes me so furious!*
2. La noticia **nos puso** tristes. *The news made us sad.*

B. 1. ¡No **te pongas** tan furiosa! *Don't get so furious!*
2. **Se pusieron** muy tristes. *They got very sad.*
3. ¿Qué hacemos si no **se pone** mejor? *What do we do if he doesn't get better?*

A. to make (him)	furious sad better complicated bigger etc.
B. to get	

poner (lo)	**furioso** **triste** **mejor** **complicado** **más grande** **etc.**
ponerse	

Poner is used for *make* in the sense of 'to bring about a change of state' (in someone else); **ponerse** is used for *to get* when the change is within oneself.

› TRANSLATION DRILL

1. Calm him down, boy!
   Calm down, boy!
2. Don't worry her!
   Don't worry!
3. They thrilled me.
   They were thrilled.
4. Then I calmed her down.
   Then I calmed down.
5. He didn't thrill us.
   He wasn't thrilled.
6. She doesn't worry me.
   She doesn't get worried.
7. They made (put) him furious.
   They got (put themselves) furious.
8. She made (put) him sad.
   She got (put herself) sad.
9. He made me furious.
   He got furious.
10. She made me sad.
    She got sad.
11. He made me sick.
    He got sick.
12. He made me serious.
    He got serious.
13. The class got boring.
    The exam got complicated.
    The boss got ridiculous.
    The strike got serious.
    The teacher got sad.

Reflexive constructions, indirect object

EXAMPLES

1. **Le quité** la corbata. *I took off the (his) tie for him.*
   Quítese la corbata. (*Take off the tie for yourself.*)
2. **Te** voy a **poner** este termómetro debajo de la lengua. *I'm going to put this thermometer under your tongue (under the tongue for you).*
   Póngase este termómetro debajo de la lengua. (*Put this thermometer under the tongue for yourself.*)
3. Mi madre **me ponía** la corbata. *My mother used to put my tie on for me.*
   Voy a **ponerme** la corbata. *I'm going to put on my tie.*
4. El médico **le lavó** las manos. *The doctor washed his hands (for him).*
   El médico **se lavó** las manos. *The doctor washed his (own) hands.*

On him ⟶ I put the shoes. (I put his shoes on for him.)	**Le** **Me** **puse** **los** **zapatos.**	⟵ On myself I put the shoes. (I put my shoes on.)

On me ⟶ he cut the face. (He cut my face.)	**Me** **Se** **cortó** **la** **cara.**	⟵ On himself he cut the face. (He cut his face).

A service or disservice done to oneself or to someone else takes the indirect-object pronoun, reflexive or nonreflexive. English generally uses a possessive for this meaning.

› TRANSLATION DRILL

1. I washed his hands.
   I washed my hands.
2. He pulled my hair.
   He pulled his (own) hair.
3. He cut my face.
   He cut his face.
4. She took off my shoes (for me).
   She took off her shoes.
5. Wash his face.
   Wash your face.
6. Put on my shirt (for me), Help me on with my shirt.
   Put on your shirt.
7. Take off my tie (for me).
   Take off your tie.

EXAMPLES

A.
1. **¿Está tomando** algo?
2. Sí, aspirinas. Ayer **me tomé** cinco. (*Yesterday I took five for myself.*)
3. **Tómese** estas pastillas.

B.
1. **Lleve** el paquete. *Carry the package.*
2. **Llévese** esta receta. *Take this prescription for yourself.*

ACTION PERFORMED
verb

ACTION PERFORMED FOR BENEFIT OF ACTOR		
verb	+	*indirect-object reflexive*

To emphasize the benefit that the actor gets from his action, a reflexive pronoun may be added; compare English *I'm going to eat* ***me*** *a sandwich.*

EXAMPLES A. 1. ¿Tomó las aspirinas? *Did you take the aspirin?*
2. Sí, **me las** tomé anteanoche. *Yes, I took them night before last.*

B. 1. ¿Me llevo los paquetes? *Shall I take the packages?*
2. Sí, llévé**selos.** *Yes, take them.*

INDIRECT-OBJECT REFLEXIVE	OTHER PRONOUN, DIRECT OBJECT
me **nos** **te** **se**	**lo** **la** **los** **las**

The reflexive pronoun precedes another pronoun.

› CONSTRUCTION SUBSTITUTION DRILL

INSTRUCTIONS: Repeat the following sentences just as you hear them. Then repeat them again, substituting an appropriate with-verb pronoun for the direct-object noun and modifiers, if any.

1. TEACHER: Ella se comió *la fruta.* *Repita.*
   STUDENT: **Ella se comió la fruta.**
   TEACHER: *Cambie.*
   STUDENT: **Ella se la comió.**
2. Nos comimos *cuatro huevos.*
3. Me lavé *la cabeza.*
4. María se compró *el traje.*
5. Se comieron *la carne.*
6. El se lavó *las manos.*
7. Me corté *el pelo.*
8. Nos tomamos *la limonada.*
9. Se compraron *los zapatos.*
10. Me tomé *dos tazas de café.*

› PATTERNED RESPONSE DRILL

A. 1. ¿Se comió usted la fruta?
   Sí, me la comí.
2. ¿Se comió ella la fruta?
3. ¿Se comieron ustedes la fruta?
4. ¿Te comiste tú la fruta?
5. ¿Se llevaron ustedes los zapatos?
6. ¿Se tomó ella las dos tazas de café?
7. ¿Se compraron ellos el coche?
8. ¿Nos tomamos él y yo la limonada?
9. ¿Se comieron ustedes la carne?
10. ¿Nos llevamos él y yo las plumas?
11. ¿Se lavó Paquito las manos?
12. ¿Te cortaste el pelo?

EXAMPLES A. 1. **Cae** la lluvia. *The rain falls.*
2. **Cayeron** muchos en ese ataque. *Many fell in that attack.*
3. **Me caí.** *I (lost my balance and) fell.*

B. 1. **Muere** el día. *The day is dying.*
2. Los policías a veces tienen que **morir.** *Policemen sometimes have to die.*
3. **Se muere** mi padre. *My father is dying.*

C. 1. Con estas pastillas la fiebre no le **sube.** *With these tablets his fever won't go up (on him).*
2. Juan **subió** por esa calle. *Juan went up that street.*
3. ¿Cómo **se subió** Juan al balcón? ¿Por la pared? *How did Juan get up to the balcony? By the wall?*

D. 1. **Quedé** muy triste. *I remained (The experience left me) very sad.*
2. La sala **quedó** sucia. *The living room was left (came out as a result) dirty.*
3. **Nos quedamos** aquí. *We're staying here.*

E. 1. **Iba** a trabajar. *He was going (was on his way) to work.*
2. Supe que usted **se iba** a trabajar al campo. (*I heard you were going off to work in the country.*)

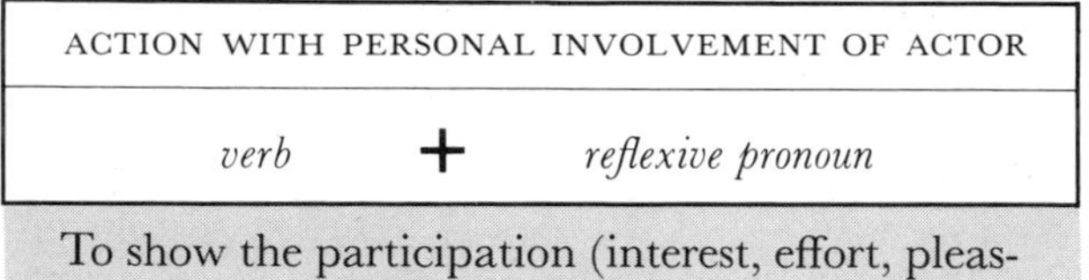

To show the participation (interest, effort, pleasure, pain, restraint, etc.) of the actor in the action, a reflexive pronoun is added.

› TRANSLATION DRILL

1. TEACHER: He took aspirin (as a remedy).
   STUDENT: **Tomó aspirina.**
   TEACHER: He took those aspirins.
   STUDENT: **Se tomó esas aspirinas.**
2. He carried the package.
   He carried off the package.
3. He ate the beans.
   He ate up the beans.
4. Something dropped (fell) into the cup.
   The man fell down.
5. The day is dying.
   The man is dying.
6. I remained sad.
   I stayed a week.
7. He's going to work.
   He's going off to work.

› DISCUSSION

The last set of examples contains verbs without direct objects (intransitive verbs) accompanied by reflexive pronouns. Certain verbs, such as **caer** and **morir,** are more often than not used in this way. The difference that adding the reflexive pronoun makes is rather subtle.

An action may be viewed as a historical unit, with the actor being carried along as part of it. Or the action may be viewed as a developing something, with the actor in a position to affect the course of developments: to make them inevitable by his carelessness, slower by his resistance, possible by his efforts, pathetic by his suffering, etc. To express the latter view, Spanish adds a reflexive pronoun. For example, to imply that a body is affected by gravity or swept down by force, we use the simple verb **caer;** but to imply that the body in the act of falling fails to keep erect, or fights to hold its balance, or gives in to an impulse to fall, we use the reflexive **caerse:** the body is a partner in what happens to it or in what it causes to happen. English has no single device parallel to this, but certain rough approximations can be listed: **ir** *to go,* **irse** *to get on one's way, pick up and go, go off, go away,* **quedar** *to remain,* **quedarse** *to stay;* **caer** *to fall,* **caerse** *to go (come) tumbling down.*

Now that the last of the with-verb pronouns have been introduced we can summarize their position with respect to one another when two occur in sequence (see Unit 12, Section 59):

se	me nos te	lo la los las le les

The **se** here is either the reflexive **se** (direct or indirect) or the **se** for **le, les.** Rarely do more than two of these appear in combination.

80 Reflexive for unplanned occurrences

EXAMPLES

1. **Se me** olvidó su nombre. *I forgot his name (His name slipped my mind, forgot itself on me).*
2. **Se me** ocurrió la idea. *The idea popped into my head.*
3. **¿Se te** cayeron (rompieron) las tazas? *Did you drop (break) the cups (Did the cups fall, break, for you)?*
4. **Se nos** quedaron las herramientas en casa. *We left our tools at home (The tools stayed, got left, home on us).*
5. **Se me** rompió la camisa. *I tore my shirt (my shirt tore, got torn, on me).*

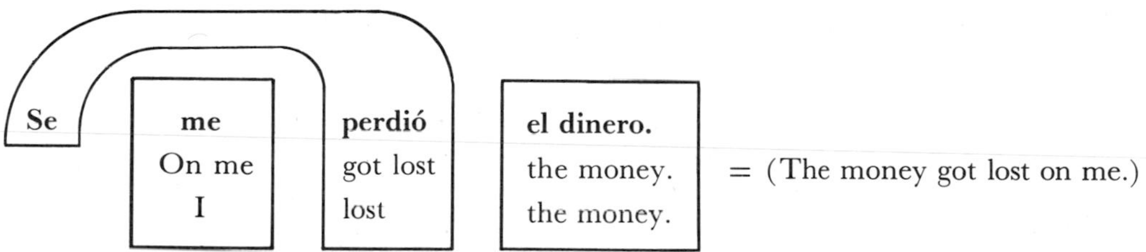

Where English uses *It fell, It broke, It got away from me,* etc., to make a happening appear to occur on its own without any premeditation, Spanish uses a reflexive construction for the verb and adds an indirect object referring to the person.

PERSON-NUMBER SUBSTITUTION DRILL

1. *A mí* se me olvidó la dirección.
   (a él, a nosotros, a ellos, a ti, a usted)
2. *A Juan* se le cayó una taza de café.
   (a ellos, a mí, a ti, a ella, a nosotros)
3. Se le rompió la taza.
   (a ellos, a mí, a ti, a ella, a nosotros)
4. Se nos quedaron los libros en casa.
   (a mí, a Pablo, a ustedes, a ti, a ella)
5. *A mí* se me rompió la camisa.
   (a ustedes, a ti, a usted, a nosotros, a ellos)
6. Se me ocurrió una idea magnífica.
   (a nosotros, a usted, a ti, a ellos, a ella)

ITEM SUBSTITUTION DRILL

1. Se me rompió la *camisa.*
   (zapatos, libro, corbata, discos, taza, juguetes, flecha)
2. Se nos olvidó el *número.*
   (recados, lista, noticias, edad, colores, fecha, cuentas)

3. Se le cayó una *taza.*
(tijeras, paquete, peine, recibos, pan, frijoles)
4. Se les quedaron las *pastillas* en la sala.
(receta, termómetro, periódicos, recibo, cuenta, lista)
5. Se me ocurre *una cosa.*
(algo, una idea, otra cosa, algo fantástico, un tema)

› PATTERNED RESPONSE DRILL

A. 1. ¿Qué se le olvidó a usted?
Se me olvidó la corbata.
2. ¿Qué se me olvidó a mí?
3. ¿Qué se le olvidó a él?
4. ¿Qué se les olvidó a ustedes?
5. ¿Qué se nos olvidó a él y a mí?
6. ¿Qué se te olvidó a ti?

B. 1. ¿Se les olvidaron a ustedes las corbatas?
Sí, se nos olvidaron.
2. ¿Se le olvidaron a él las corbatas?
3. ¿Se te olvidaron a ti las corbatas?
4. ¿Se nos olvidaron a él y a mí las corbatas?
5. ¿Se les olvidaron a ellos las corbatas?
6. ¿Se me olvidaron a mí las corbatas?

C. 1. ¿Se le cayó a usted el libro?
Sí, se me cayó.
2. ¿Se les rompieron a ellas las tazas?
3. ¿Se te olvidó a ti la receta?
4. ¿Se les rompieron a ustedes los discos?
5. ¿Se les cayeron a ustedes los lápices?
6. ¿Se le cayó a usted el arroz?
7. ¿Se le rompió al médico el termómetro?
8. ¿Se nos olvidaron a nosotros las aspirinas?

D. 1. ¿Qué le pasó al libro de usted?
Se me cayó y se me rompió.
2. ¿Qué les pasó a los discos de ustedes?
3. ¿Qué le pasó al termómetro del médico?
4. ¿Qué les pasó a las tazas de ellas?

› GUIDED CONVERSATION

R. *Raimundo* M. *Médico*

R. (*hablando por teléfono*) Con el Doctor Castillo, por favor... Gracias, señorita... Doctor Castillo, le habla Raimundo Mendoza, hermano de Ricardo que estuvo en su oficina[2] ayer.
M. Ah claro, ahora ______________
R. Acabo de llegar a mi oficina, pero creo que tengo una fuerte gripe, igual que mi hermano. Me duele todo el cuerpo.
M. Pues como le dije a él, con este invierno ______________
R. ¿Entonces no es nada muy serio?
M. A ver. Primero ______________
R. Como unas dos o tres horas no más. Y tengo un poquito de fiebre.
M. Entonces tiene que ______________
R. ¿Y me tomo las mismas pastillas que Ricardo?
M. Sí, cada tres o cuatro horas tómese ______________
R. Gracias, doctor.

› PATTERNED RESPONSE REVIEW DRILL

Nominalized demonstratives.

1. TEACHER: ¿Cuál es mi libro? (*holding up a book*)
STUDENT: **Ese.**
TEACHER: ¿Este?
STUDENT: **Sí, ése.**

2. ¿Cuál es su lápiz?
Este.
¿Ese?
Sí, éste.

[2] *office*

3. ¿Cuáles son sus libros?
4. ¿Cuáles son mis libros?
5. ¿Cuáles son tus lápices?
6. ¿Cuáles son mis lápices?
7. ¿Cuáles son mis zapatos?
8. ¿Cuál es tu dinero?
9. ¿Cuál es mi peine?

❯ ITEM SUBSTITUTION REVIEW DRILL

Ser and **estar** with adjectives.

A. 1. Este policía es bruto.
2. La criada ______
3. ______ enferma
4. Mi amigo ______
5. ______ equivocados
6. Mis compañeras ___
7. ______ extranjeras
8. Los cónsules ______
9. ______ nuevo
10. Los tocadiscos ______
11. ______ portátil
12. Estos radios ______
13. ______ descompuestos
14. El teléfono ______
15. ______ grande
16. Las pinturas ______
17. ______ americanas
18. La alumna ______
19. ______ contenta

B. 1. La sala es sencilla.
2. ______ sucia
3. ___ zapatos ______
4. ______ azules
5. ___ pastillas ______
6. ______ necesarias
7. ___ café ______
8. ______ caliente
9. ___ leche ______

C. 1. El abogado es moderno.
2. ______ resfriado
3. ___ médicos ______
4. ______ juntos
5. ___ familia ______
6. ______ respetable
7. ___ muchacho ______
8. ______ furioso
9. ___ toro ______
10. ______ argentino

reading

Una visita al médico

P. *Pablo* R. *Ricardo, amigo de Pablo*

P. Buenos días, Ricardo. ¿Qué tal?
R. Hola, Pablo, ¿cómo estás?
P. Muy bien, ¿y tú?
R. Así, así; tenía gripe hace unos cuantos días, pero ya estoy recobrando la salud.

unos cuantos *a few*

P. ¡Qué lástima! ¿Viste al médico?
R. Sí, pero tú conoces a esos matasanos.[3] Le hacen a uno esperar en una antesala elegantemente adornada y ricamente amueblada; le preguntan a uno qué siente... si sé lo que siente, ¿para qué debo ir al médico, eh?

matasanos *charlatans, quacks*

[3]The word is derived from **mata** and **sanos; matar** means *to kill,* and **sanos** means *healthy.*

P. Yo me acuerdo de una visita...

R. (*con el aire insistente de un hombre que va a decirlo todo*) Cuando entré, estaba la enfermera sentada en la antesala...

P. ¿Era bonita?

R. ¡Ni en pintura! Bastante vieja, demasiado gorda... De todos modos, me preguntó si quería ver al doctor... ¡qué diablos! ¿Para qué creía que estaba allí?... Le dije que sí, y le recordé que tenía hora con él para las once. Entonces me preguntó cómo me llamaba. ¡Caramba! Si tengo gripe, fiebre, dolor de cabeza o cualquier otra cosa, ¿qué puede importar mi nombre? Pero al fin se acordó de que yo tenía hora con el médico, y me admitió a la presencia de Su Señoría...

De...modos *At any rate*

Su Señoría *His Lordship*

P. ¿Y entonces?

R. ¡No me apures!... —Tenga la bondad de sentarse, me dijo. Así que tuve la bondad de sentarme. Me preguntó cómo me sentía. Le dije que tenía gripe, que me dolía todo el cuerpo. Me contestó que con este invierno todo el mundo está resfriado, y que a todos les duele la cabeza y la garganta. —¿Qué debo hacer? le dije. Entonces me preguntó que cuánto tiempo llevaba sintiéndome así, que si estaba tomando algo y otras cosas por el estilo. Me quité la corbata y la camisa y me puse un termómetro debajo de la lengua.

apurar *to hurry*

cuánto...sintiéndome *how long I'd been feeling*

P. ¿Tenías fiebre?

R. Sí, pero sólo un poquito. Tuve que irme a casa y acostarme, lo que no quería hacer; tomé unas pastillas con una limonada bien caliente. ¡Una limonada caliente, figúrate! No pude protestar; no hay pero que valga con estos médicos. Y además, hay que pagar la cuenta. La vida es dura, ¿verdad?

¡figúrate! *imagine!*

Buenos Aires: Pharmacy

UNIT 15

The Kidnaping

M. *Manuel* E. *Emilio*

M. OK, I know they're traitors. But they won't kill an *ambassador.*

E. Don't you remember that [the (matter) of the] French correspondent, the one they kidnaped about three years ago? At the hour announced, pow! Dead!

M. Yes, but don't forget the reaction there was. And not only here, everywhere!

E. But don't you see that nobody's opinion is worth two cents [a whistle] to these scoundrels?

M. Well I say that the government has got to stand [maintain itself] firm.

E. That's precisely why we're in this mess [to that this mess owes itself], pal. They had just arrested [seized prisoner] Soto, (the) leader of the National Liberation Army, when the ambassador disappeared.

* * *

M. They freed the ambassador? Is it certain?

E. Yes, they just said so over the radio. An agreement was reached to hand over just Soto and another ringleader in exchange for the ambassador.

M. Some agreement! They're nothing but a bunch of despicable enemies of the country. And now turned loose!

E. You're right [of agreement], but on the other hand, the life of the ambassador has been spared.

El secuestro

M. *Manuel* E. *Emilio*

M. Hombre, yo sé que son traidores. Pero a un embajador no lo van a matar.

E. ¿No recuerdas lo del periodista francés, aquél que secuestraron hace como tres años? A la hora anunciada, ¡pum! ¡Muerto!

M. Sí, pero no olvides la reacción que hubo. Y no sólo aquí, ¡en todas partes!

E. ¿Pero no ves que a estos canallas no les importa un pito la opinión de nadie?

M. Pues yo digo que el gobierno debe mantenerse firme.

E. Precisamente a eso se debe este lío, hombre. Acababan de coger preso a Soto, líder del Ejército de Liberación Nacional, cuando desapareció el embajador.

* * *

M. ¿Soltaron al embajador, dices? ¿Es cierto?

E. Sí, acaban de decirlo por radio. Se llegó a un acuerdo de entregar sólo a Soto y a otro cabecilla, a cambio del embajador.

M. ¡Vaya un acuerdo! No son más que unos miserables enemigos de la patria. ¡Y ya libres!

E. De acuerdo, pero en cambio se le ha salvado la vida al embajador.

M. All right, but now what about the other embassy officials?
E. Nonsense! The police can protect them.
M. Some protection! If they couldn't do it before, how can they now? Look, this is a matter of the security of all the diplomats.
E. Things have got to improve [themselves] toward the end of the agrarian reform. By then there can't be as much violence as (there is) now.
M. But meanwhile the foreign press keeps talking about how anarchy's reigning in this country. And they're not far from the truth [they don't fail to be right].

M. Bien, pero ahora ¿qué de los otros diplomáticos de las embajadas?
E. ¡Qué va! La policía puede protegerlos.
M. ¡Bonita protección! Si no pudieron hacerlo antes, ¿cómo pueden ahora? Fíjate que se trata de la seguridad de todos los diplomáticos.
E. Deben mejorarse las cosas a fines de la reforma agraria. Para entonces no debe haber tanta violencia como ahora.
M. Pero mientras tanto la prensa extranjera sigue hablando de que en este país reina el anarquismo. Y no dejan de tener razón.

› WRITING EXERCISE

The use of the letter **h.** INSTRUCTIONS: Write the following lists of words from dictation.

haber
hablar
hacer
hambre
hombre
hasta
himno
hora
historia
hermano

a**h**ora
a**h**ito
des**h**onra
de**h**esa
re**h**usar
re**h**acer
a**h**ondar
a**h**ogar
in**h**alar
in**h**umano

hiedra
hielo
hiena
hierba
hierro
hiel

hueco
hueso
huevo
huelgo
huerta
huésped

hijo
hoja
hijuelo
higiene
a**h**ijado
héjira

The letter **h** represents no sound at all in present-day Spanish. Its use is partly an inheritance from Latin (e.g., Spanish **h** may represent a Latin *h* as in **haber** from Latin *habere*) and partly a relic of Old Spanish (originally the *h* of **hacer,** from Latin *facere,* was pronounced like English *h*).

Note that the letters **j** and **g** in the last column above have the value [x], but that **h** in these words is silent.

The fact that **h** is silent has brought about variant spellings of some words, for example, **harmonía** and **armonía, hujier** and **ujier, harpa** and **arpa.**

81 Nominalization with the neuter article *lo*

EXAMPLES

A. 1. No podemos hacer **lo imposible.** *We can't do the impossible.*
2. **Lo poco** que hice. *The little (that) I did.*

B. 1. Hay que respetar **lo sagrado.** *One must respect what is sacred.*
2. **Lo mío** es mío. *What's mine is mine.*

C. 1. **Lo pesado** de la clase son los exámenes. *The unpleasant part of the class is the exams.*
2. **Lo inútil** de la filosofía es **lo peor.** *The useless nature (uselessness) of philosophy is the worst part.*

Lima, Peru: Presidential Palace

D. 1. Esto es **lo bueno** de mi profesión.
   2. Es **lo único** que sé. *It's the only thing I know.*
   3. La pronunciación es **lo principal.** *Pronunciation is the main thing.*
   4. **Lo primero** es trabajar. *The first thing is to work.*

A. the	impossible little	
B. what is	sacred mine	
C. the	unpleasant useless	part –ness (*nature*)
D. the	nice only main first	thing

lo	**imposible** **poco** **sagrado** **mío** **pesado** **inútil** **bueno** **único** **principal** **primero**

To nominalize an adjective that refers to a known noun, the articles **el, la, los,** and **las** are used. (See Unit 12, Section 61.) To nominalize an adjective that does not refer to a known noun, the neuter article **lo** is used. The English equivalent usually adds a cover word such as *part, side, aspect, thing,* or the suffix *–ness.*

▸ ITEM SUBSTITUTION DRILL

1. Lo *mejor* de la casa es la sala.
   (bueno, malo, típico, peor, moderno)
2. No nos gusta nada lo *ridículo.*
   (sucio, complicado, anticuado)
3. Hay que respetar lo *sagrado.*
   (profesional, viejo, fuerte, bueno)
4. Lo *bonito* de la casa son los muebles.
   (admirable, malo, viejo, horrible)
5. Espere un momento; ahora viene lo *importante.*
   (fantástico, serio, triste, bueno)
6. Lo *primero* es defenderse.
   (difícil, necesario, imposible, último)
7. Lo *pasado* se debe olvidar.
   (personal, equivocado, presente, fácil)
8. Eso es lo *infame* de la situación.
   (tremendo, horrible, principal, grande)
9. Esto es lo más *probable.*
   (posible, inútil, desgraciado, fenomenal, relativo)
10. Lo *importante* es no olvidar nada.
   (difícil, principal, bueno, mejor)

EXAMPLES

1. ¿No recuerdas **lo del** periodista francés?
2. Aprendí de memoria **lo de** Sócrates.
3. ¿Y qué me dices de **lo de** ayer? *And what do you say about yesterday's business?*
4. **Lo de** Juan fue peor. *That Juan thing (business) was worse.*

the business matter affair concern stuff etc.	of about

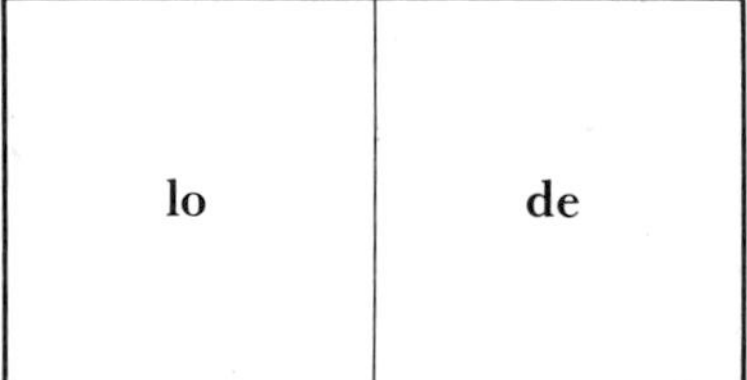

lo	**de**

Prepositional phrases with **de** may also be nominalized. Again English uses cover words.

EXAMPLES

1. **Lo de usted** es sencillo; **lo mío** no. *Your part is easy; mine isn't.*
2. Esto es **lo de Juan.** *This is Juan's concern (business).*
3. **Lo de ellos** (**lo suyo**) no es mucho. *What's theirs (their part) isn't much.*

my part what is mine	**lo mío**
your part what is yours etc.	**lo tuyo** **etc.**
x's part what is x's	**lo de x**

Possessives with **de,** as well as the other possessives of Unit 12, Section 63, may be nominalized with **lo.** English cover words include *what is, part,* etc.

EXAMPLES

1. Sea **lo que** sea. (*Let be that which may be.*)
2. Haga **lo que** yo. *Do what I do.*
3. **Lo que** dices es ridículo. *What you're saying is ridiculous.*

what that which	**lo que**

What (noninterrogative) and *that which,* when they have no specific noun as their referent, are equivalent to **lo que.**

› PATTERNED RESPONSE DRILL

INSTRUCTIONS: Answer the questions, following the model.

A. 1. Lo que pasó ayer fue horrible, ¿no?
Sí, lo de ayer fue horrible.
2. Lo que hizo Juan fue una barbaridad, ¿no?
3. Lo que dijo Alfredo no está bien, ¿verdad?
4. Lo que hicieron en el cementerio fue horrible, ¿no?
5. Lo que preguntaron en el examen estuvo difícil, ¿no?

B. 1. ¿Qué traigo?
Traiga lo que tiene.
2. ¿Qué mando?
3. ¿Qué vendo?
4. ¿Qué llevo?
5. ¿Qué como?

C. 1. ¿Qué es ridículo?
Lo ridículo es lo que usted dice.
2. ¿Qué es imposible?
3. ¿Qué es fantástico?
4. ¿Qué es fenomenal?
5. ¿Qué es horrible?

D. 1. ¿Tú dijiste eso?
No, eso no fue lo que dije.
2. ¿Tú mencionaste eso?
3. ¿Tú olvidaste eso?
4. ¿Tú mandaste eso?
5. ¿Tú preguntaste eso?

› TRANSLATION DRILL

1. That business about standing firm is very important.
2. That business about the kidnapping is very serious.
3. That stuff about the profit is a lie.
4. That business about the salary is a lie.
5. This is Alvaro's part.
6. This is my stuff.

› DISCUSSION

Like the definite articles **el, la, los, las** which show number and gender (see Unit 12, Section 61), the neuter article **lo** is used to nominalize adjectives. English has something similar in phrases like *the good, the true,* and *the beautiful,* but Spanish extends the process to virtually all adjectives.

Attaching **lo** to an adjective amounts to giving your hearer these instructions: "Treat this adjective as a noun and make its meaning cover as broad an area as the context will permit." So in **lo sagrado** without further qualification the meaning covers EVERYTHING that is sacred. But in **lo sagrado de este lugar** the meaning is *whatever-is-sacred about this place* or *the sacredness of this place* or *the sacred part of this place,* depending on context, for now **lo sagrado** is limited.

Since **de** phrases and **que** clauses are used as adjectives (they modify nouns), attaching **lo** to them is a part of the same nominalizing process as attaching **lo** to any other adjective. But it is convenient to treat **lo de** and **lo que** as units, **lo de** with the meaning *the business* (*the concern,* etc.) *of* (or *the part of, ———'s part* when the **de** is possessive) and **lo que** with the meaning *what* or *that which.* Remember that **lo** is neuter, whence *that which* when equivalent to **lo que** cannot refer to anything already mentioned in the form of a specific noun. If we say *My money and that which* (*what*) *you have* **Mi dinero y el que usted tiene,** *that which* or *what* refers to *money,* **el dinero,** a masculine singular noun, and consequently **el que,** not **lo que,** is the equivalent. *Do only that which* (*what*) *is right* uses **lo que** in the Spanish.

82 Comparatives

EXAMPLES A. 1. ¿Qué te gusta **más,** leer o dormir?
2. Creo lo que dice, **más** o **menos.**

B. 1. Hay **más camisas** en este paquete. *There are more (most) shirts in this package.*
2. **Menos elecciones, menos manifestaciones.** *Fewer elections, fewer demonstrations.*

C. 1. Va a ser la planta **más moderna** de Latinoamérica.
2. La oposición tiene un partido mucho **más fuerte.**
3. Ahora la reunión es **menos pesada.** *Now the meeting is less (least) unpleasant.*

D. 1. Lo voy a terminar **más adelante.** *I'm going to finish it later on.*
2. En esta religión, Dios parece **menos cerca.** *In this religion God seems less (least) near.*

COMPARATIVES WITH **más** AND **menos**			
more —er most —est	**más**	less fewer least fewest	**menos**

The usual way of showing a greater or lesser degree or amount of something—verb (Examples A), noun (B), adjective (C), or adverb (D)—is with the words **más** (corresponding to *more, most*) and **menos** (corresponding to *less* or *fewer, least* or *fewest*).

› ITEM SUBSTITUTION DRILL

1. No puedo *comer* más.
   (hablar, prometer, contestar, comprar, faltar)
2. Es la planta más *moderna* de Latinoamérica.
   (complicada, importante, grande)
3. Después *comió* menos.
   (peleó, recordó, alcanzó, tardó, salió)
4. Ahora hay menos *dólares.*
   (fotos, competencia, ganado, ganancia)
5. Esta huelga es menos *interesante.*
   (horrible, libre, necesaria, personal)
6. Dígalo más *tarde.*
   (claro, adelante, pronto)

› TRANSLATION DRILL

A. 1. This exam is easier.
2. His hair is shorter.
3. His body is stronger.
4. These are bigger.

B. 1. Biology is more difficult.
2. Wool costs more.
3. Education is more important.
4. Religion is more sacred.
5. Bullfighting is more respectable.

C. 1. These messages are less admirable.
2. The total is less ridiculous.
3. The headlines are less fantastic.
4. The events are less complicated.
5. The situation is less serious.

EXAMPLES 1. Lo de hablar **mejor** o **peor** es algo muy relativo. *This business of speaking better or worse is a very relative matter.*
2. ¿Qué **mejor** clase que ésta? *What better class than this (one)?*
3. Yo soy la **menor.**
4. Es mi hermano **mayor.** *He's my older (oldest) brother.*

THE **-or** COMPARATIVES	
better, best	**mejor**
worse, worst	**peor**
older, oldest (greater, greatest; bigger, biggest)	**mayor**
younger, youngest (smaller, smallest; lesser, least[1])	**menor**

These are the only comparatives not formed with **más** or **menos:** Spanish **mejor** is like English *better* in place of *more good.* In place of **mayor** and **menor, más grande** and **más pequeño** are preferred when physical size is emphasized.

› PATTERNED RESPONSE DRILL

INSTRUCTIONS: Answer the following as in the model, using the antonym of the adjective.

A. 1. ¿Está mejor?
No, estoy peor.
2. ¿Sigue peor?
3. ¿Ella es la menor?
4. ¿Se siente mejor?
5. ¿Usted es el mayor?
6. ¿Se siente peor?

B. 1. ¿Tienen los mejores toros?
No, tienen los peores.
2. ¿Venden la peor ropa?
3. ¿Vienen los mejores atletas?
4. ¿Ofrecen la menor cantidad?

› TRANSLATION DRILL

A. 1. He works better now.
2. I feel worse today.
3. Luis is my younger brother.
4. Elena is my elder sister.

B. 1. They use the best bulls.
2. They sell the worst cows.
3. She is the youngest.
4. I am the oldest.

› DISCUSSION

English has two ways of forming comparatives, the words *more* and *less* (with verbs, nouns, adjectives, and adverbs) and the suffix *-er* (with certain adjectives and adverbs). In Spanish all comparatives are formed with **más** and **menos,** except for a remant of four forms, **mejor** and **peor** (which may be either adjectives or adverbs) and **mayor** and **menor** (adjectives).

English has two distinct forms with divided functions: *-er, more* and *-est, most.* Spanish has only the comparatives listed in the boxes above, relying where necessary on context for the difference in meaning. Sometimes this means adding a bit of context. To distinguish between *He does it better*

[1] *Least* in size or importance; *least* in amount is **menos.**

and *He does it best,* for example, the latter may appear as **El lo hace mejor que nadie** (*He does it better than anyone*).

The words **mayor** and **menor** when referring to age are relative, not absolute. To imply that someone is "really old" or "really young" the words **viejo** and **joven** are used. **Soy más viejo que usted** *I am older than you* means that we are both along in years; **Soy mayor que usted** *I am older than you* might be spoken equally by a five-year-old or by a seventy-year-old. In this sense **mayor** and **menor** follow the noun: **Es mi hermano mayor** (**menor**) *He is my older* (*younger*) *brother.*

Both **menor** and **menos** translate *least.* **Menor** refers to importance or size, as in **No tengo la menor idea** *I haven't the least* (*slightest, smallest*) *idea* or in **El menor ruido me preocupa** *The least* (*smallest, slightest*) *noise worries me.* **Menos** refers to amount, as in **¿Cuál va a ser menos trabajo?** *Which is going to be least* (*less*) *work?* or **Prefiero el cuarto con menos ruido** *I prefer the room with least* (*less*) *noise.*

Except when **mayor** and **menor** refer to age, the adjectives **mayor, menor, mejor,** and **peor** more often precede the noun than follow it. **Más** and **menos** always precede it.

83 Comparison of inequality

EXAMPLES

A. 1. Hay más **de** diez heridos.
2. Me prometió menos **de** una cuarta parte. *He promised me less than a fourth.*
3. No quiere trabajar más **de** lo poco que le exigimos. *He won't work more than the little that we require of him.*

B. 1. El puede hacer más **que** yo. *He can do more than I* (*can*).
2. Ella es más bonita **que** usted. *She is prettier than you* (*are*).
3. La oposición tiene un partido mucho más fuerte **que** el del gobierno.
4. Algo mejor **que** un empleado de banco.
5. Compré más leche **que** ayer. *I bought more milk than* (*I did*) *yesterday.*
6. Bebí más leche **que** agua. *I drank more milk than* (*I did*) *water.*

C. 1. No hay más remedio **que** hacer una huelga general. (*There's no more* [*other*] *remedy than to call a general strike.*)
2. No son más **que** unos miserables enemigos de la patria.
3. No tengo más **que** seis pesos. *I have only* (*no more than*) *six pesos.*
4. Necesito algo más **que** dinero. *I need something more than money.*
5. Estoy más **que** furioso. *I'm more than furious.*

A. COMPARING DIFFERENT AMOUNTS OR DEGREES OF THE *Same* THING			
	COMPARATIVE AMOUNT OR DEGREE		AMOUNT OR DEGREE IT IS COMPARED WITH
Hay	**más [heridos]**	**de**	**diez heridos.**
Me prometió	**menos**	**de**	**una cuarta parte.**
No quiere trabajar	**más**	**de**	**lo poco que le exigimos.**

When both the amount or degree compared and the amount or degree that it is compared with are specifically mentioned, and both refer to amounts or degrees of the same thing (wounded, quantity of work, etc.), the equivalent of *than* is **de.**

B. COMPARISONS IN WHICH THE PRIMARY AMOUNT OR DEGREE (THE AMOUNT OR DEGREE WITH WHICH THE COMPARISON IS MADE) IS LEFT OUT				
	COMPARATIVE AMOUNT OR DEGREE		AMOUNT OR DEGREE IT IS COMPARED WITH	
El puede hacer	**más**	**que**		**yo.**
Ella es	**más bonita**			**usted.**
Tiene un partido mucho	**más fuerte**			**el del gobierno.**
Algo	**mejor**			**un empleado de banco.**
Compré	**más leche**			**ayer.**
Bebí	**más leche**			**agua.**

When one pole of the comparison is left out the equivalent of *than* is **que.** For example, in the second sentence there is no word or words telling *how pretty* you are; in the fourth sentence there is no word or words telling *how well off* a bank employee is.

C. COMPARING DIFFERENT THINGS			
	WHAT IS COMPARED		THE DIFFERENT THING IT IS COMPARED WITH
No hay	**más remedio**	**que**	**hacer una huelga general.**
No son	**más**		**unos miserables enemigos de la patria.**
Necesito	**algo más**		**dinero.**
Estoy	**más**		**furioso.**

When the comparison is between two different things the equivalent of *than* is **que.** For example, *something more* (*than money*) might refer to *love* or something of the kind: *more* is *other than*. **No... más... que** *No more than* commonly means *only, merely*.

› TRANSLATION DRILL

A. 1. TEACHER: There are more than ten photos.
STUDENT: **Hay más de diez fotos.**
2. There are fewer than twenty employees.

B. 1. There's more than one tyrant in this world.
2. There's less than a kilo of beans.

C. 1. I don't have more than ten dollars; I have eight.
No tengo más de diez dólares; tengo ocho.
2. I don't have less than ten dollars; I have twelve.

D. 1. Her lies are more complicated than mine.
Sus mentiras son más complicadas que las mías.
2. His car is newer than Carlos's.
3. His sister is younger than Josefina.

E. 1. I eat later than the family.
2. I go to bed later than Rosa.
3. We work fewer hours than you.
4. I have less money than Olga.

F. 1. When he goes to the city, he buys more than anyone (no one).
2. When she goes to the market, she haggles more than anyone.

G. 1. To talk is better than to argue.
2. To be a coward is worse than to die.

H. 1. There's more cattle for milk than for meat.
2. There's more time for sleeping than for studying.

I. 1. I'm more than furious.
2. I'm more than sad.
3. He lost more than money.
4. He lost more than time.

J. 1. That coward is more than (a) tyrant.
2. That assassin is more than infamous.
3. His speech was no more than an excuse.

K. 1. All they did was (They did nothing more than) ask what the exchange was.
2. All he did was stand firm.

L. 1. I have only (no more than) ten cows.
2. She has only a fourth part of the profit.
3. It is only (not more than) one o'clock.
4. It is only five o'clock.

› DISCUSSION

The chief problem in the comparison of inequality is the choice of **que** or **de** for *than*. Consider the preceding boxes in reverse order.

1. **Que** is used when the comparison is between two *different* things, that is, when the phrase *more than* implies *other than* (as we might expect, *other than* is **otro que**). **No hay más remedio** means *There is no other remedy* (*There is nothing else to do*). There are places where **que** and **de** contrast in this sense of *other* and the more usual sense of *more*. In **Perdió más de mil dólares** *He lost more than a thousand dollars* we infer that he lost, say, a thousand plus two hundred; we are comparing two different amounts of the same thing, i.e., dollars. But in **Perdió más que mil dólares** we infer *He lost* (*something*) *more* (*important*) *than a thousand dollars*—in addition to losing the money he lost, say, his reputation. He lost something *other than* dollars. In negative sentences with quantities **que** is commonly used in the sense of *only:* **No tengo más que seis** means *I have no other amount than six,* that is, *I have only six* (but I do have six). **No tengo más de seis** means *I don't have more than six* (maybe I have only four—I don't necessarily have six).

2. **Que** is used when the primary amount or degree—that is, the amount or degree with which the comparison is made, that serves as the standard of the comparison—is not embodied in an explicit word. In *I have more than John* the *more* that I have is measured against *what* John has, but there is no word—*fifty, a hundred, several,* or just the word *what* itself—to make this measuring stick explicit. In *You have a longer workday than I* (*have*) the comparative *longer* is included, but there is no other explicit word referring to an amount of length.

3. **De** is used when this primary amount or degree is explicitly given. In *I have less than fifty* the comparative *less* is included and so is the amount against which it is measured: fifty. The amount or degree need not be precise so long as there is a word for it. Thus *I have more than that amount* is **Tengo más de esa cantidad,** using just the noncommittal word *amount* itself. The **de** actually has its fundamental meaning of *from* or *of,* for we are saying *I have upwards of* (an amount *up from*) *that amount.*

Lo with compared adverbs

EXAMPLES 1. Vuelva **lo** más pronto **posible.**
2. Lo dije **lo** más claro **que pude.** *I said it as clearly as* (*the most clearly*) *I could.*

	COMPARED ADVERB	FURTHER MODIFICATION
lo	**más pronto**	**posible**

When an adverb with **más** (or **mejor** or **peor** used as an adverb) is further modified, **lo** precedes it.

TRANSLATION DRILL

A. 1. TEACHER: He came back as soon as possible.
STUDENT: **Volvió lo más pronto posible.**
2. She came back as late as possible.
3. He spoke as clearly as possible.
4. He came as near as possible.
5. I went as far as possible.

B. 1. I put it as high as I could.
Lo puse lo más alto que pude.
2. I put it as far away as I could.
3. I put it as near as I could.
4. I put it as [far] ahead as I could.
5. I put it as [far] back as I could.
6. I put it as [far] outside as I could.

C. 1. He did it the best he could.
Lo hizo lo mejor que pudo.
2. He did it the worst he could.
3. He did it the soonest he could.

85 Comparison of equality

EXAMPLES

A. 1. Tiene **tantos** toros **como** vacas. *He has as many bulls as cows.*
2. Lo hice **tantas** veces **como** él. *I did it as many times as he (did).*
3. No saqué **tantas** fotos **como** él. *I didn't take as many photos as he (did).*

B. 1. Para entonces no debe haber **tanta** violencia **como** ahora.
2. Hay **tanta** oposición **como** antes. *There's as much opposition as before.*
3. No trabajan **tanto como** nosotros. *They don't work as much as we (do).*

C. 1. El es **tan** buena persona **como** su hermano. *He's as fine a person as his brother (is).*
2. Un gobierno **tan** malo **como** éste jamás ha existido.
3. Hablamos **tan** bien aquí **como** en España. *We speak as well here as (they do) in Spain.*

as many . . . as	**tantos, -as... como**
as much . . . as	**tanto, -a... como**
as . . . as	**tan... como**

The first *as* is **tan(to),** the second **como.** As in the comparison of inequality, the tagged *is, do,* and the like normally have no equivalent in Spanish.

ITEM SUBSTITUTION DRILL

1. Pero no debes *comer* tanto como tu papá.
(hablar, discutir, pelear, dormir)
2. Yo no tengo tanto *dinero* como Bernardo.
(plata, tiempo, ropa, suerte)
3. Hay tantos *problemas* aquí como en Latinoamérica.
(barbaridades, periodistas, abogados, profesoras)

Lima, Peru: Main post office

4. Perdí tantas *camisas* como trajes.
   (vestidos, corbatas)
5. El vendedor no es una persona tan *buena*.
   (mala, seria, difícil, inocente, admirable)
6. Un gobierno tan *malo* como éste nunca ha existido.
   (bueno, fuerte, horrible, equivocado)
7. No hablamos tan *bien* como en España.
   (mal, perfectamente, infamemente, desgraciadamente)

› PATTERNED RESPONSE DRILL

INSTRUCTIONS: Answer the questions, following the model.

A. 1. ¿Tiene usted más fotos que él?
   No, tengo tantas como él.
2. ¿Tiene usted más camisas que él?
3. ¿Tiene usted más trajes que él?
4. ¿Tiene usted más suerte que él?
5. ¿Tiene usted más tiempo que él?

B. 1. ¿Tiene usted más camisas que vestidos?
   No, tengo tantos vestidos como camisas.
2. ¿Tiene más tíos que tías?
3. ¿Tiene más primos que primas?
4. ¿Tiene más lápices que plumas?

 Comparison of identity

EXAMPLES A. 1. Yo tengo **la misma** cantidad. *I have the same amount.*
2. Estos periódicos no son **los mismos que** los de ayer. *These newspapers are not the same as yesterday's.*
3. Llegó a **la misma** hora **que** ayer. *He arrived at the same time as yesterday.*
4. Ellos van a morir **lo mismo que** nosotros. *They are going to die the same as we (are).*

B. 1. Yo tengo **igual** cantidad. *I have the same amount.*
2. Estos periódicos no son **iguales que** los de ayer. *These newspapers are not the same as yesterday's.*
3. Es **igual que** todas las demás materias. (*It's the same as all the other subjects.*)
4. Hablan casi **igual que** en el Paraguay.

A. ABSOLUTE IDENTITY		
the	same	as
el **la** **los** **las** **lo**	**mismo** **misma** **mismos** **mismas** **mismo**	**que**

B. CLOSE SIMILARITY		
the	same	as
	igual **iguales**	**que**

Mismo is used when two things are matched as identical (they are one and the same); **igual** is used when two things are compared for similarity (one is *like* the other). The adverb forms are **lo mismo** and **igual,** without inflection for number or gender.

› PATTERNED RESPONSE DRILL

INSTRUCTIONS: Answer the questions, following the models.

A. 1. ¿El y usted tienen el mismo nombre?
Sí, su nombre es el mismo que el mío.
2. ¿El y usted tienen el mismo grupo?
3. ¿El y usted tienen las mismas ideas?
4. ¿El y usted tienen los mismos discos?
5. ¿El y usted tienen el mismo jefe?
6. ¿El y usted tienen la misma enfermera?

B. 1. ¿Sus autos son iguales?
Sí, su auto es igual que el mío.
2. ¿Sus corbatas son iguales?
3. ¿Sus recetas son iguales?
4. ¿Sus trajes son iguales?
5. ¿Sus tazas son iguales?
6. ¿Sus cuentas son iguales?
7. ¿Sus recibos son iguales?

› DISCUSSION

English blends two senses of the word *same:* absolute identity, as in *It's the same man I saw yesterday* ($x = x$), and close similarity, as in *He's the same as his brother* ($x = y$). Spanish distinguishes them, using **mismo** for the first and **igual** for the second.

Mismo and **igual** overlap somewhat. **La misma cantidad** and **igual cantidad** are practically equivalent: in the first the speaker thinks of your amount, say *five,* as identical with my five ($x = x$); in the second he thinks of two separate things, *yours and mine* ($x = y$). But when there is real identity, as in the example *It's the same man I saw yesterday,* only **mismo** may be used.

Certain uses of the indefinite article: identification and individualization

EXAMPLES A. 1. Es pariente del Jefe. *He's a relative of the Chief.*
2. Eres hombre respetable.
3. Usted es norteamericano.
4. Dicen que es extranjero.

B. 1. Es **una** planta magnífica.
2. Fue **un** gran filósofo. *He was a great philosopher.*
3. Ese viaje fue **un** maratón. *That trip was a marathon.*

A. *mere identification*	**Ortega y Gasset es filósofo.** **Armando Vega es atleta.**	Ortega y Gasset is a philosopher. Armando Vega is an athlete.
B. *individualization*	**Juan es un filósofo.** **Juan es un atleta importante.**	Juan's a philosopher. Juan's an important athlete.

In the first pair (**es filósofo, es atleta**) we classify: Ortega y Gasset belongs to a class of persons known as philosophers, and Armando Vega is a professional athlete. In the second pair we individualize: Juan is for the moment being philosophical, or his status as an athlete makes him distinctive.

› TRANSLATION DRILL

1. Rafael is a philosopher.
   Rafael es filósofo.
   Rafael is a *philosopher!*
   ¡Rafael es un filósofo!
2. Luis is an administrator.
   Luis is *an administrator.*
3. Chalo is a student.
   Chalo is *a student.*
4. Alberto is a doctor.
   Alberto is a good doctor.
5. Don Francisco is a Spaniard.
   Don Francisco is an old Spaniard.
6. José is a friend of María Elena.
   José is a real friend of María Elena.
7. Olga is a cousin of Pepe's.
   Olga is a pretty cousin of Pepe's.
8. Mr. Romero is a clerk.
   Mr. Romero is a good clerk.

EXAMPLES A. 1. Tuvimos examen en filosofía.
2. Tengo hora con él.
3. ¿Tengo fiebre?
4. Busco casa. *I'm house-hunting.*
5. ¿Hay médico aquí? *Is there a doctor here?*
6. Salió sin corbata. *He went out without a tie.*
7. Necesito una casa con cocina. *I need a house with a kitchen.*

B. 1. Tengo **un** hambre feroz. *I've got a ferocious appetite.*
2. Aquí traigo **un** paquete con ropa.
3. No recibimos **un** traje y **un** vestido que ustedes quedaron en mandar.
4. Ayer hubo **una** reunión grande.
5. Se considera como **un** verdadero arte.

A. STRESSING THE MERE EXISTENCE OF SOMETHING		
tener **haber** **buscar** **sin** **con** **etc.**		*noun*

When the question is merely about the existence or nonexistence (occurrence or nonoccurrence) of something, the indefinite article is not used.

B. FOCUSING ON AN INDIVIDUAL THING OR THINGS		
verb *preposition* (*or other relator*)	**un, -a**	*noun*

In the sense *one of those,* or *a certain,* when something is individualized, the indefinite article is used.

› TRANSLATION DRILL

1. I'm house-hunting.
   I'm looking for a house.
2. I need clerical help.
   I need a clerk.
3. I didn't have a reaction.
   He had a bad reaction.
4. Is there a doctor here?
   Is there a good doctor here?
5. Do I have fever?
   Do I have a very high fever?

› DISCUSSION

After the verb **ser** Spanish does not use the indefinite article when the purpose is merely to identify a person or thing by attaching some conventional label. It does use the article when the purpose is not merely to identify but to make the person or thing stand out. A noun used as a figure of speech (e.g., *She is an angel* or *He is a pirate,* meaning he is a sharp businessman) therefore calls for the article, as do most combinations in which there is an enhancing adjective such as *great, wonderful, despicable,* etc.

Similarly, the indefinite article is not used in Spanish when a noun in object position is considered merely in the light of its existence or nonexistence. The verbs whose meaning refers fundamentally to existence, **tener** and **haber,** and the prepositions that refer to presence or absence, **con** and **sin,** are the commonest situations in which the article is not used. But if the purpose is to focus on something already considered to be in existence (*one of those*) and to make it stand out, the indefinite article is used.

English has this identical contrast in the plural though not, as we have seen, in the singular. Thus if we say *We have examinations* we mean merely that examinations take place where we are concerned—we refer to the existence, or occurrence, of the examinations. But if we say *We have some examinations,* the attention is immediately drawn to particular examinations. Likewise, though in the singular we require *a* in *John is a lawyer,* nothing similar is required in the plural: *John and Henry are lawyers.*

Unos is simply the plural of **un.** Both **unos** and **algunos** are translated *some.* Their difference in meaning is the same as the difference between their respective singulars: just as **un hombre** *a man* makes a more specific reference than **algún hombre** *some man* (none in particular), so **unos hombres** is more specific than **algunos hombres.**

GUIDED CONVERSATION

R. *Repórter* M. *Ministro*[2] *de Seguridad Pública*

R. Señor Ministro, ¿quiere usted comentar sobre el acuerdo que acaba de efectuarse[3] con los radicales?
M. Sí, en el último momento llegamos a un acuerdo ______________
R. ¿Pero no le importa a usted que se encuentren ya en libertad tales personas?
M. Sí que me importa.[4] Pero me importa más que ______________
R. ¿Cree usted sinceramente que ellos son capaces[5] de matar a un embajador?
M. Señor, no olvide usted lo del periodista ______________
R. ¿Ha tomado usted en cuenta[6] lo que puedan opinar[7] contra su partido en otras partes?
M. ¡Claro! Pero a estos canallas ______________
R. Bien, señor Ministro. ¿Puede usted garantizar[8] la seguridad del país?
M. Cómo no. Deben mejorarse ______________

PATTERNED RESPONSE REVIEW DRILL

Imperfect verb forms.
INSTRUCTIONS: Answer the questions, following the model.

A. 1. El trabaja y come mucho ahora, ¿no?
Sí, y antes también trabajaba y comía mucho.
2. El estudia y aprende mucho ahora, ¿no?
3. El habla y escribe mucho ahora, ¿no?
4. El entra y sale mucho ahora, ¿no?
5. El compra y vende mucho ahora, ¿no?

B. 1. Nosotros trabajamos y comemos mucho ahora, ¿no?
Sí, y antes también trabajábamos y comíamos mucho.
2. Nosotros estudiamos y aprendemos mucho ahora, ¿no?
3. Nosotros hablamos y escribimos mucho ahora, ¿no?
4. Nosotros entramos y salimos mucho ahora, ¿no?
5. Nosotros compramos y vendemos mucho ahora, ¿no?

reading

Problema de pronunciación

P. *Profesor* M. *Señor Moreno, estudiante*

P. Todos ustedes saben la historia del norteamericano que fue a cazar a una selva de Sud América. (*En efecto, la clase ya la ha oído dos veces durante el semestre, pero es la historia favorita del profesor.*) Este cazador se detuvo delante de una casa situada cerca de

fue a cazar *went hunting* **selva** *forest*
oído *heard*
delante de *in front of*

[2]*Minister* [3]*has just been worked out* [4]*Sure it matters to me.* [5]*capable* [6]*taken into account* [7]*what opinion they might hold* [8]*guarantee*

la selva y llamó a la puerta. Apareció el dueño de la casa, y le preguntó al cazador qué deseaba. Este respondió: ¿Aquí se caza, señor? El dueño, señalando a sus tres hijas, de edad avanzada para el matrimonio, contestó rápido: Sí, señor, elija usted a cualquiera. (*risa complaciente de parte de la clase*) Muy bien, señores, ¿quién puede explicarme esta historia? ...¿Señor Moreno?

M. Pues se trata de la pronunciación de la zeta. Las palabras *casar* y *cazar* se pronuncian del mismo modo en Hispanoamérica. Nosotros decimos [kasár] en vez de [kaθár], como debemos...

P. No, no, señor Moreno, nada de "como debemos". En primer lugar, nadie tiene que disculparse del modo de hablar de su propia lengua. Si el español de Puerto Rico, por ejemplo, es un poco diferente, en algunos aspectos, del de Castilla, eso no quiere decir que sea inferior. El de Puerto Rico es tan "correcto" para los que lo hablan como el de Castilla para los castellanos. En segundo lugar, en cuanto a diferencias de pronunciación tales como [kaθár] en la mayor parte de España y [kasár] en Andalucía e Hispanoamérica, tales detalles han sido muy discutidos por los eruditos. Sólo puedo decir que se trata de consideraciones históricas y sociales muy complejas, y debemos dejar tales asuntos para los especialistas... que no siempre están de acuerdo.

dueño *owner*
elegir *choose*
risa *laugh* **complaciente** *polite*
zeta *letter* **z**
nada de *let's not have any of that*
disculparse...modo *to apologize for his way* **propia** *own*
sea *it is*
en cuanto a *as for*
han sido *have been*
asuntos *matters*

Spain: Street in Cádiz

Puerto Rico: Luquillo beach

UNIT 16

Early at the Office

S. *Secretary* B. *Boss*

S. Mrs. Méndez called about a raffle or something [for a matter of a raffle]. How that woman can talk!

B. Yes, she'll talk your head off [even through the elbows].

S. She's raffling off a fur coat at a hundred pesos a ticket for the benefit of her neighborhood church [chapel].

B. What?! A hundred pesos! If she calls again, tell her I'm not in.

S. The mail's finally come; here it is, two magazines and several bills. And a letter for me. Wonderful!

B. Let me see those bills: rent, electricity . . . Pay the electric bill first; if we don't, they'll shut it off on us.

* * *

S. Do you know who wrote me? Ana Guadalupe Martínez, the girl who worked here two years ago.

B. Oh yes, of course, Lupita, the girl with the green eyes. We sure do miss her! What does she have to say?

S. She's getting married to Lorenzo, that Spanish fellow who was her boy friend for so long.

B. Really? I'm delighted to hear it!

Temprano en la oficina

S. *Secretaria* J. *Jefe*

S. Llamó la Sra. Méndez para un asunto de una rifa. ¡Cómo habla esa señora!

J. Sí, hasta por los codos.

S. Está rifando un abrigo de pieles a cien pesos el número, a beneficio de la capilla de su barrio.

J. ¡¿Qué?! ¡Cien pesos! Si vuelve a llamar, dígale que no estoy.

S. Por fin llegó el correo; aquí está, dos revistas y varias cuentas. Y una carta para mí. ¡Qué bueno!

J. Déjeme ver esas cuentas: alquiler, electricidad (1)... Pague primero la de la electricidad; si no, nos la cortan.

* * *

S. ¿Sabe quién me escribió? Ana Guadalupe Martínez, la que trabajó aquí hace dos años.

J. Ah, claro, Lupita, la de los ojos verdes. ¡Cómo la echamos de menos! ¿Qué cuenta?

S. Que se casa con Lorenzo, el español, su novio de años (2).

J. ¿De veras? ¡Cuánto me alegro!

Mexico City: Cathedral of Guadalupe

S. She says he's already asked [her hand (from)] her father.

B. And when's the wedding? I'd like to send them a nice present.

S. They're going to wait until after Holy Week.

* * *

B. By the way, I must go to communion one of these days. I have to please my wife.

S. She's right. You've got to do your duty by the Church at least during Lent.

B. Do you go to communion often?

S. Almost every Sunday.

B. My gosh! And to think that I almost never go to mass. But my wife goes all the time and prays for both of us. Well, let's get to work.

S. Dice ella que él ya le pidió la mano a su padre.

J. ¿Y cuándo es la boda? Quisiera mandarles un buen regalo.

S. Van a esperar hasta después de Semana Santa.

* * *

J. A propósito, debo ir a comulgar uno de estos días. Tengo que complacer a mi mujer.

S. Tiene razón ella. Hay que cumplir con la iglesia por lo menos en Cuaresma.

J. ¿Usted comulga muy a menudo?

S. Casi todos los domingos.

J. ¡Caramba! Y pensar que yo casi nunca voy a misa. (3) Pero mi mujer va siempre y reza por los dos. Bueno, señorita, vamos a trabajar.

cultural notes

(1) Personal matters, such as domestic bills, often form part of the routine in Latin-American business offices.

(2) Long courtships are quite general because young men usually wait until they become established before they marry.

(3) Latin-American women take religion more seriously than do men, who are often only nominal church members. An illustration of this difference of attitude is the long tradition of anticlericalism among Hispanic men, addressed mainly against the temporal power of the Church.

› WRITING EXERCISE

INSTRUCTIONS: Following are pairs of words containing the sound /b/ spelled **b** in one word and **v** in the other. Write them from dictation, remembering that they sound exactly alike regardless of the spelling:

basta	**v**asta	**b**ocal	**v**ocal
baso	**v**aso	**b**otar	**v**otar
baca	**v**aca	**b**ocear	**v**ocear
Baco	**v**aco	**b**alaca	**v**alaca
bello	**v**ello	ca**b**o	ca**v**o
biga	**v**iga	to**b**a	to**v**a
bino	**v**ino	sa**b**ia	sa**v**ia
bagar	**v**agar	re**b**otar	re**v**otar

INSTRUCTIONS: Write the following words from dictation as the teacher reads first one spelled with **mb** and then one spelled with **nv.**

e**mb**astar	e**nv**asar
co**mb**inar	co**nv**idar
e**mb**estir	i**nv**estir
e**mb**icar	e**nv**iar
co**mb**atir	co**nv**ertir
i**mb**erbe	i**nv**erne
A**mb**eres	a**nv**erso

The letters **b** and **v** represent both the stop and fricative variants of /b/ in present-day Spanish. The distinction, which is merely orthographic, is generally due to the etymology of the word (e.g., **beber** derives from Latin *bibere,* and **vivir** from Latin *vivere*). Up to the sixteenth century **b** and **v** indicated two different sounds for many writers, but this distinction was later lost.

88 Nominalization of numerals and indefinites

EXAMPLES

A. 1. Ella tiene **uno** portátil. *She has a portable one* (*one* [*that is*] *portable*).
2. Necesito **cinco** más grandes. *I need five bigger ones* (*five* [*that are*] *bigger*).

B. 1. Se tomó una aspirina, y diez minutos más tarde se tomó una **segunda.** *He took an aspirin, and ten minutes later he took a second one.*
2. Al comerse el churrasco, Ricardo pidió un **segundo** más grande. *Having eaten* (*Upon eating*) *the steak, Ricardo ordered a second one* (*that was*) *bigger.*

C. 1. ¿No tiene usted **otro** azul? *Don't you have a blue one* (*another* [*that is*] *blue*)?
2. Tráeme **otras** mejores. *Bring me some better ones* (*others* [*that are*] *better*).

D. 1. ¿Mataron a **alguno?**
   2. ¿Conoce usted **alguno** menos complicado? *Do you know any less complicated one (any [that is] less complicated)?*

E. No hay **ninguno** peor. *There's no worse one (none [that is] worse).*

F. Hay **pocos** modernos. *There are few modern ones (few [that are] modern).*

G. Encontré **muchos** más fáciles. *I found many easier ones (many [that were] easier).*

H. **Cualquiera** bueno sirve. *Any good one (Any [that is] good) is all right.*

a (one) some ten another (some) other some (any) no few many	portable bigger blue better etc.	one(s)

uno, -a **unos, -as** **diez** **otro, -a** **otros, -as** **alguno, -a, -os, -as** **ninguno, -a**[1] **pocos, -as** **muchos, -as**	**portátil, -es** **más grande, -s** **azul, -es** **mejor, -es** **etc.**

In Spanish the numerals (both cardinals and ordinals) and indefinites may be nominalized directly and may be modified by adjectives without the addition of any equivalent of *one: ten better ones* **diez mejores,** *a (one) better one* **uno mejor.**

ITEM SUBSTITUTION DRILL

1. Ella tiene uno *portátil.*
   (regular, complicado, sencillo, anticuado)
2. Necesito unas más *grandes.*
   (modernas, importantes, profesionales, fuertes)
3. ¿No tiene usted otros *azules?*
   (negros, verdes, mejores, nuevos)
4. No hay ninguno *mejor.*
   (peor, fácil, importado, nacional, viejo)
5. ¿Tiene alguno menos *complicado?*
   (difícil, grande, sucio, ridículo)
6. Hay pocos *profesionales.*
   (heridos, infames, inocentes, libres)
7. Encontré muchos más *fáciles.*
   (miserables, altos, horribles, juntos)

TRANSLATION DRILL

A. 1. I have a portable one at home.
   2. I have a better one at home.
   3. I have a new one at home.
   4. I have a magnificent one at home.

B. 1. There's another wounded one.
   2. There's another invited one.
   3. There's another bad one.

C. 1. In this world there are few innocent [ones].
   2. In this world there are few simple [ones].
   3. In this world there are few respectable [ones].
   4. In this world there are few free [ones].
   5. They gave me twelve longer [ones].

[1] See footnote 2, p. 209, for the plurals **ningunos, -as.**

EXAMPLES 1. Disparó contra una manifestación de estudiantes, **algo** horrible.
2. La cuenta del banco está **algo** baja. *The bank account is a bit (somewhat) low.*
3. Los juegos fueron **algo** ridículos. *The games were rather ridiculous.*

something good somewhat (rather) good	**algo bueno** **algo bueno, -a, -os, -as**

Algo *something,* like the other indefinites, may be modified by an adjective, which then takes the same form as the masculine singular. **Algo** *somewhat, rather,* being an adverb, modifies the adjective, which in turn agrees with its noun (e.g., **baja** with **cuenta,** Example 2).

› TRANSLATION DRILL

1. TEACHER: Those matters are something fantastic.
   STUDENT: **Esos asuntos son algo fantástico.**
   TEACHER: Those matters are somewhat fantastic.
   STUDENT: **Esos asuntos son algo fantásticos.**
2. The chapel is something new.
   The chapel is somewhat new.
3. Electricity is something necessary.
   Electricity is somewhat necessary.
4. This magazine is something modern.
   This magazine is somewhat modern.
5. This raffle is something ridiculous.
   This raffle is somewhat ridiculous.
6. This church is something old.
   This church is somewhat old.

EXAMPLE Trajo algo para **cada uno** (**una**) de ustedes. *He brought something for each (one) of you.*

each (one)	**cada uno** **cada una**

The adjective **cada** cannot be nominalized. In the example above it modifies the nominalized **uno, -a.**

› TRANSLATION DRILL

1. I have a gift for each one of the boys.
   I have a fur coat for each one of the girls.
2. Each of the games was short.
   Each of the letters was long.
3. Each of the receipts was necessary.
   Each of the prescriptions was important.
4. I saw each one of the races.
   I saw each one of the sports.

› DISCUSSION

The nominalization of numerals and indefinites is like that of the definites (see Unit 12, Section 61) in that no equivalent of *one* is used (**cada** is an exception). It differs, however, when an adjective is added. With the definites, what is nominalized is the adjective: **el nuevo** means *the new one.* With the indefinites, what is nominalized is the indefinite word: **uno nuevo** means *one (that is)* *new;* **otros nuevos** means *others (that are) new.* This is why we find **uno nuevo** and not **un nuevo, alguno nuevo** and not **algún nuevo,** etc. English sometimes does the same: *There's none better (no better one), There are ten wounded.* (When an adjective has already become a noun in its own right then we do find the shortened forms: **un general** means *a general,* while **uno general** means *one [that is] general* or *a general one.* Note the example with **portátil:** since this adjective has not, unlike the English *portable,* become a noun in its own right, we must say **uno portátil** *a portable one* rather than the literal equivalent of *a portable.*)

The *each-other* construction

EXAMPLES

1. Llegó este policía y **nos peleamos.** (*This policeman arrived, and we fought each other.*)
2. Sea lo que sea, no **nos entendimos.**
3. **Nos encontramos** en el Club de la Unión. (*We met each other at the Union Club.*)
4. ¿Van a **verse** mañana? *Are you going to see each other tomorrow?*
5. Todos **nos compramos** regalos. *We all buy one another presents.*

verb	+	each other one another

nos *or* **se**	+	*verb*

Each other (two persons) and *one another* (more than two) are additional meanings of the reflexive pronouns **nos** and **se.** There is no difference between direct and indirect objects.

EXAMPLES

1. No queremos hablar mal **uno del otro.** *We don't want to speak ill of each other.*
2. Ricardo y su hermana no pueden hacer nada **uno sin el otro.** *Ricardo and his sister can't do anything without each other.*
3. Hablaron **unas con otras.** *They (Women) talked with one another.*

preposition	each other one another

uno (**una**) **unos** (**unas**)	*preposition*	**el otro** (**la otra**) **otros** (**otras**)

When *each other* (*one another*) is the object of a preposition, the formula is **uno con (para, contra,** etc.) **el otro (unos con otros)** without **nos** or **se.** When both sexes are involved the masculine is used for both pronouns.

PATTERNED RESPONSE DRILL

1. ¿Ustedes dos se pelearon?
   Sí, nos peleamos.
2. ¿Ustedes dos se entendieron?
3. ¿Ustedes dos se compraron regalos?
4. ¿Ustedes dos se conocieron?
5. ¿Ustedes dos se mandaron regalos?
6. ¿Ustedes dos se ofendieron?

TRANSLATION DRILL

1. TEACHER: Finally we understood each other.
   STUDENT: **Por fin nos entendimos.**
2. The ladies are going to see each other tomorrow.
   We bought each other presents.
   Why did they kill one another?
3. They can't do anything without each other.
   They can't study without each other.
   They can't go to communion without each other.
   They can't eat without each other.
4. They don't want to speak against one another.
   They don't want to say anything against one another.
   They don't want to argue against one another.
   They don't want to fight against one another.

DISCUSSION

Each other (*one another*) adds one more meaning to the reflexive pronouns in Spanish. Thus:

1. **Se mataron** *They killed themselves,* literally committed suicide.

2. **Se mataron en un accidente** *They got killed in an accident.* (In Section 40 this was limited to nonpersonal subjects, but it may also be used with personal ones if the context or circumstances make the meaning clear.)

3. **Se mataron** *They killed each other* (*one another*).

Normally, context and circumstances prevent any confusion. The *each-other, one-another* meaning can be clarified, however, by saying, for the above example, **Se mataron uno al otro** (**unos a otros**), with the personal **a** used in the same type of construction as the other prepositions illustrated in the second box. This is given here for information, not for practice.

Equivalents of *that, which, who,* and *whom*

EXAMPLES

A. 1. Primera y última vez **que** vengo aquí.
2. Mi sobrina **que** vive en México.
3. El papel en **que** escribo. *The paper I write on* (*on which I write*).
4. El abogado **que** escogieron. *The lawyer* (*that, whom*) *they picked.*

B. 1. ¿Ellas son las muchachas de **quienes** me hablabas anoche? *They're the girls* (*that, whom*) *you were telling me about last night?*
2. Yo no soy la persona a **quien** se[2] lo dio. *I'm not the person he gave it to* (*to whom he gave it*).

A. IN MOST SITUATIONS	
that which who whom	**que**

The word that most frequently carries the meanings of *that, which, who,* and *whom* is **que. Que** is not normally omitted as the English equivalents often are.

B. AFTER A PREPOSITION	
that (*person*) whom	**quien, quienes**

After a preposition **quien** (plural **quienes**), not **que** is used for persons. The required indirect object form is **a quien** (**a quienes**).

[2] Relative **quien** like interrogative **quién** when used as an indirect object calls for an added with-verb pronoun. See Unit 11, Section 58.

› TRANSFORMATION DRILL

INSTRUCTIONS: Combine the following pairs of sentences into one sentence, as in the model.

A. 1. TEACHER: Lupita es la chica. Tiene los ojos verdes.
   STUDENT: **Lupita es la chica que tiene los ojos verdes.**
2. Lorenzo es el español. Se casa con Lupita.
3. Ahí va la secretaria. Trabajó aquí el año pasado.
4. Ahora viene esa señora. Habla hasta por los codos.
5. Ese es el muchacho. Ganó en las carreras.

B. 1. Estas son las casas. Las voy a comprar.
   Estas son las casas que voy a comprar.
2. Estas son las cuentas. Las quieren pagar.
3. Este es el abrigo. Lo tiene que vender.
4. Este es el correo. Lo debemos leer.
5. Esta es la capilla. La acaban de terminar.

C. 1. Esa es la rubia. Te hablaba de ella anoche.
   Esa es la rubia de quien te hablaba anoche.
2. Esos son los compañeros. Estudiaba con ellos.
3. Esas son las amigas. Salía con ellas.
4. Ese es el viejo. Rezamos por él.
5. Esa es la sobrina. Compré el regalo para ella.

D. 1. Aquí está el abogado. Le vendí el coche.
   Aquí está el abogado a quien le vendí el coche.
2. Aquí está el señor. Le ofrecieron el puesto.
3. Aquí está el español. Le pedimos el favor.
4. Aquí están los extranjeros. Les exigieron una multa.
5. Aquí están los profesores. Les quitaron las clases.

› TRANSLATION DRILL

1. Where are the bills I gave you?
2. Which is the magazine that you mentioned?
3. Olga is the clerk who sold me the bed.
4. Lupe is the secretary that we miss.
5. He's the doctor (whom) I need.
6. He's the journalist (whom) I wait for.
7. She's the girl (whom) we were speaking of.
8. The businessman we sold it to is American.
9. The administrator we spoke to is Spanish.

EXAMPLES

1. Las dos chicas **que están** en la sala.
2. Una casita verde **que está** en la esquina.
3. El periódico **que está** debajo del paquete. *The newspaper (that is) under the package.*

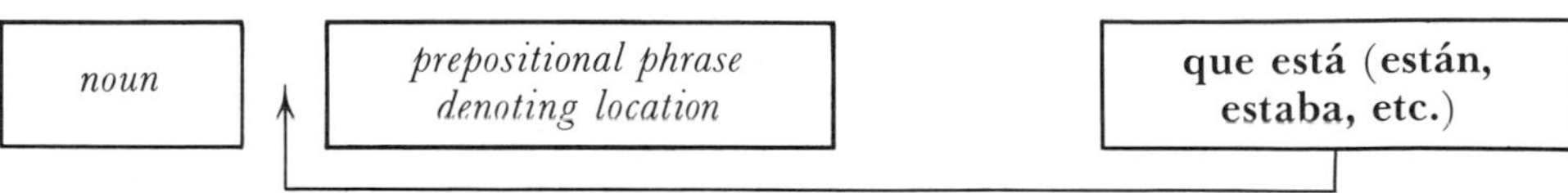

Whereas English may modify a noun directly by means of a prepositional phrase denoting location, Spanish normally adds **que** plus a form of **estar.**

› TRANSLATION DRILL

A. 1. Who are the two girls in the living room?
2. Who are the two maids in the kitchen?
3. Who are the two boys in the patio?
4. Who are the three boys on the corner?

B. 1. The newspapers under the package.
2. The messages under the telephone.
3. The documents under the painting.
4. The tools under the car.
5. The sheep under the tree.

› DISCUSSION

As a direct object referring to persons, **a quien** (**a quienes**) may replace **que,** although this point is not included in the drills: *the man I respect* **el hombre que respeto, el hombre a quien respeto.**

Spanish almost never omits relative words as English does: *The man I saw* **El hombre que vi;** and prepositions are joined directly to relatives: *The house* (*that*) *I live in* **La casa en que vivo.**

91 Word order

EXAMPLES

A.
1. Llamó la señora **Méndez.**
2. Por fin llegó el **correo.**
3. Llegó este **policía.**
4. ¿Por qué anda toda la gente **corriendo?**
5. Y eso ¿qué **importa?**
6. Tiene razón **ella.**

B.
1. Sólo de **eso** se habla. (*Only of* ***that*** *do they speak.*)
2. ¡Qué buen **café** es éste! (*What a good* ***café*** *this is!*)
3. Cómo **habla** esa señora. (*What a* ***talker*** *that woman is.*)

X = the center of attention or most informative element, carrying the major stress of the sentence
y = some other informative element
z = an element with very little attention, already spoken about or obvious from the context, carrying least stress

A. CLIMACTIC WORD ORDER		**B.** ANTICLIMACTIC WORD ORDER		
y	X	(y)	X	z

Corresponding to the type *A* ***policeman*** *came up, The* ***telephone*** *rang, The* ***mail*** *arrived,* with order Xy in English, Spanish normally has order yX: *Came a* ***policeman.*** These are Examples A above.

As in English a sentence may be made more "relaxed" by putting some unstressed element at the end and uttering it at a low pitch. These are Examples B above.

› PATTERNED RESPONSE DRILL

1. TEACHER: ¿Quién llamó?
   STUDENT: **Llamó la señora Méndez.**
   TEACHER: ¿Qué hizo la señora Méndez?
   STUDENT: **La señora Méndez llamó.**
2. ¿Quién salió?
   ¿Qué hizo la señora Méndez?
3. ¿Quién terminó?
   ¿Qué hizo la señora Méndez?
4. ¿Quién desapareció?
   ¿Qué hizo la señora Méndez?
5. ¿Quién llegó?
   ¿Qué hizo la señora Méndez?
6. ¿Quién comió?
   ¿Qué hizo la señora Méndez?

› TRANSLATION DRILL

INSTRUCTIONS: Translate the following sentences, placing the emphasized words last.

1. The opinion *changed.*
   The opinion changed.
2. The opposition *lost.*
   The opposition lost.
3. The police *arrived.*
   The police arrived.
4. The maid *swept.*
   The maid swept.

› FRAME SUBSTITUTION DRILL

INSTRUCTIONS: Repeat the following sentences just as you hear them. Then repeat them again, following the intonation shift illustrated by the model.

A. 1. TEACHER: Es difícil la filosofía. *Repita.*
STUDENT: **Es difícil la filosofía.**
TEACHER: *Cambie.*
STUDENT: **Es difícil la filosofía.**
2. Es horrible el tránsito.
3. Es importante la Cuaresma.
4. Es ridículo el discurso.
5. Es necesario cumplir.
6. Es anticuada la casa.
7. Es imposible terminar.

B. 1. Sin falta se lo traigo.
2. ¡Cuánto lo siento!
3. De veras lo digo.
4. A menudo los compra.
5. Inmediatamente se lo presto.
6. Seguí sus órdenes.

C. 1. Por eso lo digo.
2. Por eso lo menciono.
3. Por eso lo exagero.

› DISCUSSION

The fact noted in connection with questions in Unit 3, Section 10, is true to some extent of most other sentences in Spanish: the item that is the center of attention and carries the major stress of the sentence tends to be shifted to the end.

In English this shift is not always possible because word order is needed more often than in Spanish for making some grammatical distinction. We cannot shift *Méndez* to the end of the sentence in *Mrs. Méndez called,* even if it is the most stressed word, because in *Called Mrs. Méndez* it would appear to be the object rather than the subject. In Spanish this problem is taken care of by the personal **a,** and **Llamó la señora Méndez** (stressing **Méndez**) is the usual order to tell "what Mrs. Méndez did." The difference between the two languages shows up most sharply in brief sentences in which the subject is stressed and precedes the verb in English but follows it in Spanish: *The telephone rang* **Sonó el teléfono.**

The effect of shifting the position of the stressed element, where English can manage, it is the same in both languages, though English may have to reword slightly. Compare the climactic *There came a blinding flash, They talk about nothing but that* with the anticlimactic *A blinding flash came, It's only that that they talk about.* In Spanish no rewording is necessary, and the stressed element can come early in the sentence (the less usual position) or at the end (the usual position): **Sólo de *eso* se habla, Sólo se habla de *eso*.**

Though less so than in English, word order in Spanish is restricted in certain ways. The sentence **Cómo habla esa señora** would not be normal with the subject **esa señora** between **Cómo** and **habla** since interrogative words (Unit 3, Section 10) are normally followed by the verb.

Position of adjectives with *qué*

EXAMPLES A. 1. ¡**Qué buen** café es éste!
2. ¡**Qué mala** cara trae!

B. 1. ¡**Qué** cosa **más** (**tan**) **ridícula!** *What a ridiculous thing! (What thing more [so] ridiculous!)*

qué +	*adjective* + *noun* OR *noun* + **más** (**tan**) + *adjective*

› ITEM SUBSTITUTION DRILL

A. 1. **¡Qué buen café es éste!**
2. _____ leche _____
3. _____ magnífica _____
4. _____ toro _____
5. _____ bonito _____
6. _____ ganado _____
7. _____ mal _____
8. _____ mantequilla _____
9. _____ buena _____
10. _____ papas _____

B. 1. **¡Qué mala cara trae!**
2. _____ tiene
3. _____ bonita _____
4. _____ pelo _____
5. _____ largo _____
6. _____ zapatos _____
7. _____ grandes _____
8. _____ manos _____
9. _____ fuertes _____
10. _____ cuerpo _____
11. _____ perfecto _____
12. _____ vida _____
13. _____ mala _____
14. _____ costumbres _____

C. 1. **¡Qué cosa más ridícula!**
2. _____ costumbre _____
3. _____ anticuada
4. _____ idea _____
5. _____ sencilla
6. _____ gente _____
7. _____ moderna
8. _____ señor _____
9. _____ importante
10. _____ persona _____
11. _____ fantástica
12. _____ invitación _____
13. _____ aburrida
14. _____ cuestión _____
15. _____ difícil
16. _____ tema _____

D. 1. **¡Qué tío tan bueno es usted!**
2. _____ padre _____
3. _____ malo _____
4. _____ profesor _____
5. _____ amable _____
6. _____ abogado _____
7. _____ bruto _____
8. _____ médico _____
9. _____ anticuado _____
10. _____ administrador _____
11. _____ serio _____
12. _____ empleado _____
13. _____ complicado _____
14. _____ abuelo _____
15. _____ respetable _____
16. _____ hombre _____
17. _____ moderno _____
18. _____ técnico _____

E. 1. **¡Qué carrera tan fenomenal!**
2. _____ cantidad _____
3. _____ astronómica
4. _____ número _____
5. _____ horrible
6. _____ tema _____
7. _____ importante
8. _____ persona _____
9. _____ equivocada
10. _____ jefe _____
11. _____ malo
12. _____ sistema _____
13. _____ diferente

F. 1. **¡Qué foto más admirable!**
2. ______________ tremenda
3. _____ vida ________________
4. ______________ tranquila
5. _____ juego ________________
6. ______________ complicado
7. _____ materia ________________
8. ______________ exacta
9. _____ sistema ________________
10. ______________ diferente

93 Singular for "one each"

EXAMPLES A. 1. A todos les **duele la cabeza y la garganta.**
2. Nos ponemos **la corbata.** *We put on our ties.*
3. Lo tuvieron en **la mano derecha.** *They held it in their right hand(s).*

B. 1. Levantaron **las manos.** *They raised (both) their hands.*
2. Vamos en **nuestros coches.** *We're going in our cars.*

Lima, Peru: Wedding reception

	PLURAL OF POSSESSOR		SINGULAR OF THING POSSESSED
A	**todos les**	**duele**	**la cabeza y la garganta.**
	Nos ponemos		**la corbata.**
Lo	**tuvieron**	**en**	**la mano derecha.**

A.

To link more than one possessor with a single thing possessed, normally the thing is expressed in the singular.

PLURAL OF POSSESSOR		PLURAL OF THING POSSESSED
Levantaron		**las manos.**
Vamos	**en**	**nuestros coches.**

B.

To link the possessors with more than one thing apiece (or with just one if the singular would be ambiguous), the thing is expressed in the plural.

› PATTERNED RESPONSE DRILL

1. ¿Quiénes tienen coche? ¿Los estudiantes?
   Sí, todos los estudiantes tienen coche.
2. ¿Quiénes tienen novio? ¿Las rubias?
3. ¿Quiénes tienen corbata? ¿Los profesores?
4. ¿Quiénes levantan la mano? ¿Los estudiantes?
5. ¿Quiénes tienen secretaria? ¿Los jefes?
6. ¿Quiénes tienen tijeras? ¿Los barberos?
7. ¿Quiénes se lavan las manos? ¿Los niños?
8. ¿Quiénes tienen los ojos negros? ¿Las morenas?
9. ¿Quiénes tienen pieles? ¿Las señoras?

› DISCUSSION

English and Spanish both use the singular for "one each," though English wavers: *They pledged their honor* (not *honors*), *The crash carried fifty passengers to their death* (or *deaths*). Spanish extends it to all situations where the result is not ambiguous: **Todos los alumnos tienen coche** can only mean "one car apiece" (English *have cars* might mean one or more than one apiece). If, however, the singular is ambiguous, Spanish uses the plural just as English does: *We are going in our cars* **Vamos en nuestros coches** (**Vamos en nuestro coche** would suggest one car owned by several persons, a family, for instance).

94 Idioms with *tener* and *dar*

EXAMPLES

A.
1. **Tiene razón** ella. Hay que cumplir con la Iglesia.
2. **Tienes razón.** Para café bueno no hay como este lugar.
3. Otra cosa que **tengo ganas** de ver es una buena corrida de toros. (*Another thing that I have a desire to see [desires of seeing] is a good bull-fight.*)
4. **Tengo hambre;** voy a ir a comer algo.

B.
1. **Tengo muchas ganas** de ir.
2. **Tengo un hambre feroz.** *I have a ferocious appetite.*
3. **¿Qué edad tiene** ella? (*What age does she have?*)
   Debe **tener unos veintiún años.**
4. ¡Ella **tiene tanta suerte!** *She's so lucky!*

A.

to be right	**tener razón**
to be eager	**tener ganas**
to be hungry	**tener hambre**
to be ten years old	**tener diez años**
How old are you?	**¿Cuántos años tienes?** / **¿Qué edad tienes?**

The English equivalents of the **tener** idioms usually contain the verb *to be.*

B.

FORM OF *be*	ADVERB MODIFYING THE ADJECTIVE	ADJECTIVE
I am	very	eager.
I am	ferociously	hungry.

FORM OF **tener**	ADJECTIVES MODIFYING THE NOUN	NOUN	
Tengo	**muchas**	**ganas.**	
Tengo	**un**	**hambre**	**feroz.**

In these idioms, when the adjective in English is modified by an adverb, the noun in Spanish is modified by an adjective.

› PERSON-NUMBER SUBSTITUTION DRILL

1. *Ella* tiene razón en eso.
   (usted, nosotros, tú, ustedes, yo, ellos, él)
2. *Yo* tengo ganas de ver una buena corrida de toros.
   (nosotros, ella, ellos, ustedes, usted, tú, él)
3. Tenemos unas ganas tremendas de ir.
   (él, yo, ellas, ustedes, tú, usted, ellos)
4. Tengo muchísima hambre.
   (ella, nosotros, ellos, tú, ustedes, usted)
5. *Ella* tiene unos veintiún años.
   (tú, él, ustedes, ella, usted, ellos, Susana)

› TRANSLATION DRILL

1. TEACHER: She's right.
   STUDENT: **Ella tiene razón.**
   TEACHER: She's very right.
   STUDENT: **Ella tiene mucha razón.**
2. I'm eager to go.
   I'm very eager to go.
3. We're hungry.
   We're very hungry.
4. She's twenty years old.
   She's approximately twenty years old.
5. I'm hungry.
   I'm so hungry.
6. She's eager.
   She's so eager.
7. He's hungry.
   He's ferociously hungry.

EXAMPLES

1. **Tenga cuidado** de no romper nada.
2. Tú **tienes** más **suerte** que yo. *You're luckier than I am.*
3. No **tenga cuidado,** doña Beatriz.
4. Con la **suerte** que **tengo** yo, eso tenía que pasar. *With* **my** *luck* (*the luck I have*), *that was bound to happen.*
5. ¿Quién **tiene** la **culpa?** *Whose fault is it* (*Who is to blame*)?
6. **Tenga** la **bondad** de sentarse.

to be careful, worry	**tener cuidado**
to be lucky, have luck	**tener suerte**
It's my fault.	**Yo tengo la culpa.**

Not all **tener** idioms are necessarily matched by *to be* expressions in English.

TRANSLATION DRILL

A. 1. I'm always careful not to break anything.
2. We're always careful not to break anything.
3. Don't worry, Doña Beatriz.
4. Don't worry, ladies.

B. 1. No, sir, with *our* luck.
2. No, sir, with *their* luck.
3. You're never very lucky.
4. We're never very lucky.

C. 1. It's his fault.
2. It's their fault
3. It's our fault.

D. 1. Please sit down, sir.
2. Please sit down, gentlemen.
3. Please sit down, ladies.

EXAMPLES 1. Ese rosbif le **da hambre** a toda la familia. *That roast beef makes the whole family hungry.*
2. Los exámenes me **dan ganas** de quedarme en casa. *Exams make me feel like staying home.*
3. El ser fuerte no te **da razón.** *Being strong doesn't make you right.*

FORM OF *to make*	OBJECT	ADJECTIVE
It makes	the family	hungry.
It makes	you	right.

INDIRECT OBJECT	FORM OF **dar**	NOUN	
Le	**da**	**hambre**	**a la familia.**
Te	**da**	**razón.**	

Most of the nouns used with **tener** may also follow **dar** with the meaning *to make.*

ITEM SUBSTITUTION DRILL

1. Ese *rosbif* le da hambre a toda la familia.
(frijoles, carne, pan)
2. Estos *exámenes* me dan ganas de quedarme en casa.
(examen, manifestaciones, huelga, discursos)
3. El *ser moderno* no te da razón.
(ser viejo, estar aburrido, ser extranjero)

▸ TRANSLATION DRILL

1. TEACHER: I'm hungry.
   STUDENT: **Tengo hambre.**
   TEACHER: It makes me hungry.
   STUDENT: **Me da hambre.**
2. He's right.
   It makes him right.
3. We're very eager.
   It makes us very eager.
4. I'm very lucky.
   That makes me very lucky.
5. It's not my fault.
   That doesn't make it my fault.

▸ DISCUSSION

In a number of expressions in which English has *to be* plus an adjective, Spanish has **tener** plus a noun. English, too, often uses its verb *have* in ways that compare with *be: He has all the luck* is similar to *He is always lucky,* and *Have courage* is like *Be brave;* the problem is one of remembering the particular expressions in which English uses one form and Spanish the other.[3] An additional problem is the modifiers: in English they are adverbs (*I am **very** hungry*); in Spanish they are adjectives (**Tengo *mucha* hambre,** literally *I have **much** hunger*).

Tener cuidado normally means *to be careful,* i.e., to have care in the sense of taking pains. **No tener cuidado** means *to be carefree,* i.e., not to have cares or worries, hence *not to worry.*

Many of the same nouns that serve as objects of **tener** are also found with **dar;** here the person *acquires* the quality or state referred to. **Tengo hambre** (*I have hunger, I'm hungry*) refers to being in the condition or having it; **Me da hambre** (*It gives me hunger, It makes me hungry*) refers to getting that way.

 *Hacer* in expressions of time

EXAMPLES

A. 1. **Hace** como **cuatro años que vive** allá. *It's been* (*It makes*) *about four years that he has lived there.*
Vive allá **hace** como **cuatro años.** *He has lived there* (*for*) *about four years.*
2. Dígame **cuánto tiempo hace que se siente** así.

B. 1. Llegó **hace una hora. Hace una hora que** llegó. *He arrived an hour ago.* (*It's been an hour since he arrived.*)
2. Ana Guadalupe Martínez, la que trabajó aquí **hace dos años.**
3. **¿Cuánto hace** que comieron? *How long ago did you eat?*

A.

FORM OF *have*	*–ed* FORM OF VERB		PERIOD OF TIME
She has	lived	there	four years.

hace	PERIOD OF TIME	que	PRESENT TENSE OF VERB	
Hace	**cuatro años**	**que**	**vive**	**allá.**

To express the time during which something has been going on (*y has been going on for x time*), Spanish prefers the equivalent of *It makes x time that y goes on.*

[3] Other examples are the Spanish equivalents of *to be warm, cold, in a hurry, ashamed, afraid, thirsty, successful, sleepy,* and a very few others. Elsewhere, English *to be* matches Spanish **ser** and **estar:** *He is sick* is matched with **Está enfermo,** not with a literal equivalent of *He has sickness.*

B.

x time	*ago*

hace	*x* time

For the meaning *ago* Spanish uses the equivalent of *it makes:* e.g., *two years ago* = *it makes two years* **hace dos años.**

› TRANSFORMATION DRILL

1. TEACHER: Ha vivido allá cuatro años. (*He has lived there [for] four years.*)
   STUDENT: **Hace cuatro años que vive allá.**
2. Ha estado aquí dos semanas.
3. Ha vivido en México seis meses.
4. Ha esperado aquí dos horas.
5. Ha existido ese problema por catorce años.
6. Me he sentido enfermo por tres días. (*I have felt sick for three days.*)

› PATTERNED RESPONSE DRILL

A. 1. ¿Cuánto tiempo hace que comió usted?
   Hace una hora que comí.
2. ¿Cuánto tiempo hace que comió ella?
3. ¿Cuánto tiempo hace que comieron ustedes?
4. ¿Cuánto tiempo hace que comimos él y yo?

B. 1. ¿Cuánto tiempo hace que llegaron ustedes a la clase?
   Hace quince minutos que llegamos a la clase.
2. ¿Cuánto tiempo hace que llegaste tú a la clase?
3. ¿Cuánto tiempo hace que llegaron ellos a la clase?
4. ¿Cuánto tiempo hace que llegó usted a la clase?

› CONSTRUCTION SUBSTITUTION DRILL

INSTRUCTIONS: Repeat the following sentences just as you hear them. Then repeat them again, reorganizing the order of the elements of the sentence in the pattern of the model.

1. Hace tres años que Guadalupe trabajó aquí.
   Guadalupe trabajó aquí hace tres años.
2. Hace una hora que Lorenzo llegó.
3. Hace un año que volví de Colombia.
4. Hace mucho tiempo que entró al país.
5. Hace dos meses que celebré mi aniversario.
6. Hace ocho días que me prometió el puesto.
7. Hace quince días que encontré un trabajo.
8. Hace años que hubo una revolución.

› DISCUSSION

Hacer is found in two different contexts referring to time. The first has to do with how long something that is now going on has been going on. When English looks at the past duration and says *She* ***has lived*** *there four years,* Spanish prefers to look at the present continuation and say **Hace cuatro años que *vive* allá,** literally *It makes four years that she* ***lives*** *there,* with the verb in the present tense. The second context measures the time between the moment of speaking and some event in the past, usually expressed in English with *ago: He arrived an hour ago* **Llegó hace una hora,** literally *He arrived it makes an hour.*

Although the word order as given in the last two examples is more usual, the position of **hacer** can be reversed in both contexts: **Vive allá hace cuatro años, Hace una hora que llegó** (**que** is added whenever the **hacer** phrase comes first). Only the latter, the "ago" formula, is offered for practice in both positions: **Llegó hace una hora** *He arrived an hour ago,* **Hace una hora que llegó** *It's been an hour since he arrived.*

The presence of **cuánto** forces the **hacer** phrase to come first: **¿Cuántos años hace que vive allá?** *How many years has he (is it that he has) lived there?* **¿Cuánto (tiempo) hace que llegó?** *How long ago did he arrive? (How long has it been since he arrived?)*

› GUIDED CONVERSATION

C. *Concepción Márquez* R. *Rodrigo Márquez*

C. Hola cariño.[4] ¿Mucho trabajo en la oficina hoy?
R. Sí, Conchita, como siempre. Primero llamó la señora Méndez ______________
C. ¡A mí me lo dices![5] Me llamó a mí también.
R. ¿Te dijo que estaba rifando ______________
C. Sí. Y yo le dije a ella que no me costó más de cien pesos el abrigo que llevo ahora. Bueno, ¿había mucho correo?
R. Lo de siempre.[6] Sólo ______________
C. Pero no podemos pagarlas todas. La cuenta del banco[7] está algo baja.[8]
R. Ya lo sé. Pagué sólo ______________
C. ¿Y no me dijiste algo por teléfono de una boda?
R. Sí, la de Ana ______________
C. ¿Y cuándo es la boda? Quisiera mandarles un buen regalo.
R. Van a ______________
C. Hablando de Semana Santa, debes ir a comulgar conmigo uno de estos días.
R. Tienes razón ______________
C. ¡Pensar que tú casi nunca vas a misa y que yo voy casi todos los domingos!
R. Menos mal que tú vas ______________

› PATTERNED RESPONSE REVIEW DRILL

The **usted** command forms.

A. 1. TEACHER: ¿Llego mañana?
   STUDENT: **No, no llegue.**
2. ¿Contesto mañana?
3. ¿Llamo mañana?
4. ¿Estudio mañana?
5. ¿Pago mañana?
6. ¿Trabajo mañana?
7. ¿Corro mañana?
8. ¿Discuto mañana?
9. ¿Barro mañana?
10. ¿Escribo mañana?
11. ¿Salgo mañana?
12. ¿Sigo mañana?
13. ¿Vuelvo mañana?
14. ¿Vengo mañana?

B. 1. ¿La apago?
   No, no la apague.
2. ¿La arreglo?
3. ¿Las cambio?
4. ¿Lo celebro?
5. ¿Los invito?
6. ¿Los llevo?
7. ¿Los mando?
8. ¿Lo paso?
9. ¿La contesto?
10. ¿La barro?
11. ¿Lo discuto?
12. ¿Lo prometo?

[4] *dear* [5] *You're telling me!* [6] *The same as usual.* [7] *bank account* [8] *low*

C. 1. ¿Le doy el termómetro?
   No, no me lo dé.
2. ¿Le presto la maquinilla?
3. ¿Le llevo el café?
4. ¿Le mando la comida?
5. ¿Le cierro la puerta?
6. ¿Le digo la verdad?
7. ¿Le ofrezco pan?
8. ¿Le prometo la oportunidad?
9. ¿Le traigo el coche?
10. ¿Le vendo la casa?

reading

Orden de las palabras

E. *Estudiante* P. *Profesor* S. *Segundo estudiante* T. *Tercer estudiante*

E. Señor profesor, usted nos dijo ayer algo sobre el orden de las palabras. A mi parecer, los libros de gramática nos enseñan muy poco acerca de esto, y yo lo encuentro algo enredado.

acerca de *about, concerning*
enredado *confusing*

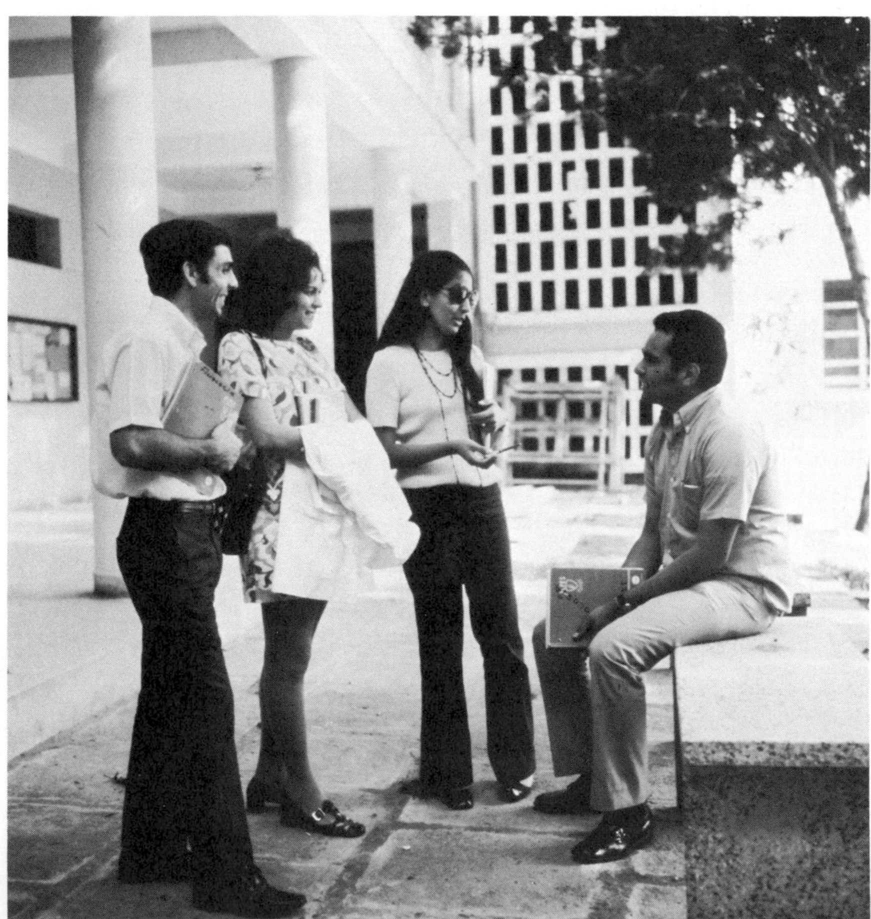

Mérida, Venezuela: Students at Universidad de los Andes

P. Usted tiene razón, y voy a repetir algunas de mis observaciones de ayer, usando ejemplos nuevos. Vamos a empezar con frases sencillas, o independientes. Por ejemplo, en una afirmación el orden común es sujeto-verbo-complemento, ¿no es verdad? Si le pregunto a usted: "¿Qué hizo la señora Méndez?" ¿qué me responde?

E. Pues, digo: "La señora Méndez hizo tal cosa."

P. Muy bien: La señora Méndez llamó, o habló, rifó un abrigo, o volvió a llamar, etc. Lo importante en estos casos es lo que *hizo* la señora Méndez, en contestación a la pregunta "¿Qué hizo?" Pero si le pregunto: "¿Quién llamó?" ¿qué me contesta?

E. "Llamó la señora Méndez."

P. Exactamente. Es decir, que la información nueva que se busca se halla al final de la frase, ¿cierto? Miren ustedes la primera frase del diálogo. Lo fundamental es la señora Méndez, y no la acción de llamar... Ahora... Miren la segunda. Una vez más, lo importante es que *la señora Méndez,* concretamente *esa señora,* habla mucho... ¿Quién puede mostrarme otros ejemplos en el diálogo?

final *end (e.g., of something written)*

mostrar *to show*

S. La secretaria, en su tercer discurso, dice: "Por fin llegó el correo." La cosa más importante es *el correo,* y no la llegada.

P. Bien. ¿Otros ejemplos?

T. Hacia el final del diálogo la secretaria dice: "Tiene razón ella." Esto quiere decir que es la esposa la que tiene razón, y no el jefe, ¿no es así?

Hacia *toward* **querer decir** *to mean*

P. ¿Comprenden todos?

UNIT 17

Problems of Growing Up

P. *Pedrito* M. *Mom* D. *Dad*

P. Pass me the meat, Mom.
M. Just a minute, Pedrito; your father hasn't been served.
D. Where's María Elena?
M. She ate early and went to the movies with Luis Alberto.
D. Again? They've already been [gone] twice this week. Who's with them [Who are they out with, With whom do they go around]?
M. I let them go alone since all of us here have already seen that picture.

* * *

D. I don't know, Alicia, but it seems to me that girls shouldn't be allowed to go out alone at night. I hope they get back early.
M. Don't worry. Anyway, Luis Alberto is a fine boy and comes from a fine family.
D. I know, it's not that; it's just that I've never gone along with these modern customs.
M. But Jorge, it's ridiculous nowadays for girls to have to take a chaperone everywhere.
D. Call it [It can be] ridiculous or anything you like, but in my day . . .

Problemas del crecer (1)

P. *Pedrito* M. *Mamá* PA. *Papá*

P. Pásame la carne, mamá.
M. Un momentito, Pedrito, tu papá no se ha servido.
PA. ¿Y dónde está María Elena?
M. Comió temprano y se fue al cine con Luis Alberto.
PA. ¿Otra vez? Ya han ido dos veces esta semana. ¿Con quién andan?
M. Los dejé ir solos porque ya aquí todos hemos visto esa película.

* * *

PA. No sé, Alicia, pero me parece que las muchachas no deben salir solas de noche. Ojalá que regresen temprano.
M. No te preocupes. Además, Luis Alberto es un buen muchacho y de muy buena familia (2).
PA. Ya lo sé (3), no es eso; es que yo nunca he estado de acuerdo con estas costumbres modernas.
M. Pero Jorge, hoy día es ridículo que las muchachas tengan que llevar chaperón a todas partes.
PA. Puede ser ridículo o lo que tú quieras, pero en mis tiempos...

Buenos Aires: Movie theater

M. Yes, yes, yes, I know . . . in your day. Things change [Everything changes]. Only you haven't changed.

* * *

D. Maybe you don't remember that when we were going together, we weren't allowed to go out alone even as far as the front door.

M. Yes . . . and how you fumed.

D. That has nothing to do with it.

M. All right, all right, let's not get on [touch] that subject; we've already discussed it many times.

P. Mommy, will you pass me a little bit of meat, please?

M. Sí, sí, sí, ya lo sé... en tus tiempos. Todo cambia. Sólo tú no has cambiado.

* * *

PA. Tal vez ya no recuerdes (4) que cuando tú y yo éramos novios, no nos dejaban salir solos ni a la puerta.

M. Sí... y cómo rabiabas.

PA. Eso no tiene nada que ver.

M. Bueno, bueno, no toquemos ese tema; ya lo hemos discutido muchas veces. (5)

P. Mamacita, ¿me pasas un poquito de carne, por favor?

cultural notes

(1) The article accompanies the infinitive here as it accompanies any other noun to emphasize "all of something": *Growing-up-in-general.* (See Unit 13, Section 72.) Remember that the infinitive is a verbal noun. (See Unit 8, Section 36.)

(2) The reference to Luis Alberto's family is an instance of widespread social stratification and the tendency among Spaniards and Latin Americans to regard family background as an important factor in evaluating people.

(3) The object pronoun **lo,** referring to an idea expressed in a preceding clause, is often used after such verbs as **saber, decir, preguntar,** and **creer.** Sometimes **lo** may be rendered by English *it* or *so* (*He's sick but he doesn't look it, If you want them say so*), but often there is no equivalent.

(4) After **tal vez** either the subjunctive (**recuerdes**) or the indicative (**recuerdas**) may be used. (See Unit 18, Section 102.)

(5) Except for the respect she receives in her home and as a mother, the Spanish-American woman generally remains in the background. Though old customs are giving way, the typical family is still patriarchal, but the wife often gets her way indirectly.

› WRITING EXERCISE

The written representation of /y/ by **ll** or **y.** INSTRUCTIONS: Write the following lists of words from dictation, remembering that those in the first column are written with **ll** and those in the second column, with **y.** Note also that the pairs of words in group A are pronounced identically.

A.	halla	haya	sallo	sayo	B.	llaga	yaba
	valla	vaya	pollo	poyo		llano	yambo
	malla	maya	bollo	boyo		llave	yate
	falla	faya	olla	hoya		lluvia	yuyuba
	ralla	raya	bullo	buyo		llena	yema
	salla	saya	tulla	tuya		llora	yola
	gallo	gayo	calló	cayó		taller	ayer
	rallo	rayo				llegar	yeguar

In most dialects of Spanish **ll** and **y** represent the same sound, which more often than not is the voiced palatal semiconsonant /y/. The distinction is maintained in writing on the basis of etymology. For example, Spanish **caballo** derives from Latin *caballus,* Spanish **llave** from Latin *clavis,* Spanish **llama** (*flame*) from Latin *flamma,* and Spanish **llorar** from Latin *plorare;* Spanish **mayo,** however, derives from Latin *maius.*

In certain dialects of Spanish, spoken in particular regions of Spain and Spanish America, a distinction is made, **ll** generally representing a voiced palatal lateral and **y** a voiced palatal fricative. In such areas the **ll** and **y** in the paired words of A and B above represent different sounds.

96 The *-do* form as an adjective

EXAMPLES

A. 1. Es un trabajo muy **complicado.**
2. Esas son ideas **anticuadas.**
3. Claro que podemos; **encantados.**

B. 1. Fue un árbol **caído.**[1] *It was a fallen tree.*
2. ¿Cuál es la religión **preferida?** *Which is the preferred religion (religion preferred)?*

C. 1. Cuestan más los muebles **cubiertos.** *Covered furniture costs more.*
2. ¿Está **abierta** la embajada? *Is the embassy open?*

[1]The same verbs that have the accent mark on **-ido** have it on **-iste** and **-imos.** See Unit 7, footnote 1.

THE **-do** FORM OF REGULAR VERBS	
hablar: habl- -ado	**comer: com- } -ido** **vivir: viv- } -ido**

Most verbs are regular in the **-do** form.

VERBS IRREGULAR IN THE **-do** FORM			
escribir	**escrito**	**romper**	**roto**
abrir	**abierto**	**ver**	**visto**
cubrir	**cubierto**	**poner**	**puesto**
morir	**muerto**	**suponer**	**supuesto**
volver	**vuelto**	**hacer**	**hecho**
envolver	**envuelto**	**decir**	**dicho**
disolver	**disuelto**		

These are the verbs thus far encountered in the dialogs that have irregular **-do** forms.

a broken arrow	**una flecha rota**
the leader chosen	**el líder escogido**
the work done	**el trabajo hecho**
my lost pills	**mis pastillas perdidas**

Used as an adjective, the **-do** form agrees with the noun like any other adjective. It follows the noun almost without exception, regardless of the position in English.

ITEM SUBSTITUTION DRILL

1. Tiene un *sistema* muy complicado.
   (receta, tema, empleo, filosofía)
2. Esas son *ideas* anticuadas.
   (asuntos, revistas, trajes, vestidos, costumbres)
3. Esto fue el *mes* pasado.
   (semana, año, vez, lunes, Cuaresma)
4. ¡Qué *clase* más aburrida!
   (elecciones, grupo, persona, barrios, ciudad)
5. Mire. Aquí hay una *flecha* rota.
   (termómetro, tazas, zapatos,[2] camisa, juguete, herramientas, discos)

EXAMPLES A. 1. Los temas nuevos y **los discutidos.** *The new subjects and the ones discussed.*
2. ¿Cuál puerta, **la abierta** o **la cerrada?** *Which door, the open one or the closed one?*
3. **Los solteros** no piensan lo mismo que **los casados.** *Bachelors do not think like married men.*
4. ¿Cuál árbol? **¿Ese caído** que está ahí? *Which tree? That fallen one over there?*

[2] When referring to shoes **roto** means *worn, worn out* but to other articles of clothing, *torn.*

B. 1. **Lo conseguido** fue bastante poco. *What was accomplished was mighty little.*
2. No voy a recibir ni un centavo de **lo pagado.** *I'm not going to get even a cent of what was paid.*

A.	the wrapped ones, the ones wrapped which wrapped one? these wrapped ones	**los envueltos** **¿cuál envuelto?** **estas envueltas**
B.	what was (is, has been) wrapped, the wrapped stuff	**lo envuelto**

The **-do** form may be nominalized like any other adjective. (See Unit 12, Section 61 and Unit 15, Section 81.)

› CONSTRUCTION SUBSTITUTION DRILL

INSTRUCTIONS: Repeat the following sentences just as you hear them. Then repeat them again, omitting the noun indicated, thus nominalizing the accompanying **-do** form.

1. TEACHER: Los señores invitados están aquí. *Repita.*
   STUDENT: **Los señores invitados están aquí.**
   TEACHER: *Cambie.*
   STUDENT: **Los invitados están aquí.**
2. Aquí están las *lentejas* importadas.
3. Los *estudiantes* heridos están mejor.
4. Las *novias* preocupadas no duermen bien.
5. El *paquete* envuelto son zapatos.
6. Los *toros* muertos eran importados.
7. Esa *camisa* rota no sirve.

› TRANSLATION DRILL

A. 1. What's known isn't much.
   Lo sabido no es mucho.
2. What's united is strong.
3. What's written is old-fashioned.
4. What's sold isn't the best.

B. 1. This is what's complicated.
   Esto es lo complicado.
2. This is what's bought.
3. This is what's produced.
4. This is what's arranged.

› DISCUSSION

The **-do** form, traditionally called the past participle, parallels in almost all respects the related *-ed* form in English:

1. As an adjective: *imagined earnings* **ganancias imaginadas,** *written documents* **documentos escritos.**

2. As a "passive voice" (explained in the next section): *The city was attacked* **La ciudad fue atacada.**

3. As part of the constructions termed "perfect tenses" (Section 98 below): *They have come* **Han venido.**

As an adjective the **-do** form readily nominalizes. In addition quite a number of words that now are nouns in their own right have come from it; among those encountered thus far in the dialogs are **entrada** (from **entrar**), **ganado** (from **ganar**),[3] **empleado** (from **emplear** *to employ:* the English *-ee* suffix corresponds to Spanish **-do**).

[3] For a similar semantic shift compare English *capital–chattel–cattle.*

97 The *-do* form with *ser* and *estar*

EXAMPLES

A. 1. ¿Cómo **fueron heridos** tus padres? *How were your parents wounded?*
2. Un gobierno como ése nunca va a **ser aceptado** por nadie. *A government like that is never going to be accepted by anyone.*
3. La policía **fue atacada** por los estudiantes. *The police were attacked by the students.*

B. 1. La puerta **está abierta.** *The door is open.*
2. Sí, pero **está descompuesto.**
3. Las luces **están apagadas.** *The lights are out (extinguished).*
4. El radio **estaba puesto.** *The radio was on (turned on).*
5. El policía **estaba enojado** conmigo. *The policeman was mad at (angry with) me.*

ACTION HAPPENING	ACTION ENDED (ITS RESULT CONTINUING)
ser + **-do** *form*	**estar** + **-do** *form*

When English uses *is* (*was*, etc.) ———*ed,* Spanish may use **ser** ———**do** if the reference is to the happening of an action but must use **estar** ———**do** if the happening is over and only the result is referred to.

ITEM SUBSTITUTION DRILL

A. 1. El *policía* fue atacado a tiros.
(oposición, presidente, agricultores)
2. La *policía* fue obligada a defenderse.
(jefe, chica, administrador, latinoamericanos, estudiantes)
3. La *carta* fue escrita por él.
(libro, noticias, periódico, revista, diálogos, invitación)

B. 1. Mi *tío* está enojado conmigo.
(tía, primo, novia, cuñado, amigas, abuelos, compañeras, padres)
2. La *muchacha* está resfriada.
(alumno, cónsul, alumna, señoras, señores, profesoras, agricultor)
3. El *tocadiscos* está descompuesto.
(maquinilla, radio, coches)
4. Por fin la *sala* está arreglada.
(cuarto, cocina, patio, fincas)
5. El *banco* está abierto.
(puertas, cine, flor, colegios)

DISCUSSION

English *is* (*was,* etc.) plus *-ed* has two distinct functions: *The chair was cracked* may mean that the chair got cracked (*The chair was cracked by the weight that was put on it*) or that it was in a cracked state (*I didn't sit on the chair because it was cracked*). These two functions call for **ser** and **estar,** respectively. Sometimes English does not use its *-ed* form but some other word corresponding to Spanish **-do** with **estar,** e.g., *The door is open* (rather than *opened*) or *The meeting was over* (rather than *finished*).

The construction with **ser** competes with the reflexive (see Unit 8, Section 40) and is somewhat infrequent in speech. It is usually limited to subjects not viewed as being so helpless or unimportant that they can be easily pushed around. In *The door was opened* (*came open*) there is very little that the door can do about it, and we normally find **se abrió.** Also, in *The wounded were taken to the hospital* **Los heridos se llevaron al hospital,** we readily find **se llevaron** because the wounded are viewed impersonally, as more or less inert. But in *We weren't invited* **No fuimos invitados** and in *His ideas are respected* **Sus ideas son respetadas,** the **ser** construction is normal because the person or thing acted upon is important. More often than not such grammatical subjects are persons.

98 Present perfect

EXAMPLES

A. Nunca **he estado** de acuerdo.

B. Sólo tú no **has cambiado.** (*Only you haven't changed.*)

C. 1. Tu papá no se **ha servido.**
2. Un gobierno tan malo como éste jamás **ha existido.**
3. Se le **ha salvado** la vida. *His life has been spared* (*to him*).

D. 1. Todos **hemos visto** esa película.
2. Ya lo **hemos discutido** muchas veces.

E. Ya **han ido** dos veces.

he **has** **ha** **hemos** **han**	**-do** *form*

The present perfect is composed of the present tense forms of **haber** plus the **-do** form with nothing else between them. The feminine and plural of the **-do** form never appear in this construction.

› PERSON-NUMBER SUBSTITUTION DRILL

1. *Yo* nunca he estado de acuerdo.
(ellos, nosotros, ustedes, tú, él, él y yo, usted)
2. Ya han tomado limonada.
(nosotros, él, tú, yo, ella, ustedes, mi hermano mayor)
3. No hemos comido en este restorán.
(usted, él, yo, él y yo, tú, nosotros, los estudiantes)
4. *El* no ha recibido cartas.
(ustedes, tú, ella, ellos, nosotros, yo, el jefe)
5. No hemos ido al cementerio.
(ellos, yo, usted, ella y yo, ustedes, tú, esos cobardes)
6. Hemos hecho la comida temprano.
(ella, ustedes, tú, usted, yo, ellos, la criada)
7. *Ellos* no han visto esa película.
(yo, usted, nosotros, ella, tú, ellos, mi novia)
8. ¿Dónde han puesto el correo?
(yo, él, tú, nosotros, usted, la secretaria)

TENSE SUBSTITUTION DRILL

INSTRUCTIONS: Repeat the following sentences just as you hear them. Then repeat them again, changing the present tense form of the verb to present perfect.

A. 1. ¡Ay, que me tira del pelo!
¡Ay, que me ha tirado del pelo!
2. Nosotros comulgamos casi todos los domingos.
3. No les importa un pito.
4. Yo corro en la carrera de maratón.
5. El no merece otra cosa.
6. No celebran el aniversario.
7. Siempre vivimos en el norte.
8. Pablo no me deja en paz.
9. Mario sigue por la avenida.

B. 1. Siempre perdemos en todo.
2. Esa mujer habla hasta por los codos.
3. ¡Cómo la echamos de menos!
4. El barbero me corta muy poco atrás.
5. No les importa la opinión de nadie.
6. Todos van excepto mi sobrina.
7. ¡Cómo rabia mi hermano mayor!
8. Me duele la cabeza y la garganta.

C. 1. Siempre me acuesto a las diez.
2. Nos levantamos a las siete.
3. Alfredo se baña todos los días.
4. Nunca se acuerdan de mí.
5. No me siento muy bien hoy.

PATTERNED RESPONSE DRILL

A. 1. TEACHER: ¿Ya habló usted?
STUDENT: **No, todavía no he hablado.**
2. ¿Ya terminó usted?
3. ¿Ya comulgó usted?
4. ¿Ya aceptó usted?
5. ¿Ya contestó usted?
6. ¿Ya esperó usted?
7. ¿Ya ganó usted?
8. ¿Ya jugó usted?
9. ¿Ya pagó usted?

B. 1. ¿Ya comió usted?
No, todavía no he comido.
2. ¿Ya durmió usted?
3. ¿Ya escribió usted?
4. ¿Ya pidió usted?
5. ¿Ya siguió usted?
6. ¿Ya volvió usted?

C. 1. ¿Rifó el abrigo?
No, no lo he rifado.
2. ¿Celebró el aniversario?
3. ¿Pasó la carne?

D. 1. ¿Envolvió la ropa?
No, no la he envuelto.
2. ¿Escribió la carta?
3. ¿Trajo el auto?
4. ¿Cambió las llantas?
5. ¿Recibió el paquete?

E. 1. ¿Se mantuvo firme?
No, no se ha mantenido firme.
2. ¿Se entusiasmó el jefe?
3. ¿Se arregló la rifa?
4. ¿Se discutió el asunto?
5. ¿Se peinó el señor?
6. ¿Se disolvió la manifestación?

DISCUSSION

The present perfect is a two-word construction as in English: the forms of **haber** correspond to English *have,* and Spanish **-do** corresponds to English *-ed.* The chief difference is that English sometimes divides the construction (*Have **they** gone? They have **never** gone*), but Spanish does not (**¿Han ido *ellos?* Ellos *nunca* han ido**). With-verb pronouns precede the inflected form of **haber: *Lo* hemos discutido.**

Whereas English makes a dual use of its verb *have* (*have* in *I have gone* does not mean the same as *have* in *I have money*), Spanish uses two different verbs: *I have gone* = *I've gone* **He ido,** *I have money* = *I've got money* **Tengo dinero.**

English and Spanish use the present perfect in similar ways. It may safely be used in Spanish wherever English has it. (Review Unit 16, Section 95, for an exception to this.)

Forms of the present subjunctive; subjunctive after *ojalá*

EXAMPLES
1. Ojalá que **regresen** temprano.
2. No **toquemos** ese tema.
3. Es ridículo que las muchachas **tengan** que llevar chaperón.

REGULARLY FORMED PRESENT SUBJUNCTIVE				
	INFINITIVE	FIRST-PERSON SINGULAR PRESENT		SUBJUNCTIVE ENDINGS
regular **-ar**	**hablar**	**habl-**	**-o**	**-e** **-es** **-e** **-emos** **-en**
regular **-er** *and* **-ir**	**comer** **vivir**	**com-** **viv-**	**-o**	**-a** **-as** **-a** **-amos** **-an**
verbs irregular in the first-person singular	**conocer** **parecer**[4] **producir**[5] **tener** **venir** **poner**[6] **valer** **salir** **caer** **traer** **hacer** **decir** **oir** **incluir** **ver**	**conozc-** **parezc-** **produzc-** **teng-** **veng-** **pong-** **valg-** **salg-** **caig-** **traig-** **hag-** **dig-** **oig-** **incluy-** **ve-**	**-o**	

In almost all verbs the present subjunctive is based on the first-person singular of the present indicative. (See Unit 5, Section 23, for the **usted, ustedes** forms used as commands.)

PRESENT SUBJUNCTIVE OF VERBS WITH CHANGES IN THE STEM	
recordar	**pensar**
rec**ue**rde	p**ie**nse
rec**ue**rdes	p**ie**nses
rec**ue**rde	p**ie**nse
recordemos	pensemos
rec**ue**rden	p**ie**nsen

[4]Similarly most other **-ecer** verbs, e.g., **ofrecer** and **merecer.** [5]Similarly all other **-ducir** verbs. [6]Similarly all other **-poner** verbs, e.g., **suponer.**

PRESENT SUBJUNCTIVE OF VERBS WITH CHANGES IN THE STEM (*cont'd*)	
poder	**querer**
pueda puedas pueda podamos puedan	quiera quieras quiera queramos quieran
dormir[7]	**sentir**[8]
duerma duermas duerma durmamos duerman	sienta sientas sienta sintamos sientan
	pedir[9]
	pida pidas pida pidamos pidan

The stem changes in the present subjunctive resemble those in the present indicative (see Unit 4, Section 17) except that the subjunctive adds a change in the first-person plural of **-ir** verbs. Endings are regular.

IRREGULARLY FORMED PRESENT SUBJUNCTIVES		
dar		dé des dé demos den
estar		esté estés esté estemos estén
ser ir haber saber	se- vay- hay- sep-	-a -as -a -amos -an

These verbs do not base the present subjunctive on the first-person singular of the present indicative. Endings, however, are regular.

[7] Similarly **morir.** [8] Similarly **preferir** and a few other verbs. [9] Similarly **seguir, conseguir, servir,** and a few other verbs.

EXAMPLES 1. Ojalá que **regresen** temprano.
2. Ojalá que **haya** venido. *I hope he has come.*
3. Ojalá **haya** algún beneficio. *I hope there is some benefit.*

	They get back	early.		**Regresan**	**temprano.**
I hope	they get back	early.	**Ojalá (que)**	**regresen**	**temprano.**

The subjunctive is used after **ojalá (que).**

› PERSON-NUMBER SUBSTITUTION DRILL

1. Ojalá que trabajemos aquí.
   (él, ellos, yo, tú, usted, ustedes)
2. Ojalá que no paguen nada.
   (nosotros, él, yo, tú, ella, ellos)
3. Ojalá que **yo** venda la casa.
   (ellos, nosotros, él, ustedes, tú, mis padres)
4. Ojalá que no maten al embajador.
   (ustedes, yo, nosotros, él, usted, ellas)
5. Ojalá que **usted** reciba una carta hoy.
   (yo, nosotros, ellos, ella, tú, ustedes)
6. Ojalá que no discutamos ese asunto.
   (ellos, él, tú, usted, ustedes)
7. Ojalá que **usted** vea esa película.
   (yo, nosotros, ellos, tú, ustedes, ella)
8. Ojalá que **yo** sepa su opinión.
   (ellas, nosotros, Pablo, los alumnos, usted, tú, ustedes)
9. Ojalá que **tú** recuerdes todo.
   (ellos, yo, nosotros, usted, Cecilia, ustedes, tú)
10. Ojalá que **me** sienta mejor.
    (su hija, nosotros, usted, ellos, tú, ustedes)

› CONSTRUCTION SUBSTITUTION DRILL

INSTRUCTIONS: Repeat the following sentences just as you hear them. Then say them again, preceding them with **ojalá que,** which will change the verb to the present subjunctive.

1. TEACHER: Ella hace la comida. *Repita.*
   STUDENT: **Ella hace la comida.**
   TEACHER: *Cambie.*
   STUDENT: **Ojalá que ella haga la comida.**
2. Ellos conocen a alguien.
3. Va temprano.
4. Pone dinero en el banco.
5. Su cumpleaños cae en sábado.
6. A ella le parece bien.
7. El oye mejor.
8. Mañana no hay clase.
9. Yo nunca pierdo.
10. Producen mucho maíz.
11. Están adentro.
12. Nos dan una comida.
13. Ellos pueden ir.
14. Voy a México.
15. No saben todo.
16. No piensa lo mismo.
17. El es mi profesor.
18. Usted dice la verdad.
19. Quiere comer con nosotros.

› PATTERNED RESPONSE DRILL

A. 1. ¿Vienen las muchachas ahora o esta noche?
   Ojalá que vengan ahora (**esta noche**).
2. ¿Llaman el lunes o el martes?
3. ¿Traen el auto viejo o el nuevo?
4. ¿Incluyen la electricidad o el gas?
5. ¿Esta tarde hay exámenes o clase?

B. 1. ¿Van a ver la película?
   Si no la han visto, ojalá que la vean.
2. ¿Van a repetir el programa?
3. ¿Van a mandar los trajes?
4. ¿Va a pedir él ese puesto?
5. ¿Va a barrer ella el comedor?

C. 1. ¿Vino Cecilia?
No sé, ojalá haya venido.
2. ¿Estudió Susana?
3. ¿Volvió Roberto?
4. ¿Ganó Josefina?
5. ¿Barrió Rosa?
6. ¿Pagó Patricio?
7. ¿Regresó María Elena?
8. ¿Se casó Lupita?

DISCUSSION

The subjunctive and indicative are two different sets of verb forms. All the verb forms thus far studied, except the infinitive, the **-ndo,** the **-do,** and commands, have been forms of the indicative. The **usted, -es** commands (Unit 5, Section 23) are special uses of the subjunctive.

The subjunctive endings are roughly the reverse of those in the indicative, in the way they are associated with **-ar** verbs on the one hand and **-er, -ir** verbs on the other: the indicative **-ar** endings are now attached to **-er, -ir** verbs, and the indicative **-er** endings are now attached to **-ar** verbs. The exception is the first person, which in the subjunctive is the same as the third.

As in the indicative, stem changes in the verbs that have them are associated with stress. (See Unit 4, Section 17.) The changes occur when the vowel is stressed. In addition **-ir** verbs have the same changes in the first-person plural that they have in the third-person preterit and the **-ndo** forms (Unit 10, Section 47), namely, **o → u** and **e → i: durmamos, sintamos, pidamos.**

The present subjunctive of **haber** (**haya, hayas,** etc.) is used to form the present perfect subjunctive exactly as the present perfect indicative is formed. (See Section 98.) In addition its third singular, **haya,** is the equivalent of *there is, there are,* and *there will be* in the subjunctive. (See Unit 8, Section 39.)

Ojalá que, meaning *I* (*we*) *hope that,* is always followed by the subjunctive. The **que** is often omitted. **Ojalá** is derived from Arabic (wàsălá) and literally means *May Allah grant.*

100 Equivalents of *-ly*

EXAMPLES

A. 1. **Exactamente,** una casita verde que está en la esquina.
2. Saludos a todos.
Igualmente.
3. **Desgraciadamente** vamos a perder en todo.
4. ¿Quién va a ganar los Juegos? ¿Los americanos?
Probablemente.
5. **Principalmente** para lana.

B. 1. Lo conozco **personal y profesionalmente.** *I know him personally and professionally.*
2. **Exacta y perfectamente.** (*Exactly and perfectly.*)

A.

adjective	-ly

feminine singular of adjective	**-mente**

The usual equivalent of the English *-ly* is **-mente,** attached to the feminine singular of the adjective.

B.

adjective	-ly	+	*adjective*	-ly

adjective	+	*adjective*	**-mente**

Where English repeats *-ly* with each member of a series, Spanish attaches **-mente** only to the last member.

EXAMPLES 1. Lo llamaron cobarde, y **con razón.** *They called him a coward, and no wonder (rightly).*
2. Hágalo **con cuidado.** *Do it carefully.*
3. Me lo ofreció **con mucha bondad.** *He very kindly offered it to me.*

(very)	*adjective*	–ly

con	**(mucho, –a)**	*noun*

Spanish frequently prefers a noun with **con** where English has an adjective with *–ly.* The equivalent of *very* is then **mucho, –a** before the noun.

› SUBSTITUTION DRILL

1. TEACHER: Lo dijo perfectamente.
   STUDENT: **Lo dijo perfectamente.**
   TEACHER: Exacto.
   STUDENT: **Lo dijo exactamente.**
2. *Desgraciadamente* tenemos que pagar.
   (probable, último, difícil)
3. *Probablemente* es lo mismo.
   (posible, general, regular)
4. *Principalmente* para lana.
   (igual, fácil, probable)
5. Habla *perfectamente.*
   (amable, horrible, serio, inocente)
6. Es *igualmente* respetada.
   (total, nuevo, sencillo)

› TRANSLATION DRILL

A. 1. He said it, and rightly (with reason).
2. He did it, and carefully (with care).
3. He accepted it, and gladly (with pleasure).
4. He ate it, and hungrily (with hunger).
5. He fixed it, and competently (with competence).

B. 1. They attacked fiercely and furiously.
2. They attacked uselessly and ridiculously.
3. They attacked openly and freely.
4. They attacked easily and professionally.
5. They attacked regularly and personally.

› DISCUSSION

The usual equivalent of *–ly,* with which English makes adverbs out of adjectives, is **-mente,** attached to the feminine singular of an adjective. Where two or more occur in a coordinate series, **-mente** is attached only to the last.

Rather more than in English one finds phrases with **con** used instead of adverbs with **-mente.** This is not unknown to English, of course; we say *easily* but cannot say *difficultly*—for the latter, we use *with difficulty.* Thus there are two equivalents for *carefully:* **cuidadosamente** (**cuidadosa** *careful* + **-mente**) and **con cuidado** *with care,* of which the latter is probably heard oftener.

› GUIDED CONVERSATION

L. *Luis* M. *María*

L. Pero, María, ¿por qué se preocupa tanto tu padre? ¿No sabe que soy de muy buena familia?
M. No es eso; es que ________________
L. ¿Qué costumbres?
M. La de los chaperones principalmente. A él le parece que ________________
L. Pero ustedes han hablado de eso antes, ¿verdad?

M. Sí, ya lo hemos ____________
L. ¿Y cómo se lo has explicado[10]?
M. Le he dicho que hoy día ____________
L. ¿Y qué dice de eso?
M. Sólo que cuando él y mi madre eran ____________
L. Sí, sí. Y yo apuesto a que él rabiaba como un león.[11]

› TRANSLATION REVIEW DRILL

Unemphatic *some, any.*

A. 1. TEACHER: Give me some rice.
STUDENT: **Déme arroz.**
2. Give me some coffee.
3. Give me some butter.
4. Give me some milk.
5. Give me some bread.
6. Give me some corn.
7. Give me some potatoes.

B. 1. Have you got any meat?
¿Tiene carne?
2. Have you got any beans?
3. Have you got any fruit?
4. Have you got any corn?
5. Have you got any eggs?
6. Have you got any onions?
7. Have you got any wheat?
8. Have you got any aspirins?

reading

A la mesa

PAQ. *Paquito* E. *Elena, su hermana mayor* M. *Madre* ABA. *Abuela*
P. *Padre* ABO. *Abuelo*

PAQ. Elena, pásame los frijoles.

E. (*como hermana mayor*) Paquito, ya te he dicho muchas veces cómo se deben pedir las cosas. Tienes que decir: Ten la bondad de pasarme la carne, o bien: ¿Quieres pasarme el pan? o bien: Haz el favor de pasarme la mantequilla; o bien... — **o bien** *or else*

PAQ. Pero no quiero carne ni pan ni mantequilla; quiero los frijoles na más. — **na más** *just*

E. Esa palabra es *nada,* no *na: na–da.* ¿Cuándo vas a hablar correctamente? A tu edad...

PAQ. A tu edad Tía Julia estaba casada y tenía tres hijos. ¿Cuándo te vas a casar tú?

M. Niños, niños, por favor: dejen de pelearse. Paquito, come tu comida. Elena, no atormentes a tu hermanito... Y pásale los frijoles, por favor... ¿Sales?

E. Sí, madre, con permiso. Tengo que ver a alguien.

[10] *explained* [11] *lion*

Mexico City: Family at dinner

PAQ. ¿A quién?

E. Si es que te importa, a Rodney Ramsbottom, un joven inglés que conocí la semana pasada.

PAQ. ¿Ese tipo?

E. (*No dice nada, pero la mirada que le da a su hermanito es muy expresiva. Sale.*)

ABA. ¿Adónde va Elena con su amigo?

M. Al cine. Hay una película que no han visto.

ABA. ¿Quién los acompaña?

M. (*Tenemos la impresión de que la familia ya ha discutido este asunto muchas veces, puesto que Elena es una joven muy bonita.*) Nadie, abuela.

ABA. Ay, estas costumbres modernas no me gustan. Cuando yo era joven...

PAQ. ¿Cuántos años tienes, abuelita?

P. (*escandalizado*) ¡Paquito! ¡A tu abuelita no tienes que hacerle esa pregunta! Y mira, a las señoras nunca se les pregunta la edad. (*Habla tan fuerte que despierta al abuelo, que se ha caído dormido en su silla, y ha empezado a roncar.*)

ABO. (*despertando de un salto*) ¿Eh? ¿Qué fue eso?

ABA. Abuelo, ¿cuántas veces he tenido que decirte que no debes roncar cuando duermes, y que no debes dormir cuando comes?

ABO. ¡Pobre de mí! No puedo roncar, no puedo dormir... ¡tan pocos placeres que tiene un viejo!

tipo *fellow, guy, creep*
mirada *look*
puesto que *since, because*
despertar *to awaken*
silla *chair* **roncar** *to snore*
de un salto *with a start*

UNIT 18

Politics in the Home

R. *Ramón* F. *Father* M. *Mother*

R. Well, no matter what they say [Let them say what they may say], Vargas Campo is the man of the hour [day].

F. Don't talk foolishness. He's an idealistic fool who wants to change everything. Our people will never accept him.

R. In spite of what you say, Dad, I don't agree with you.

M. Please don't talk about politics any more. Let's change the subject.

R. What do you want us to talk about, Mom? Clothes?

M. You two never agree. You always end up in an argument.

* * *

F. Let's drop the subject. Anyway, I wanted to talk to you about something more important, your studies.

R. Please, don't insist that I study medicine.

F. We won't stand in the way of your choice [oppose ourselves to what you choose]. You're the one to decide. But . . .

M. The only thing we ask is that you don't study law.

La política en la casa

R. *Ramón* P. *Padre* M. *Madre*

R. Pues digan lo que digan, Vargas Campo es el hombre del día.

P. No digas tonterías. Es un loco idealista que todo lo (1) quiere cambiar. Nuestro pueblo (2) jamás lo va a aceptar.

R. A pesar de lo que tú digas, papá, no estoy de acuerdo contigo. (3)

M. Les ruego que no discutan más de política. Cambiemos de tema.

R. ¿De qué quieres que hablemos, mamá? ¿De vestidos?

M. Es que ustedes dos nunca se ponen de acuerdo. Siempre terminan en un pleito.

* * *

P. Dejemos ese tema. De todos modos, quería hablarte de otra cosa más importante, tus estudios.

R. Por favor, no insistan en que estudie medicina.

P. No nos vamos a oponer a lo que tú escojas. Tú eres el que decides. Pero...

M. Lo único que te pedimos es que no estudies para abogado. (4)

R. What's so bad about that?

M. There are so many lawyers that it's difficult to make a name for yourself in that field.

F. Unless one gets into politics, and we hope you won't do [dedicate yourself to] that. Let somebody else [others] do it.

M. Well, talk it over. I'm going to see how dinner's coming.

R. . . . Look, Dad, about that other matter, what do you really have against Vargas Campo? Why do you hate him?

F. Because I don't want to see our country ruined [in ruins]. And let's not discuss it any further. You young people won't listen to anybody [Nobody can convince you young people].

R. ¿Qué hay de malo en eso?

M. Es que hay tantos abogados que es muy difícil destacarse en ese campo.

P. A menos que uno se meta en la política; y ojalá que tú no te dediques a eso. Que lo hagan otros.

M. Bueno, sigan ustedes hablando de eso. Voy a ver cómo anda lo de la comida.

R. ...Mira, papá, volviendo a lo otro, sinceramente, ¿qué tienes tú en contra de Vargas Campo? ¿Por qué lo odias?

P. Porque no quiero ver a nuestra patria en la ruina. Y no discutamos más. A ustedes los jóvenes no los convence nadie.

San José, Costa Rica: The University campus

cultural notes

(1) The pronoun **lo** is generally used with **todo** *everything,* when **todo** is the object of a verb. It makes the *everything* more concrete and emphatic. When the **todo** comes before the verb (this position makes it still more emphatic), the accompanying **lo** shows that **todo** is the object of the verb and not its subject. Compare English *He knows everything* and *He knows it all.*

(2) *People* in the sense of group of persons (e.g., *There were many people at the meeting*) is **gente** in Spanish; in the sense of nation, race, or body of persons united by a common culture (e.g., *A characteristic trait of the Spanish people is individualism*) **pueblo** is used.

(3) The transition from childhood to adulthood in Spanish America is abrupt. Children in their teens become acquainted with adult problems and decisions, including those of politics, at a time when their combination of idealism and inexperience may lead them to extremes.

(4) Whereas English says *study for the bar* (study law), *study for the priesthood,* etc., Spanish says **estudiar para abogado, estudiar para cura,** *study for lawyer, study for priest,* i.e., study to be a lawyer, priest, etc.

The professions with the greatest prestige in Latin America are medicine, engineering, and law, although others such as architecture and economics are gaining ground. The field of law, which is overcrowded, is one of the avenues to a political career. Many law students have no intention of practicing their profession, and a large number aspire to government positions, which in some countries afford considerable security and always confer prestige. The fact that professions as a whole are held in higher esteem than trades accords with the Latin American's view of manual labor as menial (see Unit 9, Cultural Note 1).

In contrast to American students, who enter professional schools of law, medicine, and the like around the age of twenty-one, after a three- or four-year undergraduate preparation, the Latin-American student at the age of seventeen or eighteen goes directly to a professional school after completing secondary-school education (see Unit 10, Cultural Notes 4 and 5). He thus has to decide upon a career several years sooner than does his American counterpart.

› WRITING EXERCISE

The written accent mark with attached pronouns and with adverbs in **-mente.**

INSTRUCTIONS: Write the following paired forms from dictation.

1.	diga	dígame	hablando	hablándome	2.	decir	decírmelo
	hable	háblenos	levantando	levantándonos		dar	dárselo
	pregunte	pregúntele	leyendo	leyéndolo		enviar	enviármelo
	conteste	contésteles	muriendo	muriéndose		preguntar	preguntárselo
	vaya	váyase	preguntando	preguntándome		di	dímelo
	levante	levántese	diciendo	diciéndolo		pon	póntelo

Verb forms (command forms, infinitives, and **-ndo** forms) follow precisely the rules for the accent mark given in Unit 10. When attaching pronouns to these forms results in a word that is stressed on any syllable other than the next to the last, the written form calls for an accent mark on the stressed vowel. This occurs (1) when one or more pronouns are attached to a command form having more than one syllable or to an **-ndo** form (which always has at least two syllables), or (2) when two pronouns are attached to an infinitive form (which is always stressed on its last syllable) or to a one-syllable command form (e.g., **di, pon**).[1]

INSTRUCTIONS: Write the following pairs of words from dictation.

cortés	cortésmente
fácil	fácilmente
cómodo	cómodamente
íntimo	íntimamente
último	últimamente
único	únicamente

[1] In a few instances attaching a pronoun results in loss of the written accent mark: **estate, deme.**

101 Indicative and subjunctive in noun clauses

EXAMPLES

A. Es que **hay** tantos abogados. (*It's that there are so many lawyers.*)

B. 1. Sé que **hay** más de diez heridos.
2. Yo sé que **viven** cerca del Parque Central.
3. ¿Sabes que mañana **es** la inauguración?

C. ¿No ve que **soy** su padrino?

D. 1. Yo digo que el gobierno **debe** mantenerse firme.
2. Dígale que no **estoy.**

E. 1. Tal vez ya no recuerdes que no nos **dejaban** salir solos.
2. No olvide que la oposición **tiene** un partido mucho más fuerte.

F. Creo que **tengo** gripe.

G. 1. Parece que cada vez que abro la boca, **meto** la pata. *It seems that every time I open my mouth, I put my foot in it.*
2. Me parece que las muchachas no **deben** salir solas.

H. Apuesto a que **ganamos.** *I bet we win.*

I. Supongo que **va** a ir mucha gente importante.

J. Me imagino que **deben** tener ovejas y cerdos.

VIEWING WHAT FOLLOWS AS INFORMATION		THE INFORMATION
Es	que	**hay tantos abogados.**
Sé	que	**viven.**
Dígale	que	**no estoy.**
Me parece	que	**no deben salir.**
Apuesto a	que	**ganamos.**

When what the noun clause says is viewed as straight information its verb is in the indicative. Usually the main verb gives the point of view: whether the information is held (*know, believe*), found out (*see, discover, learn*), or given (*say, predict*).

TRANSLATION DRILL

A. 1. I know that he's an idealist.
2. It seems to me that he's an idealist.
3. They say that he's an idealist.
4. I'll bet that he's an idealist.
5. It's that he's an idealist.
6. Tell him that he's an idealist.

B. 1. I know he's going home.
2. It seems to me he's going home.
3. They say he's going home.
4. I'll bet he's going home.
5. It's that he's going home.
6. Don't forget that he's going home.

EXAMPLES

1. Les ruego que no **discutan** más de política. (*I beg you that you not argue more about politics.*)
2. Lo único que te pedimos es que no **estudies** para abogado.
3. No insistan en que **estudie** medicina.
4. ¿De qué quieres que **hablemos?** (*About what do you want us to* [*that we*] *speak?*)
5. Merece que lo **odiemos.** *He deserves that we hate him.*

6. ¿Qué sugieres que **hagamos?** *What do you suggest that we do?*
7. Prefiero que **rifes** otra cosa. *I'd rather you raffled (I prefer that you raffle) something else.*
8. Es muy temprano para que **lleguen** ahora. *It's too early for them to arrive now.*
9. Me dice que lo **haga** después. *She tells me to do it later.*

AN INFLUENCE BROUGHT TO BEAR		WHAT IS INFLUENCED
Les ruego	**que**	**no discutan.**
Prefiero	**que**	**rifes.**
Es muy temprano para	**que**	**lleguen ahora.**

When the main idea tends to affect the course of what happens in the clause (to cause it, encourage it, prevent it, discourage it), the verb of the clause is in the subjunctive.

EXAMPLES

1. Me gusta que **sigas** mis consejos. *It pleases me that you are following my advice.*
2. Sentimos que no **hayas** decidido. *We're sorry you haven't decided.*
3. Ojalá que tú no te **dediques** a eso.
4. Es ridículo que las muchachas **tengan** que llevar chaperón. (*It's ridiculous that girls have to take a chaperon.*)
5. Se oponen a que lo **cambiemos** tanto. *They're opposed to our changing it so much.*
6. No creo que **haya** nada de malo en eso. *I don't think there's anything wrong in that.*
7. No están convencidos de que **sea** importante. *They're not convinced that it's important.*

AN ATTITUDE OF LIKE-DISLIKE OR ACCEPTANCE-REJECTION		WHAT IS LIKED OR DISLIKED OR ACCEPTED OR REJECTED
Me gusta	**que**	**sigas mis consejos.**
Sentimos	**que**	**no hayas decidido.**
Es ridículo	**que**	**tengan que llevar chaperón.**
No creo	**que**	**haya nada de malo.**

When the main idea shows a positive or negative bias, often tinged with emotion, the verb of the clause is in the subjunctive.

› PERSON-NUMBER SUBSTITUTION DRILL

INSTRUCTIONS: Repeat the following sentences just as you hear them. Then repeat them again, substituting the suggested subjects for the second verb.

1. ¿De qué quieres que hablemos, mamá? (yo, ellos, ella, él y yo, él)
2. Susana quiere que *yo* le compre un abrigo de pieles. (ellas, nosotros, ustedes, tú, usted, Lorenzo)
3. ¿Desean los señores que *yo* entre? (nosotros, ellas, él, ellos, ella, el periodista)

4. Prefiero que no exageres tanto.
(ustedes, él, ellos, usted, tú, las señoras)
5. El merece que *nosotros* lo odiemos.
(yo, ellos, ella, tú, tú y yo, el pueblo)
6. Mis padres sugieren que *yo* siga otra carrera.
(nosotros, él, tú, ustedes, él y yo, mi hermano mayor)
7. Nadie se opone a que *yo* estudie para abogado.
(él, ustedes, nosotros, ellos, tú, ella)
8. No aceptan que *ustedes* discutan la decisión.
(nosotros, yo, tú, usted, ellas, él)
9. No pidan que salgamos otra vez.
(yo, ellos, él, Alberto y yo, ella, los señores)
10. Yo no dejo que *mis hijas* vayan ahí.
(ella, ustedes, Elena, las chicas, tú, ellas)
11. El profesor dice que abramos el libro.
(usted, ustedes, tú, yo, ellos, ella)
12. Ellos necesitan que *yo* les haga la comida.
(nosotros, él, tú, ella, ustedes, usted)
13. Ella espera que llegues a una decisión pronto.
(yo, ustedes, usted, ellos, él, nosotros)
14. Siento que *usted* no pueda cambiar mis dólares.
(ustedes, él, ellos, tú, el empleado)
15. Me alegro que no tenga que comprar otra batería.
(nosotros, ustedes, él, tú, ellos, Ricardo)
16. Me gusta que *tú* sigas mis consejos.
(él, ellos, usted, ustedes, mi sobrina)
17. Ojalá que *tú* no te dediques a la política.
(él, ellos, usted, ustedes, nosotros, yo)
18. Es ridículo que *las muchachas* tengan que llevar chaperón.
(ella, nosotras, ellas, tú, usted, ustedes, yo)
19. Es mejor que no rabies tanto.
(yo, ustedes, usted, nosotros, ellos, él)
20. Es bueno que *Olga* estudie el español.
(ustedes, tú, usted, yo, ellos, nosotros)
21. Es difícil que *Pablo* haga eso.
(yo, nosotros, tú, ellos, ella, ustedes)
22. Es importante que estudiemos.
(Julio, ellas, yo, tú, ustedes, usted)
23. Es probable que *ellos* salgan esta noche.
(yo, ustedes, tú, nosotros, ella, los muchachos)
24. Es necesario que esperes un momento.
(nosotros, ella, ustedes, usted, ellos, yo)
25. Lástima que *yo* no sepa jugar.
(usted, ellos, nosotros, tú, él, ustedes)
26. No importa que no paguen ahora.
(usted, tú, yo, ellos, nosotros, él)
27. El paquete es muy grande para que *Paquito* lo lleve.
(tú, usted, ustedes, nosotros, ellas, el niño)
28. Son muy jóvenes para que *nosotros* los dejemos salir de noche.
(ella, yo, ellos, tú, usted, mis padres)

INSTRUCTIONS: Repeat the following sentences just as you hear them. Then make the with-verb pronoun agree with the cue. The subjunctive verb form in the noun clause must be made to agree with the person and number of the pronoun.

1. *Les* ruego que no discutan tanto.
(a usted, a ellos, a ella, a los jóvenes, al muchacho)
2. *Nos* dice que tomemos un bus.
(a ustedes, a mí, a usted, a ti, a ellos, a él)
3. *Me* sugiere que cambie los dólares.
(a nosotros, a usted, a ti, a ustedes, a ella, a ellas)
4. *Les* pide que estén ahí sin falta.
(a mí, a usted, a ti, a ustedes, a nosotros, a él)
5. *Te* mando que no vayas sin permiso.
(a usted, a ustedes, a él, a ellos, a ella, a ellas)
6. *Me* escribe que vaya la otra semana.
(a ellas, a él, a nosotros, a ellos, a ti, a ella)

› CONSTRUCTION SUBSTITUTION DRILL

INSTRUCTIONS: Repeat the following sentences just as you hear them. Then repeat them again, preceding them with the expressions indicated and changing the verb from indicative to subjunctive.

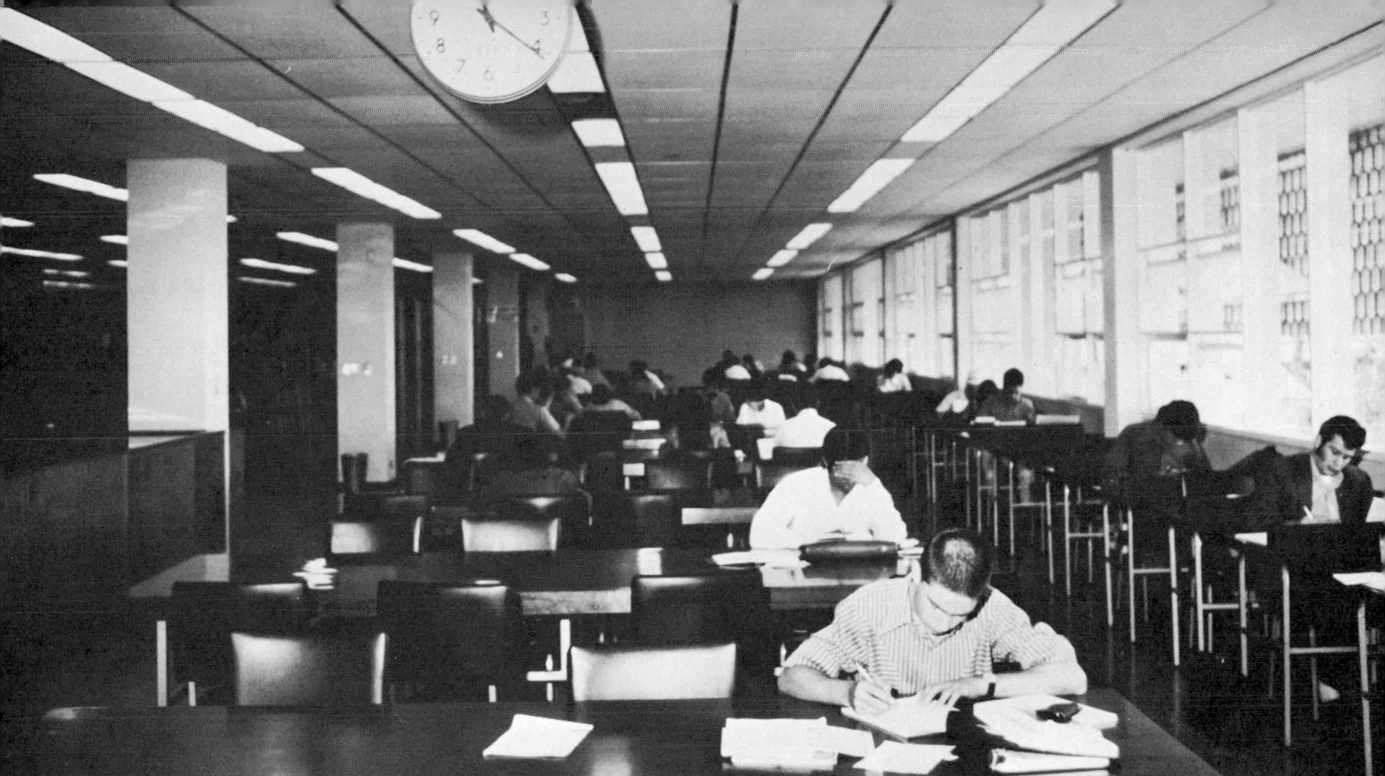

San José, Costa Rica: The University library

1. Me cambian los pesos en el banco.
   (quiero que, prefiero que, espero que)
2. Vendo el ganado en el invierno.
   (me exigen que, me sugieren que, me piden que)
3. Las chicas viven allí.
   (me alegro que, me preocupa que, me opongo a que)
4. Seguimos otra carrera.
   (es importante que, es mejor que, es necesario que)
5. Pides un café bien caliente.
   (sugiero que, prefiero que, quiero que)
6. Don Rafael conoce bien el centro.
   (espero que, me alegro que, ojalá que)
7. Nosotros salimos para el Club de la Unión.
   (ruegan que, les duele que, no les gusta que)
8. Aquí no hay electricidad.
   (es probable que, es difícil que, es ridículo que)
9. Mi patria está en la ruina.
   (siento que, no creo que, lástima que)
10. No hay más remedio que aceptar.
    (es imposible que, lástima que, parece fantástico que)
11. Ellas salen solas de noche.
    (me preocupa que, no estoy de acuerdo que, parece fantástico que)

› CHOICE-QUESTION RESPONSE DRILL

A. 1. ¿Quiere que salgamos o prefiere que tomemos algo?
2. ¿Quiere que le demos una parte o prefiere que le paguemos?
3. ¿Desea que nos vayamos al cementerio o prefiere que nos quedemos aquí?
4. ¿Desea que consigamos otras llantas o prefiere que compremos éstas?

B. 1. ¿Quiere que yo vaya al cine o prefiere que me quede en casa?
2. ¿Quiere que yo estudie química o prefiere que consiga un empleo?
3. ¿Quiere que yo sirva la carne ahora o prefiere que espere un rato?
4. ¿Desea que yo mande los documentos o sugiere que los lleve?

FORMING A NOUN CLAUSE IN SPANISH TO CORRESPOND TO ENGLISH INFINITIVE OR *-ing* FORM
(*Asterisks indicate unacceptable expressions, included here for comparison only.*)

MAIN CLAUSE	NOUN PHRASE	INFINITIVE OR *-ing* FORM WITHOUT ITS OWN SUBJECT	USUAL ENGLISH INFINITIVE OR *-ing* FORM WITH ITS OWN SUBJECT	EQUIVALENT CLAUSE CONSTRUCTIONS
to want, not to want *and equivalents:*				
She wants (desires)	quiet.	to be quiet.	us to be quiet.	that we be quiet.
Quiere	**tranquilidad.**	**callarse.**	—	**que nos callemos.**
She doesn't want	an argument.	to argue.	us to argue.	that we argue.
No quiere	**un pleito.**	**discutir.**	—	**que discutamos.**
We insist	on a hot coffee.	on ordering a hot coffee.	on his bringing us a hot coffee.	that he bring us a hot coffee.
Insistimos	**en un café caliente.**	**en pedir un café caliente.**	—	**en que nos traiga un café caliente.**
message-bearing equivalents of to want (to tell, to write, to phone, to wire, *etc.*):				
She keeps telling			me to come early.	*that I come early.
Sigue diciendo			—	**que venga temprano.**
It's ridiculous	that schedule of his.	to get up so early, getting up so early.	for him to get up so early, his getting up so early.	that he get up so early.
Es ridículo	**ese horario suyo.**	**levantarse tan temprano.**	—	**que se levante tan temprano.**
It's too early (It's awfully early)	for lunch.	for eating lunch, to eat lunch.	for us to eat lunch.	*that we eat lunch.
Es muy temprano	**para el almuerzo.**	**para almorzar.**	—	**para que almorcemos.**
They're opposed	to the change.	to changing.	to our changing.	*that we change.
Se oponen	**al cambio.**	**a cambiar.**	—	**a que cambiemos.**
I'm not convinced	of its importance.		of its being important.	that it's important.
No estoy convencido	**de su importancia.**		—	**de que sea importante.**

In general when English has an infinitive or an *-ing* form with its own subject the Spanish equivalent is a clause. Note that if Spanish uses a preposition before a noun, then it uses the same preposition before the infinitive or the clause. (See Unit 9, Section 41.)

PATTERNED RESPONSE DRILL

A. 1. ¿El va a *venir* temprano?
Sí, dígale que venga temprano.
2. ¿El va a ir a la plaza?
3. ¿El va a traer las revistas?
4. ¿El va a arreglar el carburador?
5. ¿El va a usar otro coche?

B. 1. ¿*Vengo* con mi novia?
Sí, ella quiere que venga con su novia.
2. ¿Estudio física?
3. ¿Hago la comida?
4. ¿Salgo ahora?
5. ¿Como más?

C. 1. ¿*Van* al cine?
No, es muy tarde para que vayan al cine.
2. ¿Jugamos fútbol?
3. ¿Apuesto ahora?
4. ¿Llamamos a la tintorería?
5. ¿Hago las preguntas?

D. 1. ¿*Venimos* otra vez?
No, ellos se oponen a que vengamos otra vez.
2. ¿Apostamos más?
3. ¿Trabajamos todo el día?
4. ¿Estudiamos química?
5. ¿Abrimos los libros?
6. ¿Compramos las materias?

USING A WORD-ORDER TEST IN ENGLISH TO DISTINGUISH BETWEEN INDICATIVE AND SUBJUNCTIVE IN SPANISH NOUN CLAUSES
(*Asterisks indicate unacceptable forms.*)

ENGLISH, NORMAL ORDER	*that* DELETED, MAIN CLAUSE SHIFTED	SPANISH
The fact is that there are so many lawyers.	There are so many lawyers, the fact is.	**Es que hay tantos abogados.**
I know that they are living.	They are living, I know.	**Sé que viven.**
Tell him that I'm not in.	I'm not in, tell him.	**Dígale que no estoy.**
It seems to me that they shouldn't go out.	They shouldn't go out, it seems to me.	**Me parece que no deben salir.**
I bet that we'll win.	We'll win, I bet.	**Apuesto a que ganamos.**
I beg (of) you that you not argue.	*You not argue, I beg (of) you.	**Les ruego que no discutan.**
I prefer that you raffle.	*You raffle, I prefer.	**Prefiero que rifes.**
I like (it) that you follow my advice.	*You follow my advice, I like (it).	**Me gusta que sigas mis consejos.**
We're sorry that you haven't decided.	* You haven't decided, we're sorry.	**Sentimos que no hayas decidido.**
It's ridiculous that they have to take (along) a chaperon.	*They have to take (along) a chaperon, it's ridiculous.	**Es ridículo que tengan que llevar chaperón.**

Where English can drop *that* in a noun clause and move the main verb to the right with no change in the meaning of the sentence, Spanish uses the indicative. Where this shift is not permitted in English, Spanish uses the subjunctive.

DISCUSSION

The most important uses of the subjunctive in Spanish (apart from its use in the **usted, -es** commands) are in subordinate clauses. A subordinate clause has its own subject and verb and fits into and becomes part of a larger sentence. It occupies the same place that might be occupied by a word. In the following sentence pairs note how the clause performs essentially the same function as the single word it is compared to:

1. He deserves that people hate him. (subject *people,* verb *hate*)
   He deserves *hatred.* (no subject, no verb)
2. Do you admire someone *who works hard?* (subject *who,* verb *works*)
   Do you admire someone *industrious?*
3. I saw him when he came. (subject *he,* verb *came*)
   I saw him *yesterday.*

The first of these clauses functions as a noun and is therefore called a noun clause; just like the single word *hatred,* the clause *that people hate him* is the object of the main verb *deserves.* The second clause functions like the adjective *industrious* and is called an adjective clause. The third clause functions like the adverb *yesterday* and is called an adverb clause.

Noun clauses are more frequent in Spanish than in English; in English the infinitive and the *–ing* form compete with the clause, as seen in the large box above. But in the few instances where the English subjunctive survives, it closely resembles Spanish. The noun clauses in *I recommend that he try harder, I insist that he stop,* and *I move that it be tabled* have the subjunctive forms *he try, he stop, it be* rather than the indicative forms *he tries, he stops, it is.* These correspond to the examples at the top of page 293, in which an influence is brought to bear.

In order to use the Spanish subjunctive in noun clauses correctly, an English speaker must learn to adapt the infinitive or *–ing* form to a clause construction. The most frequent circumstances requiring this transformation are as follows:

1. With the verb *to want* or *not to want* (or an equivalent, such as *to command, to entreat, to desire,* or *to forbid*) or *to tell* (someone to do or not to do something). Since *to tell* (and its message-carrying equivalents *to write, to wire, to phone,* etc.) means roughly "to communicate a want," these verbs are all closely related by their function of exerting influence. In most instances these verbs are used with the infinitive construction in English:

> She wants us to be there at three o'clock sharp.
> The union forbids them to unload the cargo until a settlement is reached.

And some verbs of this family may (and sometimes must) take the *–ing* construction:

> Do you always allow his wandering in like that, unannounced? (Do you always allow him to wander in like that, unannounced?)
> I oppose his delaying the decision for a week.

(With a verb of the *want* family it often happens that *for* is inserted as a "buffer" to prevent the main verb and the personal object from occurring side by side: *I hate [don't want] for you to work so late.*)

2. With the impersonal *It is . . .* construction, in which *it* functions as a dummy subject. The usual form is *It is . . . for* [noun or pronoun] *to* [infinitive]:

> It's downright impossible for me to make it through all that traffic.
> It's ridiculous for a girl to have to take a chaperon everywhere.

In these sentences the *for* functions merely as the grammatical signal for the subject of the infinitive. Compare the following (the asterisk indicates an unacceptable sentence):

> It's too early for dinner.
> *It's impossible for dinner.

The *for* with *early* indicates the appropriateness of the time *for* having dinner; it is a true preposition. The *for* with *impossible* is nonsense. This contrast involving nouns in English applies also to infinitives in Spanish:

It's too early to eat. **Es muy temprano para comer.**
It's impossible to eat. **Es imposible comer.**

Now apply what you know about prepositions before nouns and infinitives; Spanish requires that the same preposition appear before a clause:

It's too early for us to eat. **Es muy temprano para que comamos.**

3. With certain verbs of the acceptance-rejection variety (some with obligatory preposition) which allow only the *-ing* form:

They disapprove of my taking five courses, but it's my tuition money.
I'm opposed to his being appointed to the committee.

Other verbs, particularly those of feeling, may permit the *-ing* construction, often with the addition of an appropriate preposition:

The union forbids their unloading the cargo until a settlement is reached.
I don't like your having to work so late.
I'm really sorry about his having failed the exam.
Frankly, they are afraid of the auditor's walking in on them again.

To summarize the problem of clause formation, Spanish consistently uses a noun clause with a subjunctive, even when the equivalent English expression may allow or even require an infinitive or *-ing* construction. And *for* should not be translated if it functions merely as a "buffer" (as in *I love for him to play that piece*) or as a subject-indicator (as in *It's rough for an old man to keep up this pace*). "True" prepositions which occur in the main clause should be retained in the Spanish noun clause construction: *They're opposed to our changing* **Se oponen a que cambiemos.** One can generally tell whether a preposition is a true preposition by substituting a simple noun; thus we don't say **I'd love for a drink*, even though English uses a *for* in *I'd love for you to have a drink.* But in *He insists on the truth* the *on* with the simple noun carries over to the clause in Spanish: *He insists that I tell the truth* **Insiste en que diga la verdad.**

Spanish organizes its indicative-subjunctive contrast in noun clauses around the point of view that the main verb takes toward the content of the clause. If the main verb is one of the expressions we use when we report information—*to know, to be sure, to say, to tell, to find out, to reveal, to state, to assert, to think, to assume, to realize, to conclude, to decide; it seems, it is true, it is a fact, it is evident*—then the content of the clause is generally viewed as no more than information, and the verb of the clause is indicative. The corresponding English sentence will allow *that* to be dropped and the subject and verb of the main clause to be moved to the right, as noted in the rule above. Considered another way, the dependent clause becomes the important information of the sentence, with the original main clause a kind of appendage—in effect a sentence adverb—that is retained more as a comment: *I am sure he can go, Assuredly he can go.* As with sentence adverbs, there is a freedom of placement, with the possibility of location after the rest of the sentence: *He can go, I am sure; He can go, assuredly.*

If the main part of the sentence, especially the main verb, is one of the expressions we use to show our desires, hopes, or feelings toward what the clause says, then the verb of the clause is subjunctive and the English expression will not allow the main clause to be right-shifted. It does not matter that the content actually is to some extent informative. For example, *I am sorry that he is sick* (**Siento que esté malo**) would inform a third party that the person in question is sick, but the verb is nevertheless subjunctive because *to be sorry* does not convey a report but an emotion; we could not say in English, **He is sick, I am sorry.* By way of contrast, the expression *I hear that he is sick* (**Oigo que está malo**) uses *I hear* that is common in straight reporting, and the verb of the clause in indicative in Spanish. The main clause can again be right-shifted: *He is sick, I hear.*

Whether the information in the subordinate clause is true or false, real or imagined, makes no difference when the main idea is one of *conveying* it. In **Apuesto a que ganamos** the speaker uses *I* *bet* as a way of conveying a prediction; he does not say how he feels about it or try to make it happen but simply foresees it (*We'll win, I bet*). In *I dreamed that I was queen* the speaker reports the content of the dream; the verb is indicative despite its unreality. Furthermore, the speaker may be quite vehement in his assertion of the information. He may thump his fist and say *I declare,* but this does not affect the verb; it is still indicative.

The kind of emotion that calls for subjunctive is one that views the idea in the noun clause as something to be welcomed or spurned. *To accept, to be glad, to approve,* and *to applaud* are notions of welcoming; *to disapprove, to be sorry, to disbelieve,* and *to dislike* are notions of spurning. Certain expressions in this group sometimes express the "conveying information" point of view. In *I didn't know that he was here* (**que estaba aquí**) the speaker reports his ignorance of a piece of information, and **estaba** is indicative; in *Oh, I don't know that it's so good* (**que sea tan bueno**) the speaker spurns the idea of its being good, and **sea** is subjunctive. (The main verbs *not to know, not to think,* and *not to believe* constitute an exception to the right-shift rule.) In *I don't think it's true* the indicative will be used if the speaker implies "This item of information is conveyed as false" (positive denial): **No creo que es la verdad.** But the subjunctive will be used if he implies "I'm dubious about the idea (I'm inclined to reject it)": **No creo que sea la verdad.** In statements like this, which suggest that someone is being contradicted, the subjunctive is preferred because it is more polite.

The "influence" notion admits of no alternative; the verb in this case is always subjunctive.

102 Subjunctive or indicative with *tal vez*

EXAMPLES

A. 1. Tal vez ya no **recuerdes.** *Maybe you don't remember now.*
2. Tal vez no **hayan** contestado. *Maybe they haven't answered.*
3. Tal vez **haya** algún beneficio. *Maybe there'll be some benefit.*

B. 1. Tal vez **puedo** ir.
2. Tal vez no lo **entendiste** tú. *Maybe you didn't understand him.*

C. 1. **Viene** mañana, tal vez. *He's coming tomorrow, maybe.*
2. No lo **entendiste** tú, tal vez.
3. **Enseñan** alemán aquí, tal vez. *They teach German here, maybe.*

	INDICATIVE	SUBJUNCTIVE
tal vez precedes the verb	√	√
tal vez follows the verb	√	

When **tal vez** appears after the verb, the verb is in the indicative; when it appears before the verb, the verb may be either indicative or subjunctive.

› PERSON-NUMBER SUBSTITUTION DRILL

A. 1. Tal vez trabajemos aquí.
(él, ellos, yo, tú, usted, ustedes)
2. Tal vez *ella* enseñe ahí.
(tú, yo, ellos, nosotros, ustedes, él)
3. Tal vez no olvidemos nada.
(yo, ellos, usted, tú, ella, ustedes)
4. Tal vez llame ahora.
(tú, yo, ustedes, nosotros, él, ellos)
5. Tal vez ganen otra vez.
(nosotros, usted, tú, yo, ustedes, él)
6. Tal vez paguemos algo.
(él, ustedes, yo, tú, ella, ustedes)

B. 1. Tal vez *yo* venda la casa.
(ellos, nosotros, él, ustedes, tú, mis padres)
2. Tal vez aprendamos algo.
(yo, ustedes, ella, tú, ellos, usted)
3. Tal vez secuestren al diplomático.
(usted, ellos, tú, ella, ustedes, yo)
4. Tal vez reciba una carta.
(nosotros, yo, ellos, tú, usted, ustedes)
5. Tal vez compre un restorán.
(nosotros, ellos, usted, tú, él, ellos)
6. Tal vez escriban esta noche.
(yo, tú, usted, ellas, nosotros, ustedes)
7. Tal vez no discuta ese asunto.
(nosotros, ellos, él, tú, usted, ustedes)

C. 1. Tal vez *yo* conozca a alguien.
(él, tú, nosotros, usted, ellos, el jefe)
2. Tal vez produzcan más.
(él, ustedes, tú, yo, usted, nosotros)
3. Tal vez *él* no tenga tiempo.
(ellos, tú, usted, nosotros, ella, ustedes)
4. Tal vez *Juan* venga mañana.
(ellas, nosotros, tú, yo, él, los otros)
5. Tal vez no tengamos que llevar chaperón.
(ella, tú, ellas, yo, usted, las muchachas)
6. Tal vez salgamos esta noche.
(yo, ustedes, ella, él y yo, ellos, tú)
7. Tal vez hagamos una comida.
(tú, ellos, ella, ustedes, yo, nosotras)
8. Tal vez digas la verdad.
(usted, ellos, ella, ustedes, nosotros, él)
9. Tal vez oiga mejor.
(ustedes, tú, él, nosotros, ellos, yo)

D. 1. Tal vez puedan ir.
(yo, tú, él, ustedes, nosotros, usted)
2. Tal vez *tú* ya no recuerdes.
(usted, ustedes, nosotros, ella, ellas, yo)
3. Tal vez pierdan hoy.
(él, ustedes, nosotros, tú, yo, ellos)
4. Tal vez no quiera venderlo.
(ellos, usted, tú, nosotros, ustedes, yo)
5. Tal vez no piensen lo mismo.
(nosotros, él, ustedes, yo, tú, usted)

E. 1. Tal vez durmamos en casa.
(yo, ellos, tú, él y yo, ustedes, él)
2. Tal vez se sientan mejor hoy.
(usted, ellos, ella, ustedes, tú, yo, nosotros)
3. Tal vez pidamos fruta.
(él, ustedes, tú, ellos, yo, él y yo)
4. Tal vez sirva bien.
(ustedes, tú, él, nosotros, ellos, yo)

F. 1. Tal vez no estén ahí.
(ella, ellos, él, tú, yo, nosotros)
2. Tal vez no vayan mañana.
(nosotros, él, ustedes, tú, ella, yo)
3. Tal vez no hayan entendido bien.
(ustedes, usted, ellos, tú, nosotros, yo)
4. Tal vez no sepamos todo.
(yo, tú, usted, él, ustedes, ellos)

› CONSTRUCTION SUBSTITUTION DRILL

INSTRUCTIONS: Repeat the following sentences just as you hear them. Then repeat them again, shifting **tal vez** to the end of the sentence and changing the verb from subjunctive to indicative.

A. 1. Tal vez llegue mañana. *Repita.*
Llega mañana, tal vez.
2. Tal vez no necesites una corbata.
3. Tal vez esté adentro.
4. Tal vez desee la muerte.
5. Tal vez cambie el mercado.
6. Tal vez no la preste.
7. Tal vez no lo exijan.

B. 1. Tal vez no salgan extras.
2. Tal vez haya algún beneficio.
3. Tal vez no sea tan aburrido.
4. Tal vez la conozcan.
5. Tal vez no produzcan maíz.
6. Tal vez no diga la verdad.
7. Tal vez no haya reforma.

› PATTERNED RESPONSE DRILL

A. 1. ¿Viene Juan?
No sé, tal vez venga.
2. ¿Estudia Elena?
3. ¿Participa don Rosario?
4. ¿Sale Felipe?
5. ¿Vuelve Carlos?
6. ¿Espera Fernando?
7. ¿Gana Rosa?
8. ¿Sigue el señor Alonso?

B. 1. ¿Vino Cecilia?
No sé, tal vez haya venido.
2. ¿Estudió Susana?
3. ¿Participó don Pepe?
4. ¿Salió Patricio?
5. ¿Volvió Roberto?
6. ¿Esperó doña Mercedes?
7. ¿Ganó Josefina?
8. ¿Discutió el barbero?

› TRANSLATION DRILL

1. Perhaps he'll come today.
Tal vez viene hoy.
Perhaps he may come today.
Tal vez venga hoy.
2. Maybe he's mistaken.
Just possibly he may be mistaken.
3. Perhaps it'll arrive too late.
Perhaps it may arrive too late.
4. Maybe he'll do it.
He just may do it.
5. Perhaps it's the other one.
Perhaps it may be the other one.
6. Maybe it's not ridiculous nowadays.
Could be it's not ridiculous nowadays.
7. Perhaps he has an appointment.
Perhaps he may have an appointment.

› DISCUSSION

After **tal vez,** Spanish uses the subjunctive to express greater uncertainty than is expressed by the indicative in a similar sentence. English usually makes this distinction by tone of voice or by using other qualifying words like *possibly, just:* **Es hoy tal vez** *It's today, maybe;* **Tal vez es hoy** *Perhaps it's today, Quite possibly it's today;* **Tal vez sea hoy** *Perhaps it's today, Possibly it's today.* Note that when **tal vez** follows the main verb it has a purely adverbial function, simply modifying the action of the sentence rather than exerting any "influence." This is analogous to the right-shifting of the noun phrases in the preceding section; those phrases tend to behave like adverbs, modifying rather than influencing the action of the main clause.

As the example **Tal vez haya algún beneficio** indicates, the present subjunctive includes future meanings. Thus **Tal vez no valga más** may mean, depending on context, either *Maybe it isn't worth more* or *Maybe it won't be worth more.*

103 Indirect commands

EXAMPLES

1. Que lo **hagan** otros.
2. **Digan** lo que digan.
3. Que **espere.** *Let him (He can just) wait.*
4. Que **pasen.** *Have them come in.*
5. Que se **vaya.** *Let him go (He can go for all I care).*
6. Que ella los **lleve** (Que los **lleve** ella). *Let* ***her*** *carry them.*
7. Que no **estudie** medicina. *Don't let (have) him study medicine.*

Let Have	him her them	do it.	
Que	**(él)** **(ella)** **(ellos, -as)**	**lo haga.** **lo hagan.**	**(él).** **(ella).** **(ellos, -as).**

Indirect commands, like **usted, -es** commands, use the present subjunctive third-person singular and plural. Except in a few set phrases (Example 2), they are introduced by **que.** With-verb pronouns precede the verb, and subject pronouns, as usual, are normally included only for emphasis.

› PATTERNED RESPONSE DRILL

A. 1. TEACHER: ¿Rosa va a comprar la carne?
STUDENT: **Sí, que la compre.**
2. ¿Patricio va a pedir el cambio?
3. ¿Don Pepe va a contar la ganancia?
4. ¿Fernando va a arreglar la comida?
5. ¿Chalo va a discutir la cuestión?
6. ¿Alvaro va a traer los libros?
7. ¿La criada va a llevar los vestidos?
8. ¿Josefina va a apagar el radio?

B. 1. Acuéstense ustedes.
Nosotros no; que se acuesten otros.
2. Váyase usted.
Yo no; que se vaya otro.
3. Levántense ustedes.
4. Siéntese usted.
5. Báñense ustedes.
6. Acuérdese usted.
7. Alégrense ustedes.
8. Quédese usted.
9. Cálmense ustedes.

C. 1. Tráigame el libro.
Yo no; que se lo traiga otro.
2. Véndame la camisa.
3. Lléveme los paquetes.
4. Mándeme las fotos.
5. Láveme el coche.
6. Déme los recibos.
7. Cómpreme las pastillas.

› CHOICE-QUESTION RESPONSE DRILL

A. 1. TEACHER: ¿Vengo yo o viene él?
STUDENT: **Que venga él.**
2. ¿Corro yo o corre él?
3. ¿Disparo yo o dispara él?
4. ¿Escojo yo o escoge él?
5. ¿Pregunto yo o pregunta él?
6. ¿Rezo yo o reza él?
7. ¿Termino yo o termina él?
8. ¿Sigo yo o sigue él?

B. 1. Vamos nosotros o van ellos?
Que vayan ellos.
2. ¿Comemos nosotros o comen ellos?
3. ¿Hablamos nosotros o hablan ellos?
4. ¿Rifamos nosotros o rifan ellos?
5. ¿Escribimos nosotros o escriben ellos?
6. ¿Jugamos nosotros o juegan ellos?
7. ¿Pedimos nosotros o piden ellos?
8. ¿Volvemos nosotros o vuelven ellos?

› PATTERNED RESPONSE DRILL

A. 1. ¿Rosa va a lavar las tazas?
Sí, que las lave.
2. ¿Josefina va a barrer el cuarto?
3. ¿Ana va a sacudir los muebles?
4. ¿Alfredo va a traer el coche?
5. ¿El barbero va a usar las tijeras?

B. 1. ¿Van ellos a comprar el pan?
Sí, que lo compren.
2. ¿Van ellos a mantenerse firmes?
3. ¿Van ellos a pagar la multa?
4. ¿Van ellos a trabajar?
5. ¿Van ellos a venir?

C. 1. ¿A dónde va a ir ella? ¿Al cine?
Sí, que vaya al cine.
2. ¿Dónde va a comer ella? ¿En la cocina?
3. ¿Qué va a contar ella? ¿Los libros?
4. ¿Cuándo va a volver ella? ¿Mañana?

› **DISCUSSION**

To convey an indirect command or permission Spanish uses the present subjunctive. The English equivalents *let* and *have* are somewhat stronger than the Spanish implies. The *let* of *Let him go* when in the Spanish form **Que se vaya** does not suggest releasing him from restraint (this would be **Deje que se vaya** with **dejar** for *let*) but merely *He may go if he wants to. Have them come in* in the form **Que pasen** does not necessarily imply compulsion but only *They may come in,* anywhere between urging and permitting.

English at one time abounded in such expressions of commanding, permitting, or wishing, and a number of idiomatic expressions still survive, especially those with religious associations. The words *may* and *let* are frequent: (*May*) *God bless you, May they rest in peace, May* (*Let*) *the best man win, Heaven help us, Just let him try it! Let the record show that three abstained.*

104 Present subjunctive for *let's*

EXAMPLES

A. 1. **Cambiemos** de tema.
2. **Dejemos** ese tema.
3. **Sentémonos.** *Let's sit down.*
4. **Hagámoslo** ahora. *Let's do it now.*

B. 1. **Vamos** allá ahora. *Let's go there now.*
2. **Vámonos.** *Let's get going. Let's go.*

C. 1. No **discutamos** más.
2. No **toquemos** ese tema.
3. No nos **sentemos.** *Let's not sit down.*
4. No lo **hagamos** ahora. *Let's not do it now.*
5. No nos **vayamos.** *Let's not go.*

	LET'S		LET'S NOT
	discutamos		**no discutamos**
with **-nos**	**sentémo-**	**-nos**	**no nos sentemos**
with other with-verb pronouns	**hagámos-**	**-lo**	**no lo hagamos**

The present subjunctive first-person plural is used for *let's.* (**Vamos, Vámonos** is an exception in that the form of the indicative is used.) As with the direct commands (Unit 6, Section 28) the with-verb pronouns precede when the verb is negative and follow when it is affirmative. When **-nos** follows the verb the final **s** of the verb is dropped.

› **PATTERNED RESPONSE DRILL**

A. 1. TEACHER: Hable usted.
STUDENT: **No, hablemos nosotros.**
2. Entre usted.
3. Termine usted.
4. Espere usted.
5. Pague usted.

6. Coma usted.
7. Escriba usted.
8. Salga usted.
9. Siga usted.
10. Venga usted.
11. Vuelva usted.

B. 1. Acuéstese usted.
No, acostémonos nosotros
2. Quédese usted.
3. Acuérdese usted.
4. Levántese usted.
5. Siéntese usted.
6. Báñese usted.
7. Lávese usted.
8. Sírvase usted.
9. Váyase usted.

C. 1. ¿Pagamos la cuenta?
Sí, paguémosla. No, no la paguemos.
2. ¿Felicitamos a los diplomáticos?
3. ¿Tomamos la casa?
4. ¿Rifamos el abrigo?
5. ¿Miramos a las chicas?
6. ¿Dejamos los zapatos?
7. ¿Discutimos el asunto?
8. ¿Traemos la receta?
9. ¿Vendemos los libros?
10. ¿Escribimos las cartas?

D. 1. ¿Le prestamos la plata?
Sí, prestémosela.[2] **No, no se la prestemos.**
2. ¿Le llevamos el tocadiscos?
3. ¿Le contamos las mentiras?
4. ¿Le apagamos el radio?
5. ¿Le quitamos el abrigo?
6. ¿Le arreglamos los frenos?

› CHOICE-QUESTION RESPONSE DRILL

A. 1. TEACHER: ¿Estudiamos o hablamos?
STUDENT: **Hablemos.**
2. ¿Entramos o regresamos?
3. ¿Regateamos o salimos?
4. ¿Seguimos o volvemos?
5. ¿Contestamos o esperamos?

B. 1. ¿Nos quedamos o nos vamos?
Quedémonos.
2. ¿Nos sentamos o nos levantamos?
3. ¿Nos acostamos o nos vamos?
4. ¿Nos lavamos o nos bañamos?

C. 1. ¿Vendemos la casa o la arreglamos?
Vendámosla.
2. ¿Traemos a los niños o los dejamos?
3. ¿Llevamos las cartas o las mandamos?
4. ¿Servimos los huevos o los cambiamos?
5. ¿Cerramos la puerta o la abrimos?
6. ¿Usamos el coche o lo prestamos?

› DISCUSSION

In addition to **vamos a** plus infinitive (see Unit 8, Section 37) Spanish uses the present subjunctive first-person plural to express the meaning *let's*. The subjunctive is the only way of saying *let's not* (while **Vamos a hacerlo** may mean *Let's do it,* **No vamos a hacerlo** can only mean *We aren't going to do it*).

105 Colors

EXAMPLES 1. Dos cafés **negros** bien calientes.
2. Montañas, nubes, cielo **azul.**
3. Una casita **verde** que está en la esquina.

[2] **prestémossela.** The **ss** is reduced to **s.**

NEUTRALITY	
white	**blanco**
gray	**gris**
black	**negro**

INTENSITY	
light	**claro**
dark	**oscuro**

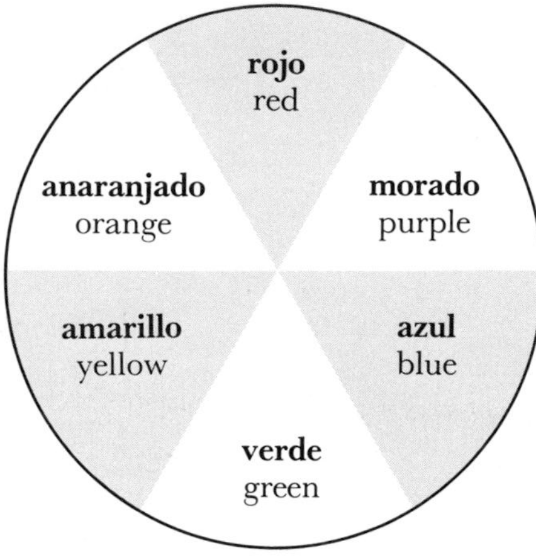

LOS COLORES

The primary colors are **rojo, amarillo,** and **azul.** The secondary colors are **anaranjado** (from **naranja** *orange*), **verde,** and **morado.**

➤ ITEM SUBSTITUTION DRILL

1. Aquí hay varios libros *negros.*
   (amarillos, rojos, azules, anaranjados)
2. ¿Dónde está mi camisa *blanca?*
   (azul, gris, verde, morada)
3. ¡Qué bonitas son esas flores *rojas!*
   (moradas, amarillas, anaranjadas, azules)
4. Me gusta el color *verde* claro.
   (azul, rojo, morado, anaranjado)
5. Ana prefiere el *rojo* oscuro.
   (azul, anaranjado, verde, morado)

➤ ITEM SUBSTITUTION DRILL

1. Compré un traje gris.
2. ________ corbata ________
3. ________________ negra
4. ________ auto ________
5. ________________ azul
6. ________ casa ________
7. ________________ roja
8. ________ maquinilla ________
9. ________________ verde
10. ________ plantas ____
11. ________________ amarillas
12. ________ paquete ____
13. ________________ anaranjados
14. ________ camisa ____
15. ________________ moradas
16. ________ flor ________
17. ________________ oscuras

Nouns with first- and second-person verbs

EXAMPLES A. 1. **(Nosotros) los americanos** no pensamos así. *We Americans don't think that way.*
2. **Ustedes los abogados** discuten demasiado. *You lawyers argue too much.*

B. 1. A **ustedes los jóvenes** no los convence nadie.
2. Creen que casa y comida son bastantes para **nosotras las viejas.** *They think that room and board are enough for us elderly women.*

A.

SUBJECT PRONOUN	DEFINITE ARTICLE	SUBJECT NOUN	VERB
(Nosotros)	**los**	**americanos**	**pensamos.**
Ustedes	**los**	**abogados**	**discuten.**

As the subject in this construction **nosotros, -as** is optional because the verb identifies the meaning as *we,* but **ustedes** is required. The definite article is used because of the meaning *all.* (See Unit 13, Section 72.)

B.

	OBJECT PRONOUN	DEFINITE ARTICLE	OBJECT NOUN
para	**nosotras**	**las**	**viejas**
a	**ustedes**	**los**	**jóvenes**

As an object both **ustedes** and **nosotros, -as** are required.

› TRANSLATION DRILL

A. 1. We technicians drink too much coffee.
Nosotros los técnicos tomamos demasiado café.
2. We government officials work hard.
3. We barbers talk a lot.
4. We businessmen buy lots of things.

B. 1. You lawyers argue too much.
Ustedes los abogados discuten demasiado.
2. You students need to study more.
3. You idealists shouldn't exaggerate so much.

C. 1. There's not much for us elderly women.
No hay mucho para nosotras las viejas.
2. There's very little for us athletes.
3. No one expects much from us servants.

D. 1. No one can convince you young people.
A ustedes los jóvenes no los convence nadie.
2. No one can convince you idealists.
3. No one can protect you ambassadors.
4. No one can comprehend you administrators.
5. No one can teach you journalists.

DISCUSSION

The Spanish equivalent of the type *you soldiers, we doctors, us students* differs in two ways from the English. First, the definite article is required with the noun, since ***We doctors*** *have licenses* generalizes in the same way as ***Practicing doctors*** *have licenses.* Second, whereas in English both *we* (*us*) and *you* always accompany the noun, in Spanish **nosotros, -as** as subject of an explicit verb is not required, unless for emphasis, because the verb ending tells that *we* is the meaning: **Los americanos no pensamos así.** But **nosotros, -as** as an object is expressed as in English, and **ustedes** is expressed regardless of its grammatical function.

GUIDED CONVERSATION

J. *Jacinto* R. *Ramón*

J. ¿Pero por qué se oponen tus padres a que estudies para abogado?
R. Dicen que hay tantos ______________
J. Entonces ¿ellos insisten en que estudies medicina?
R. No, *insisten* no. Dicen que no se van a ______________
J. A menos que sea la política, ¿verdad?
R. Sí, y cuando hablamos de política nunca nos ______________

Buenos Aires: The University Law School

J. ¿Por qué? ¿A tu padre no le gusta Vargas Campo?
R. Lo odia. Dice que es un loco ______________
J. ¡Claro que quiere cambiarlo todo! ¿Pero qué hay de malo en eso? ¡Debe cambiarse!
R. Mi padre dice que no quiere ver ______________
J. ¿Pero no ve que ya está en la ruina? A los viejos no los convence nadie.

› TRANSLATION REVIEW DRILL

The required relator **que.**

1. I think she is American.
2. I think she speaks Spanish.
3. It seems to me she is Spanish.
4. It seems to me she speaks English.
5. She says no.
6. She says it's a horror.

› PATTERNED RESPONSE REVIEW DRILL

The required relator **que.**

A. 1. ¿Es embajador?
Sí, creo que es embajador.
2. ¿Habla ella español?
3. ¿Es ella soltera?
4. ¿Va ella a la escuela?

B. 1. ¿Habla ella inglés?
Sí, parece que habla inglés.
2. ¿Estudia ella filosofía?
3. ¿Le gusta a ella la política?
4. ¿Prefiere ella el invierno?
5. ¿Se siente ella mejor?
6. ¿Gana ella mucho en las carreras?

C. 1. ¿Es ella española?
Sí, dice que es española.
2. ¿Tiene ella hambre?
3. ¿Está ella contenta?
4. ¿Está ella de acuerdo?

reading

Escojamos una carrera

E. *Estudiante* P. *Profesor* S. *Secretaria del profesor*

E. Profesor, quiero que usted me dé unos consejos.
P. Con mucho gusto. Pasemos a mi oficina... Aquí estamos... Sentémonos... Bueno, ¿en qué puedo servirle?
E. Profesor, mis padres me han dicho que piense en escoger una carrera.
P. Y tienen razón. ¿Cuántos años tiene usted?
E. Diecinueve, señor.
P. ¿Ah? ...Yo siento una corriente de aire aquí. ¿Le molesta si cierro una ventana?
E. De ninguna manera. ¿Quiere usted que le ayude?
P. Gracias... ¿Por qué no es posible, en esta época de progreso científico, que los constructores hagan una ventana que funcione? (*Llaman a la puerta.*) ¡Pase!

ventana *window*
ayudar *to help*

Valparaíso, Chile: Mechanical engineering students at Universidad Técnica Federico Santa María

S. (*entrando*) Hay una señorita aquí afuera que quiere hablarle.

P. Que vuelva. ...¿Una señorita, dice?... Pues, que espere. No voy a tardar mucho. Que espere, que espere.

S. Muy bien, señor. (*Sale.*)

P. ¿En dónde estábamos?

E. Mi carrera, profesor.

P. Ah, sí. Su carrera. ...Pues, ¿no quiere ser ingeniero? Puede inventar una ventana que se cierre y se abra con facilidad. ¿Cómo van las matemáticas?

E. Muy mal. Salí reprobado en álgebra el año pasado.

Salí reprobado *I failed*

P. Entonces no debe ser ingeniero... Usted puede perder su regla de cálculo. ¿Por qué no escoge usted la carrera de abogado?

regla de cálculo *slide rule*

E. Ay, señor, hay tantos abogados ahora que es difícil destacarse en ese campo.

P. Pero el abogado puede meterse en la política, ¿no?

E. Sí, señor, pero no toquemos ese tema. Yo soy muy idealista para meterme en la política.

P. Hmm... Pues usted es el que decide. ¿Qué quiere ser usted?

E. (*corta pausa*) Poeta, señor.

P. ¡Dios mío!... Pero, mire: lo de ser poeta... no es carrera, ¡es una condición de la mente!... Usted sí que es un idealista. Pero, si quiere escribir, si sabe escribir... entonces... escriba... Dios sea contigo,[3] hijo mío... Yo también quise ser poeta...

sí que es *are indeed*

[3]**sea** rather than **esté** because more than location is involved: *May God be active on your behalf.*

UNIT 19

A Businessman

S. *Mr. Suárez* J. *Juanita, his secretary* V. *Víctor*

It is eleven A.M. Mr. Suárez has just arrived at the office.

S. Anything new, Juanita?
J. The brochures have finally arrived from the printer's.
S. Good, because we'll need them when the board of directors meets next week.
J. But look, Mr. Suárez. The cover is printed upside down.
S. Then we've got to send them back to be redone. I'll call them before we return them to them. They've got to prepare them so that they'll arrive before the fifteenth.

(*The telephone rings.*)

J. Mr. Suárez's office . . . Yes, ma'am . . . Just a moment, please.
S. Who is it?
J. Mrs. Suárez. She says that she locked the car and that now she can't open it. The keys got locked [left] inside. And with so many packages she can't make it on foot even to the bus stop.
S. What a woman! Tell her to leave the car there and return in a taxi. I'll see later how I'm going to take care of that.

* * *

Un hombre de negocios

S. *Señor Suárez* J. *Juanita, su secretaria* V. *Víctor*

Son las once de la mañana. El señor Suárez acaba de llegar a la oficina.

S. ¿Alguna novedad, Juanita?
J. Por fin han llegado los folletines del impresor.
S. Bueno, porque los necesitaremos cuando se reuna la junta directiva la semana que viene.
J. Pero mire usted, señor Suárez. La cubierta está impresa al revés.
S. Entonces tenemos que mandarlos a rehacer. Yo los llamaré antes de que se los devolvamos. Tienen que prepararlos para que lleguen antes del quince.

(*Suena el teléfono.*)

J. Oficina del señor Suárez... Sí, señora... Un momento, por favor.
S. ¿Quién es?
J. La señora Suárez. Dice que cerró el coche y que ahora no puede abrirlo. Que se le quedaron las llaves adentro. Y que con tantos bultos no puede ir a pie ni hasta la parada de autobuses.
S. ¡Qué señora! Dígale que deje el coche allí y vuelva en taxi. Ya veré cómo arreglo eso.

* * *

San Juan, Puerto Rico: Business street

(Mr. Suárez goes out to the street)

v. Hello, Don Domingo! Don't get away from me again! I've never seen anyone as busy as you are!

s. Hi there, Víctor! Say, I'm sorry. I had completely forgotten that you were coming to see me.

v. Don't worry. Do you have just a minute right now?

s. Well, right now I'm on my way to the Exchange Commission, but if you want to, come along. When I've finished there, we'll have time for a cup of coffee. But let's look for a place that's more quiet than on the main street.

v. Wonderful, just so it's no bother to you, Don Domingo.

s. What do you mean! When it comes to [has to do with] talking about a fishing trip, there's always time.

(El señor Suárez sale a la calle.)

v. ¡Hola, don Domingo! ¡No se me escape otra vez! ¡Parece que no hay nadie que sea tan ocupado (1) como usted!

s. ¡Qué hubo, Víctor! Hombre, perdóneme. Se me había olvidado totalmente que iba a venir a verme.

v. No se preocupe. ¿Tiene un minutito ahora mismo?

s. Hombre, ahora voy a la Comisión de Cambios, (2) pero si quiere, venga conmigo. Cuando haya terminado allí, tendremos tiempo para un cafecito. Pero busquemos un lugar que sea más tranquilo que en la calle mayor.

v. Magnífico, pero con tal que no le sea molestia, don Domingo.

s. ¡Qué va! Cuando se trata de hablar de un viaje de pesca, siempre hay tiempo.

cultural notes

(1) By using **ser ocupado** Víctor classifies Mr. Suárez as a *busy man;* **estar ocupado** would suggest being busy now.

(2) The **Comisión de Cambios** is a governmental agency that regulates foreign exchange and the issuance of export and import permits.

107 Indicative and subjunctive in adverb clauses

EXAMPLES A. 1. **Como** no se **siente** tranquila, no puede dormir. *Since she doesn't feel calm, she can't sleep.*
2. Los dejé ir solos **porque** ya aquí todos **hemos visto** esa película.
3. Llegamos después de las cinco, **pues** no **salimos** hasta las doce. *We got there after five because we didn't leave until twelve.*
4. **Puesto que vale** tanto, no lo vamos a vender. *Since it's worth so much, we aren't going to sell it.*
5. **Ya que va,** ¿puede mandarme una taza de café?
6. **Ahora que** lo **conocemos** mejor, lo respetamos más. *Now that we know him better, we respect him more.*
7. No lo he visto **desde que** le **presté** mi coche. *I haven't seen him since I lent him my car.*
8. **Aunque esperamos** dos horas, no nos llamaron. *Though we waited two hours, they didn't call us.*

B. 1. **Antes que** me **olvide.**
2. Bueno, **con tal que** no le **sea** molestia.
3. Trabajemos **para que haya** más plata. *Let's work so that there will be more money.*
4. ¿Puede hacerlo **sin que** lo **sepamos?** *Can he do it without our knowing it?*
5. **A menos que** uno se **meta** en la política.

A. CONJUNCTIONS THAT TAKE INDICATIVE		
expressing cause	since, as because since, because since, inasmuch as since, now that	**como**[1] **porque** **pues**[2] **puesto que** **ya que**
	now that since (*time*) though, although	**ahora que** **desde que** **aunque**

When they have the meanings listed above these conjunctions take the indicative in Spanish.

B. CONJUNCTIONS THAT TAKE SUBJUNCTIVE	
before provided so that, in order that without unless	**antes (de) que** **con tal (de) que** **para que** **sin que** **a menos que**

[1] **Como** in this sense is usually at the beginning of the sentence.

[2] **Pues** in this sense is usually in the middle of the sentence.

› PERSON-NUMBER SUBSTITUTION DRILL

1. Antes que *yo* me olvide, es necesario escribir la carta.
   (tú, usted, nosotros, él, ellos, ella, ustedes)
2. No, a menos que *uno* se meta en la política.
   (yo, ustedes, usted, tú, él, nosotros, ellos)
3. Con mucho gusto, con tal que no estudiemos biología.
   (yo, ustedes, él, ellos, tú, usted, ellas)
4. Y temprano, para que llegues a tiempo.
   (ustedes, yo, ella, nosotros, usted, ellos, él)
5. No es posible ir sin que *él* lo sepa.
   (nosotros, ella, tú, ustedes, yo, ellos, usted)

› CONSTRUCTION SUBSTITUTION DRILL

INSTRUCTIONS: Repeat the following sentences just as you hear them. Then repeat them again, replacing each preposition with the indicated conjunction plus subject.

1. Llámeme *antes de* salir.
   ______ antes que Julio ______
   Llámeme antes que Julio salga.
2. Voy a hacer lo posible *para* volver mañana.
   ______ para que Cecilia ___
3. No podemos ganar *sin* jugar.
   ______ sin que usted ______
4. *Con tal de* venir, no hay problema.
   Con tal que Rafael ______
5. Comemos temprano *para* ir al cine.
   ______ para que las chicas ___
6. Estoy esperando *para* participar.
   ______ para que tú ______
7. No podemos progresar *sin* trabajar.
   ______ sin que todo el mundo ___

› PATTERNED RESPONSE DRILL

A. 1. TEACHER: ¿Van a discutirlo con él?
   STUDENT: **Sí, antes que se vaya.**
   2. ¿Van a discutirlo con ellos?
   3. ¿Van a discutirlo con ella?
   4. ¿Van a discutirlo con nosotros?
   5. ¿Van a discutirlo con usted?
   6. ¿Van a discutirlo contigo?
   7. ¿Van a discutirlo conmigo?
   8. ¿Van a discutirlo con ustedes?

B. 1. ¿Se lo han dicho a él?
   Sí, para que se informe.
   2. ¿Se lo han dicho a ellos?
   3. ¿Se lo han dicho a ella?
   4. ¿Se lo han dicho a usted?
   5. ¿Te lo han dicho a ti?
   6. ¿Se lo han dicho a ustedes?

C. 1. ¿El se va mañana?
   Sí, a menos que no se sienta bien.
   2. ¿Ellos se van mañana?
   3. ¿Ella se va mañana?
   4. ¿Nosotros nos vamos mañana?
   5. ¿Usted se va mañana?
   6. ¿Tú te vas mañana?
   7. ¿Yo me voy mañana?
   8. ¿Ustedes se van mañana?

D. 1. ¿Lo supo él?
   No, lo han arreglado sin que lo sepa.
   2. ¿Lo supieron ellos?
   3. ¿Lo supo ella?
   4. ¿Lo supieron ellas?
   5. ¿Lo supo usted?
   6. ¿Lo supiste tú?
   7. ¿Lo supieron ustedes?

E. 1. ¿Va a pedir él los folletines?
   Sí, con tal que los necesite.
   2. ¿Van a pedir ellos los folletines?
   3. ¿Va a pedir ella los folletines?
   4. ¿Vamos a pedir nosotros los folletines?
   5. ¿Va a pedir usted los folletines?
   6. ¿Vas a pedir tú los folletines?
   7. ¿Voy a pedir yo los folletines?
   8. ¿Van a pedir ustedes los folletines?

F. 1. ¿Van a discutir la cuestión con él?
   Sí, para que pueda hacer algo.
   2. ¿Van a discutir la cuestión con ellos?
   3. ¿Van a discutir la cuestión contigo?
   4. ¿Van a discutir la cuestión con usted?
   5. ¿Van a discutir la cuestión con nosotros?
   6. ¿Van a discutir la cuestión conmigo?
   7. ¿Van a discutir la cuestión con ustedes?

TRANSLATION DRILL

1. They're coming (in order) to study.
   They're coming so we can study.[3]
2. Call me before eating.
   Call me before the children eat.
3. I'm not going without knowing.
   I'm not going without my family knowing.
4. They're coming to celebrate.
   They're coming so we can celebrate.
5. Before deciding, write me.
   Before they decide, write me.
6. We get up early to go to school.
   We get up early so the girls can go to school.

EXAMPLES

A. 1. **Cuando** tú y yo **éramos** novios no nos dejaban salir solos.
   2. Los necesitaremos **cuando** se **reuna** la junta directiva.

B. 1. Toman las pastillas **hasta que** se **sienten** mejor. *They take the pills until they feel better.*
   2. Siga tomando las pastillas **hasta que** se **sienta** mejor. *Keep on taking the pills until you feel better.*

C. 1. **Tan pronto como llegaron** le avisé. *As soon as they arrived I advised him.*
   2. **Tan pronto** (**como**) **lleguen** avíseme.

D. 1. Lo voy a hacer **según** me **dice.** *I'm going to do it the way (according to what) he tells me.*
   2. Lo voy a hacer **según** me **diga.** *I'm going to do it the way (according to what) he tells (may tell) me.*

E. 1. Dílo **como** lo **entiendes.** *Tell it the way you (do) understand it.*
   2. Dílo **como** lo **entiendas.** *Tell it the way (whatever way) you (may) understand it.*

F. 1. Compra **donde dan** más. *Buy where they give more.*
   2. Compra **donde den** más. *Buy wherever they give more.*

G. 1. Me gusta, **aunque es** inútil. *I like it, even though it's useless.*
   2. Me gusta, **aunque sea** inútil. *I like it, even though it may be (even if it's) useless.*

CONJUNCTIONS THAT TAKE INDICATIVE OR SUBJUNCTIVE			
CONJUNCTIONS		INDICATIVE	SUBJUNCTIVE
when until as soon as	**cuando** **hasta que** **tan pronto** (**como**) **en cuanto**	*something that has happened, is happening, or happens regularly*	*something yet to happen*
the way, as the way, according to what where	**como** **según** **donde**	*something known*	*something unknown*
even though even if	**aunque**	*something conceded as true*	*something unproved or not conceded as true*

The indicative covers real happenings and things regarded as factual; the subjunctive covers things that are pending and regarded as nonfactual.

[3] The meaning of *can* is included in the Spanish subjunctive form.

› PERSON-NUMBER SUBSTITUTION DRILL

1. El Consejo Estudiantil lo va a decidir cuando llegue *Felipe*.
   (tú, usted, ellos, yo, nosotros, ustedes, ella)
2. Van a esperar aquí hasta que *nosotros* vengamos.
   (él, tú, usted, usted y yo, ella, ustedes, yo)
3. Sí, señor, tan pronto como nos escapemos.
   (tú, él, ellos, usted, don Domingo y yo, ella, yo)
4. En cuanto vuelvas, va a estar todo arreglado.
   (yo, ustedes, usted, nosotros, él, ellos, el tirano)
5. Lo voy a hacer según me digan *ellos*.
   (usted, tú, él, ustedes, ella, ellas)
6. Es verdad, aunque *tú* no lo creas.
   (ustedes, nosotros, usted, ellos, yo, ellas)

› CONSTRUCTION SUBSTITUTION DRILL

INSTRUCTIONS: Repeat the following sentences just as you hear them. Then repeat them again with an **ir a** future for the verbs indicated, changing the other verb from indicative to present subjunctive.

1. Lo compré cuando lo vi.
   __ voy a comprar ____
   Lo voy a comprar cuando lo vea.
2. No le mandaron el folletín hasta que lo pidió otra vez.
   ____ van a mandar ________________
3. Estudié mucho cuando estaba aquí.
   Voy a estudiar __________
4. Lo hice tan pronto como acabé mi carrera.
   __ voy a hacer ______________
5. Lo convencimos en cuanto le dijimos lo de la huelga.
   __ vamos a convencer ______________
6. No aceptaron esa decisión aunque vieron a su patria en la ruina.
   __ van a aceptar ______________________
7. La rubia no fue hasta que le dijeron.
   ______ va a ir ________
8. Tan pronto como llegué escribí una carta.
   _____________ voy a escribir __
9. Lo vieron cuando fue a la Comisión de Cambios.
   __ van a ver __________________
10. El tirano salió del país aunque tuvo que hacerlo de noche.
    ____ va a salir ____________________
11. Felicité a Enrique aunque no me dejó entrar.
    Voy a felicitar _______________
12. Llegó al poder aunque fue a palos y a tiros.
    Va a llegar ________________
13. En cuanto hubo una novedad, me la contaron.
    ___________________ van a contar.
14. Nunca salgo hasta que estoy totalmente preparado.
    ____ voy a salir _________________
15. Cuando algo de importancia sucede, sale una extra.
    ___________________ va a salir __
16. Compro zapatos tan pronto como los necesito.
    Voy a comprar ________________
17. Aunque no lo pagas, te lo doy.
    _____________ voy a dar.

PATTERNED RESPONSE DRILL

A. 1. TEACHER: ¿Cuándo viene Víctor?
STUDENT: **Viene cuando pueda.**
2. ¿Cuándo vienen las compañeras?
3. ¿Cuándo viene la hermana menor?
4. ¿Cuándo viene usted?
5. ¿Cuándo vienen ustedes?
6. ¿Cuándo vienes tú?
7. ¿Cuándo vengo yo?
8. ¿Cuándo venimos nosotros?

B. 1. ¿Cuándo van ustedes a contestar?
Tan pronto como decidamos.
2. ¿Cuándo va usted a contestar?
3. ¿Cuándo van los señores a contestar?
4. ¿Cuándo va él a contestar?
5. ¿Cuándo vamos a contestar?
6. ¿Cuándo vas a contestar?

C. 1. ¿Pablo va a ser médico?
No, no puede, aunque se dedique a estudiar medicina.
2. ¿Ellos van a ser médicos?
3. ¿Usted va a ser médico?
4. ¿Ustedes van a ser médicos?
5. ¿Tú vas a ser médico?
6. ¿El va a ser médico?

TRANSLATION DRILL

A. 1. Leave it wherever you want.
Déjelo donde quiera.
2. Leave it whenever you want.
3. Leave it any way (however) you want.
4. As you wish.

B. 1. Work the way he tells you.
Trabaje como le diga él.
2. Work where he tells you.
3. Work when he tells you.
4. Work until he tells you [to stop].

C. 1. Study when they leave.
Estudie cuando salgan.
2. Study as soon as they arrive.
3. Study until they come.
4. Study even though they don't want [you to].

DISCUSSION

The use of the indicative or subjunctive forms in adverb clauses is determined by whether or not the content of the clause squares with the facts. In *When he comes I'm going to see him* the clause states *he comes,* but this is not a fact, for he has not come and may not come; so Spanish uses the subjunctive: **Cuando venga lo voy a ver.** But in *When he came I saw him* the clause states *he came,* and this squares with the facts as the speaker knows them; the Spanish equivalent has indicative, **Cuando vino lo vi.** Similarly in *When he comes I see him* the *he comes* is something that he regularly does, so that this squares with the facts; the Spanish equivalent again has indicative, **Cuando viene lo veo.**

Similar to clauses with **cuando** are all clauses of time in which the content of the clause refers (1) to something unaccomplished or unfulfilled, something that has not happened or is yet to happen—here the verb is subjunctive, or (2) to something that has already happened or is happening now or happens regularly—here the verb is indicative. The conjunction **antes (de) que** always takes the first point of view and is followed by the subjunctive. The other temporal conjunctions lend themselves to either point of view.

Adverb clauses that do not refer to time follow the same general principle. The expression of purpose, for example, is always contingent—our purpose may not be carried out—so in the type **para que haya más plata** the subjunctive is always encountered. The reason one gives for one's actions, however, is regarded as real, and clauses with **puesto que,** for example, always call for the indicative even when the meaning is future: *Since I'm not going to like it* **Puesto que no me va a gustar.**

The entire situation may be moved into the past without altering the conditions that call for indicative or subjunctive. In *I wanted to see him as soon as he came* the *he came* does not square with any facts: from the past point of view it is something unfulfilled, yet to happen, and the verb is subjunctive. But in *I was there when he came* the *he came* does square with the facts.

Both conjunctions and prepositions are relator words that link subordinate elements to the rest of the sentence. Conjunctions perform this function for the elements that we term *clauses* (containing, among other things, a verb form other than the infinitive, **-ndo,** or command); prepositions perform it for the elements termed *phrases* (containing no verb form other than the infinitive). The conjunctions that begin adverb clauses are closely related to prepositions; many are derived from prepositions by adding **que:**

before eating	**antes de comer**	without waiting	**sin esperar**
before he eats	**antes (de) que coma**	without their waiting	**sin que esperen**
until six	**hasta las seis**	since yesterday	**desde ayer**
until it is six	**hasta que sean las seis**	since I arrived	**desde que llegué**
in order to open it (for opening it)	**para abrirla**	according to Pablo	**según Pablo**
in order that it may open	**para que se abra**	according to what Pablo said	**según dijo Pablo**

108 Indicative and subjunctive in adjective clauses

EXAMPLES	THE THING DESCRIBED IS PREDETERMINED		THE VERB IS INDICATIVE	
A. 1. Las dos	chicas que		están	en la sala.
2. Es un	loco idealista que	todo lo	quiere	cambiar.
3. Lo	único que	te	pedimos.	
4. Este	policía que	no me	entendió.	
5. En casa de	Olga, que		tiene	unos discos nuevos.
B. 1. Primera y última	vez que		vengo	aquí.
2. Cada	vez que		abro	la boca.
C. 1. Tú eres	el que		decides.	
2. Ana Guadalupe Martínez,	la que		trabajó	aquí.
3. Yo no fui	la que		recibí	esta ropa.
D. 1. Es un	deporte del que	yo no	sé	ni papa.
2. El	lugar sagrado donde		estaban.	

When the speaker has in mind a particular thing or things to which he applies his description, the verb of the clause is indicative.

EXAMPLES	THE THING DESCRIBED IS UNDETERMINED		THE VERB IS SUBJUNCTIVE	
1. Vamos a buscar un	lugar que		sea	más tranquilo.
2. A pesar de	lo que	tú	digas,	papá.

	THE THING DESCRIBED IS UNDETERMINED		THE VERB IS SUBJUNCTIVE	
3. Estudia	lo que	más te	guste.	
4. No nos vamos a oponer a	lo que	tú	escojas.	
5. No hay	nadie que		sea	tan ocupado.

> When the speaker does not have in mind a particular thing or things to which his description applies, the verb of the clause is subjunctive.

› PERSON-NUMBER SUBSTITUTION DRILL

1. No hay nada aquí que *él* pueda entender.
   (yo, nosotros, ellas, usted, tú, ella, ustedes)
2. ¿Hay aquí una iglesia que *yo* no conozca?
   (nosotros, él, ellos, ella, ustedes, usted, tú)
3. Busco una película que *nosotros* entendamos.
   (yo, ellos, ella, él y yo, tú, ustedes, usted)
4. No se van a oponer a lo que *tú* escojas.
   (yo, ustedes, usted, ellos, nosotros, ellas, él)
5. No se puede terminar hoy, a pesar de lo que *él* diga.
   (ellos, usted, tú, ella, ustedes, nosotros, yo)

› CONSTRUCTION SUBSTITUTION DRILL

INSTRUCTIONS: Repeat the following sentences just as you hear them. Then repeat them again, substituting the indefinite or negative expression for the definite one and changing the second verb from indicative to present subjunctive.

1. Busco *al profesor* que entiende biología.
   _____ un profesor __________
   Busco un profesor que entienda biología.
2. ¿Dónde encuentro *a la secretaria* que habla inglés?
   __________ una secretaria __________
3. Invitemos *a los alumnos* que son buenos atletas.
   _____ unos alumnos __________
4. Vamos a escoger *los que* producen más.
   __________ unos que _____
5. Voy *al restorán* donde sirven comida española.
   ___ a un restorán __________
6. Vamos *al país* donde hay corridas de toros.
   _____ a un país __________
7. Quiero conocer *a la morena* que habla castellano.
   __________ una morena __________
8. Necesito encontrar *al señor* que vende autos importados.
   __________ un señor __________
9. Llamemos *al estudiante* que se dedica a estudios sociales.
   _____ un estudiante __________
10. ¿Cuándo me presentas *a la muchacha* que comulga todos los días?
    __________ una muchacha __________
11. *Hay una calle* que es demasiado larga.
    No hay calle __________
12. *Hay un abogado* que dice la verdad.
    No hay abogado __________
13. *Hay una cosa* que sirve.
    No hay cosa _____
14. *Hay algo* que yo puedo usar.
    No hay nada _____
15. *Hay alguien* aquí que compra ropa vieja.
    No hay nadie __________
16. *Hay algo* que merece respeto.
    No hay nada _____
17. *Hay alguien* aquí que sabe regatear.
    No hay nadie __________

› PATTERNED RESPONSE DRILL

A. 1. TEACHER: ¿Qué busca?
   STUDENT: **Busco una casa que sea bastante grande.**
2. ¿Qué quiere?
3. ¿Qué necesita?
4. ¿Qué desea?

5. ¿Qué espera encontrar?
6. ¿Qué quiere comprar?

B. 1. ¿Tiene un peine?
No, no tengo ninguno que sirva.

2. ¿Tiene una maquinilla?
3. ¿Tiene unas tijeras?
4. ¿Tiene un periódico?
5. ¿Tiene una revista?

› TRANSLATION DRILL

1. TEACHER: They're going to raffle the ones that are here.
   STUDENT: **Van a rifar los que están aquí.**
   TEACHER: They're going to raffle whichever ones are here.
   STUDENT: **Van a rifar los que estén aquí.**
2. We send you the ones (letters) that we like best (most).
   We're going to send you whichever ones we like best.
3. We ask for the one (part) that we deserve.
   We're going to ask for whichever one we deserve.
4. In spite of what you are saying, no.
   In spite of what you may say, no.
5. Do what he says.
   Do whatever he says.
6. No matter what they say, it's OK.
   Digan lo que digan, está bien.
   No matter what they bring, it's OK.
   No matter what they want, it's OK.
   No matter what they ask for, it's OK.
   No matter what they do, it's OK.
   No matter what they think, it's OK.
   No matter what they have, it's OK.
7. Be that as it may, I don't agree.
   Sea lo que sea, no estoy de acuerdo.
   Let come what may, I don't agree.
   Let follow what may, I don't agree.
   Let happen what may, I don't agree.

› DISCUSSION

Adjective clauses pose a choice between the use of indicative and subjunctive regardless of whether the clause is attached to a noun as in **este policía que no me entendió** or is a nominalization like **lo que tú le diste,** and regardless of the connecting words (**que, donde,** etc.).

The indicative is used when the speaker has in mind something predetermined to which the clause is to apply. In *He's buying a house that has ten rooms* **Compra una casa que tiene diez cuartos** the choice has settled on a particular house. The subjunctive is used when what the clause is to be applied to is undetermined. In *I want a house that has ten rooms* **Quiero una casa que tenga diez cuartos** the specifications for the house have been set up, but it is not known whether house *x* or house *y* will meet them.

Other examples: *I know someone who is going to the inauguration* **Conozco a alguien que va a la inauguración**—*x*, an identifiable person. *Let's find someone who is going to the inauguration* **Busquemos a alguien que vaya a la inauguración**—it is not known whether *x* or *y* will be the one to go. *The one who wins deserves the prize* **El que gana merece el premio**—the speaker states a general truth about the winners in his experience. *The one who wins* (in the contest tomorrow) *deserves the prize* **El que gane merece el premio**—*x, y,* and *z* are taking part; there is no way to tell to which one *who wins* will apply. *In spite of what you say* **A pesar de lo que tú dices**—refers to what you have just said or are saying. *In spite of what you* (may) *say* (In spite of anything you say) **A pesar de lo que tú digas**—nothing has yet been said; there is no particular remark *x* or *y*.

109 Mass nouns and countables

EXAMPLES
1. Sacuda todos los **muebles.**
2. Un hombre de **negocios.**
3. ¿Recibiste alguna mala **noticia?**
4. No digas **tonterías.**

SINGULAR MASS	=	PLURAL COUNTABLE
furniture		**muebles**
business		**negocios**
news		**noticias**
foolishness		**tonterías**

MASS WITH A COUNTER	=	SINGULAR COUNTABLE
piece of furniture		**mueble**
piece of business		**negocio**
piece (item, bit) of news		**noticia**
piece of foolishness		**tontería**

In certain nouns the English singular matches the Spanish plural, while the English with *piece of, bit of,* and similar counters matches the Spanish singular.

› TRANSLATION DRILL

A. 1. There's another piece of furniture.
Hay otro mueble.
2. There's another item of news.
3. There's another piece of business.
4. There's another piece of foolishness.

B. 1. There's more furniture.
Hay otros muebles.
2. There's more news.
3. There's more business.
4. There's more foolishness.

› DISCUSSION

In English we say *this popcorn* but *these beans* to refer to a mass or quantity and *this kernel of popcorn* but *this bean* to refer to a single item. We have concepts that can be referred to in two ways:

machinery	machines	piece of machinery	machine
poetry	poems	piece of poetry	poem
jewelry	jewels	piece of jewelry	jewel
anger	flareups	fit of anger	flareup
strife	quarrels	outbreak of strife	quarrel

The mass noun is singular in form but akin to plural in meaning. To make it singular in meaning we prefix a counter such as *piece of, bit of, grain of,* or *item of.*

In matching words across languages it often happens that mass nouns fail to line up with mass nouns and countables with countables. Then, just as we can "translate" *machinery* to *machines* and *piece of machinery* to *machine,* we are obliged to equate the mass noun in one language with the plural countable of the other, and the mass noun with a counter in the one with the singular in the other. In matching English and Spanish the commonest problem occurs when English mass nouns correspond to Spanish countables in the plural and English nouns with *piece of* and the like correspond to Spanish countables in the singular.

› GUIDED CONVERSATION

v. *Víctor* s. *Señor Suárez*

v. Entonces salimos para el viaje de pesca el dieciséis. A propósito, vi a su mujer cargada de[4] bultos esperando un taxi. ¿Está malo su coche?
s. No, es que ella cerró ______________
v. Y eso con las muchas otras cosas que lo tienen tan preocupado.
s. Sí, y ¿recuerda aquel folletín, el que voy a necesitar ______________
v. Ah, claro. El informe sobre el estado de cuentas[5] de la compañía.

[4] *loaded down with* [5] *financial report*

s. Eso es. Pues esta mañana me dijeron que la cubierta ______________

v. ¿Y qué se puede hacer?

s. No hay más remedio que mandar ______________

v. ¿Y para cuándo deben tenerlos preparados?

s. Tienen que ______________

v. Ah, la reunión es el quince. Por eso no salimos de viaje hasta el día dieciséis.

› TRANSLATION REVIEW DRILL

English verb-preposition equivalent to Spanish verb.

A. 1. Let's look for the bus.
   2. Let's wait for the bus.
   3. Let's look at the bus.
   4. Let's ask for the bus.

B. 1. I'm going to look for the book.
   2. I'm going to wait for the book.
   3. I'm going to look at the book.
   4. I'm going to ask for the book.

Quito, Ecuador: Plaza of the Church of San Francisco

reading

¿Necesita usted empleo? *(El Universal,* México, D. F.)

ANUNCIO muy importante: Deje de buscar trabajos que no le convienen. Venga a vernos con la seguridad de que aquí se quedará. Entrevistas de 8.30 a 10 y de 5 a 7 P.M. Correspondencia No. 17 "A". Colonia Postal.

convenir *to suit*
se quedará *you will remain* **entrevistas** *interviews*

AAA. Solicitamos agentes que quieran aumentar sus ingresos. Radio América. Argentina No. 72.

AAA *A-one* **ingresos** *incomes*

NECESITAMOS dos señoritas mecanógrafas que tengan velocidad y presentación. Palma Norte No. 518, despacho 503.

mecanógrafas *typists*

SE SOLICITAN dependientes de abarrotes que sepan trabajar y con cartas de recomendación. Inútil presentarse sin estos requisitos. La Santanderina. Roldán 4.

abarrotes *grocery clerks*

SOLICITO empleados ágiles, jóvenes, que sepan el ramo. Zapatería "Rodolfo". Argentina 6. México, D. F.

ramo *line of goods*

SOLICITO agente de ventas, conozca mercado llantas, con coche. Autos Munguía, S. A., Av. Chapultepec 376.

ventas *sales*
S.A. = Sociedad Anónima *Incorporated*

SOLICITO señorita que haya trabajado en café para trabajo en restaurante. Covarrubias 45, Tacubaya.

SE SOLICITA señorita que hable inglés, para atender niños de las 14 a las 20 horas. Teléfono 14-79-80.

SOLICITAMOS joven que sepa escribir bien a máquina. Claudio Bernard 43, pinturas.

escribir...máquina *to type well*

TINTORERÍA necesita planchador. Iturbide No. 33.

planchador *ironer*

URGENNOS vendedores que estén conectados con farmacias y doctores, gastos pagados. Fray Servando Teresa de Mier 505, de 9 a 1.30 y de 3 a 6.

Urgennos *We need*
gastos *expenses*

[6] Want ads in Spanish language newspapers exhibit the same telegraphic style as our own. Typical here is the omission of the relative pronoun, the definite article, and the preposition ([**que**] **conozca** [**el**] **mercado** [**de**] **llantas**).

[7] **Urgir** patterns like **faltar, gustar,** etc. (see Unit 11, Section 58).

UNIT 20

The New Manager

W. *Mr. Wright, the new manager* D. *Mr. Delgado*
R. *Rosa* S. *Susana* E. *Esperanza*

W. Mr. Delgado, day before yesterday I asked you to speak to the employees about the matter of punctuality. Did you do it?
D. Yes, Mr. Wright, and yesterday before they left I reminded them again.
W. Then what's going on? It's already twenty-five to nine and they still haven't all arrived.
D. I don't know. It's just that they've always been accustomed to arriving between 8:30 and 8:45.
W. Well even if that was the custom before I came, we're going to change it right now.
D. I wish you would speak to them personally, if you could.
W. As the new manager, the first thing I require is that everybody be on time.
D. One other thing, you told me to consult the employees about the change in time schedule.
W. Yes. I'd like to reduce lunch to one hour.
D. Well, the majority are against it because they have to have their siesta.

* * *

R. Mr. Wright is hopping mad because you came in ten minutes late.

El nuevo gerente

W. *Mr. Wright, el nuevo gerente* D. *Señor Delgado*
R. *Rosa* S. *Susana* E. *Esperanza*

W. Señor Delgado, anteayer le pedí a usted que les hablara a los empleados sobre el asunto de la puntualidad. ¿Lo hizo?
D. Sí, Mr. Wright, y ayer antes que salieran les volví a recordar.
W. Entonces, ¿qué pasa? Ya faltan veinticinco para las nueve y todavía no han llegado todos.
D. No sé. Es la costumbre que han tenido de llegar siempre entre ocho y media y nueve menos cuarto.
W. Pues si antes que yo viniera existía esa costumbre, ahora vamos a cambiarla. (1)
D. Ojalá que usted les hablara directamente, si pudiera.
W. Como nuevo gerente, lo primero que exijo es que todo el mundo sea puntual.
D. Otra cosa, me dijo usted que consultara con los empleados sobre el cambio de horario.
W. Sí. Quisiera reducir el almuerzo a una hora.
D. Pues, la mayoría se opone porque les hace falta la siesta. (2)

* * *

R. Mr. Wright está enojadísimo porque ustedes llegaron diez minutos tarde.

Guatemala City: Business office

S. Yes, I've already noticed it without your telling me. As if *we* were to blame . . . ! It's those awful buses.

E. Besides, what's ten minutes? What an old grouch [How disagreeable is that man]!

R. Don't believe it; he's very nice. It's just that he's strict.

E. The only thing I can say is that I'm so sorry Mr. Roberts resigned.

S. Yes. Mr. Roberts didn't mind whether we were a little late as long as we did our work right.

S. Sí, ya me di cuenta sin que me lo dijeras. ¡Como si nosotras tuviéramos la culpa...! Son esos cochinos autobuses.

E. Además, ¿qué son diez minutos? ¡Qué antipático es ese señor!

R. No creas; él es muy simpático. Lo que pasa es que es exigente.

E. Lo único que digo yo es que siento tanto que Mr. Roberts haya renunciado al puesto.

S. Sí. A Mr. Roberts no le importaba que llegáramos un poquito tarde con tal que le hiciéramos bien el trabajo.

cultural notes

(1) Mr. Wright is obviously eager to introduce American ideas of efficiency, which disrupt the informal nature of Latin-American business.

(2) The **siesta** traditionally was a period of about two hours during the middle of the workday when one might relax or take a nap. Today in those places where it is still in vogue it serves mainly to allow employees to go home for lunch. Many industrial communities have reduced the lunch period to an hour or less. The **siesta** often means closing all stores and offices for the period, but to compensate for this the closing hour for the day is later. (The origin of **siesta** is Latin *sexta* in *hora sexta,* "sixth hour," i.e., 12:00 noon counting from 6:00 A.M. —the period when heat was greatest in Mediterranean countries and a recess from work was needed.)

110 Imperfect subjunctive

	INFINITIVE	THIRD-PERSON PLURAL PRETERIT		SUBJUNCTIVE ENDINGS
regular verbs	**hablar** **comer** **vivir**	**habla-** **comie-** **vivie-**		
verbs with stem changes in preterit	**dormir** **pedir**	**durmie-** **pidie-**	**-ron**	**-ra** **-ras** **-ra**
verbs irregular in preterit	**estar** **haber** **poner** **hacer** **decir**	**estuvie-** **hubie-** **pusie-** **hicie-** **dije-**		**-'ramos**[1] **-ran**

The imperfect subjunctive is formed from the third-person plural of the preterit, as shown. There are no exceptions.

EXAMPLES

A. 1. Quisiera que lo **pensara** bien. *I'd like you to think it over carefully (that you should consider it well).*
2. Me dijo que **buscara** otro empleado. *He told me to look for another employee.*
3. Les rogó que no **discutieran** más de política. *She begged them not to argue about politics any more.*
4. Sugirieron que lo **cogiera** preso. *They suggested that he arrest him.*

B. 1. A Mr. Roberts no le importaba que **llegáramos** un poquito tarde. (*It didn't matter to Mr. Roberts that we arrived a little late.*)
2. Era ridículo que las muchachas **tuvieran** que llevar chaperón. *It was ridiculous that the girls should have to take a chaperon.*

AN INFLUENCE BROUGHT TO BEAR		WHAT WAS INFLUENCED
Les rogó	**que**	**no discutieran.**

AN ATTITUDE OF LIKE-DISLIKE OR ACCEPTANCE-REJECTION		WHAT WAS LIKED OR DISLIKED, ACCEPTED OR REJECTED
Era ridículo	**que**	**tuvieran que llevar chaperón.**

In noun clauses the imperfect subjunctive is used under the same conditions as the present subjunctive, except that the point of view is in the past.

[1] There is a written stress in the first-person plural: **habláramos, dijéramos.** The same syllable is stressed in all the forms of the imperfect subjunctive, and the conventions of writing require that it be marked in first-person plural forms.

› PERSON-NUMBER SUBSTITUTION DRILL

1. Susana quería que *yo* le comprara un abrigo de pieles.
   (ellas, nosotros, usted, tú, ustedes, Víctor)
2. Preferían que *ella* no saliera sin permiso.
   (nosotros, usted, ellos, tú, yo, ustedes)
3. El mereció que *ella* lo odiara.
   (tú, ustedes, usted, ellos, nosotros, yo)
4. Mis padres sugirieron que *yo* siguiera otra carrera.
   (él, ustedes, nosotros, ellos, tú, ella)
5. Mi madre se oponía a que *yo* renunciara.
   (ellos, él, tú, ustedes, él y yo, mi hermano)
6. Exigió que *todo el mundo* fuera puntual.
   (nosotros, yo, ellos, ella, ustedes, él)
7. Era necesario que fuéramos a la oficina.
   (yo, ustedes, usted, tú, ellos, él)
8. *Nos* sugirió que nos mantuviéramos firmes.
   (a mí, a ellos, a ti, a ustedes, a él, a ellas)
9. *Nos* dijo que no discutiéramos más.
   (a ellos, a ella, a mí, a ti, a usted, a ustedes)
10. Fue bueno que le dieras algunas flores a la secretaria.
    (ustedes, usted, ellos, nosotros, yo, ellas)
11. Fue fantástico que *él* se escapara otra vez.
    (ellos, ella, ellas, usted, ustedes, nosotros)
12. Sentí mucho que *ella* se fuera.
    (ustedes, usted, ellos, ellas, tú)
13. A *nosotros* no nos perdonaba que saliéramos tan temprano.
    (él, ellos, mí, ustedes, ti, ella)

› TENSE SUBSTITUTION DRILL

1. Francisco desea que yo le pague.
   ______ deseaba ________
2. Sugiero que nos quedemos.
   Sugerí ________
3. Me dice que abra los ojos.
   ___ dijo ________
4. El jefe no quiere que ponga el radio.
   ______ quería ________
5. Espero que se sienta mejor.
   Esperaba ________
6. No creo que venga ese cochino autobús.
   ___ creía ________
7. Me alegro que no haya ninguna novedad.
   ___ alegré ________
8. Siento que no podamos ganar.
   Sentí ________
9. Me alegro que el asunto no sea tan complicado.
   ___ alegré ________
10. Siento que le duela tanto la cabeza.
    Sentía ________
11. Es ridículo que suceda una cosa tan seria.
    Fue ________
12. No es bueno que pares todo el tráfico.
    ___ fue ________
13. Es importante que vendamos pronto estas pieles.
    Era ________
14. Es necesario que paguen la cuenta.
    Fue ________
15. Es difícil que siempre lleguemos a las ocho.
    Era ________

› CONSTRUCTION SUBSTITUTION DRILL

INSTRUCTIONS: Repeat the following sentences just as you hear them. Then repeat them again, preceding them with the expressions indicated and using imperfect subjunctive in place of indicative.

1. El gerente cambió el horario.
   (querían que, preferían que, esperaban que)
2. La mayoría se oponía al cambio de la siesta.
   (fue imposible que, fue ridículo que, no importaba que)
3. Anteayer soltaron al embajador.
   (me alegré que, esperaba que, fue bueno que)
4. Su cuñado no pagó el alquiler.
   (sentí que, no creí qué, lástima que)
5. La señora Méndez rifó el abrigo.
   (no les gustó que, no importó que, fue una lástima que)
6. Les hacía falta la misa.
   (no creía que, era probable que, sentía que)

7. Lo dijo admirablemente.
   (esperaban que, se alegraban que, era bueno que)
8. Ella no pudo contestar su carta.
   (sintió que, fue ridículo que, fue probable que)
9. Fuimos a ver al médico.
   (nos sugirió que, nos dijo que, insistió en que)
10. Le dolía todo el cuerpo.
   (me preocupaba que, parecía fantástico que, no creía que)

› PATTERNED RESPONSE DRILL

A. 1. TEACHER: ¿Qué fue difícil?
   STUDENT: **Fue difícil que dejara el puesto.**
2. ¿Qué era necesario?
3. ¿Qué era probable?
4. ¿Qué fue ridículo?
5. ¿Qué parecía fantástico?

B. 1. ¿Qué sentía ella?
   Sentía que no la invitáramos.
2. ¿Qué prefería ella?
3. ¿Qué esperaba ella?
4. ¿En qué insistió ella?
5. ¿Qué sugirió ella?

C. 1. ¿Qué quería usted?
   Yo quería que usted me acompañara.
2. ¿Qué sugería usted?
3. ¿Qué prefería usted?
4. ¿Qué deseaba usted?
5. ¿En qué insistía usted?

D. 1. ¿Qué deseaba usted?
   Deseaba que él pagara.
2. ¿En qué insistía usted?
3. ¿Qué esperaba usted?
4. ¿Qué quería usted?

E. 1. ¿Qué esperaba él?
   Esperaba que entráramos.
2. ¿En qué insistía él?
3. ¿Qué deseaba él?
4. ¿Qué quería él?

F. 1. ¿Qué les pidió usted? ¿Venir?
   Sí, les pedí que vinieran.
2. ¿Qué les rogó usted? ¿Salir?
3. ¿Qué les sugirió usted? ¿Renunciar?
4. ¿Qué les exigió usted? ¿Escribir?

G. 1. ¿Qué nos pidió él? ¿Llamar?
   Sí, nos pidió que llamáramos.
2. ¿Qué nos exigió él? ¿Volver?
3. ¿Qué nos rogó él? ¿Comer?
4. ¿Qué nos sugirió él? ¿Esperar?

EXAMPLES

	CONJUNCTION THAT TAKES SUBJUNCTIVE		IMPERFECT SUBJUNCTIVE	
A. 1.	Antes que		salieran	les volví a recordar.
2. Si	antes que	yo	viniera	existía esa costumbre.
3. Ya me di cuenta	sin que	me lo	dijeras.	
4. No le importaba	con tal que		hiciéramos	bien el trabajo.

	CONJUNCTION THAT TAKES INDICATIVE OR SUBJUNCTIVE		INDICATIVE	IMPERFECT SUBJUNCTIVE
B. 1. Lo iba a hacer	según	me	decía.[2]	
2. Lo iba a hacer	según	me		dijera.[3]

In adverb clauses the imperfect subjunctive is used under the same conditions as the present subjunctive, except that the point of view is in the past.

[2] *I was going to do it the way he told me* (he was telling me then).

[3] *I was going to do it the way he told me* (it might turn out that he would tell me).

PERSON-NUMBER SUBSTITUTION DRILL

1. Tuve que escribir la carta antes que saliera *ella.*
   (ellas, él, ustedes, tú, ellos, la secretaria)
2. Volvimos temprano para que *ellos* pudieran estudiar.
   (ella, ustedes, tú, usted, ellas, yo)
3. Ya me di cuenta sin que *tú* me lo dijeras.
   (usted, ustedes, ella, ellos, él, ellas)
4. Don Domingo iba a la Comisión de Cambios con tal que *yo* fuera también.
   (ustedes, nosotros, tú, ella, ellos, el director)
5. No era posible a menos que *ellos* le dieran permiso.
   (él, ustedes, usted, tú, nosotros, el gerente)
6. Iban a decidir cuando llegara *Pablo.*
   (ellos, él, tú, yo, ustedes, nosotros)
7. Iban a esperar hasta que *yo* me sintiera mejor.
   (nosotros, ustedes, usted, tú, las chicas, Julio)
8. Tan pronto como *tú* volvieras, íbamos a salir.
   (él, ellos, ella, ustedes, usted, ellas)
9. Lo iba a hacer según me dijeran *ellos.*
   (usted, ellas, él, tú, ustedes, ella)
10. Era verdad aunque *tú* no lo creyeras.
    (ustedes, nosotros, usted, ellos, yo, ellas)
11. Roberto iba a salir en cuanto le dijeran *ellos.*
    (él, tú, ustedes, yo, nosotros, usted)

TENSE SUBSTITUTION DRILL

1. Salgo antes que llame ese antipático.
   Salía ______________________
2. Entro sin que ellos se den cuenta.
   Entré ______________________
3. Te sigo con tal que no me lleves a una clase aburrida.
   ___ seguía ______________________
4. Voy temprano para que pongamos unos discos.
   Fui ______________________
5. Ella no viene a menos que él también venga.
   ______ venía ______________________
6. Voy a escribir esa carta antes que salga el correo.
   Iba a escribir ______________________
7. Los dejo ir con tal que vuelvan temprano.
   ___ dejé ______________________
8. No lo vamos a ver, para que no nos pregunte otra vez.
   _____ íbamos ______________________
9. No voy a menos que se me quite esta fiebre.
   ___ iba ______________________
10. Me doy cuenta sin que tú me lo digas.
    Me dí cuenta ______________________

PATTERNED RESPONSE DRILL

A. 1. ¿Cuándo iba a llamar José?
   Tan pronto como pudiera.
   2. ¿Cuándo iban a llamar ustedes?
   3. ¿Cuándo iban a llamar ellos?

B. 1. ¿Iba a ir usted al teatro?
   Sí, con tal que no tuviera que pagar.
   2. ¿Iban a ir ustedes al teatro?
   3. ¿Iban a ir ellas al teatro?

C. 1. ¿Para qué vino Pepe a ver a Rosa?
   Para que Rosa lo consultara.
   2. ¿Para qué vino Pepe a ver a las chicas?
   3. ¿Para qué vino Pepe a verte a ti?
   4. ¿Para qué vino Pepe a verlos a ustedes?

D. 1. ¿Iba Fernando a escribirle a Ana?
   No, a menos que Ana se lo pidiera.
   2. ¿Iba Fernando a escribirles a las cuñadas?
   3. ¿Iba Fernando a escribirles a ustedes?

E. 1. ¿Mandaste tú el horario?
Sí, sin que tuviera que cambiarlo.
2. ¿Mandó Roberto el horario?
3. ¿Mandaron ustedes el horario?

F. 1. ¿Alicia llamó a Felipe?
Sí, pero él salió antes que ella llamara.
2. ¿Los abogados llamaron a Felipe?
3. ¿Ustedes llamaron a Felipe?

G. 1. ¿Tiene usted que levantarse temprano?
Sí, aunque yo no quisiera.
2. ¿Tienen ellos que levantarse temprano?
3. ¿Tienen las criadas que levantarse temprano?

EXAMPLES 1. Ibamos a buscar un lugar que **fuera** más tranquilo. *We were going to look for a place that was quieter.*
2. Le dije que estudiara lo que más le **gustara.** *I told him to study what he liked best.*
3. No había nadie que **fuera** tan ocupado como él. *There was no one who was such a busy man as he (was).*

	THE THING DESCRIBED IS UNDETERMINED	THE VERB IS SUBJUNCTIVE	
Ibamos a buscar un	**lugar que**	**fuera**	**más tranquilo.**

In adjective clauses the imperfect subjunctive is used under the same conditions as the present subjunctive, except that the point of view is in the past.

› PERSON-NUMBER SUBSTITUTION DRILL

1. No había nada ahí que *él* pudiera entender.
(yo, nosotros, ellas, usted, tú, ellas)
2. El deseaba un negocio que *todos* aceptaran.
(usted, nosotros, ellos, tú, yo, ustedes)
3. No había un jefe que *ella* respetara.
(ustedes, usted, tú, él, nosotros, yo)
4. No se iban a oponer a lo que *tú* escogieras.
(yo, ustedes, usted, ellos, nosotros, él)
5. No se podía terminar, a pesar de lo que *él* dijera.
(ellos, usted, tú, ella, ustedes, nosotros)

› TENSE SUBSTITUTION DRILL

1. Deseo una novia que tenga ojos verdes.
Deseaba ______________________________
2. Necesito un tocadiscos que sea portátil.
Necesitaba ___________________________
3. Quiero una reforma que resulte bien.
Quería ______________________________
4. Busco un barrio donde no haya tanto ruido.
Buscaba _________________________________
5. Ahí no hay empleado que no sea inteligente.
______ había ______________________________
6. ¿Dónde hay un bus que vaya a la embajada argentina?
______ había ____
7. No hay nadie que tenga un hambre tan feroz como la mía.
___ había ____

8. Quicro cncontrar un banco que cambie un cheque personal.
   Quería ______________________________
9. Necesito un criado que no sea tan bruto.
   Necesitaba ____________________
10. No hay médico que no tenga gripe.
   ___ había ____________________
11. Busco un lugar donde sirvan limonada.
   Buscaba ____________________

› PATTERNED RESPONSE DRILL

1. Había una señora que barría, ¿verdad?
   No, no había ninguna señora que barriera.
2. Había una chica que era extranjera, ¿verdad?
3. Había una secretaria que traducía bien, ¿verdad?
4. Había una tintorería que mandaba la ropa, ¿verdad?
5. Había una muchacha que salía sin chaperón, ¿verdad?
6. Había una escuela que estaba cerrada, ¿verdad?

› DISCUSSION

The imperfect subjunctive is used in noun, adjective, and adverb clauses under the same conditions as the present (and present perfect) subjunctive, except that the point of view is in the past. Note the following parallels:

I'm sorry you ***feel*** *bad.*	Siento que te **sientas** malo.
I was sorry you ***felt*** *bad.*	Sentía que te **sintieras** malo.
There's nobody who ***knows*** *it.*	No hay nadie que lo **sepa.**
There was nobody who ***knew*** *it.*	No había nadie que lo **supiera.**
I'm not going unless he ***goes*** *along.*	Yo no voy a menos que él me **acompañe.**
I wasn't going unless he ***went*** *along.*	Yo no iba a menos que él me **acompañara.**

The English infinitive and *-ing* form carry no sign of tense, which must therefore be inferred from the main verb (in *He ate while working* we infer *while he worked,* not *while he works*). The Spanish equivalent shows the tense:

He tells me ***to work.***	Me dice que **trabaje.**
He told me ***to work.***	Me dijo que **trabajara.**
I catch on without ***your telling*** *me.*	Me doy cuenta sin que me lo **digas.**
I caught on without ***your telling*** *me.*	Me di cuenta sin que me lo **dijeras.**

There is another imperfect subjunctive, not used by all speakers but quite common in written Spanish, that is the same in form as the one described here except that **-se-** replaces **-ra-**. Examples: **dijeses** in place of **dijeras, hablásemos** in place of **habláramos.**

111 Present and present perfect subjunctive after a verb in the present

EXAMPLES

1. Espero que **sigas** mis consejos. *I hope you are following (will follow) my advice.*
2. Vamos a buscar un lugar quc **sca** más tranquilo. *Let's find a place that is (will be) quieter.*

PRESENT	PRESENT OR FUTURE
I hope	you're following. you'll follow.

PRESENT		PRESENT
Espero	**que**	**sigas.**

In Spanish the present subjunctive covers both present and future meanings.

› **TRANSLATION DRILL**

1. TEACHER: I hope you are following my advice.
   STUDENT: **Espero que sigas mis consejos.**
   TEACHER: I hope you'll follow my advice.
   STUDENT: **Espero que sigas mis consejos.**
2. I prefer that she wash the clothes today.
   I prefer that she wash the clothes tomorrow.
3. I hope they are at the park.
   I hope they'll be at the park.
4. We're eating early so the girls can go to the movies.
   We're eating early so the girls will be able to go to the movies.
5. Is there someone here that buys old clothes?
   Is there someone here that will buy old clothes?

EXAMPLES A. 1. Siento que no te **hayas sentido** bien anoche. *I'm sorry you didn't feel well last night.*
2. Es posible que **haya estado** allí. *It's possible he was there.*
3. Buscan a alguien que **haya estado** en Bogotá en 1902. *They're looking for someone who was in Bogota in 1902.*

B. 1. Siento que no te **hayas sentido** bien hoy. *I'm sorry you haven't felt well today.*
2. Buscan a alguien que **haya estado** en Bogotá este año. *They're looking for someone who has been in Bogota this year.*

PRESENT	PAST, OR PRESENT PERFECT
I'm sorry	you felt. you've felt.

PRESENT		PRESENT PERFECT
Siento	**que te**	**hayas sentido.**

When the main verb is in the present tense the meanings of both the present perfect and the past in English are normally carried by the Spanish present perfect in noun and adjective clauses that require the subjunctive.

› **TRANSLATION DRILL**

1. TEACHER: I'm sorry you didn't feel well last night.
   STUDENT: **Siento que no te hayas sentido bien anoche.**
   TEACHER: I'm sorry you haven't felt well today.
   STUDENT: **Siento que no te hayas sentido bien hoy.**
2. I hope you studied a lot last night.
   I hope you've studied a lot today.
3. I'm glad you wrote yesterday.
   I'm glad you have written today.
4. It's possible he was here day before yesterday.
   It's possible he's been here today.

5. It's probable that the country progressed a lot last year.
It's probable that the country has progressed a lot this year.

6. I'm looking for some man who was here last night.
I'm looking for some man who has been here three hours.

7. I prefer someone who was here before.
I prefer someone who has been here all day.

› DISCUSSION

When a main verb in the present is followed by a noun clause or an adjective clause with its verb in the subjunctive, normally the latter verb occurs in one of two tenses: present for meanings corresponding to the English present and future (**Espero que estén allí** *I hope they're there* or *I hope they'll be there*), and present perfect for meanings corresponding to the English present perfect and past (**Es posible que haya estado allí** *It's possible he has been there* or *It's possible he was there*). Context usually clears up any confusion.

112 Equivalents of *as if* and *I wish*

EXAMPLES

1. **¡Como si** nosotras **tuviéramos** la culpa!
2. Anda **como si estuviera** enfermo. *He walks as if he were sick.*
3. **¡Como si hubiera** árboles aquí! *As if there were (would [might] be) trees here!*

	VERB IN THE PAST OR WITH *would* OR *might*
as if	we were (had) he were there would (might) be

	IMPERFECT SUBJUNCTIVE
como si	**tuviéramos** **estuviera** **hubiera**

EXAMPLES

1. **Ojalá** (que) **supieran** lo que yo sé. *I wish they knew what I know.*
2. **Ojalá pudiéramos** reducirlas a una.
3. **Ojalá** que usted les **hablara** directamente.

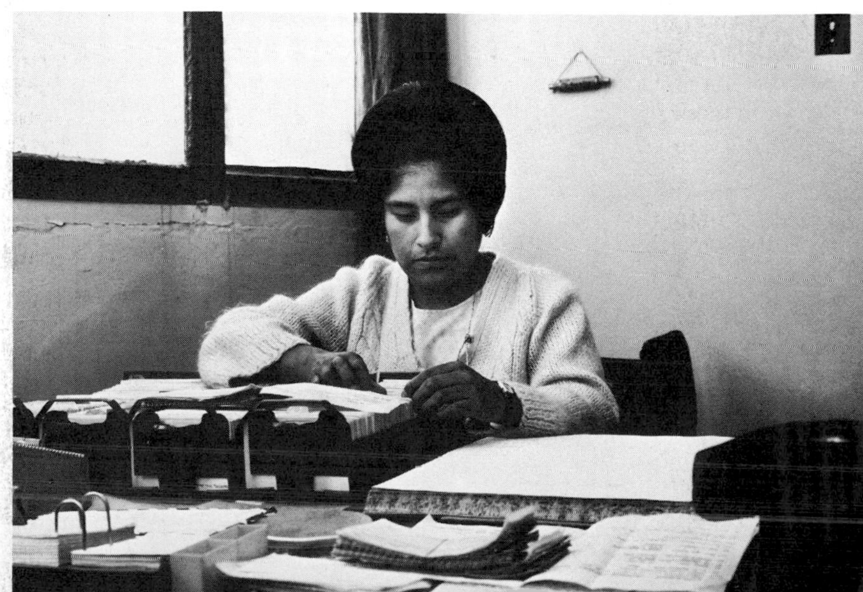

La Paz, Bolivia: Office clerk

	VERB IN THE PAST OR WITH *would* OR *might*
I wish	they knew. we could. you would speak.

	IMPERFECT SUBJUNCTIVE
Ojalá (que)	**supieran.** **pudiéramos.** **hablara.**

› CONSTRUCTION SUBSTITUTION DRILL

INSTRUCTIONS: Repeat the following sentences just as you hear them. Then repeat them again, preceding them with the expressions **como si** or **ojalá** (**que**), which will change the verb from indicative to imperfect subjunctive.

1. Nosotras teníamos la culpa.
   Como si ______
2. Había mucho ruido aquí.
   Como si ______
3. Le dolía todo el cuerpo.
   Como si ______
4. Apenas llegaba a la entrada.
   Como si ______
5. Por eso tenía que peinarse.
   Como si ______
6. Eso era lo de menos.
   Como si ______
7. Ellos sabían lo del radio descompuesto.
   Ojalá que ______
8. Me echaban de menos.
   Ojalá que ______
9. Ellos no salían furiosos de la reunión.
   Ojalá que ______
10. No pasaba nada malo.
    Ojalá que ______
11. Pedrito no tenía la cara sucia.
    Ojalá que ______
12. No estaba equivocado.
    Ojalá que ______

› DISCUSSION

In both English and Spanish a past tense is frequently used not to indicate past time but to indicate something unreal or unlikely now or in the future: *Let's suppose he* **died** (*should die*) *tomorrow* **Vamos a suponer que *se muriera* mañana.** In Spanish the past tense used for this purpose is always the past *subjunctive,* which combines the meanings of nonfactuality and remoteness from the present, thus lending itself to notions of unreality.

When in English we use the expression *as if* (*as though, like*) we are normally "pretending" something: *He walks as if he* ***were*** *sick* (but he isn't, really). Similarly when we *wish,* we wish for something we do not actually have: *I wish I knew*—but I don't know (note the past *knew* rather than the present *know*). *As if* and the verb *wish* are typical instances that call for the past in English and past subjunctive in Spanish.

(Spanish lacks an exact equivalent for *as if* with the present tense, an expression often encountered in English when unreality is not emphasized: *He walks as if he* ***is*** *sick*—perhaps he really is. **Como si** always implies unreality.)

113 Diminutive suffix *-ito*

EXAMPLES
1. Un **momentito, Pedrito.**
2. Una **casita** verde.
3. Es un hombre muy **chiquito.** *He's a very small man.*

BASE FORM	SUFFIXED FORM
Paco	**Paquito**
Pedro	**Pedrito**
momento	**momentito**
minuto	**minutito**
poco	**poquito**
chico	**chiquito**
Juana	**Juanita**
(Guada) lupe	**Lupita**
casa	**casita**

To indicate smallness or cuteness or to use a nickname of endearment the suffix **-ito, -ita** is attached to many words, especially nouns and adjectives. The gender normally remains the same.

› DIMINUTIVE SUBSTITUTION DRILL

INSTRUCTIONS: Repeat the following sentences just as you hear them. Then repeat them again, using the diminutive forms of the items indicated.

A. 1. TEACHER: Es una *casa* verde. *Repita.*
STUDENT: **Es una casa verde.**
TEACHER: *Cambie.*
STUDENT: **Es una casita verde.**
2. Es un *libro* verde.
3. Es una *cama* verde.

B. 1. ¿Tiene un *minuto?*
2. ¿Tiene un *lápiz?*[4]
3. ¿Tiene una *taza?*[5]
4. ¿Tiene un *disco?*

C. 1. Aquí hay dos *libros.*
2. Aquí hay un *bulto.*
3. Aquí hay una *planta.*
4. Aquí hay un *toro.*

D. 1. ¿Hay una *carta* para mí?
2. ¿Hay una *cosa* para mí?
3. ¿Hay un *cuarto* para mí?
4. ¿Hay una *casa* para mí?
5. ¿Hay un *regalo* para mí?

E. 1. Hola, *abuela.*
2. Hola, *amigo.*
3. Hola, *Pedro.*
4. Qué hubo, *Paco.*

F. 1. ¿Dónde está la *señora?*
2. ¿Dónde está mi *hijo?*
3. ¿Dónde está mi *sobrina?*
4. ¿Dónde están los *chicos?*
5. ¿Dónde está *Juana?*

G. 1. Es un vestido *corto.*
2. Es un vestido *azul.*
3. Es un vestido *español.*
4. Es un vestido *igual.*
5. Es un vestido *negro.*

H. 1. Vuelvo después de un *rato.*
2. *Ahora* viene.
3. Hasta *luego.*

› DISCUSSION

Like the English suffix of smallness and endearment in *baby, cutie, laddie, sonny, girlie,* Spanish has a suffix **-ito, -ita** with similar meanings. Some words carrying this suffix have a long history in the language, such as **bonito** *pretty* (compare English *bonny*) and **señorita** *miss* (based on **señora**), but **-ito** is rather freely used in making new derivatives.

[4] The diminutive is spelled **lapicito.** See p. 190.

[5] The diminutive is spelled **tacita.**

Alternate forms of this same suffix are **-cito** and **-ecito;** e.g., **cafecito** (**café**), **mujercita** (**mujer**), and **nuevecito** (**nuevo**).

While **-ito** probably is the most widely used of all the diminutive suffixes, certain regions have their own preferences, e.g., **-ico** in Costa Rica.

Next in frequency to **-ito** is the diminutive suffix **-illo,** encountered in the dialogs in the words **mantequilla** *butter* (from **manteca** *lard*), **maquinilla** *little machine* (**máquina** *machine*), and **pastilla** *pill, tablet* (**pasta** *paste*). The suffix **-illo** is less freely used in making new word formations.

114 Singular and plural verb forms with collective nouns

EXAMPLES

A. 1. **Va** a ir mucha **gente** importante.
2. ¿Por qué **anda** toda la **gente** corriendo? (*Why are all the people running?*)
3. Nuestro **pueblo** jamás lo **va** a aceptar.
4. La **policía** los **atacó** infamemente.

B. 1. **Parte** de los **heridos murieron.** *Some* (*Part*) *of the wounded died.*
2. La **mayoría** de los **empleados** se **oponen.**

C. 1. Buena **parte** del **pueblo** no **quiere** elecciones libres. *A good part of the people don't want free elections.*
2. La **mayoría** se **opone.** *The majority is* (*are*) *opposed.*

A.

gente pueblo policía	*singular verb*

The nouns **gente, pueblo,** and **policía**[6] regularly take a singular verb.

B.

FRACTION		PLURAL WHOLE		PLURAL VERB
Parte La mayoría	de los de los	heridos empleados	 se	murieron. oponen.

C.

FRACTION		SINGULAR WHOLE OR NONE		SINGULAR VERB
Buena parte La mayoría	del	pueblo	no se	quiere. opone.

When the collective noun represents a fraction of a plural whole and the plural whole is expressed, the verb is regularly plural; otherwise it is singular.

[6]Meaning *police* (see Unit 7, Cultural Note 1). We have also encountered **el policía** in the sense *the policeman;* the plural of **el policía** would be **los policías** *the policemen* and would, of course, take a plural verb.

TRANSLATION DRILL

A. 1. TEACHER: The people are wrong.
STUDENT: **La gente está equivocada.**
2. Our people are organized.
Nuestro pueblo está organizado.
3. The police are here.
La policía está aquí.

B. 1. The people of this school are very nice.
La gente de esta escuela es muy simpática.
2. The people of this country are very idealistic.
3. The police of the United States are very strict.

C. 1. Nowadays people are quite sincere.
2. Nowadays the police are quite respectable.

D. 1. People are complicated.
2. Our people are strict.
3. The police are punctual.

E. 1. Part of the wounded died.
2. Part of those invited came.
3. Part of the students left.
4. Part of the employees stayed.

F. 1. The majority of the employees are opposed.
2. The majority of the secretaries want to leave early.
3. The majority of the young girls want to go out without a chaperon.

G. 1. A good part of the people want Vargas Campo.
2. The majority of the people want a new leader.
3. The majority want a change of government.

H. 1. A good part of the police have already forgotten the kidnaping.
2. The majority of the police have already studied the situation.
3. The majority have already had the exam.

DISCUSSION

Formal agreement between subject and verb is more closely followed in Spanish than in English. Collective nouns like *people* and *police* regularly take plural verbs in English (*The people* ***are*** *ready; The police* ***are*** *after him*), and many others have the option of doing so (*My family* ***are, is*** *all with me now*), but this is done less frequently in Spanish. One place where it may and usually does occur is with a collective noun that signifies a fraction of the whole, when the whole is expressed by means of a plural noun. Compare English *Part of the people* ***are*** *wounded.*

GUIDED CONVERSATION

E. *Esperanza* D. *Señor Delgado*

E. Señor Delgado, ¿usted quiere vernos antes que salgamos?
D. Sí, Señoritas. Mr. Wright me pidió que ______________
E. ¿Pero qué son diez minutos más, diez minutos menos?
D. Yo sé que a Mr. Roberts no le importaba ______________
E. Claro. Siempre hemos tenido la costumbre de llegar un poquito tarde.
D. Pues si antes que Mr. Wright ______________
E. ¿Qué antipático es ese señor, estar enojado porque llegamos unos pocos minutos tarde!
D. No crean, él es ______________
E. Sí, ya nos dimos cuenta de eso antes que nos lo dijera usted.
D. Bueno, recuerden ustedes que él es gerente, y como gerente, lo primero ______________

❯ TRANSLATION REVIEW DRILL

Variants of the present progressive.

A. 1. TEACHER: The people are running.
STUDENT: **La gente está corriendo.**
2. The people are out running.
La gente anda corriendo.
3. The people are running along (busy running).
La gente va corriendo.
4. The people are still running.
La gente sigue corriendo.
5. The people come running.
La gente viene corriendo.

B. 1. The students are studying.
2. The students are out studying.
3. The students are studying away.
4. The students are still studying.
5. The students come studying.

C. 1. The manager is organizing the elections.
2. The manager is out organizing the elections.
3. The manager is setting about organizing the elections.
4. The manager is still organizing the elections.
5. The manager comes (around) organizing the elections.

D. 1. The poor [man] is begging (asking).
2. The poor [man] is out begging.
3. The poor [man] is busy begging (begging away).
4. The poor [man] is still begging.
5. The poor [man] comes begging.

Montevideo, Uruguay: Bank

reading

La puntualidad

E. *Esperanza* R. *Rosa*

E. ¡Rosa, figúrate! ¿Sabes lo que ha hecho el nuevo gerente?
R. ¿Mr. Wright?
E. Sí, ése.
R. No, ¿qué ha hecho?
E. Pues, te acuerdas de que el señor Delgado nos habló anteayer sobre el asunto de la puntualidad.
R. Sí, lo recuerdo.
E. Bueno, ésa no fue idea del señor Delgado.
R. Ya lo sé.
E. No, fue idea de Mr. Wright... Ahora, insiste en que todos lleguemos al trabajo a las ocho y media *en punto.*

en punto *sharp, on the dot*

R. No entiendo. Es lo que hacemos ahora.
E. No, no. No comprendes. Mr. Wright dice que algunas veces no llegamos antes de las nueve menos cuarto.
R. Ah, eso es verdad, pero... ¡Qué diablo! Una no es máquina, como un reloj. Por ejemplo, si te digo que voy a encontrarte a las cinco para el té, no es como si te dijera que estuvieras allí precisamente a las cinco. Pudieras llegar a las cinco y cinco, o a las cinco y diez, o aun a las cinco y cuarto, sin que yo me preocupara de ello.

reloj *clock, watch*

sin...ello *without my worrying about it*

E. Sí, sí, sí: todo lo que dices es verdad, y es eso lo que disgusta a Mr. Wright. (*Imitando con voz muy grave*) "Y cuando digo las ocho y media, digo las ocho y media en punto, y no las nueve menos veintinueve." ...¡Figúrate eso!
R. ...¡Ay, la pobre mujer!
E. ¿Cómo? ¿Quién?
R. Pues Mrs. Wright... si existe.
E. ¡Ojalá que no! ¡Quién querría casarse con un autómata!
R. Estoy perfectamente de acuerdo... ¡Ojalá que Mr. Roberts volviera...!

querría *would like*

UNIT 21

The Lottery

G. *Guillermo* A. *Alberto, a friend* W. *Woman*

G. Did you hear the news about Raúl? I'd like to be in his shoes.
A. Yes, indeed; he won the grand prize in the lottery. A hundred thousand pesos.
G. What a lucky guy! And all because of a lucky break.
A. I wonder how it happened?
G. They say he was standing in the doorway of a restaurant one day when an old woman came by selling tickets.
A. I bet he bought them all.
G. No, how could he? He didn't even have a dime in his pocket.
A. How was it, then?
G. Well, the old woman pestered him so much that, when a friend happened to come by, he borrowed twenty pesos from him and bought a whole ticket.
A. And now he won't even look at anybody. I can just imagine how he must feel.
G. I'd like to see how you'd be! The same thing would happen to anybody.
A. Not to me, never.
G. And why not?
A. Because I'll never play the lottery.
G. Never say "never" ["of this water I won't drink"].
A. Only if they gave me a ticket!

La lotería

G. *Guillermo* A. *Alberto, un amigo* M. *Mujer*

G. ¿Supo lo de Raúl? Me gustaría estar en su lugar.
A. Sí, hombre; se sacó el gordo de la lotería (2). Cien mil pesos.
G. ¡Qué suerte tiene ese tipo! Y todo por una casualidad.
A. ¿Y cómo sería?
G. Dicen que un día estaba parado en la puerta de un café cuando pasó una vieja vendiendo billetes.
A. Apuesto a que se los compró todos.
G. No, qué va. No tenía ni un diez en el bolsillo.
A. ¿Y cómo, entonces?
G. Que la vieja le insistió tanto que cuando pasaba un amigo, le pidió veinte pesos y compró un entero (3).
A. Y ahora ni mirará a nadie. Me imagino cómo estará.
G. ¡Quisiera verlo a usted! A cualquiera le pasaría lo mismo.
A. ¿A mí? Nunca.
G. ¿Y por qué no?
A. Porque yo jamás jugaré a la lotería.
G. Nunca diga "De esta agua no beberé."
A. ¡Sólo que me regalaran el billete!

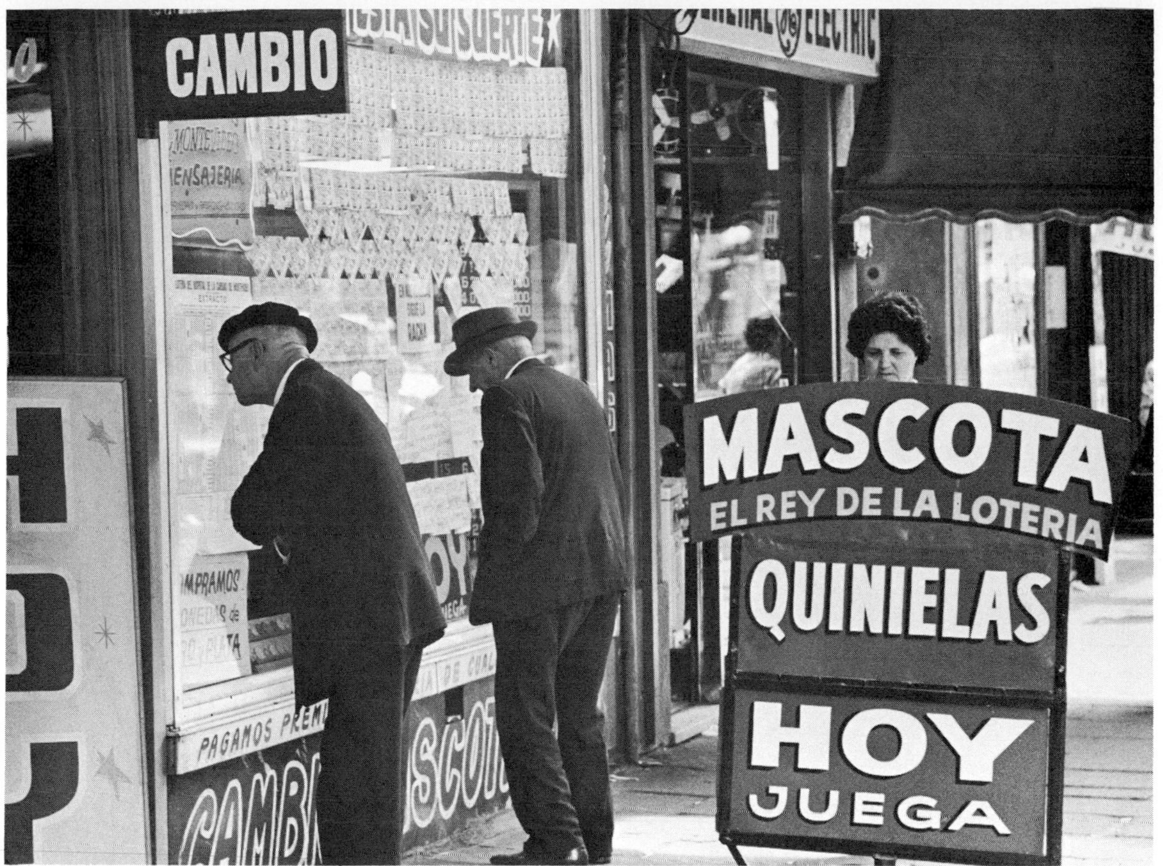

Montevideo, Uruguay: Lottery agency

G. And if it turned out to be the lucky one [rewarded], what would you do with the money?	G. Y si saliera premiado, ¿qué haría con la plata?
A. Perhaps we'd take a trip to Europe . . . The children would have everything, but . . .	A. Quizá haríamos un viaje a Europa... Los niños tendrían de todo, pero...
W. Lottery! Lottery tickets for sale!	M. ¡Lotería! ¡Se juega la lotería!
A. Look, Memo, uh . . . could you lend me twenty pesos?	A. Mire, Memo (4), este (5)... ¿podría prestarme veinte pesos?

cultural notes

(1) The lottery is a fund-raising institution organized by the state as a supplement to taxation. It supports public and charitable works such as medical centers and the Red Cross.

(2) **El gordo** or **el premio gordo** means *the fat prize,* i.e., the first or grand prize.

(3) The **entero** *whole ticket* is also referred to as **billete entero** or **número entero.** It is a long sheet often containing ten **décimos** *tenths,* all having the same serial number. Since a **décimo** is the usual *share* or *ticket* purchased, Raúl, in buying an **entero,** was playing for much higher stakes and was thus able to win ten times as much as if he had held only a **décimo.**

(4) **Memo** is a common nickname for **Guillermo.** See Unit 3, Cultural Note 5, on the nickname **Pepe.**

(5) **Este** is the most common hesitation word in spoken Spanish.

115 Future

EXAMPLES

A. 1. Yo jamás **jugaré** a la lotería.
2. De esta agua no **beberé.**

B. ¿Qué **dirás?** *What will you say?*

C. 1. Ahora no **mirará** a nadie.
2. **Habrá** más tiempo mañana. *There'll be more time tomorrow.*

D. No **podremos** dormir. *We won't be able to sleep.*

E. **¿Comprenderán?** *Will they understand?*

VERBS REGULAR IN THE FUTURE	
INFINITIVE STEM	ENDINGS
hablar– **comer–** **vivir–** **ser–** **traer–** **etc.**	**–é** **–ás** **–á** **–emos** **–án**

The straight infinitive serves as the stem of the future of almost all verbs.

VERBS IRREGULAR IN THE FUTURE		
INFINITIVE	MODIFIED INFINITIVE STEM	ENDINGS
haber	**habr–**	
poder	**podr–**	
querer	**querr–**	
saber	**sabr–**	**–é**
poner[1]	**pondr–**	**–ás**
tener	**tendr–**	**–á**
venir	**vendr–**	
salir	**saldr–**	**–emos**
valer	**valdr–**	**–án**
decir	**dir–**	
hacer	**har–**	

In these verbs a modified form of the infinitive serves as the stem of the future.

› PERSON-NUMBER SUBSTITUTION DRILL

1. *Yo* jamás jugaré a la lotería.
   (nosotros, él, ellos, tú, ella, ustedes)
2. *La señorita* volverá dentro de un rato.
   (ellos, nosotros, él, yo, tú, ustedes)
3. Comeremos esta noche en casa.
   (yo, él, tú, ellos, ella y yo, usted)
4. Un momentito, ya verás.
   (nosotros, ustedes, usted, ellos, él, yo)
5. *El gerente* reducirá las horas.
   (ellos, yo, nosotros, usted, tú, el jefe)
6. ¿Seguirán *ustedes* estudiando español?
   (ellos, usted, ellas, ella, tú, él)
7. Servirá una comida fantástica.
   (ellas, nosotros, tú, ustedes, usted, yo)
8. Podrán organizar unos juegos.
   (nosotros, usted, tú, ellos, usted y yo, yo)

[1] Also **oponer** and other derivatives of verbs in this list.

9. Sí, pero ¿todavía querrá esto mañana?
(nosotros, ellos, usted, yo, tú, ustedes)
10. No sabremos la verdad hasta el domingo.
(yo, tú, ellos, él, ustedes, usted)
11. Pondré las flores en la sala.
(nosotros, ellos, usted, ustedes, tú, ella)
12. Tendrá veintidós años la semana próxima.
(yo, tú, ella, ustedes, nosotros, él)
13. Vendremos mañana.
(yo, ella, ustedes, tú, usted, ellos)
14. Saldrán para los Juegos Olímpicos el domingo.
(ella, nosotros, yo, ellos, usted, tú)
15. No diremos nada.
(yo, él, ellos, ella, tú, usted)
16. Harás más dinero en ese puesto.
(usted, ustedes, él, yo, ellos, nosotros)

› CONSTRUCTION SUBSTITUTION DRILL

INSTRUCTIONS: Repeat the following sentences just as you hear them. Then repeat them again, substituting an equivalent future tense form for the **ir a** construction.

A. 1. Lo del secuestro *va a pasar* muy pronto.
Lo del secuestro pasará muy pronto.
2. Ese tipo se *va a sacar* el gordo de la lotería.
3. *Vamos a vivir* en el norte.
4. *Vas a ver* un cielo muy azul.
5. *Van a prometer* demasiado.
6. La *va a encontrar* en el café.
7. *Voy a ver* a mi padrino.
8. Sí, pero le *va a gustar* mucho.

B. 1. *Va a haber* corridas.
2. No *vamos a poder* oponernos.
3. Ellas no *van a querer* ir.
4. El *va a saber* regatear.
5. ¿Y tú te *vas a poner* el vestido azul?
6. *Voy a tener* mucha suerte en este país.
7. *Vamos a venir* en un día feriado.
8. A ver; *voy a salir* a las ocho de la mañana.
9. Nunca *voy a decir* otra mentira.
10. *Va a hacer* un traje.

› TENSE SUBSTITUTION DRILL

INSTRUCTIONS: Repeat the following sentences just as you hear them. Then repeat them again, substituting a future tense form for the present or imperfect.

A. 1. TEACHER: Mañana compro un entero. *Repita.*
STUDENT: **Mañana compro un entero.**
TEACHER: *Cambie.*
STUDENT: **Mañana compraré un entero.**
2. Mañana vemos una película extranjera.
3. Mañana podemos encontrar agua potable.
4. Mañana hay una reunión del Consejo Estudiantil.
5. Mañana te regalo unos zapatos.
6. Mañana consigo el empleo.

B. 1. Después ella te miraba con horror.
2. ¿Tomaba usted el autobús?
3. Nos encontrábamos en el Club de la Unión.
4. Nos veíamos muy a menudo.
5. Ellos seguían estudiando castellano.
6. Ella nunca comprendía.
7. Yo no podía llevarla.
8. Había mucha gente.

› CHOICE-QUESTION RESPONSE DRILL

A. 1. ¿Se levantará temprano mañana o se quedará en la cama?
2. ¿Le mandará una carta o la llamará por teléfono?
3. ¿Le exigirá una multa o lo dejará escapar?
4. ¿Trabajará todo el día o jugará por la tarde?
5. ¿Doblará en esa esquina o seguirá adelante?

B. 1. ¿Saldrá mañana o podrá esperarme?
2. ¿Vendrá conmigo o querrá quedarse a estudiar?
3. ¿Dirá la verdad o pondrá un pretexto?
4. ¿Sabrá arreglarlo o no tendrá tiempo?

DISCUSSION

The future tense is used somewhat less frequently in Spanish than in English. In both languages the future must compete with the **ir a** *going to* construction (see Unit 8, Section 37); but the Spanish future must also compete, more than the English future, with the present tense used with future meanings. (See Unit 4, Section 18.)

The future is the prediction of a coming event, detached from the present. In **¿Cuándo llegan?** *When do (will) they arrive?* the speaker uses a present tense to imply a future tense, suggesting that the time, whatever it is, has already been decided on: "When are they supposed to arrive?" In **¿Cuándo van a llegar?** *When are they going to arrive?* the speaker implies a future event growing out of present conditions or intentions: "When is it their intention to be here?" In **¿Cuándo llegarán?** *When will they arrive?* the speaker asks to have something foreseen, without tying it to the present.

The Spanish future is proper wherever English uses its regular future with *will* (review Unit 4, Section 18).

Mexico City: Headquarters of the national lottery

116 Conditional

EXAMPLES
1. A cualquiera le **pasaría** lo mismo.
2. Quizá **haríamos** un viaje a Europa.
3. Los niños **tendrían** de todo.

VERBS REGULAR IN THE CONDITIONAL	
INFINITIVE STEM	ENDINGS
hablar– **comer–** **vivir–** **ser–** **traer–** **etc.**	**–ía** **–ías** **–ía** **–íamos** **–ían**

VERBS IRREGULAR IN THE CONDITIONAL		
INFINITIVE	MODIFIED INFINITIVE STEM	ENDINGS
haber **poder** **querer** **saber** **poner**[2] **tener** **venir** **salir** **valer** **decir** **hacer**	**habr–** **podr–** **querr–** **sabr–** **pondr–** **tendr–** **vendr–** **saldr–** **valdr–** **dir–** **har–**	**–ía** **–ías** **–ía** **–íamos** **–ían**

The stem of the conditional is the same as that of the future. The endings are the same as in the imperfect indicative of **–er** and **–ir** verbs.

› PERSON-NUMBER SUBSTITUTION DRILL

1. En esa situación *yo* sería más puntual.
   (ellos, usted, tú, él, nosotros, ustedes)
2. Además, *nosotros* estaríamos contentos.
   (yo, ellas, tú, usted, ustedes, él)
3. *Ellos* no venderían los cueros.
   (él, ustedes, usted, tú, nosotros, yo)
4. Si no, *ella* se levantaría muy tarde.
   (ellas, usted, ustedes, tú, nosotros, yo)
5. Es que *él* no sabría.
   (ustedes, ella, nosotros, ellos, tú, yo)
6. *Ellos* no podrían arreglarlo.
   (usted, ustedes, nosotros, yo, tú, él)

[2] Also **oponer** and other derivatives of verbs in this list.

7. ¿En este caso, vendría *usted?*
   (ustedes, nosotros, yo, tú, él)
8. *Ellos* saldrían para México.
   (usted, ustedes, él, ellas, ella, tú)
9. *Yo* no pondría el radio tan fuerte.
   (usted, tú, nosotros, ella, ustedes, él)
10. Bueno, *yo* no diría eso.
    (nosotros, él, ellos, ella, ellas, él y yo)
11. Quizá haríamos un viaje a Europa.
    (yo, ustedes, él, tú, ellos, usted)

› TENSE SUBSTITUTION DRILL

INSTRUCTIONS: Repeat the following sentences just as you hear them. Then repeat them again, substituting a conditional tense form for the present or imperfect.

A. 1. TEACHER: A cualquiera le pasa lo mismo. *Repita.*
   STUDENT: **A cualquiera le pasa lo mismo.**
   TEACHER: *Cambie.*
   STUDENT: **A cualquiera le pasaría lo mismo.**
2. Compran una casa en el campo.
3. No tomo ese cochino autobús.
4. Lupe se casa con Lorenzo.
5. Ustedes dos nunca se ponen de acuerdo.
6. Hacemos un viaje a Europa.

B. 1. Iba a la reunión del Consejo Estudiantil.
2. Nos veíamos muy a menudo.
3. Había mucha gente en la plaza.
4. Todo lo quería cambiar.
5. Ese barbero me presta el peine.

› CONSTRUCTION SUBSTITUTION DRILL

INSTRUCTIONS: Repeat the following sentences just as you hear them. Then repeat them again, substituting an equivalent conditional tense form for the **ir a** construction.

A. 1. TEACHER: Dijo que *iba a trabajar* mañana. *Repita.*
   STUDENT: **Dijo que iba a trabajar mañana.**
   TEACHER: *Cambie.*
   STUDENT: **Dijo que trabajaría mañana.**
2. Dijo que *iba a comprar* la leche.
3. Dijo que *iba a preguntar* su edad.
4. Dijo que me *iba a cortar* el pelo atrás y a los lados.
5. Dijo que el ganado *iba a dejar* bastante ganancia.
6. Dijo que los estudiantes *iban a ir* al parque.
7. Dijo que las muchachas *iban a llevar* chaperón.
8. Dijo anteayer que les *iba a hablar.*

B. 1. Dijo que *iba a salir* a las siete y media.
2. Dijo que *iba a poner* las flores en la sala.
3. Dijo que *iba a venir* temprano.
4. Dijo que no *iba a poder* venir.
5. Dijo que su hermano mayor no *iba a tener* tiempo.
6. Dijo que el gerente *iba a decir* algo.
7. Dijo que *iba a hacer* una comida.

› PATTERNED RESPONSE DRILL

A. 1. TEACHER: ¿Qué discutirías?
   STUDENT: **Yo discutiría la política.**
2. ¿Qué estudiarías?
3. ¿Qué atacarías?
4. ¿Qué preferirías?
5. ¿Qué seguirías?
6. ¿Qué mencionarías?

B. 1. ¿Qué traerían ustedes?
Traeríamos el coche.
2. ¿Qué comprarían ustedes?
3. ¿Qué venderían ustedes?
4. ¿Qué llevarían ustedes?
5. ¿Qué buscarían ustedes?
6. ¿Qué desearían ustedes?
7. ¿Qué ofrecerían ustedes?
8. ¿Qué prometerían ustedes?
9. ¿Qué regalarían ustedes?

› DISCUSSION

The conditional is to the past what the future is to the present. Note the following parallels:

I know it will change.	**Sé que se cambiará.**
I knew it would change.	**Sabía que se cambiaría.**
He says it will be enough.	**Dice que será bastante.**
He said it would be enough.	**Dijo que sería bastante.**

The usual English equivalent is *would*.[3]

117 Additional progressives

EXAMPLES 1. ¿Dónde **han estado viviendo?** *Where have they been living?*
2. No **estaremos trabajando.** *We won't be working.*
3. ¿Qué **estaría pensando** ahora? *What would he be thinking now?*
4. Tal vez **estén practicando.** *Perhaps they are practicing.*
5. Dudaba que **estuviera dictando** a esas horas. *I doubted that he was dictating at that time.*
6. Espero que no **hayan estado siguiéndonos.** *I hope they haven't been following us.*

form of **estar**	**-ndo** *form*
Any form of **estar** may be used with the **-ndo** form of another verb to make a progressive. (See Unit 9, Section 44, and Unit 11, Section 55.)	

› CONSTRUCTION SUBSTITUTION DRILL

INSTRUCTIONS: Repeat the following sentences just as you hear them. Then repeat them again, substituting the present perfect progressive for the present progressive.

A. 1. TEACHER: ¿Dónde están viviendo?
Repita.
STUDENT: **¿Dónde están viviendo?**
TEACHER: *Cambie.*
STUDENT: **¿Dónde han estado viviendo?**
2. ¿Dónde está trabajando?
3. ¿Dónde estás comiendo?
4. ¿Dónde están estudiando?
5. ¿Dónde estás jugando?

B. 1. No estoy haciendo nada.
2. No está viviendo aquí cerca.
3. No estamos estudiando álgebra.
4. No están esperando a Roberto.
5. No están trabajando en la planta.

[3] *Would* has several different meanings. See the discussion of Unit 11, Section 54, for *would = used to.* Compare also *He wouldn't (didn't want to, refused to) do it* **No lo quiso hacer,** where *would* is the past of *will* (*be willing*).

INSTRUCTIONS: Repeat the following sentences just as you hear them. Then repeat them again, substituting the future progressive for the future.

C. 1. No trabajaremos esta tarde.
No estaremos trabajando esta tarde.
2. Esperaré aquí esta tarde.
3. Jugarán esta tarde.
4. Compraré un regalo esta tarde.
5. Correrá en la carrera esta tarde.

INSTRUCTIONS: Repeat the following sentences just as you hear them. Then repeat them again, substituting **dijo** for **dice,** which will cause a change in the form of **estar** from future progressive to conditional progressive.

D. 1. Dice que estará estudiando a esa hora.
Dijo que estaría estudiando a esa hora.
2. Dice que estará comiendo a esa hora.
3. Dice que estará barriendo a esa hora.
4. Dice que estará leyendo a esa hora.
5. Dice que estará discutiendo a esa hora.
6. Dice que estará trabajando a esa hora.

INSTRUCTIONS: Repeat the following sentences just as you hear them. Then repeat them again, putting **tal vez** at the beginning and changing the verb to subjunctive.[4]

E. 1. Están practicando, tal vez.
Tal vez estén practicando.
2. Se está organizando un grupo, tal vez.
3. Está haciendo algo con esas herramientas, tal vez.
4. Está trabajando en el ministerio, tal vez.
5. Están lavando el auto, tal vez.
6. Está escribiendo la carta, tal vez.
7. Están viviendo lejos de aquí, tal vez.

INSTRUCTIONS: Repeat the following sentences just as you hear them. Then repeat them again, substituting **dudaba** for **dudo,** which will cause a change in the verb of the clause from present subjunctive progressive to imperfect subjunctive progressive.

F. 1. Dudo que estén dictando.
Dudaba que estuvieran dictando.
2. Dudo que esté jugando.
3. Dudo que estén estudiando.
4. Dudo que se esté muriendo.
5. Dudo que estén escribiendo.
6. Dudo que esté sirviendo.

INSTRUCTIONS: Repeat the following sentences just as you hear them. Then repeat them again, substituting the present perfect subjunctive progressive for the present subjunctive progressive.

G. 1. Espero que no estén siguiéndonos.
Espero que no hayan estado siguiéndonos.
2. Espero que no esté estudiando.
3. Espero que no estén durmiendo.
4. Espero que no esté bebiendo.
5. Espero que no estén pidiendo.
6. Espero que no esté esperando.

› DISCUSSION

Any form of **estar,** including those with **haber** (**han estado, hayamos estado,** etc.), may be used in a progressive construction. Even **estando** is possible: **Estando viendo el juego** *While seeing the game* (literally, *being seeing the game*).

The meaning covers what is actually going on, not what is planned. English *Tomorrow I'll be working here* may be taken in the sense "Tomorrow I plan to be working here." The Spanish for this sense is **Mañana trabajo aquí** (see Unit 4, Section 18). **Estaré trabajando** would be appropriate in the context *What will you be doing when I get there?—I'll be working* (engaged at that moment in the act of working).

[4] Either the subjunctive or the indicative may be used after **tal vez.** The indicative expresses less uncertainty.

118 Additional perfects

EXAMPLES 1. No **habíamos dicho** nada. *We hadn't said anything.*
2. Para entonces se **habrán ido.** *By then they'll have gone.*
3. Sé que **habría sido** mejor. *I know it would have been better.*
4. Dudo que **hubiera sido** mejor. *I doubt that it would have been better.*
5. ¿Dónde **habían estado** viviendo? *Where had they been living?*
6. **¿Ha habido** huelga? *Has there been a strike?*

form of **haber**	**-do** *form*

All the perfect constructions in English have parallels in Spanish, in which a form of **haber** combines with the **-do** form of a verb.

› TENSE SUBSTITUTION DRILL

INSTRUCTIONS: Repeat the following sentences just as you hear them. Then repeat them again, substituting the past perfect for the preterit.

A. 1. TEACHER: No dijimos nada. *Repita.*
STUDENT: **No dijimos nada.**
TEACHER: *Cambie.*
STUDENT: **No habíamos dicho nada.**
2. No hicimos nada
3. No trajimos nada.
4. No tuvimos nada.
5. No supimos nada.
6. No pudimos hacer nada.
7. No quisimos hacer nada.
8. No tuvimos que hacer nada.

INSTRUCTIONS: Repeat the following sentences just as you hear them. Then repeat them again, substituting the future perfect for the future.

B. 1. Mañana se irán.
Mañana se habrán ido.
2. Mañana saldrá.
3. Mañana volverán.
4. Mañana regresará.
5. Mañana llamará.
6. Mañana consultarán.
7. Mañana se discutirá.

INSTRUCTIONS: Repeat the following sentences just as you hear them. Then repeat them again, substituting the conditional perfect for the present.

C. 1. Sé que es mejor.
Sé que habría sido mejor.
2. Sé que vienen mañana.
3. Sé que no puede.
4. Sé que lo hacen otra vez.
5. Sé que sigue derecho.
6. Sé que saben la lengua española.
7. Sé que no les hace falta la siesta.

INSTRUCTIONS: Repeat the following sentences just as you hear them. Then repeat them again, substituting past perfect subjunctive for present perfect subjunctive.

D. 1. Dudo que haya sido mejor.
Dudo que hubiera sido mejor.
2. Dudo que hayan venido el año pasado.
3. Dudo que no haya podido.
4. Dudo que lo hayan hecho.
5. Dudo que haya seguido adelante.
6. Dudo que hayan sabido la lengua inglesa.
7. Dudo que hayan sido muy puntuales.

INSTRUCTIONS: Repeat the following sentences just as you hear them. Then repeat them again, substituting past perfect progressive for imperfect progressive.

E. 1. ¿Dónde estaban viviendo?
¿Dónde habían estado viviendo?
2. ¿Dónde estaba trabajando?
3. ¿Dónde estaban reuniéndose?
4. ¿Dónde estaban peleando?
5. ¿Dónde estaba esperando?
6. ¿Dónde estaban durmiendo?

› DISCUSSION

Any tense, indicative or subjunctive, of the verb **haber** may combine with the **-do** form of a verb (the preterit is rarely so used, however). This includes even combinations with **haber** itself in the sense *there to be* (see Unit 8, Section 39): **ha habido** means *there has (have) been;* **había habido** means *there had been;* **habría habido** means *there would have been,* etc.

The perfect constructions are referred to by the name of the form of **haber** used: if **haber** is in the present tense, we have the present perfect; if in the future, we have the future perfect, etc. To avoid the expression "imperfect perfect" the combination of the imperfect of **haber** with the **-do** form is called the "past perfect."

119 Future of probability; *deber*, must, ought

EXAMPLES 1. Me imagino cómo **estará.**
2. ¿Qué hora **será?** *What time do you suppose it is?*
3. **Habrá** algunas desventajas. *There probably are some disadvantages.*
4. **Estará rabiando** como siempre. *He's probably fuming as usual.*

probablemente	**está** **es** **hay** **está rabiando**	=	**estará** **será** **habrá** **estará rabiando**

The future is often used to express probability in the present. The English equivalents use expressions like *probably, do you suppose, can . . . be* (e.g., *What can he be thinking?*), etc.

EXAMPLES A. 1. **Debe** estar en la cocina.
2. **Debe** tener unos veintiún años.
3. Me imagino que **deben** tener ovejas y cerdos también.

B. 1. ¿Qué **debo** hacer, doctor?
2. Las muchachas no **deben** salir solas.

must should ought	to	*infinitive*

deber	*infinitive*

Deber plus infinitive is the equivalent of English *must, ought,* and *should* plus infinitive (without *to* except for *ought to*) to express either obligation or probability.

› CONSTRUCTION SUBSTITUTION DRILL

INSTRUCTIONS: Repeat the following sentences just as you hear them. Then repeat them again, replacing **probablemente** and the present tense form with the future tense form.

A. 1. TEACHER: *Probablemente está* en la cocina. *Repita.*
STUDENT: **Probablemente está en la cocina.**
TEACHER: *Cambie.*
STUDENT: **Estará en la cocina.**
2. *Probablemente es* la criada.
3. *Probablemente son* las dos y media.
4. *Probablemente hay* algunas desventajas.
5. *Probablemente es* muy simpático.
6. *Probablemente tiene* mucha hambre.
7. *Probablemente hace* algo.
8. *Probablemente están* rabiando.
9. *Probablemente está* enojado.

INSTRUCTIONS: Repeat the following sentences just as you hear them. Then repeat them again, replacing the future tense form with the present tense of **deber** plus the infinitive.

B. 1. TEACHER: Julio *estará* en la cocina. *Repita.*
STUDENT: **Julio estará en la cocina.**
TEACHER: *Cambie.*
STUDENT: **Julio debe estar en la cocina.**
2. *Tendrá* unos treinta años.
3. *Serán* las siete y media.
4. *Tendrá* ovejas y cerdos también.
5. *Será* muy puntual.
6. *Estarán* durmiendo a estas horas.
7. *Habrá* ciertos problemas.
8. *Estará* en la misa.
9. *Tendrá* un recibo.
10. Tú *tendrás* un jefe muy antipático.

› TRANSLATION DRILL

A. 1. Do you suppose he remembers me?
¿Se acordará de mí?
2. Do you suppose it's the truth?
3. Do you suppose they walk to school?
4. Do you suppose he's dictating right now?
5. Do you suppose she takes communion every day?
6. Do you suppose it's their fault?

B. 1. TEACHER: Mario must remember the address.
STUDENT: **Mario debe recordar la dirección.**
TEACHER: Alicia should remember the address.
STUDENT: **Alicia debe recordar la dirección.**
TEACHER: Alfredo ought to remember the address.
STUDENT: **Alfredo debe recordar la dirección.**
2. Rosa must know that.
Pepe should know that.
Olga ought to know that.
3. We must sell the car.
We should sell the house.
We ought to sell the café.
4. They must finish the schedule.
They should write the letters.
They ought to send the prescription.
5. I must order (ask for) the tickets.
I should call María Elena.
I ought to leave a message.
6. You must go home.
You should go to bed.
You ought to take these pills.

› DISCUSSION

English occasionally uses the future to express probability in the present: *By now they'**ll be worrying** themselves sick.* The implication is what will turn out to be true on later verification. In Spanish this use of the future is more frequent, especially with the verbs **ser, estar, tener,** and **haber.**

A stronger probability is expressed by **deber** plus infinitive. It verges on the meaning of "obligation," and the same verb, **deber,** is used in both senses. Ordinarily when it is used with a verb of action, e.g., **no deben salir,** the meaning is obligation; with other verbs the meaning is probability, e.g., **Debe estar en la cocina.** English *must* shares the same range of meanings: *You must always ask permission,* obligation; *He must be in the kitchen,* probability.

120 Clauses with *si,* if

EXAMPLES

A. 1. Si **sale** premiado, ¿qué hará con la plata? *If it turns out to be the lucky one, what will you do with the money?*
2. Si **vienes,** ¿puedes traer tu tocadiscos?
3. Si **vuelve** a llamar, dígale que no estoy.

B. 1. Si **tenía** el dinero, debe haberlo perdido. *If he had the money, he must have lost it.*
2. Dijo que estaba bien, si **era** necesario.
3. Si antes que yo viniera **existía** esa costumbre, ahora vamos a cambiarla.

C. Si **llegaste** primero, ganaste. *If you got there first, you won.*

D. Si **ha estado** en Buenos Aires, ha visto el Teatro Nacional. *If he's been in Buenos Aires, he's seen the National Theater.*

NEUTRAL *if* CLAUSES			
if	it turns out to be	si	**sale**
	you come		**vienes**
	he had		**tenía**
	you arrived		**llegaste**
	he's been		**ha estado**

In neutral *if* clauses Spanish uses the indicative; the tenses correspond to the meanings (present form = present meaning; past form = past meaning) as in English.

EXAMPLES

A. 1. Si **saliera** premiado, ¿qué haría con la plata?
2. Si **vinieras,** ¿podrías traer tu tocadiscos? *If you should come, could you bring your record player?*
3. Si **volviera** a llamar, dígale que no estoy. *If she should call again, tell her I'm not in.*
4. Si **tuviera** el dinero lo perdería. *If he had the money he'd lose it.*
5. Si **llegaras** primero, ganarías. *If you got (should get, were to get) there first, you'd win.*
6. No hablaría así si yo **fuera** usted. *I wouldn't talk like that if I were you.*

B. 1. Si la policía no **hubiera disuelto** la manifestación, los estudiantes no habrían hecho la huelga. *If the police hadn't broken up the demonstration, the students wouldn't have called the strike.*
2. ¿Lo habría ofrecido si lo **hubiera tenido?** *Would you have offered it if you'd had it?*

	UNLIKELY AND UNREAL *if* CLAUSES			
A.	if	it should turn out to be	si	**saliera**
		you should come		**vinieras**
		he had		**tuviera**
		you arrived (were to arrive)		**llegaras**
		I were		**fuera**
B.	if	they hadn't broken up	si	**no hubieran disuelto**
		you had had		**hubiera tenido**

To suggest something unlikely of fulfillment or contrary to fact English uses *should* or *were to* (past forms that are NONPAST in meaning) and the past perfect. The corresponding Spanish forms are the imperfect and past perfect subjunctive.

› TENSE SUBSTITUTION DRILL

INSTRUCTIONS: Repeat the following sentences just as you hear them. Then repeat them again, changing the verb after **si** from present indicative to imperfect subjunctive.

A. 1. TEACHER: Si vuelve a llamar, dígale que no estoy. *Repita.*
STUDENT: **Si vuelve a llamar, dígale que no estoy.**
TEACHER: *Cambie.*
STUDENT: **Si volviera a llamar, dígale que no estoy.**
2. Si sales premiado, dale gracias a Dios.
3. Si él tiene bastante dinero, véndale el coche.
4. Si puede venir, dígale que traiga su tocadiscos.
5. Si llegas primero, espérame.
6. Si viene el profesor, dele el libro.
7. Si pregunta, contéstele.

› PATTERNED RESPONSE DRILL

INSTRUCTIONS: The teacher will describe a situation and then ask a question about it. Answer all questions with **sí** (i.e., affirmatively) plus an unlikely or unreal *if* clause, basing the answer on the situation that was described.

A. 1. TEACHER: (No tienes ni papel ni lápiz.) ¿Escribirías la carta?
STUDENT: **Sí, si tuviera papel y lápiz.**
2. (No tienes periódico.) ¿Leerías las noticias?
3. (No tienes dinero.) ¿Comprarías el traje?
4. (La ropa no está sucia.) ¿Lavarías ahora?
5. (No tienes tiempo.) ¿Lavarías las camisas?
6. (El no se acuerda de nosotros.) ¿Nos llamaría él?
7. (Está enfermo.) ¿Iría a la oficina?
8. (¡El nuevo gerente es tan exigente!) ¿Trabajarías en esa oficina?
9. (A Ricardo le falta dinero.) ¿Pagaría la cuenta de la electricidad?

B. 1. (No han lavado el auto.) ¿Habrían ido al cine?
Sí, si hubieran lavado el auto.
2. (El gerente no la ha escrito.) ¿Habríamos recibido la carta?
3. (No has comprado el billete.) ¿Habrías ganado el premio gordo?
4. (No has tenido bastante dinero.) ¿Habrías comprado unos zapatos?
5. (Luis ha pagado la cuenta.) ¿Habrían cortado la electricidad?
6. (El ha sido muy antipático.) ¿Te habría gustado?
7. (Has hecho bien el trabajo.) ¿El gerente habría estado enojado contigo?

INSTRUCTIONS: Answer the following questions with a complete statement as in the models.

C. 1. TEACHER: Si usted tuviera un millón de pesos, ¿haría un viaje o compraría coche?
STUDENT 1: **Si yo tuviera un millón de pesos, haría un viaje** (**compraría un coche**).
TEACHER: ¿Qué harías tú (ellos, ustedes)?
STUDENT 2: **Si yo tuviera un millón de pesos, compraría un coche** (**haría un viaje**).
2. Si su casa estuviera sucia, ¿usted la barrería o se pondría triste?
3. Si su novia entrara ahora, ¿usted se levantaría o se quedaría sentado?
4. Si hoy fuera el cumpleaños de ella, ¿usted la invitaría a comer o le daría un regalo?
5. Si hoy hubiera una huelga, ¿usted iría o estudiaría?

› RESPONSE DRILL

1. ¿Qué haría usted si tuviera tres días libres?
2. ¿Qué haría usted si estuviera en la ciudad de México ahora?
3. ¿Qué haría usted si tuviera mucho dinero?
4. Si alguien le regalara un viaje, ¿a qué países iría?
5. ¿Qué haría usted si se sacara la lotería?

› PATTERNED RESPONSE DRILL

1. TEACHER: Si usted hubiera tenido un millón de pesos, ¿habría hecho un viaje o habría comprado un coche?
STUDENT 1: **Si yo hubiera tenido un millón de pesos, habría hecho un viaje** (**habría comprado un coche**).
TEACHER: ¿Qué habrías hecho tú (ellos, ustedes)?
STUDENT 2: **Si yo hubiera tenido un millón de pesos, habría comprado un coche** (**habría hecho un viaje**).
2. Si su casa hubiera estado sucia, ¿usted la habría barrido o se habría puesto triste?
3. Si su novia hubiera entrado ahora, ¿usted se habría levantado o se habría quedado sentado?
4. Si hoy hubiera sido el cumpleaños de ella, ¿usted la habría invitado a comer o le habría dado un regalo?
5. Si hoy hubiera habido una huelga, ¿usted habría ido o habría estudiado?

› RESPONSE DRILL

1. ¿Qué habría hecho usted si hubiera tenido tres días libres?
2. ¿Qué habría hecho usted si hubiera estado en la ciudad de México?
3. ¿Qué habría hecho usted si hubiera tenido mucho dinero?
4. Si alguien le hubiera regalado un viaje, ¿a qué países habría ido?
5. ¿Qué habría hecho usted si se hubiera sacado la lotería?

➤ DISCUSSION

The notion of unreality often found in the imperfect subjunctive (Unit 20, Section 110) is extended to sentences containing *if* clauses. Of course, all *if* sentences are unreal in one sense: the very use of *if* implies something that has not happened or that is regarded as not necessarily true; but using imperfect subjunctive increases the unreality. English uses a similar device, that of verbs past in form but nonpast in meaning: *If you talked (should talk, were to talk) that way you'd lose the position* **Si hablara así perdería el puesto** contrasts with *If you talk that way you'll lose the position* **Si habla así perderá el puesto.**

If clauses that are contrary to fact are simply an extreme case of unlikelihood or unreality, and again the past subjunctive forms (imperfect or past perfect) are used. The English parallels are close: *If I were you* (but I'm not) **Si yo fuera usted,** *If he had gone* (but he didn't) **Si hubiera ido.**

The past forms in English are ambiguous. We cannot tell, except by viewing the sentence as a whole, whether a form like *you lost* corresponds to the indicative **perdiste** or the subjunctive **perdieras.** In *If you lost your money we can't buy them* **Si perdiste tu dinero, no los podemos comprar,** the *lost* is a past form that is past in meaning. In *If you lost (should lose, were to lose) your money we couldn't buy them* **Si perdieras tu dinero, no los podríamos comprar** the *lost* is a past form that is nonpast in meaning ("if you lost your money tomorrow," for example). The past form is used to give a shade of unreality to something that is really present or future in meaning and without the unreality would be expressed *If you lose your money we can't (won't be able to) buy them* **Si pierdes tu dinero no los podemos (podremos) comprar.**

In Spanish the future and conditional forms and the present subjunctive, with their corresponding progressive and perfect constructions, are excluded in an *if* clause. English has similar restrictions as in *If they lose* (not *will lose*) *the game they will regret it.* In *If they will lose the game we can win* the *will* means *are willing to* (**Si quieren perder**) and is not the *will* of futurity.

EXAMPLES

A. 1. Quién sabe **si aceptarán.** *Who knows if (whether) they'll accept.*
2. Nos preguntó **si sería** una molestia para nosotros. *He asked us if (whether) it would be a bother to us.*

B. 1. **Si quiere,** venga conmigo.
2. No **sé si** hubo muertos.

Buenos Aires: Display of lottery tickets

	si if	**si** if, whether
future indicative		√
conditional indicative		√
present subjunctive		√
other forms of verb	√	√

In *if* clauses implying *whether*, usually occurring after verbs of knowing, doubting, wondering, and asking, any form of the verb may be used. The future and conditional indicative and the present subjunctive may not be used in other *if* clauses.

› PATTERNED RESPONSE DRILL

A. 1. ¿Ya aceptó él?
No, ni sabemos si aceptará.
2. ¿Ya renunció él?
3. ¿Ya volvió él?
4. ¿Ya salió él?
5. ¿Ya corrió él?

B. 1. ¿No dice si viene?
No, no dijo si vendría.
2. ¿No dice si vende la casa?
3. ¿No dice si compra los billetes?
4. ¿No dice si trae la ropa?
5. ¿No dice si renuncia?
6. ¿No dice si corre?

› DISCUSSION

When **si** means *whether* (or *if* in the sense of *whether*) there are no restrictions on what form of the verb may follow it: *I don't know whether he'll be working at this time of day* **No sé si estará trabajando a estas horas;** *Who knows whether they've said it* **Quién sabe si lo hayan dicho,** etc.

121 Softened requests and criticisms

EXAMPLES A. 1. **¿Podría** prestarme veinte pesos?
2. **¿Tendría** usted tiempo para almorzar conmigo? *Would you have time to lunch with me?*
3. Se **diría** que nos odiaba. *You might say he hated us.*
4. **Habría** sido mejor esperar. *It would have been better to wait.*

B. 1. **¿Pudiera** usted aceptar menos? *Could you possibly accept less?*
2. **Quisiera** mandarles un buen regalo.
3. **Quisiera** que lo pensara por algunos días. *I'd like you to think about it for a few days.*
4. No **debieras** enojarte. *You shouldn't lose your temper.*
5. **Hubiera** sido mejor esperar. *It might have been better to wait.*

TWO DEGREES OF SOFTENING	
the speaker is ingratiating	*the conditional of any verb*
the speaker is more ingratiating	*the imperfect subjunctive of* **deber, haber, poder,** *and* **querer**

Both the conditional indicative and the imperfect subjunctive are used for toning down a request or a criticism. The imperfect subjunctive is almost apologetic and is seldom used in this way except with the four verbs listed.

› TENSE SUBSTITUTION DRILL

INSTRUCTIONS: Repeat the following sentences just as you hear them. Then repeat them again, replacing the present with the conditional.

A. 1. TEACHER: ¿*Puede* prestarme veinte pesos? *Repita.*
   STUDENT: **¿Puede prestarme veinte pesos?**
   TEACHER: *Cambie.*
   STUDENT: **¿Podría prestarme veinte pesos?**
2. ¿*Tiene* usted tiempo para almorzar?
3. ¿Me *acompaña* a la Comisión de Cambios?
4. ¿*Da* usted algo en beneficio de la capilla?
5. ¿*Dice* usted que es una buena idea?
6. ¿*Viven* ustedes en ese barrio?
7. ¿Me *explica* usted la situación?
8. ¿Me *lleva* al mercado?

B. 1. Bueno, yo no *digo* esto.
2. Bueno, yo no *hago* esto.
3. No, yo no *traigo* al gerente.
4. No, yo no me *enojo* por esto.
5. Pues yo no *pago* esa cuenta.
6. Pues yo no *juego* con ese equipo.
7. Pues yo no *toco* ese tema.

INSTRUCTIONS: Repeat the following sentences just as you hear them. Then repeat them again, substituting an appropriate imperfect subjunctive form in place of the present.

C. 1. TEACHER: ¿*Puede* usted aceptar menos? *Repita.*
   STUDENT: **¿Puede usted aceptar menos?**
   TEACHER: *Cambie.*
   STUDENT: **¿Pudiera usted aceptar menos?**
2. ¿*Quiere* usted tener un recibo?
3. ¿*Puedes* venir a la reunión?
4. ¿Pero *debemos* esperar tanto tiempo?
5. ¿*Podemos* comer juntos esta noche?
6. ¿*Pueden* entrar pronto?
7. ¿*Quieres* prestarme tu coche?

D. 1. *Quiero* darles un buen regalo.
2. *Podemos* comprar unas camisas nuevas.
3. *Debemos* mandar los trajes a la tintorería.
4. *Queremos* ver al jefe.
5. No *debes* enojarte por eso.
6. *Puedo* por lo menos felicitarla por su buena suerte.
7. *Quiero* pedirte un favor.

› TRANSLATION DRILL

A. 1. Could you lend me ten pesos?
   ¿Podría prestarme diez pesos?
2. Could you give me a newspaper?
3. Could you leave me fifteen minutes?
4. Would you have time to see me?
5. Would it be possible to hear it?
6. I would prefer coffee.

B. 1. Would you lend me fifty pesos?
¿Quisiera prestarme cincuenta pesos?
2. Would you follow me to the patio?
3. Would you make me a dinner?
4. Should we finish today?
5. Should we leave before ten?
6. Could you finish today?

GUIDED CONVERSATION

M. *Margarita* R. *Raúl*

M. ¡Raúl!
R. ¡Qué!
M. ¡Tú, sin dinero, sin trabajo... comprando un billete de lotería!
R. Ah sí, lo encontraste. Pues esta mañana estaba parado ______________
M. ¡Pero un entero! ¿Por qué no un décimo, sólo para complacer a la vieja?
R. Que la vieja ______________
M. ¡Huy! ¡Otro préstamo[5]!
R. Sí, de Enrique. Pero Margarita, si saliéramos ______________
M. ¿Por qué no podríamos ir a la luna[6] donde no hay lotería?
R. Pero te hablo en serio. Quizá ______________
M. O quizá pagaríamos esos préstamos.

DISCUSSION

In place of *Can I have a second helping?* one often finds, as a more polite request, *Could I have a second helping?* or, toning it down further, *Might I have a second helping?* There are two devices in Spanish for this kind of toning down: (1) the conditional for partial softening such as one might use in asking something that has a good chance of being fulfilled or in asking or criticizing something that one feels one has a right to ask or criticize; (2) the imperfect subjunctive for softening to the point of diffidence or apology, as in asking something or criticizing something which one does not have (or pretends not to have) the right to ask or criticize.

The conditional may be used as a softener with any verb. The imperfect subjunctive is normally used in this way only with the verbs **deber, haber, poder,** and **querer.** With **haber,** of course, the past perfect subjunctive of any verb becomes possible: **Hubiera perdido menos haciéndolo de otro modo** *You would (might) have lost less doing it another way,* **¿Quién lo hubiera pensado?** *Who would have thought it?* etc.

A caution is needed about the verb **poder** when the English equivalent is *could.* Note the following parallels:

I said I could.	*I said I was able.*	**Dije que *podía*.**
I said I could.	*I said I would be able.*	**Dije que *podría*.**
I wish I could.	*I wish I might be able.*	**Ojalá *pudiera*.**

The second of these implies a condition, e.g., *I said I could (would be able) if they gave me the chance.*

PATTERNED RESPONSE REVIEW DRILL

Preterit verb forms.

1. ¿Qué hizo él ayer? ¿Llegar, salir?
Sí, él llegó y salió.
2. ¿Qué hizo él ayer? ¿Trabajar, comer?

[5] *loan* [6] *moon*

3. ¿Qué hizo él ayer? ¿Practicar, aprender?
4. ¿Qué hizo él ayer? ¿Esperar, perder?
5. ¿Qué hicieron ellos ayer? ¿Llamar, salir?
6. ¿Qué hicieron ellos ayer? ¿Comprar, vender?
7. ¿Qué hizo usted ayer? ¿Entrar, comer?
8. ¿Qué hizo usted ayer? ¿Llegar, salir?
9. ¿Qué hizo usted ayer? ¿Hablar, escribir?
10. ¿Qué hizo usted ayer? ¿Estudiar, aprender?
11. ¿Qué hicieron ustedes ayer? ¿Pagar, seguir?
12. ¿Qué hicieron ustedes ayer? ¿Entrar, volver?
13. ¿Qué hicieron ustedes ayer? ¿Hablar, beber?

reading

Sinfonía: Conjugación del verbo "amar"

Pedro Antonio de Alarcón[7]

CORO DE ADOLESCENTES Yo amo, tú amas, aquél ama; nosotros amamos, vosotros amáis,[8] ¡todos aman!

CORO DE NIÑAS (*a media voz*) Yo amaré, tú amarás, aquélla amará; ¡nosotras amaremos!, ¡vosotras amaréis![9] ¡todas amarán!

UNA FEA Y UNA MONJA (*a dúo*) ¡Nosotras hubiéramos, habríamos y hubiésemos amado!

UNA COQUETA ¡Ama tú! ¡Ame usted! ¡Amen ustedes!

UN ROMÁNTICO (*desaliñándose el cabello*) ¡Yo amaba!

UN ANCIANO (*indiferentemente*) Yo amé.

UNA BAILARINA (*trenzando delante de un banquero*) Yo amara, amaría... y amase.

DOS ESPOSOS (*en la menguante de la luna de miel*) Nosotros habíamos amado.

UNA MUJER HERMOSISIMA (*al tiempo de morir*) ¿Habré yo amado?

UN POLLO Es imposible que yo ame, aunque me amen.

EL MISMO POLLO (*de rodillas ante una titiritera*) ¡Mujer amada, sea usted amable, y permítame ser su amante!

UN NECIO ¡Yo soy amado!

UN RICO ¡Yo seré amado!

UN POBRE ¡Yo sería amado!

UN SOLTERON (*al hacer testamento*) ¡Habré yo sido amado?

UNA LECTORA DE NOVELAS ¡Si yo fuese amada de este modo!

UNA PECADORA (*en el hospital*) ¡Yo hubiera sido amada!

EL AUTOR (*pensativo*) ¡Amar! ¡Ser amado!

aquél *he*
a media voz *in a whisper* **aquélla** *she*
fea *ugly woman* **monja** *nun*
desaliñándose *disarranging* **cabello** *hair*
trenzando *prancing* **Yo...amase.** *I would love...and might love.*
menguante *waning* **luna de miel** *honeymoon*
pollo *clever young man*
rodillas *knees* **titiritera** *female puppeteer*
necio *fool*
solterón *old bachelor*
pecadora *magdalene, prostitute*

---

[7] Well-known Spanish novelist and playwright (1833–91), best known in the United States for his novel **El sombrero de tres picos,** *The Three-Cornered Hat* (Boston: Ginn, 1952).
[8] The **vosotros** verb forms, ending in **-is,** are still used in Spain but have been replaced in Spanish America by the **ustedes** forms. (See Unit 2, footnote 1.)
[9] See footnote 8.

UNIT 22

Mourning

R. *Ramírez* F. *Alberto Fernández* M. *Doña María* C. *Doña Carmen* E. *Mrs. Esparza*

R. What do you think [Imagine]! Roberto Esparza just died!
F. What? I knew he was sick, but I didn't think he was that sick.
R. He had heart trouble; you know how treacherous those things [illnesses] are.
F. Poor Don Roberto! He had such zest for living [attachment to life]!
R. Especially poor Marta; so young and already a widow, and with four children . . . Well . . . the time comes for every man . . .
F. When will the funeral be?
R. Tomorrow afternoon at four. That reminds me, I've got to order a wreath.
F. Then the wake is tonight. I'll give her my condolences there.

* * *

F. How is Marta?
M. Very sad. I saw her crying her eyes out [bitterly].
C. I heard her cry too, and it really broke my heart [rent my soul].
M. She looks so pale dressed in black!

De duelo

R. *Ramírez* F. *Alberto Fernández* M. *Doña María* C. *Doña Carmen* E. *Señora Esparza*

R. ¡Figúrese, que se acaba de morir Roberto Esparza!
F. ¿Cómo? Yo sabía que estaba enfermo pero no creí que estuviera grave.
R. Estaba enfermo del corazón; ya sabe usted qué traicioneras son esas enfermedades.
F. ¡Pobre don Roberto! ¡Le tenía tanto apego a la vida!
R. Sobre todo pobre Marta; tan joven y ya viuda y con cuatro hijos... En fin... a cada uno le llega el día.
F. ¿Cuándo va a ser el entierro?
R. Mañana (1) a las cuatro de la tarde. Eso me recuerda que tengo que encargar una corona (2).
F. Entonces esta noche es el velorio (3). Ahí le doy el pésame.

* * *

F. ¿Cómo está Marta?
M. Muy triste. La vi llorando amargamente.
C. Yo también la oí llorar y me partió el alma.
M. ¡Se ve tan pálida vestida de negro!

Mexico: Cemetery

C. And she'll have to wear mourning two years. Poor girl! Here she comes.
F. Madam, my deepest sympathy.
E. Many thanks, Alberto. Please excuse the disorderly appearance of the house.
F. Don't even think of it!

* * *

F. Pardon me for leaving, but it's very late.

E. Thanks, many thanks, Alberto . . .

C. Y tendrá que estar de luto dos años. ¡Pobre señora! Ahí viene.
F. Señora, mi más sentido pésame.
E. Muchas gracias, Alberto. Le ruego que me perdone por el desorden de la casa.
F. ¡No faltaba más, señora!

* * *

F. Perdóneme que la deje, pero ya es muy tarde.

E. Gracias, muchas gracias, Alberto...

cultural notes

(1) Burial normally takes place the day after death.

(2) This is one of several formalized funeral procedures, which include the ordering of a wreath (**corona**), close relatives dressing in black, mourning by the widow for two years, the offering of standard expressions of sympathy (**dar el pésame, mi más sentido pésame**).

(3) The **velorio** is an all-night wake or vigil over the deceased before burial during which the family usually prays and receives visitors.

122 Indicative or subjunctive in exclamations

EXAMPLES
1. Qué bueno que **llamaste** (**hayas llamado**). (*How good that you called.*)
2. ¡Qué suerte que yo no **fui** (**haya ido**)!
3. Lástima que yo no **hablo** (**hable**) inglés.
4. Gracias a Dios que nada te **ha** (**haya**) **pasado.** *Thank goodness nothing's happened to you.*

¡———	(*indicative or subjunctive*)!

A noun clause after an exclamation may have its verb in the indicative or in the subjunctive.

TENSE SUBSTITUTION DRILL

INSTRUCTIONS: Repeat the following sentences just as you hear them. Then repeat them again, substituting present perfect subjunctive for preterit.

A. 1. TEACHER: ¡Qué bueno que llamaste! *Repita.*
STUDENT: **¡Qué bueno que llamaste!**
TEACHER: *Cambie.*
STUDENT: **¡Qué bueno que hayas llamado!**
2. ¡Qué malo que perdiste!
3. ¡Qué lástima que faltaste!
4. ¡Qué suerte que terminaste!
5. ¡Qué horror que renunciaste!
6. ¡Qué barbaridad que pagaste!
7. ¡Qué triste que peleaste!
8. ¡Qué ridículo que contestaste!
9. ¡Qué tontería que lloraste!

B. 1. ¡Qué suerte que no fui!
2. ¡Qué lástima que no estuve!
3. ¡Qué tontería que no terminé!
4. ¡Qué horror que no paré!
5. ¡Qué barbaridad que no gané!
6. ¡Qué tontería que no lo traje!
7. ¡Qué triste que no lo mandé!
8. ¡Qué ridículo que no lo envolví!
9. ¡Qué malo que no lo acepté!
10. ¡Qué bueno que no lo perdí!

C. 1. ¡Qué horror que mataron a los estudiantes!
2. ¡Qué suerte que tuvieron un día feriado!
3. ¡Qué ridículo que llevaron a los niños!
4. ¡Qué lástima que murió el presidente!

TENSE SUBSTITUTION DRILL

INSTRUCTIONS: Repeat the following sentences just as you hear them. Then repeat them again, substituting present subjunctive for present indicative.

A. 1. TEACHER: ¡Qué lástima que no hablo inglés! *Repita.*
STUDENT: **¡Qué lástima que no hablo inglés!**
TEACHER: *Cambie.*
STUDENT: **¡Qué lástima que no hable inglés!**
2. ¡Qué triste que no escribo bien!
3. ¡Qué horror que no recuerdo la dirección!
4. ¡Qué suerte que vamos los dos!
5. ¡Qué bueno que tenemos razón!
6. ¡Qué tontería que no comemos temprano!

B. 1. ¡Qué bueno que está aquí Guillermo!
2. ¡Qué malo que se va Alicia!
3. ¡Qué horror que vienen todos!
4. ¡Qué lástima que a los profesores no les pagan este mes!

› DISCUSSION

After exclamations containing expressions of the "welcoming-spurning" group (see Unit 18, Section 101), the indicative as well as the subjunctive may be used. Thus it is permissible to say either **Lástima que yo no *hablo* inglés** or **Lástima que yo no *hable* inglés.**

See Unit 20, Section 111, for the correspondence of the preterit with the present perfect subjunctive, for example, **llamaste** with **hayas llamado.**

123 Perceived actions

EXAMPLES A. 1. Yo también la oí llorar.
2. La vi llorando amargamente.
3. Lo oímos decir adiós. *We heard him say goodbye.*
4. Las vimos arreglando sus coches. *We saw them fixing their cars.*
5. Oyeron a Marta llamar a Luis. *They heard Marta call Luis.*
6. Oí a los dos muchachos discutiendo política. *I heard the two boys discussing politics.*

B. 1. Oí que acababan de llegar. *I heard that they had just arrived.*
2. Vieron que compraba los billetes. *They saw that she was buying the tickets.*

C. 1. Vieron que Olga la escribió. *They saw Olga write it.*
2. Vieron que Olga la estaba escribiendo (estaba escribiéndola). *They saw Olga writing it.*
3. Vi que se lavó. *I saw him wash (himself).*
4. Vi que se estaba lavando. *I saw him washing (himself).*

CONSTRUCTION WITH INFINITIVE OR *-ing*		
	SUBORDINATE VERB	NOUN OBJECT, IF ANY
I saw them	pass passing	the meat.

A. CONSTRUCTION WITH INFINITIVE OR **-ndo**		
	SUBORDINATE VERB	NOUN OBJECT, IF ANY
Los vi	**pasar** **pasando**	**la carne.**

B. CONSTRUCTION WITH CLAUSE		
	SUBORDINATE VERB	NOUN OBJECT, IF ANY
Vi que	**pasaron** **estaban pasando**	**la carne.**

When the subordinate verb does not have a with-verb pronoun object Spanish makes the same contrast as English between an infinitive and an **-ndo** form or instead may use a clause.

CONSTRUCTION WITH INFINITIVE OR *-ing*		
	SUBORDINATE VERB	PRONOUN OBJECT
They saw Olga	write writing	it.
I saw him	wash washing	himself.

C. CONSTRUCTION WITH CLAUSE		
	WITH-VERB PRONOUN	SUBORDINATE VERB
Vieron que Olga	**la**	**escribió.** **estaba escribiendo.**
Vi que	**se**	**lavó.** **estaba lavando.**

When the subordinate verb has a with-verb pronoun object a clause is preferred in Spanish.

› PATTERNED RESPONSE DRILL

A. 1. ¿A quién viste llegar, a Cecilia?
Sí, vi llegar a Cecilia.
¿La viste llegar?
Sí, la vi llegar.
2. ¿A quién oiste hablar, al jefe?
¿Lo oiste hablar?
3. ¿A quién viste llorar, a Marta?
¿La viste llorar?
4. ¿A quién viste salir, a Elena?
¿La viste salir?
5. ¿A quién viste jugar, a los americanos?
¿Los viste jugar?

B. 1. ¿A quién viste comprar la ropa, a María y a Juan?
Sí, vi a María y a Juan comprar la ropa.
¿Viste que la compraron?
Sí, vi que la compraron.
2. ¿A quién viste sacudir los muebles, a Rosa y a Olga?
¿Viste que los sacudieron?
3. ¿A quién viste lavar el auto, a Bernardo y a Julio?
¿Viste que lo lavaron?
4. ¿A quién viste arreglar el tocadiscos, a Rafael y a Miguel?
¿Viste que lo arreglaron?
5. ¿A quién viste pagar la multa, a Fernando y a Roberto?
¿Viste que la pagaron?

› TRANSFORMATION DRILL

1. Vi a Olga escribiendo la carta.
Vi que la estaba escribiendo.
2. Vi a Bernardo cambiando las llantas.
3. Vi a Rosa lavando las tazas.
4. Oí a Víctor llamando a la criada.
5. Oí a Roberto ofendiendo al policía.
6. Oí a Paquito repitiendo los números.

› DISCUSSION

The verbs of perception that may be followed by the infinitive or **-ndo** form in Spanish correspond closely to those that may be followed by the infinitive (without *to*) or *-ing* in English. They are the common ones like **ver** *see* and **oir** *hear,* not the less common ones like **notar** *notice* or **contemplar** *contemplate;* we can say *I saw him come* but not *I perceived him come.*

The principal difference between the two languages is that Spanish tends to avoid a with-verb pronoun at the end in this construction. Instead of *They saw Olga writing it* we find the equivalent of *They saw that Olga was writing it* **Vieron que Olga la estaba escribiendo** (**estaba escribiéndola**). (See Unit 9, Section 45, for the choice between **la estaba escribiendo** and **estaba escribiéndola.**)

Tenses are used as explained in previous units: *I used to hear him get up at six* **Oía que se levantaba a las seis.** (See the discussion in Unit 11, Section 54.) Ordinarily if a clause is called for by the above rules, when English uses an infinitive (*I heard her call us*) Spanish uses the preterit (**Oí que nos llamó**)—the calling is a single event with its termination. But if English uses *-ing* (*I heard her calling us*) then Spanish uses the past progressive (**Oí que nos estaba llamando**).

124 *El* and *un* with feminine nouns

EXAMPLES

A. 1. Me partió **el alma.**
2. **El álgebra** del sistema es difícil. *The algebra of the system is hard.*
3. ¿Y si cae **al agua?** *And if it falls in the water?*
4. En estos días hay **un hambre** de paz. *In these days there is a hunger for peace.*

B. 1. Es **la** complicada **álgebra** de estos problemas de física. *It's the complicated algebra of these physics problems.*
2. Es **una** verdadera **hambre** de paz. *It's a real hunger for peace.*

C. 1. **Las almas** de los muertos. *The souls of the dead.*
2. Si es extranjero, no puede trabajar en **las aguas** nacionales de los Estados Unidos. *If he's a foreigner he can't work in the national waters of the United States.*

	A. DIRECTLY BEFORE A FEMININE SINGULAR NOUN BEGINNING WITH STRESSED [a]	B. BEFORE A FEMININE SINGULAR NOUN UNDER ANY OTHER CIRCUMSTANCES	C. BEFORE A FEMININE PLURAL NOUN
the	**el**	**la**	**las**
a, an, some	**un**	**una**	**unas**

› TRANSFORMATION DRILL

A. 1. Las aguas.
El agua.
2. Las almas.
3. Las amigas.
4. Las haciendas.

B. 1. El hambre.
Un hambre.
2. El alma.
3. La amiga.
4. La avenida.

› CONSTRUCTION SUBSTITUTION DRILL

1. TEACHER: Tiene un hambre de paz. *Repita.*
STUDENT: **Tiene un hambre de paz.**
TEACHER: verdadera
STUDENT: **Tiene una verdadera hambre de paz.**
2. Esta es el agua para beber. (mejor)
3. No me gusta el álgebra de Einstein. (complicada)
4. Tiene un alma. (verdadera)
5. El hambre es traicionera. (verdadera)
6. Nos dieron el agua que tenían. (única)

› DISCUSSION

The **el** that appears in **el alma, el hambre,** and with other feminine nouns is not, historically speaking, the masculine article that appears in **el hombre, el lugar,** etc., though identical with it in form. Instead it is a separate development of the Latin demonstrative *ĭlla,* which, when it came before stressed [a], preserved its first syllable rather than its second: the *-a* was, so to speak, swallowed up in what followed, leaving only *el.* A descendant of the full form of *ĭlla* is the pronoun **ella.**

The **un** that appears under similar conditions before feminine nouns is a more recent development, the **-a** of **una** having fused with the following **a-: una͡alma → un alma.**

125 *De* and *por* for *by* after a *-do* form

EXAMPLES A. 1. Recibí un paquete **acompañado de** una carta. *I received a package accompanied by a letter.*
2. Resfriado, **seguido de** gripe—lo he tenido todo. *Cold, followed by flu—I've had everything.*

3. Estas palabras están **seguidas de** muchos ejemplos. *These words are followed by many examples.*
4. La ciudad está **rodeada de** barrios pobres. *The city is surrounded by run-down suburbs.*
5. Ella está **rodeada de** sus compañeras. *She is surrounded by (is among) her companions.*

B. 1. El cónsul entró **acompañado por** otros bolivianos. *The consul came in accompanied (escorted) by other Bolivians.*
2. Salí **seguido por** mis padres. *I left followed by my parents.*
3. El tirano estaba **rodeado por** los estudiantes. *The tyrant was surrounded by (under the threat of) the students.*
4. El tirano estaba **rodeado por** sus policías. *The tyrant was surrounded by (under the protection of) his policemen.*

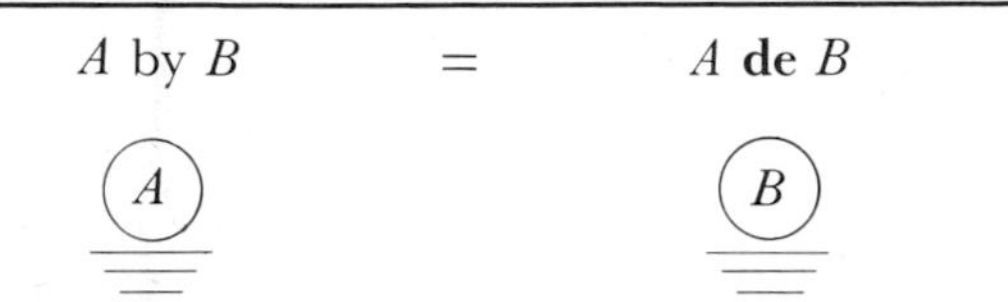

When *B* is in a POSITIONAL relationship to *A* the equivalent of *by* is **de.**

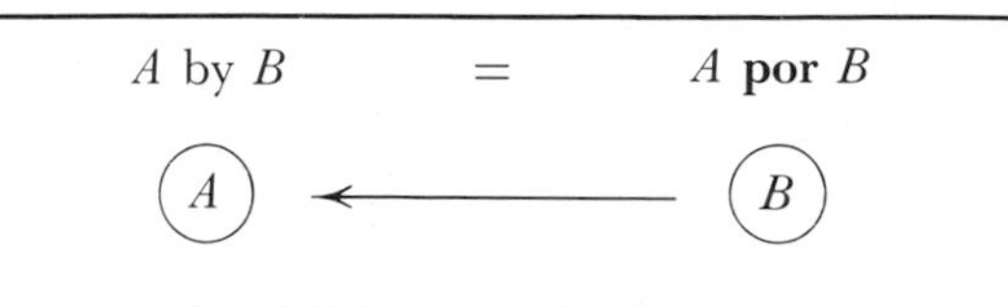

When *B* is in an ACTIVE relationship to *A* the equivalent of *by* is **por.**

› TRANSLATION DRILL

A. 1. Some books arrived accompanied by a bill.
Llegaron unos libros acompañados de una cuenta.
2. Some papers arrived accompanied by some photos.
3. Some documents arrived accompanied by a message.

B. 1. My niece arrived accompanied by her friends.
Mi sobrina llegó acompañada por sus amigos.
2. My nephew arrived accompanied by his friends.
3. My nieces arrived accompanied by their friends.

C. 1. I had a headache followed by fever.
2. We had a meeting followed by a dinner.
3. There were speeches followed by a strike.

D. 1. The consul left followed by several government officials.
2. The lawyer left followed by several businessmen.
3. The professor left followed by several students.

E. 1. He's surrounded by (in the company of) many friends.
2. The city is surrounded by mountains.
3. The houses were surrounded by fields.

F. 1. The students were there surrounded (hemmed in) by the police.
2. The bull was there surrounded by the boys.
3. The traffic chief was there surrounded by the students.

G. 1. The new plant will be dedicated by the president.
La nueva planta será dedicada por el presidente.
2. The new refineries will be dedicated by the president.
3. The demonstration was seen by everyone.
4. The headlines were seen by everyone.
5. The leaders were attacked by the police.
6. The foreigners were attacked by the people.

› DISCUSSION

Both **de** and **por** are equivalents of English *by*. The difference between them is that **de** is RELATIONAL while **por** is ACTIVE. **De** shows position in space or time; **por** shows exertion. To say, for example, that *A* is surrounded by *B* **de** would be used if we merely pictured *A* with *B* around it (*The girl is surrounded by her companions* **La niña está rodeada de sus compañeras**), but **por** would be used if the meaning is *hemmed in* or *protected* (*She is surrounded by the police* **Ella está rodeada por la policía**).

An extreme case of the active relationship is the passive voice (see Unit 17, Section 97). Thus **El tirano fue rodeado por los estudiantes** would mean that he GOT surrounded by them. **El tirano estuvo rodeado por los estudiantes** would mean that he was there with the students around him in some posture (e.g., threatening or protective) other than mere position relative to him. **Por** is used in both because more than position is involved.

126 *De* as equivalent of *with* and *in*

EXAMPLES

A. 1. Estaba todo cubierto **de** polvo. *He was all covered with dust.*
2. Lo llenaron **de** regalos. *They filled it with gifts.*

B. 1. ¡Se ve tan pálida vestida **de** negro!
2. Me gusta vestirme **de** lana. *I like to wear (dress myself in) wool.*
3. ¿Vas a vestirte **de** otro color? *Are you going to wear another color?*
4. Mire las montañas envueltas **de** nubes. *Look at the mountains wrapped in clouds.*
5. Tendrá que estar **de** luto dos años. *She'll have to be in mourning two years.*

C. 1. No quiero ensuciarlo **con** este polvo. *I don't want to dirty it with this dust.*
2. Algunos de los pobres tuvieron que vestirse **con** periódicos. *Some of the poor people had to dress themselves in newspapers.*
3. Volvió a casa envuelto **en** una sábana. *He came back home wrapped in a sheet.*

object of the preposition	*affects appearance or condition*	with / in	**de**
	makes possible the action	with in	**con** **en, con**

De is used to show one thing as affecting the appearance or condition of another (referring to the Examples, a woman has black clothes ON, box has presents IN IT, etc.). **Con** or **en** is used, depending on the sense, to show that a thing serves as the means to an action (something dirtied as a result of dust, a man clad during an emergency with whatever was quickly at hand).

› TRANSLATION DRILL

1. He arrived covered with dust.
   She arrived covered with dust.
2. They filled the cup with water.
   They filled the cup with milk.
3. Let's see. She's the lady with the red dress.
   Let's see. He's the gentleman with the gray suit.
4. She seems so pale dressed in black.
   He seems so sad dressed in black.

5. She'll have to be in mourning two years.
He'll have to be in mourning one year.
6. The mountains are wrapped in clouds.
The trees are wrapped in clouds.
7. Don't dirty it with that dust.
Don't dirty it with that butter.
8. He did it with his hand.
He did it with his foot.
9. He stuffed (filled) his pockets with old papers.
He stuffed (filled) his pockets with old tickets.
10. He was wrapped in a sheet.
She was wrapped in a sheet.
11. I brought the records wrapped in paper.
I brought the ties wrapped in paper.
12. He sent the documents written in English.
He sent the letters written in English.

› DISCUSSION

De is used to show the appearance or condition of something affected by what is on it or in it. When we say **Llegó cubierto de polvo** *He arrived covered with dust* the paramount idea is his appearance or condition. English has a similar device in the form of a compound with noun plus participle—*a dust-covered figure, a gift-filled package, the blood-spattered dress.* When we say **Llegó cubierto con una toalla** *He arrived covered with a towel* we are not primarily referring to the fact that he wore a towel but that he was *covered*—the towel was a MEANS of covering himself when the telephone summoned him from his shower.

In the same way **vestida de negro** refers to an appearance (compare *black-garbed figure*). Likewise **Lo llenaron de papel** *They filled it with paper* refers to the resultant condition of being full *of* paper. **Lo llenaron con papel** would refer to having the paper there as a means, perhaps to keep the container from being flattened or to protect contents such as glassware.

127 *En* and *a* for *at*

EXAMPLES

A. 1. Con los acontecimientos de esta mañana **en** el cementerio.
2. ¿Qué hacen **en** casa? *What do they do at home?*

B. 1. Vengo **a** las cuatro. *I'll come at four o'clock.*
2. **Al** principio la llamé cada dos o tres días. *At first I called her every two or three days.*
3. ¿**A** cómo estaba el cambio? (*At how much [what rate] was the exchange?*)
4. **A** cuarenta kilómetros de aquí.

C. 1. Llamaron **a** la puerta. (*They knocked at the door.*)
2. Se sentó **al** teléfono. (*He sat down at the telephone.*)
3. Está ahí, **a** la entrada del comedor.
4. ¿Lo quiere corto atrás y **a** los lados? (*Do you want it short in back and at the sides?*)
5. **A** la izquierda está el Café Brasil. *At (On, To) the left is the Brazil Café.*

<table>
<tr><td rowspan="2">at</td><td>place in which (no motion toward)</td><td>en</td></tr>
<tr><td>point in space, time, or on a scale
place to or toward which</td><td>a</td></tr>
</table>

En is the equivalent of *at* when the place (or event) is thought of as having dimensions within which something is located (or occurs). In most other instances the equivalent of *at* is **a.**

TRANSLATION DRILL

A. 1. TEACHER: The girls are in the living room.
STUDENT: **Las chicas están en la sala.**
2. The boys are in the patio.
3. The children are in the garden.
4. The teacher is in the school.
5. The consul is in the Ministry.
6. The widow is in the house.
7. My aunt is in the chapel.
8. My uncle is in the government.

B. 1. What happened at the cemetery?
¿Qué pasó en el cementerio?
2. What happened at the theater?
3. What happened at the meeting?
4. What happened at the office?
5. What happened at the church?
6. What happened at the funeral?
7. What happened at the wake?

C. 1. Anything new at the office?
¿Alguna novedad en la oficina?
2. Anything new at the ministry?
3. Anything new at the plant?
4. Anything new at the refinery?
5. Anything new at the club?
6. Anything new at the market?
7. Anything new at the house?

D. 1. We live ten kilometers from the city.
Vivimos a diez kilómetros de la ciudad.
2. The cleaner's is fifty feet from the corner.
3. The house is two blocks from the park.

E. 1. He came by at four.
Pasó a las cuatro.
2. He ate at six.
3. He came at the exact time.
4. He left at the end (**al final**).
5. He arrived at the beginning.

F. 1. He arrived at the door.
Llegó a la puerta.
2. He called at the door.
3. He arrived at the office.
4. He paid at the entrance.
5. He left it at the entrance.
6. He waited for it at the entrance.
7. He sat down at the table (**mesa**).

G. 1. He was in the doorway.
Estaba en la puerta.
2. He used to play in the doorway.
3. He used to work in the doorway.
4. He used to study in the doorway.
5. He used to wait in the doorway.
6. He used to sleep in the doorway.

DISCUSSION

English and Spanish divide the *in-at* semantic range in similar ways but different proportions. Essentially *in* and **en** refer to something having dimensions that can be thought of as encompassing the object placed in reference to it. *At* and **a** conceptually shrink the locus to a point. Where the two languages differ is in how far they are willing to go in this mental shrinkage. We would not say *The two rivers meet at Kansas,* for we cannot cut a whole state down to one point, but we readily say *The two rivers meet at Kansas City,* as if Kansas City were a point on a map. Spanish cannot go this far. When motion is involved, the place where motion stops can be thought of as a terminal point, and size does not matter: **Llegaron a Lima** *They arrived at Lima.* When something is really a point or an edge, such as a point of time or space (**a las seis** *at six,* **al principio** *at the beginning*) or a point or line on a scale (**a dos kilómetros** *at two kilometers*), there is no problem. In between is an area where **a** may be used if one thinks of moving (oneself or just one's eyes or attention) in the given direction or where **en** may be used if one thinks of being stationed within the place: **a la puerta, en la puerta;** compare English *at the door* (perhaps being only poised there in readiness to go in or out) and *in the doorway.*

An instance of **a** referring to a point of time is **al** plus infinitive. (See Unit 8, Section 38. See also Unit 12, Section 64, for other instances of **a** with time.)

GUIDED CONVERSATION

T. *Teresa* A. *Alberto*

T. Alberto, mira esta noticia del periódico. Que se murió Roberto Esparza.
A. ¿Cómo? Yo sabía ______________
T. Menciona algo de "haberse agotado todos los recursos de la ciencia médica.[1]"
A. Sí, estaba enfermo ______________
T. Además, yo recuerdo que en un cóctel[2] estaba fumando[3] como un loco. Pobre don Roberto.
A. Sobre todo pobre Marta. ______________
T. Sí, pero lástima que a algunos les llegue tan pronto.

PATTERNED RESPONSE REVIEW DRILL

Sequence of tenses: review of preterit.

A. 1. TEACHER: ¿No va usted a estudiar?
STUDENT: **Ya estudié.**
2. ¿No va usted a empezar?
3. ¿No va usted a jugar?
4. ¿No va usted a llamar?
5. ¿No va usted a preguntar?
6. ¿No va usted a comer?
7. ¿No va usted a beber?
8. ¿No va usted a escribir?

B. 1. ¿No va él a lavar el auto?
Ya lo lavó.
2. ¿No va él a dictar la carta?
3. ¿No va él a cambiar el dinero?
4. ¿No va él a pagar la cuenta?
5. ¿No va él a vender el coche?
6. ¿No va él a barrer la sala?
7. ¿No va él a abrir las puertas?

C. 1. ¿Cuándo me va a lavar la ropa?
Ya se la lavé.
2. ¿Cuándo me va a arreglar el bolsillo?
3. ¿Cuándo me va a traer las pieles?
4. ¿Cuándo me va a sacudir los muebles?
5. ¿Cuándo me va a vender la cartera?
6. ¿Cuándo me va a contestar la carta?

D. 1. ¿Cuándo van ustedes a traerlo?
Ya lo trajimos.
2. ¿Cuándo van ustedes a hacerlo?
3. ¿Cuándo van ustedes a darlo?
4. ¿Cuándo van ustedes a tenerlo?
5. ¿Cuándo van ustedes a ponerlo?
6. ¿Cuándo van ustedes a producirlo?
7. ¿Cuándo van ustedes a decirlo?
8. ¿Cuándo van ustedes a reducirlo?

---
[1] *every recourse of medical science having been exhausted* [2] *cocktail party* [3] *smoking*

Entre Ríos province, Argentina: Cemetery

reading

Muere un destacado miembro del foro

destacado *distinguished*
foro *Bar*

†

El señor
ROBERTO ESPARZA ALONSO

falleció ayer a las 13.30 horas en el Seno de Nuestra Madre de la Santa Iglesia Católica, Apostólica Romana, confortado con todos los auxilios espirituales.

Su inconsolable esposa, madre, hijas, hermanos, hermana, hijo político y demás parientes, lo participan a usted con el más profundo dolor y le ruegan eleve sus oraciones a Dios Nuestro Señor por el eterno descanso del alma del finado.

México, D. F., 4 de octubre de 1965.

falleció *died* **Seno** *Bosom*
auxilios *assistance*
hijo político *son-in-law*
descanso *rest* **finado** *deceased*

Muere don Roberto Esparza

Después de prolongada enfermedad dejó de existir el distinguido licenciado en Derecho y Notario Público, don Roberto Esparza Alonso.

5 de octubre de 1965.—A las 13.30 horas del día 3 de octubre dejó de existir en esta ciudad, después de haberse agotado todos los recursos que la ciencia médica aconsejó, el distinguido abogado Roberto Esparza Alonso, notario público Núm. 2, quien gozaba de general estimación en todos los círculos sociales.

El cadáver fue velado en su domicilio calle de Providencia número 864, teniendo lugar ayer a las 15 horas las solemnes honras fúnebres, trasladándos a continuación el cuerpo al Panteón Americano. Debemos hacer constar que innumerables personas de todos los sectores sociales estuvieron en la velada, resultando insuficiente la amplia residencia y teniendo que estar gran cantidad de gentes en la calle y en el pequeño jardín que se encuentra frente al referido domicilio.

Por lo que respecta a las ofrendas florales, han sido de igual manera numerosas, no habiendo materialmente lugar donde colocarlas.

El abogado Esparza fue catedrático del Instituto de Ciencias y Artes del Estado, y desempeñó además las funciones de juez en distintos distritos, dedicándose finalmente a la notaría, cargo que desempeñó hasta el momento de su muerte, contando con la estimación de todos quienes lo trataron.

(Adapted from *El Universal.*)

licenciado en Derecho *Bachelor of Laws*
después...aconsejó *after every attention called for by medical science had been exhausted*
gozaba de *enjoyed*
El...velado *The wake was held*
trasladándos *being transferred* **a continuación** *immediately afterward*
Panteón *Cemetery*
hacer constar *make it part of the record*
pequeño *little*
Por...a *With regard to*
materialmente *literally* **colocar** *to place*
catedrático *professor*
desempeñó *performed, fulfilled*
juez *judge*
cargo *position*
contando con *enjoying*

UNIT 23

The Burglary

A. *Alicia* D. *Diego* L. *Lieutenant* S. *Sergeant*

A. Diego! Stop snoring! Wake up!
D. What? How's that?
A. Wake up! I heard some noises downstairs.
D. It must have been the cat. Let me sleep, woman.

CRASH!!

A. You see? There it is again. It's burglars. Diego, call the police.
D. Sh . . . ! I wonder where I put my pistol.
A. Where are you going? Don't leave me here alone . . .
D. Quiet, woman, you make me nervous.

* * *

A. (*talking with the officer*) They took the silver service, the clock . . .
L. Just one moment. Let's begin at the beginning. What time does the patrol go by?
D. About 4 A.M., I think.
L. Hmm. How many servants are there in the house?
A. Right now, two: the cook and the maid. We let the gardener go yesterday.
D. He was with us only a few days. We didn't like him because he was so lazy.

El robo

A. *Alicia* D. *Diego* T. *Teniente* S. *Sargento*

A. ¡Diego! ¡Deja de roncar! ¡Despierta!
D. ¿Qué? ¿Cómo?
A. ¡Despierta! Oí unos ruidos abajo.
D. Habrá sido el gato. Déjame dormir, mujer.

¡¡CATAPLUM!!

A. ¿No ves? Otra vez. Son ladrones. Diego, llama a la policía.
D. ¡¡Sh...!! ¿Dónde habré dejado la pistola?
A. ¿Adónde vas? No me dejes sola...
D. Cállate, mujer, que me pones nervioso.

* * *

A. (*hablando con el Sr. Oficial*) Se llevaron la vajilla de plata, el reloj...
T. Un momentito. Empecemos por el principio. ¿A qué hora pasa la ronda (1)?
D. Como a las cuatro de la mañana, creo.
T. Hmm. ¿Cuántos empleados hay en la casa?
A. Por ahora, dos: la cocinera y la criada. Al jardinero lo despedimos ayer.
D. Estuvo apenas unos días con nosotros. No nos gustaba por perezoso.

Mexico City: Private residence

S. This looks suspicious. He had a key to the house?

A. Oh good Lord! Of course! Now that I think of it, I forgot to ask him for it when he left.

S. Esto está sospechoso. ¿El tenía llave de la casa?

A. ¡Jesús María! ¡Claro! Ahora que recuerdo, se me olvidó pedírsela cuando se fue.

* * *

L. Can you give us a description of him?

D. Yes, he's a thin fellow, not very tall, in fact, on the short side.

A. Also dark, and he had a scar on his face.

T. ¿Puede hacernos una descripción de él?

D. Sí, es un hombre delgado, no muy alto, más bien bajo.

A. También es moreno, y tenía una cicatriz en la cara.

L. Ah, I know who he is now: the famous Juan Pérez, alias "The Mouse."
A. He didn't seem like a bad sort, at least according to his references and his good conduct certificate from the police.
L. Madam, you can be sure that those documents were all forged.

T. Ah, ya sé quién es: el famoso Juan Pérez, alias "El Ratón".
A. No parecía mala persona, al menos según sus referencias y certificados de buena conducta (2) de la policía.
T. Señora, tenga la seguridad de que todos eran documentos falsificados.

cultural notes

(1) The **ronda** or night patrol is a protection provided by private agencies hired to keep watch on residences and buildings. In other countries different terms may be found. For example, in México *night watchmen* are often called **veladores,** and the patrol is called **la vigilancia.**

(2) The good conduct certificate, which might be necessary to get a job or to obtain a visa, is one of several papers that certain Latin-American countries require citizens to carry. (See Unit 7, Cultural Note 3.)

128 Probability in past time

EXAMPLES

A. 1. ¿Dónde **habré dejado** la pistola?
2. **Habrá sido** el gato. (*It was probably the cat.*)

B. 1. ¡Qué suerte tiene ese tipo! Y todo por una casualidad. ¿Y cómo **sería?**
2. **Serían** las dos. *It was probably two o'clock.*
3. **Tendría** unos veinte años. *She was somewhere around twenty years old.*

probablemente he dejado **probablemente dejé**	=	**habré dejado**
probablemente eran	=	**serían**

Probability corresponding to present perfect or preterit is expressed by future perfect; probability corresponding to imperfect is expressed by the conditional.

› TENSE SUBSTITUTION DRILL

INSTRUCTIONS: Repeat the following sentences just as you hear them. Then repeat them again, substituting future perfect for present perfect, thus suggesting probability.

A. 1. TEACHER: Ha muerto el gato. *Repita.*
STUDENT: **Ha muerto el gato.**
TEACHER: *Cambie.*
STUDENT: **Habrá muerto el gato.**
2. Ha vuelto la cocinera.
3. Ha estudiado el teniente.
4. Han escrito los oficiales.
5. Ha apostado el sargento.
6. Ha terminado el jardinero.
7. Han salido los ratones.

B. 1. ¿Ha pasado la ronda?
2. ¿Ha dejado buenas referencias?
3. ¿Han robado los documentos?
4. ¿Ha pedido un certificado de buena conducta?
5. ¿Han tenido poca seguridad?
6. ¿Ha despedido al señor de la cicatriz?
7. ¿Han dado una descripción sospechosa?
8. ¿Lo han echado de menos?
9. ¿Han progresado bastante?
10. ¿Ha hablado hasta por los codos?
11. ¿La ha dejado en paz?
12. ¿Se han escapado los ladrones?

› TENSE SUBSTITUTION DRILL

INSTRUCTIONS: Repeat the following sentences just as you hear them. Then repeat them again, substituting future perfect for preterit, thus suggesting probability.

A. 1. TEACHER: Rosa dejó la ropa en el patio. *Repita.*
STUDENT: **Rosa dejó la ropa en el patio.**
TEACHER: *Cambie.*
STUDENT: **Rosa habrá dejado la ropa en el patio.**
2. Roberto estuvo en el patio.
3. Memo tuvo hora para las once.
4. Don Rafael roncó toda la noche.
5. Carmen perdió una cantidad de dólares.
6. Ellos encargaron una corona para el entierro.
7. Esos fueron documentos falsificados.

B. 1. ¿Qué fue ese cataplum?
2. ¿Cómo está impresa la cubierta?
3. ¿Qué dijo de la cabeza y la garganta?
4. ¿Quién tuvo la bondad de llenar mi taza?
5. ¿Quiénes le dieron el pésame?

› TENSE SUBSTITUTION DRILL

INSTRUCTIONS: Repeat the following sentences just as you hear them. Then repeat them again, substituting conditional for imperfect, thus suggesting probability.

1. TEACHER: Era Juan Pérez, alias "El Ratón". *Repita.*
STUDENT: **Era Juan Pérez, alias "El Ratón".**
TEACHER: *Cambie.*
STUDENT: **Sería Juan Pérez, alias "El Ratón".**
2. Era ese periodista loco.
3. La viuda estaba muy nerviosa.
4. Estaban en el velorio.
5. Tenían mucho apego a la vida.
6. Tenía una fiebre bastante alta.
7. Había dos clases de biología.
8. No había más remedio.

› PATTERNED RESPONSE DRILL

A. 1. TEACHER: ¿Qué estaba comprando él?
STUDENT: **Quién sabe. Estaría comprando un coche.**
2. ¿Qué estaba llevando él?
3. ¿Qué estaba vendiendo él?
4. ¿Qué estaba buscando él?
5. ¿Qué estaba pidiendo él?

B. 1. ¿A quién vio Memo?
No sé. Habrá visto a Marta.
2. ¿A quién llevó Memo?
3. ¿A quién invitó Memo?
4. ¿A quién prefirió Memo?
5. ¿A quién siguió Memo?
6. ¿A quién felicitó Memo?

› TRANSLATION DRILL

1. TEACHER: I wondered what they would be wanting.
STUDENT: **Me preguntaba qué desearían.**
2. I wondered what they would be doing.
3. I wondered what they would be thinking.
4. I wondered what they would be asking for.
5. I wondered what they would be buying.
6. I wondered what they would be believing.
7. I wondered what they would be supposing.

In addition to probability corresponding to the perfect (*He has probably seen them* **Los habrá visto**), the future perfect is also used for probability corresponding to the preterit (*He probably saw them yesterday* **Los habrá visto ayer**). The conditional is similarly used for probability corresponding to the imperfect (*Why didn't they answer? They probably weren't home that early* **¿Por qué no contestaron? No estarían en casa tan temprano**).

The English equivalents are as in Unit 21, Section 119: *What could he be thinking?* **¿Qué estaría pensando?** *What do you suppose they did?* **¿Qué habrán hecho?** *I wondered what they would be wanting* **Me preguntaba qué desearían.**

As with the future of probability, the verbs most often encountered with the conditional of probability are **ser, estar, tener,** and **haber.** The future perfect of probability, however, may be freely used with any verb.

129 Meanings of *por*

imprecise location	through down along around by way of at	Vamos **por** esta calle. Anduvieron **por** la pared. *They walked along the wall.* Paseamos **por** el parque. *We strolled around (through) the park.* Empecemos **por** el principio.
duration	for	**Por** ahora, dos. (*For the time being, two.*) Fue a España **por** dos años. *He went to Spain for two years (a two-year stay).*
substitution: proxy and exchange	for (in place of) to	Mi mujer va siempre y reza **por** los dos. Estoy dictando **por** el jefe. *I'm dictating for (in place of) the boss.* No se deje dar gato **por** liebre. ¿A cómo estaba el cambio? A treinta **por** uno. Le doy dos dólares **por** todo. *I'll give you two dollars for the lot.*
corres-pondence	for per	Me sale un pelo blanco **por** cada día que paso allí. *I get (There comes out on me) a gray hair for every day I spend there.* Tienen seis materias **por** año. *They have six subjects per year.* El diez **por** ciento de los folletines no llegaron. *Ten per cent of the brochures did not arrive.*

cause, motive, and duty	for because of on account of through on after (to get) to	Le ruego que me perdone **por** el desorden de la casa. (*Please excuse me for the disorder of the house.*) **Por** eso la invitación, ¿eh? Todo **por** culpa de él. (*All because of his fault.*) Tenían que quedarse aquí **por** el colegio. Y todo **por** una casualidad. No nos gustaba **por** perezoso. Se murió **por** trabajar tanto. *He died because of working so hard.* Le escribo para felicitarla **por** su cumpleaños. Nosotros pasamos **por** ti. Estudia medicina **por** su padre. *He's studying medicine for his father* (*because his father wants him to, as a favor to him*). Vamos al parque **por** darles gusto a los niños. *We're going to the park to please* (*because that will please*) *the youngsters.*
agency	by	Será dedicada **por** el presidente. *It will be dedicated by the president.* (See Unit 22, Section 125.)

EXAMPLES

1. Es la más importante **por ahora.**
2. Ay, Paquito, **por Dios,** no hagas eso.
3. **Por ejemplo.** *For example.*
4. Trigo, lentejas, maíz, papas, cebollas y cosas **por el estilo.**
5. **Por eso** la invitación, ¿eh?
6. **Por favor,** no insistan en que estudie medicina.
7. **Por fin** llegó el correo.
8. **Por lo menos** en Cuaresma.
9. **Por lo visto,** los agricultores no la pasan mal, ¿eh?

for now, for the time being, for the present	**por ahora**
for Heaven's sake (etc.)	**por Dios**
for example	**por ejemplo**
like that, of the same sort, along those lines	**por el estilo**
that's why, therefore, for that reason	**por eso**
please	**por favor**
finally, at last	**por fin**
at least	**por lo menos**
apparently	**por lo visto**
why?—because	**¿por qué?—porque**

These are among the numerous set phrases with **por.**

TRANSLATION DRILL

A. 1. TEACHER: Let's go down this street.
STUDENT: **Vamos por esta calle.**
2. Let's go along this avenue.
3. Let's go through this door.
4. Let's go around the park.
5. Let's go by way of the school.
6. Let's go across the patio.
7. Let's go this way (through here).

B. 1. He went to Spain for a few days.
Fue a España por unos días.
2. He went to his room for a few moments.
3. He went to the country for a few days.
4. He went abroad for a few months.
5. We stopped traffic for ten minutes.
6. We studied medicine for six years.
7. We waited on the corner for half an hour.

C. 1. My wife prays [enough] for the two of us.
Mi mujer reza por los dos.
2. My wife eats [enough] for the two of us.
3. My wife drinks [enough] for the two of us.
4. My wife talks [enough] for the two of us.

D. 1. Don't let them give you a cat in place of a rabbit.
No se deje dar gato por liebre.
2. Don't let them give you water in place of lemonade.
3. Don't let them give you books in place of documents.
4. Don't let them give you algebra in place of physics.

E. 1. I'll give you two dollars for the book.
Le doy dos dólares por el libro.
2. I'll give you four pesos for the wallet.
3. I'll give you one hundred dollars for the painting.
4. I'll give you twenty thousand bolivianos for the car.

F. 1. There are two buses per hour.
Hay dos buses por hora.
2. There are three films per week.
3. There are two demonstrations per month.
4. There is ten per cent per year.

G. 1. Excuse me for the disorder of the house.
Perdóneme por el desorden de la casa.
2. Excuse me for the change of the schedule.
3. Excuse us for bringing bad news.
4. Excuse me for having arrived late.
5. Excuse me for having broken the thermometer.
6. Excuse me for getting nervous.

H. 1. And all because of a lucky break.
Y todo por una casualidad.
2. And all because of a long sickness.
3. And all because of that policeman.
4. And all because of a bad philosophy.
5. And all because of a treacherous memory.

I. 1. He's going to go by for his papers.
El va a pasar por sus papeles.
2. She's going to go by for her letter.
3. They're going to go by for their dresses.
4. We're going to go by for you at eight o'clock.

J. 1. It was dedicated by the president.
Fue dedicado por el presidente.
2. It was found by the technician.
3. It was sent by the lieutenant.
4. It was broken up by the police.

K. 1. For the time being he's not coming.
Por ahora, no viene.
2. For goodness' sake, don't come.
3. For example, he's coming.
4. That's why he's coming.
5. Please come early.
6. At last he's coming.
7. At least he's coming.
8. Apparently he's coming.
9. Why is he coming?

DISCUSSION

Prepositions enter intimately into combinations with other words in much the same way as prefixes and suffixes. They often become so stereotyped in these combinations that it is hard to trace any common core of meaning. This is strikingly true of **por** in Spanish. It has given rise to a great variety of set phrases each of which must be learned for itself. At the same time, however, it has kept the power to make free combinations with areas of meaning that can be outlined rather clearly:

1. Imprecise location. *Down* the street, *along* the beach, *through* the house, *across* the bridge, etc., are all expressed with **por.** The context tells us which of the English equivalents is appropriate. Imprecise location in time also calls for **por:** *It will be finished around 1976* **Se terminará por 1976.**

2. Duration. **Por** is like *for* in English and may be omitted under the same conditions: *He came for three weeks* **Vino por tres semanas,** *He was there (for) three weeks* **Estuvo allí (por) tres semanas.**

3. Substitution. When one person acts *for* another, or one thing is given *for* another, **por** is the equivalent of *for:* **Nosotros hablaremos por usted** *We'll speak for you (in your stead).*

4. Correspondence. Where English has *for* or *per* showing two things in a kind of reciprocal relationship, Spanish uses **por:** *One doctor for every 500 persons* **Un doctor por cada 500 personas.**

5. Cause, motive, and duty. When something acts to bring about an effect, English uses a variety of prepositions: *for, because of, through,* etc.: *I got the job through my brother* **Conseguí el empleo por mi hermano.** The influence toward the action is conceived as compelling, often being tinged with a suggestion of duty, for example, *I went in very carefully so as not to wake them* **Entré con mucho cuidado por no despertarlos** (it was a duty not to wake them). Spanish shows here a curious merging of push and aim. If the thing that one aims at is at the same time a motive for taking aim, then *(in order) to* is expressed by **por.** For example, the parents in a family feel a duty to satisfy their children; so "because of satisfying the children" is the reason for going to the park, and one says **Vamos al parque por darles gusto a los niños,** where purpose and cause coalesce.

6. Agency. See Unit 22, Section 125.

Most set phrases show their ultimate relationship to the free meanings of **por.** For example, **por lo visto** literally means *by what is seen,* i.e., the evidence of the visible, hence *apparently.*

130 Meanings of *de*

source	from	**¿De** dónde son?
possession and belongingness	———'s of to in	En casa **de** Olga. (See Unit 4, Section 21.) ¿El tenía llave **de** la casa? Va a ser la planta más moderna **de** Latinoamérica. Se sacó el gordo **de** la lotería. Es la una **de** la tarde. (See Unit 12, Section 64.)
identification	with	Lupita, la **de** los ojos verdes.
theme	about concerning	**¿De** qué quieres que hablemos, mamá? **¿De** vestidos?
substitution		Cambiemos **de** tema. (*Let's have a change of subject.*) Quiero cambiar **de** empleo. *I want to change jobs.*
partitive	of (*or nothing*)	¿Me pasas un poquito **de** carne, por favor? Necesito un poco **de** dinero. *I need a little money.* ¿Qué hay **de** malo en eso? Hay algo **de** bueno en esta revolución? *Is there anything good about this revolution?* Los niños tendrían **de** todo. Nunca diga "**De** esta agua no beberé".

comparison	than	Hay más **de** diez heridos. (See Unit 15, Section 83.)
capacity	as for	¿Y cuándo aceptó este trabajo? **De** administrador, ¿verdad? ¿Qué me ofreces **de** comida? *What do you offer me for dinner?* No quiero servir **de** profesor aquí. *I don't want to serve as professor here.*
position	by	Recibí un paquete acompañado **de** una carta. (See Unit 22, Section 125.)
appearance or condition	with in	La cubrieron **de** flores. *They covered it with flowers.* ¡Se ve tan pálida vestida **de** negro! (See Unit 22, Section 126.)

The central meanings of **de** are *of* and *from*. Peripheral meanings range as far as mere "connectedness."

EXAMPLES

1. No estoy **de acuerdo** contigo.
2. Nunca se ponen **de acuerdo.**
3. **De nada.**
4. No deben salir solas **de noche.**
5. **De todos modos,** quería hablarte de otra cosa.
6. —Se casa con Lorenzo.
   —¡De veras!

agreed in agreement	**de acuerdo**
you're welcome	**de nada**
at night	**de noche**
anyway	**de todos modos**
really	**de veras**

These are among the numerous set phrases with **de.**

› TRANSLATION DRILL

A. 1. TEACHER: Are you from Mexico?
   STUDENT: **¿Es usted de México?**
2. Are you from Panama?
3. Is he from Brazil?
4. Is he from Argentina?
5. Is she from Spain?
6. Is she from Colombia?
7. Are they from Venezuela?
8. Are they from Chile?
9. Is Diego from Europe?

B. 1. This house is Olga's.
   Esta casa es de Olga.
2. This book is Juanita's.
3. This wallet is Felipe's.
4. This bill is Alvaro's.
5. These scissors are the barber's.
6. These flowers are the secretary's.

C. 1. Here's the key to the house.
Aquí está la llave de la casa.
2. Here's the key to the car.
3. Here's the door to the living room.
4. Here's the door to the kitchen.
5. Here's the entrance to the bank.
6. Here's the entrance to the theater.

D. 1. It's the most modern plant in the country.
Es la planta más moderna del país.
2. It's the best team in the competition.
3. He's the laziest student in the world.
4. She's the prettiest girl in the class.
5. He's the oldest man in the city.
6. It's the last flower in the garden.

E. 1. Where's the girl with the green eyes?
¿Dónde está la chica de los ojos verdes?
2. Where's the man with the gray suit?
3. Where's the man with the red tie?
4. Where's the woman with the yellow dress?
5. Where's the man with the new car?
6. Where's the woman with the cat?

F. 1. Did you talk much about dresses?
¿Hablaron mucho de vestidos?
2. Did you argue much about politics?
3. Did you study much about the country?
4. Did you worry much about the revolution?
5. Did you mention anything about the money?
6. Did you say anything about the schedule?
7. Did you find out (know) anything about the robbery?

G. 1. Let's change the subject.
Vamos a cambiar de tema.
2. Let's change the hour.
3. Let's change the date.
4. Let's change books.[1]
5. Let's change classes.
6. Let's change teachers.
7. Let's change managers.
8. Let's change positions.

H. 1. I'm going to change clothes.
Voy a cambiarme de ropa.
2. I'm going to change shirts.
3. I'm going to change ties.
4. I'm going to change dresses.
5. I'm going to change coats.
6. I'm going to change cars.
7. I'm going to change shoes.

I. 1. He gave me a little rice.
Me dio un poco de arroz.
2. He gave me a little money.
3. I need a million pesos.
4. I need a million things.
5. We bought a dozen eggs.
6. We bought a dozen shirts.
7. I bought half a dozen ties.

J. 1. Is there anything bad in that?
¿Hay algo de malo en eso?
2. Is there anything good in the book?
3. Is there anything new in the house?
4. What's new?
5. There's (a little) of everything.
6. He has a little of everything.
7. He gave me a little of everything.

K. 1. They offered more than was asked.
Ofrecieron más de lo pedido.
2. They offered more than was desired.
3. They offered more than was necessary.

L. 1. He works as an administrator.
El trabaja de administrador.
2. He works as a manager.
3. He serves as a technician.
4. He serves as a leader.
5. We serve meat and potatoes for dinner.

M. 1. He goes out at night.
El sale de noche.
2. He returns at night.
3. He studies at night.
4. He practices at night.
5. He works at night.
6. He sleeps by day.

N. 1. He said, "Agreed."
Dijo, "De acuerdo".
2. He said, "You're welcome."
3. He said, "Anyway."
4. He said, "Really?"

[1]When the exchange is one-for-one, Spanish uses the singular: **cambiar de libro.** If more than one book is exchanged for more than one book, then plural, **cambiar de libros.**

› DISCUSSION

Like English *of,* Spanish **de** cannot be assigned a clearly delimited area of meaning. The central meanings of source and belongingness fade at the edges to merely relational functions like the one in *the city of Buenos Aires* **la ciudad de Buenos Aires,** where *city* = *Buenos Aires,* or in *the habit of arriving late* **la costumbre de llegar tarde,** where *habit* = *arriving late.*

Some of the special uses of **de** have already been studied. (See the references to earlier units in the table of examples above.) Other special uses are the following:

1. Belongingness (English *to* and *in*). When English uses *the key to the door, the door to the house,* Spanish uses **de: la llave de la puerta, la puerta de la casa.** When English uses *in* but refers to a thing that is not merely located in a place but belongs there, Spanish uses **de:** *the students in the class* **los alumnos de la clase** (**en la clase** would suggest perhaps casual visitors and in any case would probably be said **que están en la clase;** see Unit 16, Section 90), *the best team in the United States* **el mejor equipo de los Estados Unidos.**

2. Identification (English *with, in, on,* etc.). English has archaic expressions with *of* (e.g., *The House of the Seven Gables*) in which nowadays we would probably use *with: the house with the blue shutters.* Spanish uses **de:** *the man with the green tie* **el hombre de la corbata verde,** *the man in* (*with*) *the big car* **el hombre del coche grande.** These are a kind of belongingness in reverse: the tie actually belongs to the man, not he to it, but we can identify him by it just as we can identify *the paint on the house* **la pintura de la casa,** where the paint does "belong to" the house.

3. Substitution. When change involves substitution Spanish adds **de: cambiar de ropa, cambiar de tema.** Compare English *a change of subject, a change of clothes.*

4. Partitive. In the sense *a little,* **de** is added after **poco** (and **poquito**), e.g., **un poco de azúcar** *a little sugar;* compare English *a little bit of, a lot of,* and Spanish **un millón de.** (See Unit 6, Section 29.) In addition the indefinites **algo, nada,** and **¿qué?** may take **de** before adjectives, e.g., **Tiene algo de loco** *He's a little bit cracked.* The adjectives **bueno, malo,** and **nuevo** are especially frequent: **¿Qué hay de nuevo?** *What's new?* The phrase **de todo** occurs without any expressed indefinite, especially with the verbs **haber, tener,** and **dar: Hay de todo** *There's a little bit of everything,* **Nos dio de todo** *He gave us a little bit of everything.*

5. Capacity (English *as* and *for*). Applied to the occupation or position that a person holds, this refers to official capacity. Thus **Estoy aquí de gerente** *I am here as manager* implies that this is my official job. **Trabaja allí de administrador** *He works there as administrator* means that he has been duly appointed to the position; **Trabaja allí como administrador** has a more general sense—he might be filling in temporarily, or there might exist no official position. (**Como un administrador** means *like an administrator.*) Applied to things this **de** refers to what fills a pre-existing slot. For example, what is DINNER going to be?—*We serve meat and rice for* (*as*) *dinner* **Servimos carne y arroz de comida.** (**Carne** and **arroz** are items on the menu but not the whole meal.) A thing filling an appointed slot and a person filling an appointed job are semantically the same.

Among the set phrases, **de noche** calls for comment. We have already met **por la noche** with the meaning *at night* (Unit 12, Section 64). The difference is that **de noche** is like an adjective meaning *nocturnal.* **Llegó de noche** means *He made a nocturnal arrival.* The now almost obsolescent English *by day* and *by night* are close equivalents: *The owl hides by day and flies by night.* **Por la noche** normally refers to a particular night: **"Llegó ayer"—"¿Por la noche?"** *"He arrived yesterday"—"At night?"* The same contrast exists between **de día** and **por el día.**

131 The *-do* form for postures

EXAMPLES

1. Un día estaba **parado** en la puerta de un café.
2. ¿Ves aquel tipo **sentado** allá? *Do you see that fellow sitting over there?*
3. Están **acostados.** No los despiertes. *They're lying down. Don't wake them.*
4. La ropa está **colgada** en el patio. *The clothes are hanging in the patio.*

standing	=	planted, erect	**parado**
sitting	=	seated	**sentado**
lying down	=	stretched out, recumbent	**acostado**
hanging	=	hung	**colgado**

When an *-ing* form in English refers to a posture already assumed that is now merely being sustained, Spanish uses a **-do** form.

TRANSLATION DRILL

A. 1. TEACHER: My niece is sitting in the living room.
STUDENT: **Mi sobrina está sentada en la sala.**
2. My nephew is sitting in the dining room.
3. My nieces are sitting in the kitchen.
4. My nieces and nephews are sitting in the patio.

B. 1. He was standing on the corner.
2. She was standing on the corner.
3. They (*m*) were standing in the doorway.
4. They (*f*) were standing in the doorway.

C. 1. He's lying down.
2. She's lying down.
3. They're (*m*) lying down.
4. They're (*f*) lying down.

D. 1. He's up early, as usual.
2. She's up early, as usual.
3. They're (*m*) up early, as usual.
4. They're (*f*) up early, as usual.

E. 1. The clothing's hanging in the patio.
2. The suit's hanging in the patio.
3. The shirts are hanging in the patio.

DISCUSSION

English *They are seated* and *They are sitting* mean essentially the same thing. Ordinarily English favors an *-ing* form in referring to postures, picturing the person (or thing) as "doing something" when he maintains the posture. Spanish, however, prefers the *-ed* view of the posture and accordingly uses its **-do** form: once the housewife finishes hanging the clothes, they are no longer *hanging* but *hung*. (If **colgando** were used rather than **colgado,** it would mean *swaying*—action rather than posture.)

Related meanings that call for **-do** forms are *leaning* (*She stood leaning over the crib*), *hugging* (in each other's arms), *crouching, huddling, hiding,* etc.

132 *Tener, haber,* and *estar* without complements

EXAMPLES

A. 1. Me dijeron que don Pepe tenía mucho ganado en esa finca.
Sí, todavía **tiene.**
2. ¿No es sólo en España donde hay corridas de toros?
No, hombre, en Perú, Colombia, Ecuador, Venezuela y Panamá también **hay.** (*No, indeed; in Peru, Colombia, Ecuador, Venezuela, and Panama there are too.*)

B. 1. Mamá, dame diez centavos. *Mom, give me ten cents.*
No **tengo.** *I don't have it.*
2. Dice un señor que si hay ropa vieja para vender.
Dile que no **hay.**
3. Para café bueno no **hay** como este lugar. (*For good coffee there isn't anything like this place.*)

FORM OF *have* OR *there to be*	COMPLEMENT
we have there is etc.	it any some anything something

FORM OF **tener** OR **haber**	COMPLEMENT
tenemos **hay** **etc.**	

Spanish is free to omit the complement of **tener** or **haber** when it may be clearly inferred from the context. English sometimes omits (Examples A), sometimes not (Examples B), under similar circumstances.

EXAMPLES
1. Buenas tardes, doña Mercedes. **¿Está** Julio?
2. Si vuelve a llamar, dígale que no **estoy.**
3. Fui a verlos, pero no **estaban.** *I went to see them, but they weren't there.*

to be	here there in around

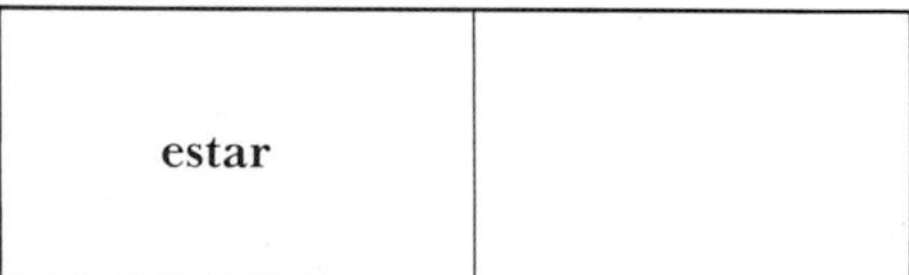

estar	

Where a location is clearly understood from the context, Spanish is free to use **estar** without adding **aquí, allí,** etc.

› PATTERNED RESPONSE DRILL

A. 1. TEACHER: ¿Hay ropa vieja para vender?
STUDENT: **No, no hay.**
2. ¿Tiene usted ropa vieja para dar?
3. ¿Tienen ellos regalos para los niños?
4. ¿Había ropa vieja para vender?
5. ¿Tenía usted periódicos viejos para dar?
6. ¿Tenían ustedes dinero para la capilla?
7. ¿Tenía ella tiempo para comer?

B. 1. El tenía mucho ganado, ¿verdad?
Sí, y todavía tiene.
2. Tú tenías muchos toros, ¿verdad?
3. Ellos tenían muchas vacas, ¿verdad?
4. Ellos tenían muchos gatos, ¿verdad?
5. Ustedes tenían muchos cerdos, ¿verdad?
6. Había muchas ovejas, ¿verdad?

C. 1. Ella quiere verlo a usted.
Dígale que no estoy.
2. Ella quiere ver a Elena.
3. Ella quiere ver a Julio y Pablo.
4. Ella quiere verlos a ustedes.

D. 1. Ayer te llamé pero tú no contestaste.
Es que no estaba.
2. Ayer los llamé a ellos, pero no contestaron.
3. Ayer la llamé a ella, pero no contestó.
4. Ayer los llamé a ustedes, pero no contestaron.

› DISCUSSION

English restricts the omission of complements after *to have* and *there to be* to cases of REPETITION. In *Does he* ***have*** *the money? Yes, he* ***has*** (*the money*), *has* repeats *have.*[2] Spanish restricts it to cases of INTELLIGIBILITY. When the mother replies **No tengo** to Paquito's request for ten cents, we know that

[2]Not only *to be* but also other auxiliary verbs in English show this sort of omission of something known from context: *Would you go?—Yes I would* (*go*); *Was he sick?—Well, he might have been* (*sick*); *Could you have helped them?—No, I couldn't* (*have* [*helped them*]).

the reference is to *money.* The omitted complement ordinarily refers to something indefinite or quantitative: *any(thing), some(thing), a lot, a few,* etc. (If it were pinpointed, Spanish, like English, would require a complement: *Please return that book I lent you.—I don't have* ***it*** **No *lo* tengo.**)

Whereas English only occasionally omits an adverb of place after *to be* (*They had been and gone* for *They had been* ***there*** *and gone*)—Spanish does so quite commonly: *I called but they weren't in* **Llamé, pero no estaban.**

GUIDED CONVERSATION

T. *Teniente* G. *Señora de Gómez-Blanco*

T. Cálmese señora. Empecemos por el principio. Estaba diciéndome por teléfono algo de un jardinero y un robo.
G. Acabamos de volver de un viaje y no hemos leído los periódicos de aquí últimamente.[3] Y esta tarde despedimos a un jardinero que cuidaba[4] la casa unas dos horas diarias.[5] Luego supe de los robos por acá.
T. ¿Puede hacernos una descripción de él?
G. Sí. ______________
T. ¿Ha estado con ustedes mucho tiempo?
G. No, estuvo ______________
T. ¿Y cómo se llamaba, según sus certificados?
G. José Prieto. Pero pidió un salario[6] tan bajo y no me parecía ______________
T. Señora, estoy seguro que es Juan Pérez. Ahora dígame, ¿él tenía llave de la casa?
G. ¡Jesús María! ______________
T. No se preocupe señora. Vamos a poner guardia[7] en su casa las veinticuatro horas. Y si ustedes oyen ruidos por la noche, sólo tienen que encender[8] y apagar muy rápidamente las luces de su cuarto. "El Ratón" no se nos escapará esta vez.

PATTERNED RESPONSE REVIEW DRILL

Sequence of tenses: review of present perfect.

A. 1. TEACHER: ¿Ya estudió usted?
STUDENT: **No, todavía no he estudiado.**
2. ¿Ya olvidó usted?
3. ¿Ya aceptó usted?
4. ¿Ya contestó usted?
5. ¿Ya regateó usted?
6. ¿Ya habló usted?
7. ¿Ya renunció usted?
8. ¿Ya terminó usted?

B. 1. ¿Ya comiste?
2. ¿Ya barriste?
3. ¿Ya dormiste?
4. ¿Ya prometiste?
5. ¿Ya saliste?
6. ¿Ya serviste?

C. 1. ¿Ya te peinaste?
2. ¿Ya te bañaste?
3. ¿Ya te lavaste?
4. ¿Ya te sentaste?
5. ¿Ya te casaste?
6. ¿Ya te entusiasmaste?
7. ¿Ya te dormiste?

D. 1. ¿Ya lo escribieron ustedes?
2. ¿Ya lo abrieron ustedes?
3. ¿Ya lo cubrieron ustedes?
4. ¿Ya lo envolvieron ustedes?
5. ¿Ya lo disolvieron ustedes?
6. ¿Ya lo rompieron ustedes?
7. ¿Ya lo vieron ustedes?
8. ¿Ya lo hicieron ustedes?
9. ¿Ya lo dijeron ustedes?

[3] *lately* [4] *cared for* [5] *daily* [6] *salary* [7] *surveillance* [8] *turn on*

Mexico City:
Private guard on patrol

reading

Noticia del día

M. *Marta* A. *Alicia*

M. Alicia, ¿qué es esto que oigo de un robo en tu casa hace unos días?

A. Ay, Marta, ¡qué susto tan grande! No pude dormir en dos noches.

¡qué...grande! *I was scared speechless!*

M. Vi la pequeña noticia en el periódico, pero no daba los detalles. Dímelos tú.

A. Pues fue así: Diego y yo estábamos acostados. El estaba roncando, pero yo no podía dormir y estaba en la cama con los ojos abiertos... Tú sabes que cuando una está despierta por la noche...

M. Sí, sí. Una oye todos los ruidos de la noche... y se imagina otros.

A. Eso es... Pues, como digo, allí estaba yo, y de repente oí unos ruidos abajo. En seguida sacudí a Diego, diciéndole que despertara. El murmuró que habría sido el gato, que yo lo dejara dormir. ¡Figúrate eso!... Entonces otra vez... ¡cataplum!

de repente *suddenly*
En seguida *Immediately*

M. ¿Y te creyó Diego esta vez?

A. ¡Claro! Diego también oyó el ruido... Le pedí que llamara a la policía.

M. ¿Tiene Diego una pistola en la casa?

A. Sí, pero se le había olvidado dónde la había dejado... Sea lo que sea, las pistolas me dan miedo.

dan miedo *frighten*

M. ¿De modo que llamaron a la policía?

De modo que *So*

A. ¡Cómo no!... El resto tú lo sabes por el periódico. Vinieron a casa esos dos policías, un teniente y un sargento, quienes nos hicieron preguntas sobre lo que faltaba, sobre los criados, etcétera.

M. Sí, ya sé todo eso. ¿Y crees tú que fue el jardinero... ¿cómo se llama?

A. Juan Pérez.

M. Sí. ¿Fue ése el ladrón?

A. Creo que sí. Es bien conocido por la policía, según su descripción, y no creo que tarden mucho en arrestarlo.

M. Supongo que no. Pero me sorprendió saber que era él. Siempre me pareció buena persona.

sorprendió *it surprised*

A. Sí, yo participaba de tu buena opinión de él... pero no es oro todo lo que reluce... ¡qué lástima!

no...reluce *all that glitters is not gold*

UNIT 24

Celebrating Independence

M. *Mariana* R. *Rosalba* S. *Second Lieutenant Ramos* T. *Second Lieutenant Torres*

M. The parade's just now beginning, and they said it would get under way at noon!

R. Mariana, look at the artillerymen at that streetcorner.

M. What a good-looking second lieutenant, the one with the gold medal! And see the look he's giving us!

R. Look at all the flowers and streamers they're throwing at the cadets from the Military College.

M. Are you going to the party at the presidential palace tonight?

R. Am I! I wouldn't miss that dance for anything in the world.

M. Then we'll see each other there—oh, good heavens! It's starting to rain. We'd better get going; without an umbrella we'll get soaked.

* * *

(*at the dance*)

R. What a lovely dance!

M. Did you see me dancing with the second lieutenant that we saw this morning [Did you see that the second lieutenant of this morning picked me (took me out) to dance]? He told me how he won that decoration.

Celebrando la Independencia

M. *Mariana* R. *Rosalba* S. *Subteniente Ramos* T. *Subteniente Torres*

M. Ya empieza el desfile, ¡y decían que era a mediodía!

R. Mariana, mira a los artilleros por aquella bocacalle.

M. ¡Qué subteniente tan guapo, el de la medalla de oro! ¡Y fíjate en la mirada que nos está echando!

R. Mira todas las flores y serpentinas que les están echando a los cadetes del Colegio Militar.

M. ¿Tú vas a ir esta noche a la fiesta del palacio presidencial?

R. ¡Que si voy! Ese baile no me lo pierdo por nada del mundo.

M. Entonces allá nos vemos. ¡Ay Dios! Está empezando a llover. Mejor vámonos; sin paraguas nos vamos a empapar.

* * *

(*en el baile*)

R. ¡Qué lindo está el baile!

M. ¿Viste que me sacó a bailar el subteniente de esta mañana? Me contó cómo se ganó esa condecoración.

Santiago de Chile: Independence Day parade

R. Lucky girl! I can see him over there talking with another fellow. Say, they're looking this way [toward here].

M. I think they're coming over to the table again. Let's pretend not to notice [make ourselves the pretenders].

R. ¡Dichosa! Allá lo veo hablando con otro. Fíjate, están mirando hacia acá.

M. Creo que vienen para la mesa otra vez. Hagámonos las disimuladas.

* * *

(talking with the officers)

S. Listen to the lively [Hear what pretty] marches the infantry band is playing! Want to go out on the balcony?

R. All right, let's go; then we can [take the opportunity to] see the fireworks that are about to begin.

(hablando con los oficiales)

S. ¡Oigan qué bonitas marchas está tocando la banda de la infantería! ¿Quieren asomarse al balcón?

R. Bueno, vamos y así aprovechamos para ver los fuegos artificiales que ya van a comenzar.

T. You go ahead; Mariana and I want to see the folk dances.	T. Vayan ustedes porque Mariana y yo queremos ver los bailes típicos.
M. The dancers are forming a semicircle. I think they're going to dance a *zapateado.*	M. Los bailarines están formando un semicírculo. Creo que van a bailar un zapateado. (1)
R. Let us know when they get ready to do the contradance and also . . .	R. Avísennos cuando vayan a bailar la contradanza (2) y también...
S. Sh . . . ! The national anthem! The president's coming in.	S. ¡Sh...! ¡El himno nacional! Viene entrando el presidente.

cultural notes

(1) The **zapateado,** a fast tap dance in 6/8 time performed by a pair of dancers, is common to all Latin America and comes from a popular Andalusian dance of the same name.

(2) The **contradanza,** like the French *contredanse,* derives from the seventeenth-century English *country dance.* Brought to America from Spain, the **contradanza** became the source of a number of Latin-American dances, e.g., the **habanera** and **danzón** in Cuba and the **tango** in Argentina.

133 Meanings of *para*

direction in space and time	toward for } = toward to } = toward on } = toward	Creo que vienen **para** la mesa otra vez. ¿**Para** dónde va? *Where are you heading (for)?* Ya faltan veinticinco **para** las nueve. Van **para** las dos. *It's going on two.* Va **para** la una. *It's going on one.*
action directed toward a goal	for to be a	Estudia **para** (ser) médico. *He's studying to be a doctor.* Lo único que te pedimos es que no estudies **para** abogado. (*The only thing we ask is that you don't study to be a lawyer.*) Trabajo **para** otra compañía. *I work for another company.*
object directed toward a goal or recipient	for	Ah, y una carta **para** mí. Fue un pretexto **para** discursos contra el Presidente. Eso de dos horas **para** el almuerzo no me parece bien.
action or object directed toward a goal that is itself an action	to in order to for so that I can } *with change of subject* for me to } *with change of subject*	Vamos por esta calle **para** llegar a la Plaza de Mayo. Una herramiento **para** cambiar llantas. *A tool for changing (to change) tires.* Dice un senor si hay ropa vieja **para** vender. ¿De parte de quién, **para** decirle? Ven acá **para** decirte una cosa. *Come here so I can (in order to) tell you something.* Espere **para** envolvérselos. (*Wait for [me] to wrap them for you.*)

time *deadline*	for by	Ella no dijo que era **para** ayer. ¿**Para** cuándo los quiere? (*By when do you want them?*) La ropa interior y las camisas **para** el martes y la de cama **para** el sábado. Estaré allí **para** las dos. *I'll be there by two.*
comparison: "by the standard of"	for	Eres muy grande **para** tu edad. *You're very big for your age.* **Para** médico, sabe poca medicina. *For a doctor, he knows very little medicine.*

The meanings of **para** cluster about the notions of direction, destination, and goal. (Review Unit 9, Section 41, and Unit 12, Section 60.)

› TRANSLATION DRILL

A. 1. TEACHER: I think they're coming toward the door.
STUDENT: **Creo que vienen para la puerta.**
2. I think they're coming toward the park.
3. I think they're coming toward the garden.

B. 1. Where are you headed? For the balcony?
2. Where are you headed? For the palace?
3. Where are you headed? For the corner?

C. 1. It's already going on one o'clock.
2. It's already going on eleven o'clock.
3. It's already going on noon.

D. 1. He's studying to be a doctor.
2. He's studying to be a lawyer.
3. He's studying to be a technician.

E. 1. He works for another group.
2. He plays for another team.
3. He writes for another newspaper.

F. 1. Is there a letter for me?
2. Is there a pretext for a strike?
3. Are there medals for the cadets?

G. 1. Two hours for lunch is enough.
2. Four hours for the dance is enough.
3. Three days for the trip is too much.

H. 1. I have until tomorrow to pay the fine.
2. We came to the plaza to hear the presidential address.
3. To see the fireworks you have to come out on the balcony.

I. 1. Come here so I can give you something.
2. Be quiet so I can bring you something.
3. Wait so I can wrap them for you.

J. 1. When do you want them for? For tomorrow?
2. I'll be there by two.
3. We'll be there by Monday.

K. 1. She's very tall for her age.
2. He's very young for this job.
3. For a professor he doesn't know much.

L. 1. He's too (very) nervous to be [a] doctor.
2. He's too old to be [a] manager.
3. She is too pretty to be [a] nurse.

› DISCUSSION

One of the principal uses of **para,** that of "purpose" with an infinitive, has already been studied in Unit 9, Section 41. We have also seen **a** used with infinitives after verbs of motion (Unit 8, Section 36). With these verbs, **a** is usually preferred: **Voy a ver** means *I'll go see* or *I'll go and see;* **Voy para ver** means *I'll go in order to see.*

The meanings of **para** are all related to a single fundamental meaning: that of aim or "towardness." **Para** may have as its object both things and actions. Sometimes, as in the example **Para café bueno no hay como este lugar,** the object is a thing with an action implied: *in order to get good coffee, if your aim is good coffee.*

For the meanings *to study* (*prepare oneself,* etc.) *to be a doctor* (*lawyer, technician,* etc.), Spanish may use or omit the verb **ser: Estudia para** (ser) **médico** (**abogado, técnico,** etc.) *He's studying to be a doctor* (*lawyer, technician,* etc.). (See Unit 18, Cultural Note 4.)

134 *Para* versus *por*

EXAMPLES

1. Vamos **para** el parque. *Let's head for the park.*
   Vamos **por** el parque. *Let's go through the park.*
2. Voy allá **para** dos semanas de vacaciones. *I'm going there for two weeks' vacation* (*to have fun*).
   Voy allá **por** dos semanas. *I'm going there for two weeks* (*to spend the allotted time*).
3. Se terminará **para** 1976. *It will be finished by 1976.*
   Se terminará **por** 1976. *It will be finished around 1976.*
4. Me dio el dinero **para** los muebles. *She gave me the money for the furniture* (to buy it with).
   Me dio el dinero **por** los muebles. *She gave me the money for the furniture* (I sold it to her).
5. Hice todo ese trabajo **para** esto. *I did all that work for this* (*result*).
   Hice todo ese trabajo **por** esto. *I did all that work for this* (*recompense*).
6. Lo hicimos **para** Juan. *We made* (*or did*) *it for Juan* (directed our efforts toward him).
   Lo hicimos **por** Juan. *We did it for Juan* (for his sake, from a sense of duty toward him, because of him).
7. Es grande **para** su edad. *He's big for his age.*
   Es grande **por** su edad. *He's big because of his age.*
8. Habla **para** tu papá. *Speak for your daddy* (perform for him).
   Habla **por** tu papá. *Speak for your Dad* (because you owe it to him, or on his behalf, or in his place).
9. Entré con cuidado **para** no despertarlos. *I came in carefully in order not to wake them* (to carry out this purpose).
   Entré con cuidado **por** no despertarlos. *I came in carefully in order not to wake them* (it was a duty, my precautions were in exchange for not waking them).

Por penetrates or pushes; the medium is in contact with the actor.

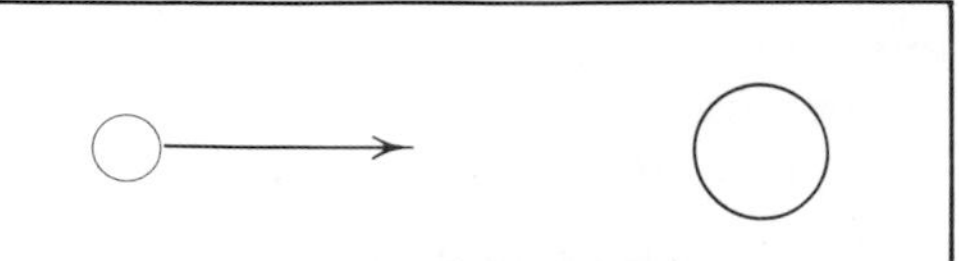

Para aims; the goal is separated from the actor.

› TRANSLATION DRILL

1. Let's head for the avenue.
   Let's go along the avenue.
2. We're headed for Panama.
   We're going by way of Panama.
3. I'm leaving for the garden.
   I'm leaving through the garden.
4. We're going to Europe for (to spend) our vacation.
   We're going to Europe on account of our vacation.
5. He's headed for the café.
   He's going for the coffee.

6. Head for the car.
Go for the car.
7. I made it for my mother.
I did it because of my mother.
8. She gave me the money for (to buy) the eggs.
She gave me the money for (in exchange for) the eggs.
9. He gave me a radio for (to install in) the car.
He gave me a radio for (in exchange for) the car.
10. I worked for the manager.
I worked in the manager's place.
11. I worked for Diego (he paid me).
I worked for Diego (took his place).
12. I wrote a letter for (to be sent to) the boss.
I wrote a letter for (in place of) the boss.
13. Speak for your grandpa (show him you can).
Speak for your grandpa (in his place).
14. He's strong for his age.
He's strong because of his age.
15. That's the purpose you bought it for (for that you bought it), eh?
That's why you bought it, eh?
16. I bought these flowers for Marta (to keep).
I bought these flowers for Marta (she wasn't able to buy them herself).
17. I bought the pistol for my uncle (it was a gift).
I bought the pistol because of my uncle (he influenced me).

› DISCUSSION

The root of the contrast between **por** and **para** lies in the way they are used for relationships in space and time. (This is fundamental to all prepositions: *on, at, under, by, from, with,* etc., have as their primary meanings some kind of positional relationship between the things they connect.) In **Fuimos por el parque** *We went through the park,* the actor is in direct contact with the thing—he must be in order to penetrate it. In **Fuimos para el parque** *We headed for the park,* the actor is separated from the park and only pointed in its direction. The extended, or what we might call figurative, meanings of **por** and **para** carry out this motif of "contact" versus "aim-with-separation":

1. "Proxy" and "exchange"—one thing displaces another as if pushing it out of its place—calls for **por.** "Correspondence," two things occupying analogous places, is a further extension of this.

2. "Cause"—something stimulates or is otherwise responsible for an action—calls for **por.** We usually think of causation in terms of one thing exerting pressure on another, hence pushing, hence contact. Even when **por** is used with an infinitive as a kind of purpose it is as if the thing aimed at had somehow got around behind the actor and given him a push. In a sense this is also a sort of "exchange": **Vamos a la plaza por darles gusto a los niños** might be thought of as "We'll make the effort (bothering to go there) in exchange for the pleasure (that it will give the children)," just like *I'll give a dollar for the lot,* trading *A* for *B.* On this account, **por** when used for purpose often gives the impression of being grudging: the actor does not look ahead toward doing it, as with **para,** but responds to a push.

3. "Goal," "recipient," and "purpose" are all manifestations of the towardness of **para.** Where action is concerned the actor, instead of being pushed, makes his way of his own volition with a conscious aim and choice. In **Llamó la señora Méndez para un asunto de una rifa,** Mrs. Méndez was busily directing her efforts toward the goal of that raffle. Had the remark been **Llamó la señora Méndez por un asunto de una rifa,** we would have understood that she was perhaps acting just from a sense of duty; something impelled her. In **La criada está arreglando los muebles para los invitados** *The maid is arranging the furniture for the guests,* we see the maid creating a new arrangement for the benefit of the people who are coming; in **La criada está arreglando los muebles por los invitados** she is doing it because of the guests, that is, because of the obligation they impose, and she is quite likely grumbling at the job. In **Me regalaron un radio para mi cumpleaños** *They gave me a radio for my birthday,* the gift was designed for or aimed at the birthday; the same wording but with **por mi cumpleaños** would suggest that the birthday was one of those occasions on which giving a gift is expected, i.e., *because of my birthday.*

135 Equivalents of English nouns modifying nouns

	NOUN WITH NO PARTICULAR REFERENT					NOUN WITH NO MODIFIER
1. a	fur	coat	**un**	**abrigo**		**pieles**
2. the	gold	medal	**la**	**medalla**		**oro**
3. a	dining room	table	**una**	**mesa**		**comedor**
4. high	government	officials	**altos**	**funcionarios**		**gobierno**
5. a	student	demonstration	**una**	**manifestación**	**de**	**estudiantes**
6. a	bank	employee	**un**	**empleado**		**banco**
7. the	petroleum	refinery	**la**	**refinería**		**petróleo**
8. the	marathon	race	**la**	**carrera**		**maratón**
9. some	business	men	**algunos**	**hombres**		**negocios**

When English identifies a noun by modifying it with another noun (naming what it is made of or by, or naming something with which it is regularly associated), Spanish uses a **de** phrase with the equivalent noun. In the above examples the modifying noun does not refer to any particular thing or things, and accordingly Spanish uses no article or other modifier with it. (See Unit 15, Section 87.)

NOUN WITH A PARTICULAR REFERENT				NOUN WITH A PARTICULARIZING MODIFIER
her neighborhood	church	**la capilla**		**su barrio**
the living-room	table	**la mesa**	**de**	**la sala**
our office	door	**la puerta**		**nuestra oficina**

When the modifying noun does refer to a particular thing or things, the appropriate adjective (normally article, demonstrative, or possessive) is used with it. As a rule an article also appears with the modified noun.

› ITEM SUBSTITUTION DRILL

A. 1. Compré un *traje* de lana.
(vestido, corbata, camisa)
2. Tiene una *medalla* de oro.
(llave, pluma)
3. Hubo una huelga de *barberos.*
(médicos, profesores)

B. 1. El es el *presidente* de un banco.
(gerente, jefe)
2. ¿Dónde está el *gerente* de la oficina?
(secretaria, jefe, empleada)
3. Es la *lista* de la clase.
(número, reunión)
4. ¿Sabes el número de la *casa?*
(cuarto, calle, coche)
5. Ahí viene el *médico* de la escuela.
(bus, cocinero, presidente)
6. ¿Dónde está el *parque* de la ciudad?
(banco, policía)
7. Sacuda los muebles del *comedor.*
(sala, clase, oficina)

› TRANSLATION DRILL

A. 1. Have you seen the football team?
¿Ha visto el equipo de fútbol?
2. Have you seen the chemistry exam?
3. Have you seen the algebra problem?
4. He's a bank employee.
5. He's a bank manager.

B. 1. It's a student group.
Es un grupo de estudiantes.
2. It's a student parade.
3. It's a student meeting.

C. 1. It's a dining room table.
Es una mesa de comedor.
2. It's a car key.
3. They are government officials.

D. 1. This is the pocket watch that I lost.
Este es el reloj de bolsillo que perdí.
2. This is the theater ticket that I found.
3. This is the country house that I bought.

E. 1. There's the car (car's) tire.
Ahí está la llanta del auto.
2. There's the bus schedule.
3. There's the dining room door.
4. There are my car keys.
5. There's our group leader.

› DISCUSSION

With rare exceptions Spanish does not modify nouns directly by nouns. It has a limited number of adjectives that serve the same purpose, for example **universitario** in **los estudiantes universitarios** *university students.* But for the most part the Spanish equivalent of an English noun that modifies another noun is a phrase with **de.** This device is familiar enough in English too, of course: *medal of gold = gold medal.*

The problem is how to manipulate the number (singular or plural) of the modifying noun and any adjective that may be present. As a rule the English parallel with *of* gives a clue. Thus for *student demonstration* we get *demonstration of students,* since obviously more than one are involved, and the Spanish equivalent is **manifestación de estudiantes.** Similarly *our office door* becomes *the door of our office* with the Spanish equivalent **la puerta de nuestra oficina.** *An aspirin package* would probably be **un paquete de aspirinas,** since presumably it contains aspirin, plural; *an aspirin tablet* would be **una pastilla de aspirina,** with aspirin now a substance, hence singular.

The office telephone, however, might refer to either of two things: a particular model for offices (perhaps with special attachments that distinguish it from other models) or the telephone in a particular office—i.e., *the telephone of* **the** *office*—whether or not it is different from any other model. The first is equivalent to **el teléfono de oficina,** the second to **el teléfono de la oficina.** In *Did they bring the dining room table that I bought?* **¿Trajeron la mesa de comedor que compré?** the speaker refers to a dining room table in contrast to a library table or a work table; in *Dust the dining room table* **Sacuda la mesa del comedor,** the reference is to the table in THE dining room. Compare the phrase **Este vestido de la señora y este traje del señor** *This lady's dress and this man's suit* in the dialog in Unit 12: the reference is to the dress belonging to THE lady and the suit belonging to THE man of the house; *a lady's dress* not related to a particular possessor would be **un vestido de señora.** *The car tires* for sale at the automotive-supply house are **las llantas de auto;** all we need **de auto** for is to distinguish the tires from truck tires—they are not associated with any particular car; but *the car tires need replacing* calls for **las llantas del auto** if the phrase means the tires of THE car that belongs to me or is otherwise particularized. *A bank president* is **un presidente de banco** if we think of an official who is typical of banks rather than universities or business firms; it is **el presidente de un banco** if *bank* is in any way particularized (e.g., in *It would be a good idea for us to have a bank president on our committee* if the speaker is thinking of the prestige of the bank rather than of the traits of the man).

Note the difference between *the Spanish class* **la clase de español,** where *Spanish* refers to the *Spanish language* and is a noun, and *the Spanish class* **la clase española,** where *Spanish* is an adjective and the meaning is perhaps "a class in Spain, with students who are Spaniards" but in which the course studied might be mathematics or engineering.

Cali, Colombia: Festival

136 Infinitive phrases and noun clauses as modifiers

EXAMPLES

A. 1. Tenga la bondad **de sentarse.**
2. Tenga cuidado **de no romper** nada.
3. Es la costumbre que han tenido **de llegar** siempre entre ocho y media y nueve menos cuarto. (*It's the habit they've had of always arriving between 8:30 and 8:45.*)
4. Otra cosa que tengo ganas **de ver.**
5. Dio la orden **de disparar.** *He gave the order to shoot.*
6. Es hora **de salir.** *It's time to leave.*

B. 1. Estas materias son imposibles **de estudiar.** *These subjects are impossible to study.*
2. Sus razones son difíciles (fáciles) **de comprender.** *Your reasons are hard (easy) to understand.*
3. Esas cosas son buenas **de comer.** *Those things are good to eat.*

C. 1. ¿Quién fue el primero **en mencionarlo?** *Who was the first to mention it?*
2. Él es siempre el último **en decidirse.** *He's always the last to make up his mind.*
3. No quiero ser el único **en atacarlo.** *I don't want to be the only one to attack him.*
4. Ese muchacho es muy rápido **en contestar.** *That boy is very quick to answer.*

NOUN	INFINITIVE PHRASE
the order **la orden**	to shoot **de disparar**

Where English has an infinitive phrase modifying a noun, Spanish uses a phrase with **de.**

	IMPLIED OBJECT OF INFINITIVE		ADJECTIVE	INFINITIVE PHRASE TAKING IMPLIED OBJECT
It's a **Es un**	job **trabajo**		difficult **difícil**	to finish. **de terminar.**
	He **(El)**	is **es**	easy **fácil**	to convince. **de convencer.**
Those **Esas**	things **cosas**	are **son**	good **buenas**	to eat. **de comer.**

When a noun or pronoun is modified by an adjective which in turn is modified by an infinitive phrase taking the noun as its implied object, the preposition **de** is used in the infinitive phrase. In *a hard job to finish* (*a job difficult to finish*), *job* is the implied object of *finish.*

	IMPLIED SUBJECT OF INFINITIVE		ADJECTIVE	INFINITIVE PHRASE TAKING IMPLIED SUBJECT
That **Ese**	boy **muchacho**	is very **es muy**	quick **rápido**	to answer. **en contestar.**
	You **Tú**	are always the **eres siempre el**	last **último**	to make up your mind. **en decidirte.**

If instead the noun or pronoun is the implied SUBJECT of the infinitive (other conditions remaining the same), the preposition of the infinitive phrase is **en.** In *He is quick to answer* we imply that he answers.

› TRANSLATION DRILL

A. 1. TEACHER: Please come in.
   STUDENT: **Tenga la bondad de pasar.**
2. Please wait a minute.
3. Please let us know.

B. 1. Be careful not to break anything.
2. Be careful not to lose anything.
3. Be careful not to touch anything.

C. 1. I don't like the custom of arriving late.
2. I don't like the custom of starting early.
3. I don't like the custom of giving condolences.

D. 1. We're eager to arrive at a decision soon.
2. I'm eager to consult them about the change.
3. She's eager to give us a description of the robber.

E. 1. He gave the order to shoot.
2. He gave the order to go to bed.
3. They gave the order to follow the cadets.

F. 1. It's time to go to the dance.
2. It's time to look for the cat.
3. It's time to eat.

G. 1. This argument is impossible to understand.
Este pleito es imposible de entender.
2. These problems are impossible to understand.
3. This problem was impossible to arrange.

H. 1. The letter was hard to write.
2. The references were easy to get.
3. The address was easy to find.

I. 1. It's a good book to read.
Es un libro bueno de leer.
2. It's a bad thing to do.
3. It's a sad thing to say.

J. 1. He was the first to leave.
El fue el primero en salir.
2. He was the first to take his shirt off.
3. She was the first to get nervous.

K. 1. He was the only one to finish.
2. She was the only one to remain calm.
3. He was the only one to get soaked.

L. 1. She's crazy to say those things.
Ella es loca en decir esas cosas.
2. She's nice to invite us.
3. She's quick to understand.

EXAMPLES

A. 1. Recibí la noticia **de** que habías salido. *I received the news that you had left (gone away).*
2. Ella nunca creyó la mentira **de** que hablabas contra mí. *She never believed the lie that you were talking against me.*
3. Respetaron la orden **de** que todo el mundo se callara. *They respected the order that everyone should keep quiet.*
4. No merecen nada por la casualidad **de** que fueron los primeros en llegar. *They don't deserve anything for the accident that they were the first to arrive.*
5. Es hora **de** que se vayan. *It's time for them to go.*
6. Tenga la seguridad **de** que todos eran documentos falsificados. *Have the assurance that all were forged documents.*

B. 1. Recibí la noticia que habías dejado. *I received the news that (which) you had left.*
2. Ella nunca creyó la mentira que decías contra mí. *She never believed the lie that (which) you were telling against me.*
3. Respetaron la orden que les dimos. *They respected the order that (which) we gave them.*

NOUN	NOUN CLAUSE ATTACHED TO THE NOUN		
the news		that	you had left (gone)
la noticia	**de**	**que**	**habías salido**

NOUN	ADJECTIVE CLAUSE ATTACHED TO THE NOUN		
the news		(that) (which)	you had left (left behind)
la noticia		**que**	**habías dejado**

When English has a noun clause attached to a noun Spanish puts **de** before its corresponding noun clause. Noun clauses may be distinguished from adjective clauses in English by the word *that,* which normally begins the noun clause but in an adjective clause may be changed to *which* or dropped.

TRANSFORMATION DRILL

A. 1. TEACHER: Dijo una mentira: que habías hablado contra mí.
STUDENT: **Dijo la mentira de que habías hablado contra mí.**
2. Dijeron una mentira: que yo me había sacado el gordo de la lotería.
3. Recibí una noticia: que habías salido.
4. Recibí una noticia: que se había muerto don Roberto.
5. Me dieron una noticia: que te habías casado.
6. Respetaron la orden: que todo el mundo saliera.
7. Respetaron la orden: que no preguntaran por qué.
8. No creí esa mentira: que habías insultado al policía.
9. No creí esa mentira: que habías ido al entierro.

B. 1. Tengo la seguridad. Todos eran documentos falsificados.
Tengo la seguridad de que todos eran documentos falsificados.
2. Tengo la seguridad. Todos son estudiantes sinceros.
3. Tengo la seguridad. Es una secretaria fantástica.
4. Tengo la seguridad. Han aprendido mucho.
5. Tengo la seguridad. Les va a gustar mi país.

C. 1. Tú dejaste un recado. Yo lo recibí.
Recibí el recado que tú habías dejado.
2. Lavaste una camisa. Yo me la puse.
3. Compraste el libro. Yo lo leí.
4. Usted pidió una revista. Yo la mandé.
5. Escribió una carta. Yo la leí.
6. Abrió las puertas. Yo las cerré.

DISCUSSION

In the previous section we noted that Spanish is not free to use nouns to modify other nouns. The same is true of infinitives, which are nouns in function (see Unit 8, Section 36), and noun clauses: Spanish turns them into prepositional phrases, usually with **de** or **en,** to make them modifiers. English sometimes does the same, using *-ing* instead of an infinitive: *my hope to be rewarded* is like *my hope of being rewarded.* Note the parallel use of **de** in all three of the following: **La noticia de su salida** *The news of their departure,* **La noticia de haber salido ellos** *The news of their having left,* **La noticia de que habían salido** *The news that they had left.*

When the infinitive phrase modifies an adjective, there are two different treatments. If the noun or pronoun modified by the adjective is itself the implied object of the infinitive, the preposition **de** is used: *That's hard to understand* **Eso es difícil de comprender.** If it is the implied subject of the infinitive, **en** is used: *He was the first to speak* **Fue el primero en hablar.** The adjectives most commonly met in the first group are **posible, imposible, fácil,** and **difícil.** The most common ones in the second group are **único** and adjectives of order: **primero, segundo, tercero . . .** and **último.**

Note the use of indicative and subjunctive in the noun clauses of the illustrative sentences: **la noticia de que habías salido** conveys information, while **Es hora de que se vayan** brings an influence to bear. (See Unit 18, Section 101.)

137 Masculine form referring to both sexes

EXAMPLES
1. Buenos días, **señores.**
2. Tengo muchos **parientes** en el extranjero.
3. Tienen muy buenos **atletas.**
4. Los **bailarines** están formando un semicírculo.
5. No conozco a sus **padres.** *I don't know his father and mother.*

MIXED GROUP	MASCULINE
Mr. and Mrs. Castro	**los señores Castro**
my brothers and sisters	**mis hermanos**
the father and mother the parents	**los padres**
the (men and women) athletes	**los atletas**

Where individuals of both sexes are combined in a group that can be referred to by a single name, Spanish uses the masculine plural of that name. (See Unit 2, Section 2.)

PATTERNED RESPONSE DRILL

1. ¿Usted tiene dos hermanos y tres hermanas?
   Sí, tengo cinco hermanos en total.
2. ¿Usted tiene tres tías y un tío?
3. ¿Usted tiene un primo y ocho primas?
4. ¿Usted tiene nueve sobrinas y cuatro sobrinos?
5. ¿Usted tiene una hija y dos hijos?

TRANSLATION DRILL

A. 1. Good morning, ladies and gentlemen.
   2. Good morning, boys and girls.
   3. Good afternoon, friends.
   4. Good-by, fellows (companions).
   5. Good morning, cousins.

B. 1. How many brothers and sisters do you have?
   ¿Cuántos hermanos tiene usted?
   2. How many sons and daughters do you have?
   3. How many uncles and aunts do you have?
   4. How many nieces and nephews do you have?
   5. How many friends do you have?

DISCUSSION

The use of masculine plural to refer to both sexes is characteristic of Spanish, even in pairs or groups like **los reyes** *the king and queen,* where a single term referring to both male and female would seem odd in English. When it is necessary to separate the sexes Spanish can use the masculine with exclusively male reference, as in the following: **—Yo tengo nueve *hermanos*. —¿Tú tienes nueve *hermanos*? —Sí, cinco *hermanos* y cuatro *hermanas*.**

138 *¿Cuál?* and *¿qué?* for *what?*

EXAMPLES 1. **¿Cuál** es la llave de la casa? *Which is the house key?*
2. —**¿Qué** es su hermano? *What is your brother?*
—Es abogado. *He's a lawyer.*

¿Cuál	**es el día del examen?** *What is the day of the exam?* answer: *Monday.* **es el centro de Madrid?** *What is the center of Madrid?* answer: *The Puerta del Sol.* **es su plan?** *What is your plan?* answer: *To leave early.*

¿Cuáles	**son los días del examen?** *What are the days of the exam?* answer: *Monday, Tuesday, and Wednesday.* **son los centros de Madrid y de México?** *What are the centers of Madrid and Mexico City?* answer: *The Puerta del Sol and the Zócalo.* **son sus planes?** *What are your plans?* answer: *To leave early and take our lunch.*

English *what is* (*are, was,* etc.)? is equivalent to **¿cuál es (cuáles son, cuál fue,** etc.)? when the answer called for is the individual thing or things that fit a definition.

¿Qué	**es un tango?** *What is a tango?* answer: *It's an Argentinean dance* (it belongs to this class of things). **son esas cosas?** *What are those things?* answer: *They're insects* (they belong to this class of things).

English *what is* (*are, was,* etc.)? is equivalent to **¿qué es (son, fue,** etc.)? when the answer called for is the definition (classifying word or words) that fits an individual thing or things.

TRANSLATION DRILL

A. 1. TEACHER: What's your name?
STUDENT: **¿Cuál es su nombre?**
2. What's your age?
3. What's your address?
4. What's your job?
5. What's your telephone number?

B. 1. What's the date?
2. What's the reason?
3. What's the question?
4. What's the problem?
5. What's the remedy?
6. What's the system?
7. What's the message?
8. What's the color?
9. What's the subject?
10. What's the situation?
11. What's the truth?

C. 1. What's her idea?
2. What's her political party?
3. What's her religion?
4. What's her excuse?

D. 1. What's a *contradanza?*
¿Qué es una contradanza?
2. What's a *zapateado?*
3. What's a cadet?
4. What's an inauguration?
5. What's a certificate?
6. What's a demonstration?
7. What's a strike?
8. What's a siesta?

E. 1. What is agriculture?
   ¿Qué es la agricultura?
2. What is security?
3. What is illness?
4. What is philosophy?
5. What is Lent?
6. What is football?
7. What is luck?
8. What is truth?

F. 1. What are elections?
   ¿Qué son elecciones?
2. What are streamers?
3. What are tools?
4. What are embassies?

G. 1. What *is* the lottery?
2. What *is* the marathon?
3. What *is* the package?

› DISCUSSION

The usual equivalent of *what?* is **¿qué?** (see Unit 3, Section 9), but in the combinations *what is? what are?* etc., with a form of **ser,** it may be **¿qué?** or **¿cuál, -es?** according to meaning:

1. If we need to know *the thing,* to have it selected for us, the equivalent is **¿cuál, -es?**
2. If we need to know something *about* the thing, the equivalent is **¿qué?**

139 *¿De quién, -es?* for *whose?*

EXAMPLES

1. ¿De parte **de quién,** para decirle?
2. **¿De quiénes** son estos billetes? *Whose tickets are these?*
3. **¿De quién** es el paraguas que llevas? *Whose umbrella are you carrying? (Whose is the umbrella you're carrying?)*
4. **¿De quién** fue el dinero con que lo compraste? *Whose money did you buy it with? (Whose was the money with which you bought it?)*

	FORM OF **ser**	THING POSSESSED
De quién, -es	**son** **es** **fue**	**estos billetes?** **el paraguas que llevas?** **el dinero con que lo compraste?**

¿De quién, -es? is normally followed by a form of **ser,** with the other elements of the sentence arranged accordingly.

› TRANSLATION DRILL

A. 1. TEACHER: Whose is that coat?
   STUDENT: **¿De quién es ese abrigo?**
2. Whose is that book?
3. Whose is that cup?
4. Whose is that package?

B. 1. Whose are those toys?
   ¿De quién son esos juguetes?
2. Whose are those shoes?
3. Whose are those ties?
4. Whose are those aspirins?
5. Whose are those tickets?

C. 1. Whose coat is that?
   ¿De quién es ese abrigo?
2. Whose fruit is that?
3. Whose lemonade is that?
4. Whose record player is that?
5. Whose money is that?
6. Whose tomb is that?

D. 1. Whose idea was that?
2. Whose umbrella was that?
3. Whose ticket was that?
4. Whose schedule was that?
5. Whose message was that?

E. 1. Whose letters are you answering?
2. Whose keys did you lose?
3. Whose tools are they doing it with?
4. Whose office are you working in?
5. Whose speech are they talking about?

› DISCUSSION

English *whose?* can precede a noun: *whose hat? whose friends?* Spanish **¿de quién, -es?** has the same limitations as English *of whom?* It calls for a form of **ser** to follow it and an arrangement of the other elements to fit. This may mean the addition of a relative word such as **que** and perhaps also the moving of a preposition: *Whose house do you live in? = Of whom is the house in which you live?* **¿De quién (de quiénes) es la casa en que vives?**

› GUIDED CONVERSATION

R. *Rosalba* M. *Mariana* S. *Subteniente*

R. ¡Qué lindo está el baile!
M. Sí. Y Rosalba, mira a ese subteniente tan ______________
R. Es hijo del Ministro de Obras[1] Públicas, si no me equivoco.
M. Y ahora lo veo ______________
R. Sí. Hagámonos las disimuladas.

* * *

S. Ya empiezan los bailes típicos. ¿Quieres asomarte al balcón?
R. Bueno, vamos y ______________
S. ¿Te alegras de haber venido a la fiesta?
R. ¡Que si me ______________
S. Ni yo tampoco. Cuando te vi en la calle mañana, yo dije a mi amigo que...
R. ¡Sh...! ¡El himno nacional! ______________

› TENSE SUBSTITUTION REVIEW DRILL

Sequence of tenses: review of imperfect indicative and imperfect subjunctive. INSTRUCTIONS: Repeat the following sentences just as you hear them. Then repeat them again, substituting the preterit for the present of **decir.**

A. 1. TEACHER: Me dice que es Juan. *Repita.*
STUDENT: **Me dice que es Juan.**
TEACHER: *Cambie.*
STUDENT: **Me dijo que era Juan.**
2. Me dice que es perezoso.
3. Me dice que hay algunos beneficios.
4. Me dice que tiene una cicatriz en la cara.
5. Me dice que vive cerca del parque.
6. Me dice que van hacia la ruina.

B. 1. Dicen que está muy bien hecho.
2. Dicen que está de duelo.
3. Dicen que les duele todo el cuerpo.
4. Dicen que odia a todo el mundo.
5. Dicen que está acompañado del embajador.
6. Dicen que es un bailarín famoso.
7. Dicen que es Juan Pérez, alias "El Gato".
8. Dicen que viene hacia esta bocacalle.
9. Dicen que así es, según el médico.

[1] *Works*

C. 1. Me dice que esté aquí mañana.
Me dijo que estuviera aquí mañana.
2. Me dice que termine pronto.
3. Me dice que saque la lengua.
4. Me dice que me quite la camisa.
5. Me dice que me siente en la mesa.
6. Me dice que me vaya a la casa.
7. Me dice que me acueste temprano.
8. Me dice que me tome estas pastillas.
9. Me dice que no me levante mañana.

D. 1. Dicen que empecemos por el principio.
2. Dicen que no hablemos tan fuerte.
3. Dicen que lleguemos más temprano.
4. Dicen que hagamos bien el trabajo.
5. Dicen que comamos en una hora.
6. Dicen que consultemos con el gerente.
7. Dicen que no compremos tanto.
8. Dicen que no olvidemos lo del horario.
9. Dicen que nos callemos.

› CONSTRUCTION SUBSTITUTION REVIEW DRILL

The subjunctive tenses. INSTRUCTIONS: Repeat the following sentences just as you hear them. Then repeat them two more times, adding **quiero que** and **quisiera que** before each sentence.

A. 1. TEACHER: Tú eres amigo de ellas. *Repita.*
STUDENT: **Tú eres amigo de ellas.**
TEACHER: Quiero que tú seas amigo de ellas.
STUDENT: **Quiero que tú seas amigo de ellas.**
TEACHER: Quisiera que tú fueras amigo de ellas.
STUDENT: **Quisiera que tú fueras amigo de ellas.**
2. Son compañeros de escuela de mi hermana.
3. Es el nuevo cónsul americano.
4. Ellas saben español perfectamente.

B. 1. Está bueno el tocadiscos.
2. Ella tiene uno portátil.
3. Usamos el teléfono.
4. Habla con la tía.
5. María Elena regresa dentro de diez minutos.
6. Tú conoces a mamá.

C. 1. Me manda una taza de café.
2. La felicitan por su cumpleaños.
3. Viven cerca del Parque Central.
4. Usted sigue derecho por la Avenida Norte.

D. 1. No se deje dar gato por liebre.
2. A mí nadie me gana.
3. No tarde mucho.
4. Vuelva lo más pronto posible.
5. Déjame en paz.
6. No ponga el radio tan fuerte.

E. 1. Ve a ver quién es.
2. Ten paciencia.
3. Ponte en mi lugar.
4. Le traes el postre.

F. 1. El ve la flecha.
2. Eso no es nada serio.
3. Habla el cuñado de él.

G. 1. No me toque las patillas.
2. Se dice algo de los próximos Juegos Olímpicos.
3. Ellos tienen muy buenos atletas.
4. Nosotros participamos en básquetbol.
5. Allí hay corridas de toros.

H. 1. Eso no es un trabajo muy complicado.
2. Tú eres hombre respetable, profesional.
3. Mañana es la inauguración de la refinería de petróleo.
4. Pensamos en progresar alguna vez.

I. 1. Tenemos examen en filosofía.
2. Sólo hacen preguntas sobre Platón.
3. Es igual que todas las demás materias.
4. Vienen de todos los colegios.

J. 1. Usted se va a trabajar al campo.
2. Me promete parte de la ganancia.
3. Los agricultores no la pasan mal.

K. 1. Nos los mandan a las cinco.
2. Usted misma nos los trae.
3. Estos son los trajes suyos.
4. Espere para envolvérselos.

L. 1. Tenemos hora con él para las once.
2. A todos les duele la cabeza y la garganta.
3. Quítese la corbata y la camisa.
4. Llévese esta receta.
5. Mañana no se bañe.

M. 1. Es un pretexto para discursos contra el presidente.
2. La policía los ataca.
3. Disuelve la manifestación a palos y a tiros.
4. Las elecciones vienen pronto.

N. 1. No matan al embajador.
2. El gobierno se mantiene firme.
3. Llegan a un acuerdo.
4. La policía puede protegerlos.

O. 1. Llama la señora Méndez.
2. Por fin llega el correo.
3. Déjeme ver esas cuentas.
4. Se casa con Lorenzo, su novio de años.
5. Mi mujer va siempre y reza por los dos.

P. 1. Pásame la carne.
2. Las muchachas no salen solas de noche.
3. Tienen que llevar chaperón a todas partes.
4. No toquemos ese tema.

Q. 1. Vargas Campo es el hombre del día.
2. Ustedes dos se ponen de acuerdo.
3. Sigan hablando de eso.

R. 1. El señor Suárez llega a la oficina.
2. Deja el coche.
3. Vuelve en taxi.
4. Vamos a la Comisión de Cambios.

S. 1. El señor Delgado les habla sobre la puntualidad.
2. Hábleles directamente.
3. Todo el mundo es puntual.
4. Consultamos con los empleados sobre el horario.
5. Los empleados se oponen.

T. 1. Se saca el gordo de la lotería.
2. Se los compra todos.
3. A cualquiera le pasa lo mismo.
4. Jamás jugamos a la lotería.
5. Los niños tienen de todo.

Mazatlán, Mexico: Fireworks

Yucatán, Mexico: Temple of the Seven Dolls

U. 1. A cada uno le llega el día.
2. Perdóneme por el desorden de la casa.
3. Ahí le damos el pésame.

V. 1. Deja de roncar, Diego.
2. Llama a la policía, Diego.
3. El tiene llave de la casa.
4. Háganos una descripción de él.

W. 1. Empieza a llover.
2. No nos empapamos con esta lluvia.
3. Los bailarines forman un semicírculo.

reading

Un poquito sobre la derivación

PROFESOR: Voy a hablarles hoy sobre la derivación de las palabras. Ya empleamos la palabra *derivación* con el sentido de *origen* o *etimología* de una palabra. Ahora voy a usar la misma palabra, *derivación,* de una manera un poco diferente: es decir, la formación de una palabra nueva por medio de la adición de un sufijo. Ya hemos tenido muchos ejemplos en el libro que estamos estudiando.

Por ejemplo: los diminutivos. Ustedes todos saben que hay en español lo que llamamos sufijos diminutivos, como *-ito, -cito, -illo,* etcétera, que muestran que la idea básica o fundamental de la palabra, es decir la raíz, se nos presenta con una alteración de significado: la de pequeñez. Así es que una *casita* es una casa pequeña; un *perrito* es un perro pequeño; una *maquinilla* es una máquina pequeña, etc. Pero hay otras consideraciones. Veamos otras formas tales como *Paquito, Lupita, Juanita* y *Pedrito.* Aquí no se trata sólo de pequeñez; hay también la noción de juventud. Paquito no sólo es pequeño de estatura; es también un chico. Y una *señorita* no es necesariamente más pequeña que una señora: aun puede ser más grande. Pero por lo general una señorita es más joven que una señora, y casi siempre es soltera. Y al fin hay que añadir que el empleo de un diminutivo lleva muchas veces una noción de cariño, de intimidad: en breve, de varios grados de expresión que reflejan el *sentimiento* del que habla. Si digo que tal o cual cosa es *nuevecita,* no digo meramente que es nueva; yo digo más bien que es muy nueva, o que es de una novedad que apruebo, que me gusta. Me acuerdo de haber leído una comedia en que se describía a dos novios *juntitos en un rinconcito.* Este es un buen ejemplo de la *afectividad* en el discurso. El autor hubiera podido decir *juntos en un rincón*—pero esto podría decirse de dos muebles. El diminutivo *juntitos* sugiere un grado de intimidad personal que faltaría a la forma *juntos.* Y *rinconcito* sugiere un lugar—un lugarcito, ¿eh?—apropiado para dos novios que quieren estar solos.

Para mañana...

mostrar *to show*
raíz *root*
significado *meaning*
perro *dog*
no...de *it isn't only a question of*
juventud *youth*
soltera *unmarried* **añadir** *to add*
cariño *affection*
tal...cosa *this or that*
aprobar *to approve (of)*
rincón *corner*

Picture Credits

Abbreviation: OAS Organization of American States

3 Jim Cron, Monkmeyer
15 Rapho Guillumette
17 Monkmeyer
26 © H. W. Silvester, Rapho Guillumette
33 Carl Frank, Photo Researchers
35 Harbrace
46 Marilu Pease, Monkmeyer
56 Harbrace
61 Dieter Grabitzky, Monkmeyer
62 Harbrace
75 *both:* Harbrace
77 William Graham, Photo Researchers
78 Standard Oil Company
83 Harbrace
89 Harbrace
91 François Vikar, Foto du Monde
97 Paolo Koch, Rapho Guillumette
101 José Bermudez, OAS
105 United Nations
116 José Bermudez, OAS
118 © Sergio Larrain, Magnum
126 George Pickow, Three Lions
131 François Vikar, Foto du Monde
133 OAS
144 Harbrace
147 François Vikar, Foto du Monde
156 Fujihira, Monkmeyer
163 Marilu Pease, Monkmeyer
165 © Dr. Georg Gerster, Rapho Guillumette
172 Monkmeyer
177 Mexican National Tourist Council
182 Braniff International
184 François Vikar, Foto du Monde
201 Jim Cron, Monkmeyer
203 Jason Laure, Rapho Guillumette
209 José Bermudez, OAS
219 United Press International
221 Harbrace
236 Eduardo Comesaña, Pictorial Parade
239 Dieter Grabitzky, Monkmeyer
248 José Bermudez, OAS
253 *left:* Spanish National Tourist Department
right: Puerto Rican Economic Development Administration
255 Mexican Government Tourist Department, OAS
265 Harbrace
272 Jane Latta
275 Harbrace
288 Harbrace
290 François Vikar, Foto du Monde
295 François Vikar, Foto du Monde
308 Eduardo Comesaña, Pictorial Parade
310 Paul Conklin, Monkmeyer
312 Harbrace
322 José Bermudez, OAS
325 François Vikar, Foto du Monde
333 Fujihira, Monkmeyer
338 A. Testoni, Black Star
341 Carl Frank, Photo Researchers
344 Harbrace
355 Harbrace
361 Marilu Pease, Monkmeyer
370 Richard Wilke, Black Star
372 Marilu Pease, Monkmeyer
386 Marilu Pease, Monkmeyer
389 H. W. Silvester, Rapho Guillumette
396 Carl Frank, Photo Researchers
405 Coca-Cola Export Corporation, OAS
406 Cindy Berkow

Appendix: Verbs

Regular Verbs

Simple Tenses

INFINITIVE	**hablar** *to speak*	**comer** *to eat*	**vivir** *to live*
-ndo FORM	hablando	comiendo	viviendo
-do FORM	hablado	comido	vivido
INDICATIVE			
Present	hablo	como	vivo
	hablas	comes	vives
	habla	come	vive
	hablamos	comemos	vivimos
	habláis[1]	coméis[1]	vivís[1]
	hablan	comen	viven
Imperfect	hablaba	comía	vivía
	hablabas	comías	vivías
	hablaba	comía	vivía
	hablábamos	comíamos	vivíamos
	hablabais	comíais	vivíais
	hablaban	comían	vivían
Preterit	hablé	comí	viví
	hablaste	comiste	viviste
	habló	comió	vivió
	hablamos	comimos	vivimos
	hablasteis	comisteis	vivisteis
	hablaron	comieron	vivieron
Future	hablaré	comeré	viviré
	hablarás	comerás	vivirás
	hablará	comerá	vivirá
	hablaremos	comeremos	viviremos
	hablaréis	comeréis	viviréis
	hablarán	comerán	vivirán

[1]The **vosotros** form of the verb is included in all conjugations for completeness. See Unit 2, footnote 1.

Conditional	hablaría	comería	viviría
	hablarías	comerías	vivirías
	hablaría	comería	viviría
	hablaríamos	comeríamos	viviríamos
	hablaríais	comeríais	viviríais
	hablarían	comerían	vivirían
DIRECT COMMAND (*familiar affirmative*[2])			
tú *and* **vosotros** *forms*	habla	come	vive
	hablad[3]	comed[3]	vivid[3]
SUBJUNCTIVE			
Present	hable	coma	viva
	hables	comas	vivas
	hable	coma	viva
	hablemos	comamos	vivamos
	habléis	comáis	viváis
	hablen	coman	vivan
Imperfect (**–ra**)[4]	hablara	comiera	viviera
	hablaras	comieras	vivieras
	hablara	comiera	viviera
	habláramos	comiéramos	viviéramos
	hablarais	comierais	vivierais
	hablaran	comieran	vivieran
Imperfect (**–se**)[5]	hablase	comiese	viviese
	hablases	comieses	vivieses
	hablase	comiese	viviese
	hablásemos	comiésemos	viviésemos
	hablaseis	comieseis	vivieseis
	hablasen	comiesen	viviesen

Perfect Forms

INDICATIVE				
Present Perfect	he	hablado	comido	vivido
	has			
	ha			
	hemos			
	habéis			
	han			

[2] For negative direct commands with **tú** and **vosotros,** and for both affirmative and negative direct commands with **usted** and **ustedes,** the corresponding subjunctive verb forms are used.

s the **vosotros** form.

s the imperfect subjunctive form most generally used and the one used exclusively in the dialogs.

s another imperfect subjunctive form, found in the readings. See the discussion in Unit 20, Section 110.

Past Perfect	había habías había habíamos habíais habían	hablado	comido	vivido
Future Perfect	habré habrás habrá habremos habréis habrán	hablado	comido	vivido
Conditional Perfect	habría habrías habría habríamos habríais habrían	hablado	comido	vivido
SUBJUNCTIVE *Present Perfect*	haya hayas haya hayamos hayáis hayan	hablado	comido	vivido
Past Perfect (**-ra**)[6]	hubiera hubieras hubiera hubiéramos hubierais hubieran	hablado	comido	vivido
Past Perfect (**-se**)[7]	hubiese hubieses hubiese hubiésemos hubieseis hubiesen	hablado	comido	vivido

[6] This is the past perfect subjunctive form most commonly used.

[7] This is another past perfect subjunctive form, less commonly used than the one ending in **-ra.** Note that the two past perfect subjunctive forms parallel the two imperfect subjunctive forms.

Stem-Changing Verbs[8]

INFINITIVE	**sentar**[9] *to seat*	**contar**[10] *to tell, count*	**perder**[11] *to lose*
-ndo FORM	sentando	contando	perdiendo
INDICATIVE *Present*	**siento** **sientas** **sienta** sentamos sentáis **sientan**	**cuento** **cuentas** **cuenta** contamos contáis **cuentan**	**pierdo** **pierdes** **pierde** perdemos perdéis **pierden**
Preterit	senté sentaste sentó sentamos sentasteis sentaron	conté contaste contó contamos contasteis contaron	perdí perdiste perdió perdimos perdisteis perdieron
SUBJUNCTIVE *Present*	**siente** **sientes** **siente** sentemos sentéis **sienten**	**cuente** **cuentes** **cuente** contemos contéis **cuenten**	**pierda** **pierdas** **pierda** perdamos perdáis **pierdan**

INFINITIVE	**soler**[12] *to be accustomed to*	**sentir**[13] *to regret, feel*	**morir**[14] *to die*	**pedir**[15] *to ask for, request*
-ndo FORM	soliendo	**sintiendo**	**muriendo**	**pidiendo**
INDICATIVE *Present*	**suelo** **sueles** **suele** solemos soléis **suelen**	**siento** **sientes** **siente** sentimos sentís **sienten**	**muero** **mueres** **muere** morimos morís **mueren**	**pido** **pides** **pide** pedimos pedís **piden**

[8] See Unit 4, Section 17, and the discussion in Unit 17, Section 99. For **morir** and **pedir** see Unit 10, Section 47. The stem-changing verbs presented as formal grammatical topics are in this Appendix. Those forms in which the stem has changed are in **bold** roman type.

[9] Like **sentar** are **cerrar, comenzar, despertar, empezar,** and **pensar.**

[10] Like **contar** are **acordar, acostar, almorzar, apostar, colgar, costar, encontrar, jugar, mostrar, probar, recordar, rogar,** and **volar.**

[11] Like **perder** are **defender, detener,** and **entender.**

[12] Like **soler** are **disolver, doler, envolver, llover,** and **volver.**

sentir are **mentir, preferir,** and **sugerir.**

morir is **dormir.**

pedir are **conseguir, despedir, elegir, perseguir, reir, repetir,** and **seguir.**

Preterit	solí soliste solió solimos solisteis solieron	sentí sentiste **sintió** sentimos sentisteis **sintieron**	morí moriste **murió** morimos moristeis **murieron**	pedí pediste **pidió** pedimos pedisteis **pidieron**
SUBJUNCTIVE *Present*	**suela** **suelas** **suela** solamos soláis **suelan**	**sienta** **sientas** **sienta** **sintamos** **sintáis** **sientan**	**muera** **mueras** **muera** **muramos** **muráis** **mueran**	**pida** **pidas** **pida** **pidamos** **pidáis** **pidan**

Irregular Forms of Verbs

Of the verbs that follow only the tenses having one or more irregular forms are listed. Irregular forms are printed in **bold** roman type, and regular forms are in light roman type.

Present subjunctive forms like **caiga, diga, haga, influya, oiga, ponga, salga, tenga, traiga, valga, vea,** and **venga** are not listed because their formation is in accordance with the rules given. For the same reason imperfect subjunctive forms such as **cayera, diera, dijera, estuviera, fuera, hiciera, hubiera, influyera, produjera, pudiera, pusiera, quisiera, supiera, trajera, tuviera,** and **viniera** are not given.

Verb forms that show only a spelling change (e.g., **caído** and **cayendo**) are given in footnotes in order to separate changes in spelling from changes in sound.

References given in parentheses following the name of a verb form are to the unit and section in which that form of the verb in question is discussed.

andar *to walk, go*	
Preterit (Unit 10 §46)	**anduve, anduviste, anduvo, anduvimos, anduvisteis, anduvieron**
caer[16] *to fall*	
Present Indicative (Unit 5 §22)	**caigo,** caes, cae, caemos, caéis, caen
conocer *to know* (*be acquainted with*)	
Present Indicative (Unit 5 §22)	**conozco,** conoces, conoce, conocemos, conocéis, conocen

[16]Forms that show only a spelling change are **-ndo** (**cayendo**), **-do** (**caído**), and preterit (**caíste, cayó, caímos, caísteis, cayeron**). See Unit 9, Section 43.

dar *to give*

Present Indicative (Unit 5 §22)	**doy,** das, da, damos, dais, dan
Present Subjunctive (Unit 17 §99)	**dé, des, dé, demos, deis, den**
Preterit (Unit 7 §30)	**di, diste, dio, dimos, disteis, dieron**

decir *to say, tell*

-ndo (Unit 9 §43)	**diciendo**
-do (Unit 17 §96)	**dicho**
Present Indicative[17]	**digo, dices, dice,** decimos, decís, **dicen**
Preterit (Unit 10 §46)	**dije, dijiste, dijo, dijimos, dijisteis, dijeron**
Future (Unit 21 §115)	**diré, dirás, dirá, diremos, diréis, dirán**
Conditional (Unit 21 §116)	**diría, dirías, diría, diríamos, diríais, dirían**
Direct Command (**tú**) (Unit 6 §26)	**di**

estar *to be*

Present Indicative (Unit 3 §14)	**estoy, estás, está,** estamos, estáis, **están**
Present Subjunctive (Unit 17 §99)	**esté, estés, esté,** estemos, estéis, **estén**
Preterit (Unit 10 §46)	**estuve, estuviste, estuvo, estuvimos, estuvisteis, estuvieron**

haber *to have*

Present Indicative (Unit 17 §98)	**he, has, ha, hemos,** habéis, **han**
Present Subjunctive (Unit 17 §99)	**haya, hayas, haya, hayamos, hayáis, hayan**
Preterit (Unit 10 §46)	**hube, hubiste, hubo, hubimos, hubisteis, hubieron**
Future (Unit 21 §115)	**habré, habrás, habrá, habremos, habréis, habrán**
Conditional (Unit 21 §116)	**habría, habrías, habría, habríamos, habríais, habrían**

hacer *to do, make*

-do (Unit 17 §96)	**hecho**
Present Indicative (Unit 5 §22)	**hago,** haces, hace, hacemos, hacéis, hacen
Preterit (Unit 10 §46)	**hice, hiciste, hizo, hicimos, hicisteis, hicieron**
Future (Unit 21 §115)	**haré, harás, hará, haremos, haréis, harán**
Conditional (Unit 21 §116)	**haría, harías, haría, haríamos, haríais, harían**
Direct Command (**tú**) (Unit 6 §26)	**haz**

[17]Except for **digo,** the present indicative form of **decir** is of the stem-changing type. See Unit 4, Section 17.

incluir[18] *to include*

Present Indicative (Unit 5 §22)	**incluyo, incluyes, incluye,** incluimos, incluís, **incluyen**

ir[19] *to go*

Present Indicative (Unit 5 §22)	**voy, vas, va, vamos, vais, van**
Present Subjunctive (Unit 17 §99)	**vaya, vayas, vaya, vayamos, vayáis, vayan**
Imperfect Indicative (Unit 11 §53)	**iba, ibas, iba, íbamos, ibais, iban**
Preterit (Unit 10 §46)	**fui, fuiste, fue, fuimos, fuisteis, fueron**
Direct Command (**tú**) (Unit 6 §26)	**ve**

oir[20] *to hear*

Present Indicative (Unit 5 §22)	**oigo, oyes, oye,** oímos, oís, **oyen**

poder *to be able*

-ndo (Unit 9 §43)	**pudiendo**
Present Indicative[21]	**puedo, puedes, puede,** podemos, podéis, **pueden**
Preterit (Unit 10 §46)	**pude, pudiste, pudo, pudimos, pudisteis, pudieron**
Future (Unit 21 §115)	**podré, podrás, podrá, podremos, podréis, podrán**
Conditional (Unit 21 §116)	**podría, podrías, podría, podríamos, podríais, podrían**

poner *to put, place*

-do (Unit 17 §96)	**puesto**
Present Indicative (Unit 5 §22)	**pongo,** pones, pone, ponemos, ponéis, ponen
Preterit (Unit 10 §46)	**puse, pusiste, puso, pusimos, pusisteis, pusieron**
Future (Unit 21 §115)	**pondré, pondrás, pondrá, pondremos, pondréis, pondrán**
Conditional (Unit 21 §116)	**pondría, pondrías, pondría, pondríamos, pondríais, pondrían**
Direct Command (**tú**) (Unit 6 §26)	**pon**

producir *to produce*

Present Indicative (Unit 5 §22)	**produzco,** produces, produce, producimos, producís, producen
Preterit (Unit 10 §46)	**produje, produjiste, produjo, produjimos, produjisteis, produjeron**

[18] Forms that show only a spelling change are **-ndo** (**incluyendo**) and preterit (**incluyó, incluyeron**). Cf. **cayendo, cayó, cayeron** (from **caer**) and **oyendo, oyó, oyeron** (from **oir**). The following is a list of all the verbs with infinitive in **-uir** that have appeared in this book and that are inflected like **incluir: atribuir, constituir, construir, contribuir, distribuir, fluir, huir, influir, rehuir, sustituir.**

[19] The **-ndo** form **yendo** shows only a spelling change.

[20] Forms that show only a spelling change are **-ndo** (**oyendo**), **-do** (**oído**), present indicative (**oímos**), and preterit (**oíste, oyó, oímos, oísteis, oyeron**).

[21] The present of this verb is the stem-changing type. See Unit 4, Section 17.

querer *to wish, want*	
Present Indicative[21]	**quiero, quieres, quiere,** queremos, queréis, **quieren**
Preterit (Unit 10 §46)	**quise, quisiste, quiso, quisimos, quisisteis, quisieron**
Future (Unit 21 §115)	**querré, querrás, querrá, querremos, querréis, querrán**
Conditional (Unit 21 §116)	**querría, querrías, querría, querríamos, querríais, querrían**

saber *to know*	
Present Indicative (Unit 5 §22)	**sé,** sabes, sabe, sabemos, sabéis, saben
Present Subjunctive (Unit 17 §99)	**sepa, sepas, sepa, sepamos, sepáis, sepan**
Preterit (Unit 10 §46)	**supe, supiste, supo, supimos, supisteis, supieron**
Future (Unit 21 §115)	**sabré, sabrás, sabrá, sabremos, sabréis, sabrán**
Conditional (Unit 21 §116)	**sabría, sabrías, sabría, sabríamos, sabríais, sabrían**

salir *to leave, go out*	
Present Indicative (Unit 5 §22)	**salgo,** sales, sale, salimos, salís, salen
Future (Unit 21 §115)	**saldré, saldrás, saldrá, saldremos, saldréis, saldrán**
Conditional (Unit 21 §116)	**saldría, saldrías, saldría, saldríamos, saldríais, saldrían**
Direct Command (**tú**) (Unit 6 §26)	**sal**

ser *to be*	
Present Indicative (Unit 2 §3)	**soy, eres, es, somos, sois, son**
Present Subjunctive (Unit 17 §99)	**sea, seas, sea, seamos, seáis, sean**
Imperfect Indicative (Unit 11 §53)	**era, eras, era, éramos, erais, eran**
Preterit (Unit 10 §46)	**fui, fuiste, fue, fuimos, fuisteis, fueron**
Direct Command (**tú**) (Unit 6 §26)	**sé**

tener *to have*	
Present Indicative[22]	**tengo, tienes, tiene,** tenemos, tenéis, **tienen**
Preterit (Unit 10 §46)	**tuve, tuviste, tuvo, tuvimos, tuvisteis, tuvieron**
Future (Unit 21 §115)	**tendré, tendrás, tendrá, tendremos, tendréis, tendrán**
Conditional (Unit 21 §116)	**tendría, tendrías, tendría, tendríamos, tendríais, tendrían**
Direct Command (**tú**) (Unit 6 §26)	**ten**

traer[23] *to bring*	
Present Indicative (Unit 5 §22)	**traigo,** traes, trae, traemos, traéis, traen
Preterit (Unit 10 §46)	**traje, trajiste, trajo, trajimos, trajisteis, trajeron**

[22] Except for **tengo,** the present indicative form of **tener** is of the stem-changing type. See Unit 4, Section 17.

[23] Forms that show only a spelling change are **-ndo** (**trayendo**) and **-do** (**traído**).

valer *to be worth*

Present Indicative	**valgo,** vales, vale, valemos, valéis, valen
Future (Unit 21 §115)	**valdré, valdrás, valdrá, valdremos, valdréis, valdrán**
Conditional (Unit 21 §116)	**valdría, valdrías, valdría, valdríamos, valdríais, valdrían**

venir *to come*

-ndo (Unit 9 §43)	**viniendo**
Present Indicative[24]	**vengo, vienes, viene,** venimos, venís, **vienen**
Preterit (Unit 10 §46)	**vine, viniste, vino, vinimos, vinisteis, vinieron**
Future (Unit 21 §115)	**vendré, vendrás, vendrá, vendremos, vendréis, vendrán**
Conditional (Unit 21 §116)	**vendría, vendrías, vendría, vendríamos, vendríais, vendrían**
Direct Command (**tú**) (Unit 6 §26)	**ven**

ver[25] *to see*

-do (Unit 17 §96)	**visto**
Present Indicative (Unit 5 §22)	**veo,** ves, ve, vemos, veis, ven
Imperfect Indicative (Unit 11 §53)	**veía, veías, veía, veíamos, veíais, veían**

[24]Except for **vengo,** the present indicative form of **venir** is of the stem-changing type. See Unit 4, Section 17.

[25]Forms that show only a spelling change are preterit (**vi, vio**).

Spanish-English Vocabulary

The vocabulary includes all words except: (1) words appearing only in the pronunciation and writing exercises, (2) adverbs ending in **-mente** when the adjective form is listed, (3) regular **-do** forms used as adjectives when the appropriate meaning is listed under the infinitive, (4) words used only in examples, grammar discussions, or cultural notes, (5) most proper nouns, and (6) most exact cognates.

The words printed in extra-large **bold** type comprise the active vocabulary, that is, the words used in the dialogs and drills. Their definitions are followed by the number of the unit in which they are introduced.

The asterisk (*) indicates words treated in the grammar; see the index for the specific locations. A clue to the kind of irregularity of certain verbs (including the spelling alterations **c ↔ z, c ↔ qu, g → j, gu → gü,** and **i → y**) is given in parenthesis after the entry.

ABBREVIATIONS

abr	abbreviation	*conj*	conjunction	*pl*	plural
adj	adjective	*dim*	diminutive	*prep*	preposition
adv	adverb	*f*	feminine noun	*pron*	pronoun
		inf	infinitive	*sing*	singular
		m	masculine noun	*v*	verb

a

***a** to, at, from, by, on [1]
abajo down, under, downstairs [5]; **hacia —** (turned) down; **para —** downward; **por —** below
abarrote *m* grocery clerk
abierto,-a (*see* **abrir**) open, opened [17]
abogado *m* lawyer [9]
abrigo *m* overcoat, shelter [16]; **— de pieles** fur coat [16]
abril *m* April [10]
abrir to open [4]; **—se mucho** to be opened (wide)
abuela *f* grandmother [2]
abuelita *f dim* granny
abuelo *m* grandfather [2]; *pl* grandparents
aburrido,-a boring [10]
acá here [6]; **hacia —** this way [24]
acabar to finish, complete, end [3]; ***— de** + *inf* to have just . . . , finish . . . *-ing* [3]
accidente *m* accident
acción *f* action
aceptar to accept [10]
acerca de about
acercarse (qu) (a) to approach
aclarar to clear up
acompañar to accompany, join [20]
aconsejar to advise
acontecimiento *m* event [13]
acordarse (ue) (de) to remember [14]
acortar to cut (down), shorten [10]
acostar (ue) to put to bed [14]; **—se** to go to bed [14]; ***estar acostado** to be in bed [23]
acostumbrarse (a) to become accustomed (to)
actividad *f* activity

acto *m* act
actor *m* actor
acuerdo *m* accord [15]; **de —** agreed, in agreement, accordingly [15]; **de — con** according to, by means of; **ponerse de —** to agree [18]
adelante forward; come in [1]
además *adv* besides [11]; **— de** *prep* besides
adentro within, inside [13]
adiós good-bye [1]
adjetivo *m* adjective
administrador *m* administrator, manager [11]
administrativo,-a administrative
admirable admirable [13]
admirar to admire
admitir to admit
***¿Adónde?** Where? [3]
aeropuerto *m* airport
afirmación *f* affirmation
afuera outside [5]
agente *m* agent
ágil agile
agosto *m* August [10]
agotar to exhaust; **—se** to be worn out
agradable pleasant
agricultor *m* farmer [11]
agricultura *f* agriculture
agua *f* water [21]
ah ah, oh [3]
ahí there [3]; **por —** over there
ahora now [4]; **— mismo** right now; **— que** since [19]; **por —** for now [16]
aire *m* air [10]
***al = a + el; — +** *inf* upon + *-ing* [6]
álamo *m* poplar tree [11]
alcanzar (**c**) to attain, reach [5], manage
alegrar to cheer; **—se** (**de**) to be glad (of) [16]
álgebra *f* algebra [10]
***algo** *pron* something, anything [4]; *adv* somewhat [8]
***alguien** someone [4]
***alguno,-a** (**algún**) some, any [3]
alias otherwise, alias [23]
alma *f* spirit, soul, heart [22]
almorzar (**ue, c**) to eat lunch [21]
almuerzo *m* lunch [20]
aló hello [3]
alquiler *m* rent [16]
alto,-a tall, high [9]
alumno *m* student [1]
allá there [3]; **más — del** beyond; **por —** over there
***allí** there [11]
amabilidad *f* kindness
amable *adj* kind [2]
amante *m* lover
amar to love
amargo,-a bitter; **amargamente** bitterly [22]
amarillo,-a yellow [18]
América *f* America; **la — del Norte** North America; **la — del Sur** South America; **la — española** Spanish America; **la — hispánica** Hispanic America; **la — latina** Latin America; **las —s** the Americas
americano,-a American [2]
amigo,-a *m f* friend [2]
amplio,-a large (spacious)
amueblado,-a furnished
anaranjado,-a orange (colored) [18]
anarquismo *m* anarchy [15]
anciano,-a old; *m* old man; **los —s** the old folks
***andar** to go, walk [10]
aniversario *m* anniversary [13]
anoche last night [10]
anteanoche night before last [11]
anteayer day before yesterday [13]
anterior before, prior [6]
antes *adv* before [10]; ***— de** *prep* before, rather than [10]; ***—(de) que** *conj* before [19]
antesala *f* waiting room
anticuado,-a antiquated [9]
antipático,-a disagreeable [20]
anunciar to announce [15]
anuncio *m* announcement, ad
año *m* year [4]; **al** (**por**) **—** yearly, per year [10]
apagar (**gu**) to turn off [5]
apego *m* fondness [22]
apenas scarcely, just [8]
apostar (**ue**) to bet [7]; **te apuesto a** (**que no**) I'll bet (not)
aprender (**a**) to learn (to) [8]
aprobar (**ue**) to approve, pass a course
aprovechar to profit by, make use of; **— para** to be able to [24]
aquel, aquella that; **aquellos,-as** those [12]
aquello that (idea)
***aquí** here [2]; **por —** this way [23]
árabe Arabic; *m* Arabic (language), Arab
árbol *m* tree [11]
argentino,-a Argentinian
aritmética *f* arithmetic
arreglar to arrange, fix [7]
arriba up, upstairs, on top [5]
arroz *m* rice [5]
arte *m f* art [8]
artificial artificial [24]; **fuegos —es** fireworks [24]
artillero *m* artilleryman [24]
asesino *m* assassin, murderer [13]
así so, thus, like that [8]; **— como** just as; **— es que** this is the way that; **— que** thus
asomar to appear; **—se** to look out of (from), go out [24]
aspirina *f* aspirin [6]
astronómico,-a astronomical [9]
asunto *m* affair, matter [16]
atacar (**qu**) to attack [13]
atención *f* attention
atender (**ie**) to care for
atleta *m* athlete [8]
atormentar to tease
atrás back, in (the) back [8]
aumentar to increase
aun, aún even, still
***aunque** although, even though [19]
auto, automóvil *m* car [9]
autobús *m* bus [16]
autómata *m* automaton
autor *m* author
auxilio *m* aid
avanzado,-a advanced
avenida *f* avenue [4]
avisar to inform, advise, tell [24]
aviso *m* warning
¡ay! oh! [3]
ayer yesterday [7]; **— por la mañana** yesterday morning

ayudar to help, assist
azúcar *m* sugar
azul blue [11]

b

¡Bah! Bah! [9]
bailar to dance [24]
bailarín,-ina *adj* dancing; *m f* dancer [24]
baile *m* dance [24]
bajo,-a *adj* short [23], low; *adv and prep* under
balcón *m* balcony [24]
banco *m* bank [6]
banda *f* band [24]
banquero *m* banker
bañar to bathe [14]; **—se** (**de**) to be bathed (by), take a bath
barba *f* beard, chin
barbaridad *f* barbarity [12]; **¡Qué —!** What nonsense! [12], How terrible!
bárbaro,-a barbarous
barbería *f* barbershop
barbero *m* barber [8]
barrer to sweep [5]
barrio *m* neighborhood [16]
básico,-a basic
básquetbol *m* basketball [8]
bastante enough, a lot (of), very, a great deal, fairly [10]
batería *f* battery [9]
beber to drink [21]
belleza *f* beauty [5]; **salón de —** beauty shop [5]
bendito,-a blessed, confounded [7]
beneficio *m* benefit [16]; **a — de** for the benefit of [16]
bien *adv* well, very, good [1]; **está —** all right, OK [1]; **más —** rather [23]; *m* good
billete *m* bill (money), ticket [21]
biología *f* biology [10]
blanco,-a white [18]
boca *f* mouth
bocacalle *f* intersection (of streets) [24]
bocina *f* horn [9]
boda *f* wedding [16]
boliviano,-a *adj* Bolivian; *m* monetary unit of Bolivia
bolsillo *m* pocket [21]
bondad *f* kindness, goodness [14]; **tenga** (**ten**) **la —** (**de**) please [14]
bonito,-a pretty [2]
botín *m* booty [12]
boxeo *m* boxing [8]
brillar to shine
brutal brutal
bruto,-a *adj* crude [7]; *m* brute
***bueno** (**buen**),**-a** good, well [1]; **Buenas noches** Good evening; **Buenas tardes** Good afternoon [2]; **Buenos días** Good morning [1]; **lo —** the good part [8]
bulto *m* bundle [19]
bus *m* bus [18]
buscar (**qu**) to get, look for, look up, meet [19]

c

caballo *m* horse
cabecilla *m* ringleader [15]
cabello *m* hair
cabeza *f* head [6]; **dolor de —** headache [6]
***cada** each, every [8]
cadáver *m* corpse; **el — fue velado** the wake was held
cadete *m* cadet [24]
***caer** to fall [4]; **— bien** to suit; **—se** to fall down [14]; **dejarse —** to drop, fall
café *m* coffee, café, restaurant [4]
cafecito *m dim* cup of coffee [19]
caliente hot [10]
calmar to calm; **—se** to calm down [7]
callar(**se**) to be quiet, hush [23]
calle *f* street [4]
cama *f* bed [12]; **ropa de —** bed linen [12]
***cambiar** (**de**) to change, exchange [2]; **— de tema** to change the subject [18]
cambio *m* change, exchange [15]; **a — de** in exchange for [15]; **en —** on the other hand
camisa *f* shirt [12]
campo *m* field, country, room, land [11]
canalla *m* scoundrel [15]
cansado,-a tired
cantidad *f* quantity, amount, number [9]
capaz capable
capilla *f* chapel [16]
cara *f* face [7]
¡Caramba! My gosh! [16]
carburador *m* carburetor [9]
cárcel *f* prison
cargar (**gu**) to charge, load (down)
cargo *m* charge, responsibility
cariño *m* affection; dear
carne *f* meat [5]
carrera *f* career, race; **— de maratón** marathon race [8]
carro *m* car
carta *f* letter [16], charter
cartera *f* purse, billfold [10]
***casa** *f* house [2]; **a —** home; **— editora** publishing house; **en —** at home [3]
casado,-a married [17]
casar to marry (marry off) [16]; **—se con** to get married to [16]
casi almost [6]
casita *f dim* little house [4]
caso *m* case [9], affair; **en todo —** anyway [9]
castellano,-a *adj and m f* Castilian [10]; *m* Castilian, Spanish (language) [10]
casualidad *f* casualty, chance [21]
cataplum kerplunk, crash [23]
catedrático *m* professor
católico,-a Catholic
catorce fourteen [2]
cazador *m* hunter
cazar (**c**) to hunt
cebolla *m* onion [11]
celebrar to celebrate, observe, hold (a meeting) [4]
cementerio *m* cemetary [13]
centavo *m* cent [7]
central central [4]
cerca *adv* near [4]; **— de** *prep* near [4]
cerdo *m* pig [11]
cero zero [2]
cerrar (**ie**) to close [1]; **—se** to close
certificado *m* certificate, credential [23]
cicatriz *f* scar [23]

cielo *m* sky, heaven [11]
ciencia *f* learning, science, field of study
científico,-a scientific
***ciento** (**cien**) a (one) hundred [6]; **por** — percent
cierto,-a *adj* certain; *adv* certainly [15]
cinco five [2]
cincuenta fifty [3]
cine *m* movie, movies [17]
círculo *m* circle
ciudad *f* city [11]
claro,-a light, clear [18]; **¡Claro!** Of course! [3]; **¡ — que no!** Of course not! **— que sí** of course [4]
clase *f* class [2], kind, kinds
club *m* club [11]
cobarde *m* coward [13]
cobrador *m* bill collector [6]
cocina *f* kitchen, cooking [2]
cocinero,-a *m f* cook
cóctel *m* cocktail (party)
coche *m* car [6]
cochino,-a filthy [20]; *m* pig
codo *m* elbow [16]; **hablar por los —s** to chatter [16]
coger to seize [15]; **— preso** to arrest [15]
colegio *m* school [10]
colgar (**ue, gu**) to hang (up) [23]
colocar (**qu**) to place
color *m* color [4]; **de —es** colored
comedia *f* comedy, play
comedor *m* diner, dining room [3]
comenzar, (**ie, c**) to begin [24]
comer to eat [4]
comida *f* dinner, meal [4]; **de —** for dinner [5]; **hacer una —** to have a dinner (party); **hora de la —** dinner time
comisión *f* commission [19]
***como** like, as, how, about [4]; **no hay —** there's nothing like [9]
***¿Cómo?, ¡Cómo!** What? [1], How?; **— no** of course [1]
compañero,-a *m f* companion, colleague; **— de escuela** (**clase**) classmate [2]
compañía *f* company

competencia *f* competition [8], competence
complacer to please [16]
complicado,-a complicated [9]
***componer** (*like* **poner**) to compose
composición *f* composition
comprar to buy [5]
comprender to understand [21], comprise
compromiso *m* engagement
compuesto,-a *adj* (*see* **componer**) composed; *m* compound
comulgar (**gu**) to go to communion [16]
común, comunes common; **por lo —** usually
***con** with, by [1]; **— tal** (**de**) **que** provided [19]
conceder to allow, grant [14]; **—se** to be bestowed
condecoración *f* decoration, badge, medal [24]
condición *f* condition, position
conducta *f* conduct [23]
conferencia *f* conference, lecture
confortado,-a comforted
conjugación *f* conjugation
conmigo with me [4]
***conocer** (**zc**) to know, be acquainted with, meet [1]; **—se de** to be known to; **dar a —** to make known
conseguir (*like* **seguir**) to get [7], manage, accomplish
consejo *m* advice; council [10]; *pl* advice [18]
conservador,-ra conservative
consideración *f* consideration
considerar to consider [8]
consigo with them, with her, with him, with you, with it
constar to be clear, be on record
cónsul *m* consul [2]
consulta *f* consultation
consultar to consult [20]
contar (**ue**) to tell, count [6], relate; **— con** to enjoy; **¿Qué cuenta?** What does she say? [16]; **¿Qué me cuenta** (**de**) . . . ? How about . . . ? What's the news?
contento,-a happy
contestación *f* answer

contestar to answer [2]
***contigo** with you [7]
***contra** against [7]; **en — de** against [7]
contradanza *f* quadrille, cotillion, contredance [24]
convencer (**z**) to convince [18]
convenir (*like* **venir**) to suit, be proper
conversación *f* conversation [3]
coqueta *f* flirt
corazón *m* heart [22]
corbata *f* necktie [14]
coro *m* chorus
corona *f* crown, funeral wreath [22]
correo *m* mail [16]
correr to run, chase, travel [6]
correspondencia *f* correspondence department (in an office)
corrida *f* course; **— de toros** bullfight [8]
corriente *adj* current, day-by-day; *f* current; **— de aire** draught
cortar to cut (off) [8]
corto,-a short, narrow [8]
cosa *f* thing [4]; **— de** a matter of; **una —** something
costar (**ue**) to cost [9]; **— muy caro** to be very expensive
costumbre *f* custom, way [10]; **como de —** as usual [10]
crecer (*like* **parecer**) to grow [17]; *m* **el —** growing up [17]
***creer** (**y**) to believe [3]; **Ya lo creo** Yes, indeed [11]
criado,-a *m f* servant, maid [5]
crianza *f* breeding, raising
cuadra *f* block [4]
cual: el —, la —, los cuales, las cuales which; **por lo —** therefore
***¿Cuál?** Which?, What? [3]
***cualquier**(**a**) any, some, anyone [10]
***cuando** when [15]
***¿Cuándo?** When? [3]
cuanto,-a all (the); **en — a** as for, as regards [19]; **tantos . . . cuantos** as many . . . as; **unos cuantos** a few
***¿Cuánto,-a?** How much? [3]
cuarenta forty [6]
Cuaresma *f* Lent [16]

cuarto,-a fourth [10]; *m* room [2], a fourth [10]
cuatro four [2]
cuatrocientos,-as four hundred [6]
cubierto,-a (*see* **cubrir**) (**de**) covered (with) [17]; *f* cover (of a book) [19]
cubrir to cover [17]
cuenta *f* account, count, bill [10]; — **corriente** checking account; **darse** — (**de**) to realize [20]; **por su** — on one's (their, his, her, your) own; **tomar en** — to take into account
cuento *m* story
cuero *m* hide, leather [11]
cuerpo *m* body, group, corps [14]
cuestión *f* question [10]
cuidado *m* care [5]; **con** (**mucho**) — (very) carefully [11]; **¡Cuidado!** Be careful!; **no tengas** (**tenga**) — don't worry [5]; **tenga** — (**de**) be careful (to) [5]
cuidar to care for, tend
culpa *f* blame, fault [7]; **tener la** — to be to blame [20]; **todo por** — **de él** it was all his fault [7]
cultivar to cultivate, grow
cumpleaños *m* birthday [4]
cumplir to accomplish, attain, carry out, doe one's duty [16]
cuñado *m* brother-in-law [7]
cuyo,-a whose

ch

chaperón,-ona *m f* chaperon [17]
cheque *m* check [17]
chico *adj* small [2]; *m* boy; *f* girl [3]; **¡Chica!** My dear!
chiquito,-a *dim of* **chico,-a**
churrasco *m* barbecued meat, steak

d

***dar** to give, make [5]; — **exámenes** to take exams; —**la vuelta** to turn around, return; —**se cuenta** (**de**) to realize [20]
***de** of, from, to, as, concerning, by, with [1]
***debajo de** under, below [14]
deber to owe, ought, must [2]; —**se** to be due; *m* duty
decidir(**se**) (**a**) to decide [18]
décimo,-a *adj* tenth [10]; *m* lottery ticket [21]
***decir** to say, tell [3]; —**se** to mean [1]; **digo** I mean; **es** — that is; **querer** — to mean; **se le dice** it is said
dedicar (**qu**) to dedicate, use [18]
defender (**ie**) to defend [15]
***dejar** to let, permit [3], leave [6], put down; — **de** to stop, fail to [15]; — **en paz** to leave alone [6]; —**se caer** to drop, fall
***del** = **de** + **el** [3]
delante de in front of
delegado *m* delegate
delgado,-a slender [23]
demás: los —, **las** — the others, the rest [10]
demasiado too much, too [10]
demostrar (**ue**) to display, show
dentro *adv* within [3]; — **de** *prep* within, inside of [3]
dependienta *f* clerk [12]
dependiente *adj* dependent; *m* clerk [12]
deporte *m* sport [8]
derecho,-a *adj* right [4], straight; *adv* straight ahead; *m* right; **a** (**hacia**) **la derecha** to the right [4]
derivación *f* derivation
derivar to derive
desaliñarse to disarrange
desaparecer to disappear [15]
descanso *m* rest
descompuesto,-a out of order [3]
describir to describe
descripción *f* description [23]
desde from, since [6]; *— **que** since [19]
desear to want [3]
desempeñar to fulfill, carry out
desfile *m* marching, parade [24]
desgraciado,-a unfortunate [8]
designar to designate
desorden *m* disorder, confusion [22]
despacho *m* office
despedir (*like* **pedir**) to fire, send off [23]; —**se** to leave, take leave
despertar (**ie**) to awaken [23]; —**se** to wake up
después *adv* afterward, later, then [2]; — **de** *prep* after [9]
destacarse (**qu**) to excel, be outstanding [18]
desventaja *f* disadvantage [21]
detalle *m* detail
***detener**(**se**) (*like* **tener**) to stop
devolver (*like* **volver**) to return, give back [19]
D.F. (= **Distrito Federal**) Federal District
día *m* day [1]; **al** — **siguiente** on the following day; **Buenos** —**s** Good morning [1]; **de** — in the daytime [23]; **del** — today's; — **feriado** holiday [4]; **hoy** — nowadays [17]; **otro** — the next day [11]; **todos los** —**s** every day [11]
diablo *m* devil; **¡qué** —**s!** the deuce!
diálogo *m* dialog [17]
diario,-a daily
diccionario *m* dictionary
diciembre December [10]
dicho,-a (*see* **decir**) said [17]
dichoso,-a happy, lucky [24]
diecinueve (**diez y nueve**) nineteen, nineteenth [6]
dieciocho (**diez y ocho**) eighteen, eighteenth [6]
dieciséis (**diez y seis**) sixteen, sixteenth [6]
diecisiete (**diez y siete**) seventeen, seventeenth [3]
diez ten [2]; **un** — a dime [9]
diferente different [9]
difícil (**de**) difficult (to) [10]
diminutivo *m* diminutive
dinero *m* money [8]
Dios God [2]; — **mío** my Heavens [2]; **por** — for Heaven's sake [5]
diplomático *m* diplomat [15]
dirección *f* direction, steering mechanism, address [4]
directivo,-a *adj* directive, managing; **junta** — *f* board of directors [19]
directo,-a direct, directly [20]

disco *m* disc, record [3]
disculparse (**de**) to make excuses (for)
discurso *m* speech, discussion [13]
discutir to discuss, argue [9]
disgustar to be furious, displeased
disimulado,-a feigned; **hacer** (**se**) **el disimulado** to pretend not to notice [24]
disolver (**ue**) to dissolve, disperse [13]
disparar to shoot [13]
disposición *f* disposition, state
disuelto,-a (*see* **disolver**) dissolved [17]
doblar to turn, fold, bend, double [4]
doce twelve [6]
docena *f* dozen [5]
doctor *m* doctor [3]
documento *m* document, identification papers [7]
dólar *m* dollar [9]
doler (**ue**) to hurt, pain [14]
dolor *m* pain [6], sadness, grief; — **de cabeza** headache [6]
domicilio *m* home
domingo *m* Sunday [10]
don,-ña *m f* title used before a given name to show respect [2], [4]
*__donde__ where [8]
*__¿Dónde?__ Where? [2]
*__dormir__ (**ue, u**) to sleep [10]
dos two [2]
doscientos,-as two hundred [6]
Dr. = **doctor** [3]
dudar (**en**) to doubt, hesitate (to) [21]
duelo *m* grief, mourning [22]; **de** — in mourning [22]
dueño,-a *m f* owner; **dueña de casa** housewife [5]
durante during
duro,-a hard

e

*__e__ and [6]
echar to throw, pour, give; — **de menos** to miss [16]; — **mirada** to glance [24]
edad *f* age [4]; — **Media** Middle Ages; **¿Qué — tiene?** How old is she? [4]
EE.UU. (= **Estados Unidos**) United States [2]
efectuar to bring about
*__¿eh?__ huh? right? hm? [3]
ejemplo *m* example [22]; **por —** for example
*__el__ the [2]
*__él__ he, him [2]; **de —** his; **— no** not he
elección *f* election [13]
electricidad *f* electricity [16]
elevar to elevate, be high, raise
*__ella__ she, her; **de —** hers [2]
*__ellas__ they, them [2]
*__ello__ it; **todo —** all of it
*__ellos__ *m* they, them [2]
embajada *f* embassy [15]
embajador *m* ambassador [15]
embargo: sin — nevertheless, but [3]
empaparse to get soaked [24]
empezar (**ie, c**) to begin [23]
empleado *m* clerk [11]
emplear to use
empleo *m* employment, job, use [7]
*__en__ in, into, on, at [1]; — **contra de** against [7]; — **cuanto** (**a**) as for;— **vez de** instead of [9]
encantado,-a (**de**) delighted (to) [4]
encargar (**gu**) to charge, order [22]
encender to turn on, to light
encontrar (**ue**) to find, encounter [11]; —**se** to meet, find oneself, be [11]
enemigo *m* enemy [14]
enero *m* January [10]
enfermarse to get sick
enfermedad *f* sickness, illness [22]
enfermera *f* nurse [14]
enfermo,-a sick [10]
enfrentarse (**con**) to meet
enojadísimo,-a very angry [20]
enojar to anger [21]
enredado,-a complicated
enseñar to teach, show [6]
ensuciar to dirty [22]; —**se** to get dirty
entender (**ie**) to understand [4], intend; —**se** to be understood
entero,-a *adj* entire, complete; **el —** *m* the lottery ticket [21]
entierro *m* burial, funeral [22]
entonces then [2]
entrada *f* entrance, doorway [3]
entrar (**a**) (**en**) to enter, come in [2]
*__entre__ between, among [11]; **por —** from
entregar (**gu**) to hand over [15]
entrevista *f* interview
entusiasmar to make enthusiastic [11]; —**se** to become enthusiastic [11]
envolver (**ue**) to wrap [12]
envuelto,-a (**de**) (*see* **envolver**) wrapped (in) [17]
época *f* age, time, epoch
equipo *m* team, equipment [8]
equivocado,-a mistaken [3]
equivocarse to be mistaken
escandalizado,-a shocked
escapar(**se**) to escape, run away [19]
escoger (**j**) to draw, select, choose [18]
escribir to write [4]; — **a máquina** to type
escrito,-a (*see* **escribir**) *adj* written [17]; *m pl* writings
escuchar to listen (to) [2]
escuela *f* school [2]
*__ese, esa__ that; **esos,-as** those [7]
*__ése, ésa__ that, that one; **ésos, -as** those [12]
eso that [3]; **por —** therefore, for that reason, that's why [3]
España Spain [8]
español,-la *adj* Spanish; *m* Spanish (language) [1]; *m f* Spaniard [16]
esperar to wait (for) [2], expect, hope
esposa *f* wife
esposo *m* husband; *pl* husband and wife
esquina *f* corner [4]
estado *m* state [2], office; *(**los**) **Estados Unidos** (the) United States [2]
*__estar__ to be [1]
estatura *f* height
este, esta this [4]; *__esta noche__ tonight [5]; **estos, -as** these
este *m* east
éste, ésta this, the latter [8]; **éstos,-as** these, the latter [8]

estilo *m* style; **por el —** of that kind [11]
estimación *f* esteem
esto this [7]; **en —** at this moment
estómago *m* stomach
estudiante *m f* student [14]
estudiantil *adj* student, of students [10]
estudiar to study [2]
estudio *m* study [18]
E.U. = Estados Unidos (*also* **EE. UU.**) [2]
Europa *f* Europe [6]
exacto,-a *adj* exact [4]; *adv* exactly
exagerar to exaggerate [9]
examen *m* examination [10]; **dar** (**sufrir**) **exámenes** to take exams
excelente excellent
excepto except [4]
exigente strict [20], discriminatory
exigir (**j**) to require, take, demand [7]
existir to exist [13]; **dejar de —** to die
explicar (**qu**) to explain
expresión *f* expression
expresivo,-a expressive
extra extra [13]
extranjero,-a *adj* foreign [4]; *m* foreigner; **del —** from abroad; **en el —** abroad [4]

f

***fácil** (**de**) easy (to) [4]
falsificar (**qu**) to falsify, forge [23]
falta *f* lack [12]; **hacerle —** to need [20]; **sin —** without fail [12]
faltar to miss, be lacking [4], need, be missing, fail; **faltan veinticinco para las nueve** it is twenty-five minutes to nine [20]; **no faltaba más** don't think of it [22]
fallar to fail [9]
fallecer (*like* **parecer**) to die
familia *f* family [2]
famoso,-a famous [23]
fantástico,-a fantastic [8]
farmacia *f* drugstore
favor *m* favor [1]; **hágame el —** (**de**) will you please?; **por —** please [1]; **si me hace el —** please [3]
febrero *m* February [10]
fecha *f* date [4]
felicitar to congratulate [4]
fenomenal phenomenal [8]
feo,-a ugly; *f* ugly woman
feria *f* fair
feriado,-a: día — holiday [4]
feroz fierce, ferocious [15]
fiebre *f* fever [14]
fiesta *f* party, feast [24]
figurar(**se**) to figure, imagine [22]; **se le figura** he imagines
fijar to fix [15]; **—se** to imagine, look [15]
filosofía *f* philosophy [10]
filosófico,-a philosophical
fin *m* end; **a —es de** at the end of [15]; **en —** in short [22]; **por** (**al**) **—** finally [16]
final *m* end
finca *f* farm, ranch [11]
firme firm, solid [15]
física *f* physics [10]
flecha *f* arrow [7]
flor *f* flower [13]
folletín *m* brochure, pamphlet [19]
forma *f* form
formar to form, make (up) [24]; **—se** to grow
formidable formidable
foto *f* picture
fragmento *m* fragment
francés,-esa *adj* French [15]; *m* Frenchman, French (language)
frase *f* phrase, sentence
freno *m* brake [9]
frente *f* face, forehead; **— a** facing, in the presence of, in front of
frijol *m* bean [5]
fruta *f* fruit [5]
fuego *m* fire [24]; **—s artificiales** fireworks [24]
fuerte strong, loud [5]
fumar to smoke
función *f* duty, **—** (**de**) function (as)
funcionar to function, work
funcionario *m* official [9]
fúnebre *adj* funeral
furioso,-a furious [7]
fútbol *m* football [8]

g

gana *f* (**de**) desire (to) [3]; **tener —s** (**de**) to want to [8]
ganado *m* livestock [11]; **— vacuno** cattle
ganancia *f* gain, profit [11]
ganar to gain, earn, win [8], beat [5]
garantizar to guarantee
garganta *f* throat [14]
gasto *m* expense
gato *m* cat [5]; **no se deje dar gato por liebre** don't let them cheat you [5]
general general [10]; **por lo —** usually
***gente** *f* people [9]
gerente *m* manager, boss [20]
gesto *m* gesture [13]
gobernar (**ie**) to govern
gobierno *m* government [9]
golpe *m* strike, hit
gordo,-a fat; **premio —** first prize [21]
gozar (**c**) (**de**) to enjoy
gracia *f* grace; *pl* thank you, thanks [1]
grado *m* degree
gramática *f* grammar
***grande, gran** large, great, big [2]
grave grave, serious [22]
gripe *m* grippe, flu [14]
gris gray [18]
grito *m* shout
grupo *m* group [8]
guapo,-a handsome [24]
guardar to keep, protect
guardia *m* guard; *f* guard (corps)
***gustar** to be pleasing, like [2]; **me gusta** I like it
gusto *m* pleasure [1], taste; **con mucho —** gladly [1]; **el — es mío** it's my pleasure; **mucho — en** (**de**) **conocerlo**(**la**) I'm glad to meet you [1]

h

***haber** to have, be [8] **— de** to be to, must; **hay, hubo, había, etc.** there is (are), was (were), etc.; **hay que** it is necessary [13]; **¿Qué hubo?** Hi there [19]

hablar to speak, talk [2]; **modo de —** way of speaking; **oir — de** to hear about
***hacer** to do, make, perform [3]; **hace como cuatro años** for about four years [4]; **hace dos años** two years ago, for two years [16]; **— compras** to shop; **— pregunta(s)** to ask (a) question(s) [10]; **— una comida** to give a dinner [4]; **—se** to become, be made; **—se tarde** to be getting late; **me hará el favor** will you please; **si me hace el favor** please [3]
***hacia** to, toward [24]; **— abajo** downward; **— acá** this way [24]; **— afuera** out; **— arriba** upward; **— fines** toward the end
hacienda *f* hacienda, estate [11]
hallar to find; **—se** to be, find oneself, be found
hambre *f* hunger [4]; **tener —** to be hungry [4]
***hasta** to, as far as, until, even [1]; ***— que** *conj* until [19]
hay (*see* **haber**) there is (are) [5]
hecho,-a (*see* **hacer**) *adj* done, made [13], already made; *m* fact
herido,-a *adj* wounded [13]; *m* wounded man
hermana *f* sister [2]
hermanito *m dim* little brother
hermano *m* brother [2]; *pl* brothers (and sisters) [2]
hermoso,-a beautiful
héroe *m* hero
herramienta *f* tool [9]
hija *f* daughter [2]
hijo *m* son [2]; *pl* sons (and daughters) [2]
himno *m* hymn [24]
hispánico,-a Hispanic
historia *f* history, story
histórico,-a historical
hmm hum [7]
hola, holá hello [3]
hombre *m* man [5]; **— del día** man of the hour [18]
honra *f* honor, reverence
honrado,-a honored, honest
hora *f* hour, time [3]; **¿Qué — es?** What time is it? [3]; **tener —** to have an appointment [14]
horario *m* schedule [20]
horrible horrible [13]
horror *m* horror [11]
hoy today [5]; **— día** nowadays [17]
huelga *f* strike [10]
huevo *m* egg [5]
humano,-a human

i

idea *f* idea [3]
idealista *adj* idealistic [18]; *m f* idealist
iglesia *f* church [16]
***igual** equal, (the) same [15]; ***— que** as well as, the same as [10]; **sin —** unequaled
igualmente the same (to you) [1]
imaginación *f* imagination
imaginar(se) to imagine [11]
importancia *f* importance [19]
importante important [9]
importar to matter [9], import [10]
imposible (de) impossible (to) [12]
impresión *f* impression
impreso,-a *adj* printed [19]
impresor *m* printer [19]
inauguración *f* inauguration [9], opening
incierto,-a uncertain
***incluir (y)** to include [5]
independencia *f* independence [24]
indiferente indifferent
infame *m* scoundrel [13]
infantería *f* infantry [24]
inferior inferior
infestar to infest
informe *m* information, item, report
ingeniero *m* engineer
inglés,-esa *adj* English; *m* English (language), Englishman [2]
inmediato,-a immediate [16]; **de —** immediately
inocente innocent [13]
insistente insistent
insistir (en) to insist (on) [18]
institución *f* institution
instituto *m* institute, (high) school
insuficiente insufficient
inteligente intelligent
interesante interesting
interior *adj* interior [12]; **ropa —** underwear [12]; *m* interior
intimidad *f* intimacy
inútil useless [13]
inventar to invent
invierno *m* winter [11]
invitación *f* invitation [3]
invitado *m* guest [5]
invitar to invite [4]
***ir** to go [3]; **— de compras** to go shopping; **—se** to go out (away) [1]; **¡qué va!** nonsense! [9]; **vámonos** let's be going [10]; **vamos a** let's [2]
izquierdo,-a left [4]; **a la izquierda** to the left [4]

j

***jamás** never, ever [13]
jardín *m* garden, yard [5]
jardinero *m* gardener [23]
jefe *m* boss, chief [7]
Jesús Jesus [23]
joven *adj* young [18]; *m* young man; *f* young lady
juego *m* game [8]
jueves *m* Thursday [5]
juez *m* judge
jugador *m* player
jugar (ue,gu) to play [5]; **—se con** to fool with
juguete *m* plaything, toy [5]
julio *m* July [10]
junio *m* June [10]
junto,-a *adj* united; *pl* together [7]; **— a** near, together with; **— con** together with
jurar to swear [6]
justicia *f* justice
juventud *f* youth

k

kilo *m* kilogram (about 2.2 pounds) [5]
kilómetro *m* kilometer (about 0.62 mile) [11]

l

*__la__ the [1], her, you, it [4]
__lado__ *m* side [8]; __al — de__ along with; __dar —__ to give way; __del — de__ with
__ladrón__ *m* thief [23]
__lana__ *f* wool [11]
__lápiz__ *m* pencil [1]
__largo,-a__ *adj* long [8]; *m* length; __a todo lo — de__ all along
*__las__ the [2], them, you [4]
*__lástima__ *f* shame, pity [2]; __— que__ it's too bad that [2]
__latín__ *m* Latin
__latino,-a__ *adj* Latin; *m* Latin
__Latinoamérica__ *f* Latin America [9]
__latinoamericano,-a__ Latin-American
__lavar__ to wash [9]; __—se__ to wash [9]
__le__ him, you, to him, to her, to you, to it [1]
__lección__ *f* lesson
__lector,-ra__ *m f* reader
__leche__ *f* milk [4]
__leer__ (__y__) to read [13]
__lejos__ far, far away [4]
__lengua__ *f* language, tongue [14]
__lentejas__ *f pl* lentils [11]
__león__ *m* lion
*__les__ to them, to you [4]
__levantar__ to raise, build; __—se__ to get up, be raised [14]
__levemente__ slightly, lightly
__libertad__ *f* liberty; __poner en —__ to free
__libre__ free [13]
__libro__ *m* book [1]
__licenciado__ *m* lawyer; licentiate (in Europe, a university degree intermediate between bachelor's and doctor's); __— en Derecho__ Bachelor of Laws (degree)
__líder__ *m* leader [13]
__liebre__ *f* hare [5]; *see* __gato__
__limonada__ *f* lemonade [14]
__linda__ *f* lovely [24]
__lindo,-a__ pretty, quaint [24]
__línea__ *f* line
__lingüístico,-a__ linguistic
__lío__ *m* confusion, fight, mix-up [7]
__lista__ *f* list, roster [5]
*__lo__ it, him, you [1], the [1]; *__— de__ the matter of [10]; *__— que__ what [15]
__loco,-a__ *adj* crazy [6]; *m* fool [18]
*__los__ them [4]
__lotería__ *f* lottery [21]
__luego__ then, later [4]; __hasta —__ so long, until later; __— que__ as soon as
__lugar__ *m* place [6]; __tener —__ to take place
__luna__ *f* moon
__lunes__ *m* Monday [5]
__luto__ *m* mourning [22]; __de —__ in mourning [22]
__luz__ *f* light; __traje de luces__ bullfighter's costume

ll

__llamar__ to call [3], knock (at the door) [2];__—se__ to be named, be called [2]
__llanta__ *f* tire [9]
__llave__ *f* key [19]
__llegada__ *f* arrival
__llegar__ (__gu__) (__a__) to arrive, reach, come, go [2]; __— a ser__ to become; __no — a tanto__ not to go that far, not to be so bad as that
__llenar__ to fill [22]
__llevar__ to carry, take, wear, have, be [5]; __— una vida__ to live, lead a life; __—se__ to carry away, take [14]
__llorar__ to weep [22]
__llover__ (__ue__) to rain [24]

m

__madre__ *f* mother [2]
__magnífico,-a__ magnificent, wonderful [9]
__maíz__ *m* corn [11]
__mal__ *adj* ill, bad [10]; *adv* badly [11]; *m* evil
*__malo,-a, mal__ bad, sick, out of order [3]; __de —__ bad [18]
__mamá__ *f* mother, mom [2]
__mamacita__ *f dim* mommy
__mandar__ to send, order [4]
__manera__ *f* manner, kind; __de ninguna —__ by no means; __de una —__ in a manner; __la — de__ in a way that
__manifestación__ *f* manifestation, demonstration [13]
__mano__ *f* hand [7]; __a —__ by hand
__mantener__ (*like* __tener__) to support, keep [15]
__mantequilla__ *f* butter [5]
*__mañana__ *f* morning [1]; *adv* tomorrow [4]; __ayer por la —__ yesterday morning; __de la —__ A.M. [19]
__máquina__ *f* machine; __escribir a —__ to type
__maquinilla__ *f dim* little machine; clippers [7]
__maratón__ *m* marathon [8]
__marcha__ *f* march [24]
__martes__ *m* Tuesday [5]
__marzo__ *m* March [10]
*__más__ more, most [4]; __lo — pronto posible__ as soon as possible; __— de__ (__que__) more than [13]; __— tarde__ later [3]; __no hay — remedio que__ there's nothing to do but [15]; __no —__ just, only [15]; __¡Qué cosa — ridícula!__ How ridiculous! [9]
__matar__ to kill [14]
__matasano__ *m* quack doctor
__matemáticas__ *f pl* mathematics
__materia__ *f* course, matter, material [9]
__matrimonio__ *m* matrimony, married couple
__mayo__ *m* May [10]
*__mayor__ *adj* greater, greatest, older, oldest [15]; *m pl* __mayores__ the elders; __la — parte de__ most of
__mayoría__ *f* majority [20]
*__me__ me, to me [3]
__mecanógrafa__ *f* typist
__medalla__ *f* medal [24]
__medias__ *f pl* hose
__medicina__ *f* medicine [18]
__médico,-a__ *adj* medical; *m* doctor [9]
__medio,-a__ *adj* half (a) [3], middle; *m* means, way; __Edad — Middle Ages__; __en — (de)__ in the midst (middle) (of); __por — de__ by means of

mediodía *m* noon [24]
***mejor** better, best [5]; **muy — que** much better than
mejorar to improve, better [15]
melón *m* melon
memoria *f* memory [10]; **de —** by memory, by heart [10]
mencionar to mention [9]
***menor** younger, less, lesser, least, youngest [2]
menos less, except [10]; ***a — que** unless [18]; **al —** at least [23]; **echar de —** to miss [16]; **en (a) — de** in less than; **las nueve — cuarto** a quarter to nine [20]; **lo de —** the least important thing; **lo — posible** as little as possible; **por (a) lo —** at least [16]
mente *f* mind
mentir (ie, i) to lie [6]
mentira *f* lie.
menudo: a — often [16]; **muy a —** very often
mercado *m* market [5]
merecer (*like* **parecer**) to merit, deserve [13]
mero,-a mere
mes *m* month [4]; **al —** per month; **hace algunos meses** some months ago
mesa *f* table [24]
meter to put, place [7]; **—se** to get, put oneself [7]
mexicano,-a *adj and m f* Mexican
***mi** my [2]
***mí** me [5]
miembro *m* member
***mientras** while [11]; **— tanto** meanwhile
miércoles *m* Wednesday [4]
mil thousand [6]
militar military [24]
***millón** *m* million [6]
ministerio *m* ministry [7]
ministro *m* minister
minutito *m dim* minute [19]
minuto *m* minute [3]
***mío,-a** my, (of) mine [2]; **Dios —** my heavens [2]
mirada *f* look [24]
***mirar** to look (at) (upon) [10]
misa *f* mass [16]
***mismo,-a** same, self [12]; **lo —** the same thing, the same to you; **— que** same as; **por lo —** therefore; **(por) lo — que** (just) the same as; **yo —** I myself
moderno,-a modern [9]
modo *m* way, manner; **de este —** in this way; **de todos —s** to make a long story short, anyway [18]; **del mismo —** in the same way
molestar(se) to bother
molestia *f* bother, trouble [19]
momentito *m dim* moment [15]
momento *m* moment, minute [18]; **de —** momentarily
monja *f* nun
montaña *f* mountain [11]
morado,-a purple [18], brown
moreno,-a dark, brunette [2]
morir (ue, u) to die [10]
mostrar (ue) to show
mozo *m* servant, waiter, boy
muchacha *f* girl
muchacho *m* boy [7]; *pl* boys (and girls)
muchísimo,-a much, very much [11]; **muchísimas gracias** thank you very much
***mucho,-a** *adj* much, many [1]; *adv* a great deal, too long (much) [5]
mueble *m* (piece of) furniture [19]; *pl* furniture [5]
muerte *f* death [13]; **dar — (a)** to kill
muerto,-a (*see* **morir**) *adj* dead [13]; *m* dead person [13]
mujer *f* woman, wife [16]
multa *f* fine [7]
mundo *m* world [14]; **del —** in the world; **todo el —** everybody [14]
murmurar to mutter, gossip
muy very, too [1]

n

nacional *adj* national [7]
***nada** *f pron* nothing, anything [5]; *adv* at all [7]; **de —** don't mention it [1]
***nadie** nobody, anybody [5]
natación *f* swimming [7]
necesario,-a necessary [11]
necesitar to need [2]
necio,-a foolish, fool
neerlandés,-esa *adj* Dutch; *m f* Dutch person
negocio *m* (piece of) business [19]; *pl* business [9]
negro,-a *adj* black [10]; *m* Negro
nervios *m pl* nerves
nervioso,-a nervous [23]
***ni** nor, or [5]; **—. . .—** neither . . . nor, either . . . or; **— papa** absolutely nothing [8]; **no . . .—** not even
***ninguno,-a, ningún** any, no, none [10]
niña *f* girl [11]
niño *m* boy [11]; *pl* children [11]
***no** no, not [1]; **— más** only, no more, just [15]
***noche** *f* night [5]; **de —** at night, by night [12]; **esta —** tonight [5]; **por la —** in the evening [12]
nombre *m* name [14], noun
norte *m and adj* north, northern [4]
Norteamérica *f* North America
norteamericano,-a North American
***nos** us, to us, ourselves [4]
***nosotros,-as** we, us [2]
notar to notice, note
notario *m* notary
noticia *f* (piece of) news [7]; *pl* news [19]
novecientos,-as nine hundred [6]
novedad *f* novelty, something new [19]
novela *f* novel
noveno,-a ninth [10]
noventa ninety [6]
novia *f* sweetheart, girl friend [16]
noviembre *m* November [10]
novio *m* lover, boy friend [16]
nube *f* cloud [11]
***nuestro,-a** our, ours [4]
nueve nine [2]
nuevo,-a new [2]; **de —** again
número *m* number [3]
numeroso,-a numerous
***nunca** never, ever [4]

O

*o or [2]; —. . .— either . . . or

obligado,-a forced, obligated [17]

observación *f* observation

obtener (*like* **tener**) to obtain, get

octavo,-a eighth [10]

octubre *m* October [4]

ocupado,-a busy [19]

ocurrir to occur [14]

ochenta eighty [6]

ocho eight [2]

ochocientos,-as eight hundred [6]

odiar to hate [18]

ofender to offend [7]

oficina *f* office [16]

ofrecer (*like* **parecer**) to offer, present [11]; **¿Qué se le ofrece?** What may I do for you? [12]

ofrenda *f* offering

*__oir__ to hear [3]; **¡Oiga!** Hey!

*__¡Ojalá!__ Would that . . . , I hope . . . [17]

ojo *m* eye [16]

olímpico,-a Olympic [8]

olvidar(se) to forget, be forgotten [14]; **se me olvidó** I forgot [23]

once eleven [6]; **la clase de las —** the eleven o'clock class; **para las —** by (for) eleven o'clock [14]

onceavo,-a eleventh

opinar to be of the opinion, judge

opinión *f* opinion [15]

oponer (*like* **poner**) to oppose; **—se (a)** to resist, be opposed (to) [18]

oportunidad *f* opportunity [8]

oposición *f* opposition [13]

oración *f* prayer

orden *m* order (series); *f* order (command); **a tus órdenes** certainly [7]

organizar (c) to organize [8]

origen *m* origin

oro *m* gold [24]

orquesta *f* orchestra

oscuro,-a obscure, dark [18]

*__otro,-a__ other, another [4]; **las unas de las otras** some from (the) others, each other; **— día** the next day; **uno,-a que —** a few

oveja *f* sheep [11]

P

paciencia *f* patience [6]

padre *m* father [2]; *pl* parents

padrino *m* godfather [4]

pagar (gu) to pay (for) [7]

país *m* country [8]

palabra *f* word

palacio *m* palace [24]

pálido,-a pale [22]

palo *m* stick, pole [13]; **a —s** with clubs [13]

pan *m* bread [5]

panamericano,-a Pan-American [8]

papa *f* potato [8]; **ni —** absolutely nothing [8]

papá *m* father, dad [2]

papel *m* paper, role [1]

paquete *m* package [12]

par *m* pair, couple [6]; **sin —** unequaled

*__para__ to, for, in order to, toward, to the end that, by [3]; **— que** in order that [19]

parado,-a standing, stationed [21]; *f* stop [19]

paraguas *m sing and pl* umbrella, umbrellas [24]

paralelo *m* parallel

parar to stop [7]

*__parecer__ *m* opinion; *v* **(zc)** to seem, appear (to be) [4]; **a mi —** in my opinion; **¿No le parece?** Don't you think so?; **¿Qué le parece?** What do you think of . . . ?; **—se (a)** to resemble, be alike

pared *f* wall [2]

parejo,-a equal

pariente *m* relative [4]

parque *m* park [4]

parte *f* part [3]; **a (por) todas —s** everywhere [17]; **de (por) — de** by, on the part of [3]; **en mucha —** in great part; **gran — de** most of; **la mayor —** most

participar to participate [8], make known, share; **— de** to partake of, share

partido,-a *adj* parted; *m* party [13], faction, game, platform

partir to divide, split, break [22]; **a — de** starting from

pasado,-a *adj and m* past [4]

pasajero *m* passenger

pasar (a) to pass, enter [3], go, happen, spend, endure; **— de** to be more than; **—lo mal** to have a hard time [11]; **— por** to pass (by) for, come for [3]; **—se** to pass away

pasear(se) to walk, take a walk [22]

pastilla *f dim* pill [14]

pata *f* foot; **meter la —** to put one's foot in one's mouth, blunder

patata *f* potato

patilla *f* sideburn [8]

patio *m* patio [2]

patria *f* fatherland [15]

pausa *f* pause

paz *f* peace [6]

pecador,-ra *m f* sinner

*__pedir (i)__ to order, request, ask (for) [4], borrow

peinar to comb [8]; **—se** to comb one's hair [8]

peine *m* comb [8]

pelear(se) to fight, quarrel [7]

película *f* film [17]

pelo *m* hair [8]

pena *f* pain, grief [6]

*__pensar (ie)__ to think, intend [4]; **— en** think about [9]

pensativo,-a pensive

*__peor__ worse, worst [15]; **si pasa lo —** if worse comes to worse

pequeñez *f* smallness

pequeño,-a small

*__perder (ie)__ to miss, lose [5]; **—se** to lose, get lost [14]

perdón *m* pardon, pardon me [3]

perdonar to pardon [19]

perezoso,-a lazy [23]

perfecto,-a perfect [2]

periódico *m* newspaper [13]

periodista *m* journalist [15]

permiso *m* permission, permit [1]; **con —** excuse me [1]

permitir to permit
pero but [3]
perrito *m dim* little dog
perro *m* dog
persona *f* person [16]; **por —** per person
personal personal [15]
pésame *m* condolence [22]
pesar *m* regret; *v* to weigh, grieve; **a — de** in spite of [18]
pesca: de — fishing [19]
peseta *f* peseta (monetary unit of Spain)
peso *m* peso (monetary unit of several Hispanic countries) [5]; grief, weight
petróleo *m* petroleum, oil [9]
pie *m* foot [19]; **a —** on foot [19]
piel *f* hide; **abrigo de pieles** fur coat [16]
pintura *f* painting, paint; **ni en —** by no means [11]
pistola *f* pistol [23]
pito *m* whistle [15]; **no importar un —** not to be worth two cents [15]
placer *m* pleasure
planta *f* plant [9]
plata *f* silver; money [5]
Platón Plato [10]
plaza *f* square, marketplace [18]; **— de toros** bullring
pleito *m* lawsuit, dispute [18]
pluma *f* feather, pen [1]
pobre poor [22]; *m f* poor person; **— de mí (ti)** poor me (you)
***poco,-a** *adj* little, few; *adv* little [8]; **un — (de)** a little [8]; **unos pocos** a few; **— a —** little by little
***poder** *m* power; *v* to be able, may, can [3]
poeta *m* poet
policía *m* policeman [7]; *f* police [7], police station; politeness
político,-a political; *m* politician; *f* politics [13], policy [18]; **hijo —** son-in-law
polvo *m* dust
pollo *m* chicken, dude
***poner** to place, put, make [5]; **—se** to put on, get [14]; **—se a** to begin, get, make [14]; **—se de acuerdo** to agree [18]
poquito *dim* a very little [8]; **un —** a little bit
***por** per, by, for, through, across, during, in behalf of, on account of [1]; **¿— que?** why? [2]
***porque** because [6]
portátil portable [3]
portugués,-esa *adj and m f* Portuguese; *m* Portuguese (language)
***posible (de)** possible (to) [5]
postre *m* dessert [6]; *pl* dessert; **de —** for dessert
practicar (qu) to practice, play, engage in [9]
preciso,-a precise, exact, necessary [15]
preferir (ie, i) to prefer [4]
pregunta *f* question [10]; **hacer —s** to ask questions [10]
preguntar to ask [6]; **— por** to ask for (about)
premiado,-a *m f* winner [21]; *m* awardee
premio *m* prize, reward [21]; **— gordo** first prize [21]
prensa *f* press [15]
preocupar to concern, divert; **—se (de)** to be concerned (about) (with), worry [5]
preparar to prepare, be ready, make ready
presencia *f* presence
presentación *f* (good) appearance
presentar to present, introduce [1]; **—se** to appear, come
presente present
presidencial presidential [24]
presidente *m* president [13]
preso *m* prisoner [15]; **coger —** to arrest [15]
préstamo *m* loan
prestar to lend, give [8]
pretérito *m* preterit (tense)
pretexto *m* pretext, excuse [13]
prima *f* cousin [2], early morning
primero,-a (primer) first [10]; *adv* first [2]; **a —s de** at the first of; **el — en** the first to [24]
primitivo,-a primitive
primo *m* cousin
principal principal, main [11]
principio *m* principle, beginning [23]; **al —** at first; **a —s** at the beginning
probable probable [8]
problema *m* problem [7]
***producir (zc)** to produce [10]
profesión *f* profession [8]
profesional professional [9]
profesor *m* professor [1]
profesora *f* professor [2]
profundo,-a profound, deep
programa *m* program; **— de clase** course
progresar to progress, get ahead [9]
progreso *m* progress
prolongarse (gu) to be prolonged
prometer to promise [11]
pronto fast, soon [5]; **lo más — posible** as soon as you can [5]; **tan — como** as soon as [19]
pronunciación *f* pronunciation
propio,-a own, one's (their) own, itself, very
propósito *m* purpose; **a —** by the way [7]
protección *f* protection [14]
proteger to protect [15]
protestar to protest
próximo,-a *adj* next; *adv* next [8]
pst exclamation used to attract attention [10]
público,-a *adj* public; *m* audience
pueblo *m* people, town [18]
puerta *f* door [1]
***pues** well, then [18], since
puesto,-a (*see* **poner**) put, made [17]; *m* job, position, stall [11]; ***— que** since [19]
puntapié *m* kick; **dar —s a** to kick
punto *m* point; **dos —s** colon; **en —** sharp, on the dot
puntual punctual [20]
puntualidad *f* promptness [20]
puro,-a pure [11]

q

***que** that, who, which [2], for, than [8]; **lo —** what [10]
***¡qué! ¿qué?** what (a), how!, what? [2]; **¿por —?** why? [3]; **¿— tal?** how are you? [3]

*__quedar__ to be left, remain, be [10]; **—se** to stay [11]; **—(se) (en)** to remain, agree
*__querer__ to wish, want, love [1]; **— decir** to mean
*__quien__ who, whom, he (him) who, which [16]
*__¿quién?__ who?, whom [2]; **¿con —?** with (to) whom? [3]; **¿de —?** whose? [3]
química *f* chemistry [10]
quince fifteen [6]
quinientos,-as five hundred [6]
quinto,-a fifth [10]
*__quitar__ to take away [6]; **—se** to take off, brush off [14]
quizá, quizás perhaps [21]

r

rabiar to rave, fume [17]
radio *m* radio [5]; **poner el —** to turn on the radio [5]
raíz *f* root
ramo *m* branch, line of goods
rápido,-a rapid, rapidly
rato *m* short time, while [4]
ratón *m* mouse [23]
razón *f* reason, reasoning [10]; **con —** rightly, no wonder; **tener —** to be right
reacción *f* reaction [15]
recado *m* message, note [3]
receta *f* prescription [14], recipe
recibir to receive, meet, get [7]
recibo *m* reception, receiving, receipt [12]
recobrarse (de) to recover (from)
recomendación *f* recommendation
*__recordar(se) (ue)__ to remember, recall, remind [4]
recurso *m* recourse, resource, income
*__reducir__ (*like* **producir**) to reduce [20]
referencia *f* reference [23]
refinería *f* refinery [9]
reflejar to reflect
reforma *f* reform [15]
regalar to give [21]
regalo *m* gift [16]
regatear to bargain [5]
regla *f* rule; **— de cálculo** slide rule
regresar to return, come back [3]
regular regular, fair, usual [14]
reinar to reign [15]
relatividad *f* relativity
relativo,-a relative [15]; *m* relative; **todo lo — (a)** everything pertaining to
religión *f* religion [15]
reloj *m* clock, watch [23]
relucir (*like* **parecer**) to shine
remedio *m* remedy; **no hay más — que** there's nothing to do except [10]
remoto,-a remote, extreme
rendir (i) to render, pay
renunciar resign, renounce [20]
reparación *f* repair
repetir (i) to repeat [2]
repórter *m* reporter [15]
reprobado: salir — to fail (a course)
republicano,-a republican
requisito *m* requisite, prerequisite
resfriado *m* cold [14]; **estar —** to have a cold [14]
residencia *f* residence
respectar to concern; **por lo que respecta a** as for
respetable respectable [9]
respetar to respect [13]
respeto *m* respect
responder to answer
restaurán, restaurante *m* restaurant
restitución *f* restitution
resto *m* rest
restorán *m* restaurant [4]
resultado *m* result, outcome
reunión *f* meeting [10]
reunir to unite; **—se** to meet [19]
revés *m* reverse; **al —** backwards, upside down [19]
revista *f* review, magazine [16]
revolución *f* revolution [13]
revólver *m* revolver
rezar (c) to pray [16]
rico,-a rich, delicious; *m* rich man; **los ricos** the rich (people)
ridículo,-a ridiculous [9]
rifa *f* raffle [16]
rifar to raffle [16]
rincón *m* corner
risa *f* laughter
robar to steal, rob
robo *m* robbery [23]
rodear (de) to surround (with)
rodillas: de — kneeling
rogar (ue, gu) to ask, pray [18]
rojo,-a red [18]
romano,-a Roman
romántico,-a romantic
romper to break [5]
roncar (qu) to snore [23]
ronda *f* round, patrol [23]
ropa *f* clothes [5]; **— de cama** bed linen [12]; **— interior** underwear [12]
rosbif *m* roast beef
rotación *f* rotation; **contar en —** to count off
roto,-a (*see* **romper**) broken [17]
rubio,-a blond [2]
ruido *m* noise [3]
ruina *f* ruin, ruins [18]

s

S.A. (= **Sociedad Anónima**) Corporation
sábado *m* Saturday [10]
sábana *f* sheet [22]
*__saber__ *m* knowledge; *v* to know (how), find out, can [2]
sacar (qu) to get, take out, pull out [21]; **— una foto** to take a picture
sacudir to shake, wave, dust [5]
sagrado,-a sacred [13]
sala *f* room, living room [2]
salario *m* salary, wages
*__salir (de)__ to leave, come (go) out (of) [3]
salón *m* shop; **— de belleza** beauty shop [5]
salto *m* jump; **de un —** with a start
saludo *m* greeting [7]
salvar to save, spare [15]
santo,-a, (san) *adj* holy, saint [4]; *m f* saint; **el día del —** Saint's Day [4]
sargento *m* sergeant [23]
*__se__ (one's) self, one, to him, to her, to you, to them [1]
secretaria *f* secretary [16]
sector *m* sector, cross section, section
secuestrar to kidnap [15]
secuestro *m* kidnaping [15]

seguido,-a (de) followed (by); **en seguida** immediately.
***seguir (i, g)** to continue, follow, keep on, go on [4]; **usted sigue** you're next [8]
***según** according to (what) [19]
segundo,-a second [10]
seguridad *f* security, assurance [15]
seis six [2]
seiscientos,-as six hundred [6]
selva *f* forest
semana *f* week [4]; **la otra —** next week; **la — pasada** last week
semestre *m* semester
semicírculo *m* semicircle [24]
sencillo,-a simple [9]
sentado,-a seated [23]
sentarse (ie) to sit (down) [1]
sentido,-a *adj* hearfelt [22]; *m* sense, feeling, meaning [22]
sentimiento *m* sentiment, feeling
sentir *m* feeling [1]; *v* **(ie, i)** to feel [14], regret [12]; **(lo) siento** I am sorry [12]; **—se** to feel, be felt [14]
señor *m* Mr., sir, man, lord [1]; *pl* Mr. and Mrs., ladies and gentlemen
señora *f* Mrs., lady, wife [1]
señorita *f* Miss, lady [1]
separar to separate; **—se (de)** to leave
séptimo,-a seventh [10]
***ser** *m* being; *v* to be [2]
serio,-a serious [7]; **en —** seriously
serpentina *f* serpentine, streamer [24]
servicio *m* service
servir (i) (de) to serve (as), help [16]; **¿En qué puedo —la?** May I help you?, What can I do for you?; **sírvase** help yourself
sesenta sixty [6]
setecientos,-as seven hundred [6]
setenta seventy [6]
setiembre *m* September [10]
sexto,-a sixth [10]
shh shh [13]
***si** if, whether [3]
sí yes [1], oneself, themselves
siempre always [9]
siesta *f* siesta, nap [20]
siete seven [2]
significado *m* meaning
silencio *m* silence
silla *f* chair
simpático,-a nice, fine, charming [20]
***sin** *adv* without [3]; **— embargo** nevertheless [3]; **— que** *conj* without [19]
sincero,-a sincere [18]
sinfonía *f* symphony
sino but [7]; **no sólo . . . —** not only . . . but also [7]; **— que** but [19]
sirvienta *f* servant-girl [6]
sistema *m* system, range [7]
situación *f* situation [13]
situado,-a situated
sobre over, on, about [10]; **— todo** especially [22]
sobrina *f* niece [4]
sobrino *m* nephew
social social
Sócrates Socrates [10]
sofá *m* sofa
solemne solemn
solicitar to solicit; **se solicita** wanted
solo,-a single, mere, only, alone [5]; **café —** black coffee
sólo *adv* only [7]; **no — . . . sino también** not only . . . but also [7]
soltar to free [15]
soltero,-a unmarried
solterón *m* old bachelor
sonar (ue) to sound, ring, play [6]
sorprender to surprise
sospechoso,-a suspicious [23]
Sr. *see* **señor**
Sra. *see* **señora**
***su** his, her, your, their, its [3]
subir to go up, rise
subteniente *m* second lieutenant [24]
suceder to happen, follow [7]
sucio,-a dirty [7]
Sudamérica *f* South America
sueldo *m* salary [6]
suerte *f* luck [10], play; **¡Qué buena — la suya!** How lucky you were!
sufijo *m* suffix
sufrir to suffer, undergo; **— exámenes** to take exams
sugerir (ie, i) to suggest [18]
sujeto *m* subject
suponer (*like* **poner**) to suppose [9]
supuesto,-a (*see* **suponer**) supposed [17]
sustantivo *m* noun
sustentar to sustain, nourish
***suyo,-a** (of) his, hers, theirs, its, yours [12]

t

tal such, such a [3]; **con — que** provided [19]; **¿Qué — ?** How are you? [3], What's it like? [11]; **— (tales) como** such as; ***— vez** perhaps [3]
***también** also [2]
***tampoco** neither, either [4]; **yo —** neither do I
***tan** so, as [5]; **— . . . como** as . . . as [13]; **— pronto (como)** as soon as [19]; **— . . . que** so . . . that
***tanto,-a** *adj* so (as) much, so (as) many [2]; **mientras —** meanwhile; **otros —s** as many; **por lo —** *adv* therefore; **tantas . . . cuantas** as many . . . as; **— . . . como** *adv* both . . . and, as much as [15]
tardar (en) to delay, be late [5]
***tarde** *f* afternoon, evening [2]; **buenas tardes** good afternoon [2]; *adj* late; **se hace —** it is getting late
taza *f* cup [4]
***te** you, to you, yourself [2]
té *m* tea; **tomar —** to have tea
teatro *m* theater [7]
técnico,-a *adj* technical; *m* technician [9]
teléfono *m* telephone [3]; **por —** on the telephone [3]
tema *m* theme, subject [8]; **cambiar de —** to change the subject [18]
témprano early [16]
***tener** to have, hold, possess [1]; **— cuidado** to be careful [5]; **(no) — cuidado** (not) to worry [5]; **— de todo** to have (some) of everything [21]; **— ganas de** to want to [8];

— **hambre** to be hungry [4]; — **la bondad de** to be so kind as to [14]; *— **que** to have to [3]; — **razón** to be right [10]; —**se** to stop
teniente *m* lieutenant [23]
***tercero,-a,** (**tercer**) third [10]
terminar to finish [18]; —**se** to come to an end
termómetro *m* thermometer [14]
testamento *m* will
***ti** you [3]
tía *f* aunt [2]
tiempo *m* time, weather [14]; **en mis —s** in my days [17]
tijeras *f pl* scissors [8]
tintorería *f* cleaner's [12]
tío *m* uncle [2]
típico,-a typical [24]
tipo *m* type, guy, fellow [21]
tirano *m* tyrant [13]
tirar to pull [8]
tiro *m* shot [13]; **a —s** with shots [13]
titulares *m pl* headlines [13]
tocadiscos *m* record player [3]
tocar (**qu**) to play (a musical instrument) [17], touch, knock [6]
todavía still, yet [10]
***todo,-a** all, every [3]; **ante —** especially; **de todos modos** by all means [18]; **del —** completely; **en — caso** anyway; **hay de —** there is (some) of everything; **sobre —** especially [22]; **— el mundo** everybody [14]; **todas partes** everywhere [15]; —**s** everybody [7]
tomar to take, drink, eat [5]; **¡Toma!** Here!
tontería *f* (piece of) foolishness [7]; *pl* trifles, nonsense [19]
toreo *m* bullfighting [8]
toro *m* bull [8]
total *m* total, whole [2]; **en —** in all [2]
totalmente totally
trabajar to work [2]
trabajo *m* work, job [9]
trabalenguas *m* tongue twister
tradición *f* tradition
tradicional traditional
traducción *f* translation
traducir (*like* **producir**) to translate [2]
traductor *m* translator
***traer** to bring, carry [3], have
tráfico *m* traffic [7]
traicionero,-a treacherous [22]
traidor *m* traitor [15]
traje *m* suit, clothes [12]; **— de luces** bullfighter's costume
tranquilo,-a tranquil, quiet [16]
tránsito *m* traffic [7], existence
trasladar(se) to move
tratar to treat, discuss, have dealings; **— de** to try, to have dealings (with); —**se** (**de**) to be a question of [15]; **de que se trata** in question
trece thirteen [6]
treinta thirty [6]
tremendo,-a tremendous [7]
tres three [2]
trigo *m* wheat [11]
triste sad [7]
triunfo *m* triumph
***tu** your [2]
***tú** you [2]
tumba *f* tomb [13]
tumbar to knock down [6]
***tuyo,-a** yours, of yours [9]

U

***u** or [7]
Ud. *see* **usted**
¡Uf! Oh!
últimamente lately
último,-a last, final [4]; **por —** finally
undécimo,-a eleventh
único,-a only, unique [14]
unidad *f* unit, unity
unión *f* union [11]
universal universal
universidad *f* university [13]
universitario,-a *adj* university [13]
***uno,-a,** (**un**) a, an, one [1]; *pl* some; **la una** one o'clock; **— que otro,-a** a few
urgente urgent [6]
urgir (**j**) to be urgent, be needed
usar to use [3]
***usted** you [1]

V

vaca *f* cow [11]
vacación *f* vacation; *pl* vacation [8]
vajilla *f* dishes, table service [23]
valer to be worth [14]; **— la pena** to be worthwhile
varios,-as several [16]
Vd. = usted
veinte twenty [4]
veintiséis twenty-six [3]
veintiuno twenty-one [4]
velada *f* evening party (usually with music and literary discussion); wake (before a funeral)
velar to watch over; to hold a wake over
velocidad *f* speed
velorio *m* wake [22]
vendedor *m* paperboy, seller [13]
vender to sell [5]; **a —** for sale
***venir** to come [3]; **¿A qué viene?** How come?
venta *f* sale
ventaja *f* advantage
ventana *f* window
***ver** to see [4]; **a —** let's see [12]; **tener que — con** to have something to do with [17]; **por lo visto** apparently [11]
veras: de — truly, really [16]
verbo *m* verb
verdad *f* truth [3]; **es —** that's right; ***¿verdad?** isn't it?, aren't they? [3]
verdadero,-a true, real [8]
verde green [4]
vestido,-a (**de**) *adj* dressed (in) [22]; *m* dress [12]; *pl* clothes [18]
vestir (**i**) to dress; —**se** (**de**) to dress (in) [22]
***vez** *f* time [3]; **a la —** at the same time, at a time; **a veces** at times; **alguna —** ever, sometime [9]; ***en — de** instead of; **otra —** again; **muchas veces** often; **tal —** perhaps [3]; **una —** once; **unas** (**algunas**) **veces** sometimes
viaje *m* journey, trip [8]; **hacer un —** to take a trip [21]

vida *f* life [15]
***viejo,-a** *adj* old [5]; *m f* old person; old boy; *m pl* old folks
viernes *m* Friday [5]
violencia *f* violence [15]
visita *f* visit [14]
visitante *m f* visitor [1]
visitar to visit
vista *f* view; **hasta la —** I'll see you later
visto,-a (*see* **ver**) seen [17]; **por lo —** apparently [11]
viuda *f* widow [22]
vivir to live [4]
***volver (ue)** to return, turn [5]; **— a** + *inf* to . . . again [16]; **— loco** to drive (one) crazy; **—se** to become; **—se loco** to go crazy
vosotros,-as you (*pl*)
vuelo *m* flight
vuelta *f* change; **dar la —** to turn around, return
vuelto,-a (*see* **volver**) *adj* returned, turned [17]; *m* change
vuestro,-a your
vulgar vulgar, of the common people

Y

***y** and [1]
ya already, now, presently [1]; **¡ — lo creo!** Yes, indeed! [11]; ***—que** since [4]
***yo** I, me [2]

Z

zapateado *m* foot-tapping dance [24]
zapatería *f* shoestore
zapato *m* shoe [7]
zeta *f* the letter **z**

Index

Spanish words and their particles are in **bold** roman type, and their English equivalents are in light *italic* type; other English entries are in light roman type. The bold numbers refer to grammar sections, which are numbered consecutively throughout the book. The light italic numbers refer to pages.

ABBREVIATIONS

adj	adjective	indef	indefinite	pron	pronoun
adv	adverb, adverbial	indic	indicative	ref	refer(ring), reference(s)
art	article	inf	infinitive	refl	reflexive
cn	cultural note	interrog	interrogative	sing	singular
cond	conditional	masc	masculine	subj	subject
const	construction	obj	object	subjunc	subjunctive
def	definite	perf	perfect	vb(s)	verb(s)
fem	feminine	pl	plural	vs	versus
fn	footnote	prep(s)	preposition(s)	w/p	with-preposition
fut	future	pres	present	w/v	with-verb
imperf	imperfect	pret	preterit		

F 7
G 8
H 9
I 0
J 1

ijuana
ESTADOS UNIDOS
30°
BAJA CALIFORNIA
GOLFO DE CALIFORNIA
Ciudad Juarez
Río Conchos
Chihuahua
SIERRA MADRE OCCIDENTAL
BOLSÓN DE MAPIMÍ
SIERRA MADRE ORIENTAL
Río Bravo (Río Grande)
Nuevo Laredo
Monterrey
MÉXICO
GOLFO DE MÉ
20°
Tampico
Río Pánuco
Puerto Vallarta
Guadalajara
Río Grande de Santiago
GOLFO DE CAMPECHE
Mérida
México, D.F.
Cuernavaca
Taxco
Río Balsas
Veracruz
PENÍNSULA DE YUCATÁN
SIERRA MADRE DEL SUR
Acapulco
Oaxaca
Belmopan
BELICE
GOLFO DE TEHUANTEPEC
Puerto Barrios
Puerto Cortés
GUATEMALA
HOND
Guatemala
Tegucigalpa
San Salvador
Acajutla
EL SALVADOR
0°
OCÉANO PACÍFICO
0
500 Millas
0
500 Kilómetros
110°
100°
90°
J. P. Tremblay